# A Companion to Rawls

# Blackwell Companions to Philosophy

This outstanding student reference series offers a comprehensive and authoritative survey of philosophy as a whole. Written by today's leading philosophers, each volume provides lucid and engaging coverage of the key figures, terms, topics, and problems of the field. Taken together, the volumes provide the ideal basis for course use, representing an unparalleled work of reference for students and specialists alike.

**Already published in the series:**

# A Companion to Rawls

*Edited by*

Jon Mandle and
David A. Reidy

**WILEY** Blackwell

*Registered Office*
John Wiley & Sons Ltd, The Atrium, Southern Gate, Chichester, West Sussex, PO19 8SQ, UK

*Editorial Offices*
350 Main Street, Malden, MA 02148-5020, USA
9600 Garsington Road, Oxford, OX4 2DQ, UK
The Atrium, Southern Gate, Chichester, West Sussex, PO19 8SQ, UK

For details of our global editorial offices, for customer services, and for information about how to apply for permission to reuse the copyright material in this book please see our website at www.wiley.com/wiley-blackwell.

*Library of Congress Cataloging-in-Publication Data*

A companion to Rawls / edited by Jon Mandle, David A. Reidy.
     pages   cm
   Includes index.
   ISBN 978-1-4443-3710-5 (cloth) ISBN 978-1-119-14456-4 (paper)
1.  Rawls, John, 1921–2002. I. Mandle, Jon, 1966–   II.  Reidy, David A., 1962–
   B945.R284C66 2014
   320.51092–dc23

                                                        2013016708

A catalogue record for this book is available from the British Library.

Cover image: John Rawls' passport photo c. 1963, courtesy of Thomas Pogge

Set in 10/12.5 pt Photina by SPi Global, Pondicherry, India
Printed and bound in Malaysia by Vivar Printing Sdn Bhd

1   2016

# Contents

# Notes on Contributors

**Kenneth Baynes** is Professor of Philosophy and Political Science at Syracuse University. He has published widely on Rawls, Habermas, and Taylor, and on human rights. His next book will be on Habermas.

**Gillian Brock** is a Professor of Philosophy at the University of Auckland in New Zealand. Her most recent work has been on global justice and related fields. She is the author of *Global Justice: A Cosmopolitan Account* (2009) and editor or coeditor of *Current Debates in Global Justice* (2005); *The Political Philosophy of Cosmopolitanism* (2005); *Necessary Goods: Our Responsibilities to Meet Others' Needs* (1998); and *Global Heath and Global Health Ethics* (2011).

**Daniel Brudney** is Professor of Philosophy at The University of Chicago. He writes and teaches in political philosophy, philosophy and literature, and bioethics. He is the author of *Marx's Attempt to Leave Philosophy* (1998).

**Claudia Card**, Emma Goldman Professor of Philosophy at the University of Wisconsin, studied with John Rawls at Harvard from 1962 to 1966 and wrote her PhD thesis, on punishment, under his direction. Her books include *The Atrocity Paradigm: A Theory of Evil* (2002), *The Cambridge Companion to Simone de Beauvoir* (edited, 2003), and *Confronting Evils: Terrorism, Torture, Genocide* (2010).

**Richard Dagger** is E. Claiborne Robins Distinguished Chair in the Liberal Arts at the University of Richmond, where he teaches in the Department of Political Science and in the Program in Philosophy, Politics, Economics, and Law. He is the author of *Civic Virtues: Rights, Citizenship, and Republican Liberalism* and coauthor of *Political Ideologies and the Democratic Ideal*.

**Samuel Freeman** is Avalon Professor in the Humanities and Professor of Philosophy and Law at The University of Pennsylvania. He is the author of *Justice and the Social Contract* (2006) and of *Rawls* (2007). He has edited three volumes: *The Cambridge Companion to Rawls* (2003); *John Rawls's Collected Papers* (1999); *John Rawls's Lectures on the History of Political Philosophy* (2008); and he coedited *Reasons and Recognition: Essays in Honor of T.M. Scanlon* (2011).

**Barbara H. Fried** is the William W. and Gertrude H. Saunders Professor of Law at Stanford University. She has written widely in moral and political theory, and is the author of *The Progressive Assault on Laissez Faire: Robert Hale and the First Law and Economics Movement* (1998).

**Gerald Gaus** is the James E. Rogers Professor of Philosophy at the University of Arizona, where he directs the Program in Philosophy, Politics, Economics & Law. His most recent book is *The Order of Public Reason* (2011).

**Paul Guyer** is Jonathan Nelson Professor of Humanities and Philosophy at Brown University. He is the author of nine books on Kant, including three on Kant's moral and political philosophy, editor of six anthologies on Kant, and cotranslator of Kant's *Critique of Pure Reason*, *Critique of the Power of Judgment*, and *Notes and Fragments*. He will shortly publish *A History of Modern Aesthetics* in three volumes.

**Thomas E. Hill, Jr** studied at Harvard and Oxford, taught for 16 years at the University of California, Los Angeles, visited at Stanford University and the University of Minnesota, and is now Kenan Professor at the University of North Carolina at Chapel Hill. He is author of *Virtue, Rules, and Justice* (2012); *Human Welfare and Moral Worth* (2002); *Respect, Pluralism and Justice* (2000); *Dignity and Practical Reason in Kant's Ethics* (1992); and *Autonomy and Self-Respect* (1991).

**Aaron James** is Professor of Philosophy at the University of California, Irvine. He is author of *Fairness in Practice: A Social Contract for a Global Economy* (2012), recipient of the ACLS (American Council of Learned Societies) Burkhardt Fellowship, and was recently a fellow at the Center for Advanced Studies in the Behavioral Sciences, Stanford University.

**Alexander Kaufman** is Associate Professor of Political Theory at the Department of Political Science, University of Georgia. He is author of *Welfare in the Kantian State* (1999) and editor of *Capabilities Equality: Issues and Problems* (2006), and has published articles on Rawls, distributive justice, social contract theory, German Idealism, and philosophy of law.

**Erin I. Kelly** is Associate Professor of Philosophy at Tufts University. Her research focuses on questions about justice, the nature of moral reasons, moral responsibility and desert, and theories of punishment. Her recent publications include "Reparative Justice," in *Accountability for Collective Wrongdoing* (2011), "Equal Opportunity, Unequal Capability," in *Measuring Justice: Capabilities and Primary Goods* (2010), and "Criminal Justice without Retribution," *Journal of Philosophy* (2009). She is editor of John Rawls, *Justice as Fairness: A Restatement* (2001).

**Larry Krasnoff** is Professor of Philosophy at the College of Charleston. He is coeditor of *New Essays on the History of Autonomy* (2004) and author of *Hegel's Phenomenology of Spirit: An Introduction* (2008). His essays have appeared in the *European Journal of Philosophy*, the *Journal of Philosophy*, and the *Philosophical Quarterly*.

**Anthony Simon Laden** is Professor of Philosophy at the University of Illinois at Chicago and the author of *Reasoning: A Social Picture* (2012) and *Reasonably Radical: Deliberative Liberalism and the Politics of Identity* (2001), as well as numerous articles on Rawls's work.

**Daniel Little** is Professor of Philosophy at the University of Michigan-Dearborn and Professor of Sociology at the University of Michigan-Ann Arbor. His fields of research include the philosophy of the social sciences, the practice of democracy, and globalization. His recent books include *New Contributions to the Philosophy of History* (2010) and *The Paradox of Wealth and Poverty: Mapping the Ethical Dilemmas of Global Development* (2003). His academic blog can be found at www.understandingsociety.blogspot.com.

**S.A. Lloyd** is Professor of Philosophy, Law, and Political Science at the University of Southern California. She is the author of *Morality in the Philosophy of Thomas Hobbes: Cases in the Law of Nature* (1992), *Ideals as Interests in Hobbes's Leviathan: Mind over Matter* (1992), *The Bloomsbury Companion to Hobbes* (2013), and *Hobbes Today* (2013), as well as numerous articles on Rawls on the family and liberal feminism.

**Colin M. Macleod** is Associate Professor of Philosophy and Law at the University of Victoria in Canada. His research focuses on issues in contemporary moral, political, and legal theory with a special focus on distributive justice and equality; children, families, and justice; and democratic ethics. He is the author of *Liberalism, Justice, and Markets* (1998) and coeditor with David Archard of *The Moral and Political Status of Children* (2002).

**Jon Mandle** is a Professor in the Philosophy Department at the University at Albany (SUNY). He is coeditor with David Reidy of this volume and of the forthcoming *Rawls Lexicon*, and the author of *What's Left of Liberalism: An Interpretation and Defense of Justice as Fairness* (2000); *Global Justice* (2006); and *Rawls's A Theory of Justice: An Introduction* (2009), as well as articles on political philosophy, ethics, and their history.

**Rex Martin** is Professor of Philosophy, Emeritus, at the University of Kansas and Honorary Professor in the School of European Languages and Politics at Cardiff University. His fields of major interest are political and legal philosophy and history of political thought. He is the author of several books, including *A System of Rights* (1993) and the editor or coeditor of several more, including *Rawls's Law of Peoples: A Realistic Utopia?* (2006).

**Richard W. Miller** is Hutchinson Professor in Ethics and Public Life and Director of the Program on Ethics and Public Life in the Department of Philosophy at Cornell University. His writings in political philosophy and ethics include *Analyzing Marx* (1984), *Moral Differences* (1992), and *Globalizing Justice:The Ethics of Poverty and Power* (2010).

**Darrel Moellendorf** is Professor of International Political Theory at Goethe University Frankfurt. He is the author of *Cosmopolitan Justice* (2002), *Global Inequality Matters* (2009), and *Dangerous Climate Change: Values, Poverty, and Policy* (2013). He has been a Member of the School of Social Sciences at the Institute for Advanced Study and a Senior Fellow at Justitia Amplificata at the Johann Goethe Universität, Frankfurt and the Forschungskolleg Humanwissenschaften.

**Jonathan Quong** is Associate Professor of Philosophy at the University of Southern California. He is the author of *Liberalism without Perfection* (2011), as well as articles on political liberalism, public reason, democracy, distributive justice, and the morality of defensive harm.

**David A. Reidy** is Professor of Philosophy at the University of Tennessee. He has published widely in political and legal philosophy and has focused his work in recent years on Rawls and on issues of global justice and human rights.

**Jonathan Riley** is Professor of Philosophy and Political Economy, Tulane University, and, during 2013, Visiting J.S. Mill Chair in Social Philosophy at the University of Hamburg, Germany. He is currently completing the second edition of his *Mill: On Liberty* (1998) as well as a companion volume, *Mill's Radical Liberalism*.

**Zofia Stemplowska** is University Lecturer in Political Theory and Asa Briggs Fellow, Worcester College, University of Oxford. Her publications include the coedited *Responsibility and Distributive Justice* (2011).

**Adam Swift** is Professor of Political Theory at the University of Warwick. He is coauthor (with Stephen Mulhall) of *Liberals and Communitarians* (1996) and author of *How Not To Be a Hypocrite: School Choice for the Morally Perplexed Parent* (2003) and *Political Philosophy: A Beginners' Guide for Students and Politicians* (2013).

**Robert S. Taylor** is Associate Professor of Political Science at the University of California, Davis. He specializes in contemporary analytic political philosophy and the history of liberal political thought. He is the author of *Reconstructing Rawls: The Kantian Foundations of Justice as Fairness* (2011) as well as articles in *Philosophy and Public Affairs, Ethics, Journal of Political Philosophy, Political Theory, Journal of Politics,* and *Review of Politics.*

**Steven Wall** is Professor of Philosophy at the University of Arizona, where he is also a member of the Center for the Philosophy of Freedom. He is the author of *Liberalism, Perfectionism and Restraint* (1998) and coeditor of *Reasons for Action* (2009).

**Paul Weithman** is Professor of Philosophy at the University of Notre Dame, where he has taught since 1991. He has worked on political philosophy, the philosophy of education, religious ethics and medieval political theory. His most recent book, *Why Political Liberalism: On John Rawls's Political Turn* (2011) was recognized with the 2012 David and Elaine Spitz Prize as the best book published in liberal and democratic theory in the previous year.

**Stuart White** is Fellow in Politics at Jesus College, Oxford. His research focuses centrally on the political philosophy of economic citizenship. He is the author of *The Civic Minimum* (2003) and *Equality* (2006).

**Huw Lloyd Williams** is Lecturer in Philosophy at Cardiff University. He is the author of *On Rawls, Development and Global Justice: The Freedom of Peoples* (2011).

# Introduction

## JON MANDLE AND DAVID A. REIDY

It is now more than 10 years since John Rawls died in 2002, at the age of 81, and more than 60 years since his first publication in 1951. Yet, his work continues to occupy a unique and central position in contemporary political philosophy. Over the years it has generated an enormous secondary literature and sparked numerous interpretive and critical debates. The recent publication of Rawls's Princeton undergraduate thesis and his Harvard lectures in moral and political philosophy and the archival processing by Harvard of Rawls's unpublished papers, lectures, letters, annotated books, and so on, have only served further to stimulate interest in and debate over Rawls's work, often raising new questions, reviving debates thought to be settled, and suggesting new ways of understanding Rawls's work. With all this in mind, we were keen to produce with this volume not so much a summary of past scholarly work as a serviceable roadmap for current and future work on Rawls. Accordingly, we asked our contributors to address themselves to the themes and issues that in their view will or should occupy the attention of the scholars engaged or likely to engage in this work. As evidenced by their contributions, this scholarship is likely to range beyond issues of justice. For while Samuel Freeman is certainly correct that "Rawls devoted his entire career to one general philosophical topic and as a result wrote more on the subject of justice than any other major philosopher" (2007, x), as the essays in this collection establish, and as Freeman would readily acknowledge, to understand fully and evaluate fairly Rawls's work one must engage an immense number of related issues, just as Rawls himself did.

In Part I, David Reidy and Paul Weithman draw on materials only recently available to cast new light on Rawls's own understanding of his project and philosophical ambitions. Drawing on Rawls's undergraduate senior thesis (*BI*) and unpublished material from the Rawls archives, including papers from graduate school, Reidy (Chapter 1) gives us a series of "postcards" from Rawls's early philosophical development. Each offers a glimpse into the origin of one of the several enduring themes or concerns animating Rawls's mature work. Although *BI* is one of the few places where Rawls presents his work in an explicitly religious framework, in his *Lectures on the History of Moral Philosophy*, he notes that Kant's work,

*A Companion to Rawls*, First Edition. Edited by Jon Mandle and David A. Reidy.
© 2014 John Wiley & Sons, Inc. Published 2016 by John Wiley & Sons, Inc.

clearly a source of inspiration for Rawls, has "an obvious religious aspect" (*LHMP*, 160). Rawls sometimes acknowledged in conversation that his own work was motivated by, among others, an essentially religious concern. Weithman (Chapter 2) provides a non-theistic interpretation of when a work has a "religious aspect" and argues that this characterization applies to Rawls's work as well as to Kant's. Weithman does not argue that this characterization informs Rawls's own understanding of his work, but the possibility is clearly a live one.

The essays in Part II explore certain key ideas in Rawls's philosophical method. Both Anthony Laden and Larry Krasnoff examine the meaning and significance of Rawls's "constructivism." Laden (Chapter 3) explores the relationship between constructivism and the idea of reflective equilibrium, arguing that, contrary to commonly held views, it is the latter that captures Rawls's metaethical commitments while the former constitutes Rawls's method for theory-building. Krasnoff (Chapter 4) argues that the significance of Rawls's 1980 Dewey Lectures has been widely misunderstood. Kantian constructivism was a response to certain challenges to the ideas of the original position and reflective equilibrium. While Rawls's later turn to political liberalism set aside Kantian *moral* constructivism, he did not abandon a political form of Kantian constructivism. Another key to Rawls's method is his idea that the first subject of justice is the basic structure of society. Samuel Freeman (Chapter 5) explores the justification and significance of the methodological priority Rawls assigns to the basic structure of society, taking care to show how a failure to understand this priority leads all too easily to confusions, both exegetical and substantively philosophical. Methodologically speaking, Rawls assigns priority also to ideal theory (over nonideal theory), and in fact most of his work is within ideal theory. With this feature of Rawls's method in mind, Adam Swift and Zofia Stemplowska (Chapter 6) explore the different senses in which a theory can be "ideal" and the strengths and weaknesses of these different idealizations. Finally, Rawls's method features a now familiar "device of representation" or heuristic: the idea of the "original position." Jon Mandle (Chapter 7) traces the development of this idea in Rawls's work from his dissertation to *A Theory of Justice*, shedding light on its role in Rawls's thought and its contribution to the argument for Rawls's two principles of justice.

The essays in Part III focus on the substantive claims central to *TJ*. Foremost among these, of course, is Rawls's commitment to the lexical priority of the liberty principle over the principle of fair equality of opportunity, the difference principle, perfectionist ends, and economic efficiency. Robert Taylor (Chapter 8) argues that this priority can be justified only on the basis of a robust commitment to Kantian autonomy. If Taylor is right, this would arguably have the implication of prioritizing the protection of political liberties over civil liberties. Rawls argues that the institutional implications of his principles are properly determined through a "four-stage sequence" within which they guide first the selection of a constitution, then the enacting of laws under that constitution, and finally the application of those laws to particular cases. Colin Macleod (Chapter 9) examines the application of Rawls's principles through this process to democratic political institutions, education, health care, the family, and the economy. Central to Rawls's account of economic justice are the two parts of his second principle of justice, the principle of fair equality of opportunity and the difference principle. Together these specify for Rawls an ideal of "democratic equality." Stuart White (Chapter 10) considers this ideal and whether it is appropriately responsive to effort and whether it should and can be extended to address the concerns of severely sick and disabled individuals. One of the central substantive claims of *TJ*, advanced in its final three chapters, is that a society organized around Rawls's two principles of justice as fairness would tend to be stable and indeed more stable than a society organized around candidate alternative principles. Over the years, this claim has befuddled many commentators. Rawls's recasting in *Political Liberalism* of his claims regarding the stability of a society organized around his two principles only added to the confusion. Thomas Hill (Chapter 11) reconstructs Rawls's stability argument from *TJ* and then undertakes to sort out what does and does not survive in the transition to *PL*. Although his focus in *TJ* is on the principles of justice applicable to society's basic structure, Rawls does not entirely ignore the duties and obligations of individuals. In *PL* he addresses various civic duties related to democratic deliberation (some of the essays in Part IV of this volume, discussed below, address these duties). But in *TJ* he addresses primarily political duties and obligations related to fidelity or resistance to the law. Alexander Kaufman (Chapter 12) examines Rawls's idea of political authority and the conditions under which political institutions deserve citizens' fidelity and obedience and under which their resistance is permissible or required.

A few years after the publication of *TJ*, Rawls began to worry that the argument he had given there for the stability of a society governed by his two principles was inconsistent. It presupposed a degree of doctrinal moral consensus unlikely to arise or last under the conditions of freedom guaranteed by his principles. As he worked on a solution to this problem, one issue seemed to lead to another. By the time Rawls felt he had a solution to the problem he had developed a family of new ideas and arguments. These he gathered together under the umbrella idea of a "political liberalism," presenting them in a book of the same name. The essays in Part IV of this volume take up the ideas and arguments at the heart of Rawls's "political liberalism." One of these is the idea of the reasonable pluralism of competing and conflicting comprehensive doctrines (moral, religious, philosophical) that arises inevitably under conditions of freedom and justice. In order to explain how a society organized by his two principles, and so free and just, might prove stable, notwithstanding the reasonable doctrinal pluralism that will inevitably mark it, Rawls recasts his two principles as part of a "political conception" of justice. But Gerald Gaus (Chapter 13) argues that the very conditions that make inevitable reasonable doctrinal pluralism will also make inevitable a reasonable pluralism of competing and conflicting political conceptions of justice. The stability problem emerges, then, as deeper and more challenging than is often acknowledged. Recast as a "political conception" of justice, Rawls characterizes justice as fairness in *PL* not as a Kantian moral constructivism but rather as a "political constructivism." This move has left many wondering what exactly makes a view "constructivist" and what distinguishes "political constructivism" as a special case. Aaron James (Chapter 14) clarifies the general idea of "constructivism," analyzing it into five elements, in order to make sense of Rawls's distinction between a Kantian moral constructivism and a political constructivism.

Another idea central to Rawls's "political liberalism" is the idea of public reason, or the shared reason citizens (and officials) use when deliberating or addressing one another in their role or capacity as citizens (or officials) in order to render intelligible and evaluate or justify the constitutional essentials and fundamental justice of their society's basic social structure. A reasonable political conception of justice belongs to the public reason of citizens in a free and just society. The idea and ideal of public reason has generated both confusion and resistance from many quarters. Jonathan Quong (Chapter 15) carefully sets out the idea(l) and gives it a robust defense. Of course, Rawls allows that when deliberating over and deciding political issues citizens (and officials) will also reason from their many diverse comprehensive (moral, religious, and philosophical) doctrines. While these doctrines do not belong to their shared public reason, citizens (and officials) remain free to reason from them in political life, provided they do so consistent with the idea(l) of public reason. When citizens (and officials) reasoning from their many diverse comprehensive doctrines have reason to affirm, or at least no reason to reject, one and the same reasonable political conception of justice (or family of such conceptions), they join in what Rawls dubs an "overlapping consensus." The fact, or at least realistic possibility, of an overlapping consensus is central to the stability of a free and just society. Rex Martin (Chapter 16) provides a careful account of the role of over-lapping consensus in Rawls's political liberalism. Martin pays special attention to the much discussed question of whether utilitarianism, and if so, which species of utilitarianism, can participate in an overlapping consensus the object of which includes justice as fairness. Taken together, many of the ideas central to Rawls's political liberalism specify an idea(l) of civic virtue essential to the stability of a just and free society. Richard Dagger (Chapter 17) argues that this idea(l) of civic virtue – which constitutes something like a shared answer to the question: What is democratic citizenship for? – is in fact a unifying theme running throughout Rawls's work, the foundation of public trust and social stability. Without dissent-ing from this claim, Erin Kelly (Chapter 18) argues that in contemporary democracies like the United States inequality is a more pressing threat to public trust and social stability than the reasonable pluralism of comprehensive doctrines or the absence of a publicly shared idea(l) of civic virtue.

The essays of Part V consider Rawls's extension of political liberalism to matters of inter-national relations, especially as presented in *The Law of Peoples*. The extension is necessary to complete justice as fairness and political liberalism, for the realistic possibility of a just and stable liberal democracy depends not only on its internal structure but also on its external relations to other polities. Though eagerly awaited, Rawls's account of these relations in *LP* received an overwhelmingly negative reception from scholars. Huw Williams (Chapter 19) argues that this reception was misguided and that *LP* in fact offers a novel and principled vision of international relations that ought to be attractive to liberal democratic peoples. A key feature of Rawls's extension of political liberalism in *LP* is a conception of human rights as essential to the shared public reason through which liberal democratic and other well-ordered and decent peoples render intelligible and evaluate their relations to one another on the global stage. Gillian Brock (Chapter 20) examines Rawls's conception of human rights in light of the various responses, critical and sympathetic, it has provoked. A second key feature of the view Rawls develops in *LP* is a duty owed by liberal democratic and other well-ordered decent peoples to assist impoverished peoples in achieving the material and human resources necessary to fulfilling human rights and a basic social structure that is at least not too unjust. Among peoples able to fulfill human rights and with a basic social structure that is not too unjust there is, on Rawls's view, no substantial reason arising out of considerations of justice to constrain material inequalities. Richard Miller (Chapter 21) takes a close and careful look at Rawls's duty of assistance and his relatively permissive stance toward material inequalities among peoples and argues that Rawls fails to respond adequately to the pressing problems of global poverty and inequality. Finally, in *LP* Rawls articulates various limits on the use of coercive force, including military force, within international relations. Darrel Moellendorf (Chapter 22) takes up Rawls's views here and assesses them as a contribution to the tradition of thought known as just war theory.

While Rawls's work in *TJ*, *PL* and *LP* is focused almost exclusively on issues of justice as they present themselves within the tradition of liberal democratic thought, he pursued his work with an eye toward a number of related issues and in conversation with a variety of traditions and perspectives. The essays in Part VI of this volume engage this aspect of Rawls's work. Rawls's conversation with and sympathetic understanding of the work of John Stuart Mill dates back to Rawls's days as a graduate student. While Rawls rejected the utilitarian tradition that runs from Bentham through Edgeworth and Sidgwick, his relationship to Mill's utilitarianism was and remained over time much more friendly, a fact recently highlighted in Rawls's lectures on Mill published in his *Lectures on the History of Political Philosophy*. Jonathan Riley (Chapter 23) scrutinizes Rawls's interpretation of and relationship to Mill, arguing that Rawls seems to misunderstand either Mill's or his own view. There is, of course, in Mill's utilitarianism a rather pronounced perfectionist undercurrent. And Rawls famously deploys well-known arguments against perfectionist conceptions of justice. Setting aside what this suggests about Rawls's understanding of and relationship to Mill's work, Steven Wall (Chapter 24) takes up Rawls's antiperfectionist arguments on their own terms and finds them wanting. He argues that notwithstanding Rawls's own pronouncements, there are forms of state perfectionism compatible with Rawls's justice as fairness and political liberalism. Just as Riley and Wall complicate the relationship between Rawls's work and utilitarianism, on the one hand, and perfectionism, on the other, Barbara Fried (Chapter 25) complicates the relationship between Rawls's work and the tradition of thought referred to as libertarianism. Starting with Nozick and moving forward to later versions of libertarianism, she argues that the tensions between Rawls and his libertarian critics are sometimes more apparent than real and in any case often misunderstood and overstated. Daniel Brudney (Chapter 26) makes a similar sort of point regarding the relationship between Rawls's work and Marx's, especially the work of the younger Marx (of 1844, say). Setting aside the various species of later Marxisms, Brudney argues that there are some deep thematic points of common ground between Rawls's work and the work of the younger Marx. Irrespective of details, there can be little doubt that like Marx and Rousseau before him, Rawls sees the great evils of human history as arising in important ways out of injustice, especially institutional and political injustice. Rawls notes the connection explicitly in *LP*. Taking this link as her point of departure, Claudia Card (Chapter 27) focuses on the great evils of misogyny, especially misogynistic violence, and the lessons that might be drawn from Rawls's work by those engaged in the struggle against these evils. Moved, like Rawls, by a desire both to overcome injustice and to realize freedom, Jürgen Habermas has emerged over the last few decades, worldwide but especially in Europe, as a leading theorist and critic of the social forms of modernity, including the institutions of liberal democracy. By the mid-1990s a substantial conversation had developed between Rawls (and Rawlsians) and Habermas (and Habermasians). Notwithstanding the tendency of those engaged in this conversation to emphasize points of difference, Kenneth Baynes (Chapter 28) argues that Rawls and Habermas are much closer to one another in their views than either seems fully to appreciate.

Rawls drew from a variety of disciplines over the course of his life's work: sociology, economics, formal decision theory, the history of moral and political philosophy, and so on. In his earlier work (leading up to and including *TJ*) Rawls was especially interested in drawing on the work of and addressing himself to twentieth-century economists. Daniel Little (Chapter 29) examines Rawls's relationship to the field of economics. Of course, Rawls's interest in and debts to the greats of political economy extend far back into history and are just a piece of his interest in and debts to the greats of moral and political philosophy (of which political economy historically has been a part) more generally. The final two essays in this volume take up Rawls's understanding of and engagement with the history of moral and political philoso-phy. S.A. Lloyd (Chapter 30) argues that Rawls provides a highly attractive model for how to engage with the history of political philosophy. Without dissenting from Lloyd's central point, Paul Guyer (Chapter 31) argues that Rawls nevertheless missed some key opportunities in his conversation with the history of moral philosophy. For example, Rawls missed opportuni-ties to explore the complex relationship between substantive deontological commitments and a more basic justificatory teleology, a point of common ground, on Guyer's view, between Rawls, Kant, and Adam Smith, the latter largely and unhappily neglected by Rawls.

Obviously, other ways of grouping the chapters would have been possible. Some chapters focus primarily on internal developments in or interpretations of Rawls's work, while others develop connections to and contrasts with the work of others. Some stick closely to textual interpretations while others are more imaginative, taking Rawls as inspiration. Some defend Rawls while others are more critical. But all succeed in moving the discussion forward. We are grateful to our contributors for their participation in this project. We also would like to thank Ann Bone for her truly outstanding work as copy editor.

## Note

The works by Rawls listed below are those noted in this introduction. Each chapter lists the works by Rawls it cites, together with their abbreviations.

## Works by Rawls, with Abbreviations

*A Brief Inquiry into the Meaning of Sin and Faith, with "On My Religion"* (BI), ed. Thomas Nagel. Cambridge, MA: Harvard University Press, 2009.

*The Law of Peoples, with "The Idea of Public Reason Revisited"* (LP). Cambridge, MA: Harvard University Press, 1999.

*Lectures on the History of Moral Philosophy* (LHMP), ed. Barbara Herman. Cambridge, MA: Harvard University Press, 2000.

*Lectures on the History of Political Philosophy* (LHPP), ed. Samuel Freeman. Cambridge, MA: Harvard University Press, 2007.

*Political Liberalism* (PL), expanded edn. New York: Columbia University Press, 2005.

*A Theory of Justice* (TJ), rev. edn. Cambridge, MA: Harvard University Press, 1999.

## Other Reference

Freeman, Samuel (2007) *Rawls*. London: Routledge.

# Part I

# Ambitions

# 1

# From Philosophical Theology to Democratic Theory

## Early Postcards from an Intellectual Journey

### DAVID A. REIDY

*It is easy to kill a subject by demanding too much of it early on; a subject needs to be guided by big intuitive ideas, particularly at the start. . . . It is a delusion to think that rigorous analysis in a small area unguided by a large idea is of much value. One does not understand even a small thing in this way.*
John Rawls, 1964, to students in his moral philosophy course

## 1. Introduction

Rawls published *A Theory of Justice* in 1971, though, as he noted in the "Preface," he had been circulating and teaching from earlier drafts through much of the 1960s. But *TJ* does not really originate in the 1960s. Its roots run at least to the late 1940s and 1950s, a period covering Rawls's years as a graduate student and then lecturer at Princeton, his year (1952–1953) as a visiting fellow at Oxford during which he first saw clearly the project that would occupy him for some 50 years, and his time as a faculty member at Cornell. Indeed, in some respects, its roots run to the late 1930s and early 1940s, the time of Rawls's undergraduate study at Princeton and his work on his now published undergraduate thesis (*BI*). While it was not until the mid-1960s that Rawls had in hand all the essential elements of the "painting" he sought to share in *TJ* and to complete in later works, he was possessed of, and by, the core of the "vision" by the mid to late 1950s.[1] And he was in important ways oriented toward it even earlier than that. In several respects, then, *TJ* is an early mid-century book.

This is a fact naturally overlooked by readers. *A Theory of Justice* did not reach a general and wide philosophical audience until the 1970s, a time very different philosophically, politically and culturally from that of its origin. While *TJ* clearly addresses some concerns central to that time, for example, civil disobedience and conscientious objection, in general it is not

*A Companion to Rawls*, First Edition. Edited by Jon Mandle and David A. Reidy.

profitably read primarily against the concerns, expectations and cultural landscape of the 1970s or even the latter 1960s.

In the early mid-century many thoughtful Americans were anxious about the viability of the sort of inclusive, mass democracy that seemed to be taking root. Further, many American liberals, troubled by the ideologically motivated disasters of World War II and the Soviet system, were both eager to distance themselves from political self-understandings grounded in or animated by big ideas and inclined favorably toward more modest political self-understandings of liberal democracy as either a regulated or civilized struggle among competing interest groups or a mechanism for the rational aggregation of private preferences with an eye toward efficiency (see, e.g., Schumpeter 1942; Downs 1957).

Rawls too was anxious about the viability of the sort of inclusive mass democracy that seemed to be taking root. He worried that the country lacked the resources necessary to sustain the requisite public trust among citizens. And Rawls too was deeply influenced by the ideologically driven disasters of World War II and the Soviet system. But he worried that the modest political self-understandings on offer to Americans were not only insufficient to sustain the requisite public trust among them but also in an enduring way to draw their stable allegiance as free equals. He further worried that if internalized and effectively regulative, the political self-understandings on offer would have a corrosive effect on persons, hindering rather than helping them to realize themselves as persons in community. He sought for a polity of free and equal citizens a political self-understanding animated by a big intuitive idea capable of underwriting genuine public trust among them, reliably drawing their enduring allegiance and contributing to their self-realization as persons in community. His goal was a big intuitive idea with universal reach. *A Theory of Justice* is a giant first step toward expressing this idea.

There are aspects of this idea that account, I think, for some of its gravitational force, as it were – its capacity to draw persons into its gravitational field – that can be traced back to Rawls's very early work as an undergraduate in philosophical theology. And there are also aspects that can be traced back to his early work as a graduate student in moral philosophy. In this essay, I take up Rawls's journey from philosophical theology through moral philosophy to democratic theory and political philosophy and pause at, to reflect on, a few significant points early in the journey. My aim is to give a sense – I can offer here no more than what amounts to postcards – of some of Rawls's important early concerns and commitments that structure or at least cast significant shadows over his later work in political philosophy, *A Theory of Justice* and subsequent works.

I do not mean to suggest that Rawls's journey to *TJ* is marked by or best understood in terms of only the concerns and commitments I discuss. There are others. For example, Wittgenstein was a very important influence on Rawls for many decades – Rawls acknowledges this in several letters. I do not discuss this influence here. Nor do I mean to deny important discontinuities in the development of Rawls's thought over time. His movement in the 1950s away from both theism and from a kind of Millian utilitarianism merit mention here, as does his introduction in the 1980s of the family of ideas associated with political liberalism, though in this latter case I think there is less discontinuity than is often alleged. I mean only to suggest that *A Theory of Justice* is a more rewarding read if one attends to the aspects of Rawls's big intuitive idea that are set out here and if one keeps in mind their origins in his early-mid-twentieth century thinking.

## 2. The Philosophical Theology of the Undergraduate Thesis

As is now well-known, Rawls's Princeton undergraduate philosophy thesis, "A Brief Inquiry into the Meaning of Sin and Faith: An Interpretation Based on the Concept of Community," sits at the intersection of philosophical theology and theological ethics.[2] It argues against familiar understandings of sin and faith rooted in a conception of God as our highest good and so the proper and ultimate object of our rational desire. It argues in favor of understandings of sin and faith rooted in a conception of God as the complete, self-sufficient and eternal instantiation of personality and community, neither of which can exist without the other, as well as in our capacities for participation in personality and community, dependent for their realization on the unconditional grace of God though they may be. But it is not primarily this theological content to which I wish to draw attention here, though I do want to draw attention to Rawls's conception of personality and community. Mainly it is the methodological and meta-theological context within which Rawls works out his view that I think merits notice.

Rawls's view draws on and synthesizes aspects of two traditions in philosophical theology and theological ethics with wide currency in the early twentieth century. The first is biblical historicism. The second is the neo-orthodoxy sometimes associated with what came to be known as "theology of crisis." Biblical historicism arises in the late eighteenth and early nineteenth centuries in response to the fact that it was increasingly difficult to deny that the Bible was written by many people over an extended period of time in various contexts. Informed by these facts, those inquiring into the "meaning" of the Bible found it increasingly difficult to represent it as the articulation of a single, focal revelation that took place at one time and through one person. Biblical historicism responds to this difficulty by taking the Bible as the record of Christian experience over time and seeking through reasoned analysis of that experience, as lived in historical context, a universal truth underlying and unifying it over time and so expressing the "meaning" of the Bible or the enduring universal truth of Christianity. The Hegelian idea that Christianity expresses finally and completely the universal rational meaning of moral and religious experience is kin to nineteenth-century biblical historicism.

Neo-orthodoxy or "theology of crisis" emerges as a reaction both from within and against biblical historicism in the early twentieth century, and in particular after World War I. Skeptical of biblical historicism's ability reliably to deliver through its methods the enduring universal truth of Christianity and cognizant of the tremendous harm humans are capable of if not guided by that truth, the proponents of neo-orthodoxy put the emphasis back on the authority of the Bible as the record of a unique – one time, one person – revelation, the content of which was not accessible by human reason alone. Interestingly, some associated with neo-orthodoxy proposed an account of the content of this revelation that Rawls ultimately found quite congenial, namely that God is the complete, self-sufficient and enduring realization of personality and community, each of which requires the other; that all personal relations begin with an opening by one person to another, an invitation to community; that Christ is that invitation to communion with God; and that the invitation and our capacity to overcome pride and accept it are both functions of God's grace.

In his undergraduate thesis, Rawls appropriates this neo-orthodox account of the content of the revelation given in the Bible and argues, within a biblical historicist framework, that it best accounts for – as a kind of deep explanation of – not only Christian experience, including his own, but also the experiences of non-Christians. He pays special attention to the experiences of conversion through grace and to the forms of aloneness and despair experienced, and capacities for harm and evil exhibited, by those who have not converted. Conversion here refers to the process, itself a gift of grace, of being saved from the deep tendency in our nature toward prideful refusal of personal relations and community, of being brought to a genuine openness and orientation to both with others, including with God. Here conversion involves no affirmation of doctrinal theological content or dogma but rather a reorientation of one's moral psychology and self-understanding and so one's experience of living with others in the world. Reason and linguistic communication more generally serve as necessary media or instruments of personal relations and community, but they do not initiate or demand either. The call to personal relations and community originates elsewhere.

There are several things to notice here. One is the fact that Rawls seeks the meaning of Christianity, of sin and faith, in the best explanation – not causal explanation, but rational explanation – of Christian experience, indeed of human experience generally. Undoubtedly, he takes the Bible as an authoritative expression or record of Christian (as well as Hebrew and other) experience. But it is the experience, not the biblical text per se, that constitutes the data to be understood. And the experience is to be understood not in the space of causes, as it were, but in the space of a rational, in the sense of intelligible to a common or shared reason, moral psychology. Indeed, though Rawls does not say so explicitly, it is not unreasonable to suppose that he understood the articulation of such a rational explanation as itself a practical contribution to the realization of the universal Christian community. Without it, we cannot fully understand ourselves and so cannot with full awareness or understanding participate in communion with one another and with God.

Another thing to notice here is that notwithstanding the exclamation point that the early stages of World War II placed behind the "crisis" to which the neo-orthodox "theology of crisis" turn to the revealed authority of scripture was a response, Rawls is not drawn in his undergraduate thesis to this aspect of neo-orthodoxy. He makes no appeal to what he will a decade later in his PhD dissertation refer to as "exalted authorities." The Bible is authoritative, but it is so as a record of a certain pattern of human experience. And it is this pattern of experience that must be rendered intelligible and properly understood in the space of reasons. If there is any appeal to authority here, it is the authority of our own self-recognition and self-understanding. Effectively Rawls asks us in his undergraduate thesis whether, having heard his explanation of the experiences of Christians and others and put it side by side with the story he attributes to Augustine and Aquinas, we do not in fact more fully and completely recognize and understand ourselves in and through his story than its alternative. There is no suggestion that this self-recognition and self-understanding by itself will or can bring about the experience of "conversion" at the center of Christian experience, an experience that is itself, on Rawls's account, a gift of grace. Nevertheless, it is essential to participating with full understanding in community with others and with God.

## 3. Ethics as Science

After returning from his service in World War II, Rawls began graduate study in philosophy at Princeton. In 1946, as a first year graduate student, he wrote "A Brief Inquiry into the

Nature and Function of Ethical Theory." He begins by asking what it is that moral philosophers do. He argues that the way to answer the question is not to survey, but to observe moral philosophers. If we observe them, we find that they are engaged in a science of moral judgment. They seek to explain competent moral judgments in a way that would enable us reliably to predict them. They do not seek the meaning of moral terms, in the sense of identifying synonyms which might be substituted for them in any statement in which they appear without altering its truth value. Nor do they seek to uncover what one intends to assert or has in one's mind when one makes a moral judgment. Nor, further, do they seek to identify the logically basic objects and relations ingredient in the propositions expressed by moral judgments, or to select among rival logical or formal notations we might use in talking about those objects and relations. In short, Rawls concludes, moral philosophers do none of the things that had come to be associated mid-century with the tradition of analytic philosophy associated with Bertrand Russell, G.E. Moore and the early Wittgenstein. Instead, what moral philosophers do is to construct theoretical models to explain and predict familiar, everyday, noncontroversially competent moral judgments. Rawls refers to this work as "explication" and "ethics as science."

Of course, Rawls notes, this is work one might think more profitably done by psychologists, sociologists or anthropologists (or, today, by socio-biologists or neurologists). But moral philosophers do not approach moral judgments as mere events, mental or otherwise, to be explained and predicted within the natural causal order. Rather, they approach them as, well, *moral judgments* – as the publicly visible manifestation of the exercise or activity of practical reason by and among persons. Accordingly, Rawls maintains, the kinds of models of interest to the moral philosopher are something like "reasoning machines" – systems of definitions and axioms such that when fed determinate input regarding the sorts of familiar moral choices with respect to which we can noncontroversially distinguish competent from incompetent judgments, they yield theorems, or moral principles, that provide sufficient reasons for, and thereby render intelligible to us, all and only the competent judgments. These "reasoning machines" are not meant to represent or to be incorporated necessarily into any actual psychological process, what actually goes on in the mind of a person making a moral judgment. Rawls notes that very often we make competent moral judgments without, or without any awareness of, any deliberative thought process at all. We simply hear or express the "voice of conscience." This the moral philosopher regards as, in itself, no defect in need of correction. Instead, the moral philosopher aims to *represent* the phenomenon of competent moral judgment as a public or visible manifestation of the activity or exercise of practical reason. The moral philosopher offers us a way of understanding ourselves, of making ourselves intelligible to one another, as persons, as rational social beings with a capacity for moral judgment. He will later in his dissertation, but does not yet in this 1946 paper, take up the contribution such a self-understanding or representation makes, when not only shared but internalized by a group of persons, to the realization of personal relations in community, relations best characterized in terms of mutual justification.

Rawls does not claim that our ability to make or to identify familiar, everyday, noncontroversially competent moral judgments depends on our successfully explicating those judgments through appeal to a "reasoning machine" worked up within ethics as science. He gestures, already in 1946, to the linguistic analogy, noting that our ability to utter and identify grammatically sound sentences seems not to depend at all on our ability to represent that ability in terms of a system of grammar worked up within linguistics as science. What is at stake in ethics as science is not our ability to make or even to identify familiar, everyday, noncontroversially competent moral judgments, but rather the nature, content and implications of our self-representation and self-understanding as beings exercising this ability.

To the extent that Rawls locates ethics as science in relation to the analytic tradition associated with Russell, Moore and the early Wittgenstein, he does so by reference to Frege's work in deductive logic, which Rawls regarded as a scientific explication, within the space of reasons rather than causes, of familiar, everyday, noncontroversially competent judgments regarding valid inference. Frege successfully represented our ability to make and identify valid inferences in terms of a "reasoning machine" capable of explaining and reliably predicting our judgments regarding valid inference. In so doing, he put us in a position to understand our noncontroversially competent judgments regarding valid inference as the public or observable manifestation of the activity or exercise of our capacity for theoretical reason. Rawls took his task to be doing for noncontroversially competent moral judgments what Frege did for noncontroversially competent judgments regarding valid inference.

Rawls identifies four main activities or exercises of reason, two theoretical and two practical. There is for each a "science" within the space of reasons that is properly pursued by philosophers as persons who seek to understand themselves as rational and social animals capable of knowledge and morality. Theoretical reason expresses itself not only in the form of noncontroversially competent judgments regarding valid inference, but also in the form of noncontroversially competent judgments regarding theory confirmation. Frege developed a "science" of the former: deductive logic; J.S. Mill advanced a "science" of the latter: inductive logic. Practical reason expresses itself not only in the form of noncontroversially competent judgments regarding one's ends and the means to them, what Rawls would later call "the rational," but also in the form of noncontroversially competent judgments regarding one's relation as a person with other persons in social life, or what he would later call "the reasonable." The philosophical "science" of the former is the theory of rational choice, understood to include axiology. The philosophical "science" of the latter Rawls sought to advance through ethics as science.

Rawls characterizes his concern with and ambition for ethics as science as fully scientific in the sense associated with the Vienna Circle. That ethics as science unfolds within the space of reasons rather than causes is irrelevant to its status as science. What is crucial, Rawls insists, is that it must avoid all theoretical claims that can be neither confirmed nor refuted by publicly observable evidence, in particular the evidence constituted by familiar, everyday, noncontroversially competent moral judgments. If there is to be a sound moral science, it must proceed in this fashion. Its aims are descriptive, explanatory and predictive, rather than normative or prescriptive. Or, better, a sound moral science is normative only in the non-prescriptive sense of providing a clear and intelligible rational model or representation of noncontroversially competent moral judgments as a publicly observable phenomenon. That is, it provides us with a predictively reliable way of representing – a criterial understanding of – the distinction between noncontroversially competent moral judgments and noncontroversially incompetent moral judgments.

Rawls insists that we ought to draw no metaphysical conclusions from any success of ethics as science. From the fact that an intelligible reasoning machine generates theorems that make it possible reliably to predict all and only noncontroversially competent moral judgments, no metaphysical conclusions follow. There is no reason to think that the reasoning machine or the theorems it generates tells us anything about what ultimately or "really" makes such judgments noncontroversially competent, about the "essence" of morality or of moral rightness, about the so-called "right-making" properties of the world. Rawls dismisses inquiries into these matters as stemming from little more than the traditional "quasi-religious" character of moral language and judgment.

On the other hand, if ethics as science succeeds, then, as Rawls notes, emotivist and other noncognitivist orientations toward moral judgment thought to follow from a generally scientific philosophical orientation would be destroyed from within. So while Rawls insists there are no positive metaphysical conclusions to be drawn from the success of ethics as science, there are some negative metaphysical conclusions to be drawn. Certain possibilities are preserved. Others are ruled out. One of Rawls's earliest impulses, then, would appear to be to try to save a properly scientific philosophical orientation from various excesses to which it seemed all too easily tempted.

The shadow of the Vienna Circle and scientific philosophy more generally falls over Rawls's 1946 "Brief Inquiry" paper in another respect. Rawls takes the view that the "meaning" of any moral term is best understood as given by the explication – the "reasoning machine" and the theorems or moral principles it generates – that most reliably predicts as intelligible and justifiable all and only the noncontroversially competent moral judgments in which it figures. That is, the "meaning" of a moral term is given by the "scientific theory" – responsive only to public, observable evidence, albeit worked out in the space of reasons – that successfully accounts for the noncontroversially competent moral judgments in which it appears. It is not given by synonyms that might be substituted for it within any statement in which it appears without any change to that statement's truth value. Such inquiries into "synonymy meaning" provide no independent basis for predicting noncontroversially competent moral judgments and thus no independent basis for understanding the actual meaning of the moral terms that occur within them. The sense in which such inquiries into "synonymy meaning" shed light on the actual meaning of moral terms is shallow and of no more than linguistic interest. Nor is the actual meaning of moral terms given by some private mental content thought to be present to the mind when moral terms are competently used. The pursuit of meaning as private mental content is, Rawls insists, a hopeless pursuit.[3]

As a model for his ethics as science, Rawls invoked Hans Kelsen's "pure theory of law." Kelsen, the Austrian legal positivist, aimed at a "legal science" capable of laying out, within the space of reasons, the norms governing valid law and competent legal judgment, without moralistic assumptions or tendencies and without naturalistically reducing either phenomenon to only facts and causes. Kelsen held that as a normative social practice, the law could not be fully understood solely in terms of facts and causes, and thus could not be fully understood solely within or through the social sciences. As a normative social practice, it had to be understood also within the space of reasons, in terms of norms or principles of competent (legally valid) judgment. But to understand it within the space of reasons, one had to approach it scientifically and without moralistic assumptions or aspirations. Legal philosophy, for Kelsen, was just another name for the scientific study of law as a normative social phenomenon within the space of reasons (see Kelsen 1978 [1934]).

Rawls conceived of moral philosophy on analogous terms. Just as a "pure" theory of law would identify the most basic norms or reasons in terms of which we might, within any particular legal system, render intelligible and reliably predict noncontroversially competent legal judgments, so too a "pure" theory of ethics would identify the most basic norms or reasons in terms of which we might render intelligible and reliably predict noncontroversially competent moral judgments. Just as what makes a legal judgment noncontroversially competent is that it is a judgment universally shared or nearly so among those engaged in the practice of law and is arrived at and remains stable under favorable background conditions (a stable legal system, the absence of bribes, etc.), so too what makes a moral judgment noncontroversially competent is that it is a judgment universally shared or nearly so among those engaged in the practice of morality and is arrived at and remains stable under favorable background conditions (a free society, without disfiguring social forces, within which material and other conditions essential to moral development are secure, etc.). The task of moral philosophy is to represent rationally the competent moral judgments free and intelligent persons naturally make, not to establish for them the competency of their moral judgments.

Rawls concluded his 1946 paper by suggesting in outline an ethical theory that seemed to him promising, at least "if ethics is to be done as a science." He called it "imperative utilitarianism." The theory purports to cover only noncontroversially competent judgments of right, and then only at the level of individual actions. It represents such judgments as the result of reasoning from principles established by a reasoning machine that marks as required or forbidden action types that persons are not likely to perform or refrain from performing without significant social incentives, and with respect to which, at least in their statistically most common occurrences, social utility strongly depends on their being, respectively, performed or not performed. Of course, as Rawls acknowledges, one must feed such a reasoning machine a great deal of information provided by the natural and social sciences in order to have any chance of generating principles that would provide sufficient reasons to support noncontroversially competent moral judgments of right in this domain. The machine must be fed information about individuals' beliefs, about the statistical patterns of their behavior (with and without incentives), about the utility produced by various action types and the costs associated with making instrumental use of morality as a social incentive to induce or deter such action types, and so on. And this information will be vast and vary from society to society. But, Rawls maintains, at least in 1946, this is no defect.[4] Indeed, it is a merit insofar as the theory may be applied to any society or population, no matter what the facts about its members' conduct, utility profiles, and so on. The only question is whether once fed the relevant information the reasoning machine generates principles that make it possible reliably to predict noncontroversially competent moral judgments of right for the relevant population. If it does so across all societies or populations, then it gives us the "meaning" of right, simply *qua* right, by giving us a "scientific" (answering to public observable evidence only) theory of competent moral judgments for any society.[5]

The largely theoretical, or "scientific," orientation and concerns of Rawls's 1946 paper is one of its striking features. The paper evidences no significant or sustained interest in ethical theory as a means of improving or correcting moral judgments or of perfecting moral capacities or dispositions more generally. And while it aims at the production, via a "reasoning machine," of moral principles capable of justifying – that is, functioning as intelligible public reasons for – competent moral judgments, and so of representing competent moral judgments as rational and cognitive, it does not address the question of the justification of the principles themselves or the "reasoning machine" from which they are derived. Nor does it take up the quality of the relations realized among persons who affirm one and the same scientific representation of their capacity for competent moral judgment. These matters will come to occupy Rawls's attention within just a few years in his PhD dissertation.

16

Perhaps anxious about the largely theoretical or "scientific" orientation of the paper, Rawls notes in its final pages that, as with all theoretical scientific inquiries, so too with ethics as science: "men of affairs" will want to know its "cash value." He cites two benefits. The first arises in response to the fact that we sometimes find ourselves faced with situations so novel that we have no clear sense of what would count as a competent moral judgment – the voices of both individual conscience and the community's moral tradition are silent. In these cases, we may find value in an appeal to the principles of an ethical theory otherwise reliable as a predictor of noncontroversially competent moral judgments, for they may speak where individual conscience and community standards are silent. They may help at least to orient deliberation and discussion.

The second arises in response to the fact that people sometimes disagree in their moral judgments. When they do, it does not follow necessarily that anyone is guilty of a less than competent exercise of her moral capacities or that anyone is doing something that may not be represented as rational and cognitive. Of course, these are nevertheless possibilities. Sometimes one or both parties to a moral disagreement venture an incompetent moral judgment, one that could not be represented as rational or cognitive. Moral disagreements often arise, on one or both sides, from naked class ambition, group bias, or simple old-fashioned selfishness swamping the competent exercise of moral capacities. But there is no reason to suppose that they may not sometimes arise reasonably for other reasons. So there are reasonable moral disagreements and what we might call simple moral disagreements. But it is not always easy to distinguish the former from the latter. Yet we have compelling reasons to want to be able reliably and publicly to do so. For those driven by naked class ambition, group bias, or old-fashioned selfishness to incompetent moral judgments and so to simple moral disagreements with others will often, perhaps typically, take great pains to pretend at being reasonable. Without the ability to distinguish reliably and publicly between reasonable and simple disagreements, a community is likely, then, to misunderstand the content of its own established community standards or respected voices of conscience. An ethical theory, properly worked up within ethics as science, ought, Rawls maintains, to "enable us to say to the disputants . . . what their moral judgments really are" and "to expose moral pretense . . . for what it really is, naked class ambition, group bias, or selfishness."

Rawls does not think of the "cash value" of ethics as science in terms of replacing established community standards or respected voices of conscience as a source of moral guidance. Nor does he think of it in terms of drawing moral agreement out of the soil of genuine or reasonable moral disagreement. Morally decent people sometimes reasonably disagree. Not all moral disagreements are really disagreements rooted in naked class ambition, group bias, or selfishness merely pretending to be genuine or reasonable disagreement. Genuine or reasonable disagreements are, it seems, problems for which ethics as science is not the solution, except insofar as ethics as science contributes to our ability to distinguish them from unreasonable disagreements that merely appear, or are unreasonably made to appear, to be reasonable.

To illustrate his claim regarding the "cash value" of ethics as science, Rawls cites the postwar conflict, already significant in 1946, over the civil rights of African-Americans. A sound ethical theory, he suggests, would enable us publicly to expose this dispute for what it really is: an unreasonable disagreement arising out of the unreasonable assertion of naked class-ambition or group-bias dressed up to have the mere appearance of competent moral judgment. Those opposed to recognizing the civil rights of African-Americans, often occupying positions of power and commanding social respect, may pretend to be exercising their moral capacities. They may use moral language, talk in cool tones, and even invoke what may seem to be moral principles. But their pretense will not survive an encounter with the principles of a sound ethical theory. And it must be exposed for what it is if the community is to understand and to have confidence its own established standards and respected voices of conscience.

Rawls is confident in 1946 that a successful explication (along the lines of his favored "imperative utilitarianism") of the noncontroversially competent moral judgment of free and intelligent men and women living in more or less favorable social conditions will yield principles capable of supporting only the judgment that African-Americans must be granted full and equal civil rights. Contrary judgments may be encouraged by rhetoric, propaganda, and emotive appeals and may be voiced in a moral idiom or key. But they will not be vindicable, from the point of view of ethics as science, as competent exercises of our moral capacity understood as a rational cognitive capacity. If they pretend to this status, they are counterfeit. As a "reasonable" moral disagreement, the disagreement over the civil rights of African-Americans is counterfeit. Herein ethics as science shows its "cash value."

## 4. From Ethics as Science to Moral Philosophy

Rawls first moves beyond ethics as science to take up the question of the justification of the moral principles it establishes and the reasoning machine it puts to use in a late 1940s paper titled "Ethical Rationalism." But it is not until the 1950 dissertation that the move is largely completed and given more or less full expression. There he first indicates an interest in not only the representational capacity but also the regulative and motivational capacity, as part of an internalized self-understanding, of the moral principles and reasoning machine given by ethics as science. I focus here on the dissertation.

In his 1950 dissertation, "A Study in the Grounds of Ethical Knowledge: Considered with Reference to Judgments of the Moral Worth of Character," Rawls builds on the earlier papers discussed above and ventures a more thoroughly systematic treatment of the rationality of our moral judgments and capacities. He sets out an approach to moral philosophy which he then applies, by way of illustration, to judgments regarding the moral worth of character. He expresses his intention to extend the approach taken, in due course, to judgments regarding ends or goods (questions of value) and to judgments regarding right actions. He pays no attention to judgments regarding institutions or practices. Indeed, he seems to assume at this point that a moral theory is complete so long as it ranges over judgments of character, value and right action.[6]

Rawls distinguishes between two tasks essential to moral philosophy. The first is to explicate noncontroversially competent moral judgments in terms of general moral principles given by an intelligible reasoning machine. This is the now familiar task of ethics as science. Rawls acknowledges in his dissertation that ethics as science may yield more than one candidate explication of noncontroversially competent moral judgments. And so moral philosophy must move beyond ethics as science to include the systematic development and comparison of different candidate explications of noncontroversially competent moral judgments. This work Rawls dubs "ethical theory" or "moral theory." Ethical theory or moral theory starts with but takes us beyond ethics as science by helping us to refine and deepen our understanding of plausible candidate explications. Plausible candidate explications are worked up more fully into "moral conceptions." The aim of ethical theory or moral theory, however, is not simply to work up a more complete understanding of plausible candidate explications. It is also to put clearly into view all the features of rival moral conceptions so that their respective capacities to draw the allegiance of free and intelligent persons under favorable conditions may be fully tested. This allegiance, freely given, and manifested by way of an enduring and effective regulative self-understanding, is what justifies a moral conception.

It is not the allegiance of moral philosophers that is crucial, though it counts. Rather, it is the allegiance of free and intelligent persons capable of competent moral judgment. And this allegiance is claimed only as the final test of whether a moral conception is justified. There is no further metaphysical claim regarding the ground of justification. Moral philosophy inquires into the justification of competing moral conceptions by inquiring into their capacities to draw the relevant allegiance under the appropriate conditions and so to underwrite among persons a shared understanding and experience of their moral relations as mutually intelligible and defensible within the space of reasons. This is its second main task. Explication, of course, is the first.

Moral philosophy emerges, then, as the exercise of practical reason aimed at producing a moral conception capable over time and in light of the empirical facts of human psychology of winning the enduring allegiance of free and intelligent persons and so underwriting for them a certain kind of experience and self-understanding of, and purposeful attention to, their relations with one another. While both ethics as science (explication) and moral theory (systematic comparison of rival moral conceptions) draw on theoretical reason,[7] both are ultimately expressions of and in service of practical reason, which "seeks reasonable means to reasonable ends."[8] Here the reasonable end is a particular kind of experience and self-understanding of, and practical success with, relations among persons. While this end is a reasonable end, there is no further defense of it offered. It is simply available to practical reason as a reasonable end to be pursued by reasonable means. Moral philosophy is the exercise of practical reason in search of the reasonable means.

The foregoing helps to explain Rawls's often noticed reluctance to characterize moral principles as true or false. Truth is not the primary currency of practical reason. Practical reason aims at reasonable means to reasonable ends. Sound moral principles are reasonable means to a reasonable end. Insofar as they do justificatory work, playing a role in the justification of determinate moral judgments, they do so, in the end, not because they are "true," but because they are "reasonable" or because they belong to a "reasonable" moral conception. Of course, it does not follow that there is no sensible point of view from which moral principles or even the "reasoning machine" from which they are generated might properly be regarded as "true" or "false." Nor does it follow that there is no sensible point of view from which determinate moral judgments (justified by reference to reasonable moral principles) might properly be regarded as true or false. Truth may be the language spoken by the voice of (morally competent) conscience. Rawls takes no position on these matters one way or another. His point is simply that as reasonable means to the reasonable end of rendering mutually intelligible and acceptable the relations given or established by our noncontroversially competent moral judgments, moral principles are, on his view, reasonable rather than true. Whether they or the determinate moral judgments they justify are true also, and what it would mean for them to be so, is a question he finds himself disinclined to pursue, apparently failing to see that anything of import hangs in the balance.

With respect to explication, Rawls devotes considerable attention in his dissertation to determining the data to be explicated, noncontroversially competent moral judgments, by ethics as science. He is especially keen to avoid begging any questions. Judgments count as noncontroversially competent if and only if they are the spontaneous, and stable upon reflection, judgments of free and intelligent men or women regarding familiar or standard sorts of cases and made under favorable conditions (not the result of obvious bias, or manipulation, or propaganda; with access to and understanding of relevant information, etc.). So-called moral intuitions generated in response to wild thought experiments far removed from the sorts of cases and circumstances to which human beings have been regularly exposed over successive generations are not included in the data to be explicated. The data to be explicated is, essentially, the public observable manifestation of our moral sentiments as stable, enduring aspects of our nature developed and expressed under favorable conditions.

That there is data of this sort to be explicated by ethics as science is something that we discover. There is no a priori reason to suppose that free and intelligent persons in favorable conditions will converge in their moral judgments to any particular degree. If there is no convergence or no significant convergence, then ethics as science cannot get off the ground and moral philosophy would be stymied before it could get started. But, Rawls insists, there is significant convergence.

But it ought not be overestimated. Rawls explicitly excludes many moral judgments from the data to be explicated by ethics as science. No matter how widespread or confidently held, moral judgments arrived at within contexts characterized by widespread social manipulation, exposure to propaganda, lack of access to or refusals to consider relevant information, relations of subordination or excessive dependency, or similar circumstances, do not constitute good evidence of the shape of the moral sentiments of free and intelligent persons living under favorable conditions. And so Rawls excludes them from the data to be explicated, even if they are widely believed by those holding or making them to be noncontroversially competent. To be sure, he allows that in the end these judgments might be validated as competent moral judgments by the principles given in a successful explication arrived at through ethics as science. But ethics as science cannot start with these judgments, at least not if it aims to show that our moral nature is part of our rational nature freely expressed.

Rawls concedes that this methodological constraint may substantially diminish the data set to work from within ethics as science. The moral theorist would seem to be left with only the noncontroversially competent moral judgments of free and intelligent persons within more or less developed and reasonably just liberal democracies. But given what we know of human history, Rawls notes, we should hardly be surprised to find that we have a limited supply of evidence regarding the exercise under favorable conditions of moral capacities by, or the shape of the sentiments of, free and intelligent persons as such.

This is an important point. Moral philosophy cannot proceed, on his own account, without adequate data. To be adequate, this data must arise against certain background social conditions. These conditions include something like a reasonably just and stable constitutional liberal democracy within which free and intelligent men and women are able to give full and direct expression to their moral sentiments free of distortion by various sorts of familiar material, psychological and social forces. But then moral philosophy depends on our ability to establish, scientifically, as it were, by reference to observable evidence, the existence of these background conditions. Establishing the existence of these conditions scientifically is, like establishing the fact that our moral nature is part of our rational nature, not something that unfolds within the space of facts, events and causes. It unfolds within the space of institutions, actions and reasons. But it is scientific nonetheless, at least insofar as it answers only to publicly observable evidence. In any event, unless and until we can assure one another, publicly and by reference to publicly observable evidence, that we (or some population) in fact live under the sorts of background conditions that must be present if moral philosophy is to have the sort of data necessary to pursue ethics as science, moral philosophy is stalled in the water. There is, then, a methodological priority to political philosophy over moral philosophy. In 1950, Rawls seems to assume that liberal democracy instantiates favorable background conditions and that contemporary liberal democracies largely are what they appear to be and that we can know this scientifically, as it were, by reference to observable evidence and shared public criteria. One way to read his later work, explored below, is as an attempt to make good on these assumptions.

After devoting roughly the first half of his dissertation to the task of explication and "ethics as science" with respect to judgments regarding the moral worth of character, Rawls turns in the second half to moral philosophy's second basic concern, the issue of justification. He argues that justification ultimately terminates in what he calls "intuitive justification." By "intuitive" he does not mean to refer to the exercise of some special intellectual faculty capable of noninferentially ascertaining true moral principles. Rather he means to refer only to the point at which there is no further point to inquiring after a justification. In moral philosophy, this point is reached when free and intelligent men and women in favorable conditions find themselves not only converging in their noncontroversially competent moral judgments in this or that domain, but also drawn to one and the same explication of that domain and to internalizing it as part of their regulative self-understandings and public self-representations. An explication or moral conception so embraced and internalized is sufficient to secure and maintain mutually intelligible and acceptable, that is, justified, relations among persons, at least within its domain. Once it is in hand, there is no further point to inquiries into moral justification. There is no test of whether the relations among persons are justified beyond whether by reference to the principles of a shared moral conception they prove to be mutually intelligible and acceptable to them as free and intelligent persons under favorable conditions.

Rawls recognizes in his dissertation that it is possible for free and intelligent persons, even under favorable conditions, to err in thinking that a particular moral judgment is noncontroversially competent. We are, individually and together, morally fallible. It is tempting in light of this to think that moral philosophy must fail, for it leaves us powerless to identify such errors. Indeed, it may convince us that we are justified in our erroneous moral beliefs. It is tempting to think that the only way to avoid this possibility is for moral philosophy to inquire into what "really" makes a moral judgment "true" or what "really" makes an action "right," to get beyond justification as Rawls presents it. It is this worry, Rawls suggests, that lies behind the conception of moral philosophy as aimed at the discovery and representation of a moral order fixed prior to and independent of any exercise of practical reason or moral judgment. This is a conception of moral philosophy we should resist, on Rawls's view, not because we have good reasons to believe that there is no such order, but rather because we cannot so easily free ourselves of the burden of our practical reason.

Rawls analogizes this situation to the Supreme Court. Free and intelligent persons under favorable conditions stand to moral judgment in the same relation as the Supreme Court stands to legal judgment. The test of whether a legal judgment is valid or competent is

21

whether the Court affirms it in light of the principles given by the best explication of other noncontroversially competent legal judgments. Of course, this doesn't mean that the Court's so affirming a legal judgment is what makes it valid or competent. Nor does it mean that the Court cannot err, either in its affirming a legal judgment on review or in the identification of the data – the other noncontroversially competent legal judgments the explication of which yields the principles it draws on when affirming a legal judgment on review. It is tempting, then, as in the case of moral judgment, to suppose that judges or legal philosophers ought to inquire into what "really" makes a legal judgment "true," to somehow get beyond or behind the Court's judgment as the test or criterion of legal validity or competence. But there would be no more to be gained in making this shift in the legal case than in the moral case. Irrespective of one's metaethical or metalegal commitments, there can be no higher or further *test* of whether a legal judgment is valid or competent beyond whether the Court exercising its own best judgment affirms it as such. And there can be no higher or further *test* of whether the Court's best judgment is good enough beyond the Court's own best judgment of the matter. And so on. This does not mean, of course, that the Court is the source of, or infallible in its exercise of, its own authority. It means only that, like practical reason itself, it is the final arbiter of its own authority. There is no further test, only repeated applications of the same final test. Referring to practical reason, Rawls suggests that here lies the deep truth of the saying that you "cannot derive an ought from an is." Practical reason is the final arbiter of its own authority.

Rawls does not restrict the point here about reason as the final arbiter of its own authority to the contexts of legal and moral judgments. He generalizes it to all judgments arising out of the exercise of reason, whether practical or theoretical. There is no higher or further standard of justification within science, for example, beyond what free and intelligent persons engaged in inductive theory confirmation (in the sciences) affirm and internalize (as a reasonable means to their reasonable ends) as an explication of the judgments in these areas they take to be noncontroversially competent. And there is no higher or further standard within logic beyond what free and intelligent persons engaged in deductive inference (in philosophy, mathematics, logic, etc.) affirm and internalize (as a reasonable means to their reasonable ends) as an explication of the judgments in these areas they take to be noncontroversially competent. In each case, reason answers only to itself. And importantly, even when the judgments under examination arise out of the exercise of theoretical reason, as in the cases of inductive and deductive logic, it is ultimately practical reason that has the final word. For the criteria of competent judgments in these cases will be given by an explication of noncontroversially competent judgments in the domain that free and intelligent persons working in that domain accept and internalize as a reasonable means to their reasonable end of mutual intelligibility and justification therein. Remarkably, Rawls held these views while still committed to a roughly Millian utilitarianism. The evidence of Kantian or Wittgensteinian influences is thin. Kant's *Metaphysics of Morals* and *Critique of Practical Reason* are included in the dissertation's bibliography but are not examined in detail in the text. Wittgenstein does not appear in the bibliography.

Here lies, I suggest, the root of Rawls's idea of reflective equilibrium. An explication of competent moral judgment that is effectively regulative within a person (because it draws her allegiance and so belongs to her internalized self-understanding) brings her particular judgments and more abstract theoretical beliefs in line. An explication widely shared by persons in this way brings them, at least with respect to the relevant particular judgments and more abstract theoretical beliefs, in line with one another. Persons so aligned, and knowing publicly that they are so aligned with one another this way achieve mutually intelligible and justifiable relations with one another as rational social beings. That is, they are justified, or aligned, to one another. Of course, persons make competent moral judgments across many domains – in particular, the domains over which the four exercises of reason, two theoretical and two practical, range. Persons possessed of a shared and effectively regulative explication of competent judgment across all these domains are fully justified, or aligned, to one another as rational social beings. They share as persons a fully intelligible and mutually acceptable or at least reasonable social world. Rawls would eventually characterize these relations in terms of wide, full, general reflective equilibrium. When this state is reached, further inquiry into justification lacks point or purpose. There is no further test available to us. And ultimately it is practical reason that gives and grades the test.

It is here, all the way back in Rawls's dissertation, that we find the roots also of his later constructivism. If complete justification consists in full, wide, general reflective equilibrium, then a, perhaps the most, reasonable way to proceed in working up a reasoning machine capable of explicating noncontroversially competent judgments across one or more domains will be to organize it so that its parts reflect key elements of a familiar normative self-understanding likely to draw the allegiance of free and intelligent persons under appropriate background conditions. For example, a reasoning machine that models a familiar normative self-understanding of democratic citizenship, taken as the basic political office or relationship among persons within a society, and that in turn generates principles capable of explicating (and extending the range of) noncontroversially competent political judgments, would presumably stand a good chance of drawing the allegiance of persons over time and so contributing to their achieving the sorts of relations contemplated by wide, full, general reflective equilibrium.

## 5. From Moral Philosophy to Democratic Theory

Rawls evidenced some interest in politics and political philosophy as early as his undergraduate thesis. There he is critical of the social contract tradition, taken in its contractarian rather than contractualist form, and insistent that the problem of politics is not the reconciliation of the individual and the social, for personality and community are mutually interdependent, but rather the identification and institutional management of the various forms of "sin" that threaten both personality and community. Ultimately, of course, in the undergraduate thesis Rawls takes the view that human beings are fundamentally corrupt and incapable of achieving and maintaining personality and community without God's grace. And politics and political philosophy presumably must accept this limitation. Rawls's later work aims at a more hopeful, a reasonably hopeful, view of what human beings are capable of, both morally and politically, on their own.

Rawls's interest in politics and political philosophy is evidenced again by his discussion of the "cash value" of "ethics as science" in his 1946 paper, written early in his graduate studies and discussed above. It is further evidenced in later papers written in graduate school and in his 1950 dissertation. Rawls begins his dissertation emphasizing the links between his inquiries in moral philosophy to the possibility and justification of democracy. What had in 1946 been simply a closing remark about the "cash value" of ethics as science had become by 1950 a kind of organizing and motivating principle for his work. Rawls notes that citizens and officials very often disagree in their basic political judgments. These disagreements appear often to be, at their root, moral disagreements, disagreements about the demands of justice or right on their interactions and on their institutions. In a democracy, citizens and officials resolve these disagreements by voting, by exercising the authority of their political office. Or at least they do so when there is a felt need for collective action and the disagreements stand in the way of their acting collectively. So much is obvious.

But under what conditions do they each and all have good reason to acquiesce in collective action determined by voting? Under what conditions, for example, would citizens in the late 1940s or early 1950s each and all have good reason to acquiesce in the outcome of a democratic process concerned to address the civil rights of African-Americans. This question was undoubtedly on Rawls's mind. Most generally, the matter must be one of reasonable rather than merely simple disagreement, to use the terminology I introduced earlier. Citizens generally have no standing reason, certainly no moral reason, to acquiesce to the outcome of a vote taken to resolve a simple disagreement, a disagreement to which one or both parties bring an unreasonable view, a view unintelligible (irrational or unreasonable) in light of the principles that explicate noncontroversially competent judgments in the relevant domain. If citizens generally have a moral reason to acquiesce to the outcome of democratic processes, it is because those processes are deployed to resolve their reasonable moral (and other) disagreements over matters requiring their collective action. But then they must have some shared criteria for distinguishing reasonable from simple moral disagreements. Here moral philosophy can contribute to democratic theory. Evidencing his interest in politics and political philosophy, Rawls intends his dissertation to make, among others, a contribution of this sort. Setting out the moral principles that underwrite competent moral judgment and so demarcate the boundary of reasonable disagreement in a particular domain is a contribution to not only moral but also political philosophy or democratic theory.

This interest in contributing to political philosophy or democratic theory is signaled at the start of his dissertation. Rawls notes that (mid-century) liberal democracies are plagued by two moral outlooks, widespread but fundamentally at odds with liberal democracy. The first he refers to as positivism. Positivist views reduce morality to facts or settled patterns, natural or conventional, without any reference to the authority of practical reason over issues of justification. The positivist might do something that looks like Rawls's explication or ethics as science in order to move beyond mere description to the prediction and explanation of moral phenomena. But the positivist either pursues explication or ethics as science within the space of causes rather than reasons, or treats justification as no more than proof via an exercise of theoretical reason, ignoring the final authority of practical reason to adopt any particular candidate explication as a reasonable means to its reasonable ends. In either case, the positivist does not seek from "ethics as science" an explication of competent moral judgment within the space of reasons the justification of which is determined by whether free and intelligent persons are drawn to adopt it as a reasonable means to their reasonable end of relations of mutual intelligibility and justification within moral community. For the positivist, moral principles constitute facts of one sort or another discoverable and justifiable by theoretical reason. For Rawls, Hume qualified as a positivist. So too did the Scandinavian legal realist Axel Hagerstrom, whom Rawls had read carefully, and the German legal positivist Gustav Radbruch. So too further did the British emotivist A.J. Ayer, and his American analogue, Charles Stevenson.

The second sort of view Rawls identifies as inconsistent with a viable democratic polity is authoritarian. Authoritarian views "assert that ethical principles must be taken on authority, or posited by an act of faith, or at least presupposed." Divine command theories are paradigmatically authoritarian. But so too are those that posit moral principles justified by a transcendental metaphysical necessity discoverable through the theoretical exercise of reason alone.

Positivist and authoritarian views subordinate practical to theoretical reason. And they provide no fertile ground from which to draw a compelling vision of democratic politics capable of winning the enduring allegiance of free and intelligent persons. Rawls characterizes both positivist and authoritarian views as "appeals to exalted entities." The exalted entities he has in mind include God, nature, history, established conventions, all manner of self-proclaimed elites and authorities, theoretical reason, and metaphysics.[9] Moral views built up around appeals to exalted entities subordinate the authority of practical reason to something taken as fixed independent of and prior to any exercise of practical reason. This is a view that Rawls rejects. He insists that practical reason bows before no authority save its own, not even the authority of theoretically demonstrable transcendental or metaphysical necessity. There are no moral principles beyond rational criticism and correction in the face of practical experience and no standard of justification higher or further than the allegiance of free and intelligent men and women. On this, he is quite explicit.

But apart from their rejection of what he affirms, namely the priority and authority of practical reason, why should Rawls worry about positivist and authoritarian views of morality? How do they pose a threat to democracy? The tenor of Rawls's work as a graduate student, including his dissertation, suggests that the answer to these questions is that Rawls suspected that those who affirm positivist or authoritarian views of morality were likely to prove too easily tempted to a kind of dogmatic fanaticism within or apathetic withdrawal from democratic politics. Democratic politics is treated as either a means to their end of vindicating an exalted entity or little more than a modus vivendi or necessary evil. In either case it is hardly the sort of thing to which one pledges full and final allegiance, the sort of allegiance that must be pledged if democracy is to survive in the long run in a world likely to continue to generate threats to it, new Naziisms, new Stalinisms, etc. And so Rawls ventures in his dissertation to contribute to democratic theory, or political philosophy more generally, by taking a step toward an alternative, nonpositivist, nonauthoritarian, yet still fully cognitive, view of morality, one more congenial to a genuinely viable democratic politics. But the contribution here is still one made from within moral philosophy.

It is not until his year at Oxford, 1952–1953, as a Fulbright Fellow that Rawls begins to contemplate a more direct contribution to democratic theory or political philosophy more generally, one made from within, as it were. He departed for Oxford still working toward extending the framework of his dissertation, which focused on judgments regarding the moral worth of character, to include also judgments of value and right action, all within the broadly Millian utilitarian framework with which he was sympathetic at the time. He returned to the United States at work on what would emerge as a theory of justice. I want to conclude this essay with some comments on this transition.

During his year at Oxford Rawls spent a good deal of time thinking about Mill's various precepts of justice. These function as moral principles available to citizens to establish the reasonableness or competence of, to render intelligible and justify to one another, their political views on a wide range of issues. Of course, the precepts will permit reasonable disagreement.

Even if only one precept applies to an issue, citizens may still reasonably disagree over the particular judgment it most supports. But often more than one precept will apply to an issue, so that precepts must be weighed and balanced (or lexically ordered) for the case at hand in order to arrive at a particular judgment. And here too citizens may reasonably disagree.

Now it presumably lies within the political authority of citizens, the authority of their office in a democracy, to resolve these reasonable disagreements by voting. If citizens restrict their voting to issues requiring collective action with respect to which they reasonably disagree, and they vote only for reasonable positions, then a compelling case may be made (and will be much more easily made on the sort of nonpositivist, nonauthoritarian, cognitivist view of morality for which Rawls argues in his dissertation) for the claim that they have a good moral reason to acquiesce to the outcomes of democratic processes. But if they do not so restrict their voting, making such a case seems difficult at best. The question Rawls finds himself contemplating, then, is whether Millian utilitarianism, with its highly plausible precepts of justice, is capable of serving as a public criterion of reasonable political disagreement eligible for democratic resolution. For if it is not, then the particular moral theory he is at work on will prove, in the end, inadequate to the needs of democratic theory and fail as a contribution to political philosophy.

Rawls worries that Millian utilitarianism is not up to the task. And the reason he worries is straightforward. Consider a case in which more than one precept of justice applies so that precepts must be weighed and balanced (or lexically ordered) in light of the particularities of the case in order to arrive as a reasoned determinate judgment. There is no criterion, other than the principle of utility, to which to appeal to establish the reasonableness of any particular weighing and balancing (or lexical ordering) of the precepts. But the principle of utility places no principled constraint on the amount of information relevant to its application. Of course, every application will necessarily draw on information less than the total amount of available and potentially relevant information. Without a further criterion for distinguishing reasonable from unreasonable applications of the principle, or selections of informational input, it looks like the range of reasonable applications of the principle of utility to weigh and balance (or lexically order) Mill's precepts of justice is virtually unlimited. For any claim about how to weigh and balance (or lexically order) the relevant precepts for a particular case there will be an application of the principle of utility capable, with the right informational inputs, of vindicating its reasonableness. But this leaves the democratic authority of citizens unlimited. And surely there is no compelling moral reason to acquiesce to the outcomes of democratic processes in which citizens exercise unlimited authority or in any case cannot publicly establish for one another that they are doing otherwise. If citizens are to acquiesce willingly to the outcomes of democratic processes, those processes must involve and be publicly vindicable as the exercise of limited democratic authority. Of course, the limits may have no deeper ground than the normative self-understandings at work in wide, full and general reflective equilibrium among citizens.

Here Rawls seems quickly to recognize three key points, and they together put him on the path to what would be a theory of justice. The first is that while democratic authority must surely be limited to the resolution of reasonable disagreements, it does not extend to the resolution of all reasonable disagreements. Citizens reasonably disagree over which religion to affirm and embrace. Yet they have no standing general reason to acquiesce in collective action determined by a vote to resolve the disagreement over which religion should be affirmed and embraced. Indeed, they have a standing general reason not to do so. This is something like a provisionally fixed point within democratic self-understandings. Only certain reasonable disagreements are eligible for democratic resolution.

But which ones? Presumably only those that stand in the way of necessary or desirable collective action for the common good. But how are these notions to be understood? When is collective action necessary or desirable? And how do we give content to the idea of the common good? Even if these questions permit of more than one reasonable answer, we need criteria for distinguishing reasonable from unreasonable answers. This brings us to the second point. To contribute to democratic theory or political philosophy generally a moral theory must answer these questions. The answers given, whether in the form of the idea of the basic social structure as the logically first collective action in which citizens must necessarily engage, or in the form of the priority of certain basic liberties as a necessary feature of any reasonable conception of the common good, need not have any deeper ground than the normative self-understandings at work in wide, general and full reflective equilibrium among democratic citizens.

Taking the first two points together, we can say that Rawls saw the need to provide criteria by which to pick out reasonable disagreements over necessary or desirable action aimed at the common good. These criteria specify the limits of the authority citizens wield in a democracy. They may ultimately be constructed out of widely shared normative self-understandings. And they need pass no justificatory test other than winning the allegiance of free and intelligent citizens standing in relations of wide, full and general reflective equilibrium. But this brings us to the third point. For they must also prove sufficient, in light of observable evidence, to validating objective judgments as to whether any particular citizen is in fact acting within the scope of her authority when she advances or votes for a particular position on a political issue. Citizens and officials must be able to assure one another by reference to these criteria, in light of publicly observable evidence, that when they take official political action they are in fact acting within the scope of their authority and not illegitimately using it to advance ends they are not authorized to advance (for example, something other than the common good or their private good as part of the common good). In the absence of such assurances there remains always the possibility that what appears to be democracy is in fact counterfeit. This possibility is corrosive of the public trust upon which democracy depends. Without this public trust, democracy is at risk of collapsing into a kind of generalized prisoner's dilemma. Unwilling to be played by others as a sucker or chump, and incapable of assuring themselves that they are not being so played, citizens are willing to do no more than pretend at the authority of their office, pretend to be advancing reasonable views about necessary or desirable collective action aimed at the common good, all the while seeking to advance only ends much narrower.

During his year in Oxford, Rawls appears to have become convinced that democratic theory or political philosophy must take up these questions and establish shared public criteria for the normative structure or the authority of citizenship in a democracy. And he found himself uncertain as to whether the Millian utilitarianism he otherwise favored (over available versions of classical utilitarianism) could be developed so that it was fully up to the task. Intuitionist moral views seemed an unpromising alternative, since they offered no criterion for determining a reasonable weighing and balancing or lexical ordering of precepts of justice for any particular case other than that the person judging the case reports that she sincerely judged the matter thus. As with the principle of utility, the intuitionist's criterion for determining a particular application of the precepts of justice to be reasonable leaves the field virtually unlimited. To establish the reasonableness of any particular application of the precepts of justice I need only say that I sincerely judge it to be reasonable. There is, then, no limit to the scope of my democratic authority other than the limit I choose to place on it. Which is to say, there is no limit.

It is instructive and illuminating, I think, to view what emerged as *A Theory of Justice* as originating in the search for a viable shared public understanding of the normative structure of citizenship in a democracy, an understanding capable of sustaining objective judgments as to whether a political disagreement was in fact a reasonable disagreement properly settled by democratic procedures or was merely a simple or unreasonable disagreement masquerading as a reasonable disagreement. While Millian utilitarianism and intuitionism were clearly moral views more congenial to democracy than positivist or authoritarian views, they seemed to Rawls by the early 1950s less than ideally equipped to deliver the sort of shared public understanding of citizenship necessary to the long-term stability and vitality of a democracy. *A Theory of Justice* takes a fresh start, taking a constructivist and contractualist approach to the problem. Rawls's two principles of justice, already lexically ordered and more or less easily applied to observable evidence, establish the nature and scope of the authority citizens wield, and so mark the field of reasonable political disagreement, whether at a constitutional convention, a legislative session, a judicial decision, or a vote at the ballot box. The first principle affirms each citizen's equal claim to a system of basic liberties fully adequate to the development and exercise of her moral capacities. The second affirms each citizen's equal claim to a basic social structure within which the different offices or positions, with their different powers and responsibilities and different economic rewards, arising out of a structurally maintained division of labor are, first, open to all on terms of fair equality of opportunity and, second, such that there is no alterative scheme of offices and positions, no alternative division of labor, with a superior least desirable social position. (The social position occupied by the typical unskilled laborer is the least desirable social position, in terms of lifetime expected income, arising out of the division of labor structurally maintained in most advanced industrial democracies. This is just only if there is no alternative division of labor with a least desirable position superior to that of today's typical unskilled worker.) In a democracy an exercise of official political power is counterfeit if it is inconsistent with either of these two principles or their lexical ordering. The two principles, conjoined with the idea of the basic structure as the first subject of justice, express the criteria by which citizens can validate a particular issue as one within the scope of their political authority qua citizen. Rawls's hope, of course, is that the two principles and the original position (reasoning machine) used to generate them not only explicate what we take to be noncontroversially competent judgments regarding the nature, scope and reasonable exercise of the authority vested in democratic citizenship, but that they do so in a way, or as part of a larger political moral conception, capable of drawing our enduring allegiance as free and intelligent men and women. If he is right, then justice as fairness is a, perhaps the most, reasonable means to our reasonable end of realizing and maintaining as free equals mutually intelligible and justifiable political relations. For this end, of course, there is no argument. There is just the power of a picture – a picture, reasonable to be sure, of what we are and what we might be.

# Notes

Research for this essay was supported by, and I express my gratitude for, a Fellowship from the National Endowment for the Humanities.

1   Rawls famously often analogized his life's work to a single painting – his attempt to set out the single vision that had captured his attention for a half-century, even as he struggled to bring it into focus, attended to different elements at different times, and periodically found himself adjusting this or that feature in an attempt to get it "just right."

2   I discuss the undergraduate thesis at some length in Reidy 2010.

3   This is a point that suggests the influence of Wittgenstein. But, interestingly, throughout the later 1940s and through his dissertation in 1950, Rawls draws on figures associated with "scientific philosophy" and the Vienna Circle other than Wittgenstein.

4   By the early 1950s, Rawls began to worry about this feature of utilitarianism, at least if utilitarianism is to serve the social role of morality by supporting a shared public criterial understanding of the competent exercise of our moral faculties. Because there are no principled limits on the amount of relevant information plausibly fed into the utilitarian "reasoning machine" and because the machine's output, the theorems or moral principles it generates, will inevitably vary with the information given as input, which must always be less than all possibly relevant information, the theory's ability to serve as a reasonable means to our reasonable end of rendering our competent moral judgments mutually intelligible and justifiable seems to depend on some accidental, unexplained and probably unlikely agreement as to the portion of all relevant information to be fed into the reasoning machine. By the late 1950s or early 1960s, Rawls had concluded that this problem was sufficient to render even the most plausible sort of utilitarianism, some version of Millian utilitarianism of the sort he'd been developing, unworkable as the theoretical framework for a public theory of justice within a democracy.

5   In commenting on his proposed "imperative utilitarianism," Rawls notes that there is no reason to think that a sound scientific understanding of the effective exercise of our moral capacities or of our competent moral judgments will contribute to our more reliably acting as required by morality. There remains, he notes, the problem of the "radical evil" of human nature, a problem that cannot be overcome save through divine grace. This is a remarkable note for several reasons. First, it indicates that in 1946 Rawls was not yet fully out from under the shadow of the religious views expressed in his undergraduate thesis. Notwithstanding his recollection late in life of having abandoned his faith during or very shortly after the war, the evidence suggests that Rawls's prewar theistic commitments were slowly altered and abandoned over a period of some 10 years following the end of the war. In 1954, Rawls taught a course in Christian Ethics at Cornell. He was then still thinking very seriously about Christianity and was still in the process of finding his way to the "nontheistic" orientation on which he would eventually settle by the late 1950s or early 1960s. Second, it indicates the extent to which Rawls conceived of ethics, at least in 1946, as aimed primarily at our self-understanding as persons and not at making or improving us as persons. Over time, he would come to think of moral philosophy as making a practical contribution to our complete realization, including our improvement or education, as persons.

6   This, of course, would change in the early 1950s. The change would be announced in the paper "Two Concepts of Rules," which Rawls regarded as clearing the way for the addition of institutions and practices to the list of subjects properly evaluated by moral judgment and so properly covered by a complete moral theory.

7   Rawls emphasizes that these two inquiries at the heart of moral philosophy – one into explication and the other into justification and motivation – may be intelligently carried out without much attention being paid to the sorts of metaphysical, metaethical, and linguistic inquiries that seemed so often to distract, even to dominate the attention of, moral philosophers mid-century. One might add today that they may be so carried out without much attention to many of the empirical inquiries that seem so often to distract, even dominate, the attention of moral philosophers today.

8   Rawls characterizes reasonable ends as activities which are comprehensively satisfactory for the person whose activities they are and inclusively harmonious with the comparable activities of other persons within the community to which the person belongs.

9  Rawls includes here the sort of nonnaturalist "realism" urged by G.E. Moore. Rawls agrees with Moore in holding that "good" cannot be analyzed – in the sense of "synonymy meaning," an analysis that would preserve truth values through substitution – in purely naturalistic terms. It is, in that sense, a nonnatural or moral property. But Rawls rejects the claim that this linguistic fact entails any further fact, metaphysical or otherwise, discoverable through the exercise of theoretical reason to which practical reason must acquiesce.

## Works by Rawls, with Abbreviations

*A Brief Inquiry into the Meaning of Sin and Faith, with "On My Religion"* (BI), ed. Thomas Nagel. Cambridge, MA: Harvard University Press, 2009.

"A Brief Inquiry into the Nature and Function of Ethical Theory" (1946), Rawls Archive: Box 3, Accession 14990, Pusey Library, Harvard University.

*Collected Papers* (CP), ed. Samuel Freeman. Cambridge, MA: Harvard University Press, 1999.

"Ethical Rationalism" (late 1940s). Rawls Archive, Box 2, Accession 14990, Pusey Library, Harvard University.

"A Study in the Grounds of Ethical Knowledge: Considered with Reference to Judgments of the Moral Worth of Character." PhD dissertation, Princeton University, 1950.

*A Theory of Justice* (TJ), rev. edn. Cambridge, MA: Harvard University Press, 1999.

"Two Concepts of Rules," *Philosophical Review* 64(1) (1955): 3–32. Also in *Collected Papers* (20–46).

## Other References

Downs, Anthony (1957) *An Economic Theory of Democracy*. New York: Harper & Row.

Kelsen, Hans (1978 [1934]) *The Pure Theory of Law*. Berkeley: University of California Press.

Reidy, David A. (2010) "Rawls's Religion and Justice as Fairness." *History of Political Thought* 31: 309–343.

Schumpeter, Joseph (1942) *Capitalism, Socialism and Democracy*. New York: Harper.

# 2

# Does Justice as Fairness Have a Religious Aspect?

## PAUL WEITHMAN

In this essay, I argue that John Rawls's work on justice has a religious aspect. This claim may occasion some surprise. Rawls's recently published undergraduate thesis *A Brief Inquiry into the Meaning of Sin and Faith* is undoubtedly religious and there are interesting philosophical connections between it and *A Theory of Justice*. But *BI* is not among the writings in which Rawls developed justice as fairness and it will not be my concern here.[1] Rawls developed his conception of justice in his mature work, which does not obviously include any religious elements, at least as religion is traditionally understood.

Despite the absence of obvious religious elements, I shall try to show the religious aspect of Rawls's work using a condition of religiosity that he himself endorsed. Showing that justice as fairness satisfies this condition does not involve showing that it is theistic. Instead it involves showing that justice as fairness tries to answer some of the questions traditional religion also tries to answer. What those questions are, how they arise and why the attempt to answer them gives a view a religious aspect will become clearer by seeing what Joshua Cohen and Thomas Nagel meant by observing, in their introduction to *BI*, that Rawls's work was informed by "a religious temperament" (*BI*, 5).

In section 1, I look at the passage in which Rawls asserts his condition of religiosity – hereafter his "religiosity condition" – and I raise a number of questions about the passage. In section 2, I argue that Cohen's and Nagel's observation itself rests on a religiosity condition and that if we read Rawls as appealing to that condition, or a variant of it, we can answer many of the questions raised about the passage discussed in section 1. That passage occurs in one of Rawls's lectures on Kant published in his *Lectures on the History of Moral Philosophy*. In section 3, I show how Rawls argued that Kant satisfied the religiosity condition laid out in section 2 and why Rawls therefore thought Kant's moral philosophy has what Rawls called "a religious aspect." In section 4, I argue that justice as fairness as presented in *TJ* has a religious aspect as well. The argument proceeds by showing that justice as fairness satisfies Rawls's own religiosity condition in ways that are similar to the ways in which Rawls

*A Companion to Rawls*, First Edition. Edited by Jon Mandle and David A. Reidy.
© 2014 John Wiley & Sons, Inc. Published 2016 by John Wiley & Sons, Inc.

thought Kant's moral philosophy satisfies it. In section 5, I ask whether the religious aspect of justice as fairness survives Rawls's political turn.

# 1. What Does Rawls Think Gives a View a Religious Aspect?

I said that the condition of religiosity to be applied to Rawls's work is one that he himself endorsed in a lecture on Kant's moral philosophy. Since much of what I have to say about the condition and its application to Rawls's own work depends upon a careful reading of the passage in which Rawls asserts it, I shall quote the passage in its entirety. Rawls writes:

> I conclude by observing that the significance Kant gives to the moral law and our acting from it has an obvious religious aspect, and that his text occasionally has a devotional character. In the second *Critique*, there are two obvious examples. One is the passage beginning "Duty! Thou sublime and mighty name . . . What origin is worthy of thee?" The other is the passage beginning "Two things fill the mind . . . with admiration and awe . . . the starry heavens above me and the moral law within me."
>
> While it is a necessary condition of Kant's view to count as religious that he should hold that there are some things of far greater significance than the everyday values of secular life and our happiness as a whole, this is not sufficient to make it religious. One could give this significance to moral virtues and excellences, say, to a certain nobility and courage, and steadfastness in friendship, as Aristotle might be said to have done. This does not give his view a religious aspect, as profound as it might be.
>
> What gives a view a religious aspect, I think, is that it has a conception of the world as a whole that presents it as in certain respects holy, or else as worthy of devotion and reverence. The everyday values of secular life must take a secondary place. If this is right, then what gives Kant's view a religious aspect is the dominant place he gives to the moral law in conceiving of the world itself. For it is in following the moral law as it applies to us, and in striving to fashion in ourselves a firm good will, and in shaping our social world accordingly that alone qualifies us to be the final purpose of creation. Without this, our life, in the world, and the world itself lose their meaning and point.
>
> Now, perhaps, we see the significance of the mention of the world in the first sentence of *Groundwork* I: "It is impossible to conceive anything in the world, or even out of it, that can be taken as good without qualification, except a good will."
>
> At first it seems strange that Kant should mention the world here. Why go to such an extreme? we ask. Now perhaps we see why it is there. It comes as no surprise, then, that in the second Critique he should say that the step to religion is taken for the sake of the highest good and to preserve our devotion to the moral law.
>
> These religious, even Pietist, aspects of Kant's moral philosophy seem obvious; any account of it that overlooks them misses much that is essential to it. (*LHMP*, 160–161)[2]

This is a difficult passage to unpack. Readers of Kant will be familiar with Rawls's reference in the fifth paragraph to Kant's assertion that we must "step" from morality to religion to "preserve our devotion to the moral law." But even these readers may be brought up short by Rawls's implications in the first paragraph that Kant attached specifically religious significance to the moral law itself, that he thought our devotion to the moral law was religious devotion and that it is obvious he did so.

The job of pinning down just what Rawls meant to imply in that paragraph is complicated by the ambiguity of the word "significance," which can refer to both "importance" and "meaning." What Rawls might take to be obvious is that Kant accorded the moral law and our acting from it a degree of importance that would befit an object of religious devotion. This interpretation gains some credence from the condition asserted in the second paragraph, which requires that Kant give the moral law enough weight or importance to override everyday values and happiness. Alternatively, Rawls might take it as obvious that obedience to the moral law has a meaning or point which is in some sense religious, perhaps because it gives meaning or point to the whole of life, as religion is said to do. This interpretation seems to be supported by the last sentence of the third paragraph.

That paragraph, in which Rawls lays out his interpretive argument, is especially perplexing. It begins with Rawls's assertion of his religiosity condition. Because Rawls seems to imply that that condition picks out just what it is that "gives a conception a religious aspect," the most natural way to read him is as asserting a religiosity condition that is both necessary and sufficient. Read this way, the religiosity condition is a very strong claim. That claim might seem implausible since Judaism, Christianity and Islam surely qualify as religious views despite the fact that they do not obviously satisfy it. What qualifies them as religious, it seems, is instead that they have a conception of a *person*, namely God, who is presented as holy and as worthy of devotion and reverence. The religiosity condition also expresses a stronger premise than Rawls needs to reach his conclusion. That conclusion, which I take to be expressed by the consequent of the third sentence, concerns Kant's view. To reach it, all Rawls would have needed to do is to assert a sufficient condition of a moral view's having religious aspects and to show that Kant's view satisfies that condition.

Quite apart from its strength, the religiosity condition is difficult to understand. For a view can satisfy that condition only if it "has a conception of the world as a whole." On encountering the phrase "world as a whole," we may think of some particularly vast portion of the cosmos such as "the starry heavens above." The heavens may inspire awe or wonder, but our conception of a part, even a large part, of the world should not be mistaken for a conception of the whole. Rather, a conception of the world as whole must somehow include *all* of the natural world, perhaps under a very abstract description of the laws that govern it. But even a conception of the natural, as opposed to the human, world should not be mistaken for such a conception either. Human beings are part of the world and act in it. A conception of the world as a whole must somehow include all of the natural world, but it must include human activity as well.

And what does Rawls means when he says that a view which satisfies his condition presents the world as a whole as "worthy of devotion and reverence"? Surely he does not mean that it is conceived of as a fitting addressee of prayer and worship. But what would it be to be devoted to or to revere the world? In what conduct would such attitudes manifest themselves? As we shall see, an especially important question is this: since "the world as a whole" includes human activity, would conduct of that kind itself be included in the conception of the world which is presented as worthy of devotion and reverence?

Another puzzle about the third paragraph is that the argument Rawls offers there admits of two readings.

On one reading, the religious character of our devotion to the moral law, as attested to by the quotes from Kant's text in the first paragraph, is a premise. Kant is then said to present the world as worthy of devotion and reverence, and thereby to satisfy the religiosity condition, by presenting it using a law that is itself worthy of devotion and reverence. Thus, according to this reading, the religious significance of the moral law would be "transferred" to the world as a whole. The conclusion of the argument would then really mean "what gives Kant's view a religious aspect is the dominant place he gives to *the religious significance of* the moral law in conceiving of the world itself." The problem with this reading is that it puts considerable pressure on the religiosity condition. For if, as this first reading says, Rawls's Kant assumes that moral law has religious significance, then that would seem to be sufficient to give his view a religious aspect. It is hard to see why Rawls would think satisfaction of the religiosity condition is necessary.

According to the second reading, the religious significance Kant attaches to the moral law, and the religious tones in which he describes our devotion to it, have to be explained rather than assumed. On this reading as on the first, Rawls says Kant used the moral law to describe the world in such a way that his view satisfies the religiosity condition. Satisfaction of the condition implies that his view has a religious aspect. But according to this interpretation, the propriety of describing our devotion to the moral law as religious and of ascribing religious significance to the law follows from the fact that law plays a prominent role in Kant's satisfaction of the condition. Thus, on this reading, the religiosity of Kant's view is "transferred" to the moral law. The problem with this reading is that the role the moral law plays in Kant's presentation of the world is supposed to be explained in the fourth and fifth sentences of the paragraph, which refer to Kant's notion of a "final purpose of creation." But those sentences add to the perplexity of the paragraph since Rawls does not explain Kant's notion of a final purpose and the premises Rawls needs to move from those sentences to his conclusion in the third sentence are suppressed.

That Rawls's terminology is occasionally imprecise and that his reasoning is somewhat elliptical are not entirely surprising since the passage on Kant is drawn from lecture notes. But the imprecision and compression contribute to the difficulty of understanding why Rawls thinks Kant's view has a religious aspect and what implications his reading of Kant has for the question of whether there is a religious aspect to his own work. I believe Rawls takes the religiosity condition to be necessary as well as sufficient, and I shall therefore opt for the second of the two readings of his argument. To see the implications of Rawls's argument for justice as fairness, it is first necessary to sort through the perplexities in Rawls's text. To do that, it will help to recover a religiosity condition that is applied to Rawls by Joshua Cohen and Thomas Nagel and show that it is the religiosity condition Rawls endorses and applies to Kant in the quoted passage.

## 2. Moral Philosophy and the Religious Temperament

In their introduction to Rawls's *Brief Inquiry*, Cohen and Nagel write: "Those who have studied Rawls's work, and even more, those who knew him personally, are aware of a deeply religious temperament that informed his life and writings, whatever may have been his beliefs" (*BI*, 5). Cohen and Nagel support this observation by citing several passages from *Political Liberalism*, *The Law of Peoples* and *TJ* and then say "These and kindred reflections express an aspiration to a comprehensive outlook on the world, which is an element of what we mean by a religious temperament" (*BI*, 5). The fact that the passages Cohen and Nagel cite include some of a decidedly Kantian flavor lends some credence to my suggestion that we might learn something about the religious aspect of Rawls's view by examining its affinity to Kant's. But what is a "comprehensive outlook on the world"? What does it mean to say of a moral view like Rawls's that it "express[es] an aspiration" to such an outlook? And how does the fact that Rawls's writings are "informed" by such an outlook, or "express an aspiration" to such an outlook, show that he had a religious temperament?

In Nagel's essay "Secular Philosophy and the Religious Temperament," he says that "religious temperament" names "a disposition to seek a view of the world that can play a certain role in the inner life – a role that for some people is occupied by religion" (Nagel 2010, 2). I believe Nagel intends the phrase "a view of the world" to mean what he and Cohen mean by "a comprehensive outlook on the world." So we can make some progress in answering these questions by asking what role a comprehensive outlook on the world plays in the inner life of a religious believer. What Nagel says in the opening pages of "Secular Philosophy and the Religious Temperament" suggests the following.

Adherents of traditional monotheisms believe that God is able to survey all creation. They do not think God's standpoint is simply a point of view from which God could produce an accurate description of the world in its totality. Rather, God's view of the world is also normatively laden. Nagel does not say what content he thinks traditional theisms assign to God's view of the world. Some theists think that God has *two* conceptions of the world. One is a view of the world as whole as it might be. This is a vision of a world that has been renewed or redeemed by God's saving work. This is the world as God wants it or plans it to be. The other is a view of the world as it is. This is a world sometimes described as "broken," but with potential for renewal or redemption. Thus, as seen from the divine standpoint, the world as a whole has, or has the potential to have, an order or a harmony which is of great value.

These two "view[s] of the world" as it appears from God's standpoint, God's two "comprehensive outlook[s] on the world," play important roles in the lives of religious believers. For each person is a part of creation, and since God's viewpoint is all-surveying, the religious believer thinks that God sees her life and sees how it contributes to or detracts from the harmony, or the potential harmony, of the whole. Because it is important that the whole be as God wishes it to be, the traditional believer feels called to do her part in bringing about a renewed creation. The importance of restoring harmony to the world and the need for her to do her part in restoring it give her life a larger significance. And since the world's realization of harmony – or its failure to realize harmony – is ongoing rather than episodic or one-off, it depends upon her every action. Each action is therefore endowed with that larger significance, a significance which far exceeds the values realized in everyday life.

For the religious believer, then, the choice of every action has to be governed by how her action will be seen from the divine standpoint. Of course, regulating one's choices in this way itself requires considerable discipline. And so the religious believer strives to shape her own character accordingly, cultivating in herself the requisite habits of deliberation and choice, perhaps by prayer or spiritual formation. By doing so, she gives God's "view of the world" "a certain role in [her] inner life." Her motivation to do so can be heightened by the powerful attractions of a renewed world, so evocatively spoken of in religious texts.

Nagel thinks that the sense that there is a point of view on all the world is most familiar from traditional theisms, but that it is not exclusive to them. Crudely put, he thinks that nontheists can also have the sense that there is point of view from which their lives can be seen as a part of a world which is in, or which has the potential for, an all-embracing harmony. They too can strive to give that point of a view a role in their inner lives by allowing the importance of cosmic harmony, as seen from that point of view, to regulate their delibera-tion and choice, and by striving to give their own characters the requisite shape. And they too can find that their motivation to do so is elicited or heightened by an attractive conception of the world as it might be.

We are now in a position to see how Nagel thinks a philosophical view can "express an aspiration to a comprehensive outlook on the world" and thereby show a religious temperament.

In trying to show the role that such a view can play in the lives of theists and nontheists, I passed over the many questions that the theist and the nontheist will have to confront – questions about just how the world looks from the transcendent point of view, what kind of value its order has, what its moral demands are, why a conception of the world so ordered motivates us to comply with those demands and how the transcendent point of view from which the world is apprehended can be treated as regulative. As we saw, Nagel implies that a religious temperament is a disposition to "seek" a comprehensive view of the world. The word "seek" is important. For a reflective person with a religious temperament will be trou-bled by these questions and will seek a comprehensive view of the world as whole – under-stood now as an *account* of the world as a whole – that offers answers. The questions that trouble her are philosophical and the account she seeks will therefore be a philosophical one. A philosophical view, whether theistic or not, "express[es] an aspiration to a comprehensive outlook on the world," and shows its author's religious temperament, when it tries to provide an account that answers them. This is Nagel's "religiosity condition."

I suggest that the religiosity condition that Rawls had in mind in his lecture on Kant is the one that Nagel developed in "Secular Philosophy and the Religious Temperament."[3] This suggestion comes to the following:

- When Rawls says that a view has a religious aspect if it "has a conception of the world as a whole," we take him to be saying that a view has a religious aspect if it has an all-embracing conception of a properly ordered natural and social world.
- When Rawls adds that that conception "presents [the ordered world] as in certain respects holy, or else as worthy of devotion and reverence," we take him to be saying that the conception presents the order of the world as having an ethical value to which the appro-priate human response is "devotion and reverence."
- We read Rawls as thinking that we show the ordered world "devotion and reverence" when we accord that world a superordinate role in what Nagel calls our "inner life."

How can we treat a conception of an ordered world as superordinate? Because such a concep-tion is *all-embracing* it includes each of us. The order of the world must therefore depend upon our ongoing activity. Part of what a view with a religious aspect has to do is to identify norms each of us must follow if our activity is to help constitute and maintain the good order of the world. So I suggest:

- We take Rawls to be saying that we treat a conception of an ordered world as superordi-nate when we treat those norms as regulative of our thought and conducts, so that they govern – and thereby subordinate – our pursuit of everyday values.

- Finally, we read Rawls as thinking that – precisely because the conception of an ordered world includes each of us – to treat those norms as regulative is, in effect, to govern one's life by a transcendent conception of one's own place in the world.

In sum, I suggest we read Rawls as thinking that a view which tries to work out such an all-embracing conception of an ordered world, together with its associated values and norms, "express[es] an aspiration to a comprehensive view of the world" and has "a religious aspect." As we shall see, reading Rawls as sharing Nagel's condition makes it possible to solve the puzzles raised by the passage from Rawls's Kant lecture and to understand why Rawls thought Kant's moral philosophy has a religious aspect. Understanding that, in turn, helps us to see the religious aspect of justice as fairness.

Nagel's development of the religiosity condition implies that philosophical views which satisfy it are *responsive*. They respond to the philosopher's initial, undertheorized sense that there is a point of view from which it is possible to apprehend the world as a whole and his place in it, a point of view which must be given some role in human thought and conduct. Rawls does not explicitly build responsiveness into his statement of the condition, though I think he presupposes it in his reading of Kant. My claim that Rawls's work satisfies the religiosity condition raises the question of whether his work was itself responsive and, if so, to what. I shall close with speculative answers to these questions. If those speculations are right, then they provide further reasons for concluding that justice as fairness has a religious aspect.

This way of proceeding assumes the truth of the religiosity condition. That condition strikes me as extremely promising when it is taken as a sufficient condition, though I do not know how to make it precise and I do not have an argument for it. One way to specify the condition and to lend it some credence would be to look carefully at the details of philosophical views which seem to satisfy it and to show that those views can plausibly be described as having a religious aspect *because* they satisfy it. Since that is what I do here, my treatments of Rawls on Kant and of Rawls's own view provide indirect support for the religiosity condition. With the condition in hand, let us now return to Rawls's argument.

## 3. What Gives Kant's View a Religious Aspect?

I said that the conclusion of Rawls's argument in the passage from his lecture on Kant quoted above is to be found in the third sentence of the third paragraph:

> what gives Kant's view a religious aspect is the dominant place he gives to the moral law in conceiving of the world itself.

This conclusion is supposed to follow from the two sentences that precede it and the two that follow it. The preceding pair is:

> What gives a view a religious aspect, I think, is that it has a conception of the world as a whole that presents it as in certain respects holy, or else as worthy of devotion and reverence. The everyday values of secular life must take a secondary place.

The first sentence of this first pair asserts Rawls's religiosity condition. The second sentence clarifies or draws out an implication of the way the world is presented by religious views. For I take Rawls to mean that what the everyday values of secular life must take a secondary place *to*, according to views which satisfy the religiosity condition, is the worth or value of the world to which devotion and reverence are appropriate responses.

There are many ways in which a value can take a secondary place to something revered. Someone can be devoted to an athletic team or can be said to revere one of its star players without organizing his whole life around his interest in the team's fortunes. Such a person has many ends of which his team's success is just one that he regards as especially important. But it is clear from what Rawls says earlier in the quoted passage that the worth of the world as a whole is not, on a view which satisfies the religiosity condition, one especially important value for which a good life must make room, as steadfastness in friendship is for Aristotle or as the success of a team is for the devoted fan. Rather, according to the interpretation of Rawls's view that I suggested in the previous section, Rawls means that a view which satisfies the religiosity condition presents the world as a whole as having a worth or value which is of a different and greater order than the values of everyday life, so that the former subordinates the latter and conduct which expresses reverence for the world subordinates or frames the pursuit of everyday values.

If that is right, then the religiosity condition should be understood as saying:

> What gives a view a religious aspect is that it has a conception of the world as a whole that presents it as in certain respects holy, or as having a value to which the proper human response is devotion and reverence and to which the everyday values of secular life are subordinate.

The considerations brought forward so far should help to make the religiosity condition somewhat plausible as a sufficient condition. For to present something simply as worthy of devotion is not to present it as worthy of religious devotion, since – as the example of the devoted fan suggests – there are nonreligious kinds of devotion. But to present something as having a value of a different order than "everyday values," so that devotion to it subordinates other pursuits, is arguably to present it as worthy of a devotion that significantly resembles that which traditional theists give to the objects of their devotion.

Of course, much depends upon what Rawls would mean by "subordinate" and on how he thinks devotion to the world is to be shown on Kant's view. We shall get to these questions shortly. For now, note that if the religiosity condition is understood in the way that I have suggested, then we can see how Rawls can get to the conclusion about Kant's view that he wants to reach. He can get to it if he can show:

> Kant's moral theory has a conception of the world as a whole in which the moral law has a dominant place and, because of the dominant place of the moral law, that conception presents the world as in certain respects holy, or as having a value in virtue of which it is worthy of devotion and reverence to which the pursuit of the everyday values of secular life should be subordinate.

Let us call this claim the "intermediate step" in Rawls's argument. To understand the argument, we have to see on what grounds he takes that step. The intermediate step is a conjunction. To see why Rawls takes it, we have to see how he establishes each conjunct.

I have said that a conception of "the world as a whole" must include human beings, since we are part of the world. I have suggested we read Rawls as saying that it is a conception of an ordered world, the order of which we help to constitute and maintain by our ongoing activity that accords with norms of human conduct. Kant's moral philosophy clearly includes such a conception: the realm of ends. That conception is one in which the moral law has a "dominant place," since it is the norm by which we act in the realm of ends.

If the realm of ends is a conception of the *as a whole*, it must somehow embrace the natural, as opposed to the human, world as well. Rawls thinks Kant's conception does that. For Rawls thinks that to conceive of a realm of ends is not *just* to conceive of what he calls "our social world." Our social lives are played out against conditions set by the world of non-human nature and those conditions constrain what we can achieve. If the necessities of life were extremely scarce, if the laws of human psychology led us to return evil for good, or if causal laws frequently failed to hold, then realizing the realm of ends might be beyond our capacities. And so if the moral law is to be generally observed, then the natural world as a whole – its circumstances and its physical and psychological laws – cannot be inhospitable to the law's observation. Rawls thinks the assumption that it is not, the assumption that the natural world is hospitable, is implicit in the conception of a realm of ends. For near the end of his lectures on Kant, he says "we can believe a realm of ends is possible in the world only if the order of nature and social necessities are not unfriendly to that ideal" (*LHMP*, 319). Thus, on Rawls's reading, Kant's moral philosophy includes a conception of the world as a whole in the description of which the moral law has a dominant place.

In fact, Kant's moral philosophy – like the traditional theisms I referred to in section 2 – does not just contain one conception of the world as a whole, but two. Or it contains two conceptions of the same world. For the realm of ends is not now realized in the world, and so the conception Kant's philosophy most obviously includes is a conception of the world as the world might be. But because the realm of ends is possible according to the physical and psychological laws that govern the world, the conception of a realm of ends carries with it and makes us aware of a conception of the actual world. Once the idea of a social world in which the moral law is generally honored is made explicit, we can conceive of the actual world as a potential realm of ends. The first conjunct of the intermediate step is doubly satisfied.

What of the second conjunct? When I raised questions about the passage from Rawls's Kant lecture, I noted that when Rawls says a view with a religious aspect presents the world as worthy of devotion and reverence, he does not mean that it presents the world as a fitting addressee of prayer or worship. But what would it be to show the realm of ends super-ordinate devotion and reverence? And why think that the conception of the world as a realm of ends, or as a potential realm of ends, presents the world as holy or worthy of such a response?

To see the answers to these questions, we need to turn to the fourth and fifth sentences of Rawls's argument, which I referred to above as the second pair of sentences that is supposed to support his conclusion. Those sentences read:

> For it is in following the moral law as it applies to us, and in striving to fashion in ourselves a firm good will, and in shaping our social world accordingly that alone qualifies us to be the final purpose of creation. Without this, our life, in the world, and the world itself lose their meaning and point.

I read the beginning of the first sentence as saying what conduct manifests devotion and reverence for the conception of the world as a whole presented in Kant's moral philosophy. That conception is the realm of ends and the realm of ends is, Rawls says, an "ideal" of the world (*LHMP*, 319). In "following the moral law as it applies to us . . . striving to fashion in ourselves a firm good will, and . . . shaping our social world accordingly," we conduct ourselves as members of a realm of ends and thereby do our part to realize that ideal in the world. If our attempts "to fashion in ourselves a firm good will" and to "shap[e] our social world accordingly" are unwavering, we show that we are committed to the ideal of the realm of ends, to the world as a whole as it might be. Moreover, by doing our part to realize the ideal, we respond to the actual world as a potential realm of ends.

If we express our devotion to the realm of ends in the ways Rawls describes in the first sentence, then the expression of devotion to that ideal subordinates our other pursuits. It does not subordinate them as one end might subordinate others which are judged less weighty or important. Rather, it subordinates our other pursuits by constraining them absolutely. For if we "fashion in ourselves" a will which is "firm[ly]" or reliably regulated by the moral law and if we "follow[] the moral law as it applies to us," then all of the maxims on which we act – and hence our pursuits of all of our ends – are regulated by the law. Once we see this, we can see why Rawls thinks that the devotion to and reverence for the realm of ends are religious in character. For since we show devotion and reverence for the realm of ends by acting always from the moral law, the realm of ends is an ideal that we never trade off against other ends and that we never act against. It is to govern our will absolutely as the objects of more traditional religious devotion, such as the conception of a world renewed, are supposed to regulate the wills of believers.

The end of the first sentence, together with the second, tell us why the conception of the world as a realm of ends is worthy of such devotion, but these sentences are easy to misread. In the second sentence, Rawls might be taken to say that if we do not follow the moral law, strive to fashion a good will and shape our social world accordingly, then we will *experience* our lives and the world as meaningless. *Perhaps* this is what Rawls is saying. But even if it is, his observation that such conduct "qualifies us to be the final purpose of creation" suggests a more nuanced interpretation. It suggests Rawls thinks that according to Kant, human life and the world have – or can be presented as having – natural purposes or "point[s]" which will be frustrated if we do not regulate our conduct by the conception of the realm of ends by living as members of that realm, regardless of whether or not we actually experience those lives as lacking meaning. If that is right, then we will experience the meaningless of such lives only if we somehow grasp our purpose and realize that we have failed to fulfill it.

Consider, in this connection, why Rawls might say that according to Kant "our life, in the world . . . would lose [its] meaning and point" if we failed to act from the moral law. "*Our* life, in the world" is a human life. A human life differs from the lives of other animals because it is lived in large part by the exercise of practical reason. Kant argues in the *Groundwork* that the natural purpose of practical reason is to produce in us a good will (Kant 1997 [1785], 10). A human being who fails to act from the moral law and to "fashion in [himself] a firm good will" defeats the purpose of practical reason and fails to live as distinctively and fully human. If he experiences his life as meaningless or as frustrated, it will be because he somehow grasped his failure to live the kind of life he can and should live.

On the other hand, if everyone were to follow the moral law and the realm of ends were realized, we would live together as reasonable and rational beings and our relations with one another would express the mutual recognition of our common dignity (*LHMP*, 209–210). In the realm of ends, "people attain their mutual happiness" (*LHMP*, 312). And that is, of course, a very great good (*CP*, 508–509). A world with such great goods in it would seem to be a world eminently worth realizing. Though Rawls does not say so, I presume he thinks that we can see some significance in doing our part to realize a realm in which these goods are available to all.

What is the natural or the "final purpose" of the world and how is it frustrated if we fail to act from the moral law? Kant's idea is roughly the following.[4]

Living things are organized to attain certain ends, such as nutrition, growth and reproduction. Because they are so organized, they have "inner purposiveness." To attain these ends, they must make use of things in their environment. The presence of these things in their environments can be explained mechanically. Insofar as it can be, the coexistence of natural things is presented as pointless or without purpose, since mechanical explanations are nonteleological. But the fact that organisms use things in their environment to attain their purposes means that the things they find useful have a kind of purposiveness which Kant calls "outer purposiveness." Indeed, Kant thinks that once we have the idea of this kind of purposiveness, we can conceive of the world as an ordered "system of ends," in which the systematic connections are connections of outer purposiveness. The conception of the world as a system of ends leads naturally, Kant thought, to the questions of whether there is some final end of nature, outside the system of ends, for the sake of which the system as a whole – the world as a whole – exists and of what our place in that ordered whole might be.

Kant argues a priori that only human beings, considered as moral agents, can serve as the final end of the world as a whole. For we – and only we – are both out of the world and in it. As moral agents, we must be capable of free choice and to be capable of free choice, we must exist beyond the purview of causal laws. To consider us as moral agents is therefore to consider us as noumenal beings who exist outside the system of ends. We can realize our freedom only by acting in the world. And it is only when we act freely in the world that we serve as the world's final end. For when we set purposes for ourselves and use nature to achieve them, our purposes serve as the ends of nature. When we set and pursue our purposes autonomously – when we act from the categorical imperative – our purposes and actions are not conditional on some further aims. Chains of outer purposiveness come to an unconditioned end in our freely chosen action. We then serve as the final end of the world, that for the sake of which the whole system of ends exists. On the other hand, because only human beings can serve as the final end of the world and we serve as that end only when we act from the moral law, our failure to act from the moral law leaves chains of outer purposiveness unfinished.

Thus while the world can be described in mechanistic terms, or as a system of ends related by outer or relative purposiveness but without beings who are conceived of as noumenally free, either description of the world would be incomplete from a certain point of view on the system of ends which it is natural to us to adopt. That is the point of view from which we are naturally led ask whether the whole system exists for the sake of something outside itself. Kant's moral philosophy offers a normatively laden description of the world that appears more complete from that point of view – a conception or an ideal of the world which presents it as having a purpose that is realized when moral agents act in it autonomously, following the moral law. That ideal is, of course, the realm of ends.

Rawls does not spell out this reading of Kant, but his reliance on it would explain his summary remark at the end of the argument I am trying to parse: "[w]ithout this" – that is, unless we try to realize the realm of ends by acting from the moral law, fashioning a good will and properly shaping our social world – "our life, in the world, and the world itself lose their meaning and point." And so I read Rawls as saying that according to Kant, our life and the world will have a point, and will fully achieve their purposes, only if we allow the conception of a realm of ends a superordinate role in thought and conduct by striving to live as members of it. Whether we live as members of that realm depends upon *all* our thought and conduct. And so I read Rawls as saying that for Kant, the importance of achieving our purpose lends significance to our every action.

But how does this show that Rawls thought Kant presented the realm of ends as having a value in virtue of which it is worth realizing, as the second conjunct says? Doesn't showing *that* require showing that Kant presented the purposes of human life and the world as worth realizing? What Rawls has to show to establish the second conjunct is that Kant presents the realm of ends as having a value in virtue of which it is worth realizing *by us*, in *our* actions. That value is value from *our* point of view. Of course, the value cannot be one which depends upon our arbitrary or contingent choices, so that the end might not be worth realizing after all. So to establish the second conjunct, Rawls has to show that Kant presents the realization of the realm of ends as something we naturally see as valuable or as worth doing, given the kind of creatures we are. We will see it that way if we see that the realm of ends connects with purposes in which we take a natural interest or concern.

Rawls says Kant thinks that once we grasp the ideal of the realm of ends, we will see that it is worth realizing and will be moved by a desire to realize it. He writes:

> Just as the representation, or an exemplar, of a morally worthy action done from a steadfast regard for the requirements of the moral law apart from all advantage to oneself uplifts the soul and arouses in us a wish that we could act in the same way, so, likewise, the ideal of a realm of ends . . . arouses in us the wish that we could be a member of that world. (*LHMP*, 213)

Kant thinks the fact that the realm of ends moves us is, Rawls says, simply "a fact about persons as reasonable and rational and animating a human body" (*LHMP*, 214). Why is the desire to be part of a realm of ends natural to us?

Rawls does not describe the phenomenological character of the sentiments he says Kant thinks the realm of ends arouses in us. One description would connect the realm of ends with the goods that I said are available in it. A natural desire for those goods would then explain the desire to be part of a realm of ends. But it is tempting to connect the passage I have just quoted with the remark, quoted by Rawls, in which Kant says that the moral law fills us "with admiration and awe," and to read Rawls as saying Kant thinks the ideal of the realm of ends moves us to follow the moral law by eliciting our "admiration [for] and awe [of]" a world in which everyone follows the law.

If we read Rawls this way, then the interest Rawls thinks we take in the realm of ends seems to be of a qualitatively different character than an interest in the great goods that realm would make available. Indeed, if we read him this way, then we can see why Rawls said Kant presents the world as "holy." For the awe that Rawls's Kant thinks is inspired by the ideal of the realm of ends sounds quite like the experience of the holy so famously described by Rudolf Otto in his classic treatment of the subject (2004, chs 3 and 4).

Nagel's development of the religiosity condition suggests a way of filling in this alternative description of the interest we take in the moral law. At the end of section 2, I said Nagel's development of that condition implies that philosophical views which reveal a religious temperament are responsive to, and try to work out the questions raised by, undertheorized conceptions of the world and its order. Rawls's statement of the religiosity condition does not explicitly mention responsiveness, but the remark he quotes about the moral law filling us with admiration and awe is suggestive. It suggests to what experience Rawls might think Kant's moral philosophy responds. For Kant says that we are filled with awe, not just by "the moral law within" but also by "the starry heavens above." Rawls might say that when we behold the order and grandeur of the cosmos, we are moved to ask the questions Kant thought it natural for us to ask: the questions of whether the natural system has some end outside itself and what place each of us has in that vast system. Those questions are answered by Kant's conception of the natural and social world as a realm of ends. I believe Rawls thinks that at least part of what we find awe-inspiring about the realm of ends is that it is a conception of the world in which we act freely, rather than under the influence of alien causes. Working out this conception of the world as a whole might then be thought to heighten the awe inspired in us by the starry heavens by giving us a clearer view of what is awesome about it.

As we saw, Rawls observes that according to Kant, the laws of nature, including human nature, are "not unfriendly" to the realization of the realm of ends, and so he thinks Kant presents the world as it is as a potential realm of ends. This may not show that Kant presents the world as it is as worthy of reverence. But it is not implausible to say that he helps us to see even the world as it is as worthy of our devotion. For if we accept Kant's view, then we can conceive the world as it is as our vocation, requiring our committed action to be transformed into a realm of ends. Kant clearly gives the moral law a dominant role in conceiving the world as it is and the world as it might be. And so Rawls can establish the second conjunct of the intermediate step as well as the first. Given the religiosity condition, he can infer his desired conclusion. And once we see that his view is given its religious aspect by the place of the moral law, we can understand why Kant describes our devotion to the law in religious tones. For the moral law founds the norms from which we must act if we are to live in harmony with the order of the world as Kant's moral philosophy presents it.

This reading handles many of the puzzling features of Rawls's argument. It also solves one of the lingering puzzles about the longer quoted passage in which the argument is embedded. Recall that Rawls speaks in the first paragraph of that passage of "the significance Kant gives to the moral law." I observed that "significance" is ambiguous between "meaning" and "importance" and I implied that an interpretation of the passage should resolve the ambiguity. In the second and third paragraphs Rawls says Kant thinks that acting from the moral law is important and that its importance transcends everyday values. On the reading offered here, it transcends them by subordinating them: the moral law is to frame the pursuit of our other ends. The argument I have said Rawls would offer for the second conjunct of the intermediate step shows that according to Rawls, Kant thinks acting from the moral law has the importance it does because of its meaning – more precisely, because of its connection with the meaning or purposes of human life and the world. Those purposes can be fulfilled only if we rise above the order of causation and regulate our lives by a law we give ourselves.

Connecting the significance of the moral law with the meaning of life and the world may, however, raise worries about the argument and its relevance to Rawls's own view. For Rawls says that the significance Kant gives to the moral law "has an obvious religious aspect." The argument I have interpreted is supposed to show what gives it that aspect. But on the interpretation I have offered, it is not at all apparent that the aspect Kant's view is said to have can plausibly be described as "religious." Even if it can be, it may seem clear that no parallel argument can be used to show that justice as fairness has a religious aspect.

These worries can be made more precise by reference to the religiosity condition. That condition is supposed to be sufficient, though not only sufficient, and I have treated it as such. To show why Rawls thinks Kant's view satisfies it, I have read him as saying that Kant presents the realm of ends as having transcendent importance, as naturally inspiring our awe and as giving humanity a vocation. But, it may be said, the value Rawls says Kant attributes to realm of ends has no connection with traditional theism. Nor does it seem to be spiritual – if by "spiritual" is meant that it asserts the existence of higher, immaterial beings with whom human beings must cultivate a relationship if we are to live well. And so, it may be said, the importance of the realm of ends and the awe it inspires may be similar to religious importance and awe, but they are not instances of them and the vocation to which the realm of ends summons humanity is not a religious calling. But if that is right, then Kant's view does not really have a religious aspect after all. The only way Rawls can avoid this conclusion is to interpret the word "religious" in the religiosity condition quite weakly. Once the condition is interpreted so permissively, however, the condition may seem too weak to be plausible as a sufficient condition.

But a view need not have a theistic or a spiritual aspect to have a religious one and the religiosity condition is not, I think, implausibly weak. As Rawls reads Kant, what makes the superordinate importance of the realm of ends, the awe it inspires and the vocation it gives us all genuinely religious are the connections Kant forges with what gives significance to human life and the world. What Kant thinks each of us is called to do, on Rawls's reading, is to regulate our wills by a transcendent conception of the world and of our place in it, so that we rise above the causal order and help to realize "the final purpose of creation." When we do *that* even our daily actions, done from respect for a law which is to govern our conduct absolutely, are endowed with transcendent meaning. That seems sufficient to give Kant's view a religious aspect.

I shall not spell out this reply in further detail. For I have reconstructed Rawls's interpretive argument in order to ask whether a parallel argument can be used to show that Rawls's own work has a religious aspect. So let us turn our attention to justice as fairness.

## 4. Justice as Fairness Has a Religious Aspect

To see whether such a parallel argument is available, we need to see whether Rawls took something like the intermediate step and whether he took it for reasons that are like the reasons Rawls thought Kant took it. The Rawlsian version of the intermediate step would read:

Justice as fairness has a conception of the world as a whole in which the principles of justice have a dominant place and, because of the dominant place of the principles of justice, that conception presents the world as worthy of devotion and reverence to which pursuit of the everyday values of secular life should be subordinate.

Rawls clearly has a conception of an ordered social world in which the principles of justice have a dominant place, as Kant has a conception of the social world in which the moral law has a dominant place. Rawls's social world is the well-ordered society, in which the basic structure conforms and is known to conform to principles of justice (*TJ*, 4).[5] The well-ordered society is a modern nation-state, and not a global realm of ends. But we can take the well-ordered society to embrace the social world as a whole either by abstracting from the existence of all other societies, as Rawls does in *TJ*, or by conceiving of a world composed entirely of such societies, as Rawls does in *LP* (*TJ*, 7; *LP*, 124).

Rawls's presentation of his ideal social world, like Kant's presentation of the realm of ends, relies on claims about the natural world and its amenability to the realization of that ideal. The circumstances of justice obtain, so that justice has a place and the material or objective conditions of the world are amenable to its realization (*TJ*, 110). Human nature is amenable to its realization as well. In *TJ*, Rawls shows how the laws governing human psychology, including the three laws of reciprocity, the Aristotelian Principle and the companion effect, make it possible for us to develop a sense of justice under just institutions (*TJ*, 429–430, 374–376). And so Rawls's ideal, like Kant's, can be described as a view of the world as a whole. Since the principles have a dominant place in the specification of that ideal, the first conjunct of the Rawlsian intermediate step is true. Moreover, in Rawls's view as in Kant's and in traditional theisms, the first conjunct is doubly satisfied, since the conception of a well-ordered society carries with it a view of the actual social world as a potential well-ordered society or a potential world of such societies.

What of the second conjunct? In conceiving of the world as a well-ordered society, does Rawls present it as worthy of superordinate devotion and reverence? Let us begin by looking at how devotion and reverence for a well-ordered society could be expressed.

I suggested earlier that as Rawls reads Kant, devotion and reverence for the ideal of the realm of ends are expressed by trying to realize and maintain it, by "following the moral law as it applies to us, and in striving to fashion in ourselves a firm good will, and in shaping our social world accordingly." The well-ordered society, like the realm of ends, is an ideal. In Part III of *TJ*, Rawls assumes away problems of transition to the well-ordered society and asks whether the well-ordered society, once realized, would be stable. He thinks its members express their commitment or devotion to the ideal of a just society by doing their part to stabilize or maintain it. Rawls thinks they do *that* by following the principles of justice as they apply to them and by continually shaping the institutions of their social world so that they continue to accord with the principles. And I believe he thinks we, in the world-as-it-is, can express our devotion to the ideal by trying to shape our institutions so that they conform to the principles.

Somewhat less obvious is what Rawls says about how members of the well-ordered society express their devotion to the ideal of the well-ordered society by "striving to fashion in [them] selves a firm good will." I take it that Rawls thinks a good will is or includes a sense of justice. In *TJ*, he argues at some length that the institutions of a just society will encourage a sense of justice in those who live under them. But he also recognizes that preserving a sense of justice requires effort and commitment. Only with such effort and commitment can someone become and remain the kind of person who regularly acts from a sense of justice, so that her sense of justice is "firm." And so members of the well-ordered society have to strive to fashion a sense of justice in themselves and have to commit themselves to preserving it by incorporating such strivings into their plans of life. That is why Rawls is at pains to argue, in his discussion of stability, that members of the well-ordered society must "*plan* to preserve [their] sense of justice as governing their other aims" (*TJ*, 503, emphasis added).

We saw that for Kant, expressions of devotion to the realm of ends subordinate the pursuit of other values because we express our devotion by acting from the moral law and because in all our pursuits, we must act from maxims which satisfy the law. Similarly, Rawls thinks that devotion to the ideal of a well-ordered society is superordinate or transcendent – as is suggested by the conclusion I just quoted, in which Rawls says that members of the well-ordered society must "plan to preserve [their] sense of justice *as governing their other aims*." For he argues, in effect, that they – and we – express devotion to the ideal by being just persons. And he argues that a just person does not treat justice as one end to be balanced among others. Someone who does that, and who fails to treat the principles of justice as regulative, has thereby failed to be a just person (*TJ*, 503). Like the realm of ends and the objects of traditional religious devotion, the ideal of the well-ordered society and the associated principles of right are to govern the good will absolutely and are thereby to play a regulative role in our "inner life."

But does Rawls present the ideal of a well-ordered society as *worthy* of devotion and reverence? And does Rawls think it is worthy for reasons that are anything like the reasons Rawls says Kant thinks the ideal of a realm of ends is worthy of devotion and reverence?

I argued that on Rawls's reading, Kant establishes that the realm of ends is worthy of devotion and reverence by showing that the expression of devotion and reverence gives our lives "meaning and point" and that it does so for three related reasons. It is only by living as members of the realm of ends that we can lead fully human lives, by living as members of a realm of ends we do our part in making its very great goods available and it is only by acting from the moral law that we can serve as the final purpose of creation.

Rawls does not argue that we can realize the final purpose of creation only by living as members of a well-ordered society, though in *Political Liberalism* he does imply –in a passage to which we shall return – that finding out that a just society is possible shows why "it is worthwhile for human beings to live upon the earth" (*PL*, lx). But in *TJ*, Rawls offers a line of argument that is reminiscent of Kant's argument that human beings would have been endowed with practical reason in vain if we did not use our reason to produce a good will. The upshot of Kant's argument was that someone who fails to do that fails to live a fully human life. In a similar vein, Rawls argues that we can express our nature as reasonable and rational beings only by acting "from principles that would be chosen if this nature were the decisive determining element" (*TJ*, 222). Since our nature as reasonable and rational is the "decisive determining element" of choice in the original position, the Rawls of *TJ* argues that we can express our nature – and so live fully human lives – only by acting from principles that would be chosen there. He also thinks members of the well-ordered society would regard it as a great good to do our part in sustaining institutions which allow for diverse forms of human flourishing on a footing of equality and mutual respect (*TJ*, 462).

We also saw that as Rawls reads Kant, presenting the realm of ends as worthy of devotion and reverence was not a matter of presenting it as having intrinsic value, but of presenting it as something human beings naturally regard as worth realizing for its own sake. I believe the same is true of Rawls's own view. Rawls rarely referred to intrinsic value and it is questionable whether the notion did any real work for him. And so Rawls's view, like the Kantian view on Rawls's reading of it, can be said to have a conception of the world which it presents as worthy of devotion and reverence if it presents that conception in such a way that it connects with interests that we naturally have or that we would naturally develop under favorable conditions.

Rawls certainly hopes his view presents the ideal of the well-ordered society that way, for he writes in *TJ*:

> a theory should present a description of an ideally just state of affairs, a conception of a well-ordered society such that the aspiration to realize this state of affairs, and to maintain it in being, answers to our good and is continuous with our natural sentiments. A perfectly just society should be part of an ideal that rational human beings could desire more than anything else once they had full knowledge and experience of what it was. (*TJ*, 417–418)

And the Rawls of *TJ* and the Dewey Lectures believed he *had* presented the ideal of a well-ordered society that way to members of the well-ordered society. In the second of the original Dewey Lectures, he says that the full publicity of his view in a well-ordered society "educate[s]" its members in an ideal of their person so that that "ideal . . . can elicit an effective desire to be that kind of person" (*CP*, 340).

How the desire to be a just person is elicited, and why members of the well-ordered society would affirm that satisfying it is part of their good, are the subjects of *TJ*, sections 70–74 and 86, on the sense of justice, the moral and natural sentiments and congruence. One important strand that runs through Rawls's arguments is this. With the understanding of justice as fairness afforded by the publicity condition, members of the well-ordered society think of themselves as reasonable and rational, develop a desire to express their nature as such, and know that they can realize their nature as such only by honoring the principles of justice (*TJ*, 501, 503). Another is this. The well-ordered society realizes the ideal of a social union of social unions. By the Aristotelian Principle and the companion effect, members of that society would naturally want to uphold the principles of justice that make realization of that ideal possible (*TJ*, §79).

Rawls does not connect the desire to live up to that ideal or the "aspiration to realize" the ideal of a well-ordered society with the awe that Rawls's Kant thinks is inspired by the realm of ends. Perhaps that is because Rawls thinks there is no one thing that it is like to have one's affections engaged by these ideals. Be that as it may, he clearly thinks that these affections can be powerfully motivational. As we saw earlier, Kant thought that the realm of ends inspired our awe in part because it is an ideal of a social world in which we rise above the order of causation. The Rawls of *TJ* thinks that part of what moves us about the ideal of a well-ordered society is that it is a social world in which basic arrangements are not determined by "natural and social contingencies" (*TJ*, 62). Rather, it is one in which we conduct ourselves as free equals and thereby rise above "the contingencies and accidents of the world" (*TJ*, 503). This is not unlike the feature of the realm of ends that I said Kant found awe-inspiring.

Does Rawls present the ideal of a well-ordered society as worthy of devotion by us, his readers? I believe Rawls thinks that we who live in liberal democratic societies which are not well-ordered, and in which justice as fairness is not institutionalized and public, still conceive of ourselves as free and equal citizens and want to live as such. And I believe he thinks that the conception of society as a fair cooperative scheme has some purchase on us. Insofar as that is right, he thinks we will be moved by the specific ideals of the person and society that justice as fairness presents. As Kant's conception of the world as it might be carried with it a conception of the actual world as a potential realm of ends, so those ideals carry with them a conception of our world as having the potential to be a well-ordered society and a conception of our fellow citizens as having the potential to be fellow members of it. These potentialities are not, Rawls insists, mere logical possibilities. They are ones that we can realistically hope to actualize (*LP*, 126). And so, like the realm of ends, the ideal of the well-ordered society does not just carry with it a conception of our world as it is. It also presents us with the vocation of realizing that ideal.

I have maintained that Rawls's view "has a conception of the world as a whole that presents it as worthy of devotion and reverence" because of the way it conceives of and presents the well-ordered society. Recall that when Nagel presents his religiosity condition, he implies that part of what makes a view religious is that it has a conception of a *point of view* from which the natural and social world as a whole can be apprehended as worthy of devotion and reverence. Rawls's view has just such a standpoint: the original position. For one of the roles of the original position in Rawls's theory is to make vivid what it is to have a conception of the world as a whole. By imagining ourselves in the original position, we can grasp the relevant psychological and scientific facts, which are admitted by the veil of ignorance, conjoin those facts with the principles of justice, and see how the world as a whole might be.[6] We can, that is, grasp a natural and social world which is worthy of devotion and reverence because it is a world in which "men exhibit their freedom, their independence from the contingencies of nature and society" (*TJ*, 225).

If that point of view really affords a view of the world as a whole, it must provide a view of each person's life and its proper place in that whole – a view that each is to take as regulative of her life. In traditional theistic views according to which the view of the whole is God's, the details of each person's life are open to view. To take that all-embracing viewpoint as regulative, each of us must discern and follow God's plan for us. Parties in the original position are, of course, veiled from knowledge about particular persons. Though the original position must afford us a view of our own lives that is different from that afforded by the transcendent viewpoint associated with traditional theisms, it still enables us to view ourselves as contributing to the order of the whole when we act as we should.

To see that the original position affords us such a view of ourselves, recall that what makes the ideal of the well-ordered society worthy of devotion is that members of that society regulate their conduct by principles of right. They and we express devotion to that ideal by regulating our conduct by such principles as well. And so, in answer to a question raised above at the end of section 1, the same kind of conduct that inspires devotion to the ideal of a well-ordered society also expresses that devotion. It is worth asking why this should be.

The answer begins from the fact that the well-ordered society is an ongoing cooperative scheme. Since it is ongoing, it can remain just only if its members act from the principles in perpetuity. This happens only when members of each generation act so as to elicit in their successors a devotion for the just society they have inherited, when their successors show that devotion by "maintain[ing] [the just society] in being," and when the conduct by which they maintain it inspires similar devotion in those who follow them.[7] If our action is at once to express devotion for the world bequeathed us by our predecessors and to elicit the appreciation of those who follow us, then we must see ourselves as belonging to one among a succession of generations, all of whose perspectives we must somehow adopt in thinking about how to conduct ourselves. That means that if our conduct is both to express and inspire devotion, we must be able to adopt and act from a perspective on our own action that is, as it were, outside our own time so that a view of the world as natural, social and temporal whole regulates our conduct. This is just what Rawls says the original position enables us to do in the moving closing sentences of *TJ*, where he says that the original position enables us to see "our place in society" *sub specie aeternitatis*. For to enter the original position is, he says, "to view the human situation not only from all social but from all temporal points of view" (*TJ*, 514).

I can now sum up this stage of the argument. The Rawlsian version of what I called "the intermediate step" would read:

> Justice as fairness has a conception of the world as a whole in which the principles of justice have a dominant place and, because of the dominant place of the principles of justice, that conception presents the world as worthy of devotion and reverence to which pursuit of the everyday values of secular life should be subordinate.

We have now seen that both conjuncts of this step are satisfied. It therefore seems to follow that Rawls's view, like Kant's view on Rawls's reading of it, has a religious aspect which is due to the dominant place he gives the principles of right in working out a conception of the world as a whole.

The plausibility of the parallel argument depends upon the plausibility of the religiosity condition. In the first section, I noted that Rawls seems to put forward the condition as both necessary and sufficient. In discussing his claim that Kant's view has a religious aspect, I treated it as a sufficient condition and I argued at the end of the previous section that Rawls's conclusion does not show the condition to be implausibly weak. But the argument that justice as fairness has a religious aspect may seem to resurrect the worry of implausible permissiveness since Rawls's political philosophy is not generally thought to be religious.

But if it is plausible to say of Kant's moral philosophy that it has a religious aspect – as I argued it is – then it is plausible to say the same of justice as fairness. Rawls, like Kant, attaches a transcendent or superordinate importance to the ideal of the well-ordered society and to the principles of right he uses to conceive it, for he argues that we are to treat the principles as regulative and so as superordinate to our other pursuits. While Rawls does not say that the ideal naturally inspires our awe, he does think that the ideal exercises a very powerful hold on us. Awe of the ideal world does not seem to be a necessary condition of having a religious aspect anyway, since traditional theisms can present conceptions of a renewed or redeemed world that can be powerfully attractive without inspiring our awe.

The biggest obstacle to drawing out the parallel between Kant and Rawls seems to be that while Kant says we realize the purpose of creation when we live autonomously, Rawls says nothing like that. It was, however, the connection Rawls's Kant drew between the importance of acting from the moral law and the meaning of doing it – the connection between treating the moral law as regulative and achieving these larger purposes – that made Rawls's conclusion about Kant's view plausible enough to allay doubts about the religiosity condition. Without that connection, acts done from the principles of right may not seem to have a significance that is plausibly described as religious. But as I argued, Rawls does think we must act from the principles of right, not just to express our devotion, but also to constitute the order of the world and so to help bring about or maintain a world which is worthy of reverence. The need for each of us continually to constitute the order of the world invests our every act with a larger significance. This investment makes it plausible to say that justice as fairness has a religious aspect.

## 5. Does Political Liberalism Have a Religious Aspect?

In arguing that Rawls's view has a religious aspect, I drew almost entirely on *TJ*. It is therefore natural to ask whether the religious aspect of justice as fairness survived Rawls's re-presentation of his view as a political liberalism. It is natural to answer that it did not. For in his later work, Rawls presents justice as fairness as a "module" that citizens are to fit into various comprehensive doctrines themselves (*PL*, 12). This and much else Rawls says in *PL* seems to imply that by presenting justice as fairness as a political conception, he is eschewing the project of providing justice with any larger significance.

I do not deny that the later Rawls is eschewing that project. But I do want to suggest that even in Rawls' later work, justice as fairness has something of a religious aspect because Rawls both early and late was concerned with some of the deep existential questions that many religions have raised and tried to answer. Those questions are that of whether we can be reconciled to our life in the world as it is, that of whether human beings can be good despite what history shows about us, and that of whether the world as a whole can be good. That Rawls was moved by them shows his religious temperament. His sustained attempts to answer them give justice as fairness a religious aspect that survives his political turn.

We saw earlier that in the closing passages of *TJ*, Rawls speaks of seeing our lives *sub specie aeternitatis*. He follows a number of other philosophers in raising the possibility of seeing our lives that way. What some philosophers have meant to do in asserting the possibility of seeing ourselves *sub specie aeternitatis* is to make vivid the contrast between, on the one hand, the true insignificance of our lives and how they go and, on the other, the much greater importance we attach to them because we matter to ourselves and our lives are *ours*. Seeing this contrast, it might be thought, is the beginning of wisdom. For once we adopt a view of the world form which we can properly see our place in it, and once we give that view a superordinate place in our reflections, we can attach to our lives the insignificance that they really have. Doing so makes us less inclined to resist what befalls us and readier to accept our fate with equanimity. If facing our fate with equanimity rather than resistance is, or shows, that we are reconciled to it, then the point of inviting us to see ourselves *sub specie aeternitatis* is reconciliation of our will with our situation in the world as it is.

Such an invitation might suffice to give the view which issues it a religious aspect. Those who think that to view the world *sub specie aeternitatis* is to view it as God sees it may be especially attracted to this position. So, too, might those who deny that religion must be theistic and who instead identify religiosity with renunciation of self. For they will think that seeing the world *sub specie aeternitatis* involves independence of all that matters from our own particular point of view in the world.[8] These thinkers may believe that the original position makes such independence vivid because the veil of ignorance frees those who are behind it from the pull of their particular ends. And so, these philosophers may say, when we adopt and act from the point of view of the original position while living in the world, we live lives which are religious as they understand the term.

These are not Rawls's views. "The perspective of eternity is not," he says "the point of view of a transcendent being" (*TJ*, 514). The principles adopted in the original position are not principles of renunciation; members of the well-ordered society are not supposed to live as if they had no ends and attachments of their own. Entering the original position and acting from the principles adopted there are not supposed to reconcile us to whatever sufferings or injustices we may face in the world as it is. Yet presenting an ideal social world, and a conception of the world as it is as "not unfriendly" to that ideal, does have a reconciling function. That helps to give justice as fairness an aspect which is plausibly described as religious.

The world with which Rawls hopes to reconcile us is the social world as it is under modern conditions. Moral and religious pluralism, and widespread secularism, are irreversible features of that world. They have profoundly altered the claims traditional beliefs and traditional morality can make on public life. Modern conditions have also brought with them large institutions that establish new and morally significant human relationships (see, e.g., Scheffler 2010, 169). The institutions of the nation-state establish the relationship of "fellow citizen" among persons spread across vast geographic and social distances. Those institutions have also altered the character of local relations in myriad and obvious ways. The twentieth century demonstrated that the bureaucratic, logistic, police and military powers of those institutions enable them to visit very great evils on their citizens, sometimes with the acquiescence or the active cooperation of large numbers of those who stand in the relation of "fellow citizen" to the victims. Daily politics in societies that purport to be liberal and democratic is often self-seeking and tawdry. The scope of commercial enterprises and the externalities they generate make possible the dislocation of individual and communal lives by forces that seem distant and uncontrollable. All of this can make for profound disaffection for, and alienation from, our large social world and its inhabitants. To be reconciled to the world and its inhabitants is to overcome these attitudes.

A theory of justice for the basic structure identifies principles of right that are to regulate some of the most fundamental institutions and relationships that modern conditions bring with them. Its conception of the world as it might be is therefore a conception of those institutions and relationships as *they* might be. As presented by that conception, those basic institutions are just. They make available a number of very great moral and political goods, such as the goods of a social union of social unions discussed in *TJ* and the goods of democratic governance discussed in *PL* (202–203). The operations of these institutions are not characterized by the brutality or squalor of political life as revealed by history or current events. Moreover, according to that conception, just institutions educate those who live under them, so that they develop a sense of justice and appreciate the goods that a well-ordered society makes available.

Rawls's view of how political philosophy can fulfill the task of reconciliation changed significantly with his turn to political liberalism.[9] But both early and late, Rawls seems to have thought that if we are disaffected by or alienated from the modern social world as it is, a theory of justice can show that its institutions and relationships do not inevitably have the features which engender these attitudes. The basic structures of modern society can be just and can answer to our good as we would come to view it if we lived in a modern society that was well-ordered. Even if things were to go badly for us in a well-ordered society, and our lives do not work out as we had hoped, we could see that our fate was not the result of structural injustices. If we have lived as members of the well-ordered society, committed ourselves to regulating our plans by principles chosen in the original position, and "fashion[ed] in ourselves a firm good will," we would not regret being the kind of person who made that commitment (*LP*, 501–503).

Of course, merely showing the logical possibility of a well-ordered society would not be enough to reconcile us to life under modern conditions. But because Rawls – both early and late – presents a conception of the world as whole according to which natural and psychological laws allow for the establishment and maintenance of a well-ordered society, he shows that we can reasonably hope such a society will be realized. By presenting the world as it is as a potential well-ordered society, justice as fairness tries reconcile us to the institutions under which we live. And if history inclines us to cynicism about or contempt for those with whom we share the world – as Kant said history could (*LHMP*, 320) – then justice as fairness tries to reconcile us to *them* by presenting them as persons who would be willing to do their part sustaining such a well-ordered society, provided others will also. It presents those with whom we share the world as, in that sense, good (*CP*, 7).

Rawls does not try to reconcile us to the world as it is by providing a point of view from which we can see our own insignificance or by encouraging us to renounce our ends. When we see ourselves *sub specie aeternitatis*, we see ourselves not just as free, but also as equals. And when we act from that point of view, we do not forswear the pursuit of our ends, but regulate it by mutually justifiable principles. Nor does Rawls try to reconcile us to our circumstances by encouraging us to conform our will to the world as it is. Rather, in presenting the world as it might be, he presents a conception of one important part of the world – the basic structure – as conforming to principles we would will from that point of view. In so reconciling us to our world, to other persons and to the consequences of living a just life – and in showing that the world and those in it can be good – justice as fairness draws on principles of right to do part of what more uncontroversially religious views also try to do. This use of the principles grounds reasonable faith in the possibility of an ideal world as Rawls conceived it and is part of what give Rawls's view a religious aspect.

Though I have treated the religiosity condition as a sufficient condition, I said in section 1 that Rawls thinks it is necessary as well as sufficient. He must therefore think that religions such as Judaism and Christianity satisfy it. Seeing why he might have thought they do brings to light another reason justice as fairness can be said to have a religious aspect.

One way in which Judaism and Christianity present the world as worthy of devotion and reverence is by presenting the world as a whole as the work of a loving God who entrusts it to our care after pronouncing it "very good." Recall now that I alluded to a place in *PL* where Rawls says that if a just society is not possible, "one might ask with Kant whether it is worthwhile for human beings to live upon the earth" (*PL*, lx). As we saw, Rawls's Kant thought that human beings have a distinctive contribution to make to the world. By exercising our transcendental freedom in the world, we fulfill the world's "final purpose." That, Rawls's Kant might say, is why it is worthwhile for us to exist at all and why our general failure to act from principles of right would raise the question Rawls mentions. Rawls does not argue that we are the final purpose of creation. Why does he think the impossibility of a just world would raise that question?

We saw that Kant was led to identify a final purpose of creation because he thought it natural for us, on observing a system of ends bound by relations of outer purposiveness, to be dissatisfied with a mechanistic description of that system and to ask whether there is something that the world exists *for*. The answer is that the world is the vocation of we who are not just in the world but also out of it. Kant's question depends upon a presumption that Rawls shares: the presumption that we can entertain a conception of the world as a whole, including the human world. I believe Rawls thinks we can ask, not just about the goodness of humanity, but about whether the world as a whole, including us, is good. This question is closer to Kant's than it may first appear to be. For in Rawls's hands, this is not a question about the intrinsic value of the world. Rather, it asks whether there is a conception or description of the world which presents it as answering to the most fundamental interests of our nature as moral theory identifies them. So the question Rawls poses is not about the purpose of the world. It is about whether the world can be presented as a purpose or vocation for us, given the kind of creatures we are.

Rawls presents a conception of our highest-order interests, and a conception of the world which engages them, so that we are moved by that conception to try to realize it. He also argues that its realization is more than a theoretical possibility. By drawing on the principles of justice to present the world as our vocation, and by using the principles to answer a question about its goodness, Rawls responds to questions about the world that are implicit in the creation narrative of Genesis.[10] He thereby gives another religious aspect to justice as fairness.

The possibility of still another religious aspect is opened by asking why Rawls was interested in whether the world can be good. When I said that Rawls's Kant thought it natural to ask whether the world has an end outside itself, I said it was an implication of Nagel's treatment of the religiosity condition that philosophy which satisfies that condition is responsive. I conjectured that Kant's question arose in response to an undertheorized sense of awe at the grandeur of the world. Nagel's implication raises the question of whether Rawls's work is responsive and, if so, to what. Nagel provides a promising clue. He says that philosophy which shows a religious temperament begins with the sense that "Existence is something tremendous, and day-to-day life, however indispensable, seems an insufficient response to it" (2010, 10). Perhaps – and here we can do no more than speculate – Rawls's work responded to the undertheorized wonder at existence that Nagel identifies, and to a correlative desire to figure out what our response to it should be. The experience of wonder at the existence of the world is most famously associated with Wittgenstein (1965, 8), who said of the experience that it is "exactly what people were referring to when they said that God had created the world" (1965, 10). A number of religious thinkers influenced by Wittgenstein have identified a similar sense of wonder as the source of traditional theism.[11] If these thinkers are right, and if traditional theism and Rawls's work – both early and late – respond to similar experiences, then that too gives justice as fairness something of a religious aspect.

## Notes

1   I have discussed Rawls's undergraduate thesis, and its relation to his later writings, in Weithman 2009; 2012.

2  Extract reprinted by permission of the publisher from *Lectures on the History of Moral Philosophy* by John Rawls, edited by Barbara Herman (Cambridge, MA: Harvard University Press), pp. 160–161. Copyright © 2000 by the President and Fellows of Harvard College.

3  More precisely, I suggest that the necessary and sufficient condition Rawls has in mind is the condition Nagel develops as sufficient.

4  The following two paragraphs summarize the excellent presentation of Ginsborg 2005, section 3.5.

5  Rawls describes the well-ordered society as "an interpretation of the idea of a kingdom of ends" at *CP*, 264.

6  Rawls says "My suggestion is that we think of the original position as in important ways similar to the point of view from which noumenal selves *see the world*" (*TJ*, 225, emphasis added).

7  In *PL*, at 204, Rawls says "establishing and successfully conducting reasonably just . . . democratic institutions over a long period of time, perhaps gradually reforming them over generations . . . is a great social good and is appreciated as such."

8  See the views which are critically discussed in Thomas 1995.

9  For discussion, see Weithman 2010, 265–266.

10  See the sources cited at Weithman 2010, 368 n43.

11  See, e.g., Hauerwas 2010, 52; Clack 1999, 38; Kerr 1997, 153. Brian Davies finds Wittgenstein's wonder at existence at the roots of St Thomas's theism; see Davies 2004, 33–34.

## Works by Rawls, with Abbreviations

*A Brief Inquiry into the Meaning of Sin and Faith* (*BI*), ed. Thomas Nagel. Cambridge, MA: Harvard University Press, 2009.

*Collected Papers* (*CP*), ed. Samuel Freeman. Cambridge, MA: Harvard University Press, 1999.

*The Law of Peoples, with "The Idea of Public Reason Revisited"* (*LP*). Cambridge, MA: Harvard University Press, 1999.

*Lectures on the History of Moral Philosophy* (*LHMP*), ed. Barbara Herman. Cambridge, MA: Harvard University Press, 2000.

*Political Liberalism* (*PL*). expanded edn. New York: Columbia University Press, 2005.

*A Theory of Justice* (*TJ*). Cambridge, MA: Harvard University Press, 1999.

## Other References

Clack, Brian R. (1999) *An Introduction to Wittgenstein's Philosophy of Religion*. Edinburgh: Edinburgh University Press.

Davies, Brian (2004) *Aquinas*. New York: Continuum.

Ginsborg, Hannah (2005) "Kant's Aesthetics and Teleology." *Stanford Encyclopedia of Philosophy*. Revised 2013, at http://plato.stanford.edu/entries/kant-aesthetics/ (accessed June 2013).

Hauerwas, Stanley (2010) *Hannah's Child: A Theologian's Memoir*. Notre Dame, IN: University of Notre Dame Press.

Kant, Immanuel (1997 [1785]) *Groundwork of the Metaphysics of Morals*, trans. Mary Gregor. Cambridge: Cambridge University Press.

Kerr, Fergus (1997) *Theology after Wittgenstein*. London: SPCK.

Nagel, Thomas (2010) *Secular Philosophy and the Religious Temperament*. New York: Oxford University Press.

Otto, Rudolf (2004) *The Idea of the Holy*, trans. John W. Harvey. Whitefish, MT: Kessinger.

Scheffler, Samuel (2010) *Equality and Tradition: Questions of Value in Moral and Political Theory.* New York: Oxford University Press.

Thomas, Emyr Vaughn (1995) "Wittgensteinian Perspectives (Sub Specie Aeternitatis)." *Religious Studies* 31(3): 329–340

Weithman, Paul (2009) Review of Rawls, *A Brief Inquiry. Notre Dame Philosophical Reviews*, Aug. 18. At http://ndpr.nd.edu/review.cfm?id=17045 (accessed May 2013).

Weithman, Paul (2010) *Why Political Liberalism? On John Rawls's Political Turn.* New York: Oxford University Press.

Weithman, Paul (2012) "On John Rawls's *A Brief Inquiry into the Meaning of Sin and Faith.*" *Journal of Religious Ethics* 40(4): 557–582.

Wittgenstein, Ludwig (1965) "Wittgenstein's Lecture on Ethics." *Philosophical Review* 74(1): 3–12.

# Part II

# Method

Part II

Methods

# 3

# Constructivism as Rhetoric

## ANTHONY SIMON LADEN

The many ongoing philosophical discussions that form part of John Rawls's legacy are littered with ironies. Here is one: the man who used his Presidential Address to the American Philosophical Association in 1974 ("The Independence of Moral Theory") to deliver a broadside against the whole project of metaethics is now widely credited as one of the key early articulators (albeit through his interpretation of Kant) of constructivism, one of the main metaethical views in current debates. Rawls not only described Kant's moral philosophy as constructivist. He also described his later work, which developed through and after his lectures on Kantian constructivism, as constructivist, although he distinguished the political constructivism of *Political Liberalism* from the moral constructivism of Kant. So it has been easy for commentators to miss this irony, merely reading a perhaps restricted kind of metaethical view into his later work, and seeing most of the pieces of such a metaethics as at least existing in less theorized terms in his earlier writings. The essence of such a reading describes the argument from the original position as the heart of Rawls's constructivism and constructivism as the form of his metaethics. On this view, his metaethics is admittedly "restricted" and this may make it not really a metaethical view at all. But even in that case, one can see how even if Rawls can get away without officially committing to a robust metaethical view, his form of constructivism can easily be ramped up into a full-blown metaethics.[1]

There are, however, two basic problems with this interpretive approach. The first is that, as hinted above, it leaves Rawls's commitment to a purely political liberalism deeply unstable, because he appears unable to maintain that his commitment to constructivism is not ultimately a commitment to a particular metaethics and thus a particular comprehensive doctrine.[2] The second is that this interpretation has a hard time making sense of the central role of reflective equilibrium in Rawls's theory and the way that his thinking about reflective equilibrium as a form of justification developed over 40 years. Sharon Street, for instance, accepts that reflective equilibrium is an important part of Rawls's "restricted" constructivism, but she limits reflective equilibrium to the form that goes on within a single individual, thus

*A Companion to Rawls*, First Edition. Edited by Jon Mandle and David A. Reidy.
© 2014 John Wiley & Sons, Inc. Published 2016 by John Wiley & Sons, Inc.

ignoring the importance of what Rawls calls "general" reflective equilibrium.[3] As a result, reflective equilibrium becomes a kind of philosophical method for working out a view.

In this chapter, I explore an alternative interpretive framework, which basically inverts the roles that the construction of the original position and the reliance on reflective equilibrium play in Rawls's argument. That is, rather than treat constructivism as Rawls's metaethics and reflective equilibrium as his method for theory construction, I want to sketch out the basic contours of Rawls's thinking if we treat constructivism as his method for theory construction and reflective equilibrium as his metaethics. Doing so has two initial advantages and one intriguing consequence. The advantages, briefly put, are these. First, it makes Rawls's metaethics self-effacing, and so makes it easier to see why the working out of his view led him away from a comprehensive doctrine complete with a robust metaethics and toward the idea of political liberalism. Second, it unifies the parts of his thought that changed the most over the course of 40 years, making it clear how that thought developed. The intriguing consequence is that this interpretive approach shifts the status of the original position argument from a kind of deduction of the principles of justice and thus a foundation of the theory to a rhetorical exercise. It will be part of my aim in this chapter to suggest why that is a good thing.

The interpretation I advance in this chapter will be controversial, and I do not want to claim that it captures everything Rawls said on the matters it explores. So I won't spend a lot of time on detailed textual exegesis or responding to objections that would begin from particular passages. My claim is, rather, that my reading makes sense of some general lines of thought in Rawls's work, and the way they developed over the course of his writings, lines of thought that can be obscured by more traditional interpretations. I think the view that emerges is interesting in its own right, and so worth exploring even if it is merely suggested by Rawls's work. But I accept that to the extent that what I present here differs from the view that best captures what Rawls wrote, it may very well be that he and others have seen flaws in it that I have missed. Even if that is so, I hope that the view developed below is at least worth articulating and thinking about.

## On What Metaethics Is

As my opening comments suggest, any talk of metaethics in the context of working out an interpretation of Rawls has to proceed with caution. What, exactly, distinguishes a metaethics from a moral theory or a methodology? In "The Independence of Moral Theory" Rawls distinguishes "moral theory" from "moral philosophy" thus: "Moral theory is the study of substantive moral conceptions, that is the study of how the basic notions of the right, the good, and moral worth may be arranged to form different moral structures" (CP, 286). Moral philosophy includes moral theory but also includes such matters as a theory of the meaning of moral terms, the nature of moral knowledge and facts, and questions about the mind, self and will. Metaethics, as it has come to be called, is thus clearly a part of moral philosophy outside of moral theory. We might get clearer on what, precisely, metaethics is by exploring the analogy with metaphysics. In the "Reply to Habermas," Rawls gives this brief characterization of metaphysics: "I think of metaphysics as being at least a general account of what there is, including fundamental, fully general statements . . . So viewed, W. V. Quine is a metaphysician. To deny certain metaphysical doctrines is to assert another such doctrine" (PL,

379 n8). We might, then, begin to characterize metaethics as being at least a general account of what, morally, there is, of something like the nature of moral facts. We can remove the realist bias built into this description by focusing not on what there is, but on our moral judgments. This yields something like Street's characterization of metaethics: metaethical theories tell us in what the correctness of moral judgments consists. But though this characterization of metaethics opens up more room within metaethics for constructivist and antirealist views, it does not open things up far enough. In particular, it will not help us with the point about Quine. We need a way of understanding metaethics, such that to deny certain metaethical claims is to take a metaethical position, but such that there is some way to do moral theory without first settling metaethical claims. So I will characterize metaethics as a view about what the justification of a moral claim consists in. If we think that moral judgments admit of truth and falsity or of other forms of correctness, then justifying a moral claim will involve showing it to be true or correct. This will lead us to the kind of moral philosophical work in epistemology and the philosophies of language and mind that are familiar from work in contemporary metaethics. And it will lead us to conceive of the priority between metaethics and moral theory in precisely the way Rawls argued against. But a metaethical view might involve the denial that this is the right way to think about moral justification. If moral justification is not a matter of correctness but of how we relate to one another, then it will turn out that understanding what moral justification consists in will, as Rawls argued, have to begin with moral theory. It is in this sense that I will suggest that reflective equilibrium is central to Rawls's metaethics. And the possibility that such a metaethics is self-effacing will consist in the ability to both engage in moral justification and reflect on it without thereby having to make prior theoretical claims about what justification consists in.[4]

## The Trajectory of Rawls's Thought

Before laying out the view that I think Rawls developed, I begin by pointing to some well-known features of Rawls's work and its history that suggest why the standard reading of Rawls's constructivism should strike us as suspicious and why we should turn our attention more fully to reflective equilibrium if we wish to understand the large scale justificatory and thus metaethical structure of the theory. If one traces the development of the argument from the original position from its first statement in the 1958 "Justice as Fairness" (*CP*, 47–72), where it is called the "initial situation," through its first full development in *A Theory of Justice* (1971, rev. edn 1999), and into his final writings, including *Justice as Fairness: A Restatement* (2001), one remarkable fact about it is how relatively unchanged its basic features are over that time. Of course, he does make some changes in how he presents the argument for each of the two principles, and changes somewhat the description he gives of the status of the material he uses to motivate and lay out his constructive device, but it is nevertheless the case that one does not fundamentally misunderstand the theory or the argument in its final form if one only reads its presentation in *TJ* (or even, I think, "Justice as Fairness," where it doesn't include devices such as the "veil of ignorance"), and ignores the developments after that. On the other hand, at every major turn in the articulation of his theory there is a new or more developed account of reflective equilibrium and in particular its justificatory role in the theory.[5] Compared to shifts in clarity about where the maximin rule for choice under uncertainty is deployed in the argument or even the shift in the formulation of the first principle in response to H.L.A. Hart's criticisms, the development of the idea of a political liberalism, an overlapping consensus, public reason and the three stages of justification discussed in his "Reply to Habermas" mark enormous changes in how Rawls both understood and articulated his theory. In particular, these changes all concern how the theory squares with its conception of what moral justification consists in, that is, with Rawls's metaethics. As I will argue below, these changes can all be understood as developing not the idea of the original position, but the idea of reflective equilibrium. Moreover, while the theoretical changes alluded to here are vast and deep, they can all be seen as the systematic working out of ideas about moral justification that one can find in Rawls's earliest writings.

## The Moral Point of Reflective Equilibrium

What, then, is the point of reflective equilibrium and what role does it play in the justification of justice as fairness? When Rawls initially introduces the idea, he describes it as follows:

> In searching for the most favored description of this situation [the original position] we work from both ends. . . . By going back and forth, sometimes altering the conditions of the contractual circumstances, at others withdrawing our judgments and conforming them to principle, I assume that eventually we shall find a description of the initial situation that both expresses reasonable conditions and yields principles which match our considered judgments duly pruned and adjusted. This state of affairs I refer to as reflective equilibrium. (TJ, 18)

On its own, this description lends support to the thought that the search for reflective equilibrium is a matter of method, not metaethics. But it is important to notice the context in which this description appears, and the ways that this context leads to certain natural developments in the idea of reflective equilibrium that move it beyond a mere methodology.

First, the introduction of reflective equilibrium comes in a discussion of how to justify the particular features of the original position as the appropriate interpretation of the initial situation. Rawls thus suggests two lines of justification: "To justify a particular description of the initial situation one shows that it incorporates these commonly shared presumptions [about the conditions under which principles of justice should be chosen]. . . . There is, however, another side to justifying a particular description of the original position. This is to see if the principles which would be chosen match our considered convictions of justice or extend them in an acceptable way" (TJ, 16–17). But for Rawls, justifying a certain theory of justice is a matter of bringing others to accept it, so the value of the coherence we achieve in reflective equilibrium is not that it is directly a criterion of having the right account, but that it gives us reason to think we can justify it to others. As Rawls points out at the end of this section, the reason we should take interest in the results of this hypothetical situation, what supports our saying that "certain principles of justice are justified because they would have been agreed to in an initial situation of equality" is that, if we have described it correctly, "the conditions embodied in the description of the original position are ones that we do in fact accept. Or if we do not, then perhaps we can be persuaded to do so by philosophical reflection" (TJ, 19).

Note here that Rawls is claiming that the justification of his principles of justice rests not, ultimately, on their being chosen in the original position, but in their being the principles we would agree to, would accept, in reflective equilibrium. That is, for Rawls, justification is a matter not of following a constructive procedure but of securing agreement, and so the importance of the idea of reflective equilibrium must lie here. The connection of justification and agreement is an aspect of Rawls's view that goes deep. One finds it in one form or another across the span of his writing, and it explains, I will argue, the development of that thought, and the connection between reflective equilibrium and the key materials of the theory of justification that appear in his later writings.

First, to its depth and staying power: In Rawls's first published article, "Outline of a Decision Procedure for Ethics", published in 1951, Rawls begins by asking

> Does there exist a reasonable decision procedure which is sufficiently strong, at least in some cases, to determine the manner in which competing interests should be adjudicated, and, in instances of conflict, one interest given preferences over another; and further, can the existence of this procedure, as well as its reasonableness, be established by rational methods of inquiry? (CP, 1)

He goes on to explain that he poses the initial question this way because "the objectivity or the subjectivity of moral knowledge turns, not on the question whether ideal value entities exist or whether moral judgments are caused by emotions or whether there is a variety of moral codes the world over, but simply on the question: does there exist a reasonable method for validating and invalidating given or proposed moral rules and those decisions made on the basis of them?" (CP, 1). Now this remark is consistent with a constructivist reading whereby what is important is the existence of a method of validation, but it is also possible to place the emphasis not on the method but on its being reasonable, and thus capable of being used in our discussions with others about their moral convictions. By the 1958 paper "Justice as Fairness" it is this second feature which has clearly taken a primary role. There, he argues that a criterion of the justice of a set of institutions is that it allows people to "face each other openly" (CP, 59). That is, one of the functions of a set of principles of justice that render them just principles as well as principles about justice is that in citing them to one another as we argue about the social institutions in which we live together, we can face one another openly. This idea is then echoed in the final section of TJ, entitled, appropriately enough, "Remarks on Justification." There he says that rather than rely on first principles or nonmoral natural facts, "justification rests on the entire conception and how it fits in with and organizes our considered convictions in reflective equilibrium" (TJ, 507). And in case we were tempted not to pay attention to the "our" in that sentence, he makes a point of responding to the worry that reliance on this picture of justification "appeals to the mere fact of agreement" (TJ, 508). And his response is telling, for it lays out a theory of justification as

> argument addressed to those who disagree with us, or to ourselves when we are of two minds. It presumes a clash of views between persons or within one person, and seeks to convince others, or ourselves, of the reasonableness of the principles upon which our claims and judgments are founded. Being designed to reconcile by reason, justification proceeds from what all parties to the discussion hold in common.

If we put together the emphasis on reasonableness in "Outline" and the passage just quoted from *Theory*, with the remarks about facing each other openly from "Justice as Fairness" the outlines of the metaethical view I am attributing to Rawls begins to emerge. Part of treating others justly is being able to face them openly, and this involves being able to offer justifications for one's conduct and the principles and institutions that guide one's conduct and that one supports. Genuinely offering such justifications is not a matter of merely laying out the contents of one's own thoughts, but being open to other people's reasonable rejection of what you say. The aim of justifying one's position is reconciliation with others, finding common ground, not establishing warrant for one's position. Note that, so conceived, this view is both moral and metaethical, insofar as it lays out a basic norm of treating others, and an account of what justification consists in. Moreover, it ties these together in a manner that gives priority not to the metaethical claim but to the moral one. That is, what ultimately grounds the view about what justification consists in is not a view about what we are or the underlying structure of reason, or any other position in epistemology, the theory of meaning or the philosophy of mind, but rather a grasp of the appropriateness of treating others with whom we live according to this ideal of recognition and respect, of striving to be able to face them openly.

If this conjecture is right, then we should expect that after *TJ* changes in the account of justification should come not from changes in metaphysical or epistemological convictions, but from changes in our grasp of the moral ideal. And this is, I will briefly argue, indeed what happens. In "The Independence of Moral Theory" (1975) we get an argument for the priority of moral theory that in part treats the requirements of plurality and stability that play a big role in the argument of *TJ* not as formal matters arising from a theory of the meaning of moral terms but as part of what is involved in treating others morally (*CP*, 293–294). By the time of his Dewey lectures on "Kantian Constructivism in Moral Theory" (1980), the description of the point of justification is unabashedly practical. Justification is a matter of finding a way for people to settle together on a public conception of justice (or morality) to allow them to live together in ways that let them face each other openly (*CP*, 305). Moreover, the account of reflective equilibrium changes to include the idea of "general" as well as "wide" equilibrium (*CP*, 321). Wide equilibrium requires that a single individual not only find a way to cohere her extant considered judgments at all levels of generality but also that she confronts those judgments with alternative judgments coming from the major traditions of moral thought. It is nevertheless something that an individual (perhaps equipped with a good library) could do alone. General reflective equilibrium, in contrast, is a social notion, and involves all members of a society not only reaching wide equilibrium, but in doing so settling on the same political conception of justice.[6] It is thus tied to ideas that get developed in the full development of political liberalism: the overlapping consensus (an agreement on a political conception of justice that does not rest on more fundamental agreements), public justification, and the idea of public reason.

More could be said about each of these stages, but the point I want to draw out of this overly quick history is that the idea of what justification consists in under development here is one that ties it not to traditional forms of metaethics, but to an unfolding understanding of the kind of respect we owe to one another in our dealings with each other, primarily as fellow citizens, but we might also conjecture, as human beings. The idea here is bound up with an understanding of what it is to offer reasons to another, and this is why it generates not only a moral ideal but a metaethical position. Nevertheless, unlike the metaethical position generally described by the label "constructivism," this metaethics has a tendency to be self-effacing. That is, rather than point us toward some or other foundational claim, the metaethical position that emerges from a commitment to reflective equilibrium and public justification is one that, as it develops, gives increasing weight to the actual interaction

among citizens and fellow moral agents, and less and less to the particular metaethical doctrines that each might take to ground her actions. It provides us, I argue below, a way of
doing moral and political philosophy that is moral all the way down.

## Whither Constructivism?

Though I think the interpretation I am offering explains the development of Rawls's thought
over time, it may appear to run into two fatal problems. First, if reflective equilibrium and the
search of public justification is indeed the justificatory weight-bearing part of the view, then
why does Rawls call his theory "constructivist" and insist on the importance of the original
position in the constructivist framework? And second, if reflective equilibrium is his metaethics, what grounds this view of justification? That is, how can this position be truly self-
effacing? I take these up in turn over the next two sections. As we will see, answering them
not only staves off serious objections, but also reveals some of the further interest of Rawls's
work on this line of interpretation.

One of the most important features of a constructivist argument is that it makes bare its
presuppositions. That is, in giving an argument for a principle of morality or politics in constructivist form, we make clear not only the reasons in favor of those principles, but exactly
how we might derive them from a set of concepts or ideals or facts about the world or our
moral nature.[7] So, for instance, the argument for the two principles of justice via the original
position lays out the considerations that go into setting up the original position in a particular
way as well as the arguments that the parties might offer to one another in favor of one set
of principles over another. Moreover, one of the advantages that this approach has that comes
to greater and greater prominence is its ability to be laid out in what Rawls comes to call a
"free-standing" manner (see, i.e., PL, 10). That is, it looks like the presuppositions of the
argument can be spelled out in ways that do not rely on religious or metaphysical theories
that are controversial and thus to which we cannot expect everyone to agree. We can lay out
the argument for principles of justice via the original position by relying on shared fundamental ideas latent in our democratic culture, or in our shared understanding of the meaning
of justice. This idea of relying on premises publicly shared and available to all in a democratic
society, is, of course, one of the ideas that motivates Rawls's development of his theory in the
direction of political liberalism and the essays that come after it. Note, though, that it is also
already present in the idea of facing each other openly and the constraint of publicity on the
principles and the argument for them in TJ and the earlier essays.

But now notice that if I am, due to a commitment to justification in the form of full reflective equilibrium, concerned to make arguments about justice and principles of justice to my
fellow citizens that they might accept, then one good strategy to do so would be to put my
arguments in constructivist form. And one good test of whether my arguments are ones that
I could in good faith offer to my fellow citizens, whether I can advocate the conclusions I have
reached and the arguments for them while facing them openly, is whether these arguments
could be given such form. Note that on such a construal, the constructivist form of an argument is a way of representing the argument, not a necessary metaethical commitment. It
is, in other words, just what Rawls in fact says the original position is: "a device of representation."[8] Here, we have to understand this remark not, as many have, as referring to a
device that represents citizens or even our considered convictions, but rather a device that

represents an argument for justice in a way that makes it easier both to tell whether it could be made good to our fellow citizens, and to offer it to them.

Of course giving one's argument a form that allows it to more easily appeal to a particular audience, given what you know about the audience's background and position, is the job of rhetoric. So on the reading under development here, it turns out that constructivism is not a metaethical position, but a rhetorical strategy. This conclusion will no doubt meet with skepticism. How could it be, it will be asked, that Rawls's most famous contribution to the history of political philosophy is merely a rhetorical device? Let me answer this question by questioning two of its presuppositions. First, one upshot of the reading I am offering here is that Rawls's most important contributions to political philosophy may not come in the form of the argument from the original position, catchy and attractive as it is. Rather, it would lie in his formulation of a truly democratic articulation of a democratic political philosophy, one which abjures the grand theoretical aspirations of much of the philosophical tradition and takes seriously its place within a fully democratic society.[9] Second, and perhaps more important for the aims of this chapter, I want to counter the devaluation and skepticism of rhetoric implied by the question. That is, if we can abandon philosophy's traditional hostility to rhetoric and not treat rhetoric as just a fancy name for manipulation and insincerity, then we can appreciate the rhetorical aspiration in the original position, and the importance of that aspiration to any truly democratic form of philosophy.[10]

Much more work than I can do here would be needed to fully explore the original position as an exercise in rhetoric. But I can suggest the lines of that work by giving a general characterization of rhetoric that allows us to capture both the kind that arouses philosophers' suspicion and the kind that seems essential to democratic interaction. Rhetoric, then, can be understood as a form of communication that aims to persuade a particular audience of something. It thus aims at persuasion and is tailored to a particular audience. Now, on one natural reading of this characterization, rhetoric is purely instrumental and in danger of being manipulative. That is, if we understand the act of persuasion as something like conversion, whereby I start with a settled and unshakeable position and bring another to my view, then rhetoric will be a tool I use to bring about an end that I have (getting my audience to form a certain view) that is independent of the exercise of rhetoric. Furthermore, if I then also insist that rhetoric aims to achieve this result by being tailored to the particular features of my audience, it will look like it must be manipulative and in danger of being insincere. The orator who hopes to convince his audience of his point of view will say whatever works to convince them, whether he believes it or not, whether or not getting them to believe what he does involves getting them to believe the truth.

But we can understand these constitutive features of rhetoric differently. In adjusting what I say to my particular audience, I attend to their specificity and position, and thus reach out to them, trying to find a way to move toward where they are, rather than insist they come to me. Moreover, this willingness to adjust to my audience is itself persuasive, not in the sense that it gives me access to the levers by which I can more effectively manipulate them, but because by showing my respect for where they stand in the way I choose to address them, I give them reason to trust me and reach out to me. Rhetoric so understood can move my audience because it involves an expression on my part of a willingness to be moved, and thus an expression of a commitment to find common ground together. And so though rhetoric aims at persuasion, it need not do so in a way that treats what I say as purely instrumental. Notice, however, that this second account of how rhetoric works dovetails nicely with the picture of democratic justification toward which I have been suggesting the trajectory of Rawls's work points.

If I am committed to only adopting principles of justice that I can advocate to you openly, then working out what those principles are cannot be an exercise independent of articulating them and my reasons for them to you, and calling for your response. Since what I am willing to accept is in part dependent on what I can persuade you to accept, persuasion is not just something that comes after reflection and aims to get everyone on board. It is part of working out what the substantive moral commitment to finding shared principles commits me to. In such a case, this form of rhetoric is just the activity of communicating with one another as we work out together the guiding principles of the institutions that shape our lives together. It is, in other words, precisely the method of justification we need.[11]

My claim, then, is that the constructivist argument from the original position is an exercise in rhetoric in this second sense. Justifying a set of principles, whether moral or political ones, in a way that respects the commitment embodied by the metaethics of reflective equilibrium means that when we try to persuade others of a particular view, we need to do so in a way that addresses them where they are, and leaves open the possibility that common ground may not lie where we initially thought it did. In practically every incarnation of the argument from the original position, Rawls introduces the argument with something like this thought. To the extent that this has been obscured, it is, I think, because the argument as it is presented in *TJ* takes on features that it does not take on either before or after that, features connected to the formal language of economics and rational choice theory. The presentation of the argument there makes it look like it is a technical, quasi-deductive argument, and the language Rawls uses there (his rhetoric, one is tempted to say) emphasizes these features of the argument.

There are at least two ways to understand why he adopts this technical language in the most exhaustive and complete treatment of this argument. The first, more widely accepted, explanation is that he thought the formal tools of rational choice theory would allow him to make an airtight and final argument in favor of his principles. On this view, the ambitions of *TJ* fail and it is this failure which leads to the developments on the way toward *PL*. But if we take what I have been suggesting seriously, another possibility opens up, and that is that this choice of language is itself rhetorical, in the sense that it is aimed at a particular audience.[12] *TJ* is concerned to offer a systematic alternative to utilitarianism and in particular to the formal apparatus that a long line of utilitarian mathematicians and economists as well as moral philosophers had developed. Thus, while it works out a theory for a democratic society, there is an important sense in which its audience is not, in the first instance, Rawls's fellow citizens, but those who are attracted to the formal system of utilitarianism. To persuade this audience to take seriously his alternative, Rawls aims to show them that it is articulable with the same level of formal precision as their preferred theory. In later works, his attention is directed elsewhere, to the concerns of what he calls "citizens of faith" and to those who have lost faith in the possibility of a just constitutional democracy in the face of reasonable pluralism. It would be a rhetorical mistake to address this audience with the formal apparatus of rational choice theory, and so this language, which was never essential to the argument, is left aside. The shift in language is not, then, a recognition of the failure of an overreaching ambition, but an expression of the deep metaethical conviction that how one argues for moral principles reflects one's morality as deeply as what moral positions one argues for.

# Morality as Metaethics

This account of Rawls's rhetoric, however, still leaves my second question. How are we to understand reflective equilibrium as a metaethics, where this includes something like a grounding for an account of what moral justification consists in? And moreover, how can we understand that grounding in a way that is self-effacing, that does not commit Rawls to a particular metaethical doctrine, even one whose principal content is the denial of metaethical claims? That is, why should we think that even reasoned agreement tells us anything about which moral judgments are justified, let alone what moral truth or the moral facts consist in? The beginning of an answer lies in the recognition that the commitment to reflective equilibrium and public justification as a metaethics is moral, not theoretical.

That is, I think Rawls begins with and anchors his commitment to reflective equilibrium in the broad sense I have been using the term here in a moral insight. It is, roughly, the same moral insight that leads T.M. Scanlon (1982) and Christine Korsgaard (1996a) to say that relationships are what morality is about. It is the idea that what it is to take and treat someone as a fully free and equal moral being, to treat them as a person, is that we be able to justify what we do that affects them on terms that they accept. This is, I claim, the same insight that leads Rawls to describe justice as a condition that obtains when we can face each other openly. And my contention now is that this insight is not best thought of as the conclusion of his arguments, but the starting point of those arguments, or at least what determines that they have the shape they do. If Rawls's metaethics is grounded in anything, then, it is this moral conviction, and not, as with the other forms of constructivism classified by Street, in a metaphysical claim about our nature or the nature and structure of reason. Those attached to more traditional metaethics will feel that the claim that Rawls grounds his theory in a moral conviction cannot be a final answer, as it just sweeps the problem of what grounds his theory under the rug. That is, the moral commitment appears to wind up functioning like a kind of foot-stomping assertion of a dogmatic moral realism that refuses to speak its name, and so still leaves open the question of what grounds the moral commitment.

There is, however, another possibility, and for its inspiration we need to look not to the title of the lectures where Rawls introduces the term "constructivism" ("Kantian Constructivism in Moral Theory"), but to their occasion (the Dewey Lectures). Rawls ends his introductory remarks to these lectures with a nod toward Dewey, and in particular Dewey's affinities with Hegel's attempt to overcome various dualisms in Kant's thought. The basic insight that I want to take from Dewey and Hegel here can be put another way. It is the idea that we can ground the starting points of our theories not by working backwards to ever more fundamental and necessary premises, but by seeing how the theory develops going forward.[13]

The idea is something like this. We start with a perhaps somewhat inarticulate and not fully grounded moral insight, intuition or conviction, and try to work out its implications through figuring out what we might say on the basis of it and on its behalf to others. The result, if the initial idea turns out to have value, is that we will be able to give a theory that rests on it, and the package of insight and theory will be attractive to those who encounter it. If we thus come to find shared ground through and on top of that theory, then we will have a justification for it, but that justification will, somewhat surprisingly, also turn out to justify in the sense of vindicate our initial intuition.[14] Think, for instance, of how work in mathematics actually proceeds. Mathematicians do not typically assemble a bunch of theorems and then subject them to accepted rules of inference and see what comes out. They typically begin with a problem and an insight about what might solve it. What ultimately vindicates the insight is the proof and solution that it generates, and while part of the vindication will involve fitting the output of the insight into a preexisting formal structure, both the vindication and the more precise content of the insight are not given by a kind of prior grounding, but through what it has yielded. Similarly, I am suggesting that in doing moral philosophy, we start with problems and insights about both what might solve them and what constraints we ought to obey in working out a solution, about, for instance, what a basic moral regard demands of us. As we work out our solutions more fully, this process serves not only generate solutions to our problems, but to vindicate our initial insight. We begin with the thought that morality requires offering one another reasons, or treating others with respect, and we then come to see what we have to say in its favor in the very process of working out what reasons we have to offer others for this general insight as well as the more particular features of our moral positions that offer solutions to our various problems. On this view, then, the moral commitment that I am suggesting supports the metaethics of reflective equilibrium is not a premise that requires further grounding, but a hypothesis that is both filled out and validated by the theory it produces.

Moreover, the process of developing arguments and theories not only vindicates our initial insights but also serves to explicate them. That is, we learn what it means to have this kind of moral regard for another precisely by learning how it gives rise to these further theories or commitments. So, if we want to know what, precisely, the moral insight and commitment is that forms the basis of Rawls's view, the best way to get a handle on it is to understand how that view is an articulation of it.[15] That would involve something like the project I have been undertaking here. However, the development of insight and theory is not a static process, because as we come to understand our initial insights more clearly, we might also come to change those insights, or at least to see them differently than we had originally. There is not a bright line of demarcation between coming to see that treating a person with respect requires being able to face her openly and that this can be done through accepting an idea of public reason in political deliberation, on the one hand, and coming to see that facing one another openly is insufficient for treating a person with respect and must be replaced with a conception that includes an idea of public reason. Part of what changes as our insight is developed here is our conception of a person, and thus what respecting persons amounts to. So the process of vindication that I am describing turns out to be an ongoing and always changing one. As insights are grasped and theories developed, we come to see the nature of our initial insights differently than we did before, and this leads us not merely to different philosophical positions but to different moral and political ones. Our grasp of what it is to see and respect another as a person and our understanding of what morality demands of us in our interaction with other persons change together and in light of one another. And so these changes, in our moral theory and our grounding insights, then start up the whole process of theory development and vindication again. What I have described here is both the search for reflective equilibrium and at least one way to understand the nature of dialectic advance according to Hegel.[16]

Note that in the hands of Hegel, Dewey and Rawls, the possibility that our starting points undergo revision as we work out from them is not a source of despair or skepticism born of the thought that our theoretical edifices are built on nothing but heaps of sand, but a kind of faith and optimism that our practices of reflection are potentially self-correcting. It is, I think, this attitude that ultimately allows for the full self-effacement of the metaethical outlook I have been suggesting was Rawls's. That is, if our moral insights and convictions need not prior grounding but vindication and revision in the light of their enactment, then the very nature of moral justification is one that can do without metaethical arguments. This does not amount to a denial of metaethical claims but an eschewal of them. Either metaethical arguments turn out to be just one more way of clarifying and vindicating our basic moral positions or they are, morally speaking, beside the point. (As Rawls says in a footnote to an early, unpublished version of the class notes that became the *Restatement*, "No deep thinking here. Things are bad enough already.")[17]

## Reasoning and the Moral Life

Let me conclude this chapter by pointing toward a perhaps unexpected by-product of the interpretive approach I have been developing here. Throughout Rawls's early writings, he routinely refers to his position as a form of moral sense theory, suggesting that the point of moral theory is to work out a fuller and clearer understanding of our moral sense or sense of justice.[18] It is hard to know what to make of these remarks if one is trying to make sense of Rawls as a Kantian constructivist, searching for a well-grounded deduction of justice or the moral law. On such a view, questions of moral psychology will appear to be side issues, concerned with motivation and feasibility, not what the theory under development is about. But if something like the view developed here is right, these remarks are exactly what we should expect Rawls to say about his view. That is, working out a moral or political theory is a matter of working out what we can say to one another in the course of living our lives together, and that very process is a matter of working out the details of and trying to vindicate our basic moral insights and commitments, the deliverances, that is, of our moral sense. Doing so is not, however, a purely theoretical endeavor, best left in the hands of metaphysicians, philosophers of mind, and metaethicists. It is, rather, something we do together, in the course of making moral and political arguments, staking out positions and listening to what others say. And the result is not an abstract theory but a clearer moral vision, an improved moral sense.

Note that this is not only where the arguments of this chapter take us, but where Rawls thought the arguments of *TJ* took him and might take his readers. For the final line of that work is not about justice or the institutions of the basic structure, but about what one would achieve by taking up the point of view captured in the original position ("a certain form of thought and feeling that rational persons can adopt within the world"). It is also one final rhetorical flourish in a book that turns out to have been full of them: "Purity of heart, if one could attain it, would be to see clearly and to act with grace and self-command from this point of view" (*TJ*, 514).

## Notes

1   See, for instance, Sharon Street, "Constructivism about Reasons" (Street 2008). The term "restricted" is hers.

2   For one influential interpretation along such lines, see Habermas 1995. For some skeptical reflections of the aptness of this criticism, see Laden 2010 and 2004.

3   At various points in his work, Rawls distinguishes between various forms of reflective equilibrium, including "narrow," "wide," "full," and "general." I discuss these different forms and their various meanings below.

4   It would not, I think, be amiss to notice a distinct whiff of pragmatism here. I return briefly to Rawls's connection to Dewey below, but the full story of Rawls the pragmatist will have to wait for another essay (probably by another author).

5   The truth of this claim will depend on how broadly one conceives of the idea of reflective equilibrium, and in particular, whether one sees it as deeply connected to a set of other ideas that get developed in his later writings. I make a case for drawing such connections below.

6   Note that varieties of reflective equilibrium abound in Rawls's work. In addition to wide and general reflective equilibrium, there is narrow reflective equilibrium (reached by an individual without the library) and full reflective equilibrium, which is the achievement of a well-ordered society when all of its members are in wide and general reflective equilibrium. This taxonomy is most clearly laid out in *Justice as Fairness: A Restatement* (*JF*, 31).

7   So, for instance, Christine Korsgaard (1996b) argues for a robust form of moral constructivism partly on the grounds that it captures the truth of realism without succumbing to realism's inevitable dogmatism.

8   See, e.g., "Justice as Fairness: Political not Metaphysical" (at *CP*, 400–401).

9   For readings of Rawls that stress this feature of his work, see Dreben 2003; Rorty 1991.

10  On the importance of rhetoric to democracy, see, among others, Allen 2004; Dryzek 2010, though the latter develops his point in opposition to what he takes to be Rawls's implicit hostility to rhetoric embodied in his commitment to reason.

11  Note that understanding rhetoric this way also pushes toward a rather different understanding of the activity of reasoning with others. For a detailed description of such an understanding, see Laden 2012.

12  Note that my point here is not that every change between *TJ* and *PL* should be understood as a matter of rhetoric, but merely that changes in the language and form of the argument from the original position between the two books can be so understood.

13  For a clear articulation and development of this idea of normative grounding in historical development, see Brandom 2009.

14  I take the language of vindication here from Onora O'Neill's work on Kant. See, for instance, O'Neill 1989.

15  Note that this also provides a way of understanding constructivist arguments as a path to a shared representation of our moral nature, and not merely as a theory about the space of moral reasons or about what justification consists in. I thank David Reidy and Jon Mandle for pointing out the relevance of this other side of constructivism to the arguments here.

16  It might also remind some readers of the hermeneutic circle. If so, they would be in the good company of Sam Fleischacker, to whom I owe the point.

17  The statement occurs in a footnote explaining why Rawls doesn't employ the term "identity" to talk about the attitudes that citizens form of themselves in light of aspects of the background public culture. Identity, Rawls remarks, suggests "the profundities of metaphysics and the philosophy of mind"; "Justice as Fairness: A Briefer Restatement," 45 n27.

18  See, for instance, *TJ*, 41. Note here that Rawls means by "moral sense" something different than the idea of moral sense as it is generally understood in the work of the so-called sentimentalists of the eighteenth century. It is in no way a nonrational capacity, but, as he suggests, analogous to our sense as language users of grammaticalness.

# Works by Rawls, with Abbreviations

*Collected Papers* (CP), ed. Samuel Freeman. Cambridge, MA: Harvard University Press, 1999.

"The Independence of Moral Theory" (1975), in *Collected Papers* (236–302).

"Justice as Fairness" (1958), in *Collected Papers* (47–72).

"Justice as Fairness: A Briefer Restatement," MS, 1989.

"Justice as Fairness: Political not Metaphysical" (1985), in *Collected Papers* (388–414)

*Justice as Fairness: A Restatement* (JF), ed. Erin Kelly. Cambridge, MA: Harvard University Press, 2001.

"Kantian Constructivism in Moral Theory" (KC) (1980), in *Collected Papers* (303–358).

"Outline of a Decision Procedure for Ethics" (1951), in *Collected Papers* (1–19).

*Political Liberalism* (PL), expanded edn. New York: Columbia University Press, 2005.

"Reply to Habermas" (1995), in *Political Liberalism* (372–434).

*A Theory of Justice* (TJ) (1971), rev. edn. Cambridge, MA: Harvard University Press, 1999.

# Other References

Allen, Danielle (2004) *Talking to Strangers*. Chicago: University of Chicago Press.

Brandom, Robert (2009) *Reason in Philosophy: Animating Ideas*. Cambridge, MA: Harvard University Press.

Dreben, Burton (2003) "On Rawls and Political Liberalism." In Samuel Freeman (ed.), *The Cambridge Companion to Rawls*. Cambridge: Cambridge University Press.

Dryzek, John (2010) "Rhetoric in Democracy: A Systemic Appreciation." *Political Theory* 38(3): 319–339.

Habermas, Jürgen (1995) "Reconciliation through the Public Use of Reason: Remarks on John Rawls's Political Liberalism." *Journal of Philosophy* 92 (Mar.).

Korsgaard, Christine (1996a) "The Reasons We Can Share." In Korsgaard, *Creating the Kingdom of Ends* (275–310). Cambridge: Cambridge University Press.

Korsgaard, Christine (1996b) *The Sources of Normativity*. Cambridge: Cambridge University Press.

Laden, Anthony Simon (2004) "Taking the Distinction between Persons Seriously." *Journal of Moral Philosophy* 1(3): 277–292.

Laden, Anthony Simon (2010) "The Justice of Justification." In James Gordon Finlayson and Fabian Frayenhagen (eds), *Habermas and Rawls: Disputing the Political*. New York: Routledge.

Laden, Anthony Simon (2012) *Reasoning: A Social Picture*. Oxford: Oxford University Press.

O'Neill, Onora (1989) "Reason and Politics in the Kantian Enterprise." In O'Neill, *Constructions of Reason* (3–27). Cambridge: Cambridge University Press.

Rorty, Richard (1991) "The Priority of Democracy to Philosophy." In Rorty, *Objectivity, Relativity and Truth* (175–196). New York: Cambridge University Press.

Scanlon, T.M. (1982) "Contractualism and Utilitarianism." In Bernard Williams and Amartya Sen (eds), *Utilitarianism and Beyond*. Cambridge: Cambridge University Press.

Street, Sharon (2008) "Constructivism about Reason." In Russ Shafer-Landau (ed.), *Oxford Studies in Metaethics*, vol. 3. Oxford: Clarendon Press.

# 4

# Kantian Constructivism

## LARRY KRASNOFF

## 1. The Received History of the Dewey Lectures

In the title of his 1980 Dewey Lectures, John Rawls announced that his theory of justice as fairness could be described as an example of "Kantian Constructivism in Moral Theory" (KC). On its face, this description seemed to imply two claims. First, Rawls was saying that "constructivism" should be understood as a particular option in moral theorizing, one that should be distinguished from more familiar and traditional positions such as intuitionism, rationalism, or emotivism. Second, Rawls was saying that there was a particularly Kantian version of constructivism, one that included Rawls's own theory of justice as well as Kant's practical philosophy. Together, these two claims seemed to make the connection between Rawls's and Kant's views especially tight. Rawls was saying not only that he and Kant shared a particular conception in moral philosophy (constructivism) but also that they agreed on a particular version of this conception (the Kantian kind).

This alleged connection struck many readers, with good reason, as an important change from *A Theory of Justice*. In §40 of *TJ*, the book's most extensive discussion of Kant, Rawls argued that his procedural conception of justice could be given a Kantian interpretation. By speaking of "the Kantian interpretation of justice as fairness" in the title of this section, Rawls was clearly implying that it was possible, and even perfectly legitimate, to interpret his theory of justice in another, non-Kantian way. Because Rawls argued specifically in *TJ* §40 that the Kantian interpretation of justice as fairness meant understanding agents as acting autonomously when they acted on principles chosen in the original position, it also seemed to follow that the idea of autonomous choice was the Kantian idea that could be dispensed with in the plausible non-Kantian interpretation of justice as fairness. Since justice as fairness was a matter of what would be chosen in the original position, Rawls seemed to be saying that the content of what was chosen could be separated from a particular interpretation of how it was chosen. The controversial notion of autonomous or noumenal choice could be exchanged for a suitably naturalistic model of agents maximizing their expected gains.[1] On this alternate

---

*A Companion to Rawls*, First Edition. Edited by Jon Mandle and David A. Reidy.
© 2014 John Wiley & Sons, Inc. Published 2016 by John Wiley & Sons, Inc.

and more modest interpretation, Kant's moral philosophy could be reduced by Rawls's theory of justice to its substantive, anti-utilitarian content: not using others merely as means, as expressed in the priority of liberty and the difference principle (the subject of Rawls's next most extensive, and quite clearly separate, discussion of Kant in *TJ* §29). What Kant would have chosen to be just could thus be separated from how or why he might have chosen it. For many naturalistically inclined readers of *TJ*, the justification of Kantian moral principles without the metaphysically loaded theory of autonomy was the chief philosophical achievement of the book.

On this interpretation of *TJ*, Rawls's announcement of his commitment to Kantian constructivism in KC looked like a straightforward return to the formerly optional and hence dispensable Kantian theory of autonomy. Since constructivism was now said to be a view according to which the content of morality was nothing more than what a particular set of agents, specified in a particular way, would choose for themselves, Rawls seemed to be placing the entire weight of his view on the description of the choosing agents. If it was essential that these agents be described in a Kantian way, then it would seem that a conception of autonomous choice was now understood as essential to Rawls's theory of justice.

Unsurprisingly, those naturalistic readers of *TJ* who had preferred to opt out of the Kantian interpretation of the original position were not pleased by this new development. It was thus highly reassuring to these readers (e.g., Rorty 1991) when Rawls announced, in his next major essay ("Justice as Fairness: Political not Metaphysical," 1985), that his constructivism was "political, not metaphysical," and when he went on to distinguish explicitly in *Political Liberalism* between his merely political constructivism and Kant's moral constructivism. *PL* classified Kant's moral constructivism as a potentially controversial comprehensive doctrine, not capable of generating public consensus around its claims to moral truth. Rawls was now treating Kantian autonomy as he treated traditional religious doctrines, as relying on controversial metaphysical assumptions – which is exactly how the earlier, naturalistic readers of *TJ* had understood it all along. Reading *PL* along these lines produces an interpretation of KC as a misguided but ultimately rejected experiment with Kantian metaphysics. On this now rather familiar history, Rawls flirted around 1980 with a strong commitment to Kantian autonomy, only to abandon it as unnecessary to the justification of his theory of justice.

There are obvious problems with this kind of interpretation of Rawls's intellectual trajectory. For one thing, Rawls continued to use the term "constructivism" to describe his merely political liberalism, and he continued to speak of the central importance of autonomy, even if this autonomy was described as specifically political rather than moral (*PL*, II, §§4–5). Clearly something had changed with KC that Rawls never sought to renounce. Still, if one presses hard on the distinction between "Kantian" and "constructivism," and sees the latter – seeking to build a stable public consensus around merely political principles – as the core idea of Rawls's later work, one can nonetheless regard KC as a kind of advance, even if a metaphysically handicapped one, toward an improved (in the sense of a less Kantian and less metaphysical) theory of justice. The *locus classicus* of this kind of interpretation is William Galston's influential but ultimately misleading essay, "Two Concepts of Liberalism" (1995). In this essay, Galston distinguishes sharply between two strategies for justifying liberal political arrangements, between an "Enlightenment project" and a "Reformation project." On this distinction, Enlightenment liberals sought to ground liberalism in the politically and metaphysically contested notions of autonomy and individual choice, while

Reformation liberals sought to ground liberalism in the pragmatic and metaphysically neutral task of accommodating the plurality of comprehensive doctrines. For Galston, the appeal of Rawls's later work is its affirmation of the Reformation project, its reframing of the constraints of the original position as a practical device that could generate political agreement under conditions of reasonable pluralism. If again we understand the primacy of the practical task of generating public agreement as the essential feature of Rawls's constructivism, then we can understand the Dewey Lectures' "Kantian constructivism" as an important but nonetheless incomplete advance in the justification of Rawls's theory of justice. We can say that the Dewey Lectures first identified public consensus rather than independent moral truth as the goal of the theory, and that the subsequent work went on to ground the goal of public consensus in the pragmatic and historically specific task of the Reformation project, rather than in any sort of appeal to individual or collective choice. The gradual stripping away of the "Kantian" part of Rawlsian constructivism – a task to which Galston's essay is eager to contribute – becomes the centrally important project of Rawls's later work.

To a very large extent, this account of Rawls's intellectual development has dominated the debate over the justification of his political liberalism. One can argue, with Galston, that Rawls needs to affirm decisively the purely political constructivism of his later work, perhaps even to the point of giving up some of his professed theoretical aims (McCabe 2011). Or one can argue, against Galston, that a pragmatic or purely political liberalism can never succeed, that any justified political theory must inevitably retain certain irreducibly "metaphysical" commitments (Steinberger 2000), so that Rawls must make those commitments, perhaps even to the point of affirming a full-blown Kantianism (Taylor 2011). But in this entire debate, an opposition between the "Kantian" (and hence more strongly metaphysical) and the "merely political" (and hence more purely constructivist) elements of Rawls's work is taken for granted.

In what follows, I want to argue that this supposed opposition – and indeed the entire distinction that Galston seeks to draw – is based on a serious misunderstanding of Rawls's intellectual trajectory, and especially of the way he understands the Kantian elements of his theory. My goal is to show that, against the assumptions of the familiar debates described above, Rawls in and after KC consistently held that the practical aims of constructivism and the philosophical goal of a fully rational justification are not in any sort of tension. In fact, the rejection of such a tension is exactly the content of Rawls's "Kantianism." I will then attempt to show that Rawls's claims in *PL* and after, and especially his distinction between his political and Kant's moral constructivism, in no way undermine this argument from 1980. Read in the right way, Rawls's later work can be understood as a continual attempt to provide his theory of justice with a deeper and more fully rational justification, not a weaker and more pragmatic one. But one can understand this conception of justification only if one understands the Kantianism of KC as something quite different from a flirtation with metaphysics.

## 2. Constructivism before the Dewey Lectures

Just how and why did Rawls come in 1980 to describe his theory of justice as a form of Kantian constructivism? Though the word "constructivism" does not appear in *TJ*, Rawls does there describe his theory of justice as "constructive."[2] This description is introduced by way of a contrast with intuitionism, which Rawls defines in a very striking fashion:

> I shall think of intuitionism in a more general way than is customary: namely, as the doctrine that there is an irreducible family of first principles which have to be weighed against one another by asking ourselves which balance, in our considered judgment, is the most just. Once we reach a certain level of generality, the intuitionist maintains that there exist no higher-order constructive criteria for determining the proper emphasis for the competing principles of justice. While the complexity of the moral facts requires a number of distinct principles, there is no single standard that accounts for them or assigns them their weight. Intuitionist theories, then, have two features: first, they consist of a plurality of first principles which may conflict to give contrary directives in particular cases; and second, they include no explicit method, no priority rules, for weighing these principles against one another: we are simply to strike a balance by intuition, by what seems to us most nearly right. (*TJ*, 30)

One might think that the distinctive feature of intuitionism is its reliance on a faculty of moral intuition, on some sort of immediate capacity for perceiving moral truths. This is exactly the definition that Rawls rejects. "These characteristic epistemological doctrines are not a necessary part of intuitionism as I understand it" (*TJ*, 31). Instead Rawls defines intuitionism in terms of what might seem to be a derivative result of appealing to an intuitive capacity: the intuitionist's inability or unwillingness to settle conflicts between different intuitions. Indeed Rawls is saying that the essential feature of intuitionism is its positing of potentially competing intuitions. That there could be a single, practically dominant intuition seems ruled out from the start. "Perhaps it would be better if we were to speak of intuitionism in this broad sense as pluralism" (*TJ*, 31). Though there could in principle be a monistic form of intuitionism, an intuitionism that proclaimed the supremacy of a particular value, Rawls is arguing that such an intuitionism has, by its own lights, no way of rationally explicating the supremacy of its favored value over other, subordinate values, or over a different candidate for a supreme value. In practice, then, intuitionism amounts to a form of pluralism because the intuitive appeal to value always leaves open the possibility of equally intuitive and hence competing appeals to other values. But pluralism does not necessarily imply intuitionism: "a conception of justice can be pluralistic without requiring us to weigh its principles by intuition. It may contain the requisite priority rules" (*TJ*, 31). A priority rule is understood here as a clearly defined method for adjudicating among a plurality of potentially competing practical principles. Theories that assert priority rules thus join intuitionism in assuming the truth of pluralism, but they depart from intuitionism in going on to propose criteria for ordering a plurality of practical claims. Proposing such criteria is just what makes a theory constructive: "The only way therefore to dispute intuitionism is to set forth the recognizably ethical criteria that account for the weights which, in our considered judgments, we think appropriate to give to the plurality of principles. A refutation of intuitionism consists in presenting the sort of constructive criteria that are said not to exist" (*TJ*, 35).[3]

Rawls cites two main examples of constructive moral theories of justice: classical utilitarianism and his own theory of justice as fairness (*TJ*, 36–37). He notes that there may well be other such theories, but these two theories represent important options for adjudicating potentially conflicting claims about justice (*TJ*, 40). On the one hand, classical utilitarianism attempts to respond to the plurality of our desires or preferences, and of moral disputes about those desires or preferences, by subordinating them all to a single, aggregative standard. The principle of utility is intended to be the sole criterion for settling practical conflicts. By contrast, justice as fairness, though proposing the original position as the unique framework for political justification, famously advances from the original position two distinct principles of justice, arranged in lexical priority. A constructive reply to intuitionism must be a principled reply, but constructivism alone does not specify whether intuitions should be subordinated to a single, overarching principle, or as in justice as fairness, to some set of principles, arranged in some sort of lexical priority.

In one sense, this account of justice as fairness as constructive is quite far from the constructivism of KC. In the later account, Rawls will insist that his theory is constructivist because justified political claims are created by the choices of the parties in the original position (Krasnoff 1999, 401–402). In the earlier account, all that is required to make a theory constructive is that it advance a method for producing justified political claims in the response to potentially conflicting intuitions. Nothing in this requirement implies that the method of justification must feature persons who choose or construct principles of justice for themselves. In the terms of *TJ*, utilitarianism clearly counts as a constructive moral theory, but nothing in the principle of utility requires that the summing and weighing of desires or preferences is carried out by a set of constructors. Indeed classical utilitarianism is perfectly consistent with a realist interpretation that holds that the human good is pleasure and that what would produce the greatest pleasure for the greatest number is an independent fact that utilitarian calculators are always trying to track. Not every constructive theory (in *TJ*'s sense), then, relies (as Rawls does) on a specifically constructivist method of justification (in KC's sense).

But in another way, it is striking how clearly the account in *TJ* anticipates the themes of Rawls's later work. Specifically, Rawls identifies a constructive theory, and thus a satisfying account of justification, with a certain response to a kind of pluralism, with the specification of a method that could adjudicate among potentially competing intuitions about justice. Though Rawls has yet to formulate *PL*'s historically specific account of reasonable pluralism as the natural outcome of the exercise of practical reasoning under modern conditions, he is already in *TJ* understanding the aim of his theory as providing a principled response to a kind of pluralism. Since we have seen that *TJ* also understands utilitarianism as constructive, and thus as another possible response to this pluralism, we can see that Rawls is then left with the task of explaining why his constructive theory is superior to that of utilitarianism. In the argument of *TJ*, Rawls's answer is his insistence that utilitarianism is in conflict with certain of our moral intuitions, especially those that emphasize the separateness of persons. It thus makes good sense that Rawls immediately follows his discussion of constructive justification in *TJ* §§7–8 with his famous discussion of reflective equilibrium in *TJ* §9. Since many principled responses to pluralism are available, we need some account of what makes one ordered set of principles better than another, and *TJ*'s answer to that question is that we must constantly test our moral principles against our intuitions in particular cases. Rawls's ultimate argument in *TJ* is that the process of reflective equilibrium will cast moral doubt on utilitarianism's willingness to subordinate the interests of the individual to the aggregative good of the entire society, and will thus reveal why the original position is arranged in a way that ultimately justifies the principle of equal liberty and fair equality of opportunity and the difference principle over the principle of average utility.

Each of these claims, however, was intensely disputed in the first wave of critical responses to *TJ* during the 1970s. Early critics of Rawls attacked the second of the two claims by arguing that Rawls had saddled the parties in the original position with an unduly conservative attitude toward risk. Were the parties simply allowed to maximize their expected gains, the critics argued, they might well choose to risk being part of a small, economically disadvantaged minority in a society that had achieved a higher level of overall wealth. Only the conservative attitude toward risk justified the use of the maximin rule, and thus the difference principle, over the principle of average utility. At the same time, a different set of critics attacked the method of reflective equilibrium for treating our existing moral intuitions as a reliable guide to moral truth. These critics understood reflective equilibrium as aiming at a certain coherence of our moral convictions, and then went on to worry that we could achieve that coherence with a set of morally dubious convictions. Though these two criticisms are distinct, aiming at different aspects of Rawls's theory of justice, it is important to understand how they can and did interact with one another, putting pressure on Rawls from two sides, both theoretically and politically.

Theoretically, the first criticism targeted the characterization of the parties in the original position, seeking to deprive that characterization of its anti-utilitarian force. That put theoretical pressure on Rawls to derive his anti-utilitarianism more directly from the constraints that reflective equilibrium placed on the design of the original position. But that move just strengthens the force of the second criticism, which attacks the method of reflective equilibrium itself. To deny that reflective equilibrium is itself unduly conservative, simply ratifying a culture's existing and perhaps flawed moral convictions, Rawls had to stress the theoretical pressure that the work of formulating general moral principles puts on our existing moral convictions, which can no longer remain as they were. But that move just strengthens the force of the first criticism, which questions Rawls's ability to justify his favored principles without loading in a dubious premise about risk, which then has to be justified in reflective equilibrium as some sort of basic moral conviction. Politically, in turn, the first criticism was often favored by those (Harsanyi 1975) who wanted to attack Rawls from the right, arguing that the original position could not justify the strong egalitarianism of the difference principle over the procapitalist emphasis on overall economic growth inherent in the principle of average utility. And the second criticism was often favored by those (like Singer 1974 and Cohen 2008) who wanted ultimately to attack Rawls from the left, subjecting the received beliefs of welfare liberals to a more sweeping moral critique. Faced with these theoretical and political pressures from both sides, Rawls needed some new way of navigating between his lexically ordered principles and his method of reflective equilibrium, so as not to emphasize one at the expense of the other. What Rawls went on to propose, I will now suggest, was just the Kantian constructivism of the Dewey Lectures.

## 3. Constructivism in the Dewey Lectures

Let's review briefly. In *TJ*, Rawls understands his theory of justice as constructive because it can respond to pluralism in a principled way. But since utilitarianism also proposes its own principled response to pluralism, Rawls is left to explain how he can justify his lexically ordered principles over the principle of utility. In the light of the critical discussion between *TJ* and *KC*, it seemed that neither the original position nor the method of reflective equilibrium could guarantee this justification. In *KC*, Rawls responds by tying the entire justification of his theory to the constructive project. Rather than arguing that justice as fairness represents a morally superior constructive response to pluralism, with "morally superior" then defined in some independent sense, he now argues that the moral superiority of justice as fairness to utilitarianism just is the effectiveness of its constructive response to pluralism. In this sense, after *KC*, the method of reflective equilibrium no longer provides the justification of the superiority of Rawls's theory of justice to other constructive theories; or if it does, it is only because the proper outcome of the method of reflective equilibrium is now understood as the formulation of the properly constructive response to pluralism.

In an earlier discussion (Krasnoff 1999), I argued that Rawls's account of constructivism in *KC* has been understood in two quite different ways. On the one hand, Rawls's constructivism has been understood as contractualism or hypothetical proceduralism: a specific type of moral or political theory in which agents choose justified practical principles for themselves.[4] "What distinguishes the Kantian form of constructivism is essentially this," writes Rawls at KC, 304, "it specifies a particular conception of the person as an element in a reasonable procedure of construction, the outcome of which determines the content of the first principles of justice." On the other hand, constructivism has also been understood as the claim that a moral or political theory should play a practical rather than a theoretical role: not identifying some sort of independent truth about the good, but allowing individuals within a society to justify their relationships and claims to one another.[5] "On the Kantian view that I shall present," writes Rawls at KC, 305, "conditions for justifying a conception of justice hold only when a basis is established for political reasoning and understanding within a public culture. The social role of a conception of justice is to enable all members of society to make mutually acceptable to one another their shared institutions and basic arrangements, by citing what are publicly recognized as sufficient reasons, as identified by that conception." Though Rawls presents each of these ideas in *KC*, it is important to understand that they are not the same. A hypothetical social contract might simply be a theoretical device for justifying certain practical truths in philosophical terms; it might play no public or social role for citizens in their daily lives. And a theorist who did want his or her theory of justice to play a public or social role is not thereby committed to making that theory contractualist; it might well be that some religious or eudaemonist view might be seen as superior at allowing citizens of a particular society to justify their claims to one another. So why did Rawls link these two senses of constructivism together in *KC*? Why did he think that practical task of public justification could best be accomplished by a theory that understood citizens as choosing the principles of justice for themselves?

Before we answer this question on Rawls's behalf, we should note that an exactly parallel question arises in the interpretation of Kant's practical philosophy as constructivist. On the one hand, one can regard Kant as a constructivist because he proposes a hypothetical and procedural test, the categorical imperative, for the justification of maxims. This is the interpretation that Rawls stresses in his own account of Kant, with its emphasis on what Rawls likes to call "the CI-procedure" ("Themes in Kant's Moral Philosophy," 1989). But we can and should distinguish this operation of this practical test from the question of what sort of justification the categorical imperative itself has. There are important interpretations of Kant's practical philosophy, like that of Karl Ameriks, that answer this second question in a realist and explicitly anticonstructivist way (Ameriks 2000 and 2003). Such readings regard the moral law as having an independent rational status for Kant, and understand our autonomy as the capacity to rationally perceive the moral law and apply it (procedurally) to our own actions. But the categorical imperative seems to express a necessary condition for fully rational principles rather than being a fully rational principle itself. The maxims that survive the universal law test are possible candidates for fully justified practical principles, not fully justified principles themselves. To make sense of this difference, I have defended the view that the categorical imperative is best understood not as a principle that is independently perceived to be purely rational, but as the uniquely pure practical expression of our desire for a purely rational principle to govern our actions (Krasnoff 2013). On this view, there is a sense in which the categorical imperative is itself constructed or legislated, and our autonomy consists not simply in our ability to act on rationally justified principles, but in our imposing on ourselves the way we understand practical principles as rationally justified.

A key feature of this interpretation is that the proceduralist form of the categorical imperative (the first sense in which Kant's practical philosophy might be understood as constructivist) is dictated by the practical role that moral agents construct that principle to play (the second sense in which we might understand Kant as a constructivist). Specifically, given the multiplicity of our desires and our inability to agree on a determinate conception of happiness, we need a way of justifying our actions to one another that does not depend on any specific desire. The clearest way to do that is to allow universalizability, which is itself only a necessary condition of a fully justified practical principle, to serve also as a sufficient condition (we understand an agent's maxim as justified if it could be made into universal law). Constructivism in the first, proceduralist sense follows from constructivism in the second, strictly practical sense because of the specific practical problem that Kant takes it upon himself to solve: that in the modern world, we understand our actions as events in the natural world, and thus as driven by desires, which have no rational justification in themselves. The task is then to construct this justification for ourselves.

Now let's turn back to Rawls and look at the specific practical problem that he understands his theory of justice as intended to solve in KC. Though that problem is not yet defined as it will be in *PL*, Rawls's account is already historically specific:

> we take our examination of the Kantian conception of justice as addressed to an impasse in our political history; the course of democratic thought over the past two centuries, say, shows that there is no agreement on the way basic social institutions should be arranged if they are to conform to the freedom and equality of citizens as moral persons. The requisite understanding of freedom and equality, which is implicit in the public culture of a democratic society, and the most suitable way to balance the claims of these notions, have not been expressed so as to meet general approval. Now a Kantian conception of justice tries to dispel the conflict between the different understandings of freedom and equality by asking: which traditionally recognized principles of freedom and equality, or which natural variations thereof, would free and equal persons themselves agree upon, if they were fairly represented solely as such persons and thought of themselves as citizens living a complete life in an ongoing society? Their agreement, assuming

an agreement would be reached, is conjectured to single out the most appropriate principles of freedom and equality, and therefore, to specify the principles of justice. (KC, 305)

In this crucial passage, Rawls links the two sides of his Kantian constructivism together by explaining his theory of justice as a solution to a particular version of the problem of value pluralism: the proliferation of different, and potentially conflicting, conceptions of freedom and equality in the history of modern, democratic political culture. Since the task is to generate agreement on the proper conception of freedom and equality, the proposed solution is to represent persons as free and equal (and only as free and equal), and then to allow them to agree on principles for themselves. Rawls's hypothetical proceduralism, the set of constraints that constitute the original position, is thus justified by the practical task of securing agreement about the relation of freedom and equality.

Let's examine how this constructivist account can be understood as responding to the earlier criticism of *TJ*'s rejection of utilitarianism. The criticism was that Rawls had to justify his preference for the priority of liberty and the difference principle either by assuming an unjustifiably conservative attitude toward risk in the original position or by assuming that the process of reflective equilibrium would guarantee an anti-utilitarian outcome. Neither of these is assumed in KC's account. Rawls does start with certain historically specific moral premises, namely the priority of freedom and equality in our political culture. But he does not assume that the premises will themselves defeat utilitarianism. Instead he argues that free and equal persons could not agree on the principle of utility, since the freedom and equality of any individual would be compromised if his or her interests were sacrificed or traded off for the interests of some larger group. The preference of the parties for the maximin rule does not represent an unduly conservative attitude toward risk, because in the original position I am not in fact thinking about risking my own interests for the sake of some potentially larger reward. Rather I am thinking about whether I, as a free and equal moral person, could expect any such person to agree to a set of principles that traded off his or her interests for the chance of advancing mine (or any other's). What seems to be an assumption about risk is really, like everything else about the original position, another consequence of the need for free and equal persons to come to an agreement, to regard their political claims as justified to one another.

Citizens who do see their political claims in this way, Rawls argues, are fully autonomous. This is not because they are understood to have made any sort of uncaused or otherwise metaphysically special choice, but nor is it because they have simply chosen for themselves by maximizing their expected gains. The latter sort of choice is described by Rawls as rationally but not fully autonomous, or merely rational and not yet reasonable (KC, 314–320). To be reasonable is to propose terms of social coordination that others could freely accept. Rawlsian citizens are said to be reasonable because they affirm principles of justice that have been chosen in a reasonable way: by regarding each person as free and equal (and only as free and equal), and allowing such persons to collectively choose those principles for themselves. To be fully autonomous, on KC's account, is to act on principles that one and all others have been able to choose for themselves.[6] The need for full autonomy, in turn, is prompted by the situation of pluralism to which Rawls's theory intends to respond. Differing conceptions of freedom and equality can be reconciled, Rawls is arguing, only if our political principles are autonomously chosen: when free and equal persons construct those principles for themselves.

## 4. Constructivism after the Dewey Lectures

This connection between autonomy and an effective response to pluralism should already cast doubt on Galston's opposition between a morally or metaphysically controversial Kantianism and a more practical determination to generate political consensus. For the Rawls of KC, such a consensus is best forged by a theory of justice that understands citizens as fully autonomous. To see that Rawls never abandoned this view, however, we need to understand the constructivism of his later work; and to do that, we need to understand the way in which the constructivism of KC and after is intended to deepen the justification of TJ's justice as fairness.

Recall that although the constructivism of TJ is defined as a principled response to value pluralism, that constructivism is not understood as sufficient to determine that response. Instead Rawls needs an independent process of reflective equilibrium to justify his preference for justice as fairness over utilitarianism, and it is not clear that reflective equilibrium can do the job he needs it to do. By the time of KC, however, Rawls is linking his critique of utilitarianism to his account of pluralism and to his constructivist response. He does this by making his account of pluralism more historically specific. Rather than speaking generally about a plurality of claims about justice, as in TJ, Rawls in KC speaks of a plurality of conceptions of freedom and equality as a specific problem that emerges in the political culture of modern democracies. Kantian constructivism is then defined as a uniquely determined solution to this specific problem: free and equal persons will construct the principles of justice for themselves, and free and equal persons will not be able to justify sacrificing one another's interests on utilitarian grounds. The historical specificity of the account of pluralism is not intended to weaken Rawls's justification of his theory of justice by somehow restricting its application. Justice as fairness was always meant to apply specifically to modern democratic societies. Instead the historical specificity of Rawlsian pluralism is intended to deepen the justification of the theory, by connecting superiority of justice as fairness as a constructive theory to the constructive project itself.

With this account in mind, we can better understand the constructivism of PL and after as an even further specification of Rawls's historical account of pluralism, one that continues to deepen the justification of the theory. Why is it that we should understand the conflicts between different conceptions of freedom and equality as the central political problem of modern democratic societies? Where do these different conceptions of freedom and equality come from, and what makes them more important than other moral ideals? It is not clear that KC has answers to these questions. Rawls there simply takes the controversies among conceptions of freedom and equality to be a basic fact of modern democratic culture. But by the time of "Justice as Fairness: Political not Metaphysical" and PL, Rawls is offering a deeper explanation. On this now familiar account, the controversies over the proper understanding of freedom and equality are consequences of the larger divisions between religious traditions, and between religion and secularism, in the wake of the Reformation. These divisions have produced what Rawls calls the fact of reasonable pluralism, a condition in which we cannot reasonably expect agreement among different comprehensive doctrines, holding different conceptions of the good life. Under conditions of reasonable pluralism, it is not simply that disputes about freedom and equality are to be expected, as examples of conflicts between comprehensive doctrines. It is also that these particular disputes take on a certain priority in the political culture of modern societies. Because comprehensive doctrines are exercises of practical reason, adherents of those doctrines will seek to justify political claims, like all other practical claims, in terms their doctrines can understand as rationally acceptable. And since political claims are addressed to all competent members of a society, each of whom may affirm a different comprehensive doctrine, political claims must be reasonable: they must be expressed in terms that could be acceptable to adherents of any other (equally reasonable) comprehensive doctrine. It is from this requirement that we can explain the priority of freedom and equality in modern political culture. Citizens are free in the sense that they determine their own conceptions of the good, in the terms of their own comprehensive doctrines, and they are equal in that none of their comprehensive doctrines can have any political priority. Rawls's understanding of persons as free and equal, then, is not simply assumed as a modern political ideal; it is now explained as the historical result of the specifically modern problem of justifying political arrangements under conditions of reasonable pluralism.

In Rawls's later work, then, political constructivism is the view that since modern political arrangements must be reasonable, justifiable to adherents of other reasonable comprehensive doctrines, we can best justify political arrangements by constructing them from the idea of the reasonable itself. This construction takes place via a series of specifications: starting from the bare idea of the reasonable, moving to the idea of citizens as free and equal, to the constraints of the original position, and finally to the choice of the two principles of justice. Rawls's positive theory of justice is thus meant to be the answer to the question: what political arrangements would reasonable citizens, citizens seeking only to justify their political claims to those holding different comprehensive doctrines, choose for themselves? The political autonomy of citizens consists in their constructing reasonable political principles for themselves. Nothing in this later view alters KC's double understanding of constructivism, of the connection between autonomy and the practical problem of responding to conditions of value pluralism.[7] It is just that in the later work, that practical problem is described in terms that are more historically specific, and more tightly connected to Rawls's specific procedure of construction.

It is not, then, as Galston's reading would have it, that Rawls's later work suggests any sort of rejection of Kantian autonomy as developed in KC. In both KC and *PL*, Rawls insists on a tight connection between autonomy and pluralism, with the autonomous choices of the constructors understood as the practically effective response to conditions of pluralism. All that is resisted (though not therefore rejected) in Rawls's later work is Kant's moral constructivism, as distinguished from a merely political constructivism. Here Rawls understands Kant's moral constructivism as a comprehensive liberal doctrine, with its own secular understanding of the nature of the good. But it is important to see (*pace* Galston) that as a form of comprehensive liberalism, the distinctive feature of Kant's moral constructivism is not its emphasis on autonomy or freedom. A fully religious view is certainly capable of understanding human beings as autonomous, with our freedom explained as a gift from God. What is distinctive about Kant's moral constructivism, as I explained in the previous section, is that Kant understands our autonomy as expressed not just in the obedience to but also in the construction of practical principles, and the construction of those principles as a practical response to the problem of reconciling objective claims about the good with a modern, scientific worldview. The metaphysically controversial aspect of Kant's practical philosophy is not the value he gives to autonomy, but the way he understands that value as not theoretically perceived, but practically constructed.

In the later Rawls's terms, political constructivism is a practical response to modernity's experience of the fact of reasonable pluralism, which requires that our political arrangements be understood as fully reasonable. The specific response that Rawls proposes is that free and equal agents construct political arrangements for themselves and all others, under the hypothetical constraints of the original position. Since the choices of the free and equal parties in the original position are nothing more than a practical response to the fact of reasonable pluralism, we can say that the political autonomy of Rawlsian citizens is itself practically constructed. But we do not have to say this to affirm the value of political autonomy, and even if we do want to say it, it is crucial to see that we still need to explain why this kind of practical construction is sufficient to justify the value we give to political autonomy. Just as Kant's categorical imperative turns a necessary condition of practical rationality (universalizability) into a sufficient condition, so Rawls turns a necessary condition of modern political justification (reasonableness) into a sufficient condition of modern political justification (the value of political autonomy, understood as sufficient to determine the original position as the unique framework for justifying political claims). If political liberalism is a practical device for securing reasonable political agreement, then we (even Galston) must explain, at a deeper level, why we can give this reasonable political agreement such importance in our lives.

This question is what Rawls, since *TJ*, has called the problem of stability. It is not, as many readers have supposed in reading *PL*, another way of thinking about the practical effectiveness of political liberalism as a practical device. In asking whether his theory of justice is stable, Rawls is not asking simply whether reasonable political agreement is likely to persist over time. Rather he is asking whether we can understand the persistence of this kind of agreement as fully rational, in the light of all the things we take to be valuable (Hill 1994; Krasnoff 1998). In Part III of *TJ*, Rawls assumed that his theory of justice needed to solve this problem for itself, by developing an argument for the value of acting on the principles that we had chosen in the original position. But by the time of *PL*, Rawls understands such claims about value as issuing from particular comprehensive doctrines. The argument of Part III of *TJ* (most notably the Aristotelian principle) is intended as a contribution to any conception of the good; in the terms of *PL*, it is as if Rawls were trying to make a comprehensive claim that would be acceptable on any comprehensive doctrine. But since Rawls in *PL* understands comprehensive doctrines as independent exercises of practical reasoning, this kind of argument is quite unnecessary. The various comprehensive doctrines are both capable of explaining, and themselves driven to explain, the value that reasonable political justification should play in our lives. Kant's moral constructivism, which seeks to justify the reasonable as in fact sufficient for rationality, is just one such explanation. There are less direct explanations that might proceed from thicker (as in certain religious views) or thinner (as in certain forms of value pluralism) conceptions of practical rationality. Any of these views might be able to justify the value of merely reasonable political justification, and if there exists an overlapping consensus of views that justify political liberalism in this way, Rawls contends that political liberalism is fully justified. Indeed, his argument is that political liberalism is better justified by an overlapping consensus of comprehensive doctrines than by political liberalism. Since political liberalism is itself defined by the respect it gives to the diversity of comprehensive doctrines as exercises of practical reason under conditions of reasonable pluralism, political liberalism is ultimately justified by the agreement of the reasonable comprehensive doctrines themselves, judging in the light of their fullest conceptions of practical rationality.

In the received history of the Dewey Lectures, as we have seen, Kantian autonomy has been understood as a formerly optional feature of justice as fairness that Rawls added for purposes of deeper justification – only to abandon it in *PL* as an obstacle to practical consensus. The result has been a debate, which still dominates the current literature, about the extent to which Rawls needs more or less "Kantianism" either to deepen the rational justification of his theory, or to facilitate a more effective political consensus. My goal has been to show that the contribution of the Dewey Lectures to Rawls's intellectual development is precisely its rejection of this opposition. Even in *TJ*, Rawls identifies constructivism with the development of an effective response to value pluralism. In KC, Rawls argues that he could not justify his own constructive procedure over the principle of utility without connecting it to an argument for a more practical, more historically specific account of the nature of modern value pluralism. On this argument, the original position represents the parties as free and equal (and only as free and equal) because modern political culture is dominated by debates over the different meanings of freedom and equality. Only autonomous agents can resolve such debates, Rawls argues in KC; in this sense his Kantianism cannot be separated from his commitment to a conception of reasonable pluralism. By the time of *PL*, Rawls understands our debates about freedom and equality as derived from a deeper conflict of comprehensive doctrines. This conflict still demands a (politically) autonomous response, but that political autonomy can be fully respected only by allowing the various comprehensive doctrines to secure the stability of political liberalism on their own. This move requires that that we understand Kant's moral constructivism, the place autonomy has in a Kantian theory of reason, as just one among many potential comprehensive views. But this understanding of Kant's moral constructivism has no effect on the (political) function of Kantian autonomy in Rawls's theory of justice. Since the argument of the Dewey Lectures, that function has remained the same: to allow free and equal persons to settle practical conflicts for themselves.

## Notes

1   Indeed, for some readers of *TJ*, the model of rational choice deployed in the original position was evidence that Rawls had already rejected the Kantian conception of autonomy (Johnson 1974).
2   As has been noted by Onora O'Neill 2003, 351; see also Krasnoff 1999, esp. 401–402.
3   David Reidy points out that Rawls's doctoral dissertation treats emotivism in just the same way that *TJ* treats intuitionism: refuting it by proposing the kind of rational or cognitive account that intuitionism and emotivism claim cannot be given.
4   See most prominently Barry 1991, 264–271, and esp. 268. The term "contractualism" comes from Scanlon 1982. The term "hypothetical proceduralism" comes from Darwall et al. 1992.
5   This feature of Rawls's theory was first emphasized as "constructive" by Ronald Dworkin in his influential review of *TJ* (Dworkin 1977); there are important connections to Dworkin's own views of judicial practice. For a discussion of Dworkin's account, see Krasnoff 1999, 389–391.
6   This was already the account of autonomy sketched on Rawls's behalf in Darwall 1976, in reply to Johnson 1974.

7   For a more general account of the relation between autonomy and pluralism, see Krasnoff 2010. This account is explicitly a form of comprehensive liberalism, which might also be said to be affirmed in the anti-Platonic account of Kantian constructivism in the third lecture of KC (esp. 343–351). But as I go on to argue here, Rawls's political constructivism and its conception of political autonomy are equally compatible with the commitments of other reasonable comprehensive doctrines that reject this sort of anti-Platonism.

## Works by Rawls, with Abbreviations

*Collected Papers* (CP), ed. Samuel Freeman. Cambridge, MA: Harvard University Press, 1999.
"Justice as Fairness: Political not Metaphysical" (1985), in *Collected Papers* (388–414).
"Kantian Constructivism in Moral Theory" (KC) (1980), Dewey Lectures, in *Collected Papers* (303–358).
*Political Liberalism* (PL), expanded edn. New York: Columbia University Press, 2005.
"Themes in Kant's Moral Philosophy" (1989), in *Collected Papers* (497–528).
*A Theory of Justice* (TJ), rev. edn. Cambridge, MA: Harvard University Press, 1999.

## Other References

Ameriks, Karl (2000) *Kant and the Fate of Autonomy: Problems in the Appropriation of the Critical Philosophy*. Cambridge: Cambridge University Press.
Ameriks, Karl (2003) *Interpreting Kant's Critiques*. Oxford: Oxford University Press.
Barry, Brian (1991) *Theories of Justice*. Berkeley: University of California Press.
Cohen, G.A. (2008) *Rescuing Justice and Equality*. Cambridge, MA: Harvard University Press.
Darwall, Stephen (1976) "A Defense of the Kantian Interpretation." *Ethics* 86: 164–170.
Darwall, Stephen, Gibbard, Allan, and Railton, Peter (1992) "Toward *Fin de Siècle* Ethics: Some Trends." *Philosophical Review* 101: 139–140.
Dworkin, Ronald (1977) "Justice and Rights." In Dworkin, *Taking Rights Seriously* (150–205). Cambridge, MA: Harvard University Press.
Galston, William (1995) "Two Concepts of Liberalism." *Ethics* 105: 516–534.
Harsanyi, John (1975) "Can the Maximin Principle Serve as a Basis for Morality? A Critique of John Rawls's Theory." *American Political Science Review* 69: 594–606.
Hill, Thomas E., Jr (1994) "The Stability Problem in Political Liberalism." *Pacific Philosophical Quarterly* 75: 333–352.
Johnson, Oliver A. (1974), "The Kantian Interpretation," *Ethics*, 85: 58–66.
Krasnoff, Larry (1998) "Consensus, Stability, and Normativity in Rawls' Political Liberalism." *Journal of Philosophy* 95: 269–293.
Krasnoff, Larry (1999) "How Kantian is Constructivism?" *Kant-Studien* 90: 385–409.
Krasnoff, Larry (2010) "Autonomy and Plurality." *Philosophical Quarterly* 70: 673–691.
Krasnoff, Larry (2013) "Constructing Practical Justification: How Can the Categorical Imperative Justify Desire-Based Actions?" In Mark Timmons and Sorin Baiasu (eds), *Kant on Practical Justification: Interpretive Essays* (87–109). Oxford: Oxford University Press.
McCabe, David (2011) *Modus Vivendi Liberalism*. Oxford: Oxford University Press.
O'Neill, Onora (2003) "Constructivism in Rawls and Kant." In Samuel Freeman (ed.), *The Cambridge Companion to Rawls* (347–367). Cambridge: Cambridge University Press.
Rorty, Richard (1991) "The Priority of Democracy to Philosophy." In Rorty, *Objectivity, Relativism, and Truth: Philosophical Papers, Volume 1*. Cambridge: Cambridge University Press.

Scanlon, T.M. (1982) "Contractualism and Ethics." In Amartya Sen and Bernard Williams (eds), *Utilitarianism and Beyond*. Cambridge: Cambridge University Press.

Singer, Peter (1974) "Sidgwick and Reflective Equilibrium." *The Monist* 58: 490–517.

Steinberger, Peter J. (2000) "The Impossibility of a 'Political' Conception." *Journal of Politics* 62: 147–165.

Taylor, Robert S. (2011) *Reconstructing Rawls: The Kantian Foundations of Justice as Fairness*. University Park: Penn State University Press.

# 5

# The Basic Structure of Society as the Primary Subject of Justice

## SAMUEL FREEMAN

Rawls's focus on principles of justice for the basic structure of primary social institutions evolved from his early discussion of practices, social rules and Humean conventions, and his apparent commitment to a version of rule-utilitarianism. In his 1955 "Two Concepts of Rules" his stated aim is "to show the importance of the distinction between justifying a practice and justifying a particular action falling under it, and . . . explain the logical basis of this distinction" (CP, 20). Though Rawls claims a "logical basis" for the distinction, in later works the parallel distinction between principles for institutions and for individuals, and the primacy assigned principles of justice for the basic structure, are regarded as moral assumptions required by "the Reasonable" (CP, 316–317) that ultimately stem from ideals of persons and society. Rawls's conception of free and equal moral persons, and the social conditions necessary to realize reciprocity and citizens' fundamental interests, are integral to understanding why Rawls assigns primacy to principles of justice for the basic structure of society.

Rawls says that there are two sources for the primacy assigned to the basic structure: the profound effects of basic social institutions on persons and their future prospects, and the need to maintain background justice. I discuss the main reasons underlying these considerations for the primacy Rawls assigns to principles of justice for the basic structure. First, it is necessary to the freedom, equality and independence of moral persons (section 3 below). Second, Rawls's focus on the basic structure is a condition of economic reciprocity and the just distribution of economic powers, resources, and income and wealth (section 4). Third, the primacy of the basic structure is required by moral pluralism and the plurality of values, and by reasonable pluralism, or the plurality of reasonable conceptions of the good among free and equal persons (sections 4–5). Before addressing these issues, I discuss the meaning of the primacy of the basic structure (section 1) and the profound influence of the basic structure (section 2).

A Companion to Rawls, First Edition. Edited by Jon Mandle and David A. Reidy.
© 2014 John Wiley & Sons, Inc. Published 2016 by John Wiley & Sons, Inc.

# 1. The Primacy of the Basic Structure – What It Means

In the opening pages of *A Theory of Justice*, Rawls declares: "Our topic . . . is social justice. For us the primary subject of justice is the basic structure of society" (*TJ*, 6). The basic structure is "the background social framework within which the activities of associations and individuals take place" (*JF*, 10). More precisely it is:

> the way in which the major social institutions fit together into one system, and how they assign fundamental rights and duties and shape the division of advantages that arise through social cooperation. Thus the political constitution, the legally recognized forms of property, and the organization of the economy, and the nature of the family, all belong to the basic structure. (*PL*, 258)

The parties to Rawls's original position choose principles to apply directly to the basic structure of society, to make rules that regulate individuals' and officials' conduct. The first principle of equal basic liberties then applies to the political constitution to determine and regulate legitimate political procedures for enacting and applying laws and specify the constitutional rights of citizens; while the second principle applies to structure social opportunities and design the economic system, including ownership and control of the means of production as well as the distribution of income and wealth.

Rawls says the basic structure is the "first subject" (*PL*, 251) and the "primary subject" of principles of *social* justice (*TJ*, 6; *CP*, 156). It is not the only subject of justice, even of social justice. Here Rawls refers to "the need for the division of labor between different kinds of principles" (*PL*, 469). In addition to institutional principles of justice for the basic structure, there are also principles of justice for individuals, including the "natural duties" of justice, mutual respect, and mutual aid, and the principle of fairness determining political obligations, duties of fidelity including the keeping of promises and agreements of all kinds, etc. There are also principles of remedial and compensatory justice (TJ, 8), including societal duties to those with severe disabilities (*PL*, 20), which Rawls does not specify. Moreover, "Justice as fairness is a political, not a general conception of justice" (*JF*, 11). The principles of justice do not apply to larger and smaller-scale institutions and issues, or to "lifeboat situations" (*CP*, 156). There are, Rawls argues, different principles of international justice that regulate the relationships between different societies – The "Law of Nations" or "Law of Peoples." And there are principles of "*local justice*" (*JF*, 11) that apply to structure and regulate individual relationships and associations within political and global society; these include certain duties and norms of fairness within the family, universities, business firms and labor unions, and other nonpublic associations.

The primacy of the basic structure also does not mean that social justice is morally more important than these other forms of justice; for example, our duties of social justice do not always outweigh duties and principles of international and local justice. It would be unjust for a government to violate human rights and other requirements of international justice (the Law of Peoples) to further justice or prevent injustice within its own society. For example, the difference principle is subject to the duty of assistance owed to burdened societies. A government cannot neglect its duty to contribute its fair share to pay for the alleviation of poverty and economic development of burdened societies in order to pay larger income supplements to the least advantaged members of its own society.[1] Nor can a society violate duties of fairness in trade relations, by taking unfair advantage of vulnerable nations, in order to increase opportunities or income supplements to less advantaged members of its own society.

In saying that the basic structure is the "first subject" of justice Rawls basically means that the principles of justice for the design and regulation of basic social institutions have to be settled first, before the nature and scope of principles of justice regulating individual conduct, global society, and other private and nonbasic public institutions can be fully ascertained. "Justice as fairness starts with domestic justice – the justice of the basic structure. From there it works outward to the law of peoples, and inward to local justice" (*JF*, 11). The primacy of the basic structure means then that principles of justice for the basic structure have a kind of *methodological and regulative primacy* over other principles of justice.[2]

In recognizing a *plurality of principles of justice* that apply to different subjects and institutions, Rawls is not simply saying that different institutions and social arrangements must be regulated by different principles. Most any moral conception, including utilitarianism, recognizes that the principles and procedures applicable to political constitutions (e.g., one-person/one vote, and majority rule) would not be appropriate for regulating family life or many other associations. But utilitarianism and other universal moral conceptions see such principles as secondary, and as formulated in light of and in order to achieve the aims of a more fundamental or supreme moral principle, such as maximizing aggregate utility. In asserting the primacy of principles for the basic structure, Rawls in effect denies what Liam Murphy has called "monism," the view that there is a single moral principle (or set of principles) that applies at all levels of moral assessment, to determine the justice (or more generally the rightness and wrongness) of all actions, rules, and institutions. In saying there are "different principles for different kinds of subjects" (*PL*, 262), Rawls means there are different *first* or *fundamental principles* that apply to and are appropriate for different kinds of social arrangements and institutions. The first principles of social justice are not appropriate for regulating relations among members within families, universities, or global society itself, nor are these principles for associations directly derivable from principles of social justice. Different social arrangements require different principles. What makes these different principles for different institutions "first principles" is that they are not derivative from any principle that is universal in its scope and application.

The primacy of the basic structure presupposes then a kind of *moral pluralism* of first principles of justice, just as it presupposes evaluative pluralism, of values and conceptions of the good. There are different principles for different subjects of justice, and there are different values and moral principles that determine the role of and regulate associations within society. Again, this is a moral assumption Rawls makes, related to "the autonomy of the various elements of society" and ultimately the freedom and equality of moral persons.[3] What prevents this pluralism of first principles from becoming a kind of *intuitionism* that requires balancing of first principles of local, social and political, and global justice to determine one's duties "all things considered"? It is the method of determination and justification of these first principles, and the *methodological and regulative primacy* Rawls assigns to principles of social justice. The plurality of first principles for multiple subjects of justice are unified by an "appropriate sequence" of determination from the original position (or in the case of local justice, some other relevant moral point of view), as its conditions of agreement are adjusted to the nature and role of different kinds of social arrangements and institutions. "[T]he parties to a social contract are to proceed through this sequence with the understanding that the principles of each later agreement are to be subordinate to those of all earlier agreements, or else adjusted to them by certain priority rules" (*PL*, 262). The "regulative primacy" of the basic structure means that the principles of justice for the basic structure are to be determined first in this sequence, and that, while they do not determine the content of other first principles, they are *regulative* of their scope and content (*PL*, 257–258).[4]

In addition to the plurality of principles for different subjects, implicit in the regulative primacy Rawls assigns to the basic structure is a bifurcation between "*principles for institutions*" of the basic structure, and "*principles for individuals*" that set forth their natural duties, obligations of fairness, and other moral duties (of fidelity, charity, friendship, etc.).[5] Principles of justice for institutions directly apply to and regulate the activities of the basic social institutions, and should be used to specify or assess the many legal and other social rules (of property, contract, etc.) that individuals are required to observe pursuant to the natural duty of justice. Principles of justice for institutions do not then apply directly to regulate the conduct of individuals; rather they apply *indirectly* to individuals via the many institutional "*rules for individuals*" that they call for. Principles for institutions directly apply to determine and assess the justice of the many laws and conventional norms that constitute the basic institutions of the basic structure. These include provisions of the political constitution, including the specification of political powers, procedures and a bill of rights; the structure of the economy, including control of means of production, and therewith, laws of property, contract, and other legal measures necessary for economic production, exchange, and consumption; and certain norms that apply to the family regarding the upbringing of children.

Here it is important to emphasize that Rawls's distinction between principles for institutions and individuals does *not* mean that principles of justice do not apply to individuals' conduct. Quite the contrary, they apply *indirectly* to regulate and restrain all kinds of individual activity by settling most laws and other social rules of justice that directly apply to regulate individuals' day-to-day activities. It is important then not to confuse Rawls's distinction between *principles* for institutions vs *principles* for individuals with his different distinction between "*rules* for institutions" and "*rules* for individuals." These are not parallel distinctions.[6] The principles of justice for the basic structure are the source of *both* rules for institutions (e.g., constitutional procedures, laws specifying the form of private corporations) as well as rules for individuals (e.g., laws of property specifying individuals' rights of use, disposal, and income, or of permissible and impermissible contracts). Indeed, almost all the rules of justice for individuals are settled by the principles of justice for institutions, and not by the principles of natural duty and fairness for individuals. For example, the complicated rules of property, permissible transfers, and requirements of valid binding contracts that individuals are under a duty to observe are the result of applying the second principle of justice, including the difference principle, to specify the rules of basic institutions. That we have a moral duty to abide by these institutional rules for individuals follows from the individual duties of justice, mutual respect, and so on, which are principles for individuals; but the rules of property, contract, etc. themselves are the consequence of applying the principles of justice for the basic structure. Principles for institutions are then the source of most rules of justice for both institutions *and* for individuals.

This is important because some philosophers have made the mistake of assuming that, because the principles of justice apply directly only to institutions and not to individuals, they do not apply to individuals *at all* – which would mean they do not imply *any* particular rules or duties for individuals. This leads (as we'll see in section 5) to the mistaken argument that the reason Rawls does not apply the difference principle to regulate individual conduct is to enable individuals to selfishly pursue their economic and other self-interests without moral constraints. On the contrary, the difference principle applies indirectly to regulate and restrain individuals' conduct in all sorts of ways, via the many institutional rules for individuals that it requires.

To sum up, Rawls means at least three things in saying that principles for the basic structure are the first or primary subject of justice. First, there is a *plurality of first principles of justice* that apply to different subjects and institutions, and the principles of justice for basic institutions have "regulative primacy" over these principles. Lesser associations within the basic structure of society have standards of local justice peculiar to their purposes and role, and these are not determined by principles of justice for the basic structure. Nonetheless, these associations must adjust their requirements of local justice to the requirements that the basic structure imposes in order to establish "background justice" in society as a whole (*PL*, 261).[7] Second, within Rawls's contractarian framework, the primacy of the basic structure implies the *methodological priority* of principles of social justice to the law of peoples and principles of local justice. There is an "appropriate sequence" of determination of principles from the point of view of the original position, with the principles of social justice being determined first. Third and finally, the primacy of the basic structure is presupposed by Rawls's distinction between principles for institutions and principles for individuals: principles of justice for basic institutions provide *content* to the institutional rules for individuals that they are under a duty to comply with pursuant to their natural duties of justice and obligations of fairness; moreover these principles are necessary to maintain *background justice* as individuals freely pursue their aims and associations.

In the following sections I elaborate on these remarks, in discussing three different kinds of reasons for the primacy of principles for the basic structure. I conclude in section 5 with a discussion of some prominent objections.

## 2. The Social Nature of Human Relationships and the Profound Influence of Basic Social Institutions

Rawls discusses two main reasons for focusing on the basic structure of society: the profound influence of basic social institutions on individuals' aims, characters, and life prospects; and the importance of maintaining background justice. While the first of these is addressed by considerations relevant to both principles of justice, the second mainly concerns matters of economic justice covered by the second principle.

Before discussing these reasons and related considerations, three points should be emphasized. First, Rawls does not think that there is any particular set of considerations providing a decisive argument for making the basic structure the primary subject of justice. "No such decisive arguments are available." As is true of other controversial assumptions he makes, ultimately "everything depends on how the conception of justice hangs together as a whole" in reflective equilibrium (*JF*, 55–56).[8]

Second, like other fundamental ideas he incorporates (free and equal persons, a well-ordered society, reasonableness, reasonable agreement, reciprocity, etc.), the basic structure is not sharply defined from the outset of Rawls's argument, but rather "is initially a rough idea" (*JF*, 12) that is developed in conjunction with other fundamental ideas. "A sharp definition of this structure might have gotten in the way of fitting it into these other ideas"

(*JF*, 57). This too is related to Rawls's holistic account of justification and reflective equilibrium – of fundamental ideas being provisionally set forth, then elaborated upon and elucidated in a process of discovery and justification of principles of justice, which in turn solidify
the meaning of these fundamental ideas. It's only once the principles of justice are set forth
and explicated that a clear idea of basic social institutions and the basic structure emerges.
This is to say that, which institutions are part of the basic structure depends in part
upon the *specific content of the principles of justice*, the kinds of requirements they impose
upon governments and individuals, and ultimately the ideals of persons and society that
these principles realize.

This relates to a third preliminary point: Rawls's focus on the basic structure is integrally
tied (in ways to be discussed) to his Kantian form of contractarianism, especially to the ideal
of persons and of society that are presupposed by his theory of justice. Rawls says, "Once we
think of the parties to a social contract as free and equal (and rational) moral persons, then
there are strong reasons for taking the basic structure as the primary subject" (*PL*, 259). In
later works Rawls says that the idea of the basic structure is, along with the original position,
a "fundamental idea" that is needed to work out the details of the "fundamental intuitive
ideas" of society as a fair system of cooperation, free and equal moral persons, and a well-
ordered society (*JF*, 10). It's not immediately clear what he means by these remarks. In the
following discussion I will try to unravel the various ways in which the freedom and equality
of moral persons relates to the primacy given to principles of justice for the basic structure
of society.

Now to turn to the first general reason for Rawls's focus on the basic structure: namely,
the importance he assigns to "the social nature of human relationships" (*PL*, 278). This is
evident in his account of the social contract itself. The primary influence here is Rousseau
rather than Locke. There are significant differences in Locke's and Rousseau's natural rights
theories of the social contract, which are reflected in subsequent developments of social
contract theories. Locke and Lockean views begin with an idea of natural rights and natural
property held by fully rational free and independent persons in an apolitical state of nature.
Natural individuals are regarded as fully rational, free, independent, and self-sufficient owners
who contract to enter political society in order to protect their property in their persons and
rightful possessions. The task of the social contract is to work out a morally acceptable solution to the "inconveniences" of a state of nature that is mutually beneficial while preserving
individuals' freedom and natural property in themselves as well as their possessions.

Rousseau and his intellectual heirs reject the idea of a state of nature as a baseline for the
social contract. Indeed Rousseau debunks the state of nature as a relevant starting point for
assessing the justice of social and political institutions. Natural man, he contends, is not
rational or even aware of his natural rights, but is a "stupid limited animal" that acts on
instinct from motives of self-love and natural compassion. Natural man's capacities for reasoning and intellect are unrealized in a state of nature, since his needs are few and he has
no need to plan for his future. As such, natural man has no need for property or even the
ideas of morality and justice. It is only when men enter into society and are able to develop
their distinctly human capacities that they require concepts of "mine and thine" and other
concepts of justice. Property and economic rights are entirely products of society, responses
to the distinct needs and interests of persons living in social contexts. On Rousseau's account
of the social contract, the state of nature and natural man's preexisting endowments play
no role in determining requirements of justice, property, and individuals' entitlements.[9]

Rawls follows Rousseau in holding that the ideas of a state of nature, natural property, and the entitlements man brings to society are simply irrelevant to assessing conceptions of justice. "No sense can be made" of what persons own in a state of nature, nor consequently of "that part of an individual's social benefits that exceed what would have been their situation in another society or in a state of nature" (*PL*, 278). Likewise, since humans are social beings, "There is no question of determining anyone's contribution to society, or how much better off each is than they would have been had they not belonged to it, and then adjusting the social benefits of individuals by reference to these estimates" (*PL*, 279). In the ultimate dismissal, Rawls says the state of nature is "a historical surd, unknowable, and even if it could be known, of no significance" (*JF*, 55).[10]

The "social aspect of human relationships" (*PL*, 279) is the starting point for the primacy Rawls assigns to the basic structure of society. Like Rousseau, Rawls sees our desires and ends, our characters including virtues and vices, and many propensities to behavior as products of society. Though we do not begin life as a "blank slate," and clearly have certain natural propensities,[11] our distinctly human capacities (including language, reason, understanding, emotion, imagination) can only be developed and realized in cooperative social interaction. "We cannot view the talents and abilities of individuals as fixed natural gifts" (*PL*, 269). Though they have a "significant genetic component" they can only be developed and realized under social conditions. Moreover the particular form of the social conditions under which we live determines not only the direction of their development, but also which talents and natural propensities are realized or left undeveloped.[12] The same holds true of our desires, interests, ambitions, and final ends. None of these are fixed either. The social conditions under which we develop, including our position relative to others and the means and opportunities available to us, determine the range of options and choices we have in life, and therewith shape our interests and aims, as well as our future prospects.

Rawls regards all this as obvious, and few reasonable and informed persons would deny the effects of society and culture on people's interests and characters. The particular twist that Rawls applies to these plain truths is the fundamental role within society played by the basic social institutions (the constitution of government, property and the economy, and the family). "Everyone recognizes that the *institutional form of society* affects its members and determines in large part the kinds of persons they want to be as well as the kind of persons they are" (*PL*, 269). It's not just "society" and its multifarious influences, but the basic social institutions that form the *basic structure* of society that is fundamentally responsible for shaping as well as limiting people's ambitions and hopes, the natural talents they develop and their direction, as well as their future prospects in society.

Obviously the political constitution and the economic system under which we live have profound effects on our opportunities and future prospects. (Compare people's prospects in Western democracies with those in North Korea.) But here some have claimed that the social institutions Rawls singles out as having such a profound influence on our lives are not limited to those he mentions (see, e.g., Cohen 2008, ch. 3). For example, the religious institutions prevalent in most societies (in almost all societies until the mid-twentieth century) have an enormous effect on people's interests, aims, and characters. Why aren't religious institutions such as the Catholic Church equally if not more influential on the characters of people raised within them than the political constitution or economic class they are born into? If the profound influence of basic social institutions is the reason for making the basic structure the first subject of justice and for formulating principles that regulate these institutions, then why shouldn't other equally influential social institutions be incorporated into the basic structure and regulated by principles of social justice as well. The objection is that the class of institutions Rawls includes in the basic structure is unduly restricted and arbitrary.

The answer to this objection is that Rawls's basic social institutions are necessary for cooperation in almost any society, certainly in any complex society under modern conditions. Though religion has and continues to have enormous influence on many people's lives, it is not in general a precondition for peaceable and productive social cooperation (indeed it is often the primary source of continual civil strife). Many contemporary societies exist where religion has little or no role in maintaining socially cooperative relations (Western Europe and Communist China for example), whereas Rawls's basic social institutions are an integral and essential part of any modern society. Thus some political framework is needed in any (nonprimitive) society for making, revising, applying, and enforcing the social rules that make cooperation possible, and for adjudicating disputes arising under them. Otherwise a social group is governed by static customs and is unable to effectively respond to changing circumstances and necessities.[13] (Even prehistorical societies had leaders and procedures for making decisions and resolving disputes.) Further, in order for economic production, trade, distribution and consumption to be possible, there have to be settled rules of property governing ownership and control of land, raw materials, and other productive resources, as well as conventions (such as markets and rules of contract and sale) governing the manufacture and transfer of resources and distribution of goods. Finally, any society needs some form of the family to nurture and educate its young and reproduce society across successive generations. No matter how important other social institutions and associations – religious, educational, communications, cultural, athletic, etc. – may be to particular societies, these social institutions and associations are all dependent upon the basic social institutions that specify and secure their property claims and other entitlements, and maintain background conditions for their safe and effective functioning.

Still, the fact that we are social beings, that property is not natural but a social institution, that justice presupposes a web of social relationships, and that basic social institutions exert a profound influence on who we are, arguably is not enough to warrant making the basic structure of society the primary subject of principles of justice. Utilitarians also recognize the social nature of humanity, that property is a social convention, and so on; yet this does not prevent them from affirming a first moral principle that applies directly to assess the justice of individual conduct without the mediation of basic social institutions. An (act) utilitarian might then say: "Of course the design of basic social institutions is important, but this does not call for unique principles applying only to the basic structure. The principle of utility can just as well determine and regulate the laws and social rules that define basic social institutions as it can the rules of associations and individual conduct, and even specific actions. What's so special about the basic structure, when what ultimately matters is the maximum satisfaction of desires or interests?" (see Murphy 1998).

Rawls's claims regarding the profound influence of the basic structure cannot be taken in isolation from his other fundamental ideas and moral assumptions. It's the profound influence of basic institutions on persons conceived in a specific way – as free and equal moral persons with fundamental interests in exercising their moral powers – that warrants giving primacy to the basic structure. Here Rawls's nonconsequentialism, his contractarianism, the political values of freedom and equality, and the ideal conceptions of persons and society informing Rawls's constructivism all come into play. If all that mattered, morally,

95

was the maximization of individual utility or some other good state of affairs, then it's understandable why the basic structure of society might be of no special significance. What would then be important is promoting happiness or some other ultimate good, without special regard for society's basic structure. But Rawls rejects the consequentialist position that the fundamental issue in questions of justice is maximizing or otherwise promoting states of affairs. Rawls assumes instead that justice is fundamentally about the nature and moral quality of social relations among persons. The freedom of and equality among persons, and their cooperation on terms of reciprocity and mutual respect are relations and values of paramount importance. These values provide reasons to focus on the questions whether and how the basic social institutions governing individuals' social and political relations are to be designed so as to respect individuals as free and equal moral persons. There are indefinitely many forms of society with different basic structures within which people might find their happiness, but it is only in societies where basic institutions take certain definite forms that individuals can live freely and as equals on terms of reciprocity and mutual respect. As opposed to promoting aggregate happiness or some other good state of affairs, it is the moral quality of human relationships and the political/moral values of freedom, equality, reciprocity, and mutual respect that inform the primacy assigned to principles of justice for the basic structure of primary social institutions. These claims are further clarified in the following section.

## 3. The Basic Structure and the Ideals of Persons and Society

Rawls's constructivism in both its Kantian and its political versions is highly relevant to understanding his focus on the basic structure. Constructivism, as Rawls conceives of it, is a nonconsequentialist approach to moral values and ideals. For moral constructivists, morality and justice are fundamentally about relations among persons who interact and cooperate according to rules and institutions that appropriately realize such moral values as human dignity and moral autonomy (Kant); mutual recognition (Scanlon); and respect for others as free and as equal moral persons who cooperate on terms of reciprocity and mutual respect (Rawls). These moral values and ideals are not states of affairs that can be promoted by taking the most effective means to maximize them. Instead they are "principle-dependent" values and ideals to be realized through the interpersonal relations of individuals who interact and cooperate according to principles and rules justifiable by procedures that exemplify these values and ideals. Kant contends that dignity, respect for humanity, and moral autonomy require that we act only on rules that fully rational persons can consent to and will to become universal laws. In Scanlon's contractualism, mutual recognition among persons is realized in interpersonal relations when everyone can justify their conduct to one another by rules that no one could reasonably reject on grounds of objective personal reasons. And in Rawls, the ideal of free and equal moral persons is realized only when society and individuals respect everyone's basic rights and willingly comply with requirements of basic social institutions regulated by principles that would be unanimously agreed to by rational persons in the original position.

Rawls says the original position is a "procedure of construction" that incorporates ideals of persons and society (PL, 95). The moral powers, to be reasonable and rational, are "essential interests" of free and equal moral persons (JF, 169), but, Rawls says, it makes little sense to maximize the development and exercise of these powers. Instead, these and other values constituting Rawls's complex ideals of persons and society are "modeled" in the original position (PL, 103), and then are realized when citizens cooperate according to principles that express these values and are constructed on their basis.

Here is where Rawls's focus on the basic structure becomes relevant. Rawls says the freedom and equality of moral persons "require some public form" and have an "institutional expression" (PL, 281). "Once the parties are described in terms that have an institutional expression, then, given the role of the basic structure" – its profound influence on our person and future prospects – "it is no accident that the first principles of justice apply directly to the basic structure."[14] The complex ideal of free and equal moral persons achieves its institutional expression via the equal basic rights and liberties guaranteed by the political constitution, other measures that achieve fair equality of opportunities, and guaranteed economic entitlements satisfying the difference principle. Recall here again the crucial point that the moral conceptions of free and equal persons and a well-ordered society are not states of affairs to be instrumentally promoted or maximized; rather they are ideals to be realized by society's members cooperating according to the rules for institutions and individuals that exemplify the principles of justice constructed from these ideals. Kantian and political constructivism are based in the idea that principles of justice should incorporate the freedom, equality, and moral powers of persons, *and that these features of moral persons are to be expressed in basic social institutions themselves* in order to realize this ideal of persons and their social relations.

Accordingly, Rawls says, "Freedom [of moral persons] as applied to social institutions means a certain pattern of rights and liberties; and equal freedom means that certain basic liberties and opportunities are equal and that social and economic inequalities are regulated by principles suitably adjusted to preserve the fair value of these liberties" (PL, 280). Rawls elsewhere says that "one main reason" for focusing on the basic structure "is to secure citizens' freedom and independence" (JF, 159).[15] One way that moral persons are free is their capacity to be rational: they are capable of forming, revising, and rationally pursuing a rational plan of life, and are (held) responsible for their actions and their ends accordingly.[16] The basic liberties are the "institutional expression" of the freedom of moral persons; these liberties are among the institutions necessary to develop and exercise the capacity to be rational and individuals' formation and rational pursuit of their conception of the good. Rawls argues that equal basic liberties of conscience, association, and thought and expression are primary among the institutions that enable individuals to develop and exercise their capacity to be rational, to form and pursue a rational plan of life and take responsibility for their ends and conduct (PL, 310–315).

Another main reason for focusing on the basic structure is to guarantee the social and moral equality of persons. "It is only if the basic structure satisfies the requirements of background justice that a society treats its members as equal moral persons" (CP, 317). Moral persons are equal in that they all have the moral powers to a requisite minimal degree; the moral powers are then "the basis of equality" (TJ, §77). Equality of basic rights and liberties and of fair opportunities are the institutional expression of moral persons' equality as persons and as citizens, and the difference principle secures the worth and fair value of the basic liberties for all citizens (TJ, 179; PL, 280).

Finally, regarding the institutional expression of moral powers of justice: Equal political rights of participation and freedom of political thought and expression are institutions necessary for realizing moral capacities for a sense of justice, including our capacities for public reasoning (*PL*, 340–342). Moreover being publicly recognized as a free and equal citizen, as defined by institutional principles incorporating equal basic rights and fair opportunities, is necessary to moral persons' achieving the good of self-respect as equal citizens.[17]

It is then (Rawls suggests) the ideal of persons and society reflected in the description of the parties and the original position that requires "institutional expression" in the basic structure of society. The central point here seems to be this: It is *only* by acting within a definite institutional framework (of equal basic rights and liberties, fair equal opportunities, etc.), and acting to uphold the justice of these institutions, that we can fully realize and "express our nature as free moral persons" (*TJ*, 572) or (as Rawls puts it in *PL*) realize our political self-conception as free and equal moral persons. Realizing our "nature" (*TJ*) or our "political self-conception" (*PL*), as free and equal moral persons cooperating on terms of reciprocity and mutual respect, can be achieved *only* by affording primacy to principles of justice for the basic structure. And acting upon and for the sake of principles of justice that express our moral and rational nature or political self-conception is the fundamental idea of Rawls's Kantian and political constructivism. This seems to be the general idea behind Rawls's enigmatic claim that a "particular institutional expression" is required by the freedom and equality of moral persons, and that "the content of the two principles fulfills this expectation" (*PL*, 281).

Now to complete the comparison with utilitarianism begun earlier: While utilitarianism recognizes the social nature of human relations and the profound effects of basic social institutions, the utilitarian conception of persons does not require any particular institutional expression in the basic structure. Utilitarians take the capacity for pleasure and pain (or the capacity for desire or for happiness more generally) as the fundamental moral fact about individuals; and this capacity can be promoted and satisfied *without any specific institutional framework* and in a large variety of social forms. Rawls's (Kantian and political) ideal of persons and society, by contrast, requires a particular kind of basic structure of society to give this ideal its "institutional expression." It's the profound influence of the basic structure on persons who are conceived in a specific way – as free and equal moral persons with fundamental interests in exercising their moral powers – that ultimately is needed to make sense of Rawls's assumption of the primacy of principles of justice for the basic structure. And once this ideal conception of persons is expressed via institutional principles in the form and content of basic social and political institutions, these principles and the institutional procedures, rights, and duties that result should have regulative primacy over individuals' conduct and pursuits. Otherwise, they cannot realize these ideals or their fundamental interests as free and equal moral persons who cooperate on terms of reciprocity and mutual respect.

Let's assume these considerations support Rawls's claim of the regulative primacy of principles of justice for the basic structure over individuals' conduct within these and other institutions. Some might still insist, in spite of Rawls's constructivism and rejection of consequentialism, that he has yet to establish that his principles of *distributive justice* directly apply *only* to the basic structure and not directly to govern or assess individual conduct. Why should society but not individuals have a moral duty to maximally promote the position of the least advantaged? This brings us to the institutional division of labor and the division of moral labor, two topics discussed in the following sections, 4–5.

# 4. Distributive Justice and the Importance of Background Justice

Rawls says, "The main problem of distributive justice is the choice of a social system" (*TJ*, 242). Here again, as with respecting the freedom and equality of moral persons, a fundamental question of justice, in this case distributive justice, is transformed into a question of the design of basic social institutions. Traditionally distributive justice has been regarded as a problem of "allocative justice," the dividing up of some preexisting bundle of goods or income and wealth (*TJ*, 77). This explains the attraction of such distributive principles as: to each equally; or according to efforts, or contributions, or needs; or to maximize utility. Many classical liberals and libertarians, such as Hayek and Nozick, reject the idea of distributive justice and requirements of "patterned," "end-state," or other allocative distributions. They argue that almost *any* distribution of holdings is just so long as it is the outcome of a historical process of free exchanges and consensual transfers between free, property-owning individuals.

Since Rawls says his position is "egalitarian" it may seem odd that Rawls agrees with the rejection of allocative conceptions and in endorsing a process-based conception: just distributions are determined, he says, by "pure procedural justice" (*TJ*, §14). This means that distributions are just when they are the outcome of a process where individuals freely engage in economic activity against a background of, and in compliance with, the requirements of fair or just basic economic and legal institutions.

It is because Rawls's view is, like classical liberals and libertarians, a process-based conception that relies on markets that many on the left, most notably G.A. Cohen, have argued that Rawls's focus on the basic structure is driven by a concern to justify self-seeking within the capitalist welfare state. Rawls, it is said, agrees with classical liberals in endorsing capitalism; his difference principle is a way to moderate the vast inequalities capitalism inevitably results in, while still allowing economic agents to selfishly pursue their economic interests. A problem with this objection is that Rawls explicitly rejects capitalism, including welfare-state capitalism, since it concentrates economic powers, including ownership and control of productive resources, in the hands of a privileged class. He endorses instead property-owning democracy and liberal socialism, which both guarantee widespread distribution of economic powers and prerogatives as well as income and wealth (*TJ*, xiv–xvi).

The main reason Rawls gives for focusing on the basic structure in matters of distributive justice is that it is necessary to maintain "background justice" via a "social process" that counteracts the tendency of multiple individual transactions to distort the distribution of economic powers, income, and wealth. "Historical process" views such as libertarianism, Rawls says, have "no special role for the basic structure" (*PL*, 262). Libertarians and many classical liberals maintain that, given a historical starting point of just initial acquisitions, almost *any* configuration of holdings that results from a historical process of free exchanges and transfers is also just. Moreover distributions remain just across generations no matter how unequal the ensuing configuration of assets, so long as the rules of this historical process are uniformly complied with and any deviations are rectified.

The problem Rawls sees in historical process views is that the capitalist "invisible hand" inevitably guides distributions in the wrong direction, not toward but instead away from a fair distribution that exhibits "reciprocity at the deepest level" (*JF*, 49). A series of historical transactions that are all apparently fair and where all parties comply with their individual duties will tend over time to result in grossly unequal and often distorted outcomes (monopolies, oligopolies, destitution among the poor, etc.). This gives us reason to question the fairness of individuals' bargaining situations, and the entire historical process of distribution itself.[18]

Missing from historical process views is a conception of background justice that provides criteria for assessing the fairness of individuals' starting positions, relative bargaining power, outcomes of economic bargains and of long-term economic trends; also the just distribution of economic powers and prerogatives, and of income and wealth; and the permissible range of inequalities that may result from transactions among free economic agents. A fundamental role of the economic and legal institutions that constitute the basic structure is to establish and maintain "background procedural justice" (*JF*, 52, 171) within an "ideal social process" (*JF*, 57) of economic activity among free and equal moral persons in their capacity as economic agents. *Principles and rules for institutions* specify and regulate basic economic institutions (property, markets, the law of contracts, sales, corporations, finance, etc.) and continually adjust and rectify the inevitable tendencies of markets away from background fairness (via limits on inequalities, income supplements for the less advantaged, and other measures.). Individuals freely engage in economic activity according to the *rules for individuals* that regulate uses of property, permissible contracts and other transactions, financial instruments, etc., and prohibit fraud, duress, price fixing, and other violations of justice. Of these rules for individuals Rawls says, "They are framed to leave individuals and associations free to act effectively in pursuit of their ends and without excessive constraints" (*PL*, 268).

This is the "*institutional division of labor*" (*JF*, 54) between, on the one hand, the institutional principles and rules of justice that apply to the basic structure and maintain background justice, and, on the other hand, the moral principles and institutional rules that apply to regulate individual and associational conduct in their particular transactions. Rawls insists on this division of labor between principles and rules for institutions and for individuals in establishing distributive justice for two reasons relating, respectively, to the second and first principles of justice.

First, the institutional division of labor is necessary to maintain "pure background procedural justice" according to the difference principle (*JF*, 57). Rawls sees a free market economy as one requirement of economic justice and the difference principle, since markets effectively process limitless information regarding supply and demand and are (normally) more efficient in allocating factors of production, thereby potentially promoting everyone's advantage, including the less advantaged. Importantly, the use of markets and the price system to efficiently allocate productive resources does not require, Rawls says, the market distributions of income and wealth defended by classical liberals and libertarians (*TJ*, 239–242). Entitlements to market income depend on rules of property, which specify the extent to which people have rights of income in the resources they own and for sale of their labor. Distributions of income and wealth, along with economic powers and prerogatives, are to be determined by rules of distribution legislated to comply with the difference principle. Accordingly, market distributions of income and wealth, along with the exercise of economic powers, are to be periodically adjusted by taxation and other measures and redistributed as needed to conform to rules of distribution required by background justice (*JF*, 52).[19]

Rawls says the institutional division of labor required by pure procedural justice "allows us to abstract from the enormous complexities of the innumerable transactions of daily life and frees us from having to keep track of the changing relative positions of particular individuals" (*JF*, 54; see also *TJ*, §14). The problem addressed here is not simply that individual economic agents cannot process limitless information regarding others' economic activities and know whether their economic choices conform to an allocative end state distribution (such as maximum utility, or equality). Because of pure procedural justice, there is no such allocative end state required; instead, there is a system of background procedural justice, and it is beyond individuals' capacities to achieve and maintain via their individual transactions the system of background justice required by the difference principle (cf. Scheffler 2012, 120). I discuss this further in the following section.

The second reason for the division of labor between principles and rules for institutions on the one hand and principles and rules for individuals on the other is that this division is necessary to enable free and equal persons to freely pursue their purposes, commitments, and life plans, "secure in the knowledge that elsewhere in the social system the necessary corrections to preserve background justice are being made" (*PL*, 269). It would be unduly restrictive of individuals' free pursuit of their life plans, as well as their fulfilling special commitments and obligations and other moral duties, to impose an individual duty to promote directly the ends of distributive justice in all that they do – whether this be equality, maximum or maximin utility, or any other allocative distribution. Even if it were not beyond individuals' capacities to know whether their economic choices promote or conflict with allocative patterns, the imposition on individuals of a stringent moral duty to directly promote specific allocative distributions would occupy most, if not all, moral space.

There are two separate considerations at work here. First, there is Rawls's fundamental assumption that there are a plurality of values, moral principles, and reasons for acting in addition to those required by distributive justice. Requirements of distributive justice must accommodate the multiple values, special commitments and other moral duties and special obligations to particular individuals that we have. Second, given this plurality of values and principles, Rawls contends that essential to individuals' good is that they have the freedom to determine their values and commitments, in fashioning their own rational plan of life within the constraints that justice and personal morality impose upon them. The diversity of values and principles has been termed "value pluralism" (Scheffler 2012, 116). Rawls in *Political Liberalism* uses the term "reasonable pluralism" to refer to the diversity of permissible conceptions of the good and comprehensive moral and religious doctrines in a liberal society that respects freedom and equality. The problem is to fashion an account of distributive justice that allows for value and/or reasonable pluralism – including individuals' free pursuit of a multiplicity of (intrinsically) valuable purposes, activities, and commitments. This is what Samuel Scheffler has aptly called Rawls's "division of moral labor" between the demands of justice and the demands of other values, moral duties, and special obligations and commitments to others.[20]

Here G.A. Cohen and others have replied that the requirement that individuals in their choices and actions promote an allocative distribution such as equality, or the well-being of the least advantaged, or maximum utility, does not coercively restrict individual freedom, for it is not a legal requirement but a moral requirement on individuals' conduct. Individuals can then freely choose to comply with or (selfishly) ignore this moral duty to promote the ends of distributive justice in their choices. Hence there is no undue restriction on individuals' liberty by the imposition of a moral duty to promote a patterned allocation of income and wealth.

Even if Cohen's individual moral duty to promote a specified allocative pattern is not legally enforced, there still remains the problem that, in acting according to their freely chosen life plans, special commitments, and other moral obligations, free persons would rarely be in compliance with the strict allocative demands of distributive justice, and would be morally adjudged to be guilty of selfishly pursuing their own interests, no matter how beneficent or morally obligatory their actions otherwise might be. In addition to duties of justice, there are a multiplicity of individual moral duties and commitments imposing special obligations on us, and these can be quite demanding in their own right. Moreover there are many unselfish pursuits and valuable activities that make up individuals' freely adopted conceptions of the good. Rawls is concerned, not simply with the scope of legal liberties and external constraints, but with maintaining the diversity of values and moral principles, and the full autonomy of individuals to decide their primary ends and create and pursue their life plans in compliance with the requirements of justice and other moral duties they have. This is a primary reason for the division of labor between principles and rules that apply to the basic structure to maintain background justice vs those principles and rules that regulate individual conduct as they freely pursue valuable activities.

This further clarifies the abstract claim addressed in the preceding section, that the ideal of persons as free and equal requires "institutional expression" in the basic structure. Once again, we see that the fundamental justification for the primacy of the basic structure and division of labor between principles for institutions vs individuals is to guarantee both the plurality of values and the possibility of the *full autonomy* of free and equal moral persons – their freedom to create and pursue consistent with justice and personal morality a freely chosen life plan against a background of a plurality of (intrinsic) goods and worthwhile activities. Given Rawls's account of the fundamental interests of free and equal moral persons – to realize their rational and moral capacities – the problem is to find a way to make the moral requirements of (distributive) justice compatible with individuals being able to live according to their freely chosen rational life plans while conforming to, and even acting for the sake of, justice and other moral duties in their day-to-day activities. The "congruence" of the good and the right, or of rational and moral autonomy, would not be possible were all our actions subject to a moral demand that we maximize social utility, or promote equal (opportunity for) welfare, or promote the well-being or maximum share of primary goods of the least advantaged, or any other stringent allocative principle of justice that is directly applicable to assessments of individual conduct.[21]

# 5. Clarifications, Objections, and Responses

To clarify Rawls's assumption of the primacy of the basic structure, it may be helpful briefly to summarize and reply to some notable objections.

## 5.1 Monism vs Dualism

Liam Murphy contends that Rawls's institutional division of labor has no bearing on whether a moral principle applies to either or both the basic structure and individual actions. As opposed to what he calls Rawls's "dualism" Murphy argues for "monism," the position that fundamental principles of justice should apply directly both to the design of the basic structure and to assessments of individuals' actions. Here his position resembles G.A. Cohen's argument that the difference principle, or other egalitarian principle of justice, should apply both to basic institutions and to guide and assess individual conduct. While Cohen's position requires equalizing the consequences of luck and then rewarding people according to effort, Murphy endorses a modified utilitarian "principle of weighted benefi-cence" to design economic institutions to "maximize aggregate weighted well-being over time; likewise people . . . should act to promote the same thing . . ." (1998, 263). Murphy says that, given appropriate institutional liberties that free individuals of the burdens of promoting weighted well-being in their individual activities, individuals are left free and "can for the most part pursue their own interests" without "having to think too much about promoting general well-being" (1998, 263). Thus, Murphy, like Cohen, concludes, monism need not unduly constrain individuals' liberty or put unreasonable demands on their conduct.

Murphy's "monism" is a variation on the traditional (act) utilitarian position that the requirement to maximize aggregate utility applies to both individual conduct and also laws and social institutions. Can monism (as Murphy claims) realize the purposes of the institu-tional division of labor as Rawls conceives of it? This once again is where Rawls's ideal of justice as the regulation of social relations among free and equal moral persons plays a crucial role.

To begin with, if the main purpose of Rawls's distinction between principles for institutions and individuals is to provide for individuals' free determination of their conceptions of the good against a background of a plurality of (intrinsic) values, moral duties, and commit-ments, then it seems apparent that monism cannot accommodate Rawls's distinction; for monism, as Murphy describes it, is the denial of value and moral pluralism. There is nothing particularly liberal about not legally requiring individuals to maximize weighted well-being (or equality for Cohen) in their day-to-day decisions. Even if we grant that Murphy's (and Cohen's) account has a place for liberal rights, still when individuals act on these liberties and freely pursue their interests, they are not complying with the stringent moral require-ments of Murphy's (or Cohen's) principle of distributive justice. They are instead acting in pursuit of the values, commitments, and obligations constituting their conception of the good, which is conduct that rarely would be sanctioned by a monistic principle such as weighted utility that applies to assess all individual actions and institutional measures. Merely having the legal liberty to freely pursue one's own interests instead of conforming to the exacting moral requirements of a stringent, monistic moral principle does not render indi-viduals' free pursuit of their self-determined rational good compatible or congruent (in Rawls's sense) with justice. Personal pursuits, even if excusable on a monist view, nonetheless conflict with the demands of justice on Murphy's account.[22]

The ultimate justification for Rawls's distinction between institutional and individual prin-ciples is not simply to leave individuals *legally* free to pursue their own good, including per-sonal commitments, while leaving distributive justice up to background justice. No reasonable conception imposes a legal requirement that individuals must make economic choices that meet requirements of a monistic principle of justice. It's then no surprise that Murphy and Cohen leave individuals legally free to pursue their own interests. The problem is that there is no way both to pursue one's individual aims, commitments, and autonomously determined rational life plan and, at the same time, satisfy the stringent requirements of exacting monis-tic principles. Monistic principles leave no space for the pluralism of intrinsic values and principles, including fundamental moral duties that stem from special relationships and personal commitments, nor for the full autonomy of free and equal persons.

## 5.2 Capitalism, Incentives and the Institutional Division of Labor

G.A. Cohen and Liam Murphy also argue that Rawls's "dualism" puts no serious demands on people's behavior, and leaves people free to pursue their self-interest without requiring them to "promote justice" (conceived as equality on Cohen's account, as weighted benefi- cence for Murphy, and maximizing the well-being of the least advantaged on their allocative interpretation of Rawls's difference principle) (Murphy 1998, 267). This criticism ignores the role in regulating individual behavior of the natural duties and other moral duties and obliga- tions people have. On Rawls's account, though individuals have a duty to comply with rules of justice and promote just institutions, they are not under a constant duty always to act to maximize the share of primary goods going to the least advantaged. Why should they be, given the plurality of value and other moral duties and obligations? In addition to duties of justice, individuals are subject to duties of mutual aid and mutual respect; duties of fidelity and obligations of fairness in their dealings with others; special obligations to families, friends, associates, etc.; duties of beneficence; and many other moral duties required by Rawls's non- consequentialist, nonmonistic position. Nothing about Rawls's position precludes a moral duty not to be selfish or self-aggrandizing, or not to take advantage of others; these duties seem part of the natural duties of mutual respect, mutual aid, and beneficence to others. What moral persons are not required to do is maximize weighted beneficence, the position of the least advantaged, or equality, in all their actions and pursuits – for such individual duties would displace other moral duties and obligations we have and would make individual autonomy amid a plurality of intrinsic values, as well as most special relationships and com- mitments, morally impermissible. We do not live in a monistic moral universe.

Behind Cohen's and Murphy's argument is a serious misinterpretation of the kind of social system that is required by the difference principle. Cohen argues that the purpose of Rawls's institutional division of labor is to free people up to act on their self-interest and engage in "unlimited self-seekingness," while leaving it to principles for the basic structure to redistrib- ute wealth so as to achieve the purposes of distributive justice (G.A. Cohen 1997, 16). The purported purpose of Rawls's "dualism" is to take advantage of capitalist markets' "invisible hand," by providing incentives to people, to exercise their undeserved talents in self-interested ways that coincidentally benefit others. The difference principle, regarded purely as an insti- tutional principle, then allegedly serves as Rawls's justification for welfare state redistribu- tions within a capitalist economy.

Rawls's liberalism requires a market economy, not to accommodate "unlimited self-seek- ingness," but to guarantee freedom of occupation, association, and fair equality of opportu- nity, and to achieve efficient allocations of productive resources, which are to everyone's benefit. Markets do not however provide a substantive criterion for the just distribution of income and wealth for Rawls, unlike libertarianism and classical liberalism. It's the role of the difference principle to adjust and reallocate market distributions so that they meet requirements of background procedural justice. It is a serious misreading then to suppose that the difference principle and the institutional division of labor are intended to accom- modate capitalism. Rawls explicitly argues that capitalism, even welfare-state capitalism, is unjust, since it concentrates economic powers, including control over productive wealth, in the hands of a capitalist class, and denies economic powers and ownership of productive wealth to the majority of citizens (*JF*, 135–140). Instead of capitalism, the difference principle requires either property-owning democracy, or "liberal" or "associational socialism" (*CP*, 277). Rawls assumes that, in these economic systems satisfying the principles of justice, neither will there be opportunities for the "unlimited self-seekingness" encouraged by capitalism, nor should individuals be motivated primarily by self interest and self-aggrandizement. Instead, Rawls argues, citizens' pursuit of their aims and personal commitments will be regulated by their sense of justice, their willingness to comply with justice and other moral duties, and their desire to do their fair share in contributing to social cooperation. Under social and economic conditions that satisfy Rawls's principles, the institutions of a just society should encourage the development of aspirations that limit individuals' desires for acquisitiveness (see J. Cohen 2001).

## 5.3 Rawls's Principles of Justice Are Neither Consequentialist Nor Prioritarian

Implicit in Murphy's and Cohen's criticisms of Rawls's institutional division of labor is an assumption that the difference principle is an allocative principle and is either consequentialist and/or prioritarian. They both argue that a fundamental problem with Rawls's institutional division of labor is its implication that the best way to promote the "aim of justice" is *always* to comply with institutional requirements. But, Murphy claims, particularly in non-ideal conditions of a partially just or unjust society, it is often better to bypass institutions and act directly to "promote whatever it is that just institutions are for," whether that be increasing weighted well-being or the position of the least advantaged or some other aim (Murphy 1998, 280, 283). "Once we accept that the principles that govern the design of ideal institutions *essentially describe means to ends*, the oddness of thinking that justice describes some means to that end but not others becomes rather evident" (1998, 282, emphasis added). "It is not credible that what fundamentally matters is that the relevant institutions promote equality or well-being, rather than that equality or well-being be promoted" (1998, 283).

Cohen's criticism of Rawls's difference principle is similar: If what is ultimately important is equality, or the well-being of the least advantaged, then it is shortsighted only to apply the difference principle or similar egalitarian principles to institutions and not also to assess and guide the choices and conduct of individuals, requiring that they too promote the same ends that the principles of justice are designed to promote.

These arguments misinterpret the nature and role of Rawls's principles of justice, especially the difference principle. To begin with, Rawls's principles of justice for the basic structure are framed as principles for institutions; they are not stated in terms that would apply directly to individual conduct. This is clear in case of the basic liberties and fair equality of opportunities, which are constitutional requirements. How could I, or any individual, guarantee everyone "a fully adequate scheme of equal basic liberties" or "conditions of fair equality of opportunity"? These demands can only be satisfied institutionally. For example, fair equality of opportunity requires setting up institutions that provide universal educational and health care benefits, as well as taxation to limit inequalities of income, wealth, and economic powers. While we surely can respect others' basic liberties and not discriminate unfairly against them in hiring, etc., as required by our individual duty of justice, we cannot individually guarantee equal basic liberties and fair equal opportunities for all or take the institutional measures needed to do so. Strictly speaking, it makes no sense to say that these principles of justice should be applied by individuals in their day-to-day activities. Only if it is assumed that these principles for institutions are designed to promote some state of affairs that we are also obligated to promote in our individual conduct does this argument make sense.

Rawls however would reject this premise (Murphy's), "that the principles that govern the design of ideal institutions essentially describe means to ends." The first and second principles, including the difference principle, are neither consequentialist nor prioritarian: they are not designed to promote or maximize a state of affairs or "end-state" of equal or maximin distribution of either welfare or primary social goods. Instead the principles of justice are principles of social cooperation that structure social institutions and regulate social relations so that they express and realize an ideal of free and equal moral persons who cooperate on terms of reciprocity and mutual respect that everyone can reasonably accept. If anything is "the end of justice" (Murphy) it is this ideal of persons and of social cooperation. This ideal is not however a consequentialist end-state to be maximally promoted, but an ideal that is realized and expressed within social relationships of reciprocity and mutual respect among free and equal persons who act on and from the principles of justice for both institutions and individuals.

Were the difference principle a consequentialist principle,[23] it would imply that the well-being of others is simply a means to maximizing the well-being of the least advantaged (workers). But what reason would an individual or society have to want to maximize *only* the position of least advantaged (*workers*) at the expense of other equally reasonable aims, such as the well-being of the disabled? Rawls implicitly denies the consequentialist reading of the difference principle in saying that the difference principle is a principle of reciprocity that "expresses concern for all members of society," not simply the least advantaged (*JF*, 71).

The difference principle is also not prioritarian in Derek Parfit's sense. Prioritarianism implies that most any state of affairs in which the least advantaged are better off is preferable to one in which they are less well off. Rawls implicitly denies the prioritarian reading in saying that the difference principle is a principle of "reciprocity at the deepest level." This implies the following: starting with a just status quo, many economic measures leading to states of affairs that make the least advantaged better off are nonetheless unjust since they do not *maximally* or even primarily benefit the least advantaged by making them better off than other alternative measures would.[24] Most economic measures designed to bring about Pareto improvements to a just status quo are in this sense unjust; they unfairly deprive the least advantaged of gains that go to the more advantaged instead.

To connect this discussion up with the main point of the previous section: The difference principle, rather than promoting an end-state of maximal well-being (or maximal primary goods) for the least advantaged, is a principle of democratic reciprocity ("at the deepest level") that fairly structures economic relations (including economic powers and control over productive resources) among socially productive free and equal citizens, and then fairly distributes the social product among them. Some principle is needed for this purpose on any account of economic justice. For utilitarians, the principle of utility has traditionally played this role, with the primary focus being on economic efficiency and maximizing total productive output so as to maximize the satisfaction of consumers' desires. Utilitarianism is the traditional justification of laissez-faire capitalism, as well as modern welfare-state capitalism. Murphy's quasi-prioritarian ideal of maximizing "weighted well-being" is simply a variation on the traditional utilitarian argument, and justifies a more humane capitalist welfare state. But

Rawls is consciously trying to break with this predominant utilitarian/capitalist tradition by imposing, via the difference principle, a requirement of fair democratic reciprocity over efficiency and maximum utility in the economic relations of free and equal citizens and in the distribution of economic powers and resulting income and wealth. This largely accounts for his arguments for property-owning democracy or liberal socialism, and rejection of capitalism of all forms.

This is a complicated subject, better taken up in a discussion of the institutions required by the difference principle itself. But the failure of Cohen and Murphy to focus on Rawls's rejection of capitalism is indicative of their misunderstanding of the role of the institutional division of labor underlying the difference principle.

## 5.4 Social vs Cosmopolitan Justice

Rawls's principles of justice are for the basic structure of *society*, and do not apply to global institutions or within lesser domestic institutions. Rawls's account of justice says that, as a matter of reciprocity, a society and its members owe rights of political and distributive justice to members within their own society – to those engaged in social cooperation and subject to the rules of these basic institutions – and not to members of other societies who are subject to different social institutions. Cosmopolitans object to this as an unjustified moral discontinuity. Why should artificial national boundaries make such a difference to the distribution of income and wealth? These are historical contingencies, normally the product of (unjust) wars or ancient marriages; moreover, it is also accidental whether a person is born on one side of a boundary or another. Arbitrary contingencies should not matter to justice, since no one is responsible for them.

Some cosmopolitans argue that, since we engage in economic cooperation with much of the world, the difference principle should be extended to apply to these other societies. Utilitarians and other monists contend that even this does not resolve the problem of moral discontinuity and arbitrary contingencies; for example, some societies (e.g., Somalia and other burdened societies) have nothing to offer or are incapable of economic cooperation (see Murphy 1998, 224). Institutions, whether social or global, are simply irrelevant to fundamental principles of distributive justice.

The cosmopolitan critique of Rawls is a large topic addressed elsewhere in this volume. But insofar as it draws into question the relevance of the basic structure of society to distributive justice, this much should be said: A society has numerous duties of justice to provide benefits to members of other societies, as well as to its own, that are not duties of distributive justice. Rawls in *The Law of Peoples* addresses the problem of global poverty by imposing on societies a duty of justice (not charity) to assist burdened societies in meeting the basic needs of their members and becoming economically self-sufficient. But for Rawls this is not a question of *distributive justice* as he uses that term. Nor are a society's duties to remedy the disabilities of the mentally and physically impaired, or meet the basic needs of its own poor, or address other arbitrary contingencies (disaster relief, etc.) problems of distributive justice. Rawls conceives of distributive justice more narrowly than other contemporary views; it addresses a specific problem of economic cooperation among members of a society who are subject to its basic institutions. The basic social institutions of any society (including laws of property, contract, sales, corporations, gifts and bequests, etc.) make economic production, trade, distribution, and consumption of product among the members of that society possible.

For purposes of distributive justice, Rawls conceives of society's members as normally fully cooperative, which means that they are productive and do their fair share in contributing toward the social product. Given these assumptions, the *fundamental question of distributive justice* for Rawls is: How is a society to structure the basic social institutions that make economic production possible among socially productive agents, including the division of economic powers and opportunities and control over means of production, and then determine fair shares to the resulting social product of income and wealth that is to go to the economic agents responsible for it?

This is the question that informed the socialist critique of capitalism, with which the idea of distributive justice originates. It is a different question than the question of what a society owes its members to meet their basic needs, or to address their natural disabilities and other arbitrary contingencies; or of what a society owes to members of other societies. These questions raise entirely different issues – of redress, decency, humanitarianism, etc. – and should be addressed by different principles – of remedial or compensatory justice, principles of assistance or beneficence, and so on. The difference principle is framed to address the specific problem of distributive shares among socially productive economic agents that any conception of justice needs to respond to. The problem with "monism" is that it provides the same answer to all questions of justice and morality, regardless of their differences, and regardless of different kinds of relationships (social, productive, associational, familial, cosmopolitan, etc.) among persons.

Once the problem of distributive justice is conceived this way, and the profound influence of basic social institutions on citizens' moral personality and future prospects is taken into account, then there seems to be no "moral discontinuity" in distributing the economic powers, opportunities and income and wealth that result from socially productive activity to the members of society who fully engage in it and do their fair share in maintaining basic social institutions. Instead, assuming that a society has satisfied its duties to the disabled and the unemployed, provided educational and health care benefits, met the basic needs of its own members, and also has complied with its duties of assistance to other societies, the "moral discontinuity" would be to apply the difference principle, affording "reciprocity at the deepest level," indiscriminately to distribute economic powers, income and wealth to people who are not "fully cooperative" and engaged in socially productive activity. "Reciprocity at the deepest level" requires not simply membership in society, but also *productive reciprocity,*[25] or doing one's fair share in the assumption of social burdens and creation of social benefits.

Moreover, while there is cooperation among members of different societies, and various influential global institutions (the United Nations, World Trade Organization, International Monetary Fund, etc.), there is no global basic structure of basic economic institutions – no global property regime, etc. – to which the difference principle might be applied to fashion these institutions; nor is there a global political society or political constitution with the capacity, authority, or legal institutions to globally apply the principles of justice, or to create a comprehensive global legal and property system. The global basic structure that exists to regulate trade and other relations among peoples is instead dependent upon the political and economic institutions of different societies, and is ideally subject to their joint determination. For these and other reasons, it is for Rawls the basic structure of societies, not of the world generally, that is the source and primary subject of distributive justice.[26]

# Notes

I am grateful to the editors of this volume, and to Kok-Chor Tan and Chris Melenovsky for their helpful comments and suggestions.

1  This assumes that the basic needs of the least advantaged in one's *own* society are met. Rawls says the first principle of justice assumes that citizens' basic needs are met (*JF*, 44 n7); and that a social minimum that meets basic needs is a "constitutional essential" (*JF*, 48, 162). The difference principle, he continues, is more demanding and should not be a constitutional essential.

2  Rawls says, "the conception of justice that [applies to the basic structure] has a certain *regulative primacy* with respect to the principles and standards appropriate for other cases" (*PL*, 257–258).

3  "It is the distinct purposes and roles of the parts of the social structure, and how they fit together, that explains there being different principles for distinct kinds of subjects. Indeed, it seems natural to suppose that the distinctive character and *autonomy of the various elements of society* requires that, within some sphere, they act from their own principles designed to fit their peculiar nature" (*PL*, 262).

4  Again, to say that principles of social justice are regulative of the scope and content of other principles of justice cannot mean that considerations of social justice trump all other moral considerations. Obviously a society cannot violate the human rights or take unfair advantage of other societies in order to increase benefits to the least advantaged under the difference principle. Moreover the regulative nature of the principles of justice does not conflict with the requirement that individual shares under the difference principle are subject to a society's first having paid its fair share under the duty of assistance owed to burdened peoples.

5  The principles for individuals Rawls sets forth are the natural duties and the principle of fairness (see *TJ*, §§18–19, 51–52). Natural duties include positive duties to uphold justice, mutual aid, mutual respect, and also include negative duties not to be cruel, or injure others, or harm the innocent, or cause unnecessary suffering (*TJ*, 94, 98). The principle of fairness includes obligations of fairness, and of fidelity (to keep promises, etc.). Rawls also says we have "a natural duty to bring about a great good . . . if we can do so relatively easily" (*TJ*, 100). Rawls does not intend his lists to be exhaustive (*TJ*, 98).

6  Liam Murphy I believe makes the mistake of confusing these two distinctions and assuming that they are parallel. See section 5 below.

7  For example, while heads of families have the freedom to raise their children according to their own religious beliefs, they do not have the freedom to deny them their right to an education that teaches children their rights and opportunities as democratic citizens and enables them to develop their capacities so as to become independent and productive members of society. See *PL*, 466–474.

8  Similarly Rawls says no specific argument for the principles of justice is conclusive; rather the argument "depends on judgment – on judging the balance of reasons" (*JF*, 95; see also *JF*, 133 on the "balance of reasons" favoring the difference principle).

9  See in general Rousseau's *Discourse on Inequality*, Part I on natural man, and his *Social Contract*. See also Rawls's 'Lectures on Rousseau' (*LHPP*, 191–248).

10  Rawls is arguing in part against David Gauthier's hybrid Lockean/Hobbesian contract view, which assumes natural property and presocial endowments, and then uses these as a baseline for determining individuals' contributions to society and their entitlements to the "cooperative surplus" due to social cooperation. See *PL*, 278 n14.

11  See for example the remarks on evolution and the sense of justice (*TJ*, 440–441) and on the genetic basis for our natural talents (*PL*, 269).

12   "Developed natural capacities are always a selection, a small selection at that, from the possibilities that might have been attained" (*PL*, 270; see also *JF*, 57).

13   On this see Hart 1997, ch. 5.

14   Rawls continues, "The freedom and equality of moral persons require some public form, and the content of the two principles fulfills this expectation" (*PL*, 281).

15   In summarizing the reasons for the primacy of the justice of the basic structure, Rawls says: "This structure comprises social institutions within which human beings may develop their moral powers and become fully cooperating members of a society of free and equal citizens. . . . It also answers to the public role of educating citizens to a conception of themselves as free and equal; and when properly regulated encourages in them . . . a sense of being treated fairly in view of the public principles . . ." (*JF*, 57).

16   Because of this capacity to be rational, moral persons have a "higher-order interest" in regulating all their other interests and activities "by reason, that is by reasonable and rational principles that are expressive of their autonomy" (*PL*, 280).

17   All these arguments are in *PL*, Lecture VIII, "The Basic Liberties and their Priority."

18   "The tendency . . . is for background justice to be eroded even when individuals act fairly: the overall result of separate and independent transactions is away from and not toward background justice" (*PL*, 267).

19   Moreover, for Rawls free markets in allocating labor are a condition of freedom of occupation and choice of careers, freedom of association, and fair equality of opportunity. Markets enable citizens to freely choose their occupations, careers, and where they live and work, and to compete for open positions on fair terms with other similarly talented individuals (*TJ*, 239, 240–241).

20   In two important papers, Samuel Scheffler explains the primacy of the basic structure largely as a reflection of "the division of moral labor" that stems from the "plurality of values and principles" that Rawls's account of justice is designed to accommodate. See Scheffler 2012, 116, 125, 134, and chs 4–5 more generally. Rawls himself refers to "the division of labor between different kinds of principles" (*PL*, 469). See also Tan 2012, chs 1–2, on institutions, which is also very helpful. Value pluralism is a thesis about the nature of value and morality, and is part of a comprehensive philosophical doctrine that is consistent with assumptions made in *TJ*. In *PL* any assumption of value pluralism is replaced by "reasonable pluralism," which is not a philosophical thesis about the nature of value but an empirical assumption that in a liberal society reasonable people will inevitably affirm diverse values, commitments, and religious, moral and philosophical views that impose duties and obligations.

21   From Rawls's Kantian perspective, Cohen's remedy of "personal prerogatives" of unspecified dimensions does not solve this problem (G.A. Cohen 2008, 10–11, 61, 71); for in acting on personal prerogatives, though one may be temporarily *excused* from stringent demands of promoting just distributions, he or she is not acting on or even compatible with the duty to promote justice. See Freeman 2013.

22   Personal pursuits conflict with justice on Cohen's account as well, though sometimes we are excused from pursuing justice because of "a certain self-regarding prerogative," the scope of which he does not specify (G.A. Cohen 2008, 61, 71).

23   Murphy seems to regard both the difference principle and the individual duty of justice as consequentialist principles. "When pure procedural or 'deontological' theories of distributive justice are incorporated into people's practical lives, they seem to collapse into consequentialist theories" (1998, 289).

24   For example, start with a just distribution #1 at T1 that satisfies the difference principle, where the members of the least advantaged group (LAG) have 50 and those of the most advantaged group (MAG) have 250. Two economic regulations are proposed and voted upon by legislators: measure #2 raises the share going to the LAG to 51 with MAG at 350, while measure #3 provides the LAG with 60 and the MAG have 275. It would be an obvious injustice to enact #2 rather than

#3 under *both* prioritarianism and the difference principle. But for reasons of reciprocity, it would also be an injustice under the difference principle, but not for prioritarianism, to enact #2 rather than remain with the status quo at #1. (For the difference principle, 3 > 1 > 2 whereas for prioritarianism, 3 > 2 > 1.) According to the difference principle, while society under measure #2 may be richer and more efficient than under #1, and the LAG are better off, still it is unjust, or clearly less just than society at #1.

25  I borrow this term from Stuart White.
26  See Freeman 2007, chs 8–9, discussing the main points in this section.

## Works by Rawls, with Abbreviations

"The Basic Liberties and Their Priority" (1982), Lecture VIII in *Political Liberalism*.
*Collected Papers* (CP), ed. Samuel Freeman. Cambridge, MA: Harvard University Press, 1999.
*Justice as Fairness: A Restatement* (JF), ed. Erin Kelly. Cambridge, MA: Harvard University Press, 2001.
*Lectures on the History of Political Philosophy* (LHPP), ed. Samuel Freeman. Cambridge, MA: Harvard University Press, 2007.
*Political Liberalism* (PL), expanded edn. New York: Columbia University Press, 2005.
*A Theory of Justice* (TJ), rev. edn. Cambridge, MA: Harvard University Press, 1999.
"Two Concepts of Rules" (1955), in *Collected Papers* (20–46).

## Other References

Cohen, G.A. (1997) "Where the Action Is: On the Site of Distributive Justice." *Philosophy and Public Affairs* 26(1): 3–30.
Cohen, G.A. (2008) *Rescuing Justice and Equality*. Cambridge, MA: Harvard University Press.
Cohen, Joshua (2001) "Taking People As They Are." *Philosophy and Public Affairs* 30(4): 363–386.
Freeman, Samuel (2007) *Justice and the Social Contract*. New York: Oxford University Press.
Freeman, Samuel (2013) "Assessing G.A. Cohen's Critique of the Difference Principle." *Harvard Review of Philosophy* 19.
Hart, H.L.A. (1997) *The Concept of Law*. 2nd edn. Oxford: Oxford University Press.
Murphy, Liam (1998) "Institutions and the Demands of Justice." *Philosophy and Public Affairs* 27(4): 251–291.
Scheffler, Samuel (2012) *Equality and Tradition*. New York: Oxford University Press.
Tan, Kok-Chor (2012) *Justice, Institutions, and Luck*. Oxford: Oxford University Press.

# 6

# Rawls on Ideal and Nonideal Theory

## ZOFIA STEMPLOWSKA AND ADAM SWIFT

## 1. Introduction

The world is full of grave injustice. Though his mode of theorizing is sometimes taken to betray a lack of interest in that fact, Rawls sees himself as responding to it. He believes we cannot gain a systematic understanding of the pressing and urgent problems we confront in our nonideal circumstances unless we have a grasp of what he has called the ideal theory of justice; ideal theory is the necessary precursor of nonideal theory. He tells us right at the start of *A Theory of Justice* that his theory is intentionally constrained in two ways: it is ideal (rather than nonideal), and it focuses on the justice of the basic structure of society (rather than other social practices, or individual actions) (*TJ*, 7–8). The latter constraint is famously controversial (Cohen 2000) but the idea is intuitively easy to grasp. What are we to make of the former?

## 2. What Is Ideal Theory?

Rawls contrasts ideal theory of justice with nonideal theory of justice. Ideal theory asks which principles of justice would regulate a perfectly (or nearly perfectly) just society that is, to use his vocabulary, "well-ordered."[1] Nonideal theory in turn asks "which principles to adopt under less happy conditions" (*TJ*, 216) when perfect justice is, at best, a distant goal. So both ideal and nonideal theory are concerned with what justice requires and thus both are concerned with the "ideal" of justice. The difference is that nonideal theory asks what justice requires under nonideal conditions, while ideal theory asks what it demands when conditions are ideal enough to sustain a just, well-ordered society.

Putting aside (for now) why anyone should be interested in an ideal theory's answer to what perfect justice requires, let us first outline in more detail the three idealizing assumptions that allow ideal theory to focus on the requirements of perfect justice.

*A Companion to Rawls*, First Edition. Edited by Jon Mandle and David A. Reidy.
© 2014 John Wiley & Sons, Inc. Published 2016 by John Wiley & Sons, Inc.

First, ideal theory assumes that "(nearly) everyone strictly complies with . . . the principles of justice" (*JF*, 13). Under this assumption of strict compliance, citizens share a conception of justice and are motivated to comply with it. That ideal theory makes this assumption should come as no surprise given its aim of theorizing about perfect justice; when people do not comply with the requirements of justice, we are faced with injustice. The problem of how to respond to injustice is the task of nonideal theory, which "comprises such topics as the theory of punishment, the doctrine of just war, and the justification of the various ways of opposing unjust regimes, ranging from civil disobedience and conscientious objection to militant resistance and revolution" (*TJ*, 8).[2]

Although Rawls introduces the concept of ideal theory for the first time exclusively with reference to its assumption of strict compliance (*TJ*, 7–8), and speaks of "ideal, or strict compliance, theory" (*JF*, 13), ideal theory assumes also the presence of so-called "favorable circumstances." This idea appears in *A Theory of Justice* (216) and becomes more explicit in his later work. In *Justice as Fairness*, he explains that favorable circumstances are the "conditions that, provided the political will exists, make a constitutional regime possible" (*JF*, 101). They are favorable in that they can sustain a constitutional democracy, which is what, for Rawls, a just, well-ordered society needs to be. The relevant conditions do not include "political will," but they do include "historical, economic and social conditions," such as "economic means . . . education, or the main skills needed to run a democratic regime" (*JF*, 47). In *Political Liberalism*, he clarifies that the favorable conditions are "determined by a society's culture, its traditions and acquired skills in running institutions, and its level of economic advance (which need not be especially high), and no doubt by other things as well" (*PL*, 297).

Distinguishing social and cultural conditions from political will is tricky, but the basic point is clear: ideal theory assumes that the broad social, cultural and economic conditions (socioeconomic conditions for short) are such that they could sustain a perfectly just society should people try to have it. Nonideal theory, by contrast, deals with socioeconomic conditions that are inhospitable to such a society. Such conditions need not make its achievement impossible in the long run, but they rule it out, or make it very difficult to sustain, at present.

In short, ideal theory puts aside obstacles to perfect justice that arise due either to agents' noncompliance with the demands of justice (partial compliance) or to inadequate socioeconomic conditions (unfavorable circumstances). There is, however, a third kind of obstacle to perfect justice that Rawls considers in *A Theory of Justice*. Although he sometimes links them to "historical and social contingencies" and discusses both together, the "natural limitations and accidents of human life" (*TJ*, 215) that persist even under favorable circumstances seem importantly distinct. This category includes a variety of permanent or temporary "limitations and accidents" such as childhood and severe mental disability.

Rawls's stance on how to accommodate this category is inadequately explained – it is perhaps telling that it does not reappear in his later work. In *A Theory of Justice*, though he does discuss childhood (e.g., in the context of his developmental moral psychology), he mainly suggests that ideal theory assumes the absence of such natural limitations and accidents. Thus it is nonideal theory that deals, for example, with the "limitation on the scope of majority rule" that arises "from the permanent conditions of human life" (*TJ*, 217). And it is nonideal theory that engages with the "adjustments" necessary on account of the presence of children or the severely mentally disabled (*TJ*, 215, 219). At the same time, however, he stipulates that *ideal* theory must accommodate "the fixed constraints of human life" (*TJ*, 216).

113

So it is unclear why he immediately adds that it is nonideal theory that deals with "the more or less permanent conditions of political life" which constrain liberty "even in a well-ordered society under favorable circumstances" (*TJ*, 216). If the conditions are "more or less permanent" and persist even under favorable circumstances, why are they not the province of ideal theory? It cannot be that he means "fixed constraints" to refer only to the laws of nature as opposed to the laws of political life, since the former presumably include the "fixed" presence of children in ongoing societies, which is itself due to nature's laws precluding the birth of fully formed adults.

Another possibility is that the "fixed conditions" (said to belong to ideal theory) and the "permanent conditions" (said to belong to nonideal theory) divide, respectively, into conditions whose presence should lead us to redefine what perfect justice requires, on the one hand, and conditions whose presence blocks our achievement of justice, on the other. Given the initial identification of ideal theory with the theory of perfect justice, this would explain why it is nonideal theory that ought to deal with the latter. But this distinction seems hard to sustain. Does the fact that the severely mentally disabled or young children are not autonomous and need paternalistic protection mean that we cannot achieve perfect justice for them and their society? Simmons has defended this view, arguing that such "natural limitations and accidents" take us away from perfect justice since we must deal with "unfortunate individuals (within otherwise just societies) whose liberties must be curtailed for their own good. All [these cases] seem to involve departures from ideal principles" (2010, 16). But while it is possible to see why severe mental disability would count as "unfortunate," it is less apparent why childhood should. In any case, it is unclear why responding to the presence of such individuals would involve a limitation on justice rather than a refinement in what we take perfect justice to consist in. True, some instances of impaired agency – whether through childhood or severe mental disability – might be seen to make the persons inappropriate addressees of justice, just as inanimate objects or ants are not the type of beings to whom the requirements of justice could be addressed. But this is hardly true of all the impaired agents to whom others would owe paternalistic protection. In most cases, it might be more accurate to conclude that given the presence of children and the severely mentally disabled we must reconsider what perfect justice requires.

Rawls offers a rejoinder, however, when he points out that his primary focus is on justice understood as a set of rules applying specifically to society understood as a fair system of cooperation. To "achieve a clear and uncluttered view" of justice understood in that particular way, we "idealize and simplify" and assume "that persons as citizens have all the capacities that enable them to be cooperating members of society" (*PL*, 20). This assumption is temporary in that "we would like eventually to answer" (*PL*, 21) the question of what is owed to those who are not, or not yet, fully cooperating members of society, but to answer this question we may need to reach for a broader conception of justice or of another virtue (*PL*, 21). If so, then childhood and disabilities that prevent people from participating as fully cooperating members of society can indeed be seen, in line with Simmons's suggestion, as obstacles to perfect justice, with the latter understood in the specified sense. At the same time, however, a broader conception of justice, or another value, would make dealing with childhood and mental impairment part of its ideal theory. This means that, ultimately, we can treat the assumption of the absence of "natural limitations and accidents of human life" as a simplification that allows us to focus, in the first instance, on the justice of social cooperation (*PL*, 272 n10) rather than as an assumption that is necessary to keep us in the realm of ideal theory.[3]

Once we are prepared to complicate matters, we might attempt to design an ideal theory of justice that takes permanent natural limitations and accidents of life into account.

Our discussion of Rawls's assuming away "natural limitations and accidents" might invite similar questions about the ideal theory assumption of favorable circumstances: must such circumstances be assumed if we are to identify the requirements of perfect justice, or should we see this assumption also as merely simplificatory? Why think that unfavorable circumstances such as severe poverty, say, preclude perfect justice rather than simply changing what perfect justice requires? One answer here is the Humean one that some conditions of scarcity make the category of justice irrelevant (*TJ*, 110). In addition, however, even if there could be a kind of perfect justice for unfavorable circumstances, Rawls's explicit suggestion that his own society enjoys, and his implicit suggestion that many other societies enjoy, favorable circumstances explain his focus on that case (*PL*, 297; *JF*, 47 n12). The assumption of favorable circumstances in effect forces us to work out what perfect justice requires of us in our circumstances.

No matter what their status and rationale, let us accept that ideal theory should make the various assumptions listed above. Ideal theory might now face a different problem. Conceiving ideal theory as a vehicle to theorize about perfect justice would seem to be in tension with Rawls's explicit aim of offering a vision of a "realistic utopia" and avoiding what Simmons has called "idle utopianism" (*LP*, 6; Simmons 2010, 8).[4] A vision of a society is "realistically utopian" when "it depicts an achievable world" (*LP*, 6) that is also just. The depicted world is "achievable" when, among other things, it coheres with "the actual laws of nature" and when its principles are "workable and applicable to ongoing political and social arrangements" (*LP*, 12–13). Or, as Rawls also puts it, a "realistic utopia" must thus describe a society that "is feasible and might actually exist, if not now then at some future time under happier circumstances" (*LP*, 12).

How does Rawls reconcile premising his theory on idealizing assumptions with this will to be realistic? The answer is that he thinks of all the assumptions of ideal theory as realistically achievable. To see why, first consider strict compliance. True, no society is currently characterized by full compliance with the requirements of justice (or any other norm). But he argues that "men's propensity to injustice is not a permanent aspect of community life; it is greater or less depending in large part on social institutions, and in particular on whether these are just or unjust. A well-ordered society tends to eliminate or at least to control men's inclinations to injustice" (*TJ*, 215). So Rawls's view is that noncompliance is not inevitable and, indeed, the third part of *A Theory of Justice* is dedicated to explaining why a well-ordered society would tend to be characterized by compliance. Moreover, despite the fact that ideal theory assumes strict compliance, it must still consider whether a given principle could be complied with "only with great difficulty" given "the general facts of moral psychology" (*TJ*, 126). If complying with a principle would require moral heroism, the principle cannot be part of a good theory of justice. So although ideal theory assumes strict compliance, it must also test whether what it requires of people is such that we can reasonably expect compliance from them once they themselves do not encounter injustice in their lives.

The second assumption of ideal theory is that of favorable circumstances. That this assumption is supposed to be realistic is even more apparent since, as we have said, Rawls thinks that such circumstances are not exceptional. Indeed, he suggests in *The Law of Peoples* that very few societies lack the economic resources necessary to sustain a well-ordered society. He offers the Arctic Eskimos as a rare example of a society that suffers from too much resource scarcity (*LP*, 108 n34).[5] We can also infer from his claim that Germany between 1870 and 1945 enjoyed favorable circumstances (*JF*, 101 n23) – even though it did not capitalize on them to achieve justice – that such circumstances should be seen as relatively widespread.

This leaves the most problematic assumption: the absence of natural limitations and accidents of life. It is hardest to accept that this fits into the idea of a realistic utopia. After all, any normal society that continues over time must involve children. But as we suggested above, the role of the assumption might have been simplification of the ideal theory of justice rather than specification of something without which the theory cannot be ideal. Rawls's attempt to offer a realistic vision is a further reason to see this assumption as no more than simplifying. Simplifications won't secure realism, of course, but they may still be necessary, at least initially, if without them the problem is too complex for us to to solve.

## 3. What Is Ideal Theory Good For?

With this account of its assumptions in place, let us return to the question of the point of ideal theory. In *A Theory of Justice* Rawls claims: "If ideal theory is worthy of study, it must be because, as I have conjectured, it is the fundamental part of the theory of justice and essential for the nonideal part as well" (*TJ*, 343). Elsewhere, he suggests that ideal theory is "fundamental" in that it shows how "the nonideal scheme is to be set up" (*TJ*, 212). It thus seems that ideal theory is fundamental in that it is essential for nonideal theory. We will say more about the sense in which it is essential below, but the short answer is that it provides "the only basis for the systematic grasp of these more pressing [nonideal] problems" (*TJ*, 8).

In *A Theory of Justice* the usefulness of ideal theory turns on its link with nonideal theory.[6] In *Justice as Fairness* Rawls repeats this thought: "the idea of a well-ordered society should . . . provide some guidance in thinking about nonideal theory, and so about difficult cases of how to deal with existing injustices" (*JF*, 13). But he also identifies two further functions of ideal theory, which are independent of its relationship to nonideal theory.

On the one hand, he explains that democratic debates in liberal advanced democracies are often already about justice at the level of ideal theory and so focusing on that level allows us to intervene in such debates: "We focus on ideal theory because the current conflict in democratic thought is in good part a conflict about what conception of justice is most appropriate for a democratic society under reasonably favorable conditions" (*JF*, 13). On the other hand, ideal theory can help us reconcile ourselves to our world. Although Rawls does not make the distinction, we can talk of two different types of reconciliation here.

First, ideal theory is meant to facilitate recognition that our world is not irrevocably doomed to injustice:

> we consider whether a well-ordered democratic society is possible . . . This endeavor belongs to political philosophy as reconciliation; for seeing that the conditions of a social world at least allow for that possibility affects our view of the world itself and our attitude toward it. No longer need it seem hopelessly hostile, a world in which the will to dominate and oppressive cruelties, abetted by prejudice and folly, must inevitably prevail. None of this may ease our loss, situated as we may be in a corrupt society. But we may reflect that the world is not in itself inhospitable to political justice and its good. Our social world might have been different and there is hope for those at another time and place. (*JF*, 37–38)

In a sense, then, Rawls's emphasis that his utopia is realistic shows that he sees human nature as good, or at least as capable of being good enough to sustain a perfectly just society. This is most apparent in his regarding the assumption of strict compliance as "realistic." We humans are not, as many have thought, so fundamentally selfish or corrupt that a just society must inevitably exceed our grasp.

The second type of reconciliation with our world consists in reconciliation to particular features of our current circumstances that strike us as unwelcome. If we can show these would persist even in a well-ordered society, we may come to accept their presence now. As Rawls puts it, "the fact of profound and irreconcilable differences in citizens' reasonable comprehensive religious and philosophical conceptions of the world . . . is not always easy to accept, and political philosophy may try to reconcile us to it by showing us the reason and indeed the political good and benefits of it" (JF, 3–4). To give a simpler illustration of the same idea, if having reflected on what your ideal life partner would be like you observe that he or she would still possess a feature you find annoying in your nonideal partner (e.g., his or her occasional unavailability when you call), it might help you see this feature as more acceptable: after all, even your ideal mate would have it (Stemplowska 2008, 337).

Let us now return to the main point of ideal theory: its usefulness for nonideal theory. Rawls's claim is that the key idealization of ideal theory – the idea of a well-ordered society – "should also provide some guidance in thinking about nonideal theory, and so about difficult cases of how to deal with existing injustices. It should also help to clarify the goal of reform and to identify which wrongs are more grievous and hence more urgent to correct" (JF, 13). Thus, ideal theory contributes to nonideal theory in two ways.

On the one hand, it identifies the goal at which nonideal theory ought to aim and thereby gives nonideal theory its ultimate target (the target role). As Rawls puts it, "until the ideal is identified . . . nonideal theory lacks an objective, an aim, by reference to which its queries can be answered" (LP, 90). In its target role, then, ideal theory helps nonideal theory answer the question "where do we want to get to?"

On the other hand, ideal theory helps us assess the urgency of injustice we face in the real, nonideal world (the urgency role). It enables nonideal theory to answer the question "which of the injustices we face here and now are the most urgent?" For Rawls, the most urgent (grievous) injustices are "identified by the extent of the deviation from perfect justice" (TJ, 216). Furthermore, he argues that the more urgent injustices are to be "dealt with first" (TJ, 267). In effect, therefore, as ideal theory helps us identify the urgency of injustice, it also thereby identifies the schedule of reform. Rawls makes this suggestion more explicit and systematic by reference to "priority rules" (TJ, 266–267). As he puts it, "The lexical ranking of the principles specifies which elements of the ideal are relatively more urgent, and the priority rules this ordering suggests are to be applied to nonideal cases as well" (TJ, 216). So, for example, because ideal theory tells us that the liberty principle is lexically prior to the difference principle, in nonideal circumstances we should eliminate inequalities in the basic liberties as a matter of priority before we act to remove inequalities in income and wealth that do not benefit the worst off.

The basic idea, then, is that ideal theory both provides the target of reforms undertaken in nonideal circumstances and constrains the route for getting to it by specifying the sequence in which reforms should be undertaken. In this way ideal theory makes nonideal theory avoid the simple consequentialism of anything goes just as long as it advances us toward the target of perfect justice (Simmons 2010, 36 and before; Taylor 2009, 488–491).

Some commentators have suggested further ways in which ideal theory can constrain the trajectory of reforms undertaken in nonideal circumstances toward the target. Drawing on the work of Korsgaard (1996) and Schapiro (2003), Taylor has argued: "Whether or not the nonideal theory demands that we follow the letter of the ideal theory in any given case . . . it always insists that we act in its spirit: only by doing so can we pay due respect to those fundamental values (autonomy, democracy, and freedom . . .) that animate it" (2009, 490). The suggestion is that the values that ground an ideal theory (its "spirit") might impose constraints that differ from those implied by the principles themselves (its "letter"). According to Korsgaard, for example, in nonideal circumstances in which citizens face injustice, "civil disobedience is better than resorting to violence not just because violence is bad in itself, but because of the way in which civil disobedience expresses the democratic principles of the just society it aspires to bring about [i.e. the spirit of the ideal theory]" (Korsgaard 1996, 148, quoted in Taylor 2009, 489–490). Fidelity to the spirit of ideal theory might be thought directly to rule out a variety of methods for advancing toward the ideal target: while priority rules apply only in some instances, the need to respect democracy, autonomy, etc. might apply to a wider range of cases and actions.

Rawls probably thought that even in nonideal circumstances we are constrained by moral considerations beyond those listed in the priority rules. It would hardly be permissible, for example, for public officials to observe specific people secretly through CCTV even if such actions fell short of violating their basic liberties. He explains in *The Law of Peoples* that non-ideal theory "looks for policies and courses of action that are morally permissible and politically possible as well as likely to be effective" (*LP*, 89), and the unexplained category of "moral permissibility" might plausibly be invoked further to constrain the reforms recommended by nonideal theory. It is plausible, further, that the considerations relevant to the issue of permissibility do indeed relate to the "fundamental values" that "animate" the ideal theory. Here we are talking about what, in our final section, we will refer to as "theory of ideals" rather than "ideal theory." But Rawls does not explicitly invoke the distinction between "spirit" and "letter," nor does he explain how moral permissibility relates to "ideal theory," so his own views on this matter can only be a matter of speculation.[7]

He is clear that the priority rules constrain nonideal theory, but he is careful also to stress the limits of this thought:

> By putting these principles in lexical order, the parties are choosing a conception of justice suitable for favorable conditions . . . But even granting the soundness of these principles for this purpose, we must still ask how well they apply to institutions under less than favorable conditions, and whether they provide any guidance for instances of injustice. The principles and their lexical order were not acknowledged with these situations in mind and so it is possible that they no longer hold. (*TJ*, 216–217)

Later he says that "the ranking of the principles of justice in ideal theory reflects back and guides the application of these principles to nonideal situations. It identifies which limitations need to be dealt with first"; but he immediately acknowledges: "In the more extreme and tangled instances of nonideal theory this priority of rules will no doubt fail; and indeed, we may be able to find no satisfactory answer at all" (*TJ*, 267).

In the end, therefore, while Rawls suggests at times that ideal theory guides nonideal theory in a very specific way, his view of the actual relationship between the two is less clear-cut. He is adamant that ideal theory is fundamental for nonideal theory, but he also admits that this relationship might break down. Still, despite these uncertainties, Rawls is clear that the requirements of ideal theory are never to be followed without regard for the actual circumstances – as opposed to the circumstances assumed by ideal theory.

## 4. Should Ideal Theory Set the Target? Should It Set Priorities?

Let us start by evaluating Rawls's claim that ideal theory sets the target of reform for nonideal theory, whose task it is to work out what to do "under less happy conditions." Against this view, Amartya Sen has argued that nonideal theory can be done in a "comparative" mode rather than in the Rawlsian mode that he terms "transcendental." His core claim is that we do not need to know what perfect justice would require in a well-ordered society in order to be able to compare alternative options that are open to us here and now and select the target of our reforms. Knowing what a perfectly just society would look like is neither necessary nor sufficient to decide which option to pursue. As Sen puts it, "The characterization of spotless justice does not entail any delineation whatever of how diverse departures from spotlessness can be compared and ranked" (2006, 220; cf. 2009, 99) and "the possibility of having an identifiably perfect alternative does not indicate that it is necessary, or indeed useful, to refer to it in judging the relative merits of two other alternatives" (2009, 102). By analogy, to climb the highest mountain within range, we need to know not that Everest is the highest mountain in the world but which mountains are within range and how to compare them. Similarly, if justice not mountaineering is our aim, we can easily judge, for example, that the elimination of extreme poverty would constitute progress toward justice without knowing what principles of justice would be recommended by ideal theory. So, according to Sen, ideal theory is useless in setting the target in nonideal circumstances. Indeed, if we are concerned with urgent problems of nonideal theory such as "iniquities of hunger, illiteracy, torture, arbitrary incarceration, or medical exclusion as particular social features that need remedying" then we should focus on "the ways and means of advancing justice – or reducing injustice – in the world by remedying these inequities" rather than searching only for "the simultaneous fulfilment of the entire cluster of perfectly just societal arrangements demanded by a particular transcendental theory" (2006, 218). Sen's charge then is that focusing on "spotless justice" is unnecessary, not to say counterproductive.

But suppose that our ideal theory correctly identifies the desirable long-term goal that is also achievable, if only in the long run, perhaps the very long run. Knowing what the ultimate goal is could make a difference to the reforms we ought to undertake here and now. As Simmons (2010, 21) has pointed out, a course of action that might appear to advance justice, and might indeed constitute a short-term improvement with respect to justice, might nonetheless make achievement of the long-term goal less likely, perhaps even impossible. So when selecting a course of action, we should assess its impact not only on specific injustice but on our chances of reaching our overall target – that is the ultimate target that appropriately combines all our piecemeal goals.

Sen might respond that assessing policies in such a comprehensive way is extremely difficult and that, in any case, it is not obvious that piecemeal improvements suggested by the simpler, comparative methods will prevent us from reaching the overall target in the long run. True, given the topography of our planet, starting off, say, in Africa and reaching the local maximum (Mount Kilimanjaro) will lead us away from reaching the overall maximum (Mount Everest) and might exhaust us enough to make climbing the latter impossible. But is the roadmap to justice equally tricky? We do not know for sure, but it is plausible to suppose that it is. Marx, for one, thought so when he outlined his critique of social democracy: satisfying one set of desiderata first (better conditions for the working class) might make the satisfaction of all desiderata far harder if not impossible.

This final point might answer Sen's challenge, but it introduces two further worries about the use of ideal theory to set the overall target for reform in nonideal circumstances. The first is that the overall target of reform can be realistic, in Rawls's sense of "realistic utopia," without being empirically likely, even in the very long term. But it would be irrational to eschew certain immediate progress for the sake of a hugely ambitious vision that, though not impossible, was vanishingly unlikely ever to be realized. Perhaps this is why Rawls stipulates, in addition, that nonideal theory should look for policies that are "likely to be effective" (LP, 89). Even armed with this extra proviso, however, we may well simply lack the information needed to judge how a potential short-term improvement relates to the long-term goal. Knowing what a realistically-ideally just society would look like is one thing, assembling the social science needed for us to know how to get there is quite another; charting the route to the just society is even more hazardous than mapping the Himalayas. Again, then, skepticism about our capacity to make the relevant empirical predictions would support our taking gains where we can (Simmons 2010, 25). Moreover – and this is the second worry – even if we knew that incrementally progressive reforms would preclude our ever achieving the ideal target, it does not follow that we should refrain from taking piecemeal improvements in justice when they are available. Not to take them would be to impose avoidable injustice on some (current or proximately future people) for the sake of ideal justice for others (future generations who will benefit from ideal justice in the long term). Too much emphasis on achieving the ultimate goal, even where it is indeed known to be achievable, could involve inappropriate fetishization of the ideal, and neglect of the interests of those consigned to suffer injustice en route.

If ideal theory must take probability of success into account, and if such judgments are very difficult, then there might be little difference between using ideal theory to set the goal for nonideal theory and Sen's comparative incrementalism. But we cannot assess the remoteness or (un)likelihood of the realistic ideal without *some* sense of what that realistic ideal is. Perhaps political philosophers have by now done enough work at the level of ideal theory to give us that. If so, that does not make ideal theory useless; the claim is rather that we already have (enough of) it. In the end, then, we offer a heavily qualified defense of the importance of the ideal theory target for nonideal theory. We disagree with Sen that knowing the overall target is irrelevant in nonideal circumstances but we recognize that – just as Rawls expected – its pursuit must be weighed against other considerations.

The other way in which ideal theory is supposed to be fundamental to nonideal theory is by setting priorities – identifying injustices that "need to be dealt with first." But, as we have noted, Rawls concedes that the priority rules of ideal theory may fail in some of the more "tangled" cases of nonideal circumstances.

The most obvious difficulty is that it is hard to see why ideal theory would stand in such a relationship to nonideal theory. It seems intuitively more plausible that we will need to decide on a case-by-case basis whether the nonideal circumstances we face preserve or undermine the plausibility of the priority rules. It is not obvious, for example, that depriving a group of people of their freedom of religion for a few years in order to eliminate extremely unjust income and wealth inequality is never a price worth paying (even though the priority rules say otherwise). Addressing a similar problem, Rawls claims that "the equal political liberties cannot be denied to certain groups on the grounds that their having these liberties may enable them to block policies needed for economic growth and efficiency," but he immediately adds that his claim presupposes that adequate "economic means" and "education" are already in place (*JF*, 47). This means that the priority rules do not hold in all circumstances and it is in this sense that their application is "left importantly to intuition" (*TJ*, 216). Given this, it is unclear just when ideal theory can inform the priorities of non-ideal theory.

Even if, guided by intuition, we have reached agreement on which injustices are more urgent than others, judging which should be eliminated first seems plausibly constrained by assessments of the probability of success (*LP*, 89). Imagine for example that we agree that eliminating relatively minor infringements of some people's basic liberties is more urgent than eliminating even extremely unjust inequality of income and wealth; imagine further that we can either opt for a course of reform that has a 0.4 probability of achieving the former or go for one that has a 0.9 chance of securing the latter. Ideal theory does not guide our choice here. It might be implausible, of course, to expect it to do so, but the fact that it does not suggests that it is less fundamental than Rawls's remarks about its fundamental role seem to imply.

## 5. Is Ideal Theory Too Utopian?

Considering all these limitations on the target and urgency roles of ideal theory, there is an important sense in which ideal theory is less realistic than it might be: it aims to offer a vision of an achievable world (a realistic utopia) but it does not aim to verify if we could permissibly and successfully get there from where we are now. That observation will appeal to those who have offered a more radical critique of Rawls's ideal theory approach, seeing it as the paradigm example of, and major influence on, a prevalent tendency in contemporary political theory. The objection is that such theory fails adequately to engage with the realities of politics (Galston 2010). In our view, many realist criticisms of ideal theory simply overlook the distinction between ideal and nonideal theory and end up criticizing the former for not being the latter. We shall put such misguided objections to one side, together with challenges to "ideal theory" emanating from radical skepticism about normative philosophy.[8] The more interesting and important challenge to the Rawlsian picture goes deeper.

That picture, realists claim, looks guilty of the charge of what Bernard Williams calls "political moralism," according to which "political theory is something like applied morality" (2005, 2). For Williams, "the first political question" is the Hobbesian one: how to secure "order, protection, safety, trust, and the conditions of cooperation" (2005, 3). But not all solutions to that question are "acceptable"; to qualify as legitimate, in order to be more than successful domination, a state must be able to offer a justification of its power to each subject, including to those radically disadvantaged groups within it. Williams does not deny that this "basic legitimation demand" (2005, 4) is itself a moral principle. What it is not, he insists, is a moral principle that is prior to politics. To solve the problem of order by force alone is not to achieve a political solution; politics is, by definition, an alternative to mere force. The trouble with Rawlsian political moralism is not that it asserts moral claims *tout court*, but that it fails to recognize the specificity of the moral issue specific to, or inherent in, politics.

Of course Rawls accepts the specificity of "the political" and explicitly denies that his theory of justice should be understood as "applied moral philosophy," precisely because "[p]olitical philosophy has its own distinctive features and problems" (*JF*, 14). But, for Williams, this is not enough since he still sees Rawls's project of "political liberalism" as grounded in an over-ambitiously moralized, and idealized, conception of political relationships.

This theme of liberal political philosophy's excessive and naive ambitions pervades realist thinking. Rawls's well-ordered society, in which all citizens comply with the demands of justice and accept as legitimate the state's demands on them, is seen as utopian, aiming unrealistically high. Political philosophy in "ideal theory" mode, it is claimed, quixotically aspires to a society where citizens' inevitable disagreements do not result in conflict, one in which there is universal compliance with demanding norms of political morality; it attributes to political agents cognitive and moral powers far exceeding anything human history could lead us to regard as remotely plausible. Such idealism is not merely futile but positively dangerous. Only at our peril do we neglect the fragility of social order, fail to celebrate less lofty accomplishments as the achievements that they really are (witness Rawls's denigration of a "mere modus vivendi"), and overlook the fact that expecting too much of people tends to tyranny. In seeking the impossible, we risk losing what we have.

But we have already seen that Rawls's "ideal theory" is intended precisely to identify a "realistic utopia." It's crucial to his view not only that the goal is possible, in the literal sense that it can be achieved by human beings, but that it is possible without assuming heroic motivations. So Rawls takes issues of feasibility to be internal to the "ideal theory" project. Perhaps realist critics think he is simply wrong about what human beings are capable of; perhaps they think the kind of well-ordered society he describes is beyond the feasible set. If so, that would be a coherent objection to the content of his ideal theory; he would indeed be offering as our lodestar a target that we could never achieve, and that might perhaps be unhelpful, or even dangerous. But it would not be an objection to the project of constructing an ideal theory in his sense.

## 6. Is Ideal Theory Too Concessive to Human Nature?

Rawls has also been challenged from the other side, so to speak. G.A. Cohen, in particular, has advanced two relevant critiques. He has argued, first, that certain of Rawls's concessions to human moral psychology mean that his ideal theory fails to identify a truly just society (2000), and second, that his concern with realism means that he fails to identify genuinely fundamental principles of justice (2008). Put differently, Cohen's charges are that Rawls's well-ordered society tolerates injustice and that, even where it does not, his method fails to deliver ultimate principles of justice. Lacking the space to give both criticisms adequate attention, we will focus here on the former.[9]

Cohen objects in particular to the way in which Rawls's well-ordered society allows those with marketable talents to collect incentive payments for the work necessary to improve the position of the worst off; justice requires that the talented should do the work without the extra pay (Cohen 2008, 151–180). To be clear, the issue at stake between them is not whether in fact people will inevitably seek self-interested incentive payments. Neither Rawls nor Cohen is committed either way on that question. (For Rawls, the case of incentives payments is no more than an illustration of how an inequality might benefit the worse off; *TJ*, 67–68.) The issue is whether accommodating such requests, should they arise, would involve a compromise or sacrifice of justice.

This feature of Rawls's difference principle, though it has commanded a lot of attention, is best thought of as a particular instance of a wider issue that applies to ideal theory quite generally: his insistence, implied by his concern to identify a realistic utopia, that the strict compliance of the well-ordered society should accommodate certain facts of moral psychology. For Rawls, the assumption of strict compliance made by ideal theory

> still permits the consideration of men's capacity to act on various conceptions of justice . . . If a conception of justice is unlikely to generate its own support, or lacks stability, this fact must not be overlooked . . . [The parties in the original position] are rational in that they will not enter into agreements they know they cannot keep, or can do so only with great difficulty. Along with other considerations, they count the strains of commitment. (*TJ*, 125–126)

So Rawls thinks that a theory of justice must eventually relax the assumption of strict compliance and consider how plausible that assumption is; the system it recommends should be assessed in terms of how well it motivates the people living under it to comply with its requirements. The motivational potential of a given set of principles, so to speak, is regarded as a function of the difficulty of complying. How exactly, then, does the difficulty of compliance matter? It cannot be, for example, that we should reject a principle of antiracism simply because some members of society are so wedded to racist attitudes that it would be too difficult – either too costly, or simply beyond their skills and capacities – for them to comply. Rawls asks us to assume that people have a sense of justice. This matters because "[a] just person is not prepared to do certain things, and if he is tempted too easily, he was prepared after all" (*TJ*, 498). So considerations of the difficulty of complying with certain rules simply cannot arise. Anybody who finds it too difficult lacks the sense of justice that Rawls assumes all citizens to possess. When selecting principles of justice, we must indeed take into account how difficult it will be for people to comply with them, but the people we are thinking about are those already motivated by a sense of justice.[10]

What matters, for Rawls, is whether compliance with a candidate set of principles would be too difficult even for those with a sense of justice; whether even they would face too much temptation to disobey. This explains why it can count against utilitarianism and the morality of heroism that they are very difficult to observe since, at least for Rawls, their demands are very hard to follow even for those with a sense of justice. It explains also why he thinks that even in a well-ordered society populated by people with a sense of justice, we need some penal sanctions, and why therefore, despite his explicit claim that punishment belongs with nonideal theory, even ideal theory has to have some account of punishment.[11] As he points out,

> It is reasonable to assume that even in a well-ordered society the coercive powers of government are to some degree necessary for the stability of social cooperation. For although men know that they share a common sense of justice and that each wants to adhere to the existing arrangements, they may nevertheless lack full confidence in one another. They may suspect that some

are not doing their part, and so may be tempted not to do theirs. The general awareness of these temptations may eventually cause the scheme to break down . . . the existence of effective penal machinery serves as men's security to one another. (*TJ*, 211)

For example, being tempted not to pay one's fair share of taxes in a situation in which one lacked assurance that others were paying theirs is something to which even those with a sense of justice, who would not commit graver sins, are susceptible. Cohen has argued that Rawls's quest for principles of justice that are stable, in the sense that they take account of the temptations even just people find difficult to resist, confuses justice and stability (Cohen 2008, 327–330). If people find some temptations too difficult to resist that is not a reason to change what we require of them. Rather we should acknowledge that our pursuit of justice, *stricto sensu*, may have to be constrained by a concern to adopt a set of arrangements for society that, over time, will generate and perpetuate its own support. In effect, Rawls's ideal theory is accused by Cohen of compromising perfect justice in order to come up with less demanding principles that human beings are more likely to be willing to go along with.

What should we make of this critique? Rawls rules out only those requirements that cannot reliably be complied with even by people who are motivated to act justly. We cannot say that it would be literally impossible for them to fulfill the more demanding requirements, but for Rawls it matters that they are unlikely to be met. A respectable Rawlsian response here would be to say that his conception of ideal theory as realistic utopia means that he must identify a target that is not beyond the motivational capacities of people with a sense of justice. There may, indeed, be other, more challenging targets we could aim at but that is no reason not to be interested in what the less ambitious – but still demanding – target is.

Presumably Cohen would not deny that it would be good to know what that target looks like, and Rawls constructs his ideal theory as a way of getting at it. To some extent, it may be simply that Rawls and Cohen differ in what they understand by "principle of justice." Moreover, Rawls might respond, it is misleading to regard justice and stability as genuinely distinct considerations. The stability that he is interested in achieving, and for the sake of which he is willing to compromise (in Cohen's terms) his principles, is the stability *of a just society*. If there is a trade-off here at all, Rawls might say, it is between justice as a short-lived achievement and justice as a long-term stable state of society. To pay attention to the latter, even to the extent of tailoring one's principles with an eye to their ability to produce their own support in the long term, is hardly to put other considerations above justice; it is to take justice itself seriously.

## 7. Ideal Theory, Nonideal Theory and Action Guidance

Rawlsian "ideal theory" involves a limited number of idealizations, or idealizing assumptions: full compliance, favorable circumstances, and sometimes, "natural limitations and accidents of life." The different types of idealization raise distinct issues for nonideal theory. Situations of partial compliance are those in which some are failing to comply with the demands of justice. Nonideal theory that focuses on "[h]ow justice requires us to meet injustice" (*TJ*, 215) is crucial, and in our view underexplored, philosophical terrain. But – as Rawls emphasized – it involves quite distinct questions from those concerning what justice demands in circumstances that are unfavorable in other ways.

But in principle there are as many variants of ideal theory and of nonideal theory as there are kinds and degrees of constraint that we might assume away or take as given (Hamlin and Stemplowska 2012). We could, for example, theorize nonideally about the requirements of justice – or democracy (Tomlin 2012) or equality (Cohen 2008) or legitimacy (Mason 2010) – in many different settings. We could ask what principles would be adopted in a world where informational problems were soluble but the political will was lacking, or where full compliance was forthcoming but economic conditions were unfavorable, and so on. The various theories that such exercises produced would remain action guiding in form, even if they were not intended to guide action in our circumstances (with partial compliance and informational difficulties). Those impatient with ideal theory are not, typically, interested in that kind of more or less nonideal counterfactual; they want guidance about what to do here and now. Such guidance will typically involve complicated empirical judgments about which the philosopher has no particular expertise (LP, 93).

Rawls's claim that ideal theory is a necessary precursor to nonideal theory is clearly crucial. If he is right, then the impatience of ideal theory's critics is misplaced. Ideal theory may look utopian in the worst sense, but as long as the goal it posits is indeed a realistic utopia ideal theory should not be regarded as an optional extra; the intellectual resources devoted to it are not self-indulgent or wasteful. We argued above that ideal theory has a limited role in setting the target of reform for nonideal theory: we need to know the goal before we can form an all-things-considered evaluation of transitional steps in its direction. We also accepted that ideal theory might also sometimes set the priorities for reform – in accordance with its urgency role – but we were not persuaded that it offers us a plausible systematic way of identifying such priorities. We are doubtful that a ranking of the fulfillment of different values in ideal circumstances translates easily into the prioritization of reforms in nonideal circumstances.

That said, we cannot do without philosophy no matter what the circumstances (Swift 2008). And, when we engage in philosophy, particular forms of idealization are extremely useful in helping us to disentangle, clarify, and sometimes to weigh the competing values that can then be applied to the feasible set. We need, that is, "theory of ideals," and idealization helps us get it (Hamlin and Stemplowska 2012; Stemplowska 2008, 326–329); in our view, much philosophical work that is presented as "ideal theory" can readily be construed as contributing to the "theory of ideals." The core of the distinction here is that Rawls's "ideal theory" suggests what principles and institutions we should adopt, while "theory of ideals" helps us systematically think about our values and the relations between them. There is some artificiality to the distinction but, nonetheless, it is helpful to think of these projects as somewhat distinct. That said, we think that much of what Rawls does, and what many find compelling, consists in "theory of ideals" – an attempt to list and prioritize the values of a liberal democracy.

We end with one more distinction – and an exhortation. The complaint that contemporary political philosophy fails to engage sufficiently with our actual empirical circumstances is typically formulated as a request for policies and institutions. But to issue even a specific policy recommendation to citizens generally, or to argue that a particular institutional arrangement is required, is not to recommend a specific action to any actually existing person. Since it is only individuals that act – policies are not enacted, institutions are not established, without individual human agents doing things to bring them about – such recommendations must be seen as addressed to citizens who know how to solve the relevant coordination problems, including the philosophically crucial issue of the duties to contribute to the bringing about of the collective, political, action that fall on differentially situated individual agents. That is itself a form of idealization. Since we can know what we collectively ought to be doing without knowing what any of us individually ought to be doing, even the kind of nonideal theory that delivers concrete action-guidance for "us" remains unhelpfully ideal if it does so merely in the form of policies or institutional arrangements (Swift 2008).

We began with Rawls's observation, at the start of *A Theory of Justice*, that his theory is limited in two distinct ways: by being ideal and by focusing on the basic structure of society. But the latter is also a form of distancing from the task of offering direct solutions in nonideal circumstances. An attempt to explain how to translate the principles that regulate the basic structure into principles to guide the actions of individuals would be just as valuable – and perhaps more successful – than an attempt to formalize the relationship between ideal and nonideal theory.

# Notes

Part of this chapter draws on Stemplowska and Swift 2012. We are grateful for comments or discussion to Matthew Clayton, Timothy Fowler, Jonathan Quong, the editors of this volume, and the participants in the University College London conference "From Ideal Principles to Real Politics", June 18, 2012.

1   A "well-ordered society" is one "effectively regulated by a public conception of justice" (*JF*, 8ff.). In Rawls's later work it becomes clear that he envisages the possibility of societies that are well-ordered by an institutionally embodied commitment to conceptions of justice other than that for which he argues in *A Theory of Justice*, but that complication can be left aside here.

2   In *A Theory of Justice*, Rawls does in fact offer an extended discussion of civil disobedience and conscientious refusal (*TJ*, 308–343), so he doesn't confine himself entirely to ideal theory.

3   Here we distinguish two kinds of idealizing assumptions, both of which may be counterfactual in involving departures from the real world: *simplifying* assumptions make a complex problem more manageable, whether that problem is one of ideal or nonideal theory; *assumptions of ideal theory*, on the other hand, are those that allow us to focus on the particular question addressed by an ideal theory of justice.

4   Although the phrase "realistic utopia" does not appear in *TJ*, Rawls retrospectively explains: "Both *A Theory of Justice* and *Political Liberalism* try to say how a liberal society might be possible" (*LP*, 6–7).

5   The category of well-ordered societies in *The Law of Peoples* includes "decent" societies, as well as those that are (perfectly) just by liberal standards, but there is little reason to suppose that Rawls thought that more economic resources are needed to sustain the latter than the former.

6   As David Leopold has put it, "Rawls appears to hold that if ideal theory were construed in such a way as to lack these (or similar) links with nonideal theory, then it would cease to be worth pursuing" (2012, 28).

7   See Simmons (2010, 20–21, 34) for an interesting discussion.

8   For a summary of and answer to one set of such worries see Freeman 2009. For further discussion see Stemplowska and Swift 2012.

9   See Stemplowska and Swift 2012 for our view on the latter. See also A. Williams 2008 for an important discussion relevant to both debates.

10   There is a further profound problem of what exactly a sense of justice involves that we leave aside here.

11   Rawls might be distinguishing the theory of punishment for those with a sense of justice (ideal theory) from the theory of punishment for those too easily tempted to crime (nonideal theory).

## Works by Rawls, with Abbreviations

*Justice as Fairness: A Restatement* (*JF*), ed. Erin Kelly. Cambridge, MA: Harvard University Press, 2001.
*The Law of Peoples, with "The Idea of Public Reason Revisited"* (*LP*). Cambridge, MA: Harvard University Press, 1999.
*Political Liberalism* (*PL*), expanded edn. New York: Columbia University Press, 2005.
*A Theory of Justice* (*TJ*), rev. edn. Cambridge, MA: Harvard University Press, 1999.

## Other References

Cohen, G.A. (2000) *If You're an Egalitarian, How Come You're So Rich?* Cambridge, MA: Harvard University Press.
Cohen, G.A. (2008) *Rescuing Justice and Equality*. Cambridge, MA: Harvard University Press.
Freeman, Samuel (2009) "Raymond Geuss, *Philosophy and Real Politics*." *Ethics* 120: 175–184.
Galston, William (2010) "Realism in Political Theory." *European Journal of Political Theory* 9: 385–411.
Hamlin, Alan and Stemplowska, Zofia (2012) "Ideal Theory, Nonideal Theory and the Theory of Ideals." *Political Studies Review* 10: 48–62.
Korsgaard, Christine (1996) *Creating the Kingdom of Ends*. Cambridge: Cambridge University Press.
Leopold, David (2012) "A Cautious Embrace: Reflections on (Left) Liberalism and Utopia." In Ben Jackson and Marc Stears (eds.), *Liberalism as Ideology*. Oxford: Oxford University Press.
Mason, Andrew (2010) "Rawlsian Theory and the Circumstances of Politics." *Political Theory* 38: 658–653.
Schapiro, Tamar (2003) "Compliance, Complicity, and the Nature of Nonideal Conditions." *Journal of Philosophy* 100: 329–355.
Sen, Amartya (2006) "What Do We Want From a Theory of Justice?" *Journal of Philosophy* 103: 215–238.
Sen, Amartya (2009) *The Idea of Justice*. London: Allen Lane.
Simmons, A.J. (2010) "Ideal and Nonideal Theory." *Philosophy and Public Affairs* 38: 5–36.
Stemplowska, Zofia (2008) "What's Ideal about Ideal Theory?" *Social Theory and Practice* 34: 319–340.
Stemplowska, Zofia and Swift, Adam (2012) "Ideal and Nonideal Theory." In David Estlund (ed.), *The Oxford Handbook of Political Philosophy*. New York: Oxford University Press.
Swift, Adam (2008) "The Value of Philosophy in Nonideal Circumstances." *Social Theory and Practice* 34: 363–387.
Taylor, Robert (2009) "Rawlsian Affirmative Action." *Ethics* 119: 476–506.
Tomlin, Patrick (2012) "Should We Be Utophobes about Democracy in Particular?" *Political Studies Review* 10: 36–47.
Williams, Andrew (2008) "Justice, Incentives and Constructivism." *Ratio* 21: 476–493.
Williams, Bernard (2005) *In The Beginning Was the Deed: Realism and Moralism in Political Argument*. Princeton: Princeton University Press.

# 7

# The Choice from the Original Position

## JON MANDLE

The range of John Rawls's contribution to ethics and political philosophy is vast. At the more abstract level, he wrote about the ideas of reflective equilibrium; moral and political constructivism; public reason; and argued that moral theory is largely independent of epistemology, metaphysics and the philosophy of mind.[1] More concretely, he defended the model of a property-owning democracy; critically reflected on the US constitutional history of free speech; and argued that "both Hiroshima and the fire-bombing of Japanese cities were great evils."[2] What ties these and many other disparate concerns together is the idea of the original position. By considering the choice from the original position, Rawls holds, we can bring our more abstract commitments together to generate principles of justice that can then be applied to more concrete cases. Conversely, the original position can help ensure that our more abstract commitments are consistent with the considered particular judgments about which we are most confident. Considering the choice from the original position may "provide guidance where guidance is needed" (*TJ*, 18) and help us move in the direction of reflective equilibrium by serving as "a mediating idea by which all our considered convictions, whatever their level of generality . . . can be brought to bear on one another" (*PL*, 26; cf. *JF*, 39, 81). Justice as fairness represents "the hypothesis that the principles which would be chosen in the original position are identical with those that match our considered judgments and so these principles describe our sense of justice" (*TJ*, 42).

Although he did not introduce the idea of the original position until 1963, its roots can be found in a problem that Rawls faced in his 1950 dissertation, "A Study in the Grounds of Ethical Knowledge." There, he frames his project by noting: "Two attitudes are common in present discussions of ethical knowledge: that expressed by various authoritarian views, and [that] put forth by a variety of opinions often labeled 'positivistic'" (SGEK, 1). While the former "asserts that ethical principles must be taken on authority, or posited by an act of faith, or at least presupposed," the latter holds that ethical norms "are simply the expressions of settled emotional dispositions, and, being such, they are not the kind of things that can be submitted to rational criticism and reflection" (SGEK, 2, 3). Even though Rawls was con-

*A Companion to Rawls*, First Edition. Edited by Jon Mandle and David A. Reidy.
© 2014 John Wiley & Sons, Inc. Published 2016 by John Wiley & Sons, Inc.

cerned with ethical (as opposed to political) theory at the time, he found this choice unacceptable for a strikingly political reason that is worth quoting at length:

> Although both of these extremes stand in many ways opposed to each other, they have in common the following: they make reasoning in moral questions to no effect . . . In either case it is plain that the use of rational principles, as the only reasonable instrument of settling conflicts and guiding decisions, is given up.
>
> Now what is the effect of these two views? Plainly we all have to make decisions, and plainly we need some guide. Therefore the effect of negating rational argument is to usher in other only too well-known techniques of guiding choices and deciding social policy. The result is to encourage in social life just those elements which, in democratic countries, we have tried to get rid of: the authoritarian, the arbitrary and the irrational.
>
> The democratic conception of government looks to the law and not to the state as the primary source of authority; and it views the law as the outcome of public discussions as to what rules can be voluntarily consented to as binding upon the government and the citizens. The law is regarded as those rules which discussion has shown to be right and reasonable so far as the citizens, as a group of intelligent men, have been able to ascertain that fact. Rational discussion is not outlawed or held to be irrelevant. On the contrary, it constitutes an essential precondition of reasonable law. Democratic theory and practice must consider the process of reasoning as one of the very crucial points in its whole program. (SGEK, 7–8)

Rawls's project was to rescue moral reasoning and the possibility of moral knowledge from the antidemocratic and nihilistic choice between dogmatism and skepticism.

The idea was to ground moral knowledge in "the collective sense of right of free and intelligent men and women." The key thought was this: "Those principles of law and morals are finally authoritative which reasonable men can willingly adopt as their own, and because they feel them to be right and just after the widest inquiry has been made on the questions involved" (SGEK, 8). Although these judgments are fallible, they can serve as the basis from which to "construct" an ethical theory. Rawls discusses four necessary and sufficient criteria for an individual to be included among this group who provide the justification of principles. He or she must (1) be intellectually and emotionally mature; (2) have a reasonable degree of knowledge and education; (3) "*be* reasonable," by which he means something like being "intellectually honest" – willing to learn from evidence, for example; (4) possess "a certain amount of sensitivity for the feelings and interests of other people; and a certain sympathy and understanding for human suffering and human problems" (SGEK, 32–37). Rawls is at pains to stress that this does not involve appeal to an arbitrarily selected group of authorities. In fact, this group includes "*any* man who possesses to the requisite degree the four properties just considered, irrespective of all other properties such as wealth, class, nationality, race, creed or religion, whatever they may be" (SGEK, 39).

Not all judgments made even by this class of persons provide a suitable basis for constructing an ethical theory, and Rawls places additional requirements on the judgments themselves. For example, he says, we should rely on judgments that are relatively stable:

> it is obvious that the study of ethics, so far as it is a rational attempt to explicate common sense morality, could not exist unless there were more or less permanent patterns of judgment and appraisal to serve both as a material for theoretical construction and as a body of data against which the validity of the theory could be tested. (SGEK, 49–50)

129

And they should be those about which we are most confident: "They express our deep-seated intuitive convictions which remain on reflection . . . the feeling of certainty is not temporary, but remains with us after criticism" (SGEK, 57, 58).

The "feeling of certainty" should not be taken to indicate infallibility, however. (Perhaps the term "confidence" would be more appropriate than "certainty.") Even "the collective sense of right of free and intelligent men and women . . . is not final, or infallible" (SGEK, 8). Although these judgments serve as data for the construction of an ethical theory, they are not unalterable or foundational.

> While an explication could hardly cause us to change all our judgments, it may, after we have reflected upon it, cause us to change some of our opinions. Therefore, not only may an ethical theory provide an answer where there is a genuine conflict, and so where there is no opinion at all; but it may actually change some accepted appraisal which was originally considered a part of the subject matter. (SGEK, 92)[3]

Rawls notes that this feature marks an important contrast between ethics and natural science.[4] So, to summarize: the "data" from which Rawls proposes that we construct an ethical theory consist in the stable judgments that reasonable men and women would make, under favorable circumstances, about which they are most confident after reflection and criticism. However, even these judgments are subject to revision in light of the development of the theory. By constructing principles in this way, Rawls hopes to rescue ethical knowledge from the challenge of dogmatism and skepticism. In addition, the construction of principles in this way can help to provide "criteria to evaluate difficult and doubtful cases wherein there is, as yet, no recognized solution" (SGEK, 298). Together, these elements constitute the core of what Rawls would later identify as "reflective equilibrium," the approach that he defended and utilized throughout his career.

In order to be able to construct a theory on this basis, the data must show a certain consistency. Thus: "It is hoped, of course, that the class of reasonable men, as defined, will in fact agree in holding certain ethical opinions and agree in making certain ethical judgments. Otherwise ethical theory would have no subject matter from this source" (SGEK, 43). One obvious way in which the judgments of different people might diverge is if they failed to be impartial. Not surprisingly, therefore, in addition to the requirement that the judgments be relatively stable, Rawls also requires that they be impartial. He notes certain obvious factors which could lead to objectionable partiality, and therefore should not be present, such as "Anger, revenge, jealousy, fear and the like" (SGEK, 54). In addition to putting aside these emotions, impartiality also requires that "all of the relevant interests have been conscientiously reviewed in imagination" and the judgment "is not unwittingly or deliberately biased by a likelihood of winning personal gain" (SGEK, 54). If one's own interests are at stake, this is liable to distort the judgment away from impartiality. But Rawls apparently struggles to find a psychological mechanism that would adequately allow us to implement this requirement in real people. He notes

> two ways in which the removal of distorting interests can be achieved. First, those interests can be removed from a person's character by repression or reorientation. Second, the person's interests can be satisfied fully, so that temptations are removed . . . Since a moral judgment involves a fair adjustment of interests, a competent judge must know these interests and their satisfactions directly; and this he cannot do if he has repressed them. Therefore, regarding the legitimate and

ordinary interests which come up for adjustment, a competent judge will fully understand them only if he has made them an abiding satisfaction in his life . . . Yet on the other hand many interests, if satisfied, wreck havoc [sic] on the person himself as well as on society; and some interests of this kind come up for appraisal. Repression is the only course in such cases, and a fair weighing of them will have to depend upon our ability to know them in imagination. It is somewhat futile to urge that a fair moral judge of tyrants must be a person who has been a tyrant himself, since only tyrants know the great good of being a dictator. (SGEK, 55–56)

Although not wholly without merit, it is obvious that the methods of repression and satisfaction, in addition to introducing a host of additional problems, some of which Rawls notes, cannot guarantee impartiality and agreement among the persons on whose judgments Rawls proposes we rely.

Rawls's first publication, "Outline of a Decision Procedure for Ethics," was based on his dissertation and came out the following year. In both works, for the most part, Rawls assumes that ethical problems emerge when interests conflict.[5] While both works are concerned with ethics in general, in "Outline" he seems more willing to identify such conflicts as problems of justice.[6] A more important development concerns how impartiality is modeled. Rawls drops an explicit requirement that the judgments themselves be impartial and transfers this requirement to the "reasonableness" of the judges. The "sympathetic knowledge" that competent judges possess is of "those human interests which, by conflicting in particular cases, give rise to the need to make a moral decision" (CP, 3). A competent judge has this knowledge either by "experiencing, in his own life, the goods they represent" or "by means of an imaginative experience of it" (CP, 3). Most importantly, however:

A competent judge is required to have the capacity and the desire to lay before himself in imagination all the interests in conflict, together with the relevant facts of the case, and to bestow upon the appraisal of each the same care which he would give to it if that interest were his own. He is required to determine what he would think to be just and unjust if each of the interests were as thoroughly his own as they are in fact those of other persons, and to render his judgment on the case as he feels his sense of justice requires after he has carefully framed in his mind the issues which are to be decided. (CP, 3)

In other words, Rawls simply *stipulates* that the judges render decisions through an *impartial* consideration of the various interests. There is no mention of repression and satisfaction as the psychological instruments by which impartiality is to be achieved. Rawls's model here obviously is the traditional idea of a perfectly impartial spectator, a view that he would later associate with classical utilitarianism (TJ, 23–24, 161–164).

"Justice as Fairness," published in 1958, included several crucial developments. First, Rawls draws attention to the fact that he is concerned with justice as opposed to other moral virtues. In fact, developing his insights from "Two Concepts of Rules," published in 1955, he focuses more narrowly still on "justice only as a virtue of social institutions, or what I shall call practices" (CP, 47). Second, Rawls explicitly rejects utilitarianism (at least in its classical form) as "unable to account" for "the fundamental idea in the concept of justice," which is *fairness* (CP, 47). Instead, he proposes his "two principles of justice," which, through various revisions, he would defend for the rest of his career: a principle of equal liberty (later, an equal scheme of basic liberties) and a principle encompassing fair equality of opportunity and the difference principle (CP, 48).

His justification shifts in significant ways, as well. Rawls now imagines the judges as participants in the practice who are rational and "by and large mutually self-interested" (*CP*, 52). As rational participants with potentially conflicting interests they need to identify principles for assessing and reforming their shared practice. But they understand that any such principles that they propose will be "binding on future occasions." From this, Rawls claims, it follows that

> each will be wary of proposing a principle which would give him a peculiar advantage, in his present circumstances, supposing it to be accepted. Each person knows that he will be bound by it in future circumstances the peculiarities of which cannot be known, and which might well be such that the principle is then to his disadvantage. The idea is that everyone should be required to make *in advance* a firm commitment, which others also may reasonably be expected to make, and that no one be given the opportunity to tailor the canons of a legitimate complaint to fit his own special condition, and then to discard them when they no longer suit his purpose. (*CP*, 53)

The assumption of mutual self-interest is not intended to be "a general theory of human motivation." Rather, it reflects the fact that issues of justice emerge only when the interests of different individuals conflict (*CP*, 56). Although this choice is based on self-interested considerations, once the principles or rules of the practice are chosen, compliance is assured by the duty of fair play, which is not itself chosen by the participants. The duty of fair play requires compliance with the chosen principles whether particular applications serve one's self-interest or not. This structure, Rawls claims, reflects our moral nature since we are moved by both self-interest as well as a commitment to the impartial application of the principles. Relying on a self-interested choice of the principles has another advantage. It allows us to "view the principles of justice as the 'solution' of this highest order 'game' of adopting, subject to the procedure described, principles of argument for all coming particular 'games' whose peculiarities one can in no way foresee" (*CP*, 57). However, he emphasizes, "this highest-order 'game' is of a special sort. Its significance is that its various pieces represent aspects of the concept of justice" (*CP*, 57–58).

Rational and self-interested individuals proposing binding standards for the evaluation of their shared practice would have to consider the possibility that their circumstances might shift in unpredictable ways. It would be irrational to propose principles that favor their current situation if they also impose a high cost under conditions that they might face in the future. This leads Rawls to propose a general criterion for the justice of a practice: "A practice is just if it is in accordance with the principles which all who participate in it might reasonably be expected to propose or to acknowledge before one another when they are similarly circumstanced and required to make a firm commitment in advance without knowledge of what will be their peculiar condition" (*CP*, 63). In addition, Rawls suggests that this will lead each to accept principles as if "his enemy were to assign him his place" (*CP* 54). But this does not follow. More precisely, this follows only on the basis of heroic assumptions about social mobility and the prospect of radical change in circumstances. If we consider a rigidly hierarchical social structure which is relatively stable, there may be little or no chance that those at the top will face such an extreme reversal of fortune that they would find themselves at the bottom. In that case, it might be in their rational self-interest to propose principles that would preserve their privilege. In *A Theory of Justice*, Rawls levels a similar criticism at

Edgeworth's assumption that "the policy of maximizing utility on each occasion is most likely to give the greatest utility for any person individually." Rawls replies that

> the necessary assumptions are extremely unrealistic . . . it must be assumed either that men move from one social position to another in random fashion and live long enough for gains and losses to average out, or else that there is some mechanism which insures that legislation guided by the principle of utility distributes its favors evenly over time. (*TJ*, 147–148)[7]

Of course, without these assumptions those at the bottom will find it in their own rational self-interest to propose principles that would radically reform their institutions. In such a case, participants cannot reach consensus concerning principles with which to reform their institution, and Rawls's method fails to deliver principles of justice.[8]

A veil of ignorance, of course, would ensure impartiality and generate consensus far more effectively than either repression and satisfaction or the prospect of social mobility and change. In a pair of papers published in 1963, Rawls first refers to the mutual acceptance of principles "in an original position of equal liberty" (*CP*, 77). In the first of these, "Constitutional Liberty and the Concept of Justice," he continues to assume that "each person will be wary of proposing a principle which would give him a peculiar advantage . . . [because] he will be bound by it in future circumstances, the peculiarities of which cannot be foreseen and which might well be such that the principle is then to his disadvantage" (*CP*, 78). But in "The Sense of Justice," the "original position of equal liberty" is explained this way:

> In this position it is assumed that there is an absence of information; in particular, it is assumed that the parties do not know their social position, nor do they know their peculiar talents and abilities – that is, their native assets. Briefly, they do not know how they have fared in the natural lottery. Nevertheless, in the original position, knowing the possibility (or allowing for it) of different native endowments, it is rational for them to acknowledge the two principles of justice. (*CP*, 113)

It would be irrational for the parties to propose principles strongly tied to their particular circumstances simply because they do not know what those circumstances are. Indeed, it would be impossible for them to do so. This uncertainty, he now claims, underwrites the idea that we may think of the principles "as those which a person would keep in mind if he were designing a social system in which his enemy were to assign him his place" (*CP*, 98). We no longer need to assume high levels of social mobility or likelihood of radical change in circumstances. However, Rawls offers virtually no discussion or explanation of the features of this original position.

In his initial characterization, the veil of ignorance is fairly thin. The parties still know their full conception of the good on the basis of which they assess the proposed principles. It was only in his 1969 paper "The Justification of Civil Disobedience" that he mentions (once again, without noting or justifying the change from earlier versions) that the parties in the original position "do not know their own particular interests and preferences or the system of ends which they wish to advance: they do not know their conception of the good" (*CP*, 178). At this point, it is unclear how the parties in the original position could make their choice since the thicker veil of ignorance prevents them from knowing their good. The previous year, Rawls had introduced the notion of primary goods. However, they were initially used not as a tool for the parties in the original position to cope with their lack of knowledge, but rather as a way of identifying the least advantaged social position (representative person) (CP, 158).

The various features of the original position that had accumulated in Rawls's publications over the years without much explanation were unified and given an explicit defense in *TJ*. Also, for the first time, Rawls presents a systematic argument that the parties would choose his two principles of justice over utilitarianism. The idea of the veil of ignorance is to "nullify the effects of specific contingencies which put men at odds and tempt them to exploit social and natural circumstances to their own advantage" (*TJ*, 118). We do not want the principles tied to any particular conception of the good any more than we want them tied to any particular social position or set of natural talents and abilities. The point of the virtue of justice, after all, is to identify fair institutions to mediate the conflicts among differently situated individuals with different conceptions of the good. In fact, since we want to force the parties to make their choice "solely on the basis of general considerations" (*TJ*, 118), we deny them any information that could be used to differentiate one person from another. Further, the parties do not know "the particular circumstances of their own society," including "its economic or political situation" (*TJ*, 118). This veil of ignorance is thick (*CP*, 335–336). On the other hand, the parties do know "the general facts about human society. They understand political affairs and the principles of economic theory; they know the basis of social organization and the laws of human psychology" (*TJ*, 119). They know that they are choosing principles that will be used in a well-ordered society publicly to evaluate and potentially to reform the basic structure of society. They know that that society will likely contain a wide diversity of conceptions of the good and reasonable comprehensive doctrines. They also know that the members of the well-ordered society for whom they are selecting principles will be moral persons (or citizens): they have the capacity for a sense of justice and the capacity for a conception of the good. These two moral powers are of great importance and will be discussed below.

The parties in the original position are motivated by their conceptions of the good alone, although the veil of ignorance prevents them from knowing their specific contents. They compare and choose among the various principles based on their assessment of which will result in their doing as well as possible in terms of realizing the goals associated with their conception of the good. They "try to advance their conceptions of the good as best they can, and . . . in attempting to do this they are not bound by prior moral ties to each other" (*TJ*, 111). They choose "solely on the basis of what seems best calculated to further their interests so far as they can ascertain them" (*TJ*, 512). Although they are assumed to be "mutually disinterested," this does not mean that they are "egoists, that is, individuals with only certain kinds of interests, say in wealth, prestige, and domination" (*TJ*, 12; cf. 111). They cannot assume that their conceptions of the good have these specific contents any more than any other. The reason that we conceive the parties "as not talking an interest in one another's interests" (*TJ*, 12) is because we aim to represent the circumstances in which there is a conflict among reasonable conceptions of the good that needs to be resolved fairly. As we have seen, those are the circumstances in which the virtue of justice is required. While the parties are not (directly) concerned to promote each others' goods, we do not assume they are opposed either, so Rawls stipulates that the parties are not moved by envy (*TJ*, 124). In sum, the motivation of the parties is quite different from that of the moral persons or citizens in a well-ordered society. Unlike the individuals for whom they are selecting the principles, the parties are not directly motivated by concerns of fairness or justice. The veil of ignorance is what forces their choice to be impartial and therefore fair. This simplified motivational structure is exactly what gives the original position its power to help us reach reflective equilibrium. If the parties were to consider which principles match their sense of justice, they would simply be reiterating *our* problem in reaching reflective equilibrium. By asking which principles best serve their interests, "we have asked a much more limited question and have substituted for an ethical judgment a judgment of rational prudence" (*TJ*, 39; cf. 512). Yet, because of the veil of ignorance, the answer to this question of rational prudence, we hypothesize, will also answer our question concerning the content of the principles of justice that we should endorse in reflective equilibrium.

When Rawls made the veil of ignorance thick enough to prevent the parties from knowing their conceptions of the good it became unclear on the basis of what values they could make a choice at all. In *TJ*, social primary goods play this role in addition to being used to identify any inequalities among the relevant social positions (*TJ*, 348–349).[9]

> it is rational to want these goods whatever else is wanted, since they are in general necessary for the framing and execution of a rational plan of life. The persons in the original position are assumed to accept this conception of the good, and therefore they take for granted that they desire greater liberty and opportunity, and more extensive means for achieving their ends. With these objectives in mind, as well as that of securing the primary goods of self-respect (§67), they evaluate the conceptions of justice available to them in the original position. (*TJ*, 380; cf. 125)

Although Rawls mentions the importance of primary goods for "framing" a rational plan of life, it would be easy to assume that primary goods are identified by their instrumental contribution to achieving one's determinate ends. And this may suggest that they may be tied closely to the content and popularity of various determinate conceptions of the good. In the "Preface to the Revised Edition" of *TJ* he noted that the original account "left it ambiguous whether something's being a primary good depends solely on the natural facts of human psychology or whether it also depends on a moral conception of the person that embodies a certain ideal" (*TJ*, xiii). In fact, Rawls says, the primary goods depend on a certain ideal of moral persons as "rational beings with their own ends and capable . . . of a sense of justice" (*TJ*, 11; cf. 17, 442, 491). This ideal (or model) is mentioned throughout *TJ*, but the connection to primary goods may be unclear. Even more importantly, the parties in the original position assume that they have certain "fundamental aims and interests" such as a "religious interest" and an "interest in the integrity of the person" and "a highest-order interest in how all their other interests, including even their fundamental ones, are shaped and regulated by social institutions" (*TJ*, 131).[10] The fundamental aims and interests that the parties must be concerned with can be drawn from general sociological and psychological knowledge, for example, that many people have a deeply held religious faith. The idea of higher-order interests, however, was somewhat obscure. Apparently, his idea, as he would later put it, was that the parties would want to ensure that "their original allegiance and continued devotion to these ends are formed under conditions that are free" (*CP*, 228). As developed in his later work, the two moral powers – the capacity for a sense of justice and the capacity for a conception of the good – are presented as necessary for full participation in a scheme of social cooperation (*PL*, 19, 81, 103–104). The parties have two higher-order interests in protecting these powers so that full social participation is possible, regardless of the particular system

135

of ends that they affirm. So, although the parties do not know the determinate concep-tions of the good which they attempt to satisfy, they can rely on primary goods because they serve a wide variety of ends, including fundamental ends that they assume they might have and, most importantly, their higher-order interests associated with full participation in a scheme of cooperation.[11]

In some ways, it might seem as though the thick veil of ignorance achieves its goal of ensuring unanimity too well. As Rawls notes, "we can view the agreement in the original position from the standpoint of one person selected at random" (*TJ*, 120). What, one might ask, is left of the idea of a contract? Rawls's version of the social contract differs in a number of respects from ordinary contracts. Most obviously, the veil of ignorance means that there is "no basis for bargaining in the usual sense" (*TJ*, 120). Furthermore, ordinary contracts are binding, when they are, because they were agreed to through an act of consent. They specify certain obligations that hold only because of the agreement. For Rawls, in contrast, there is a natural duty of justice that binds everyone regardless of any voluntary agreement that they may have made. The original position is designed to help us identify the content of the virtue of social justice, rather than to establish its binding character or importance.[12]

Yet, Rawls insists on retaining the rhetoric of a contract for a number of reasons, even though the agreement in the original position departs from normal contracts in these impor-tant ways.[13] First, the idea of a contract carries with it the implication of publicity. Citizens know the outcome of the agreement and they use the principles in their public deliberations about the basic structure of their society (*TJ*, 15, 115). Second, Rawls believes that one of utilitarianism's main sources of attractions is that it relies on a maximizing conception of practical reason familiar from the context of individual choice. It does this by "extending to society the principle of choice for one man" (*TJ*, 24). However, in doing this, it "does not take seriously the distinction between persons" (*TJ*, 24). Issues of justice only arise in the context of multiple persons with potentially conflicting interests. It is important that this plurality be represented in the original position. As Rawls put it in 1968, "The initial situation must be one of group choice; it must not be that of one person, whether this person is a rational risk-taker or an impartial sympathetic spectator" (*CP*, 174). Finally, by retaining the rhetoric of a social contract, Rawls is able to emphasize that the parties in the original posi-tion must make their agreement in good faith, with the full expectation that they will be able to comply with its provisions once the veil of ignorance is lifted: "when we enter an agreement we must be able to honor it even should the worst possibilities prove to be the case. Otherwise we have not acted in good faith. Thus the parties must weigh with care wither they will be able to stick by their commitment in all circumstances" (*TJ*, 153). This is a stipulation that we make in setting up the original position, and it is essential in the justification of the two principles.

We are now in a position to examine the main grounds on which the parties in the original position would make their choice. The argument is complex, and here I can only discuss certain strands. Rawls presents his argument that the parties would accept his two principles in two stages: first, by a comparison with average utilitarianism, which focuses on his first principle, and then by a comparison with so-called "mixed conceptions," which focuses on the second principle. Rawls claims that since the veil of ignorance prevents each of the parties from winning "special advantages for himself . . . the sensible thing is to acknowledge as the first step a principle of justice requiring an equal distribution" (*TJ*, 130). But this is not at all obvious. In fact, given their goal of choosing principles that maximize their prospects for achieving their conception of the good, it might seem that a more sensible choice would be average utilitarianism. And, indeed, Rawls acknowledges that "if we waive the problem of interpersonal comparisons of utility, and if the parties are viewed as rational individuals who have no aversion to risk and who follow the principle of insufficient reason in computing likelihoods . . . then the idea of the initial situation leads naturally to the average principle" (*TJ*, 143).[14] To argue against this conclusion, Rawls must show why the parties would have a strong aversion to risk when making certain choices or when certain interests are at stake. It is not enough simply to stipulate that they would be risk averse. As he pointed out in a 1974 article, "Reply to Alexander and Musgrave," such a stipulation "would indeed have been no argument at all" (*CP*, 247).

The argument just sketched for average utilitarianism assumes that the parties know nothing about the structure or content of their preferences, interests, or ends (cf. Harsanyi 1976). On this view, "The parties are conceived as having no definite highest-order interests or fundamental ends . . . They are, we might say, bare-persons" (*TJ*, 152). This model, therefore, involves a choice from an "initial situation" that differs from the original position, where the parties are assumed to "have certain highest-order interests and fundamental ends . . . which they must try to protect. Since they know that the basic liberties covered by the first principle will secure these interests, they must acknowledge the two principles of justice rather than the principle of utility" (*TJ*, 152). The parties would be willing to sacrifice potential gains in the satisfaction of other preferences in order to avoid the chance that their fundamental and higher-order interests would not be protected. In fact, an agreement in which they risked having their fundamental interests violated unnecessarily would be one that was not made in good faith. The parties know, for example, that they have a fundamental interest in practicing their religious faith (if they have one) and being able to affirm their moral and philosophical convictions. The parties would want to choose principles that protect liberty of conscience even if that meant giving up possible economic gains that could conceivably be had from restricting the religious liberty of some. The veil of ignorance would prevent them from knowing whether it would be their faith that would be suppressed. Even if they assumed it was unlikely that they would be the ones to suffer, it would not be rational for them to risk it. As Rawls explains in *Justice as Fairness*, "Were the parties to gamble in that way, they would show that they did not take seriously the religious, philosophical, and moral convictions of the persons they represent. Indeed, they would show that they did not understand the nature of religious belief, or philosophical or moral conviction" (*JF*, 105).

The "strains of commitment" would be too great if the worst happened and their fundamental interests were not protected. This is the force of saying that certain interests are *fundamental*. Similarly, the parties would want to ensure that the conditions necessary for the development and maintenance of the two moral powers are satisfied. The parties would not risk undermining the conditions that develop their capacity to participate fully in a scheme of social cooperation. Choosing such principles risks almost completely undermining their prospects for achieving their good, and since that is the goal of the parties, they would avoid such principles at all costs.[15] When their fundamental and higher-order interests are at stake, the parties will be extremely conservative in their choice of principles. This is not due to a peculiar aversion to risk that we assign to the parties. It is because of the generic structure of their interests. If we were to model their preferences formally, we would be forced to say that "the marginal utility of these fundamental interests is infinite" (*CP*, 228).

It is true that in practice, utilitarianism might also provide protection for the basic liberties. In fact, it seems quite likely to do so if we assume that the utility functions of citizens reflect their fundamental interests and that the basic liberties protect these interests. If this is the case, that is, if utilitarianism can provide support for protection of the basic liberties, "we should be cheered" (*JF*, 107) since it shows a certain overlap between utilitarianism and justice as fairness. However, this does not show that the parties would choose average utilitarianism instead of the two principles. The principles, remember, are to be used in public deliberation about the institutions of the basic structure. Although we may assume that the protection of fundamental interests would have a very high utility, average utilitarianism would have us weigh this against the preferences that some citizens might have against the protection of the basic liberties (of others). The parties would want to protect the basic liberties directly and explicitly "rather than have them depend upon what may be uncertain and speculative actuarial calculation" (*TJ*, 139). Furthermore, the two principles contribute to stability by "announcing to one another once and for all that even though theoretical computations of utility always happen to favor the equal liberties (assuming that this is indeed the case here), they do not wish that things had been different" (*TJ*, 139). The basic liberties directly protect our fundamental interests and provide the conditions for the development and maintenance of our higher-order interests. Because of the structure of their motivation, the parties in the original position would place great weight on protecting the basic liberties. The key contrast between average utilitarianism and the two principles is that the latter, but not the former, provide a direct guarantee that the basic liberties will be protected equally.

Rawls's argument from the original position has become associated with the idea of the "maximin" rule for choice under uncertainty. It is obvious why. Going back to "Justice as Fairness" in 1958, he suggested that we think of the principles as those a person would choose "if he were designing a practice in which his enemy were to assign him a place" (*CP*, 54), and in *TJ* he states that "it is useful as a heuristic device to think of the two principles as the maximin solution to the problem of social justice" (*TJ*, 132). Furthermore, there is a structural similarity between maximin and the difference principle.[16] Yet, for all of this, Rawls's use of maximin reasoning has been widely misunderstood. Contrary to the widespread assumption, Rawls argues that "the maximin rule is not, in general, a suitable guide for choices under uncertainty" (*TJ*, 133). And as we have seen, we cannot simply posit that the parties would be risk averse; we need an argument as to why, given their situation, choosing in a way that is analogous to maximin would be rational. The strains of commitment argument sketched above depends on a particular structure of fundamental and higher-order interests. For that very reason, however, we have grounds for a conservative choice only when those interests are at stake. When Rawls talks about the parties protecting themselves against the worst possible outcome, it is not the possibility of having a below-average (or even the smallest) share of wealth and income that he is primarily worried about (as long as the share is above a certain minimum). Rather, it is the prospect of not being able to satisfy one's fundamental or higher-order interests. This may be obscured in discussions of maximin that assign numerical values (utility levels) to the various possible outcomes. Once the basic liberties have been secured and everyone is assured a minimal share of resources, the fundamental interests have been satisfied. The question is whether a basic structure satisfying a conception of justice might have "positions we could not accept" (not simply ones that we would disprefer to others). If so, the parties cannot "in good faith" agree to that conception (*JF*, 103; cf. *CP*, 250–251). But the strains of commitment argument is much weaker in selecting among conceptions that each secure our fundamental and higher-order interests.[17]

A mixed conception is one that accepts Rawls's first principle of justice but substitutes a different principle for his second. Considering the choice between the two principles and such a mixed conception allows us to assess the grounds for supporting the second principle of justice. Assuming that it provides an adequate minimum share of resources, a mixed conception will satisfy our fundamental and higher-order interests and therefore keep the strains of commitment within acceptable limits. This undercuts the grounds that we saw above for using maximin as a heuristic. The implication is that, contrary to widespread belief, "in arguing for the difference principle over other distributive principles . . . there is no appeal at all to the maximin rule for decision under uncertainty" (*JF*, 43, n3; cf. 94–95).[18] The reasons the parties would choose the second principle are very different from the grounds for selecting the first, and Rawls presents them much later in *TJ* (§49), making them easy to overlook. There, the parties are faced with the choice between the two principles and a mixed conception that (like all mixed conceptions) accepts the first principle of justice, and accepts fair equality of opportunity, but substitutes for the difference principle "the principle of average utility constrained by a certain social minimum" (*TJ*, 278).[19] Since this and many other mixed conceptions protect our fundamental and higher-order interests, it is no surprise that they "are much more difficult to argue against than the principle of utility" (*TJ*, 278). And, in fact, "some mixed conceptions are certainly adequate enough for many purposes" (*TJ*, 310). Using the terminology that he introduced only later, it seems clear that Rawls would say that this mixed conception would be a member of the "family of reasonable political conceptions of justice" (*PL*, 442; cf. xlvi–xlvii, l–li, 6). A society committed to this mixed conception could certainly be legitimate, even if Rawls believes it would not be as fully just as one committed to the two principles. Note, however, that this mixed conception is underspecified. We have not yet determined the level at which the social minimum is set. One way that we might set it is by the difference principle.[20] In that case, there is a virtually complete agreement concerning which institutions are just. Indeed, in *TJ* §43 when Rawls sketches an institutional arrangement that is designed to satisfy the difference principle, it is clear that it would satisfy the mixed conception as well.[21]

Given that the two conceptions are so similar, we must look at secondary considerations to choose between them. Here, I will mention two advantages that justice as fairness has over the mixed conception. First, even though the mixed conception differs sharply from utilitarianism, the idea of utility maximization still plays a subordinate role. This means that it must resolve longstanding issues in the definition of utility and make interpersonal comparisons (*TJ*, 281–285). This is not merely a theoretical problem, although it is that, too. The principles are to be used in public deliberations concerning the justice of social institutions. Assessments of aggregate utility are much more opaque and therefore controversial than simply identifying the prospective share of primary goods of the least advantaged social position. It also raises the prospect of requiring that we make so-called "shameful revelations" about our preferences (Wolff 1998). A second consideration is that "the difference principle includes an idea of reciprocity [that] distinguishes it from the restricted utility principle" (*JF*, 122). Starting from a baseline of equality, the difference principle allows inequalities only when everyone gains. Average utilitarianism may allow further inequalities beyond this point so that the more advantaged gain even more while the less advantaged lose (compared to the corresponding positions under the difference principle). At this point, gains are no longer reciprocal. Rawls argues that reciprocity is a deep-seated psychological tendency in human beings, and, other things equal, a conception that is able to tap into it is likely to be more stable than one that does not (*TJ*, 405–441; *JF*, 124–126). Focusing on the public application of conceptions and on their stability would not be decisive if fundamental and higher-order interests were at stake. But given that these two conceptions do secure these interests, it seems appropriate that such secondary considerations become relevant, and they both seem to favor the two principles. Thus, while there are very strong grounds for the parties to endorse the first principle (and its priority) that are revealed by a comparison with utilitarianism, there are also grounds, albeit weaker, for endorsing the second principle, revealed by a comparison with mixed conceptions.

To conclude, Rawls argues that the principles chosen from the original position

> are objective. They are the principles that we would want everyone (including ourselves) to follow were we to take up together the appropriate general point of view. The original position defines this perspective, and its conditions also embody those of objectivity: its stipulations express the restrictions on arguments that force us to consider the choice of principles unencumbered by the singularities of the circumstances in which we find ourselves. The veil of ignorance prevents us from shaping our moral view to accord with our own particular attachments and interests. We do not look at the social order from our situation but take up a point of view that everyone can adopt on an equal footing. In this sense we look at our society and our place in it objectively. (*TJ*, 453)

Although I cannot discuss the point here, when presented as a form of political constructivism in *Political Liberalism*, Rawls continues to claim that the original position establishes a form of objectivity. (See *PL*, 102–116.) The choice from the original position answers the challenge that Rawls addressed in his dissertation: how is it possible to have an objective form of moral knowledge? Rawls concluded his dissertation by claiming that he had refuted authoritarianism and positivism "by offering a counterexample; that is, by taking a class of moral judgments and showing that they can be reasoned about and justified" (SGEK, 346). Rawls remained devoted to pushing back the forces of skepticism and dogmatism. The moral knowledge that comes from considering the choice from the original position, which he considered and developed over his career, was his refutation.

# Notes

Thanks to David Reidy and Kristen Hessler for helpful comments and discussion.

1   On reflective equilibrium, see *TJ*, 18–19, 42–45; *PL*, 95–97, 381–385; *JF*, 29–32. On constructivism, see *CP*, 303–358; *PL*, 89–129. On the relationship between moral theory and other areas of philosophy, see *CP*, 286–302.

2   On property-owning democracy, see *JF*, 135–179. On free speech, see *PL*, 340–363. On Hiroshima, see *CP*, 565–572.

3   Cf. SGEK, 293–294: "unless we provided for the possibility that our common sense judgments could be reformed in the light of ethical principles, ethics would be identical with the sociology of morals."

4   Rawls is aware that some may object that "Scientific theories control their data, and exercise a coercive power over observations" (SGEK, 93). But, he argues, "there is a limit as to how far a theory can discard observations relevant to it. Otherwise, it would not be a theory at all, but an opinion stubbornly maintained in the face of contradicting reports . . . Thus, while it is true that a physical theory may control its data, the relation is entirely different from that which may exist between an ethical theory and its data" (SGEK, 94–95).

5   See, for example: "If one considers that ethics is concerned with a fair adjustment of a variety of conflicting interests, then an impartial judgment will have, as one of its characteristics, an awareness of all of the relevant interests involved" (SGEK, 53).

6   See, for example, CP, 13. In the dissertation the connection to justice, although present, was not as pronounced. See, for example: "Caring for a person's interests may result in caring for his interests irrespective of those of other people, so that acting from love may very easily lead to injustice, and what to all appearances is arbitrary favoritism. Therefore, so far as the disposition is a direct inclination to help another's interests, we cannot assign it a definite value until we know to what extent it is likely to work for injustice" (SGEK, 161).

7   See also Rawls's discussion of this issue in "Constitutional Liberty and the Concept of Justice" (1963) in CP, esp. 80–85.

8   David Gauthier faces a similar problem in chapter 7 of *Morals by Agreement*. There, he argues for a proviso that is not "the object of an agreement among rational individuals, but [is] a precondition to such an agreement" (1986, 192). This proviso "prohibits bettering one's situation through interaction that worsens the situation of another" (1986, 205). This determination requires a comparison between an individual's prospects when participating in an institution with his or her prospects without participating. Rawls rejects the idea of determining what one's prospects would be outside of society altogether, for example, in "Distributive Justice" (1967), CP, 135; cf. PL, 278.

9   See also "Fairness to Goodness" (1975), in CP.

10  Rawls wavers between referring to these as "higher-order" and "highest-order" interests. See "Social Unity and Primary Goods," CP, 365. In *Political Liberalism*, he consistently uses "higher-order" and I follow that usage.

11  Rawls argues that the basic liberties, in particular, are necessary for the protection of these higher-order interests (PL, 299–324). See also the discussion of the moral powers in Mandle 2000, 55–70.

12  It is true that in TJ, Rawls considers the justification of the natural duties from the original position (TJ, 293–301). However, this occurs after the choice of principles has already been made. Furthermore, reframed as a political conception of justice, justice as fairness would allow other justifications of this natural duty.

13  See CP, 249, for a defense of the idea of a contract or agreement rather than mere choice: "In general, the class of things that can be agreed to is included within, and is smaller than, the class of things that can be rationally chosen" (cf. JF, 102).

14  Rawls argues against the use of the principle of insufficient reason. The parties cannot rationally assign an equal probability to each possible outcome. I will simply note that the parties do not even know what the various social positions will be, let alone the likelihood of their occupying each of them (TJ, 134; CP, 248).

15  This is similar to the reason that Rawls holds that the social basis of self-respect is "perhaps the most important primary good" (TJ, 386). Self-respect is "the sense that one's plan is worth carrying out" (TJ, 155). If the parties were to choose principles that did not provide the social basis of self-respect, their prospect of successfully carrying out their plan and achieving their good, no matter what it was, would be fatally compromised. Although I cannot explore this here, Rawls argues that his two principles provide stronger support for self-respect than rival conceptions of justice (TJ, 477–480).

16  Rawls notes the importance of distinguishing these two "very different things" in "Some Reasons for the Maximin Criterion" (1974), *CP*, 225. See also the passage he added to the revised edition of *TJ* at 72: "It is undesirable to use the same name for two things that are so distinct." On the other hand, Rawls himself apparently conflates the two in the "Reply to Alexander and Musgrave," *CP*, 241.

17  This is not to say it is nonexistent. In *Justice as Fairness*, Rawls connects the ideas of reciprocity and the strains of commitment. He argues: "in asking the less advantaged to accept over the whole of their life fewer economic and social advantages (measured in terms of utility) for the sake of greater advantages (similarly measured) for the more advantaged, the principle of utility asks more of the less advantaged than the difference principle asks of the more advantaged. Indeed, asking that of the less advantaged would seem to be an extreme demand. The psychological strains that may lead to instability are bound to be greater" (*JF* 127). He then notes that the strains may result either in people who "see themselves as oppressed" and "are ready as the occasion arises to take violent action in protest" or, more mildly, result in people who "grow distant from political society" and become "withdrawn and cynical" (*JF*, 128). Presumably, the most serious violations of the basic liberties generate the first type, while more mild violations of the principle of reciprocity generate the latter. See the discussion of reciprocity below.

18  In "Some Reasons for the Maximin Criterion," Rawls seems to make a "strains of commitment argument" for the use of maximin reasoning when choosing between the two principles and a mixed conception (*CP*, 229–230). However, note that there the mixed conception he is discussing does not have a guaranteed social minimum. Therefore, fundamental interests may well be at risk.

19  Note that considering this choice will not give us a justification of fair equality of opportunity since both principles accept it. In the case of the difference principle it is important that it be paired with fair equality of opportunity because the difference principle is a structural principle. It does not apply to individuals but to social positions defined by the institutions of the basic structure. But the parties in the original position are concerned with their individual prospects. While the difference principle identifies permissible structural inequalities, fair equality of opportunity requires that *each individual* have a fair prospect of occupying the various social positions.

20  Rawls speculates that there might be an implicit reliance on the difference principle to specify this level (*TJ*, 278–279). However, see Waldron 1986.

21  On this account, in addition to securing the basic liberties and ensuring fair equality of opportunity, the government has the responsibility to keep markets functioning efficiently without the formation of monopoly powers, to bring about full employment, to provide public goods, to limit inheritance and bequests, and to ensure an appropriate "social minimum" (*TJ*, §43). "But once a suitable minimum is provided by transfers, it may be perfectly fair that the rest of total income be settled by the price system, assuming that it is moderately efficient and free from monopolistic restrictions, and unreasonable externalities have been eliminated" (*TJ*, 245).

## Works by Rawls, with Abbreviations

*Collected Papers* (*CP*), ed. Samuel Freeman. Cambridge, MA: Harvard University Press, 1999.
"Constitutional Liberty and the Concept of Justice" (1963), in *Collected Papers* (73–95).
"Distributive Justice" (1967), in *Collected Papers* (130–153).
"Fairness to Goodness" (1975), in *Collected Papers* (267–285).
*Justice as Fairness: A Restatement* (*JF*), ed. Erin Kelly. Cambridge, MA: Harvard University Press, 2001.
"The Justification of Civil Disobedience" (1969), in *Collected Papers* (176–189).
"Outline of a Decision Procedure for Ethics" (1951), in *Collected Papers* (1–19).
*Political Liberalism* (*PL*), expanded edn. New York: Columbia University Press, 2005.

"Reply to Alexander and Musgrave" (1974), *in Collected Papers* (232–253).

"The Sense of Justice"(1963), in *Collected Papers* (96–116).

"Social Unity and Primary Goods" (1982), in *Collected Papers* (359–387).

"Some Reasons for the Maximin Criterion" (1974), in *Collected Papers* (225–231).

"A Study in the Grounds of Ethical Knowledge: Considered with Reference to Judgments of the Moral Worth of Character" (SGEK), submitted to the Department of Philosophy, Princeton University, Feb. 1, 1950.

*A Theory of Justice* (*TJ*), rev. edn. Cambridge, MA: Harvard University Press, 1999.

## Other References

Gauthier, David (1986) *Morals by Agreement*. Oxford: Oxford University Press.

Harsanyi, John (1976) "Can the Maximin Principle Serve as a Basis for Morality?" In Harsanyi, *Essays on Ethics, Social Behavior, and Scientific Explanation*. Dordrecht: Reidel.

Mandle, Jon (2000) *What's Left of Liberalism*. Lanham, MD: Lexington Books.

Waldron, Jeremy (1986) "John Rawls and the Social Minimum." *Journal of Applied Philosophy* 3.

Wolff, Jonathan (1998) "Fairness, Respect, and the Egalitarian Ethos." *Philosophy and Public Affairs* 27.

# Part III

# A Theory of Justice

# 8

# The Priority of Liberty

## ROBERT S. TAYLOR

## 1. Introduction

The first priority rule (the priority of liberty) of justice as fairness reads as follows: "the prin-ciples of justice are to be ranked in lexical order and therefore the basic liberties can be restricted only for the sake of liberty" (*TJ*, 266). The basic liberties are those commonly pro-tected by liberal constitutional regimes, including "freedom of speech and assembly; liberty of conscience and freedom of thought; freedom of the person . . . ; the right to hold personal property and freedom from arbitrary arrest and seizure . . ." (*TJ*, 53). The priority of liberty regards these basic liberties as paramount and forbids their sacrifice for the sake of efficiency, utilitarian and perfectionist ideals, or even the other principles within justice as fairness (viz. fair equality of opportunity (FEO) and the difference principle (DP)), regardless of the size of the benefits that might obtain as a consequence of such sacrifice.

Two examples will illustrate the force of this priority vis-à-vis the two subordinate princi-ples of justice. Suppose that a law is proposed to punish (maybe only with fines) advocacy of racially and sexually bigoted doctrines on the grounds that their spread would hinder the implementation of FEO: the dissemination of such doctrines in a population – especially among employers – may hamper the matching of people and their talents with appropriate jobs in the basic structure. Such a law would clearly violate the priority of liberty, as liberty can be sacrificed only for the sake of liberty, and would therefore be ruled out.[1] Now suppose that a law is offered to punish advocacy of ascetic or antimaterialist doctrines (e.g., the teach-ings of Jesus in the Gospels) on the grounds that their widespread adoption would effectively undermine the DP's mandate: were such ideas to gain in popularity, economic trade and production would likely diminish and fewer resources would therefore be available to redis-tribute to the least advantaged members of society. Again, if the equal-liberty principle is lexically prior to the DP, such a law must be rejected.

The priority of liberty has always played a central role in Rawls's political theory. Rawls notes that "the force of justice as fairness would appear to arise from two things: the

*A Companion to Rawls*, First Edition. Edited by Jon Mandle and David A. Reidy.
© 2014 John Wiley & Sons, Inc. Published 2016 by John Wiley & Sons, Inc.

requirement that all inequalities be justified to the least advantaged [the DP], and the priority of liberty. This pair of constraints distinguishes it from intuitionism and teleological theories" (*TJ*, 220). As we shall see, its importance in his work has if anything increased over time. Part of the reason for this greater prominence is Rawls's growing ambivalence about the other distinctive elements of his political theory, especially the lexical priority of FEO and the DP.[2] In the absence of the former element, the priority of liberty would be the chief thing preventing the special conception of justice from collapsing into the general conception, in which all social primary goods (and presumably the interests they support) are lumped together. Rawls is deeply opposed, however, to the notion that "all human interests are commensurable, and that between any two there always exists some rate of exchange in terms of which it is rational to balance the protection of one against the protection of the other," and anything short of lexical priority for the basic liberties would countenance such trade-offs under certain circumstances (*PL*, 312).

This central component of justice as fairness has been criticized in a long line of articles, including works by Kenneth Arrow, Brian Barry, Norman Daniels, H.L.A. Hart, Russell Keat and David Miller, and Henry Shue.[3] All of these authors have found Rawls's defense of the priority of liberty deficient in some respects, and many of them have been sharply critical of the very idea of lexical priority for basic liberties. Barry considers it "outlandishly extreme" (1973, 276), while Hart deems it "dogmatic" (1989, 252; see also Arneson 2000, 240–241). In section 2 of this chapter, I will review Rawls's three arguments for the priority of liberty in *Theory* and argue that two of them do indeed fail (either in whole or in part) because of two types of error. One is Rawls's conviction that once he has shown the instrumental value of the basic liberties for some essential purpose (e.g., securing self-respect), he has automatically shown the reason for their lexical priority. I will refer to this conviction – specifically, that the *lexical* priority of the basic liberties can be inferred from the *high* priority of the interests that they serve – as the "inference fallacy." The other kind of error arises because although the interest in question may have the necessary priority, the basic liberties are not *requisite* for its protection but merely *strongly contributory* toward it. Lexical priority is such a stringent condition that a special form of justification will be necessary for its defense.

As I will also demonstrate, though, Rawls's third argument for the priority of liberty does not commit either of these two errors. This defense, which I will call the "hierarchy argument," suggests that the priority of liberty flows immediately from a certain conception of free persons. Unfortunately, the argument as presented in Rawls's work is radically incomplete, leaving a number of important questions unanswered. In section 3, therefore, I present a partial reconstruction of the hierarchy argument, showing that it can offer a compelling and attractive defense of the priority of liberty. This reconstruction explains our highest-order interest in rationality, justifies the lexical priority of all basic liberties, and reinterprets the threshold condition for the application of the priority of liberty. What had perhaps previously seemed a peculiarly disproportionate concern for the basic liberties is shown to follow quite naturally from a Kantian conception of the person.

Having demonstrated this, I turn in section 4 to an apparent problem with the scope of the hierarchy argument: it does not offer a particularly compelling defense of the priority of the basic *political* liberties, including the rights to vote and hold public office. I suggest there a solution to this problem relying upon Rawls's scattered comments on the (hierarchical) relationship between our highest-order interests in reasonableness and rationality respectively, though this solution calls into question Rawls's claim that the political and civil liberties are "of equal weight . . . with neither externally imposed on the other" and is consequentially revisionist in nature (*PL*, 412). I conclude the chapter by considering the implications of the priority of liberty for the American practice of civil libertarianism.

## 2. Three Arguments for the Priority of Liberty in *Theory*

In this section, I will examine Rawls's three arguments for the lexical priority of liberty found in the revised edition of *Theory*.[4] In the first of these three, which I will label the "self-respect argument," Rawls maintains that the priority of the (equal) basic liberties is needed to secure equal citizenship, which is itself a prerequisite for self-respect. In the second, which I will call the "equal liberty of conscience argument," Rawls argues that the integrity of our religious beliefs (and, by extension, of our moral and philosophical ones) is of such importance that liberty of conscience (and, by extension, other basic liberties) must be given lexical priority. Finally, in what I will refer to as the "hierarchy argument," Rawls maintains that the lexical priority of the basic liberties is justified by the lexical priority of a particular interest that they protect – namely, our interest in choosing our final ends under conditions of freedom. I will argue that the first and second arguments suffer from the two errors discussed above (although the second can be given a narrow construction that rescues it from the charge) but that the third argument avoids them and can therefore serve as the basis for a reconstructed defense of the priority of liberty.

### *2.1 The Self-Respect Argument*

In §67 of *Theory*, Rawls says that self-respect is "perhaps the most important primary good": without it, we will doubt our own value, the value of our plan of life, and our ability to carry it out, and we will therefore be susceptible to the siren call of "apathy and cynicism" (*TJ*, 386; cf. *PL*, 318–320). In §82 of *Theory*, as a prelude to the self-respect argument, Rawls goes on to note how self-respect is tightly linked to status, that is, to our positions in social hierarchies. Because even a just society will be characterized by various kinds of inequalities (e.g., income differentials) that might erode the self-respect of the poorly ranked, any society concerned with securing self-respect for all of its citizens must affirm equality of status along a key dimension. Rawls believes political equality, or "equal citizenship," can serve this purpose, especially when socioeconomic inequalities are kept within reasonable bounds by "just background institutions" reflecting FEO and the DP (*TJ*, 478).[5]

What is required for "equal citizenship," however? Rawls contends that equality in the provision of basic liberties is a necessary condition for equal citizenship and that such equality therefore provides a secure ground for self-respect: "the basis for self-respect in a just society is the publicly affirmed distribution of fundamental rights and liberties. And this distribution being equal, everyone has a similar and secure status when they meet to conduct the common affairs of the wider society" (*TJ*, 477). Rawls persuasively argues that citizens in a just society could never consent to less than equal basic liberties, as "this subordinate ranking in public life would be humiliating and destructive of self-esteem" (*TJ*, 477). A status

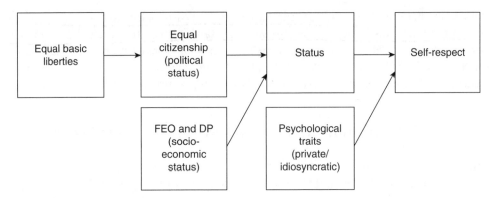

**Figure 8.1** The self-respect argument

inequality explicitly defined and enforced by the state would likely have a more devastating effect on self-respect than a socioeconomic inequality that emerges via a process merely superintended by the state. A self-respecting citizenry thus requires equal basic liberties. I summarize this multistage argument in Figure 8.1.

Up to this point, Rawls has said nothing about the priority of the basic liberties; rather, he has focused exclusively on their equal provision. Only at the end of his main presentation of the self-respect argument does he mention the priority of liberty:

> when it is the position of equal citizenship that answers to the need for status, the precedence of the equal liberties becomes all the more necessary. Having chosen a conception of justice that tries to eliminate the significance of relative economic and social advantages as supports for men's self-confidence, it is essential that the priority of liberty be firmly maintained. (*TJ*, 478)

This passage provides a good illustration of what I earlier called the "inference fallacy": Rawls tries to derive the lexical priority of the basic liberties from the central importance of an interest that they support – in this case, an interest in securing self-respect for all citizens. Without question, the self-respect argument makes a very strong case for assigning the basic liberties a *high* priority; otherwise, socioeconomic inequalities might reemerge as the primary determinants of status and therefore self-respect. What it does not explain, however, is why *lexical* priority is needed. Why, for instance, would minor restraints on the basic liberties threaten the social basis of self-respect, so long as they were equally applied to all citizens? One example might be punishing Holocaust denial for the sake of political stability. Such a restriction would involve no subordination and, being very small, would be unlikely to jeopardize the central importance of equal citizenship as a determinant of status.

Even if such minor restrictions were ruled out as too risky, we would still need to ask why self-respect is of such overwhelming importance that its social basis, an equal distribution of the basic liberties, must be given lexical priority. As noted above, Rawls maintains in §67 of *Theory* that self-respect is "perhaps the most important primary good," but he does not explain why this particular primary good should trump all others. As we shall see in the third subsection, the only way to justify something as strong as lexical priority for the basic liberties is to justify lexical priority for the interest they support, that is, assigning of such weight to an interest that it cannot be traded off for any other interest, no matter how high the rate of exchange. Securing self-respect for all citizens might be such an interest, but Rawls's arguments do not show why.

## 2.2 The Equal Liberty of Conscience Argument

In §26 of *Theory*, Rawls contends that free persons have certain "fundamental interests" that they must secure through the priority of liberty:

> I assume that the parties [in the original position, or OP] view themselves as free persons who have *fundamental aims and interests* in the name of which they think it legitimate for them to make claims on one another concerning the design of the basic structure of society. The *religious interest* is a familiar historical example; the interest in the integrity of the person is another. In the original position the parties do not know what particular forms these interests take; but they do assume that they have such interests and that the basic liberties necessary for their protection are guaranteed by the first principle. *Since they must secure these interests, they rank the first principle prior to the second.* (TJ, 131, emphasis added; cf. PL, 310–312)

Later, in *Theory* §33, Rawls further develops this argument with respect to the religious interest, among others. He explains the importance of this interest and the equal liberty of conscience that protects it as follows:

> The parties [in the OP] must assume that they may have moral, religious, or philosophical interests which they cannot put in jeopardy unless there is no alternative. One might say that they regard themselves as having moral or religious obligations which they must keep themselves free to honor . . . They cannot take chances with their liberty by permitting the dominant religious or moral doctrine to persecute or to suppress others if it wishes . . . To gamble in this way would show that one did not take one's religious or moral convictions seriously, or highly value the liberty to examine one's beliefs. (TJ, 180–181)

We might view this argument as simply another illustration of the inference fallacy: Rawls tries to derive the lexical priority of equal liberty of conscience from the fundamental importance of the interest it supports – *viz.* an interest in examining and subscribing to certain philosophical, moral, and religious beliefs. The central importance of this interest is insufficient, however, to establish the lexical priority of the liberty that supports it: one might "highly value" this interest yet still endorse small sacrifices of equal liberty of conscience and the interest it protects if such sacrifices were necessary to advance other highly valued interests. Only if the interest had lexical priority over all other interests could such trade-offs be categorically ruled out.

We can, however, interpret Rawls's argument in another way. The passages just quoted are larded with the language of compulsion: "must secure," "cannot put in jeopardy," "cannot take chances," etc. Also, when discussing the same issue in §82 of *Theory*, Rawls says that "in order to secure their unknown but particular interests from the original position, they [the parties in the OP] are led, *in view of the strains of commitment* (§29), to give precedence to basic liberties" (TJ, 475, emphasis added). Perhaps Rawls's argument here is best understood as follows: the parties in the original position, given their general knowledge of human psychology, must avoid committing to political principles whose outcomes they might not be able to accept; political principles that place fundamental interests (such as the religious interest) at even the slightest risk, by refusing lexical priority to the liberties that protect them, make the strains of commitment intolerable.

This argument seems especially powerful with regard to the religious interest. Religious persons have faith that their religious duties (e.g., acceptance of a creed, participation in certain ceremonies, etc.) are divinely mandated and that a failure to abide by these commitments may lead to divine retribution, even eternal damnation. If the parties in the original position agree to anything less exacting than the lexical priority of equal liberty of conscience, they may emerge from behind the veil of ignorance to discover that their own religious beliefs and practices have been put in jeopardy by discriminatory legislation and that they are psychologically incapable of abiding by such legislation due to an overriding fear of supernatural punishment.

This strains-of-commitment argument provides strong support for the lexical priority of equal liberty of conscience as applied to religion. Does it, however, extend to philosophical and moral commitments as well, as Rawls claims in §33 of *Theory*? Although one can point to a few important historical examples of people who were either incapable or unwilling to abide by laws that discriminated against their philosophical and moral beliefs (e.g., Galileo and Socrates), these cases are celebrated precisely because of their rarity: religious martyrs are far more common than philosophical or moral ones, as we have become uncomfortably aware in the wake of September 11 and with the spread of suicide bombing as a tactic of Islamic terrorists. Therefore, the strains-of-commitment argument, if it applies to moral and philosophical beliefs at all, is less compelling than in the case of religious belief.[6]

What of Rawls's additional claim in §33 of *Theory* that "the reasoning in this case [i.e., equal liberty of conscience] can be generalized to apply to other freedoms, *although not always with the same force*" (*TJ*, 181, emphasis added)? In some cases, this claim seems justified. Consider, for instance, Rawls's own example of "the rights defining the integrity of the person" (mentioned along with liberty of conscience in §39) (*TJ*, 217; cf. *TJ*, 53, 131). If something less than lexical priority for these rights were agreed to by the parties in the OP, they might again come out from behind the veil of ignorance to discover that their fundamental interest in bodily integrity had been jeopardized by legislation implementing, for example, compulsory live-donor organ harvesting or some radically egalitarian "slavery of the talented" for the benefit of the poor (e.g., heavy head taxes) – legislation that they might be hard pressed to obey. In other cases, though, this strains-of-commitment argument appears less compelling, as Rawls himself admits in the above quotation. Consider, for example, freedom of speech. Were freedom of speech given less than lexical priority, would the speech-curbing laws that might result lead to intolerable strains of commitment? Perhaps, though the not insubstantial variation in such legislation across stable liberal democracies (e.g., laws that check pornography, obscenity, Holocaust or Armenian-genocide denial, advocacy of race and religious hatreds, etc.) suggests otherwise. Even laws that would violate *core* protections of *political* speech on virtually anyone's understanding – for instance, restrictions on advocacy of the peaceful nationalization of industry – might not cause unbearably severe commitment strains. Parties in the original position, aware of the possible benefits of allowing such restrictions (for, say, political stability or solidarity), would be unlikely to tie the hands of agents in later stages of the four-stage sequence by assigning infinite weight to these liberties vis-à-vis other social primary goods – at least not for the reasons given here.

In summary, the strains-of-commitment interpretation of the equal liberty of conscience argument provides strong support for the lexical priority of certain basic liberties (e.g., religious liberty and the rights protecting integrity of the person) but weaker support for others (e.g., moral or philosophical liberty of conscience and freedom of speech). This result may not be especially surprising: there is no reason why the psychological strains of obeying laws that encroach upon fundamental interests should be same for each of these interests – some interests, after all, might be more fundamental than others. Hence, this interpretation of the equal liberty of conscience argument cannot by itself provide the desired support for the priority of liberty. What is needed is a defense of the priority of liberty that can justify the lexical priority of *all* basic liberties, not merely the subset whose violation creates intolerable commitment strains. Fortunately, Rawls's third argument for the priority of liberty points the way toward such a defense.

## 2.3 The Hierarchy Argument

Rawls initially presents the hierarchy argument in §§26 and 82 of *Theory*. He begins in §26 by distinguishing what he calls a "highest-order interest" from the fundamental interests that I discussed in the last subsection and by linking the former to the priority of liberty:

> Very roughly the parties [in the OP] regard themselves as having a *highest-order interest* in how all their other interests, *including even their fundamental ones*, are shaped and regulated by social institutions. They do not think of themselves as inevitably bound to, or as identical with, the pursuit of any particular complex of fundamental interests that they may have at any given time, although they want the right to advance such interests . . . *Rather, free persons conceive themselves as beings who can revise and alter their final ends and who give first priority to preserving their liberty in these matters.* (*TJ*, 131–132, emphasis added)

Rawls identifies here what he later calls a "hierarchy of interests" for free persons. Our highest-order interest (or that of our OP representatives) is in shaping our other interests, including our fundamental ones, under conditions of freedom, which we therefore assign "first priority"; this interest is identical to the highest-order interest in the development and exercise of our second moral power of rationality (*CP*, 312). Our fundamental interests, including both our religious interest and our interest in integrity of the person, come second; they are best regarded as components of the higher-order interest in "protecting and advancing [our] conception of the good," as fundamental interests are likely to be preconditions or even constituents of these conceptions (*CP*, 313). Rawls spells out the implications of the above passage more clearly in §82:

> Thus the persons in the original position are moved by a certain *hierarchy of interests*. They must first secure their highest-order interest and fundamental aims (only the general form of which is known to them), and this fact is reflected in the precedence they give to liberty; the acquisition of means that enable them to advance their other desires and ends has a subordinate place. (*TJ*, 476, emphasis added)

Thus, the lexical priority of basic liberties over other social primary goods ("means that enable them to advance their other desires and ends") can be justified by a hierarchy of interests: the highest-order interest in choosing our ends in freedom takes lexical priority ("they must first secure . . .") over an interest in advancing those ends – an interest that is secured by FEO and the DP, which provide various kinds of resources (jobs, income, etc.) for this very purpose.

In short, the hierarchy argument tries to justify a hierarchy of goods (basic liberties over other social primary goods) with a hierarchy of interests (a highest-order interest in free choice of ends over an interest in advancing those ends). Notice how this argument deftly avoids the inference-fallacy objection: by asserting the *lexical* priority of our highest-order interest in the free choice of ends, Rawls is able to defend the lexical priority of the basic liberties that are its indispensable support. The hierarchy argument seems to be a promising approach to justifying the priority of liberty.

This argument also serves as one of the key defenses of the priority of liberty in *Political Liberalism* (PL, 312–314, 335).[7] Rawls argues there that our highest-order interest in the development and exercise of rationality – both as a means to our conception of the good and as a constituent of it – must be supported by a set of basic liberties, including liberty of conscience and freedom of association. Apart from noting that liberty of conscience allows us to "fall into error and make mistakes" and thereby learn and grow as rational actors, Rawls spends little time connecting the basic liberties to this highest-order interest, nor does he really explain the underlying hierarchy of interests.

Several important questions therefore arise at this point. First, what is the exact nature of this highest-order interest, and why are some basic liberties crucial for its support? Second, what justifies the asserted hierarchy of interests? To put the question more sharply: does the hierarchy argument simply kick the problem of defending the priority of liberty up one level of abstraction (from goods to interests) without actually solving it? Third, are there goods other than the basic liberties that are indispensable buttresses for our highest-order interest (e.g., literature comparing religious faiths, which is surely necessary for intelligent "free exercise") and, if so, does this fact undermine the hierarchy argument? Rawls does not adequately address any of these questions, yet they must be answered for the hierarchy argument to be considered a full success.

In the next section, I show that all of these questions can be answered within the context of Rawls's political theory. To do so, however, I must demonstrate that our highest-order interest in the development and exercise of rationality follows naturally from the Kantian commitment to autonomy that Rawls expresses in *Theory* §40, that the basic liberties are essential institutional supports for this interest, and that the priority of liberty becomes effective only if sufficient material means are available to sustain our exercise of rationality.

## 3. A Kantian Reconstruction of the Hierarchy Argument

### 3.1 Rationality as a Form of Autonomy

Rawls defines the second moral power of rationality as the "capacity to form, to revise, and rationally to pursue a conception of the good" (CP, 312). He associates the successful execution of a plan of life, which implements our conception of the good, with happiness, and he argues that the rational pursuit of it must be consistent with principles of deliberative rationality, including "the adoption of effective means to ends; the balancing of final ends by their significance for our plan of life as a whole and by the extent to which these ends cohere and support each other; and finally, the assigning of a greater weight to the more likely consequences" (*TJ*, 359–360; *CP*, 316; cf. *TJ*, §64). The formation and revision of a plan of life, on the other hand, is the creative side of the moral power of rationality. Though it involves working with our current set of aims, interests, and desires, Rawls stresses that these elements of our conception of the good are subject to rational adherence, alteration, and even rejection; in other words, the moral power of rationality makes us the ultimate authors of our identity:

> The aim of deliberation is to find that plan which best organizes our activities and influences the formation of our subsequent wants so that our aims and interests can be fruitfully combined into one scheme of conduct. Desires that tend to interfere with other ends, or which undermine the capacity for other activities, are weeded out; whereas those that are enjoyable in themselves and support other aims as well are encouraged (*TJ*, 360–361).

Far from taking the elements of our plan of life as givens, Rawls's understanding of rationality requires us to harmonize them by trimming some and nurturing others. Exercising rationality is like tending our garden: we must work with the vegetation at hand according to certain rules, but over time we can change its composition and redirect its growth to achieve particular aesthetic or utilitarian objectives. Thus, Rawls's second moral power of rationality, which unites deliberative rationality with creative self-authorship, is simply a variation on the contemporary concept of *personal* autonomy.

This self-authorship links rationality (so understood) to Kantian *moral* autonomy, which Rawls endorses in *Theory* §40. He says there that agents in the original position "must decide . . . which principles when consciously followed and acted upon in everyday life will . . . most fully reveal their independence from natural contingencies and social accident" (*TJ*, 225). Just as one aspect of our autonomy (the first moral power of reasonableness) is the distancing from our immediate desires that is involved in acting on such principles, so another aspect (the second moral power of rationality) is the less radical distancing involved in scheduling, prioritizing, tempering, and pruning these desires in accordance with a plan of life. Both moral powers are facets of our autonomy, of our ability to detach ourselves from and reflect critically upon our desires as a prelude to self-legislation, be it moral or prudential. Failing to achieve such detachment and critical reflection is acting "as though we belonged to a lower order [of animals], as though we were a creature whose first principles are decided by natural contingencies" rather than by moral law or a plan of life; such failure is a source of shame for rational beings, which shows why our interest in maintaining such rationality must never be sacrificed for the sake of other interests (*TJ*, 225).[8]

## 3.2 Basic Liberties as Indispensable Supports for Rationality

Why does this highest-order interest in rationality and its preconditions justify something as extreme as the lexical priority of the basic liberties over other social primary goods? In short, these basic liberties are the indispensable conditions for the development and exercise of rationality, which is why agents in the OP "give first priority to preserving [our] liberty in these matters" (*TJ*, 131–132). If the parties in the OP sacrificed basic liberties for the sake of lower social primary goods (i.e., the "means that enable them to advance their other desires and ends"), they would be sacrificing their highest-order interest in rationality and thereby failing to express their trustors' nature as autonomous beings (*TJ*, 476, 493).

A concise examination of the basic liberties enumerated by Rawls will indicate why they are necessary conditions for the exercise of rationality. The freedoms of speech and assembly, liberty of conscience, and freedom of thought are *directly* supportive of the creation and revision of plans of life: without secure rights to explore ideas and beliefs with others (be it in person or through various media) and consider these at our leisure, we would be unable to make informed decisions about our conception of the good. Freedom of the person (including psychological and bodily integrity), as well as the right to personal property and immunity from arbitrary arrest and seizure, are *indirectly* supportive of rationality, as they create stable and safe personal spaces for purposes of reflection and communication, without which the free design and revision of plans of life would be compromised if not crippled. Even minor restrictions on these basic liberties would threaten the highest-order interest in rationality, however slightly, and such a threat is disallowed given the absolute priority of this interest over lower concerns. Note also that lexical priority can be justified here for all basic liberties, not just a subset of them (as was the case with the strains-of-commitment interpretation of the equal liberty of conscience argument) (*TJ*, 53).[9]

In order for these basic liberties to be truly indispensable, though, it must be the case that no compensating measures can be taken to sustain our exercise of rationality if we trade off basic liberties for lower goods; otherwise, the basic liberties lack the requisite priority. The possibility and desirability of such trade-offs vary across the two categories of basic liberties. The directly supportive basic liberties are indeed indispensable, at least along some dimensions. For example, free speech is usually consistent with so-called "time, place, and manner restrictions" because compensating measures, like additional funding for relevant media or other forums, are possible. However, it is inconsistent with content controls because, by hindering the discussion of certain topics, they reduce our ability to make informed judgments regarding them and thereby illicitly restrict our exercise of rationality. Any compensating measures that are proposed would have to either subvert the original controls or aid discussion of other, uncontrolled topics, but the latter approach would be beside the point, as a broad conception of rationality requires that all topics be open for discussion. Each and every parameter of a discussion, including especially its scope, must be revisable *from within* for a discussion to be deemed autonomous; no amount of aid can remove the stain of the original intervention, which taints all subsequent discussion and forever colors any revisions to life plans that result.

The indirectly supportive basic liberties, on the other hand, are more difficult to defend as indispensable, as compensated trade-offs would surely be possible under some circumstances. For example, a modest increase in the probability of arbitrary arrest (the result of, say, a money-saving reduction in criminal-procedural protections) might be made "rationality neutral" with an across-the-board boost to media subsidies – assuming, of course, that this increased probability of arrest were uncorrelated with one's selection of discussion topics. Still, a *minimal* provision of psychological and physical security is surely required for personally autonomous creation and revision of plans of life: for example, the continual, looming threat of violent death due to civil unrest or unchecked criminality would make the full exercise of rationality difficult, even if various compensating measures were taken. Beyond mandating a basic minimum, though, the parties in the original position are not able to say much more (due to the possibility of compensated trade-offs) and must consequently defer

156

to the judgment of those later in the four-stage sequence, who will know more about their particular societies and therefore be in a better position to judge such trade-offs.

One problem with both the reconstructed hierarchy argument and its original version, as I implied at the end of the last section, is that goods other than the basic liberties are necessary to support our highest-order interest in rationality. For example, while freedom of speech is indeed essential for the creation and revision of plans of life, so are those material goods that make this freedom effective, including assembly halls, street corners, megaphones, soapboxes, etc.; much the same could be said of other basic liberties. One potential solution to this problem would be to redefine the priority of liberty so that it supported the lexical priority of basic liberties over other goods *only when those goods were not needed to uphold the highest-order interest in rationality*. I offer a more elegant solution in the following subsection. This solution has the added advantage of elucidating the meaning of Rawls's threshold condition for the application of the priority of liberty.

## 3.3 An Interpretation of the Threshold Condition for Applying the Priority of Liberty

Rawls notes on several occasions in *Theory* that the priority of liberty comes into effect only when certain conditions are realized. For example, he begins *Theory* §82 with the following observation:

> I have supposed that if the persons in the original position know that their basic liberties can be effectively exercised, they will not exchange a lesser liberty for greater economic advantages (§26). It is only when social conditions do not allow the full establishment of these rights that one can acknowledge their restriction. The equal liberties can be denied only when it is necessary to change the quality of civilization so that in due course everyone can enjoy these freedoms. The effective realization of all these liberties in a well-ordered society is the long-run tendency of the two principles and rules of priority when they are consistently followed under reasonably favorable conditions. (*TJ*, 474–475)

His other discussions of the threshold condition in *Theory* provide little additional information, though later in §82 he adds a "degree of fulfillment of needs and material wants" to the social conditions that must be met before the priority of liberty can come into effect (*TJ*, 476; cf. *TJ*, 54–55, 132; and *PL*, 7).[10]

Rawls's description of the threshold condition can be interpreted in at least three different ways, each of which is inclusive of (and therefore more stringent than) the ones preceding it:

1  *Formal threshold*   Before the priority of liberty can apply, a society must have achieved a level of wealth sufficient for it to maintain a legal system with courts, police, etc., that can define and protect the basic liberties of citizens within the bounds of the rule of law.
2  *Weak substantive threshold*   Before the priority of liberty can apply, a society must have achieved a level of wealth sufficient for it to allow its citizens to engage in the meaningful *formation* of life plans. For example, citizens must have access to media, public forums, and schools and must have sufficient leisure time to make use of these resources and reflect on their plans.

3  *Strong substantive threshold*  Before the priority of liberty can apply, a society must
   have achieved a level of wealth sufficient for it to allow its citizens to engage in the
   meaningful *advancement* of life plans. For example, citizens must have access to professional training, start-up funds for businesses, grants for artistic, literary, and scientific
   projects, etc.

Two implications of the reconstructed hierarchy argument are clear. First, at least the formal
threshold must be met before the priority of liberty can apply: the priority of liberty would
be meaningless in a society that could not even establish the basic liberties themselves due
to social and economic conditions. All arguments for the priority of liberty, including the
reconstructed one on offer here, must take feasibility into account. Second, the strong
substantive threshold must be ruled out. Once the weak substantive threshold is met, our
highest-order interest in rationality can be fully satisfied, as all of its necessary conditions
(including the basic liberties and any other social primary goods essential for its exercise) are
then in place. Any threshold more stringent than this one, including the strong substantive
threshold, in effect sacrifices the basic liberties and the highest-order interest they protect for
the sake of advancing, not forming, our plans of life, but such sacrifice is forbidden by the
reconstructed hierarchy argument. In sum, no threshold less stringent than the formal one
or more stringent than the weak substantive one can be justified by this argument for the
priority of liberty.

Now consider the choice between the formal and weak substantive thresholds: can the
reconstructed hierarchy argument justify violations of the priority of liberty if needed to
move society to a level of wealth where the formation of life plans is meaningful? Once we
recognize that the only function of the basic liberties is to advance our highest-order interest
in rationality, the answer becomes clear: if the violation of the basic liberties is the best means
to advance the interest that they serve, then the priority of liberty must be temporarily set
aside. To insist upon the imposition of the priority of liberty under such circumstances would
be to fetishize the basic liberties. I thus conclude that the reconstructed hierarchy argument
requires a weak substantive threshold for the application of the priority of liberty.

Note how this interpretation of the threshold condition solves the problem discussed at
the end of the last subsection. Rather than modifying the definition of the priority of liberty,
we can simply stipulate that its implementation be delayed until all social primary goods
necessary for the advancement of the highest-order interest in rationality can be made available. Once this threshold is reached, however, basic liberties can no longer be sacrificed for
lower social primary goods. Thus, the reconstructed hierarchy argument, in addition to offering a strong defense of the priority of liberty, clarifies the meaning of the threshold condition
for its application.

We have now completed the reconstruction of the hierarchy argument. At the end of the
last section we asked a number of questions about the original argument, all of which have
now been answered. We have explicated our highest-order interest in preserving both rationality and the conditions of its exercise, which include basic liberties first and foremost. We
have seen that the exalted position that this interest holds in our hierarchy of interests is
justified by rationality's intimate connection to Kantian moral autonomy. Finally, we have
learned that the contribution of social primary goods other than basic liberties to this highest-order interest does not weaken the argument for the priority of liberty but rather strengthens our understanding of the threshold condition for its application.

## 4. The Special Status of the Political Liberties

Careful readers will notice that I have avoided discussing the basic *political* liberties, including the rights to vote and hold public office. I have done so because the hierarchy argument does not provide a compelling defense of their lexical priority, as they are not necessary conditions for the development and exercise of our rationality but rather means for pursuing one kind of rationally chosen end, *viz.* political engagement. If the political liberties are instrumentally valuable in the defense of the other basic liberties, however, we can build a second-order defense of their lexical priority as an extension of the hierarchy argument: if the rights to vote and hold public office are essential protections for the other basic liberties, because they empower citizens to replace rulers who abuse those liberties, then they must also receive lexical priority as the necessary conditions of the necessary conditions (the *civil* liberties) of the development and exercise of our rationality. Rawls constructs such an argument himself in *Theory* §37 and associates it with a certain strand of liberal theory, exemplified by John Locke, Benjamin Constant, and Isaiah Berlin (*TJ*, 176–177, 200–205; *PL*, 4–5, 206, 299).

Such a tight connection between political and civil liberties seems implausible, however. For example, what if in each democratic election 10 percent of the population were randomly selected and given the right to vote, whereas the other 90 percent were disenfranchised. If the selection process were truly random, then this reform would be unlikely to threaten civil liberties: expectationally, at least, the same interests would be represented, so there is little reason to think that politicians would be unleashed to violate the liberties of disenfranchised. The cost savings (in terms of the saved opportunity cost of time involved in voting, etc.) might be large. Would such an exchange of political liberty for socioeconomic benefits be ruled out by the above instrumental argument for the priority of political liberties? So long as civil liberties were protected just as well under the new scheme, it is difficult to see why it would fail to pass muster. Even if reforms of this sort diminished protection for civil liberties, so long as compensating expenditures were made to return us to the prior level of protection (e.g., diverting some of the savings into legal advocacy for the disenfranchised) the instrumental argument would have to permit diminution of political liberties.

I will sketch here an alternative, more promising approach to defending the priority of the political liberties, one with revisionist implications for Rawls's theory.[11] If the civil liberties are necessary for the pursuit of our highest-order interest in rationality (the second moral power), as the hierarchy argument maintains, perhaps the political liberties are necessary for the pursuit of our other highest-order interest, reasonableness (first moral power). In order to develop and exercise our sense of justice and our moral autonomy more broadly, we will need to provide them with an institutional medium for growth and expression. Just as moral autonomy can be understood on Kantian grounds as the legislation of morality for a kingdom of ends, so in the context of right it can be understood as participation in republican self-government, be it directly (as a legislator or bureaucrat crafting laws or regulations, respectively) or indirectly (as a voter choosing between the legislative programs of parties and candidates). Through such participation, as Rawls rightly says, we can "enlarge [our] intellectual and moral sensibilities" and exercise them in the creation of fair and impartial law for our society; political liberty, however, is not simply a means to the development and utilization of our capacity for moral autonomy, but also in some sense *is* that capacity expressed in political-institutional form (*TJ*, 206).

If such a defense of the priority of political liberty could be sustained, however, it would arguably have the revisionist implication of prioritizing political over civil liberties, contrary to Rawls's claim that they are "of equal weight . . . with neither externally imposed on the other" (*PL*, 412). Rawls himself maintains that reasonableness frames and absolutely limits rationality and that the political liberties are grounded on the first whereas several civil ones (e.g., liberty of conscience, freedom of association generally) are grounded on the second (*CP*, 317, 319; *PL*, 52, 334–335). If so, then the first moral power and its allied political liberties take priority over the second moral power and its associated civil liberties. Rawls already assigns a special weight to the political liberties (e.g., by protecting their "fair value" and emphasizing their "distinctive place" among the basic liberties); such a defense of their priority *within* Rawls's first principle of justice would make his theory more democratic than some scholars (e.g., Jürgen Habermas) have taken it to be (*PL*, 327; Habermas 1995).

## 5. Conclusion: Implications for the American Practice of Civil Libertarianism

This reconstructed hierarchy defense of the priority of liberty has significant implications for American-style civil libertarianism, especially as reflected in First Amendment jurisprudence. Consider, for example, two strands of such jurisprudence: the line of Establishment Clause cases starting in the 1960s and the string of "incitement" cases ending in *Brandenburg v. Ohio* (1969). The US Supreme Court initiated stricter enforcement of the Establishment Clause of the First Amendment ("Congress shall pass no law respecting an establishment of religion") in the early 1960s under the leadership of Chief Justice Earl Warren. A long line of decisions – including *Engel v. Vitale* (1962), *Abington School District v. Schempp* (1963), *Stone v. Graham* (1980), and *Wallace v. Jaffree* (1985) – gradually eliminated most religious content from public-school instruction. Mandatory school prayers, Bible readings, postings of the Ten Commandments, and voluntary school prayers were successively found unconstitutional. State laws either banning the teaching of evolution or mandating the teaching of "creation science" or "intelligent design" in public schools were also overturned. Finally, in *Lemon v. Kurtzman* (1971), the Supreme Court promulgated a strict three-prong test for determining the constitutionality of policies challenged under the Establishment Clause. This test has been used *inter alia* to overturn laws offering supplementary salaries to parochial-school teachers and other forms of direct economic aid to religious schools (as opposed to *indirect* aid via parentally targeted vouchers, for example, which was found constitutional in *Zelman v. Simmons-Harris*, 2002).

The string of "incitement" cases, dealing with the punishment of persons who advocate illegal conduct, begins with *Schenck v. United States* (1919). In this case, Justice Oliver Wendell Holmes articulated his famous "clear and present danger" test for incitement, which established a low threshold for the punishment of people advocating illegal conduct (in this case, resistance to the draft during wartime). A succeeding series of cases that modified this threshold (both up and down) culminated in the 1969 decision of *Brandenburg v. Ohio*, which established an extremely high threshold for punishment of incitement: "the constitutional guarantees of free speech and press do not permit a State to forbid or proscribe advocacy of the use of force or of law violation except where such advocacy is directed to inciting or producing imminent lawless action and is likely to produce such action." In practice, this decision has effectively ended punishment for incitement, thoroughly insulating those who advocate violence – even revolutionary violence.

What characterizes both of these lines of cases is the evolution of an uncompromising devotion to liberal neutrality: in the Establishment Clause cases, the Court sought to bar states from using their authority over minors to promote religious belief, whereas in the "incitement" cases, it in effect legalized the advocacy of sedition and other forms of lawless violence. What could justify such extremism in defense of (basic) liberty? The Supreme Court itself has offered many justifications, but the kind most likely to succeed is one grounded upon the inviolability of individual autonomy in matters of belief – like the justification provided by the reconstructed hierarchy argument. Only this kind of justification can provide a secure and permanent defense of the basic liberties against all political contingencies. All other justifications are ultimately held hostage to what Rawls has called "the calculus of social interests": because they are not based on the lexical priority of liberty (at the level of political principle (original position) rather than constitutional practice (constitutional/legislative stages)), their defense of basic liberties is always contingent on particular historical conditions, such as the likelihood of legislative overreach or abuse, the nature of the political culture, and the attractiveness of trading off certain basic liberties for some highly valued social good (e.g., solidarity or stability) (*TJ*, 4; *TJ*, §31). The reconstructed hierarchy argument does not hinge on such empirical circumstances: it offers a robust defense of the basic liberties that (at least when "reasonably favorable conditions" obtain) secure both them and the highest-order interest that they protect – *viz.* the development and exercise of autonomy, both personal and moral – from the depredations of eudaimonism and political expediency.

# Notes

Figure 8.1 is reproduced from my *Reconstructing Rawls: The Kantian Foundations of Justice as Fairness* (University Park: Pennsylvania State University Press, 2011), by permission.

1   The allowable sacrifices of liberty for liberty can take several forms. First, some basic liberties might be sacrificed for the sake of others: for example, free political speech (in the form of campaign expenditures) might be curtailed in order to protect the fair value of core political liberties. Second, a basic liberty might be limited for its own sake: for example, so-called "time, place, and manner" regulations on speech may help to preserve the value of speech itself by making its exercise across persons mutually consistent (by means of, say, *Robert's Rules of Order*) – see *PL*, 341. Third, a basic liberty might be *temporarily* sacrificed if doing so is a condition for its own eventual effective exercise: for example, core political liberties might be sacrificed if this were strictly necessary to increase GDP and thereby make adequate economic resources available for their effective exercise. This last variety of sacrifice falls under the rubric of nonideal theory, discussed in *TJ*, §39.

2   On his ambivalence toward the priority of FEO, see *JF*, 163 n44; on his ambivalence toward the DP, see *TJ*, xiv.

3   See Arrow 1973; Barry 1973; Daniels 1989; Hart 1989; Keat and Miller 1974; Shue 1975.

4   Rawls provides an additional argument in the original edition of *A Theory of Justice* (*TJ* 1971, 542–543) but retracts it in *Political Liberalism* (*PL*, 371 n84) because of its inconsistency with the hierarchy argument.

5   There are other determinants of self-respect, of course, some of which are private and idiosyncratic (e.g., indelible psychological traits resulting from early childhood socialization).

6   Rawls might reply here that reactions to strains of commitment can take both strong and weak forms and that the power of my examples derives from only considering the strong form. The strong form is for us to become "sullen and resentful," leading perhaps to "violent action in protest against our condition," while the weak form is for us to become "withdrawn and cynical," unable to "affirm the principles of justice in our thought and conduct . . . Though we are not hostile or rebellious, those principles are not ours and fail to engage our moral sensibility" (JF, 128). So Rawls might admit that violent resentment is indeed more probable in the religious case but still argue that cynical withdrawal is a real possibility in all of them. One can admit the force of this reply, though, and still point out that the *overall* strains in the religious case (strong plus weak) are more severe than in either the philosophical or moral cases (weak only), and this is all that I need for the above critique to do its work. All principles of justice will create *some* strains, however minor, so the strains-of-commitment argument must be understood only to rule out candidate principles that would generate especially severe, even intolerable strains – and principles that deny lexical priority to liberty of religious conscience qualify, as the long and bloody history of European Christianity amply demonstrates.

7   Though Rawls does not try to assess the "relative weights" of the various grounds he offers for the priority of liberty, he does suggest that those "connected with the capacity for a conception of the good are more familiar, perhaps because they seem more straightforward and, offhand, of greater weight"; the hierarchy argument is one such ground (PL, 324).

8   For a fuller discussion of how these two facets of autonomy are related, see Taylor 2011, ch. 2.

9   This conceptual distinction between directly and indirectly supportive basic liberties is implied by PL, 335.

10  Rawls later adds that "these conditions are determined by a society's culture, its traditions and acquired skill in running institutions, and its level of economic advance (which need not be especially high), and no doubt by other things as well" (PL, 297). Finally, he discusses these conditions a bit more in *The Law of Peoples*, §15, especially with respect to the three guidelines for assistance to "burdened societies" (LP, 106–112).

11  For a fuller discussion, see Taylor 2011, ch. 3.

## Works by Rawls, with Abbreviations

*Collected Papers* (CP), ed. Samuel Freeman. Cambridge, MA: Harvard University Press, 1999.

*Justice as Fairness* (JF), ed. Erin Kelly. Cambridge, MA: Harvard University Press, 2001.

*The Law of Peoples, with "The Idea of Public Reason Revisited"* (LP). Cambridge, MA: Harvard University Press, 1999.

*Political Liberalism* (PL), expanded edn. New York: Columbia University Press, 2005.

*A Theory of Justice* (TJ 1971), Original edn. Cambridge, MA: Harvard University Press, 1971.

*A Theory of Justice* (TJ), rev. edn. Cambridge, MA: Harvard University Press, 1999.

## Other References

Arneson, Richard (2000) "Rawls Versus Utilitarianism in Light of *Political Liberalism*." In Victoria Davion and Clark Wolf (eds), *The Idea of a Political Liberalism*. Oxford: Rowman & Littlefield.

Arrow, Kenneth (1973) "Some Ordinalist-Utilitarian Notes on Rawls' Theory of Justice." *Journal of Philosophy* 70: 245–263.

Barry, Brian (1973) "John Rawls and the Priority of Liberty." *Philosophy and Public Affairs* 2: 274–290.

Daniels, Norman (1989) "Equal Liberty and Unequal Worth of Liberty." In Norman Daniels (ed.), *Reading Rawls: Critical Studies on Rawls' A Theory of Justice*. Stanford: Stanford University Press.

Habermas, Jürgen (1995) "Reconciliation through the Public Use of Reason: Remarks on John Rawls's Political Liberalism." *Journal of Philosophy* 92: 109–131.

Hart, H.L.A. (1989) "Rawls on Liberty and Its Priority." In Norman Daniels (ed.), *Reading Rawls: Critical Studies on Rawls' A Theory of Justice*. Stanford: Stanford University Press.

Keat, Russell and Miller, David (1974) "Understanding Justice." *Political Theory*, 2: 3–31.

Shue, Henry (1975) "Liberty and Self-Respect." *Ethics* 85: 195–203.

Taylor, Robert S. (2011) *Reconstructing Rawls: The Kantian Foundations of Justice as Fairness*. University Park: Pennsylvania State University Press.

# 9

# Applying Justice as Fairness to Institutions

## COLIN M. MACLEOD

## Introduction

A great deal of Rawlsian scholarship has been devoted to analyzing the substantive principles of justice articulated by Rawls, the contractualist methodology employed in the justification of these principles and the associated conception of political philosophy reflected in the idea of political liberalism and the doctrine of public reason. Less attention has been focused on the specific character of the institutional arrangements that fidelity to justice as fairness requires in contemporary contexts. From one point of view, this is surprising because Rawls treats the basic structure of society as the subject matter of justice. The principles of justice are intended to guide evaluations of existing institutional arrangements, legislation and social policies and to help in the assessment of proposals for the reform of unjust or undemocratic institutions. So one might reasonably expect detailed proposals from those sympathetic to Rawls's theory about the kinds of institutional arrangements that need to be put in place in order to realize or at least feasibly approximate Rawls's principles. Yet despite its standing in political philosophy as the most important conception of justice developed to date, Rawls's theory has exercised relatively little influence over practical debates about the design and implementation of political institutions and social policies.[1]

However, from another point of view the inattention to the implications of Rawls's theory for institutional design is understandable for a number of reasons. First, the debates about the character and soundness of Rawls's theory remain vibrant and rich. So it is natural that they consume a great deal of intellectual energy in a way that, in practice, diverts attention away from sustained and detailed consideration of the institutional implications of Rawls's principles of justice. Second, Rawls's own remarks about institutional design and social policy are, for the most part, quite abstract and Rawls rarely comments in his published work on specific institutional proposals or social controversies in much detail.[2] Finally, determining what fidelity to Rawls's principles requires in any given polity is an extraordinarily complex matter that involves careful consideration of elements of social theory, history, economics,

*A Companion to Rawls*, First Edition. Edited by Jon Mandle and David A. Reidy.
© 2014 John Wiley & Sons, Inc. Published 2016 by John Wiley & Sons, Inc.

and psychology. As we shall see, Rawls's theory is compatible with a form of institutional pluralism: the precise character the institutions needed to realize justice can vary depending on the social, historical, geographical and demographic features of different political communities.

I cannot provide a detailed blueprint of the institutions and social policies needed to realize Rawls's conception of justice. However, Rawls's work is certainly rich enough to identify both an interesting approach for thinking about institutional design and for sketching the main contours of just institutions. Nonetheless, my approach will be selective and I will focus only on issues concerning the realization of justice in the domestic realm. I will not take up Rawls's controversial views about global justice and the kinds of institutions that should regulate relations among "peoples." Although my analysis is largely expository, it does have a critical dimension: it seeks to challenge the idea that Rawls's theory supplies the ideological foundation for the basic political, economic, educational and social institutions of contemporary liberal capitalist states.

Rawls is sometimes interpreted as offering an insufficiently critical perspective on the basic institutional arrangements that characterize contemporary liberal democratic states. On this view, fidelity to Rawls's principles of justice requires only relatively minor reforms to the liberal welfare state and democratic processes, and only modest regulation of capitalist modes of production and distribution. This view is, however, erroneous. It gives insufficient attention to the many respects in which the basic institutions of contemporary liberal states fail to harmonize with Rawls's principles of justice. Although he did not emphasize it in *A Theory of Justice*, Rawls believes justice as fairness is probably best realized through the establishment of a property-owning democracy.[3] Rawls holds that both laissez-faire capitalism and state socialism with a command economy fail to respect basic liberties and fair equality of opportunity. He quickly dismisses them as serious contenders for a model of just institutions. More importantly, Rawls expressly rejects the idea that a capitalist welfare state can be faithful to his principles. Although a capitalist welfare state and a property-owning democracy permit private ownership in the means of production, and both supply all citizens with a decent minimum standard of living, only the latter requires ownership of productive resources to be widely dispersed among citizens. Moreover, the institutions of a property-owning democracy do much more to empower citizen participation in public life than a capitalist welfare state. Finally, a property-owning democracy is directly oriented to supplying the social and material conditions in which all citizens can participate in society as free and equal persons with a robust sense of self-respect.

In this essay, I consider key ways in which fidelity to Rawls's liberal principles of justice requires significant, and in some cases, radical reforms to liberal democratic institutions. I begin with an overview of Rawls's four-stage sequence account of how to apply justice as fairness to institutions. The sequence reflects Rawls broader contractualist commitments and serves as a methodical proposal about how citizens in a civil society, concerned to achieve justice, should deliberate about different facets of the institutional realization of justice as fairness. Against this background, I then consider some of the institutional implications of the equal basic liberties principle, fair equality of opportunity and the difference principle. I shall treat these three principles[4] and the special lexical ordering of them by Rawls as comprising the substantive content of justice as fairness.

I will focus on four facets of institutional design: (1) How should basic democratic institutions and processes be structured so as to realize the fair value of the basic political liberties and to give effect to the doctrine of public reason? (2) What kinds of educational and health institutions are needed to secure fair equality of opportunity? (3) How do principles of justice apply to the family and to what extent do children's entitlement to an upbringing that facilitates development of the moral powers constrain parental authority over children? (4) What implications does the difference principle have for the structure of a market economy? I address these questions with some attention to contemporary political controversies about democracy, education, health, and government involvement in the economy. The general theme of the analysis is that genuinely liberal institutions are dramatically different than the institutions that currently masquerade as liberal. The institutions of a property-owning democracy are much more democratic and much more egalitarian than those of even a generous and well-functioning liberal welfare state.

## Institutional Design, the Four-Stage Sequence and Pluralism

The task of determining what institutions and social policies serve justice is extremely complex. We need to determine first what the basic principles of justice are, and second how to apply them to the specific social, historical and political circumstances we face.[5] To make the task of addressing these challenges more manageable, Rawls suggests that we can approach the application of justice to institutions in four stages. In each stage the heuristic device of the veil of ignorance is employed to guide our deliberations, but the epistemic constraints it imposes are progressively relaxed as we work our way through the different stages. It is crucial to emphasize that the four-stage sequence is not advanced as a practical proposal about the way in which an actual political convention among real citizens might be run in order to select a constitution, a form of government or essential pieces of legislation. Rather the sequence is meant to articulate a fruitful and normatively appropriate perspective from which to evaluate the justness of constitutional arrangements, democratic procedures, legislation, and decisions made by public officials such as judges and civil servants. At each stage in the sequence, citizens address a dimension of the general problem of devising a just basic structure for a given society by imagining themselves as occupying different roles – for example, as representatives to a constitutional convention, legislators, or judges – that are appropriate for the facet of the basic structure that is under consideration.

In order to apply principles of justice to institutions we need: (a) the fundamental principles that animate just institutions; (b) a constitutional framework that sets out a scheme for the protection of basic rights and specifies the democratic procedures through which legitimate legislation is created; (c) a conception of the kind of legislation and social policy that can secure those dimensions of justice not secured by constitutional mechanisms; and (d) a guide for the making of sound decisions by the public officials charged with interpretation and application of constitutional norms and laws.

The first stage, the *basic principles stage*,[6] is the most fundamental as it involves the identification of the principles of justice the application of which to different aspects of the basic structure is addressed at subsequent stages. Here citizens imagine themselves as parties in the original position behind the full veil of ignorance. It is at this stage that the three principles, noted above, that comprise justice as fairness are identified and justified.

The second stage is the *constitutional convention* where citizens view themselves as delegates to a convention that seeks to determine what constitutional framework can best secure

justice as fairness given general facts about the society in which they live. This involves specifying what Rawls calls the "constitutional essentials" – the elements of a society's political
basic structure that are most important and which may be enshrined in fundamental constitutional documents.[7] At this stage, the epistemic constraints imposed by the veil of ignorance are relaxed somewhat and the choice of constitutional structures is made in light of
information about the society's "natural circumstances and resources, its level of economic
advancement and political culture and so on" (*TJ*, 173). However, the participants in the
imagined constitutional convention remain ignorant about "their own social position, their
place in the distribution of natural attributes, or their conception of the good" (*TJ*, 172).
Rawls assumes that deliberation at this stage will focus on identifying the core institutional
arrangements necessary to secure the equal basic liberties principle. Thus the hypothetical
delegates at this stage mainly address the ways in which the "fundamental liberties of the
person and liberty of conscience and freedom of thought" should be afforded institutional
recognition and protection.[8] The basic democratic political structures for fairly regulating the
acquisition and exercise of political power are also determined at this stage.

Despite the strong focus on the basic liberties principle at this stage, there is some indeterminacy about the degree to which deliberation at this stage should be sensitive to fair equality
of opportunity and the difference principle. Rawls denies that mechanisms for realizing the
difference principle should be treated as a constitutional essential. However, he allows that a
social minimum (i.e., a basic level of economic support to which all citizens are entitled) is a
constitutional essential and the rationale for the social minimum is linked, in part, to the
difference principle. Similarly, Rawls allows that some dimensions of fair equality of opportunity must be treated as constitutional essentials (*JF*, 47). Moreover, what should be considered a constitutional essential may appropriately vary with features of the background
political culture and history of a society. For instance, a society seeking to overcome the
legacy of slavery, Jim Crow and legally sanctioned forms of racial discrimination may have
reason to treat fair equality of opportunity as having greater constitutional urgency than a
society that does not have such a history. Despite this indeterminacy, we can view the constitutional convention stage as providing a foundation around which other elements of a just
political structure are to be constructed.

Once the essential features of a constitutional structure that secure the basic liberties of
citizens and provide good democratic procedures for creating legislation have been determined, we move to *the legislative stage*. Here the justice of laws and social policies that will
shape the basic structure of society are assessed from the perspective of representative legislators who have detailed information about social theory and the history and present social
circumstances of their society. But, as with the first two stages, the legislators lack particular
knowledge about themselves. The hypothetical legislators determine what laws and policies
fulfill the requirements of fair equality of opportunity and the difference principle in ways
consistent with the basic constitutional structure settled upon at the previous stage. Due in
part to the complexity of social and economic issues with which parties must contend at this
stage, Rawls anticipates that it will be easier to secure agreement about suitable arrangements for the constitutional essentials than to determine what economic and social policies
best secure fair equality of opportunity and the difference principle.

The fourth stage in the sequence is the *administrative application stage* (as I will call it) in
which we determine how best to apply the rules, norms and procedures identified at the previous stages to particular cases. Here the restrictions on information imposed by the veil of

ignorance are removed entirely and judges, administrators and citizens determine what fidelity to the laws, policies and procedures that have already been identified requires in particular cases.

Rawls's extension of the original position via the four-stage sequence proceeds against the background of three kinds of pluralism that are worth distinguishing. First, there is what I shall label *doctrinal pluralism*. Rawls, especially in his later work, argues that a theory of justice must grapple with the fact that citizens can be expected to hold a wide variety of "reasonable religious and philosophical conceptions of the world" (*JF*, 3). Rawls believes there is no prospect of establishing to the satisfaction of all reasonable people which of these conceptions is true. He also holds that the basic structure of a just society can be determined without assessing the relative merits of rival reasonable comprehensive conceptions. The principles of justice must be ones that can win the endorsement of reasonable citizens who are jointly committed to societal institutions that facilitate mutually beneficial cooperation among free and equal persons. Rawls contends that the original position under the full veil of ignorance provides a compelling strategy for identifying the principles of justice that can be endorsed by all in the wake of this kind of doctrinal pluralism.

Second, there is *interpretative pluralism*. This is the idea that even when there is agreement on the basic principles of justice, there can be reasonable differences of opinion as to what institutions and policies are most likely to realize the demands of justice. For instance, people may share the conviction that income and wealth should be distributed in accordance with the difference principle, but they may disagree about whether a given tax scheme will be to the greatest advantage of the least advantaged. Our imperfect understanding of various complex social phenomena (e.g., economic behavior, moral psychology, and the social determinants of health) will often provide the basis for competing interpretations of what institutions and policies are most faithful to basic principles of justice. As noted above, Rawls thinks there is likely to be more scope for reasonable disagreement about which arrangements fulfill the demands of the difference principle and fair equality of opportunity than there is concerning the constitutional essentials that focus on the basic liberties and core democratic procedures.

Third, there is *circumstantial pluralism* that consists in the fact that there is wide variation in the demographic, sociological, geographical and historical circumstances in which different people may try to implement principles of justice. Circumstantial pluralism means that we should not expect there to be a single set of institutional arrangements that are most appropriate from the point of view of justice. For example, in a geographically large, multilingual, and multiethnic state, principles of justice might be best served by a system of federalism with a constitutionally entrenched charter of basic rights that is enforced by courts with strong powers of judicial review. By contrast, a nonfederal state without a constitutionally entrenched bill of rights might serve justice better in a small linguistically homogeneous state with a strong history of parliamentary democracy. In some historical settings, a written constitution that provides the framework for a republican form of democracy with a sharp division of powers between legislative, judicial and executive branches of government might be most suitable. In other settings, Westminster style parliamentary democracy might be more appropriate. Even though Rawls developed his theory in the context of the specifically American form of constitutionalism with which he was most familiar, there is no basis for assuming justice as fairness itself mandates a broadly American constitutional structure.

Rawls intends his account of the four-stage sequence for the application of the principles of justice to be sensitive to doctrinal, interpretative, and circumstantial pluralism. However, it is important to realize that Rawls does not accept pluralism about the basic principles of justice themselves. For the purposes of addressing the problem of institutional design, he rejects *justice pluralism* – the view that there are a variety of different and perhaps irreconcilable principles of justice that can be appealed to in the design of institutions and the choice of social policies. The point of the four-stage sequence is to provide guidance in the application of the principles that are selected in the original position and which constitute the basic normative substance of justice as fairness. At the constitutional, legislative, and administrative stages, Rawls does not think we should appeal to rival theories or principles of justice in deciding how best to design institutions and social policy.[9] Justice as fairness is not to be balanced against competing accounts of just institutions. There is, for instance, no room to allow utilitarian, libertarian or perfectionist conceptions of justice to influence deliberations about constitutional essentials. There is, of course, room for dispute about whether the original position provides a suitable device for identifying principles of justice and whether all reasonable citizens (who hold diverse comprehensive views) should endorse justice as fairness. But I will bracket such questions and consider what fidelity to the principles of justice as fairness implies for social and political institutions.

## The Basic Liberties and Democratic Institutions

Circumstantial and interpretative pluralism mean that the precise features of a property-owning democracy suitable for different societies can vary. However, we can treat some general features of a property-owning democracy as illuminating necessary features of just institutions. Three political dimensions of a property-owning democracy are worth noting at the outset. First, the democratic political structures provide special protection for the basic liberties. Rawls thinks this requires constitutional limits on the power of democratic majorities on the content of legislation. The outcome of procedurally fair democratic votes cannot legitimize curtailing the rights of political speech, political participation or freedom of conscience of a minority. Rawls favors a constitutional democracy in which there are special protections of the basic liberties over a merely procedural democracy in which legitimate democratic decisions are simply the function of the fair aggregation of votes. Second, political institutions must ensure that all citizens have fair access to meaningful participation in democratic decision-making. Formal protection of the basic political liberties is not sufficient to secure what Rawls calls the *fair value* of these liberties. Third, Rawls endorses a deliberative conception of democracy in which citizens and their representatives reason with one another and seek to justify political proposals via a conception of public reason all can accept. This means social and educational institutions must prepare citizens for participation in democratic politics where this involves the capacity and temperament to give and take public reasons in public political discourse.

Rawls is acutely aware of how interaction among political, economic and social institutions is relevant to the achievement of justice. He recognizes, for instance, that formal constitutional guarantees of basic political liberties are not sufficient to fulfill the requirements of the equal basic liberties principle. Opportunities for meaningful participation in democratic politics as free and equal citizens have crucial social and material conditions. The economic power of some citizens cannot be permitted to exclude or marginalize the participation in democratic processes of other less advantaged citizens. Similarly, educational institutions must prepare all citizens for meaningful democratic activity and not just prepare them for entry into the labor market. A property-owning democracy thus has many different interlocking facets that can be expected to work in concert in order to secure justice.

The idea that certain political liberties have a special status in democracy and merit special constitutional recognition and protection is, of course, a familiar one and is embraced, in one form or another, by most contemporary liberal democracies.[10] Rawls attaches special attention to the protection of freedom of speech and conscience and he is skeptical about content-based restrictions on political, academic, and artistic speech. These liberties have special importance for Rawls because they are closely connected to the exercise and development of the two moral powers – the capacity for a conception of the good and the sense of justice – that lie at the heart of Rawls's conception of free and equal persons. Commercial speech, by contrast, is much less constitutionally significant because it is less intimately connected with exercise of the moral powers of citizens. Rawls even allows that restrictions on advertising that does not contain useful, accurate information about products are acceptable.

Less familiar are the policies and institutions needed to secure the *fair value* of the basic political liberties. Rawls notes that "historically one of the main defects of constitutional government has been the failure to ensure the fair value of political liberty" (*TJ*, 198). Securing the fair value of political liberties has two main dimensions: eliminating unfair domination of politics by social class, and facilitating the real possibility of meaningful political participation by all citizens. First, institutions must be structured so as to ensure that political processes cannot be dominated or effectively controlled by powerful economic elites. For instance, the media should not be owned and controlled, as it currently is in many Western states, by a small number of wealthy media barons who may have narrow ideological objectives. The concentration of media ownership permits elites unfairly to set and control the agenda of political debate. It also leads to the exclusion, distortion and marginalization of pertinent political voices and ideas. Ownership of media organizations needs to be strongly regulated so as to avoid domination of the political process by powerful vested interests. Similarly, private economic interests should not be permitted to dominate electoral processes simply by outspending opponents on advertising or by making the very entry into politics prohibitively expensive for all but the wealthy (or those backed by the wealthy). So the fair value of political liberties almost certainly requires both public financing of elections and sharp restrictions on campaign financing.[11]

The absence of domination of political processes by the wealthy or social elites is not sufficient to realize the fair value of political liberty. Ordinary citizens also need the time, opportunity and wherewithal to engage in democratic activity. Ignorance, ill-health, poverty and oppressive social norms (e.g., those expressed in pervasive racist, sexist, or homophobic attitudes) can all disrupt the fair value of political liberty. So all citizens must have ready access to educational institutions that will equip them with a good understanding of political institutions and democratic processes. Education must also ensure that citizens have skills in accessing and assessing information about political issues. Moreover, given Rawls's commitment to deliberative democracy, education must provide citizens with an understanding of and sensitivity to public reason. Rawlsian civic education is oriented to preparing citizens not to press their own narrow interests in political competition but rather to articulate reasonable justifications for policies that are commensurate with basic justice and which all (reasonable) citizens can accept.

Rawls also acknowledges that appropriate democratic education involves the cultivation of a type of civic virtue (PL, 143–144). Citizens must not only have adequate opportunities to participate in democratic politics, they should also be motivated to do so. Rawls views the encouragement of widespread, vigorous and active participation by citizens in democratic politics as compatible with the tradition of classical republicanism in which the cultivation of civic virtue plays a crucial role in protecting democratic institutions from domination by powerful elites. However, Rawls is careful to distinguish the form of civic virtue he endorses from the variety favored by civic humanism in which participation in politics is integral to the leading of a good life. For Rawls, civic humanism rests on a contentious Aristotelian view of the good that citizens can reasonably reject. Participation in politics may indeed be a great good for some citizens, but for Rawls the rationale for fostering a commitment to engage in democratic politics does not depend on the idea that political activity is necessary to full self-realization. Rather the justification for encouraging political participation lies in the instrumental role that widespread participation plays in sustaining just institutions.

We can now see how the constitutional essentials which are determined at the first stage, with its focus on the equal basic liberties principle, go well beyond the basic rights protected by liberal welfare states. Adequate protection of the basic liberties and especially the fair value of political liberties requires much more than formal constitutional guarantees of basic rights of the sort common in contemporary liberal democracies.[12] Democratic majorities must not only be prevented from limiting the free exercise of basic liberties by minorities but meaningful access to and participation in democratic processes must be secured for all citizens on an equal basis. This requires that "citizens similarly gifted and motivated have roughly an equal chance of influencing the government's policy and attaining positions of authority irrespective of their economic and social class" (PL, 358).

Rawls believes that the protection of the basic liberties is more important than the realization of the other principles of justice. But he also expects that it will be easier to secure agreement about the institutions required to protect the basic liberties and the fair value of the political liberties than to achieve agreement at the legislative stage on the arrangements needed to secure fair equality of opportunity and the difference principle. However, this does not mean that the protection of the basic liberties can proceed without attention to issues about the distribution of income, wealth, and health and educational resources. A social minimum that not only meets the basic needs of citizens but also facilitates meaningful development and exercise of the moral powers is a constitutional essential. Similarly, as we shall see, the fair value of political liberty cannot be realized without the provision of universal health care and excellent education that is oriented toward equal cultivation of the moral powers of citizens. In many ways the distinction between matters addressed at the constitutional and legislative stages is not sharp.

Judged solely from the perspective of the constitutional stage where attention is on institutions suitable for protection of the basic liberties, most contemporary liberal welfare states are grossly unjust. In these societies, access to democratic processes is highly constrained by class, gender and race. Moneyed elites control the media and shape the character of political debate to suit their ideological interests. Educational institutions frequently do not prepare citizens with knowledge and critical reasoning skills needed for meaningful participation in democratic politics. Basic democratic processes themselves are not oriented toward the giving and taking of public reasons. Moreover, in many liberal democracies, there is no adequate social minimum and the basic needs of many citizens go unmet. Far from providing a sophisticated ideological apology for the liberal welfare state, Rawls's first principle of justice actually provides a damning indictment of many features of contemporary liberal democracies. Contemporary liberal states do not secure the fair value of the political liberties. Moreover, their political cultures are frequently hostile to civil, respectful and reason-regulated democratic discourse of the sort required by even a modest conception of public reason. When we turn to the legislative stage to determine what fidelity to fair equality of opportunity and the difference principle require, the contrast between the liberal welfare state and the social and economic institutions of a property-owning democracy becomes even more dramatic.

## Fair Equality of Opportunity: Education, Health and Employment

Contemporary political communities with developed economies create a wide array of jobs, careers and positions of political and bureaucratic authority. The main question posed by fair equality of opportunity concerns what fair access to these positions consists in and requires. Three dimensions of the Rawlsian answer to this question can be distinguished. First, Rawls assumes that in pursuing positions all citizens have a right to freedom of occupational choice. This does not mean that everyone has the right to the particular type of position they would most prefer to have (e.g., a particular type of job). Rawls favors open competition for positions, and success in obtaining a particular position will depend, among other things, on one's talents and willingness to work. Rather, occupational choice means that there is a diversity of positions open to all citizens, and no one is forced to hold or pursue specific kinds of employment. Second, fair equality of opportunity requires the elimination of formal obstacles to careers, offices and other social benefits that disadvantage citizens on the basis of race, sex, class, ethnicity and sexual orientation. Explicit rules or implicit social practices that either block or provide unequal access to positions and offices on the basis of irrelevant characteristics such as race, ethnicity, social class, etc. must be eliminated. Such discrimination is illegitimate even if it enjoys widespread popular political support or contributes to economic efficiency.[13] Third, and most significantly, access to positions and offices must not only be equal in the formal sense but all citizens must have a fair chance to attain positions. Rawls characterizes a fair chance in the following way: "supposing that there is a distribution of natural endowments, those with the same level of talent and ability and the same willingness to use these gifts should have the same prospects of success regardless of their social class of origin" (JF, 44).

It is obvious that educational institutions play a crucial role in ensuring that citizens enjoy fair equality of opportunity. It is through education that the knowledge and skills requisite for diverse careers and offices is primarily required. Similarly, education is indispensable to developing and nurturing the different natural talents of people. Just educational institutions must therefore adequately prepare all citizens for entry into the labor force and must contribute to conditions under which socially beneficial economic activity can take place. However, Rawls also places special emphasis on "the role of education in enabling a person to enjoy the culture of his society and to take part in its affairs, and in this way to provide for each individual a secure sense of his own worth" (*TJ*, 87). Building on the above remarks about the value of education in relation to the basic liberties and democracy, we can see that just educational institutions have at least three complementary objectives. First, they must facilitate development of the moral powers requisite to the fair value of the basic political liberties and they must equip citizens with the knowledge, capacities and disposition needed for meaningful participation in democratic deliberation and collective decision-making. Second, they must supply citizens with economically valuable skills and knowledge. Third, they must facilitate citizens' access to and appreciation of culture – for instance, art, literature, and music – in a way that helps to secure each person's sense of self-respect.

Deliberation at the legislative stage is likely to give rise to a wide variety of competing reasonable proposals both about the appropriate balance among these objectives and about the best way of structuring educational institutions (from primary schools to universities) so as to achieve them. Similarly, we can expect diversity concerning the details of the curriculum and pedagogical strategies most suited to achievement of these objectives. Moreover, on many matters concerning education, judicial authorities will not have the requisite expertise and experience to craft sound educational policies. It is not appropriate, therefore, to incorporate a detailed template defining the precise structure of just educational institutions into basic constitutional documents. Many elements of educational justice are not viewed as constitutional essentials.[14] Nonetheless, pursuit of these objectives is a requirement of justice and it is doubtful that many contemporary liberal democracies assign sufficient importance to the democratic and cultural dimensions of education. The narrow-minded focus on the economic significance of education that characterizes contemporary educational policy in many liberal democracies is a defect from the point of view of Rawls's theory. However, a much more significant failing of educational policy in liberal democracies concerns the influence of social class on access to educational goods and opportunities.

It is a familiar fact that the quality of schools, colleges and universities in many liberal democracies varies significantly and that the access that citizens have to educational opportunities and goods is significantly affected by social class. Allowing social class to influence access to education violates fair equality of opportunity both because it unfairly deprives some social classes of equal access to the intrinsic goods of education and because it disrupts fair competition for positions and offices in both the economic and democratic realm. Achieving fair equality of opportunity thus requires a dramatic reconfiguration of educational institutions so as to eliminate the influence of social class on access to primary, secondary, and postsecondary education. Rawls does not explicitly call for the elimination of advantage-conferring private schools, colleges and universities that permit affluent citizens to purchase better education for themselves or their children than is available to poorer and less affluent citizens. But it is extremely difficult to see how the private provision of education through a market can be reconciled with fair equality of opportunity. It is more plausible to think that justice requires a publicly financed school system in which ability to pay is irrelevant to citizens' access to education. The public system should be uniformly excellent in the sense that every citizen reliably receives an education that fully realizes the democratic, economic and cultural objectives noted above. Note that extinguishing the influence of social class on access to education, as required by fair equality of opportunity, goes well beyond ensuring that there is a universal access to education above some threshold of adequacy. A society in which all citizens receive at least a good education but some, in virtue of their social class, have access to significantly better educational resources violates fair equality of opportunity. Deliberation at the legislative stage is thus not simply about the appropriate quality of education but it is also essentially about securing equality of access to good education.

# Health Care

Fair equality of opportunity also has significant implications for justice in health care.[15] Preventable and treatable illnesses and diseases as well as disabilities can significantly impede the access citizens have to opportunities given their level of talent and motivation. There must, therefore, be a publicly financed health care system that adequately meets the basic health care needs of all citizens and does so in a fashion that does not place social classes at a disadvantage in relation to other social classes. In ways that parallel the case of education, the details of what constitutes adequate basic health care and the best institutional structures for the fair and effective delivery of health care are to be determined at the legislative stage in light of information about "the prevalence of various illnesses and their severity, the frequency of accidents and their causes and much else" (JF, 173). Similarly, representatives at the legislative stage must determine what fraction of the social product is appropriately devoted to health care in light of other essential social objectives such as education, provision for retirement, economic infrastructure, and national defense. A crucial consideration that animates much of the deliberation about the precise features of an adequate health care system is the conception of citizens as free and equal persons each of whom has the minimum capacities "to be normal and fully cooperating members of society over a complete life" (JF, 174).[16] Illnesses and accidents can disrupt the capacities of citizens to cooperate with others on a free and equal basis. So suitable types and levels of health care are determined in large part by considering what is needed to maintain the status of citizens as free and equal cooperators. Rawls holds that appeal to the idea of free and equal citizens helps us to determine both the relative urgency of different kinds of health care and the appropriate balance between health care provision and other social expenditures. Considerations relating to the fair value of basic rights and liberties complement the argument from fair equality of opportunity for universal basic health care. Citizens cannot be in a secure position to enjoy and exercise their basic liberties and to participate in democratic processes if they are unable meet their health care needs or if the attempt to meet them leaves them impoverished or vulnerable to exploitation. Indeed, although the appropriate configurations of a full health care system in keeping with fair equality of opportunity and the fair value of basic political liberties is left to the legislative stage, Rawls allows that a right to basic health care is a constitutional essential (PL, 407).

It is doubtful that a health care system in which health insurance is supplied in large part by private insurers in a competitive economic market can satisfy the demands of justice. Unless they are subject to wide-ranging and strict regulation, private insurers will have incentives to make insurance available at significantly different rates for different groups of persons. So those with rare or expensive medical conditions may find private insurance unavailable or prohibitively expensive. At the very least, fair equality of opportunity that is sensitive to preserving the status of citizens as free and equal cooperators must insulate citizens from the vagaries of health insurance markets as they standardly operate. Of course, without much more detailed information about the characteristics of particular societies and the range of feasible institutional structures available, it is impossible to determine how much variation in the basic design of health care systems is compatible with justice. Nonetheless, it is clear that health care systems in some liberal democracies (e.g., the United States) in which the health prospects of citizens vary dramatically with social class fall well short of meeting the demands of Rawlsian justice.

# Employment

We have seen how fair equality of opportunity requires attention to the conditions under which citizens can fairly pursue career ambitions and participate in the democratic life of a society. Rawls does not think that citizens have entitlements to particular jobs or success in their chosen careers. Against suitably fair background conditions, citizens must formulate and pursue their own career plans and they must assume responsibility for career success or failure. Nonetheless, Rawls recognizes the importance of ensuring all citizens have access to secure and meaningful work. "Lacking a sense of long-term security and the opportunity for meaningful work and occupation is not only destructive of citizens' self-respect but of their sense that they are members of society and not simply caught in it" (PL, lvii). While fair equality of opportunity does not guarantee citizens access to particular careers or types of employment, justice requires that decent and meaningful employment be available to all citizens in a readily seizable form. If markets do not supply sufficient employment for all those who wish to work or available employment is highly insecure or bereft of meaning, then the government must adopt policies to stimulate the creation of good jobs or provide suitable employment opportunities itself. Determining what constitutes meaningful and secure employment is, of course, a difficult and potentially controversial matter. But taking the standard seriously could have dramatic effects on general economic policy and the character of labor law concerning the rights of employees. For instance, the provision of long-term unemployment benefits to workers who have been "downsized" due to the response of capital to market forces would presumably not be a sufficient response. Instead, government would have a responsibility to create meaningful employment opportunities and to prepare workers with the training needed to pursue them. Similarly, it seems likely that the terms on which employment is offered would need to be sensitive not only to the needs of employers but also to the claim of employees to a work environment that is satisfying and rewarding (or provides suitable compensation for work that cannot be made meaningful). So, perhaps somewhat surprisingly, Rawls's theory has some resources to address concerns about the alienation generated by modern economies that consign many people to permanent unemployment or to dull, unpleasant or dispiriting work.

# The Family

Although Rawls recognizes the family as an important part of the basic structure of society and hence as regulated by considerations of justice, his analysis of the family is less fully developed than his discussion of other essential institutions. The family assumes importance for two related reasons. First, it is through participation in family life that many citizens pursue elements of their conceptions of the good. The opportunity to form a family provides citizens with a special opportunity to give expression to their comprehensive conceptions of value, whether religious, moral, or cultural, by sharing a life with others organized around these values. Parents, in particular, have the opportunity to transmit specific convictions, enthusiasms and practices to their children and to include children in the life of communities that share those values. The family is thus closely tied to the basic liberties that permit citizens to develop and implement their own conceptions of the good. Second, Rawls views the family as crucial to meeting the needs of children and providing them with a moral education suitable to the stable reproduction of society over time. It is largely through the family that children acquire a sense of justice and a capacity to form and pursue a conception of the good. So the family plays a central role in the creation of free and equal citizens who can support just democratic political institutions and who can respect the rights of others.

Against this background a number of questions about the appropriate structure of the family can be framed. First, we may ask who is entitled to form a family and assume responsibility for the rearing of children. Historically the right to found a family has often been restricted to heterosexual, monogamous couples.[17] Since such restrictions limit the liberty of citizens to pursue their reasonable conceptions of the good they are problematic. On Rawls's view, they cannot be defended unless it can be established that certain family structures are incompatible with the successful rearing of children as free and equal citizens or that they somehow imperil the basic rights of other citizens (e.g., the equal rights of women). Given that gay couples are just as well placed as heterosexual couples to nurture children and to foster development of the moral powers of children, there is no basis in Rawls's view to ban gay marriage or to prevent gay couples from adopting children (*JF*, 163).[18] In general, a great variety of family arrangements – for example, interfaith, interracial, intercultural, single-parent, multiple parent – must be accepted and supported by a just state.

Second, we may ask about how the internal life of families can be regulated by the state in the name of justice. Rawls's response to this matter is complex. On the one hand, the principles of justice do not apply directly to the internal life of families. For instance, families need not be democratic and resource distribution within the family need not be guided by the difference principle. Instead, the state must permit families to give expression to the values that they have adopted and seek to realize through family life. From this perspective, there seems little scope for regulation of the family. No particular division of household labor between men and women should be mandated or actively promoted by the state. Ideally, free and equal adult citizens can choose for themselves how to organize the division of labor in the domestic realm. Rawls's theory does not directly challenge the legitimacy of traditional gender roles in the family. Similarly, parents are free to teach their values, religious and otherwise, to their children and can require that children participate in activities and practices valued by their parents. Families organized around conservative religious doctrines that valorize traditional gender roles and emphasize the importance of strict obedience to religious dogma in matters of personal morality are just as legitimate as families that expressly embrace and promote liberal values of individuality and personal autonomy. In general, when it comes to the internal structure of family life the state must respect the diverse decisions citizens make about how to organize their families and it must accept, as legitimate, the resulting wide plurality of family types and the values they embody.

On the other hand, the family, like other associations in a democratic community, is subject to general constraints grounded in the basic rights and liberties and fair opportunities of all citizens. The state must ensure that families are not structured in such a way so as to deprive persons of their equal political rights or their fair access to opportunities or their knowledge of these rights or the existence of other comprehensive doctrines. Thus Rawls readily grants that "prohibitions of abuses and the neglect of children, and much else, will, as constraints, be a vital part of family law" (*JF*, 165). Similarly, the state should not respect the exercise of patriarchal power by men over women that denies women fair value of their basic rights or undermines their equal claim to pursue careers or offices on an equal basis with men. How best to address the various subtle ways in which the gendered division of labor in traditional families impedes the equal standing of men and women as citizens is a complex matter. Yet Rawls is clearly sympathetic to progressive policies that go beyond those currently in place in many liberal democracies. For example, he observes,

> If a basic, if not the main, cause of women's inequality is their greater share in the bearing, nurturing, and caring for children in the traditional division of labor within the family, steps need to be taken either to equalize their share, or to compensate them for it . . . [A] now common proposal is that as a norm or guideline, the law should count a wife's work in raising children (when she bears that burden as is still common) as entitling her to an equal share of the income that her husband earns during their marriage. Should there be a divorce, she should have an equal share in the increased value of the family's assets during that time. (*PL*, 472–473)

The constraints on the structure of the family emanating from the guarantees of political rights and fair equality of opportunity also significantly influence the nature of legitimate parental authority over the rearing of children. Parents cannot exercise their authority over children in ways that disrupt meaningful acquisition of the moral powers. Ensuring that children develop an effective sense of justice means that parents cannot seek to inculcate their children with racist, sexist, homophobic or other intolerant comprehensive doctrines that fail to suitably acknowledge the equal standing and rights of other citizens. Similarly, parents may not insulate their children from an understanding and appreciation of their own equal standing as citizens. For example, both girls and boys must be educated in such a fashion that they see women as political equals to men with the same opportunities and prerogatives as men to pursue careers and public positions. Even if Rawls does not require that children receive an autonomy-facilitating education, neither fair equality of opportunity nor the fair value of political liberty can be realized unless children receive an upbringing that permits them to appreciate the values of other citizens and to reflectively deliberate about how best to conduct their own lives.

Rawls notes that the family may present an obstacle to full realization of fair equality of opportunity. Some parents may be able to nurture their children in a way that gives them advantages over other children. For instance, highly educated parents may be able to enrich the learning environment of their children in ways that contribute to the development of valuable talents or which confer special social skills upon their children. Other parents will be unable to benefit their children in these ways. Unsurprisingly, Rawls does not think this provides a reason to abolish the family as an institution. The family's role in providing children with particularized attention of the sort needed to reliably meet their needs and facilitate their moral development along with the importance adults place on having families preclude replacing the family with a radically different institution. But whether the family poses a significant impediment to the achievement of fair equality of opportunity depends a great deal on how large the effect of differential nurturing is on the development of children's skills and motivations and whether this effect can be mitigated by suitably structured and excellent public schools. If the public education system is strong and available to all children on an equal basis and parents are prevented from purchasing advantage-conferring private education for their children then we can be optimistic that the ill effects of the family on fair equality of opportunity will be modest.

## The Economy and the Difference Principle

Designing economic institutions that satisfy the difference principle is a task primarily addressed at the legislative stage. Rawls anticipates that a property-owning democracy will rely on competitive markets to produce and allocate a wide variety of goods and services. Competitive markets are desirable both because of their allocative and productive efficiency and because they can be conducive to occupational choice.[19] But, as we have already seen, the equal basic liberties principle and fair equality of opportunity exert a great deal of prior influence on the overall character of a just economic system. Democratic institutions need to be protected from the corrosive influences of economic wealth and power. Similarly, there cannot be, in any straightforward sense, free markets in education and health care. So a great deal of the design of basic economic institutions in a property-owning democracy is already fixed by the principles that have lexical priority over the difference principle. Indeed, the institutional arrangements I have already discussed arguably provide some necessary background conditions for the fair and effective functioning of a market economy.

Subject to meeting the demands of the lexically prior principles, the main challenge for parties at the legislative stage is to determine the degree to which markets need to be regulated so as to ensure on an ongoing basis that economic inequalities work to the greatest advantaged of the least advantaged.[20] This is a complex matter that cannot be settled without careful consideration of a great deal of information drawn from economics and other social sciences. The full determination of the precise domains in which competitive markets function, the regulations to which they are subject and the way in which market-generated distributions of income should be adjusted[21] to fulfill the difference principle cannot be described here. However, there are a number of general features of Rawls's approach to basic economic institutions that are worth noting.

First, although Rawls maintains that the right to "hold and have exclusive control over personal property" (*PL*, 298) is a basic liberty that enjoys protection as a constitutional essential, he rejects a core tenet of capitalism, namely a right to private ownership of the means of production.[22] Instead, ownership of the major means of production is to be widely dispersed. Freedom of occupational choice means that citizens have a good deal of control over how they develop and deploy their skills and talents in response to the employment and investment opportunities available in a competitive market economy. Similarly, people cannot be compelled to work in socially productive ways. However, Rawls denies that there is any presumptive entitlement to ownership of all the income that can accrue to people via voluntary transactions in an unregulated free market.

Second, Rawls endorses an extensive role for government in the structuring of markets and in the management of the economy. In order to secure the conditions in which a market economy can be harnessed to serve justice in the distribution of income and wealth, Rawls suggests that government must perform four essential functions that can be viewed as the responsibility of different branches of government.[23] The allocation branch identifies and corrects defects in the basic functioning of markets. Through regulation, taxation and adjustments in the definition of property rights, it ensures that markets are competitive and economically efficient. It also guards against the "formation of unreasonable market power" (*TJ*, 244). The stabilization branch supplements and stimulates market activity so that full employment obtains in a manner that reasonably respects occupational choice. The transfer branch defines and administers a social minimum that ensures that the basic needs of citizens are adequately met. This is necessary because competitive markets cannot be relied upon to furnish everyone with the material conditions of equal citizenship. The distribution branch oversees the system of taxation necessary to preserve a distribution of wealth commensurate with the difference principle (e.g., through the imposition of inheritance taxes) and to raise the general revenue needed to adequately fund public institutions and provide essential public goods. Despite the wide latitude for management of the economy that Rawls assigns to government, he is confident that suitably regulated markets can serve the difference principle and are thus integral to a just basic structure. Yet it is striking that, unlike many contemporary liberal proponents of the market, Rawls views the importance of markets from the point of view of justice largely in instrumental terms. For Rawls, markets must be designed to serve justice and it is a contingent fact whether or to what degree particular market arrangements actually serve justice.[24] The general antipathy towards regulatory oversight, taxation and government involvement in the production of goods and services evinced by many liberal capitalists has no place in Rawls's theory.

Third, the treatment of the market illustrates an important general feature of Rawls's understanding of the nature of just institutions: when institutions are structured by appropriate principles, they exhibit pure procedural justice. This means that the fairness of the public rules structuring basic institutional processes ensure the justice of the particular outcomes they generate. In the economic realm, for instance, the overall aim of the various functions of government is to generate a set of public rules which, when followed in good faith by citizens, are conducive to meeting the requirements of the difference principle.[25] But once suitable rules structuring the market are in place, just outcomes are simply those arising out of the voluntary conduct of citizens in the economy. As Rawls puts it, "when everyone follows publicly recognized rules of cooperation, the particular distribution that results is acceptable as just whatever that distribution turns out to be" (*JF*, 54).

This view has two interesting implications. To begin with, if the complex rules structuring the economy are fair then we cannot make any process-independent judgments about the justice of particular outcomes generated by the economy. This does not mean that market-determined distributions of income and wealth are just *per se*. Rather it means that once the overall economy and other background political institutions are suitably structured so as to maximize the expectations of the least advantaged, then the distribution of resources to specific persons arising from the processes are just. Just background institutions that are part of the fair processes determining income distribution include systems of taxation and limitations on private property rights.[26] Pure procedural fairness is not an attribute of markets themselves but rather of the complex web of properly structured institutions that together comprise the basic structure of a just polity.

The second implication concerns the way in which citizens in their ordinary day-to-day life can think about their economic activity. In deciding what careers to pursue or what market investments to make, citizens need not attempt to determine what economic decisions are likely to work to the greatest advantage of the least advantaged. Rather they are free to act as rational economic actors in a competitive marketplace. This does not mean that Rawls depicts citizens as especially competitive or narrowly self-interested. Rather Rawls expects the economic activity of citizens to be shaped by pursuit of their own ends rather than any politically mandated conception of the good. The specific wages and employment opportunities of particular individuals along with the prices of many goods and services will be determined by how people respond to market signals. Citizens do, of course, have a duty to support just institutions. Moreover, their political deliberations about what scheme of cooperation is appropriate should reflect a concern for justice and the public good rather than narrow economic self-interest. Thus a citizen deliberating about just tax policy via the device of the legislative stage may endorse a tax code that does not maximally serve her actual economic interests. As a citizen concerned with the fairness of background institutions, she should lend political support to the adoption of the fair tax code. But once the fair tax code is in place, she need not guide her own economic behavior by a concern to ensure that her choices (e.g., what employment to take, what salary to accept) work to the greatest advantage of the least advantaged. It is important to note, however, that Rawls's view does not imply that when background institutions are unfair – as they are in all contemporary liberal democracies – justice permits citizens to press their economic advantage within the existing rules and structures.[27]

## Conclusion

Capitalist welfare states around the world are in crisis. Most of them are marked by profound social and economic inequalities of the sort that are corrosive to the fair value of political liberty and democracy itself. Fair equality of opportunity, in its demanding Rawlsian sense, is not even approximately realized in any state and nowhere in the world are economic institutions systematically oriented to improving the prospects of the least advantaged. But from a Rawlsian perspective, the failure of welfare state capitalism to deliver justice is not to be located simply in regrettable policies that liberals routinely criticize. To be sure, cuts to government programs of social assistance for the most vulnerable members of society, reckless deregulation of financial markets and dramatic tax cuts for the wealthy are all inconsistent with justice as fairness. The deeper failing with welfare state capitalism lies with the basic character of its institutions. They are oriented only to nominal forms of political equality and formal conceptions of equality of opportunity. They seek to secure only the basic needs of citizens. By contrast, the institutions of a property-owning democracy are directly animated by the more demanding principles of justice as fairness. Once the character of these principles is appreciated in conjunction with the four-stage sequence for thinking about institutional design, it is hard to resist the conclusion that achieving justice as fairness requires not modest tinkering with existing institutional arrangements but many kinds of radical reforms.

# Notes

I am grateful to Jon Mandle, David Reidy, and Andrew Williams for helpful feedback.

1   This is especially true in areas of social policy concerned with the distribution of income and wealth. To take but one example, discussions about tax policy among bureaucrats and economic policy analysts in the most developed economies (e.g., in the G20 countries) proceed without any attention to how the difference principle might be implemented.

2   Despite his awareness of profound racial, class and gendered injustice in his own society, Rawls has no detailed discussion of the institutional arrangements and social policies that should be adopted in the United States to address these problems. Critics divide as to whether this shows that Rawls's theory lacks the theoretical resources to deal adequately with such important matters or whether the inattention is a natural reflection of Rawls's special concern for the articulation of an ideal theory. On the more sympathetic interpretation, Rawls's theory provides an ample basis to analyze and diagnose many of the paradigmatic injustices of American history along race, class, and gendered lines.

3   Rawls allows that a form of liberal democratic socialism with a system of competitive markets might be able fulfill the aims of justice as fairness. The key difference between a liberal socialist state and a property-owning democracy is that the former has much more extensive public ownership of the means of production and natural resources than the latter. Given circumstantial pluralism of the sort described below, liberal democratic socialism may provide the economic institutions most congenial to justice as fairness in some settings (*TJ*, 242). Both regimes nourish and protect the basic liberties of citizens and secure fair equality of opportunity, and both facilitate a robust form of deliberative democracy. But Rawls devotes more attention to outlining the features of a property-owning democracy than to describing a liberal socialist economy. So I will treat a property-owning democracy as the broad institutional structure most favored by Rawls.

4   Rawls often refers to his theory as comprised of two principles. For instance, in *Justice as Fairness* he provides "a revised statement of the two principles discussed in *Theory*." The statement reads: "(a) Each person has the same indefeasible claim to a fully adequate scheme of equal basic liberties, which scheme is compatible with the same scheme of liberties for all; and (b) Social and economic opportunities are to satisfy two conditions: first, they are to be attached to offices and positions open to all under conditions of fair equality of opportunity; and second they are to be to the greatest benefit of the least-advantaged members of society (the difference principle)" (*JF*, 42–43). However, since the second principle is really comprised of two principles – fair equality of opportunity and the difference principle – and since Rawls himself frequently examines these principles independently, it is easier and clearer to characterize justice as fairness as comprised of three basic principles that are ordered in a special way.

5   Rawls notes that citizens concerned with justice and institutional design face three kinds of questions. First, what form should the basic constitutional structure through which basic rights are protected and through which democratic decisions about legislation and social policies take? Second, what kinds of legislation, social policies and administrative decisions best realize the principles of justice? Third, on the assumption that no political system will track the requirements of justice perfectly, when is it reasonable and appropriate for citizens to comply with political structures or laws that they sincerely believe to be unjust? In order to help us to address the first two questions, Rawls proposes a four-stage development of the original position device in which the epistemic constraints on the parties in the original position are progressively relaxed. Rawls treats the third question concerning the nature and extent of political obligation as belonging to "partial compliance theory" (*TJ*, 175) and in *Theory* he views it as a matter best considered after determination of ideally just institutions and policies.

6   This is my label. Oddly, Rawls did not explicitly assign a name to this stage or to the fourth stage.

7   Technically, Rawls does not insist upon a written constitution that is subject to authoritative interpretation by a judiciary. But even societies without written constitutions can, through other means, designate certain rights and democratic procedures as basic and as having special importance.

8   It is important to note that Rawls does not view protection of liberty per se as important. Only specific liberties expressly tied to the development and exercise of the two moral powers are singled out for special constitutional protection. It is better to think of the first principle as identifying a list of specific and highly valued liberties rather than as affording protection of liberty per se. The list of basic liberties includes: "freedom of thought and liberty of conscience; political liberties (for example the right to vote and to participate in politics) and freedom of association, as well as the rights and liberties specified by the liberty and integrity (physical and psychological) of the person; and finally the rights and liberties covered by the rule of law" (*JF*, 44).

9   This does not mean that all other conceptions of justice are unreasonable. Although Rawls believes that justice as fairness is the most reasonable conception of justice, he allows that there are other reasonable liberal conceptions that citizens may hold. Moreover, citizens may in good faith appeal to other reasonable liberal views in actual political deliberation. Basic institutions that depart from justice as fairness but which are shaped by other reasonable liberal conceptions can be legitimate even if they are not fully just.

10  Rawls is clearly sympathetic to the more specific idea of judicial review of legislation by a Supreme Court that has the authority to strike down laws that are deemed by the Court to violate basic rights. And in many circumstances, such an institution may provide part of the best system of protection of basic rights. It's less clear whether judicial review is required or even desirable from the point of view of justice as fairness in every society.

11  Rawls is sharply critical of the US Supreme Court rulings in *Buckley* and *First National* which declared various limitations on contributions to political campaigns unconstitutional (*PL*, 359–362). Rawls emphasizes that the First Amendment of the American Constitution should be interpreted as concerned with ensuring the fair value of political liberties and not, as the Court held, as hostile to such an idea.

12  It is important to note that under Rawls's first principle – the equal basic liberties principle – the requirement that the fair value of liberty be secured applies only to the basic political liberties. The worth of the other basic liberties is determined by the resources and opportunities secured for citizens by fair equality of opportunity and the difference principle.

13  The requirement of formal equality of opportunity need not rule out the legitimacy of programs of affirmative action that are designed to remedy historical injustices that have denied citizens fair equality of opportunity.

14  This does not mean that a judiciary charged with interpreting basic constitutional provisions can play no role in ensuring that educational institutions fulfill the demands of justice as fairness. The rights that Rawls treats as constitutional essentials do impose important parameters on acceptable educational institutions. Freedom of conscience, for instance, will sharply circumscribe the role that religion can play in public-sector schools and would justify, among other things, a constitutional prohibition of school-led prayer. Similarly, constitutionally enshrined guarantees of equal basic liberties would condemn racial or sexual discrimination in the provision of education. Rawls also allows that a minimum threshold of education sufficient to permit citizens to participate in society as equals is a constitutional essential (*PL*, 166). However, beyond these important parameters the design and implementation of just educational policies is the responsibility of the legislature.

15  Although access to health care would seem to be the kind of all-purpose good that would be valuable to all persons irrespective of their particular conception of the good, Rawls does not explicitly identify it as a primary good.

16  Rawls notes that deliberation about the appropriate level and kind of health care must consider the reasonable claims citizens have in "all phases of their life from childhood to old age" (*JF*, 174). "The idea is that the claims of those in each phase derive from how we would reasonably balance those claims once we viewed ourselves living through all phases of life" (*JF*, 174). It is arguable that this kind of deliberative requirement may provide a way of resisting the unfortunate political tendency of many health care systems to devote a disproportionate amount of health care resources to people in the last six months of their lives.

17  States have also imposed restrictions on interfaith and interracial marriage.

18  The status of polygamous marriage is potentially more complicated for Rawls since there may be a reasonable basis for thinking that legal recognition of polygamous marriages threatens the equal political standing of women. Presumably whether or not this is so is something to be determined at the legislative stage where sociological evidence of the character and effects of polygamous marriage can be considered.

19  It is doubtful that the market offers sufficient protection of occupational choice for all citizens. Citizens will not enjoy meaningful occupational choice if either there is no market demand for their labor or there is only one kind of employment available to them.

20  Here as elsewhere the phrase "the least advantaged" does not refer to particular individuals but rather to social positions of groups defined by the index of primary goods.

21  In practice this will almost certainly require a complex scheme of redistributive taxation. However, given Rawls's reliance on the idea of pure procedural justice (discussed below), the ideal is to structure economic institutions in such a fashion that the outcome of market activity will generally function to the greatest advantage of the least advantaged.

22  Rawls also rejects a conception of property associated with some forms of socialism, namely that there is a "right to property as including the equal right to participate in the control of the means of production and of natural resources, both of which are to be socially, not privately, owned" (*JF*, 114).

23  Two other economic functions of government are important. First, in order to address the problem of intergenerational justice, government must abide by a principle of just savings. This requires that sufficient resources be set aside so that a just basic structure can be maintained across generations. Second, Rawls allows that, where there is sufficient democratic support for it, government may have an exchange branch that supplies public goods favored by the citizenry but inadequately supplied by the market. The goods supplied via this branch are not required by justice but rather are ones deemed beneficial to the political community. In *A Theory of Justice*, Rawls also imposes a demanding constraint on supply of these goods: citizens must provide virtually unanimous support for the schemes through which they are funded (*TJ*, 249–250).

24  Another distinctive dimension of Rawls's view is his rejection of the idea that economic growth is an essential political virtue. He notes that the difference principle "does not require continual economic growth over generations" and he allows that a property-owning democracy is compatible with "Mill's idea of a society in a just stationary state where (real) capital accumulation may cease" (*JF*, 159).

25  The appeal to pure procedural justice does not mean that there cannot be revisions to the institutional arrangements that are used to achieve the difference principle. We may learn that the outcomes generated by some institutional arrangements are inferior, from the point of view of justice, than other arrangements. Such an observation could justify altering the rules regulating economic activity.

26  Rawls's speculative and tentative remarks about the potential attractiveness of a "tax on consumption at a constant marginal rate" (*JF*, 161) over progressive forms of taxation usually favored by liberals must be understood within the context of the broader background institutions of a property-owning democracy. It is only when the broader institutional structures of society are generally oriented toward securing the basic liberties, fair equality of opportunity and the difference

principle that a consumption tax becomes a potentially attractive way of fairly generating government revenue. There is no general endorsement of the fairness of "flat" forms of taxation.

27 Rawls's claims about how institutional arrangements can display pure procedural justice provide no justification for the self-serving economic behavior of citizens who are the beneficiaries of *unjust* background institutions. For example, in our world citizens can reasonably criticize the conduct of greedy Wall Street brokers who pursued their self-interest in ways detrimental to the public good even if the brokers did not violate any existing rules or laws.

## Works by Rawls, with Abbreviations

*Justice as Fairness: A Restatement* (*JF*), ed. Erin Kelly. Cambridge, MA: Harvard University Press, 2001.
*Political Liberalism* (*PL*), expanded edn. New York: Columbia University Press, 2005.
*A Theory of Justice* (*TJ*), rev. edn. Cambridge, MA: Harvard University Press, 1999.

# 10

# Democratic Equality as a Work-in-Progress

## STUART WHITE

*The aim is always to treat the theory as Rawls treated it: not as a magnificent machine displayed behind velvet ropes in a museum, but as a work in progress to be used and developed, as well as improved and adjusted in the light of new arguments and objections, new knowledge and technologies, and new political developments.*

Thomas Pogge, *John Rawls*, p. xi

## Introduction

What kind of economic justice should citizens of a democratic society pursue? What principles should they use to guide the design of basic economic structures so as to affirm their status as free and equal citizens?

John Rawls's answer to this question is given by his conception of justice as fairness and, more specifically, by his interpretation of justice as fairness as *democratic equality*. Democratic equality has been a hugely influential conception of justice. It challenges both utilitarianism and classical liberal and libertarian thought which continues to exert a major influence in the politics of many capitalist countries.[1] My aim in this chapter is to clarify the content of, and motivation for, democratic equality. I will also indicate how in certain respects its content remains controversial and open to both interpretative and normative debate.

We begin in section 1 with an outline of democratic equality. This section introduces and clarifies, in a preliminary way, two key elements of democratic equality: the notion of fair equality of opportunity and the difference principle. In section 2, I explain why Rawls considers democratic equality a better account of what justice requires than rival accounts (such as utilitarianism).[2]

Sections 3 and 4 then briefly review some outstanding interpretative and normative issues within democratic equality. The aim here is to be illustrative: to indicate how democratic equality remains what Catherine Audard and Thomas Pogge have rightly called a "work in

*A Companion to Rawls*, First Edition. Edited by Jon Mandle and David A. Reidy.
© 2014 John Wiley & Sons, Inc. Published 2016 by John Wiley & Sons, Inc.

progress" (Audard 2007, 16; Pogge 2007, xi). In section 3 we look at how Rawls tries to incorporate a principle of productive reciprocity into democratic equality and at the questions this raises. In section 4 we look at the question of how far democratic equality can properly incorporate the just claims of sick and disabled people (and those who care for them). Section 5 concludes.

# 1. What Is Democratic Equality?

In *A Theory of Justice* Rawls sets out to identify the conception of justice most suited to guide the shared, public reason of citizens in a democratic society. He argues that this conception is *justice as fairness* which he defines in terms of two principles:

> First: each person is to have an equal right to the most extensive scheme of equal basic liberties compatible with a similar scheme of liberties for others . . .
> Second: social and economic inequalities are to be arranged so that they are both (a) reasonably expected to be to everyone's advantage and (b) attached to positions and offices open to all. (*TJ*, 53)

Rawls uses the term "democratic equality" to refer to justice as fairness when the second principle above is given what he considers its most compelling elaboration as follows:

> social and economic inequalities are to be arranged so that they are both (a) to the greatest benefit of the least advantaged and (b) attached to offices and positions open to all under conditions of fair equality of opportunity. (*TJ*, 72)

A first feature of democratic equality, then, is that it elaborates the idea of social and economic inequalities being "attached to positions and offices open to all" and requiring "fair equality of opportunity." What is fair equality of opportunity?

Rawls argues that a just society must certainly secure "formal equality of opportunity in that all have at least the same legal rights to access all advantaged social positions" (*TJ*, 62). So, for example, there can be no laws prohibiting citizens from pursuing particular occupations on grounds such as race or gender. But *fair* equality of opportunity requires "that positions are to be not only open in a formal sense, but that all should have a fair chance to attain them" (*TJ*, 63). By a "fair chance," Rawls means "that those with similar abilities and skills should have similar life chances" (*TJ*, 63):

> More specifically, assuming that there is a distribution of natural assets, those who are at the same level of talent and ability, and have the same willingness to use them, should have the same prospects of success regardless of their initial place in the social system. In all sectors of society there should be roughly equal prospects of culture and achievement for everyone similarly motivated and endowed. The expectations of those with the same abilities and aspirations should not be affected by their social class. (*TJ*, 63)

Thus, roughly speaking, fair equality of opportunity requires that individuals' chances for occupational achievement should not be affected by the achievement of their parents. To this end, fair equality of opportunity requires measures to prevent "excessive accumulations of property and wealth" across generations and to maintain "equal opportunities of education for all" (*TJ*, 63).

Were we to stop the account here, we would perhaps think that fair equality of opportunity is essentially about making sure the naturally most gifted have fair opportunity to rise to the top of the social hierarchy. Could it allow, for example, a concentration of educational resources on the most naturally gifted neglecting the less gifted? In an important recent discussion, Samuel Freeman points out that this is not how fair equality of opportunity is to be understood (at least in the context of democratic equality). Fair equality of opportunity demands a generous education for all, within the limits of available resources, not a targeting of educational resources to the most gifted (Freeman 2007a, 93–94). This reflects a fundamental concern for the "essential primary good of self-respect" and that "a confident sense of their own worth should be sought for the least favored" (*TJ*, 91–92). Fair equality of opportunity stipulates that all citizens, regardless of their natural abilities, must have effective opportunity to develop their skills and capacities.[3]

The other component of democratic equality, part (a) in the formulation above, elaborates the idea that social and economic inequalities should be reasonably expected to work to everyone's advantage as requiring that these inequalities be to the "greatest benefit of the least advantaged." Rawls assumes here that a democratic society will be differentiated into distinct socioeconomic groups or classes. He asks us to imagine "representative individuals" for each group, and suggests that we judge the justice of the rules determining the distribution of benefits (and burdens) in the economy in terms of the long-term expectations of these group representatives (Van Parijs 2003, 211–216; *TJ*, 67). When is an inequality *in these expectations* – expectations of "life prospects" – just? According to the difference principle, inequality in expectations is just when it is such as to maximize the expected life prospects of the representative of the worst-off group: that is, the representative of the class of unskilled workers (*TJ*, 68). The idea is that by allowing higher (than average) expectations for the more market-talented or entrepreneurial, this can increase economic incentives. To the extent this generates better economic performance, and this can be harnessed for the benefit of the unskilled, the inequality can be justified. Specifically, inequality is justified to (and only at) the point where it maximizes the expected life prospects of the representative of the worst-off/ unskilled class.[4]

We are familiar in contemporary politics with arguments for inequality which appeal to incentives and to the benefits of economic growth. But it is important to appreciate the very stringent demand the difference principle makes. It will not satisfy the principle merely to show that inequality raises total or average welfare (the utilitarian view). What matters is not the *aggregate* or *average* position, but specifically that of the *worst off*. Nor will it suffice for the worst off to derive *some benefit* from inequality (as is required for so-called "trickle down"). The inequality must be of *maximal benefit* to the worst off.[5] Moreover, as we shall see in a moment, the position of the worst off is not to be evaluated wholly by reference to income and wealth. What, more exactly, does the difference principle regulate the distribution of? This requires a complex answer, but to begin answering it we need to bring more explicitly into focus Rawls's notion of "primary goods."

Any theory of justice has to include an account of the *interests* which are at stake when principles of justice are being specified. In Rawls's theory, the relevant interests are understood in terms of *primary goods*. In *Theory*, Rawls presents these as goods that it is rational to want independently of one's specific conception of the good (*TJ*, 54). In *Political Liberalism*,

Rawls elaborates this, arguing that primary goods are important because of their role in the development and exercise of citizens' two fundamental moral powers: the power to "understand, to apply and to act from the public conception of justice" and the power "to form, to revise and rationally to pursue a conception of one's rational advantage or good" (*PL*, 19; cf. 178–190). In *Justice as Fairness*, Rawls distinguishes five categories of primary goods: (1) "basic rights and liberties," such as freedom of conscience and expression; (2) freedom of movement and occupational choice "against a background of diverse opportunities"; (3) "powers and prerogatives of offices and positions of authority and responsibility"; (4) income and wealth; and, already alluded to above, (5) the "social bases of self-respect" which secure for citizens "a lively sense of their worth as persons" (*JF*, 58–59) The first principle of justice applies to (1) and elements of (2); fair equality of opportunity applies centrally to the background opportunities for the enjoyment of the freedoms mentioned in (2); the difference principle applies to (3) and (4) and is also informed (as are all the principles) by the concern for (5). The expectations of the representative of the worst-off class are thus evaluated according to an *index of primary goods* which includes (at least): income and wealth, the powers and prerogatives of office, and social factors affecting self-respect.

Particularly noteworthy here is that the difference principle does not require society to arrange economic inequality so as to maximize the income and wealth of the worst-off group. Imagine, for example, that a set of social institutions A delivers a higher long-term expectation of income for the worst off than institutional set-up B. However, under A members of the worst-off class of workers have much less autonomy in their working lives than under B, for example, they have less freedom about when to take toilet breaks at work. Then it is possible that overall, looking at the index of all primary goods relevant to the difference principle, B is better than A: overall, the worst-off class has better expectations under B than A. As Philippe Van Parijs points out, a lot consequently depends on the precise relative weighting we give to the different components of the primary goods index. Different weightings could have major implications for institutional and policy design (Van Parijs 2003, 216–222; cf. Tomasi 2012, 226–237). It is not obvious that there is clearly one single right, or most reasonable, way to weight the relevant primary goods, which implies that there might be a range of reasonable difference principles rather than a single one.[6]

Some further, important features of democratic equality should be noted. Rawls argues that the first principle of justice has priority over the second. We may not seek, for example, greater equality of opportunity, or an increase in the income and wealth of the worst-off group, at the expense of citizens' equal rights to the most extensive system of basic liberties (*TJ*, 474–480). In addition, Rawls suggests that, within the second principle, fair equality of opportunity should (probably) have a similar priority over the difference principle (*TJ*, 77–78). In other words, we may not seek to improve the economic prospects of the least advantaged by sacrificing fair equality of opportunity. These priority relationships must rest on judgments about the relative importance of the primary goods covered by the respective principles to the development and exercise of citizens' moral powers.[7] Finally, we should note that while the second principle clearly has a major role in guiding the design of social and economic institutions, so too does the first principle. In particular, the first principle includes a commitment to maintain the "fair value" of the political liberties (the rights of democratic political participation) and this commitment might have serious implications for the distribution of income and wealth. This commitment could conceivably require institutions and policies even more egalitarian than those demanded by the second principle.

# 2. Why Democratic Equality?

Hopefully we now have a preliminary sense of what democratic equality is. But what motivates it? What arguments does Rawls advance in favor of it? In moving from his initial definition of the two principles of justice in *Theory* to democratic equality, Rawls rejects three alternative ways of understanding the second principle. Looking at his reasoning here gives some insight into his case for democratic equality.

One alternative interpretation of the second principle is given by what Rawls calls the "system of natural liberty." Here the economy is "roughly a free market system" (*TJ*, 57). There is no formal limitation on entry into any occupation (the ideal of "careers open to talents"). Economic inequalities work to the advantage of all in the sense that the system is Pareto efficient: no class representative can be made better off, in terms of their expectations, without another being made worse off (*TJ*, 61). The specific efficient outcome selected under the system of natural liberty will depend, however, on the underlying distribution of marketable assets. Citizens have very unequal assets, such as marketable skills, because of differences in "accident and good fortune" (*TJ*, 63). So the Pareto efficient outcome will reflect this underlying, and morally arbitrary, inequality. As Rawls puts it: "Intuitively, the most obvious injustice of the system of natural liberty is that it permits distributive shares to be improperly influenced by these factors so arbitrary from a moral point of view" (*TJ*, 63). Rawls rejects the system of natural liberty, then, because it would allow the respective expectations of class representatives to be much too strongly shaped by these morally arbitrary endowment inequalities.

A second interpretation of the second principle, liberal equality, addresses this weakness by replacing formal equality of opportunity with fair equality of opportunity, as defined above. This somewhat reduces the extent to which citizens' prospects will depend on "social contingencies and natural fortune." However, liberal equality is unsatisfactory for two reasons. First, even if liberal equality "works to perfection in eliminating the influence of social contingencies," it leaves prospects for income and wealth strongly shaped by "the natural distribution of abilities and talents" (*TJ*, 63–64). But, as Rawls puts it: "There is no more reason to permit the distribution of income and wealth to be settled by the distribution of natural assets than by historical and social fortune" (*TJ*, 64). Second, it is anyway not feasible to perfectly eliminate the effects of different social backgrounds ("at least as long as some form of family exists"). *Fair* equality of opportunity is never going to be *perfect* equality of opportunity. So, under liberal equality, citizens' distributive shares will still be powerfully shaped by inequalities in natural endowments, combined with residual inequalities of opportunity.

To tackle this problem, Rawls proposes that we add the difference principle to our understanding of the second principle of justice. While the difference principle allows for some inequality attributable to morally arbitrary differences in natural endowment and social background, the group of workers that is least advantaged in these terms will nevertheless be doing as well as it can. Insisting on any more equality (or inequality) would only make them, the least advantaged, worse off. Intuitively, then, the worst off have no cause for complaint against the more advantaged when the difference principle is satisfied.

There is a fourth possible interpretation of justice as fairness, in addition to the system of natural liberty, liberal equality and democratic equality. This is what Rawls terms "natural aristocracy." Natural aristocracy embraces the difference principle but not the shift from formal to fair equality of opportunity. Rawls rejects natural aristocracy on similar grounds to his rejection of liberal equality: it is an "unstable" intermediate position between the system of natural liberty and democratic equality. While it corrects for the distributive impact of one morally arbitrary kind of contingency (in this case, natural endowments), it leaves another, equally arbitrary contingency (in social background) untouched (*TJ*, 64–65).

Thus far I have focused on Rawls's "intuitive" remarks which seek to "explain" democratic equality. For Rawls, however, the *argument* for democratic equality really rests with the use of the hypothetical social contract device to derive the principles of justice. Famously, Rawls proposes that we identify principles of justice by asking what principles people would choose for their society in a suitably defined "original position" (*TJ*, 15–19; *JF*, 80–83). A key feature of a suitably defined original position is that the parties there are behind a "veil of ignorance" so that they do not know what their own position in society is (or have any way of calculating probabilities on this score). Rawls claims that justice as fairness, elaborated as democratic equality, is the conception of justice parties would choose in this original position. Since the original position itself models the status of citizens as free and equal members of an ongoing, cooperative community – it is, in this sense, a "device of representation" – this gives us reason to accept the conception of justice as appropriate to a society of this kind. Some comment on Rawls's argument from the original position is necessary and helpful.[8]

Much of the critical commentary on Rawls's argument has focused on his claim that the parties in the original position would select the difference principle. A key argument Rawls gives here is that the parties in the original position must choose principles once and for all (the requirement of *finality*) and that they must therefore be confident that the principles they select can bear the "strains of commitment" (*TJ*, 153–160).[9] The parties must feel assured that once the veil of ignorance is lifted and they go on to live under the society with the principles they have chosen, they will be able to carry whatever burdens the principles place upon them. In *Theory*, Rawls presents the parties in the original position with a choice between democratic equality and utilitarianism and argues that democratic equality passes the strains of commitment test while utilitarianism does not (because maximizing average welfare is quite compatible with some groups being left very poorly off indeed).

Critics have argued, however, that there are alternatives to unrestricted utilitarianism which could also satisfy the strains of commitment test, casting doubt on the idea that the test tells decisively in favor of democratic equality. Imagine, in particular, a conception which requires us to maximize average utility subject to the proviso that all citizens have guaranteed access to a decent minimum. Since all citizens are guaranteed this minimum, wouldn't this *restricted utilitarianism* satisfy the strains of commitment requirement? (See Waldron 1993; Pogge 2007, 117–120.)

Rawls takes up this question in *Justice as Fairness*.[10] Here he distinguishes two ways in which strains of commitment can be excessive. In the first, "we become sullen and resentful, and we are ready as the occasion arises to take violent action in protest against our condition" (*JF*, 128). In the second, though not "hostile or rebellious," we "feel left out." We become "withdrawn and cynical" and "cannot affirm the principles of justice in our thought and conduct over a complete life" (*JF*, 128). Rawls argues that while restricted utilitarianism might meet the strains of commitment test in the first sense, it is still inferior to democratic equality, incorporating the difference principle, in terms of the second. Why is this?

To understand Rawls's argument at this point we must introduce the idea of *reciprocity*. The parties in the original position wish to choose principles of justice that affirm their status as free and equal. This will help secure, for each citizen, the bases of self-respect. In affirming their status as free and equal, Rawls argues, the parties must also affirm that each representative person has a presumptive right to an equal share of primary goods, including income and wealth: "they take equal division of income and wealth (equal life prospects as indexed by these primary goods) as the starting point" (*JF*, 123).[11] However, the parties will rationally want to accept inequalities where these are reciprocally beneficial; that is, where they benefit not just those most advantaged by them but also work to improve the lot of those worst off under them. According to Rawls, this principle of reciprocal benefit in turn suggests the difference principle: "taking equal division as the benchmark, those who gain more are to do so on terms acceptable to those who gain less, and in particular to those who gain the least" (*JF*, 123). In short, the difference principle captures a commitment to reciprocal benefit in moving away from a starting-point of strict equality; and this commitment itself uniquely affirms the underlying conception of citizens as free and equal.[12]

By contrast, restricted utilitarianism is inconsistent with the commitment to reciprocal benefit in moving away from a starting-point of strict equality; and, as such, is not as compatible with the underlying conception of citizens as free and equal. As a result, it cannot be expected to enlist the active support and loyalty to the society from the most disadvantaged which democratic equality, incorporating the difference principle, can. Even if it does not generate attitudes of hostility and active rebellion, it will generate cynicism and withdrawal based on a failure of the worst off to feel that their status as equal members of society has been appropriately affirmed by society's regulative principles of justice. The argument is summarized by Rawls as follows:

> We suppose citizens to view themselves as free and equal, and to regard society as a fair scheme of cooperation over time . . . We then say: if those who view themselves and their society in that way are not to withdraw from their public world but rather to consider themselves full members of it, the social minimum, whatever it may provide beyond essential human needs, must derive from an idea of reciprocity appropriate to political society so conceived. (*JF*, 130)

## 3. Productive Reciprocity

Having now set out democratic equality and sketched the argument for it, we can turn to some of the interpretative and normative debates surrounding it. Space requires that we be highly selective here. For example, the question of whether democratic equality properly has global or transnational rather than merely "domestic" application is one I bracket here. (See Beitz 1979, 125–176, and Pogge 1989, 211–280, for discussion.) Another area of debate that I will set aside here concerns whether the difference principle applies only to the design of society's basic institutions or also as a rule to be observed by individuals in their economic conduct. No one doubts that in a just society, by Rawls's standards, citizens must vote to establish, and then comply with, laws and institutions which allow inequality up to the point that maximizes the position of the worst off. But within the framework of democratically agreed laws, do the more talented citizens also have a duty, under the difference principle, to eschew higher wages for their work so as to maximize the share of social product going to the worst off (G.A. Cohen 2008; Williams 1998; J. Cohen 2001)? I also bracket here the question of how adequate Rawls's conception of democratic equality is in relation to the distribution of benefits and burdens within the family and related issues of gender equality, although our discussion of care work below is connected with this (Okin 1989, 89–109, 134–186; *PL*, 466–474).

The first issue I shall address takes us back to the notion of reciprocity and to an objection that, as presented in *Theory*, democratic equality fails to capture fully the demands of reciprocity among equals.

As we have seen, Rawls argues that differences in class background and natural ability are "arbitrary from a moral point of view" and so ought not to count in a fundamental way in determining distributive shares. However, what about differences in individual *effort*? In *Theory* Rawls argues that differences in effort are closely tied to class and natural endowments: "the effort a person is willing to make is influenced by his natural abilities and skills and the alternatives open to him. The better endowed are more likely, other things equal, to strive conscientiously, and there seems to be no way to discount their greater good fortune" (*TJ*, 274). So we ought not to try to differentiate distributive shares according to effort.

However, if entitlement to income and wealth is independent of effort then the worst-off group in terms of income and wealth could conceivably include people who are potential high-earners but who choose instead to take lots of leisure – to "surf all day off Malibu" (*JF*, 179; Musgrave 1974). It conflicts deeply with commonsensical notions of justice to hold that those who choose to work, perhaps in not so pleasant jobs, are obliged to share the fruits of their efforts with "surfers" (Scheffler 1992). Indeed, providing those who pursue this way of life the (full) social minimum guaranteed by the difference principle might seem inconsistent with the idea underpinning democratic equality – mutually affirming reciprocity among equals. Those who choose to live off the labor of others when they could work are arguably claiming a right to share in the benefits of cooperation without being fully cooperative themselves. They are implicitly claiming an "aristocratic" position in society, contrary to the ideal of reciprocity among equals (White 2003).

Rawls addresses this concern explicitly in *Justice as Fairness* (drawing on his 1974 "Reply to Alexander and Musgrave" in *CP*, 232–253). To address the surfer objection, Rawls suggests that we include leisure in the index of primary goods. We can imagine that each representative individual starts with 16 hours of leisure per day "if the standard working day is eight hours" (*JF*, 179). A citizen who chooses not to work will consequently "have eight extra hours of leisure" compared to the working citizen. This extra leisure is stipulated to be worth as much as the primary goods index of the worst-off group in employment: "we count those extra eight hours as equivalent to the index of the least advantaged who do work a standard day" (*JF*, 179). Thus one may choose not to work. But the extra leisure is, as it were, the reward: one can't also claim (at least in full) the income and wealth share of the lowest-paid group in full-time employment.

In this way, democratic equality incorporates a principle of *productive reciprocity*: in the context of otherwise fair terms of social cooperation, those who share in the goods created by the work of other citizens (assumed to be able to work) must themselves work as a condition of getting (at least in full) the income and wealth share guaranteed by the difference principle. Thus Rawls says that inclusion of leisure in the index of primary goods, in the proposed manner, is "the best way to express the idea that all citizens are to do their part in society's cooperative work" (*JF*, 179).

However, this incorporation of productive reciprocity in democratic equality remains rather undeveloped. A first question, both interpretative and normative, concerns the consequences of surfing. Does or should surfing imply loss of all income and wealth, or some fraction of the full share guaranteed under the difference principle? According to Freeman, Rawls means that the extra leisure of the surfer is equivalent to the wage of the worst-off group in full-time employment. But this wage is only a fraction of the total social minimum of income and wealth guaranteed under the difference principle (Freeman 2007a, 229–230). Say the value of this social minimum is $100 per day per person. Imagine also that the daily wage for the lowest paid in full-time employment is $48. The lowest paid in full-time employment get the $48 plus the rest of the social minimum up to a total of $100 per day. The surfers do not get the $48 wage for work: their leisure is stipulated as equivalent to this. But they would still get the balance of the social minimum: in this case, $100 − $48 = $52.

However, if this is what Rawls intends, it has some apparently odd implications. Imagine, for example, that economic conditions drive down the wage of the lowest paid, say to $40 a day. If the overall social minimum is unchanged, this has the implication that the payment to the surfers should go up to $60 a day (because $100 − $40 = $60). But why should the surfers get more income just because economic pressures make it harder to secure the full social minimum through the wage? It is hard to make moral sense of this. Alternatively, if we assume the social minimum decreases by the same amount as the wage of the lowest paid in full-time employment – in this case, from $100 per day to $92 per day – then the surfers do not get an increase in their income level but they would still see their own income level hold constant at $52 (=$92 − $40) while that of those in employment goes down (from $100 to $92). Is this fair? Similarly odd implications, but looking peculiarly unfair to the surfers, arise when we assume an increase in the wage of the lowest paid in full-time employment (Van Parijs 1991, 108–112). Were we to address the rights of the surfers more fully, then one possibility would be to consider the implications of the fact that some resources exist for use (to some degree) prior to social cooperation, for example, natural resources. Some argue that all citizens, including surfers, have legitimate claims to a share of these and relevantly similar resources and that this provides the justification for an income guaranteed to all without any requirement of productive contribution (see Van Parijs 1995; Birnbaum 2012).

Second, if we are going to stipulate that income entitlement is (to some extent) conditional on productive contribution, we need to know what counts as a contribution. Rawls refers to "work" and seems to equate work with employment. However, and to anticipate an issue to which we will return below, to what extent should forms of care work that typically go unpaid in our society also count as relevant contributions? A full elaboration of the citizen's duty of productive contribution likely requires knowledge of a given society's circumstances which is not relevant in the context of the original position where basic principles of justice are being selected. Nevertheless, a fuller elaboration of democratic equality would surely require us to offer more guidance on how to determine what counts as contributive.

As presented above, the surfer objection concerns those unwilling to make a productive contribution. A third issue arises when we acknowledge that some citizens are unable to make such a contribution or otherwise be full participants in social cooperation. We shall address this issue in the next section. We can clearly see, however, that while Rawls addresses the concern for productive reciprocity, there remain a number of important and outstanding questions about how exactly we can and should integrate this concern into democratic equality.

# 4. Disability and Mutual Care

As our discussion of productive reciprocity suggests, Rawls conceives the problem of distributive justice as the fair sharing of the benefits and burdens of social cooperation. A key assumption is that citizens are able to engage fully in cooperation: "we assume that persons as citizens have all the capacities that enable them to be cooperating members of society" (PL, 20). Thus, the analysis presented so far abstracts completely from health conditions and disabilities which stand in the way of being fully capable of cooperation in Rawls's sense. A related concern, raised in the work of Amartya Sen, is that Rawls's focus on primary goods will lead us to overlook forms of disadvantage related to health and disability. Two citizens who are equal in terms of, say, income and wealth might nevertheless have highly unequal capabilities for leading good lives because disability makes living more expensive for one of them (Sen 1990; 1992). So a challenge is posed: Can democratic equality adequately incorporate the just claims of sick and disabled people? And what of those who have responsibilities to care for severely sick and disabled people? (See Kittay 1999.) Can democratic equality properly incorporate their needs too?

Rawls explicitly abstracts from this set of issues in *Theory* and only addresses them briefly in later work. In *Political Liberalism*, he discusses "what we might call normal health care" (PL, 21). This is health care aimed at restoring those who, due to illness or accident, have fallen temporarily "below the line . . . [of having] the minimum essential capacities required to be a normal cooperating member of society" (PL, 183). Here, Rawls argues that fair equality of opportunity and the difference principle should be understood to require a right to a decent minimum level of health care for all (PL, 184; cf. JF, 173–175). Rawls refers to arguments developed in more depth by Norman Daniels (1985; 2003).[13]

Rawls's focus on "what we might call normal health care," however, leaves unaddressed the interests of those with serious and permanent health conditions and disabilities such that health care cannot bring them up to the "line" of minimum capabilities required to be "a normal cooperating member of society." Can democratic equality address their needs?

As a preliminary step in answering this question we should note that "the line" between having and not having the minimum capabilities for full social cooperation, including employment, is not simply given by people's natural endowments. In contemporary societies many people with serious long-term health conditions and disabilities find it very difficult, if not impossible, to be in employment. This is, however, in no small part a reflection of the way buildings, workplaces and job packages have been designed. It is possible to configure physical spaces, job packages and so on differently, and in this way make many jobs and offices accessible to disabled people.[14] Martha Nussbaum imagines an advocate for disabled people putting the point as follows:

> the case of citizens who are deaf, blind, and wheelchair-users is much closer to the cases of race and sex [discrimination] than people usually think. For people with impairments of this sort can usually be highly productive members of society in the usual economic sense, performing a variety of jobs at a sufficiently high level, if only society adjusts its background conditions to include them. (2006, 112–113)

To the extent this is so, the principle of fair equality of opportunity surely requires society to (re)configure physical spaces, job packages and so forth in ways that make them appropriately accessible to disabled people.

However, this point, important as it is, does not mean that democratic equality is adequate to the interests of disabled people, for at least two reasons. First, while fair equality of opportunity ensures that disabled people have fair opportunities to earn income, it does not address the separate issue that they often also have higher living costs. (This, of course, is the point Sen is making in the aforementioned critique of the primary goods metric.) Second, even if society configures spaces and institutions in the appropriately accessible way, some individuals with severe disabilities will still not be able to function as full social cooperators in Rawls's sense. Some people with severe physical disabilities, for example, will be unable to make economic contributions. People with very severe cognitive disabilities will lack the capacity to understand and follow their society's public principles of justice. Rawls himself expresses uncertainty as to whether justice as fairness can be "extended" to cover such cases and, if not, what the implications of this failure might be (PL, 21).

According to Nussbaum, this is indeed one place where Rawls's theory fails (2006, 97–223; see also Barry 1989, 241–254). Her core objection might be put like this. On the one hand, Rawls's theory aspires to capture an idea of democratic community. For a society to be well-ordered as a democratic community, we might say (these are my words, not Nussbaum's or Rawls's), it is necessary that its public principles of justice affirm the equal dignity of each community member. On the other hand, Rawls poses the problem of social justice at the outset as a problem of fair distribution amongst full social cooperators. Membership of the community of justice seems dependent on sufficient capacity for social cooperation. This apparently puts severely disabled people outside the scope of justice, which, in turn, impugns, for severely disabled people, the status of equal dignity.

Eva Kittay argues that for democratic equality to be properly sensitive to the needs of severely disabled people and carers it requires a fundamental revision. Kittay proposes, in effect, that we rethink reciprocity. More precisely, we must rethink the foundational idea of fair social cooperation by recognizing and affirming the importance of *mutual care*: of relationships in which all citizens, including people with severe disabilities, receive the care they need, while their carers also receive the care they need to carry out this role. Kittay uses the term "doulia" to capture this idea of a just society upholding an appropriate give and take of care: "*Just as we have required care to survive and thrive, so we need to provide conditions that allow others – including those who do the work of caring – to receive the care they need to survive and thrive*" (Kittay 1999, 107, emphasis in original).[15]

Building *doulia* into democratic equality calls for important changes to how we think of citizens' moral powers and primary goods. Moral powers must be understood to include not only a capacity for a conception of the good and for a sense of justice but also a capacity "to respond to vulnerability with care" (Kittay 1999, 102). Relatedly, primary goods must include the good of care: "the good *both to be cared for in a responsive dependency relation if and when one is unable to care for oneself, and to meet the dependency needs of others without incurring undue sacrifices oneself*" (Kittay 1999, 103, emphasis in original).

Can we integrate these revisions into the framework of Rawls's two principles of justice? Kittay is skeptical, suggesting that we may need a third principle.[16] My own tentative view is that we might be able to see an adequate system of public recognition and support for care as a requirement of fair equality of opportunity. People with disabilities have just claims to appropriate care under this principle to enable them to develop and exercise their abilities.[17] Carers also have claims to support under this principle, in part because without support their own opportunity range is unfairly burdened by caring responsibilities. Similarly, carers should receive (at least) the minimum income and wealth share guaranteed under the difference principle for those in full-time work. In addition, to address the important point about higher living costs we must find some way, in specifying just income and wealth shares, to appropriately multiply the income and wealth share of disabled people relative to others.[18] These are tentative (and obviously incomplete) remarks, however, and their tentativeness underscores the extent to which this set of issues, like that surrounding productive reciprocity, requires further work.

## 5. Conclusion

Having set out the basic content of democratic equality and clarified Rawls's arguments for it, my aim in this essay has been to identify and discuss some (and only some) of the areas in which there is continuing interpretative and normative debate about the content of democratic equality.

One area concerns the place of productive reciprocity in democratic equality. Rawls seems to affirm the principle that those capable of a productive contribution should make a contribution in return for the share of the social product they enjoy. But the particular way he tries to incorporate this idea into democratic equality is problematic. There is much of importance about the content of the obligations we have as a matter of productive reciprocity which remains relatively unexplored. A second area of ongoing debate concerns the extent to which democratic equality is, or, with suitable revision, can become, appropriately sensitive to the interests of disabled people and those who care for them.

Some might think that the conclusion to draw from this discussion is that Rawls's enterprise is a failure. It aspires to give democratic citizens clear principles to guide us in the design of our basic social institutions, but we find that in various ways these principles remain incomplete and contestable. But the conclusion to draw is not that of failure. Rawls saw his theory as a potentially important intervention in an ongoing history of reflection on the principles of justice appropriate to a democratic society. It succeeds insofar as it helps to move this process of collective reflection forward. In pointing to problems and controversies we do not impugn this success. We clarify some of the terrain on which we might make our own contributions.

## Notes

1   However, see Tomasi 2012 for an attempt to claim democratic equality for a classical liberal, free-market agenda.
2   My presentation of the content of, and motivation for, democratic equality draws on a number of earlier contributions. I am especially indebted to Audard 2007; J. Cohen 1989; Daniels 2003; Freeman 2007a; Nussbaum 2006; Pogge 2007; Van Parijs 2003.
3   Of course this still leaves open many questions about the just allocation of educational resources across the range of natural ability.
4   As Thomas Pogge points out (2007, 113), the difference principle does not direct us in general to introduce the institutions or policies that maximize the economic position of the worst off. More narrowly and specifically, it directs us *to allow economic inequality* to the point where it has this effect.

5   For helpful discussion to which I am indebted here, see J. Cohen 2011.

6   However, I do not think all weightings of the relevant goods are equally reasonable. For example, I think that John Tomasi's view that we should give overwhelming weight to income and wealth is implausible. See Tomasi 2012, 226–237.

7   The second priority relationship is particularly controversial. See Pogge 2007, 129–133. Van Parijs (2003, 224–226) also points out that if we take the idea of priority literally it would imply that all available resources must be used (up to the point of zero marginal benefit) to satisfy the first principle, leaving little or nothing to be distributed under the second principle. As this is obviously not what Rawls intends, we must understand the idea of priority in some weaker sense.

8   For a much more detailed and particularly helpful discussion of Rawls's arguments for democratic equality from the original position, see Audard 2007, 155–174.

9   Rawls also argues in *Theory* that selection of the difference principle is justified by the fact that it is rational for the parties in the original position to adopt a "maximin" choice rule given the limited information available to them (*TJ*, 132–135; *JF*, 97–100). However, although this argument has drawn much attention and critical comment, I am not sure it ultimately has the same status as the strains of commitment argument. As Rawls comments (*JF*, 99): "it is not essential for the parties to use the maximin rule in the original position. It is simply a useful heuristic device. Focusing on the worst outcomes has the advantage of forcing us to consider what our fundamental interests really are when it comes to the design of the basic structure." The key thing is that we imagine the parties giving their "fundamental interests" appropriate weight in their deliberation, which requires due attention to worst-case scenarios; and this is achieved by the strains of commitment test(s).

10  See also J. Cohen 1989. Rawls's response to the criticism of the original strains of commitment argument is similar to Cohen's.

11  At this point the argument from the original position seems to connect back to the "intuitive" remarks Rawls makes to "explain" democratic equality. Equality of division is the presumptive baseline, from which departures have to be justified, because the factors underlying unequal division in a market economy, e.g., differences in natural endowments, are morally arbitrary.

12  This argument requires Rawls's assumptions of "close-knitness" and "chain connection" (*TJ*, 70–73). Close-knitness requires that the position of other groups, including the worst off, always rises or falls when the position of the best off improves. If this assumption doesn't hold, then two distributive schemes might be equally good for the worst off but give different benefits to the best off. If we then choose the Pareto efficient scheme, we would be endorsing movement from equality that is not reciprocally beneficial (as the worst off do not *gain* by it, even though they do not lose by it either). See Van Parijs 2003, 205–208. Chain connection requires that improvements to both the best off and the worst off are also accompanied by improvements to intermediate social classes (where these exist). If this assumption doesn't hold, then a given move further away from equality might be beneficial to both the best off and the worst off but make an intermediate group worse off (though still leaving them better off than the worst off). It is not clear what reciprocity would require in this case.

13  Norman Daniels argues that for a particular society we can posit a "normal opportunity range": "the array of life plans that people in it find reasonable to choose, given their talents and skills" (2003, 257). Disease and disability "diminish individual fair shares of the normal opportunity range" (2003, 257). In this way, they detract from fair equality of opportunity. A system of comprehensive health care can promote "normal functioning" and, in this way, help to secure fair equality of opportunity.

14  This is the insight behind the "social model" of disability. For helpful discussion, see Barnes and Mercer 2003, 9–15, 65–87.

15  The ancient Greek *doula* signifies a servant who provides care for mothers when they care for children after birth. See Kittay 1999, 106–107.

16  Kittay suggests this "principle of social responsibility for care would read something like: *To each according to his or her need for care, from each according to his or her capacity for care, and such support from social institutions as to make available resources and opportunities to those providing care, so that all will be adequately attended in relations that are sustaining*" (1999, 113).

17  In the case of severely disabled people, Samuel Freeman argues that their interests fall under the natural duty of mutual aid in Rawls's framework. He argues that this is to be elaborated in this context "by analogy with the principle of fair equality of opportunity: we should provide those incapable of social cooperation with a reasonable degree of medical care and training designed to enable them to develop and exercise their (diminished) capacities so that they can take advantage of whatever activities are available to people with their level of disability" (2007b, 126).

18  In other words, if the class of lowest-paid workers in full-time employment has an expectation of, say, $100 per day under the difference principle, a worker in this class with a disability should expect $100 multiplied by a coefficient which tracks the higher living costs associated with this disability. In policy terms, this would imply a system of transfer payments specifically aimed at mitigating the higher living costs due to disabilities. I assume that the severely disabled who are unable to make an economic contribution have a right to the full income and wealth share guaranteed as part of the social minimum appropriately multiplied in this way.

## Works by Rawls, with Abbreviations

*Collected Papers* (CP), ed. Samuel Freeman. Cambridge, MA: Harvard University Press, 1999.
*Justice as Fairness* (JF), ed. Erin Kelly. Cambridge, MA: Harvard University Press, 2001.
*Political Liberalism* (PL), expanded edn. New York: Columbia University Press, 2005.
"Reply to Alexander and Musgrave" (1974), in *Collected Papers* (232–253).
*A Theory of Justice* (TJ), rev. edn. Cambridge, MA: Harvard University Press, 1999.

## Other References

Audard, Catherine (2007) *John Rawls*. Stocksfield, UK: Acumen.
Barnes, Colin and Mercer, Geof (2003) *Disability*. Cambridge: Polity.
Barry, Brian (1989) *A Treatise on Social Justice*, vol. 1: *Theories of Social Justice*. Berkeley: University of California Press.
Beitz, Charles (1979) *Political Theory and International Relations*. Princeton: Princeton University Press.
Birnbaum, Simon (2012) *Basic Income Reconsidered: Social Justice, Liberalism, and the Demands of Equality*. Basingstoke: Palgrave.
Cohen, G.A. (2008) *Rescuing Justice and Equality*. Cambridge, MA: Harvard University Press.
Cohen, Joshua (1989) "Democratic Equality." *Ethics* 99: 727–752. (Reprinted in Joshua Cohen, *The Arc of the Moral Universe and Other Essays*, Cambridge, MA: Harvard University Press, 2010.)
Cohen, Joshua (2001) "Taking People as They Are." *Philosophy and Public Affairs* 30: 363–386.
Cohen, Joshua (2011) "Political Philosopher John Rawls and Occupy Wall Street: A Discussion with Stanford Professor Joshua Cohen." Occupy the Airwaves, Nov. 5, at http://occupytheairwaves.com/ep6 (accessed May 2013).
Daniels, Norman (1985) *Just Health Care*. Cambridge: Cambridge University Press.
Daniels, Norman (2003) "Democratic Equality: Rawls's Complex Egalitarianism." In Samuel Freeman (ed.), *The Cambridge Companion to Rawls* (241–276). Cambridge: Cambridge University Press.
Freeman, Samuel (2007a) *Rawls*. Abingdon, UK: Routledge.

Freeman, Samuel (2007b) "Rawls and Luck Egalitarianism." In Freeman, *Justice and the Social Contract: Essays on Rawlsian Political Philosophy* (11–142). Oxford: Oxford University Press.

Kittay, Eva Feder (1999) *Love's Labor: Essays on Women, Equality, and Dependency.* London: Routledge.

Musgrave, Richard (1974) "Maximin, Uncertainty, and the Leisure Trade-Off." *Quarterly Journal of Economics* 88: 625–632.

Nussbaum, Martha (2006) *Frontiers of Justice: Disability, Nationality, Species Membership.* Cambridge, MA: Harvard University Press.

Okin, Susan Moller (1989) *Justice, Gender, and the Family.* New York: Basic Books.

Pogge, Thomas (1989) *Realizing Rawls.* Ithaca: Cornell University Press.

Pogge, Thomas (2007) *John Rawls: His Life and Theory of Justice*, trans. Michelle Kosch. Oxford: Oxford University Press.

Scheffler, Samuel (1992) "Responsibility, Reactive Attitudes, and Liberalism in Philosophy and Politics." *Philosophy and Public Affairs* 21: 299–323.

Sen, Amartya (1990) "Justice: Means versus Freedoms." *Philosophy and Public Affairs* 19: 111–121.

Sen, Amartya (1992) *Inequality Reexamined.* Oxford: Oxford University Press.

Tomasi, John (2012) *Free Market Fairness.* Princeton: Princeton University Press.

Van Parijs, Philippe (1991) "Why Surfers Should be Fed: The Liberal Case for an Unconditional Basic Income." *Philosophy and Public Affairs* 20: 101–131.

Van Parijs, Philippe (1995) *Real Freedom for All: What (If Anything) Can Justify Capitalism?* Oxford: Oxford University Press.

Van Parijs, Philippe (2003) "Difference Principles." In Samuel Freeman (ed.), *The Cambridge Companion to Rawls* (200–240). Cambridge: Cambridge University Press.

Waldron, Jeremy (1993) "John Rawls and the Social Minimum" (1986). In Waldron, *Liberal Rights* (250–270). Cambridge: Cambridge University Press.

White, Stuart (2003) *The Civic Minimum: On the Rights and Obligations of Economic Citizenship.* Oxford: Oxford University Press.

Williams, Andrew (1998) "Incentives, Inequality, and Publicity." *Philosophy and Public Affairs* 27: 97–122.

# 11

# Stability, a Sense of Justice, and Self-Respect

## THOMAS E. HILL, JR

A major aim of the third part of *A Theory of Justice* is to argue for the relative stability of a well-ordered society with a basic structure that satisfies Rawls's two principles of justice (*TJ*, 347). Rawls regarded his arguments for the relative stability of justice as fairness (compared, for example, with utilitarianism) to be an important confirmation of his earlier arguments (in Part I) for his two principles of justice. Those initial arguments offered reasons why his two principles of justice rather than utilitarian (and other) principles would be chosen by rational persons when reasoning from the morally appropriate point of view (the "original position") for assessing the relative merits of competing conceptions of justice. An independent argument for the relative stability of a society structured by his two principles of justice was necessary to complete the earlier arguments because those earlier arguments simply presupposed that members of the original position were assessing the relative merits of competing principles of justice for the basic structure of *ongoing* well-ordered societies (*TJ*, 123–126, 441). A well-ordered society is one in which more or less all of the citizens accept and conform to the principles of justice that are their public charter (*TJ*, 4–5, 397–399), and in the original position members must agree upon principles as final and "in perpetuity" (*TJ*, 127, 153). Initially the members of the original position do not consider principles of justice for societies that are deeply diverse and divided about matters of justice, nor do they concern themselves with how the well-ordered societies were created or how they could survive if abuses and dissension began to threaten their agreement-based order. In other words, in the initial arguments from the original position it is taken for granted provisionally, without argument, that achieving and maintaining the relative stability of a just society is not a problem.

If, however, doubts were to arise about the relative stability of societies structured by Rawls's principles, then the initial arguments would be called into question because they were based on a presupposition that now we may suspect to be false. The relative instability of such (Rawlsian) just societies would mean that (compared to societies structured by other principles) they are less likely to survive the inevitable internal strains and disruptions that any

*A Companion to Rawls*, First Edition. Edited by Jon Mandle and David A. Reidy.
© 2014 John Wiley & Sons, Inc. Published 2016 by John Wiley & Sons, Inc.

social order will encounter. If the societies in question lack the stabilizing forces to confront and readjust to such challenges, and return them to a just "equilibrium" state, then this would (at least partially) undermine their appeal to a rational person with the motivations that Rawls stipulates for members of the original position (*TJ*, 103, 399–401). It would also weaken our practical interest as citizens in using Rawls's conception of justice as a model for social reform, for at best successful reform would leave us with a fragile and unsustainable system. If, to the contrary, structuring societies by Rawls's principles would tend to make them more stable than societies structured by utilitarian (and other) principles, then from both the perspective of the original position and our perspective as citizens, this would strengthen the case for affirming Rawls's principles over the alternative ones. At least for these reasons, stability matters.

Rawls's concern in arguing for stability, however, was not simply a practical interest in the *durability* of a Rawlsian just society. Several points should be noted here.

*First*, it matters how stability is achieved and maintained. Most obviously, the means used to stabilize the system cannot be in violation of the two principles of justice. Hobbes's sovereign, for example, can use draconian punishment and arbitrary rule to ensure the stability of justice as Hobbes defines it, but these are unacceptable means under Rawls's first ("liberty") principle (*TJ*, 435). Besides this, in Rawls's view, the way in which citizens acquire a stabilizing sense of justice should be such that citizens will naturally affirm it when they reflect on how it was acquired (see, esp., *TJ*, §§72, 86). Stability acquired "in the right way" – by just means and through the citizens' properly developed sense of justice – would presumably be deeper and firmer as well as in itself morally preferable to stability acquired through force or indoctrination.

*Second*, as becomes clear in *Political Liberalism*, it was not merely for practical reasons that Rawls wanted to show that it is *possible* for a society based on justice as fairness to be made stable in the right way. This possibility matters even if it will never actually be realized. Like Kant, Rawls thought that an important but difficult task for philosophy is to establish the possibility that various fundamental beliefs and hopes are rationally sustainable. For Rawls, I think, to establish the *possibility* of a stable just society based on his principles was, in effect, to show that there are sufficient reasons for any rational and reasonable citizen to freely endorse justice as fairness, thereby satisfying a liberal and Kantian requirement for the full justification of the use of coercive state power.[1] In Rawls's view, an ideally just state may be hard to achieve and, even if achieved, it might be short-lived because of external historical forces, but he thought that any use of coercive power in accord with its principles will lack full justification if its stability for the right reasons is not at least *possible* in his sense.

In what follows I try to explain these initial remarks. More specifically: *First*, I summarize briefly what Rawls meant by stability, the role it plays in *TJ*, and the outline of his main strategies for showing that a well-ordered society based on his principles of justice would be relatively stable. *Second*, I comment on Rawls's use of developmental moral psychology in support of his claim that societies based on justice as fairness would be relatively stable. My focus here is on Rawls's conception of the relation between ethics and empirical psychology and on the potential value of his discussion of a sense of justice independently of the particular developmental story that he proposes (drawing on psychologists Piaget, Kohlberg, and others). *Third*, I discuss Rawls's conception of self-respect, its role in his arguments for justice as fairness, and whether it is subject to a certain Kantian objection that echoes in our contemporary political culture. *Finally*, pulling threads together, I respond to a natural concern that many of Rawls's readers today may have: that is, the suspicion that Rawls's reasons for abandoning his argument for stability in Part III of *TJ* completely undermine its value. In other words, if Rawls's turn to an overlapping consensus of reasonable comprehensive doctrines as the basis of stability in *PL* was well motivated, then why not quietly bypass the earlier work on a sense of justice and self-respect simply as an acknowledged failure?

## 1. Stability, Its Role, and Rawls's Two Lines of Argument: A Brief Summary

A scheme of social cooperation is stable, in Rawls's sense, when it is "more or less regularly complied with and its basic rules willingly acted upon; and when infractions occur, stabilizing forces should exist that prevent further violations and tend to restore the arrangement" (*TJ*, 6). Stability is not stagnation but is compatible with reasonable adjustments in social and legal institutions in response to new conditions. A system based on Rawls's principles of justice can be stable even when its institutions change, provided the altered institutions also conform to the basic principles of justice. To be stable, according to Rawls, a just social system need not be perfect or impervious to serious abuses. As he often says, stability depends on whether a system has generated within it forces that tend to restore it when such abuses occur. He argues that civil disobedience that appeals to citizens' sense of justice can be such a stabilizing force in a nearly just democracy marred by racial discrimination (*TJ*, 335–343).

Rawls regards stability, along with justice and efficiency, as virtues of social systems, but justice has priority as the first virtue (*TJ*, 3–10). This means at least that in choosing between just and unjust institutions, even if the latter are relatively more stable, this stability would not normally be sufficient grounds for adopting them. The primacy of justice over stability is not as extreme as this may suggest, however, because in Rawls's theory whether a particular conception of justice represents our best account of what justice is partly depends on the relative stability of societies based on that conception. In other words, to determine what the most defensible principles of justice are we need to take into account the degree to which alleged principles of justice (for example, Rawls's two principles, utilitarian principles, or perfectionist principles) would tend to generate stabilizing forces. Nevertheless, once he makes his full case for his principles of justice, bringing together all his arguments including relative stability, then Rawls apparently regards justice as trumping stability with regard to particular issues. For example, governments must not suppress dissenting speech, *in violation of the liberty principle*, just to make it to some degree less likely that corrupt individuals may gain office. What counts as a violation of the principles of justice, however, requires interpretation; for example, the liberty principle itself permits restrictions of some liberties for the sake of other liberties or for preservation of the whole system of just liberties (*TJ*, 178–180, 293).

Rawls has two main strategies for showing that societies based on his principles would tend to be more stable than societies based on competing (e.g., utilitarian or perfectionist) principles. The first (primarily in *TJ*, ch. VIII) is an attempt to show that when the basic structure of a well-ordered society conforms to his two principles of justice the citizens will tend to develop *a sense of justice* – a desire to maintain and live by the principles – that helps to bring the system back to justice whenever it begins to deviate. This tendency, he argues, follows from plausible principles of moral psychology and it is a relatively stronger stabilizing tendency than would be generated by well-ordered societies based on utilitarian and other conceptions of justice. The second main strategy (especially in *TJ*, chs VII and IX) is an attempt to show that for citizens in a well-ordered society based on Rawls's principles, living a just life would tend to be recognizably a good life for them as individuals. This second ("congruence") strategy aims to show that once citizens have developed a sense of justice, they would tend to find that having and reliably acting on that sense of justice is congruent with their own good (as defined by the thin theory of the good or goodness as rationality). In arguing for this general convergence of living justly with a rational pursuit of one's own ends, Rawls appeals to various psychological principles together with a rich account of goodness as rationality, rational deliberation, self-respect, happiness, and the value of social unions.

These arguments play two important roles in Rawls's complex methodology for deriving and justifying his two principles of justice (at least as superior to traditional competing conceptions of justice). First and most explicitly, the arguments for the stability of well-ordered societies based on his principles serve *to confirm the initial selection of the principles by members of the original position* by showing, on grounds accessible to them, that citizens in those (Rawlsian) societies would tend to develop a stabilizing sense of justice and would normally find that living justly converges with living well from their own point of view. The arguments depend on alleged general facts of human psychology, not on historical particulars, and so should be available to members of the original position despite their stipulated veil of ignorance. The second role for the arguments for stability is *to win the support of ordinary readers* who are trying to assess the merits of justice as fairness in the light of all available facts and arguments in their effort to reach "wide reflective equilibrium" about justice (*TJ*, 18–19, 42–45, 507–508). In seeking wide reflective equilibrium we try to take into account all the relevant facts, reasons, and arguments that we can, and Rawls's arguments regarding stability (for the right reasons) include morally relevant considerations that can be acknowledged by readers with quite different moral and religious perspectives. Apart from the special idea of an original position, most readers can be expected to care about two considerations that Rawls offers for favoring his principles – *first*, that in a natural way, without manipulation or indoctrination, citizens living under the principles would tend to develop a stabilizing sense of justice; and *second*, that most would normally find that living justly is a good life for them, which is an important consideration in its own right apart from its connection with stability.

## 2. Moral Psychology and a Sense of Justice

In Chapter VIII of *TJ* Rawls explains what a sense of justice is and how it might be expected to develop (see also "The Sense of Justice" and *JF*, Part V). Here I will briefly summarize his account, call attention to some conceptual distinctions in it, and then highlight his ideas about the relations between moral theory and empirical psychology. I suggest that, whether or not his conjectural psychological hypotheses are confirmable in their present form, his discussion points the way toward promising projects for cooperation between psychologists and philosophers.

First, what is a sense of justice? According to Rawls, a sense of justice is "a normally effective desire to apply and act upon the principles of justice, at least to a certain minimum degree" (TJ, 442). It "shows itself" by leading us "to accept the just social institutions that apply to us and from which we and our associates have benefited" and "to work for (or at least not oppose) the setting up of just institutions, and for the reform of existing institutions when justice requires it" (TJ, 415). A sense of justice motivates us to treat others in accord with the principles of justice, regardless of any special ties (for example, of friendship) that we may have with them. The *capacity* for a sense of justice is one of the "two moral powers" that Rawls attributes to human beings prior to particular social influences (TJ, vii–viii, 44). In JF he defines it as "the capacity to understand, to apply, and to act from (and not merely in accordance with) the principles of political justice that specify the fair terms of social cooperation" (JF, 18–19). A sense of justice, then, is not merely a sensuous feeling or desire. As Rawls explains, "The sense of justice (as a form of moral sensibility) involves an intellectual power, since its exercise in making judgments calls upon the powers of reason, imagination, and judgment" (JF, 29). A sense of justice is also distinct from what Rawls calls "natural attitudes" (such as love), although its development presupposes these. If we act against our sense of justice, we tend to feel guilt of a kind that we explain by reference to principles of justice (TJ, 415–416).

In making his case for the relative stability of justice as fairness, Rawls offers an explanation of how citizens in a Rawlsian just society might come to develop a sense of justice. Here is a brief summary of his explanation. The important background assumption is that the citizens understand, accept, and generally follow his principles of justice as their "public charter." And they know that other citizens do as well. When children grow up in such a society, Rawls conjectures, their moral development would proceed in three main stages, governed by three psychological laws that represent "tendencies" that are "effective other things equal." These are:

> First law: given that family institutions express their love by caring for his good, then the child, recognizing their evident love of him, comes to love them.
>
> Second law: given that a person's capacity for fellow feeling has been realized by acquiring attachments in accordance with the first law, and given that a social arrangement is just and publicly known by all to be just, then this person develops ties of friendly feeling and trust toward others in the association as they with evident intention comply with their duties and obligations, and live up to the ideals of their station.
>
> Third law: given that a person's capacity for fellow-feeling has been realized by his forming attachments in accordance with the first two laws, and given that a society's institutions are just and are publicly known by all to be just, then this person acquires the corresponding sense of justice as he recognizes that he and those for whom he cares are the beneficiaries of these arrangements. (TJ, 429-430)[2]

These proposed psychological laws are drawn from various sources (TJ, 404 n8), including William McDougall, Jean Piaget, and Lawrence Kohlberg, but they are formulated in ways appropriate for Rawls's theory and reflecting his conception of how philosophy and psychology are related.

The proposed laws are really hypotheses that incorporate certain moral concepts and cannot be tested, or even understood, without reference to them. For example, the laws (most explicitly the second and third) presuppose a background of just institutions – family, associations, and basic social structure.[3] They are formulated appropriately for use with Rawls's theory, not in any illicit way that favors his theory over alternatives, but simply because they lay out one way in which, Rawls conjectures, it might be psychologically possible for a Rawlsian just society to be stabilized consistently with its basic values of liberty, mutual respect, etc. The proposal, or empirical hypothesis, is that a stabilizing sense of justice would tend to develop in those who grow up in a society well-ordered *by Rawls's principles of justice*. Different hypotheses, Rawls suggests, would be more suitable for utilitarians (and others) who are concerned to explain how citizens in a well-ordered society with *their* principles as its public structure might develop a sense of justice – or develop some other stabilizing motivations (TJ, 417, 437–441). Rawls's proposed laws are also especially appropriate for his theory of justice because Rawls's theory (especially on the Kantian interpretation) affirms values deeply opposed to stabilizing measures (such as force, manipulation, and deception) that could be acceptable under other conceptions of justice (e.g., Hobbes's contractualism or various forms of utilitarianism).[4] Each competing theory of justice needs some account of how, consistent with its principles, it can be stable; in other words, why it is feasible and realistic to think that if its principle(s) were the public charter of well-ordered societies they would tend to generate their own stabilizing support. Rawls acknowledges, quite rightly, that ultimately we can assess the *relative* stability of competing conceptions of justice only after each has developed the hypotheses (or conjectural laws) appropriate to that theory. And, in the end, a comparative assessment must depend partly on which, if any, of the psychological explanations are confirmable or at least congruent with the best psychological theories applicable to the issue.

As I emphasize later, Rawls has much more to say about moral psychology than is contained in his explanation of how a sense of justice might develop, but this explanation is sufficient to illustrate his views about the relations between moral theory and empirical psychology.[5] His ideas here are important especially in the contemporary context where many seem to think that empirical work (brain studies, student questionnaires, and context-sensitive experiments) can confirm or refute significant normative claims. Rawls's main point, broadly speaking, is that moral theory and empirical psychology need each other. On the one hand, claims about what is just are normative claims that make use of concepts (justice, rights, obligation, etc.) that cannot be reduced to empirical psychological claims. Psychology cannot tell us what is just. Psychology is relevant to the comparative assessment of theories of justice, for example, by confirming or undermining their claims that societies based on those theories would be stable, but empirical psychology cannot even begin to contribute to debates on that issue unless they are willing to formulate, review, and test hypotheses that incorporate moral concepts. On the other hand, systematic moral theories aim to answer many questions that depend on whether our beliefs about human sentiments, thoughts, and motives – real and possible – are true. Neither wishful thinking nor casual observation is sufficient to settle what the relevant empirical facts are. So moral theory at its best needs the results of empirical work in psychology provided this is well framed to be relevant to the issues at hand. Rawls's conjectures on the development of a sense of justice (as he conceives of this) are just an illustration of these general points that, in my view, seem undeniable.

# 3. Self-Respect and the Kantian Interpretation

## Rawls's Conception of Self-Respect and Its Social Bases

Among the primary goods that are supposed to determine the rational choice of members of the original position are the social bases of self-respect. At times Rawls says that self-respect itself is a primary good, even "perhaps the most important primary good" (*TJ*, 386), but he later makes clear that what is to count as the relevant primary good in the original position is having the *social bases* of self-respect (*TJ*, 54, 478; *JF*, 60). This is because self-respect is a (subjective) attitude whereas the social bases of self-respect, like other primary goods, have an "objective character" needed to function in Rawls's arguments from the original position to his principles (*JF*, 60). Whether individuals have the attitude of self-respect depends on many factors besides the basic structure of their society, and this attitude (like "happiness") cannot be objectively identified, measured, and socially controlled. The social bases of self respect are "those aspects of basic institutions normally essential if citizens are to have a lively sense of their worth as persons and to be able to advance their ends with self-confidence" (*JF*, 59). These social bases, Rawls says, are "things like the institutional fact that citizens have equal rights, and the public recognition of that fact and that everyone endorses the difference principle" (*JF*, 60). These are features of the basic structure of society that help to support our fundamental interest in preserving self-respect (*JF*, 60 n27).

Rawls treats self-respect as a kind of self-esteem. Specifically, he defines self-respect (or self-esteem) as having two aspects: First, "it includes a person's sense of his own worth, his secure conviction that his conception of the good, his plan of life, is worth carrying out. And, second, self-respect implies a confidence in one's ability, so far as it is within one's power, to fulfill one's intentions" (*TJ*, 386). To have a social structure with features (the "social bases") that tend to foster and preserve self-respect is a primary good, something rational to want whatever one's plan of life, because, as Rawls says, "Without [self-respect] nothing may seem worth doing, or if some things have value for us, we lack the will to strive for them. All desire and activity becomes empty and vain, and we sink into apathy and cynicism" (*TJ*, 386).

Rawls's definition of self-respect stimulated an extensive literature in which various kinds of self-respect and self-esteem are distinguished,[6] but for his purposes the crucial points are that self-respect is good or rational for anyone to want to have, that having it is a necessary psychological condition for enjoying other goods, and that whether or not members of a society have self-respect is significantly influenced by the basic structure of its institutions and its public rationale. That self-respect (or self-esteem) is desirable for a person to have is generally taken for granted by philosophers, but no one has emphasized more than Rawls that a lack of self-respect undermines a person's potential for a meaningful and enjoyable life. Again, though political philosophers have often argued that unjust social conditions tend to make people unhappy, resentful, or alienated, part of Rawls's originality was to argue systematically for a theory of justice by treating the effect of social systems on the self-esteem of citizens as one of the main criteria for assessing the relative merits of such theories.

## The Significance of Self-Respect for Rawls's Theory

Rawls's claims about self-respect play several roles in his complex argument for the superiority of justice as fairness over utilitarian (and other) theories of justice. *First*, most obviously, given that having the social bases of self-respect is a primary good that all persons have reason to want, *a directly supporting argument* for the thesis that members of the original position would choose Rawls's principles of justice over other traditional principles is that a basic social structure that conforms to justice as fairness would better support the citizens' self-respect. By definition, members of the original position base their choice of principles on whether corresponding social structures are likely to secure for themselves the best possible mix of primary goods, including the social bases of self-respect as well as liberties, opportunities, wealth, income, etc. That Rawls's principles tend to provide the social bases of self-respect better than alternative principles of justice, then, must be at least one direct reason for Rawls's principles to be favored from the perspective of the original position.

*Second*, if this thesis is correct, as Rawls argues, then a society the basic structure of which publicly affirms and conforms to justice as fairness would tend to be more stable, other things equal, than societies based on other conceptions of justice. By promoting the self-respect of its members, the social structure based on Rawls's principles would tend to promote for those living under the system the convergence of a good life and a just life. Seeing that justice as fairness tends to promote their own good (in addition to appealing to their sense of justice, a separate consideration), they would naturally want to stabilize that social structure, helping to support it and restore it when it deviates from justice. This second argument, that by affirming citizens' self-respect, justice as fairness *promotes its relative stability*, offers further reason for members of the original position to favor justice as fairness over other conceptions of justice. This argument, together with other considerations favoring the stability of societies structured by Rawls's principles, supplements and completes Rawls's initial arguments that his principles would be chosen in the original position. The supplement was needed because the initial arguments simply stipulated that the various principles to be assessed were going to govern well-ordered societies that were tentatively assumed to be stable.

*Third*, presumably Rawls's claims about the social bases of self respect implicitly serve a third role in Rawls's overall defense of his principles. That is, insofar as they are justified, Rawls's claims *offer his readers prudential and moral reasons* for accepting justice as fairness that are partially independent of thoughts of stability and the original position. Suppose we (the readers) set aside arguments addressed specifically to members of the original position and take up our standpoint as actual persons seeking to achieve wide reflective equilibrium on the merits of Rawls's principles of justice. As normal human beings we do care that we ourselves have enjoyable and meaningful lives grounded (if Rawls is right) in self-respect, and as even minimally moral human beings we also care to some extent that others can have similarly enjoyable and meaningful lives. Given this, if true, Rawls's claim that his principles secure to citizens the social bases of self-respect, would provide us with both moral and prudential reasons to endorse his theory. Even those who have doubts about his definition of the original position and arguments from that perspective could see good reason to favor his principles over those, such as utilitarianism, that do not guarantee us the social bases of self-respect. The values of actual individual readers of *TJ* differ in many respects, of course, but it would be a rare person who would altogether deny that it is a merit of a social system that it tends to preserve the self-respect of citizens – as Rawls defines this. Ordinary people, in the real world, have reason to want what helps to preserve their own self-respect and typically, at least when not engaged in particular partisan conflicts, they are not indifferent to whether or not it supports or diminishes the self-respect of others.

Rawls's arguments depend on empirical claims about the effects of different social structures on the attitudes of citizens. In this respect his arguments regarding self-respect are similar to his argument that societies structured by his principles would be relatively stable because of his hypothesized psychological laws governing the development of citizens' sense of justice. All of these arguments make use of hypotheses of empirical psychology, but they are not hypotheses that can be tested or even understood without reference to the normative ideas of justice proposed by Rawls and other theorists. For example, the thesis that justice as fairness supports citizen's self-respect better than utilitarianism concerns the effects of structuring basic social institutions according to these different conceptions of justice. The alternative conceptions of justice, expressed by different principles, must be understood and incorporated into the psychological hypotheses to be tested. For example, the hypothesis needed to show the relative superiority of Rawls's principles regarding self-respect must be in conditional form, such as this: "Provided that a society is well-ordered and *the basic structure conforms to Rawls's principles of justice and everyone knows this*, then those who grow up in that society will tend to develop a secure self-respect to a greater extent than they would had the basic structure been based on utilitarian, perfectionist, or other principles of justice." If psychological studies ignore differences in how citizens understand justice, they cannot provide evidence relevant to Rawls's claims. Also, because we do not now have any actual well-ordered societies structured purely by Rawls's principles, utilitarian principles, or perfectionist principles, the relevant psychological search for confirming evidence must be indirect. Rawls's psychological conjectures seem quite plausible, but, as he suggests, to find such evidence we would need new subtly designed research projects that involve the cooperation of moral philosophers and psychologists.

Leaving such projects for others, I turn now to a different issue raised by Rawls's discussion of self-respect. Despite Rawls's endorsement of a Kantian interpretation of his theory, his idea of self-respect *as a product of social institutions* is strikingly different from self-respect as understood by Kant and contemporary Kantians. And the contrast leads to an apparent objection that may resonate broadly in our current political culture.

## Kantian Conceptions of Self-Respect: A Troublesome Contrast?

A prominent feature of Kant's ethics is his belief that we have duties to ourselves as persons whose "humanity" (or "rational nature") is an end in itself (Kant 2002, 228–233 (Ak: 427–433)).[7] For example, he argued that we have duties to ourselves to avoid degrading and self-destructive behavior and to develop our useful capacities and earnestly seek moral self-improvement (Kant 1996, 173–196 (Ak. 417–447)). The source of these duties is not a contract with ourselves or a natural desire for our own happiness but rather our basic humanity – our nature as persons with reason and the capacity for autonomy and morality. The moral law is metaphorically represented as the voice of the ideally rational "human being as such" within each of us. In Kant's view a kind of *basic self-respect* – respect for ourselves as moral agents – is inevitably forced from all responsible human beings, both good and bad, because this kind of self-respect is equivalent to (or follows from) the respect for the moral law within us. There could be no duty to have self-respect in this sense, for it is a pervasive feature of our humanity rather than something that we voluntarily acquire or that is instilled in us by prevailing social structures (see, i.e., Kant 1996, 162 (Ak. 402–403)).

Kant also held, however, that we do have a pervasive duty to live in a way that is worthy of our moral agency, that is, to treat our humanity as an end in itself, never merely as a means. This second kind of self-respect, or moral self-regard, is something that all moral agents *ought* to have, though many do not.[8] To have it is to choose to live in a self-respecting way, expressing a proper regard for one's humanity in one's acts (e.g., preserving and developing one's rational capacities) and one's attitudes (e.g., readiness to affirm and honor one's moral status of dignity and equality as a person). Kant's background assumption is that our basic life-governing attitudes and conduct must be seen, at least from our practical standpoint as agents, as freely chosen or "up to us" in a sense that makes us responsible for them. It is this second idea of self-respect that resonates with a familiar strand of thinking in the contemporary political culture. The modest version is just that normally individuals should take responsibility for developing a life worthy of respect, affirming and standing up for it, and maintaining the attitudes and psychological stability needed to live accordingly. The extreme version is that individuals should be held completely responsible when they fall short of this ideal, and so citing social determinants as explanations of shortcomings is simply illegitimate excuse-making, blaming society for personal failures.

Like Rawls's ideas about self-respect, the Kantian ideas have prompted a valuable follow-up literature, but the contrast raises an issue of broad contemporary interest apart from its connection with Kant and the Kantian interpretation of *TJ*. Empirically minded philosophers, including admirers of Rawls, may deplore the Kantian idea that we freely adopt our self-regarding attitudes. On the other side, Kantians and others, including some admirers of Rawls, may object that Rawls (apparently) treats important self-regarding attitudes, such as self-respect, as causally determined by social conditions for which individual agents are not responsible. It may seem as if Rawls thinks that the basic social structure, along with particular social facts, either *make* us self-respecting or *deprive* us of self-respect. The individual responsibility to live in a self-respecting way, even in an unjust society, may appear to be implicitly denied or disregarded. The objection is not just that Rawls does not address the question whether or not individuals have the responsibility to be self-respecting, but, even more, that he writes as if it is the responsibility of the social structure to mold citizens so that they will think they have worth – not because they do but because thinking so will enable them to be happy.

## A Possible Rawlsian Response

It is undeniable that in *TJ* Rawls is not working with an unmodified Kantian moral psychology, and, contrary to an individualistic ("conservative") strand in contemporary political culture, he does not hesitate to attribute substantial responsibility for undesirable social attitudes to defective social structures. To anyone inclined to see these as objectionable aspects of Rawls's theory, one might respond on Rawls's behalf as follows.

*First*, although Rawls proposes "a Kantian interpretation" of justice as fairness, he explicitly explains that his theory differs from Kant's moral and political theory in several important respects, not the least of which is Rawls's rejection of Kant's attempts to establish the fundamental principles a priori. Kant's abstract theory, he suggests, was in need of interpretation that employed empirical hypotheses not just to make it more appealing and applicable for twentieth-century readers but because of deep unresolved problems in Kant's theory (*TJ*, 221–227).

*Second*, although Rawls maintains that social structures have a pervasive causal influence on social attitudes, to the extent that this tendency is in fact supported by good evidence, there should be no objection, and we should note that Rawls does not say, or need to assume, that social factors completely determine individuals' attitudes. His arguments regarding relative stability and the benefits of having self-respect only require assumptions about the general tendencies of different types of social structure to promote or diminish self-respect.

*Third*, although Rawls does not argue (as Kant did) that it is a duty or responsibility of individuals to be self-respecting in their attitudes and conduct, his theory does not deny this. The morality of self-regarding attitudes is not a matter of justice, not even the obligations and natural duties of individuals that Rawls considers briefly in *TJ* (*TJ*, 93–101, 293–308).

*Fourth*, and perhaps most important, although the causal influence of social structures on the self-respect of citizens is important for Rawls's argument for relative stability, there is a different kind of argument available to Rawls when addressing readers seeking wide reflective equilibrium regarding justice as fairness. We may say that basic social institutions structured by Rawls's principles *affirm* and *express* the self-respect of citizens better than other theories do without claiming that they have a stronger causal influence in generating the attitude.[9] If we understand self-respect in the more or less Kantian way, then self-respecting persons are morally committed to maintaining themselves as rational, responsible, and equal in basic worth to any other. What kind of social structure would such self-respecting persons see as best affirming and expressing their moral attitudes? Arguably, the principles of justice as fairness do so better than alternative theories, for example, utilitarianism, because of the ways in which justice as fairness makes the opportunities and basic welfare of each individual necessarily prior to other concerns, such as aggregate welfare.

## 4. Values Not Lost in the Move to *Political Liberalism*

Rawls's views evolved over the years, and famously his conception of his main project shifted between the publication of *TJ* and *PL*. His explanation of why he thought these changes were needed may have led some to think that he completely abandoned the ideas in Part III of *TJ*. He did in fact acknowledge that he had "quite different" aims in the later book and that "a serious problem" in his account of stability had required "extensive revisions" and "basic readjustments" (*PL*, xv–xvii). The problem, he said, was that "the account of stability in Part III of *Theory* is not consistent with the view as a whole" (*PL*, xv–xvi). The argument in Part III that a well-ordered society based on his principles could be both just and (relatively) stable was "unrealistic" because, given the liberty guaranteed in his first principle, reasonable citizens could be expected to develop and affirm a plurality of comprehensive moral and religious doctrines.[10] Thus we must not suppose they would all continue to accept Rawls's principles as the principles of justice. Even if they once had a well-ordered society based on Rawls's principles, it could not be stabilized by a sense of justice the genesis of which presupposed full agreement on Rawls's principles as true, metaphysically grounded, or the most morally fundamental standard of justice for basic social institutions. The problem is not merely that it seems empirically unlikely that there will actually be just and stable societies structured by Rawls's principles. The special problem is that liberal political theory is supposed to respect the variety of opinions on moral and religious matters that reasonable people with freedom of thought and discussion can be expected to develop. Stability cannot consistently be based on citizens' continuous agreement on the superiority of Rawlsian moral theory, given that a plurality of reasonable but incompatible doctrines is to be expected. Considered as a partially comprehensive moral doctrine, justice as fairness appears to be just one among many reasonable doctrines competing for adherence in the free marketplace of ideas.

In response to the problem, Rawls explicitly limited his aim in *PL*. The aim is not to offer even a partially comprehensive *moral* theory but rather to develop a defensible "*political* conception of justice." A political conception, in contrast to comprehensive moral doctrines, draws from common ideas in our political culture, concerns a restricted range of political questions, and *explicitly* forgoes any claim to metaphysical truth but instead offers arguments for objectivity and justification of a different kind.[11] A political conception is "self-standing" rather than derivative from a larger worldview. Because political conceptions of justice do not deny the truth or deep foundations of reasonable comprehensive moral and religious doctrines, it is possible that a suitably developed political conception could gain the principled support of adherents of those doctrines for limited purposes of conducting our political affairs.[12] This, of course, was Rawls's aim. The new strategy to secure the stability of a just society based on Rawls's *political* principles was to argue that there are sufficient reasons for rational and reasonable people with different moral and religious convictions to form "an overlapping consensus" on the use of his principles for certain political purposes (*PL*, 131–172).

Many questions have been raised about this shift to the "political conception," for example, how radical the changes were, whether they were necessary, and what was lost and what gained in the transition. My brief concluding remarks concern the extent to which the aspects of Part III of *TJ* discussed above can survive the transition to Rawls's reframed project in *PL*. The issues here are complex and many, and my aim is just to call attention to some points that may be neglected and to raise some questions that may merit further attention. Here are four points to consider.

*First*, to what extent did Rawls himself repudiate Part III of *TJ* when he moved to *PL?* What is clear is that he turned to a new, reframed, or clarified project, expressed in part by the question "How is it possible that deeply opposed though reasonable comprehensive doctrines may live together and all affirm *the political conception* of a constitutional regime?" (*PL* xviii, emphasis added). As reformulated, Rawls's aim was not, and perhaps never unambiguously was, to find the correct or most defensible *moral* conception of justice. For that purpose it may not be necessary to argue for the stability of societies that adhere to it. Rather, the new or clarified aim is to articulate and defend a workable political conception of justice that can be stable despite profound disagreements among citizens about morality, philosophy, and religion. The change means that the previous argument for the relative stability of justice as fairness is no longer adequate for the purpose at hand, but this is not to deny that his psychological principles and rich discussion of self-respect and the moral sentiments have a significant role in *moral* theory where stability may not be a central issue.[13] How these aspects of Part III are important for moral theory remains a relatively neglected question, a legacy for others resulting from Rawls's turn to the "political conception."[14]

*Second*, are the psychological principles that in *TJ* he proposed to explain the development of a sense of justice still relevant to *PL?* It may seem that by projecting an overlapping consensus of reasonable moral and religious doctrines as the way to make a just society stable,

Rawls gave up the idea that psychological principles (or "laws") of the sort he proposed could explain the development of a sense of justice that would help to stabilize any well-ordered society based on his principles. With his changed strategy in *PL*, he cannot rely on the psychological laws as previously understood because they refer to background conditions in which the basic structure and other associations "are publicly known by all to be just" *by Rawls's principles*, which (we are now to suppose) were seen as part of a comprehensive moral doctrine. In a pluralistic world with many reasonable comprehensive moral doctrines, we cannot expect a shared common understanding of justice if justice is defined by any particular one of such doctrines.

If, however, the psychological laws were adjusted to presuppose only a common *political conception* of justice, then they could still be relevant in explaining the possible stability of a well-ordered society that is just according to Rawls's political conception of justice. Appeal to the psychological principles could not replace the new argument from overlapping consensus among reasonable comprehensive doctrines, but it might supplement it. Suppose, as Rawls projected, such a consensus were to develop gradually on the employment of justice as fairness for political purposes. Then there would be a politically just society structured by Rawls's political principles and increasingly becoming well-ordered and stabilized by the overlapping consensus. With this background of a common understanding and acceptance of Rawls's political conception of justice, appropriately reformulated psychological laws might explain how citizens might develop *a political sense of justice* that could supplement the consensus in stabilizing the politically just order. The proposed reformulated laws would state that citizens would tend to develop a normally effective desire to abide by Rawls's political principles, provided their society conforms to these principles and the citizens understand the principles as justified for political purposes by an overlapping consensus of reasonable comprehensive doctrines, including their own. Unless we can find societies where this background condition is satisfied, any evidence for the hypothesized laws would have to be indirect and limited – perhaps observable tendencies among various small-scale societies as they approximate the condition to various degrees. At least it is more realistic to suppose we can find approximations to the condition where agreement and conformity are based on overlapping consensus than to Rawls's initially stipulated condition that all citizens accept and conform to his principles as the principles uniquely justified by practical reason.

*Third*, how much of his innovative account of the social bases of self-respect in *TJ* survives and proves useful after the transition to *PL*? His claims about the way justice as fairness supports self-respect obviously cannot apply without modification to the world of *PL* where the basic equality of persons may not be affirmed (or interpreted in the same way) by all of the reasonable comprehensive moral and religious doctrines that join a consensus on Rawlsian political principles. Those who accept utilitarianism as the ultimately true comprehensive moral doctrine, for example, can say that "each person counts for one" in the sense that their pleasures and pains count equally with comparable pleasures and pains in others, but such utilitarians cannot affirm with Rawls, Kant, and others that each individual has a moral status with basic rights that are not conditional on what serves the aggregate welfare. Thus assuming that such comprehensive utilitarianism and various other moral and religious doctrines count as "reasonable," then if there is a plurality of such reasonable comprehensive doctrines, we can expect that the self-respect of citizens will not be as fully affirmed and supported as it would be if Rawls's account of justice were accepted by all as belonging to the superior comprehensive moral doctrine.

Nevertheless, if an overlapping consensus were to develop on justice as fairness as the shared political conception of justice, then at least the basic political, legal, and economic institutions at work in the society would treat citizens as free and equal persons with rights not to be sacrificed for the aggregate welfare. Even if some would cite God's will as the ultimate reason for joining the consensus, and others would appeal to utility or perfectionist ideals, and so on, we can conjecture that the just and stable political institutions framed by Rawls's principles would tend to support and affirm citizens' self-respect better than institutions directly shaped by utilitarian and other moral principles. As before, we have a modified empirical conjecture about the psychological effects of social institutions structured by different principles. It may be less plausible to expect the desired effects on self-respect when Rawls's principles are only accepted as the best political conception for a world with many reasonable comprehensive moral and political doctrines, but perhaps it is more realistic to think that psychology could provide confirming evidence for the modified conjecture because it concerns a possible world closer to our own than the more idealized world of TJ is.

*Finally*, we should not forget that Rawls's turn from moral theory to a self-standing political theory leaves much of his valuable work in Part III intact. Although presented as instrumental to his argument for relative stability of justice as fairness, his account of natural attitudes, moral sentiments, basic desires, and complex human relationships and ideals remains an inspiration and challenge for further work in moral theory and moral psychology. Rawls understood moral psychology, as did most great moral philosophers, to be essential to systematic moral theory and not reducible to either the study of ordinary language or empirical studies divorced from moral concepts. As Hume emphasized, the sources of moral psychology and moral theory include human experiences throughout history. As Wittgenstein and J.L. Austin taught, ordinary language is rich with valuable distinctions that are often lost in the artificial terminologies of philosophers and social scientists. As Aristotle and Kant illustrated, we do well to think systematically but not to lose our first-person perspective as moral agents concerned with how we ought to live. Drawing from the best of these and other sources, in Part III of *TJ* Rawls made a major contribution to moral theory independently of the special issue about stability that dominated much of his later work.

# Notes

1   In previous work I argued that this was Rawls's understanding in *PL*, but now it seems evident to me that the same idea is implicit in *TJ* (see Hill 1994). Rawls confirms this reading, at least regarding the later book, in his "Reply to Habermas" (*PL*, 390 n26).

2   The statement of the first law was inadvertently changed in the revised edition of *TJ*. This is the correct quote, taken from the original edition, p.490. Thanks to Samuel Freeman for clarification of this issue.

3   That the associations and basic social structure are assumed to be just is evident in the second and third laws, and the assumption regarding the family is explained later. See *JF* 10, 162–166.

4   To be fair, we should keep in mind that the "act utilitarianism'" of ethics textbooks is not what is at issue here. Rawls is comparing well-ordered utilitarian societies with well-ordered societies based on his own principles of justice. In both cases it is assumed that the relevant principles (utilitarian or Rawlsian) are publicly known and accepted. So we are not considering societies ruled by a utilitarian elite that hides its basic principle and pretends to uphold a different (e.g.,

rights based) standard. Nevertheless, those publicly known to be operating on utilitarian principles may use deception, manipulation, and force on particular issues. Citizens would have more reason than Rawls's citizens to distrust their officials' pronouncements about their particular aims and methods, but the openly utilitarian officials can consistently use methods that officials in Rawlsian well-ordered societies could not.

5  See also *JF*, 195–197, and *PL*, 86–88. Rawls typically uses the term "moral philosophy" broadly for the aims and disciplines of thinking that produced traditional "moral theories" (such as utilitarianism and social contract theories) and seek to reach a "wide reflective equilibrium" concerning their overall relative merits and weaknesses. A "moral theory," more narrowly, is a particular attempt to describe our moral capacities by constructing an account of justice (and other duties and virtues) designed to make sense of our common considered moral judgments and, if possible, to find bases of agreement where none is initially evident. In constructing, comparing, defending, motivating and explaining justice as fairness as a moral theory, of course, Rawls was engaged not only in moral theory but in moral philosophy broadly conceived.

6  See, for example, the essays collected and cited in Dillon, *Dignity, Character, and Self-Respect*, New York: Routledge, 1995.

7  Ak. numbers refer to pages in the standard Prussian Academy edition of Kant's works, now cited in the margins of most translations.

8  Although Kant does not call this a duty to respect oneself, this seems implicit in his discussion of duties to oneself (1996, 173–197 (Ak. 417–447)).

9  Rawls often writes of the *effects* of basic structures on the self-respect of citizens, for example, they can "support" and "secure" it, or "undermine" it; but he also implies that in a just society the social bases of self-respect are the fundamental institutions that publicly *affirm* the equal status of citizens (*TJ*, 386ff., 478). "[A] desirable feature of a conception of justice is that it should publicly express men's respect for one another. In this way they insure a sense of their own value" (*TJ*, 156). Arguably, the public expression or affirmation of each person's equal status is morally desirable – what Kantian self-respecting agents would want – independently of the causal effects that Rawls usually emphasizes.

10  For Rawls's account of "reasonable," see *PL*, 48–61.

11  In *PL* Rawls concedes that *TJ* may be seen as proposing a partially comprehensive moral doctrine but not that it claimed to be a metaphysically grounded true account of social justice. He explained why he regarded his theory as justified, at least relative to competing traditional conceptions of justice, by the method of reflective equilibrium, but tried to remain noncommittal about metaethical questions about moral truth and metaphysical grounding.

12  The aim is the *principled* support of reasonable comprehensive doctrines in contrast with the tentative and potentially temporary support that they might offer in a modus vivendi. See *JF*, 192, 194–195, and *PL*, xxxixf., lviii, 146f.

13  Also note that Rawls said that, apart from changes required to resolve the special problem about his argument for stability, "Otherwise, these lectures take the structure and content of *Theory* to remain substantially the same" (*PL*, xvi).

14  When I asked Rawls about the residual value of *TJ* in my comments at the American Philosophical Association in Los Angeles, 1994, he just replied "The book is still on the shelf."

## Works by Rawls, with Abbreviations

*Collected Papers* (CP), ed. Samuel Freeman. Cambridge, MA: Harvard University Press, 1999.
*Justice as Fairness: A Restatement* (JF), ed. Erin Kelly. Cambridge, MA: Harvard University Press, 2001.
*Political Liberalism* (PL), expanded edn. New York: Columbia University Press, 2005.

"Reply to Habermas" (1995), in *Political Liberalism* (372–434).
"The Sense of Justice" (1963), in *Collected Papers* (96–116).
*A Theory of Justice* (*TJ*), rev. edn. Cambridge, MA: Harvard University Press, 1999.

# Other References

Dillon, Robin S. (ed.) (1995) *Dignity, Character, and Self-Respect*. New York: Routledge.
Hill, Thomas E., Jr (1994) "The Problem of Stability in Political Liberalism." *Pacific Philosophical Quarterly* 75: 333–352. Reprinted in Hill, *Respect, Pluralism, and Justice: Kantian Perspectives* (237–259). Oxford: Oxford University Press, 2000.
Kant, Immanuel (1996) *The Metaphysics of Morals*, ed. and trans. Mary Gregor. Cambridge: Cambridge University Press.
Kant, Immanuel (2002) *Groundwork for the Metaphysics of Morals*, ed. Thomas E. Hill, Jr and Arnulf Zweig. Oxford: Oxford University Press.

# 12

# Political Authority, Civil Disobedience, Revolution

## ALEXANDER KAUFMAN

The notions of duty and obligation constitute the central focus of Rawls's account of political authority. Rawls begins his discussion of the foundations of political authority by attempting to answer the question: What principle(s) should regulate the relation between citizens of a just society and their political institutions? The appropriate principles, Rawls asserts, are those of duty and obligation. Citizens have a *duty* to create and maintain just political institutions and an *obligation* to do their part within those institutions if they have voluntarily accepted and intend to continue to accept benefits produced by those institutions. Where such duties and obligations are effective, political institutions possess the authority to exercise coercive legal and political power. Rawls's account of political authority thus emerges from his investigation of the appropriate relation between citizens and just political institutions.

Rawls develops his account of political authority in Chapter VI of *A Theory of Justice*. Part Two (Chapters IV, V, and VI) of *TJ* develops an account of the forms of political institutions that are consistent with and realize the practical implications of the principles of justice that are identified and justified in Part One. In order to work up an account of just institutions, Rawls argues, a framework is necessary to guide our judgments in applying the principles of justice to institutions. Persons reflecting about justice must, Rawls asserts, make three different kinds of judgments about justice. First, they must judge the justice of legislation and social policies. Second, since even members of a well-ordered society may disagree regarding the desirability of enacting particular pieces of legislation, they must decide which constitutional arrangements provide the most acceptable basis for selecting which political opinions are to be enacted into law. Finally, they must determine under what conditions the enactments of the majority must be complied with and under what conditions they must be viewed as so unjust that they are no longer binding – that is, they must determine "the grounds and limits of political duty and obligation" (*TJ*, 172).

In order to describe frameworks in which reliable judgments regarding these issues may be made, Rawls describes an elaboration of the original position to make possible a division of labor between stages in which persons deal with different kinds of issues of justice. After the principles of justice are selected in the original position, the veil of ignorance is progressively weakened in order to specify appropriate points of view from which certain issues are to be considered. In the first (constitutional) stage, the parties are to know both the principles of social theory and the general facts about their society. In the second (legislative) stage, the parties are provided with the full range of general economic and social facts. Moreover, in the second and third stages, the choices of the parties are designed to realize the two principles chosen in the first stage. Their motivations, therefore, are no longer guided simply by economic rationality; rather, the choices of the parties in the later stages are guided by a moral motivation that is not effective in the first stage. Finally, in the third (judicial and administrative) stage, the parties have complete access to all the facts.

Part Two of *TJ* contains Rawls's most sustained and best developed account of just institutions, and many issues relating to authority receive their definitive treatment in this section. In particular, Rawls develops his most precise account of the institutional implications of the liberty principle in Chapter IV and his only sustained account of conscientious refusal in Chapter VI.

In this chapter, I will examine Rawls's accounts of (1) the justification of political authority; (2) the essential elements of a just constitutional regime; (3) the conditions under which resistance to just institutions is permissible or required; and (4) the conditions under which institutions cease to deserve fidelity and obedience.

# 1. Political Authority and the Duty to Support Just Institutions

Rawls develops his account of political authority from an examination of the concepts of duty and obligation. Rawls's argument works from the assumption that if citizens have a duty to obey institutions or an obligation to respect the authority of the rules of those institutions, then the institutions possess legitimate political authority. This section will examine Rawls's accounts of duty and obligation as they relate to political authority. In particular, the section will discuss Rawls's accounts of (1) the duties and obligation of citizens; and (2) the duty to obey unjust laws.

## 1.1 Duty and Obligation

Rawls first emphasizes the distinction between natural duties and social obligations. Social obligation (*TJ*, 96) is the condition of being required to obey the rules of an institution or practice, and a social obligation applies if two requirements are met: (i) the institution or practice is just or fair; and (ii) the person has voluntarily accepted benefits provided by the institution. All obligations, Rawls argues, arise from the principle of fairness which holds that a person is obligated to "do his part" under the rules of a just or fair institution if he or she "has voluntarily accepted the benefits of the scheme or has taken advantage of the opportunities it offers to advance his interests" (*TJ*, 301). A person who fails to acknowledge an obligation when the two specified conditions are met, Rawls argues, is a free rider attempting to benefit from the cooperation of others without doing his or her fair share. Obligations, Rawls notes, have three characteristic features. They arise from our voluntary acts; the content of the obligation is defined by the rules of the institution or practice; and the obligations generated are to specific persons, in particular, the other persons cooperating within the institution or practice.[1]

While obligations exist within just institutions, however, basing our political ties on a principle of obligation would – Rawls argues – lead to serious complications. First, if our social ties rested solely upon a principle of obligation, then citizens would only be bound to respect the authority of a just constitution if they have voluntarily accepted and intend to continue to accept the social benefits that the constitution produces. Yet citizens who are born into and begin their lives under a constitution could reasonably question the degree to which their acceptance of benefits should be viewed as voluntary. If political ties were based solely upon a principle of obligation, Rawls concludes, concerns of this sort would undermine public acceptance of the state's authority and legitimate governments might be forced to employ significant coercive force in order to secure stability. Rawls therefore concludes that a complementary principle – the principle of natural duty – provides a better foundation for an account of political authority than a principle of obligation.

In contrast to obligations, natural duties apply to persons irrespective of their voluntary acts. Nor do duties have any necessary relation to the rules of institutions or practices. A person may be subject to a duty, then, even if she has not acted in a way that might justify claims against her by others. Nor are natural duties owed to definite individuals – they are, rather, owed to all others "as equal moral persons" (*TJ*, 99). Examples of natural duties, Rawls notes, include the duty to help others in need, the duty not to harm others, and the duty not to cause unnecessary suffering. Our most reliable considered judgments, Rawls suggests, confirm that a person need not commit a voluntary act in order to become subject to such duties. In fact, as Rawls notes, "a promise not to be cruel is normally ludicrously redundant" (*TJ*, 98). Natural duties, rather than deriving from acts or practices, reflect the requirements of the principles for social behavior that rational persons would accept in the original position. As in the case of other questions of justice, Rawls suggests, the judgments of rational persons in the original position provide a reliable guide for moral and political judgment. In fact, reflection in the original position provides the most reliable accounts of both duty and obligation.

*Authority and legitimacy*   In addition to the duties to avoid cruelty and to help others in need, Rawls notes, the most fundamental natural duties include a duty to support just institutions that exist and to further just arrangements when they are absent. Since persons have a duty to support just institutions, those institutions may be properly viewed as possessing legitimate political authority. The foundation of political authority is thus the natural duty to support just institutions. As discussed below, however, Rawls does not argue that citizens have a duty only to support institutions that are perfectly just – rather, he argues that citizens may have a natural duty to support and maintain a regime that is moderately unjust. Unless citizens have a duty to obey the moderately unjust legislation of a normally just regime, Rawls appears to assume, the stable maintenance of a just constitution may not be feasible. Rather, Rawls argues, if institutions and laws *could* have been generated through a just process and do not invade fundamental liberty interests, they satisfy the minimum criterion of legitimacy: "if the law actually voted is, so far as one can ascertain, within the range of those that could reasonably be favored by rational legislators conscientiously trying to follow the principles of justice, then the decision of the majority is practically authoritative, though not definitive" (*TJ*, 318).

In *Political Liberalism*, Rawls extends and generalizes this criterion of political legitimacy: "our exercise of political power is proper and hence justifiable only when it is exercised in accordance with a constitution the essentials of which all citizens may reasonably be expected to endorse in light of principles and ideals acceptable to them as reasonable and rational" (*PL*, 217). This criterion of legitimacy, Samuel Freeman emphasizes, does not simply constitute an interpretation of the *formal* notion of legitimacy as a standard governing the proper enactment of laws and conferring of powers upon officials. Rather than requiring merely that authority must be conferred in accordance with recognized procedures, Rawls's criterion of legitimacy provides a "moral/political standard" to be employed in evaluating the degree to which laws and institutions satisfy the minimum moral requirements that must be met before an institution, official, or law may be viewed as possessing legitimate authority (Freeman 2007, 376). In particular, Rawls's criterion requires that laws and institutions must satisfy a specific substantive requirement: they must be consistent with the substance of a constitution that could reasonably be accepted by democratic citizens.

*An ambiguous account?*　Sebastiano Maffettone thus fails to recognize the essentially substantive character of Rawls's principle of legitimacy when he argues that "Rawls' concept of legitimacy [in *PL*] oscillates ambiguously between two notions" (2010, 225). One of these notions, Maffettone suggests, corresponds to the formal notion of legitimacy deriving from the Weberian tradition; while the second notion imposes specific substantive requirements before a regime may be viewed as legitimate. In support of the claim that Rawls sometimes employs a purely formal Weberian notion of legitimacy, Maffettone cites the following language from Rawls's "Reply to Habermas": "we may think 'legitimate' and 'just' the same. A little reflection shows that they are not. A legitimate king or queen may rule by just and effective government, but then they may not . . . Their being legitimate says something about their pedigree: *how they came to their office*" (Maffettone 2010, 226, emphasis added). In insisting that legitimacy is a weaker requirement than justice and one that focuses on pedigree, Maffettone asserts, this passage in Rawls must refer to a purely formal notion of legitimacy. Thus, Maffettone concludes, Rawls in some cases employs a purely formal notion of legitimacy.

Maffettone, however, misunderstands the passage that he cites from the "Reply to Habermas," because he incorrectly assigns a purely formal meaning to the phrase "how they came to office." As discussed above, Rawls argues that a law or institution is legitimate if it falls "within the range of those that could reasonably be favored by rational legislators conscientiously trying to follow the principles of justice" (*TJ*, 318). Thus, a regime may be viewed as coming to office in a manner that justifies its legitimacy only if it could have been contracted into during a process of historical change that evolved among reasonable and rational persons deliberating under fair conditions. Rawls's account of legitimacy therefore requires not merely that a regime came to power in a manner consistent with recognized procedures, but rather that a legitimate regime could have come to power through a process in which reasonable and rational persons conscientiously trying to follow the principles of justice consented to the introduction of those institutions. Far from describing a purely formal notion of legitimacy, then, the language that Maffettone cites sets out a normative account of legitimacy. Maffettone thus fails to provide evidence that Rawls employs a purely formal Weberian notion of legitimacy. Maffettone's argument that Rawls's concept of legitimacy in *PL* oscillates ambiguously between two notions of legitimacy therefore fails.[2]

## 1.2 The Duty to Obey Unjust Law

In order to develop his account of political authority, Rawls first focuses on a problematic implication of the duty to support just institutions – if just institutions enact unjust legislation, the duty to support just institutions would appear to require obedience to those unjust laws. Rawls's analysis in Chapter VI of *TJ* thus begins by focusing on the following question: If social institutions are for the most part just, what should a citizen with a sense of justice do when confronted with an unjust law? Rawls immediately reframes the issue as a question to be examined from the perspective of the second (constitutional) stage of the original position: Could a rational person in an initial position of equality consent to a constitutional rule that would require obedience to unjust laws? In particular, how could a free rational person consent to institutions that would bind him to accept as authoritative laws that give effect to opinions that he views as unjust?

Once the question is restated in this form, Rawls argues, "the answer is clear enough" (*TJ*, 311). Among the limited number of feasible political institutions that we could adopt, none would always produce legislation that each individual views as just. The choosers know the standard of justice that they aim to realize – the standard defined by the two principles of justice as fairness. No form of constitution, however, could ensure that this standard will be fully realized. Political institutions under feasible constitutions are particularly prone to injustice, Rawls notes, because any acceptable form of constitution must respect the principle of majority rule by assigning legislative power to a democratically elected representative body. The first principle of justice, Rawls has argued in Chapter IV, requires that each citizen possess as close as possible to equal opportunity to influence the resolution of questions of public justice and policy. In addition, a form of politics that permitted minority rule could provide no acceptable criterion to determine which minority is to exercise power. But while justice requires democratic government, Rawls notes, "[t]here is nothing to the view . . . that what the majority wills is right" (*TJ*, 313). As Rawls notes, "none of the traditional conceptions of justice have held" such a view (*TJ*, 313). Majorities of voters are bound to make mistakes of judgment due to lack of information, faulty inferences, and partial or self-interested views. Thus, while it is appropriate for the citizens of a well-ordered society to accept democratic decisions as authoritative, "they do not [and should not] submit their judgment to it" (*TJ*, 314). The best feasible constitution, then, will predictably lead to the enactment of unjust legislation. Nevertheless, the best feasible constitution provides the basis for the closest approximation of justice.

Rawls contrasts the character of *imperfect* procedural justice under the best feasible constitution with that of an ideal market process. First, Rawls notes that an *ideal* market process – unlike the best feasible constitution – constitutes a *perfect* procedure for the realization of efficiency. The standard to be realized is set in advance by efficiency theory, and the procedure (assuming ideal conditions are satisfied) is perfectly designed to satisfy that standard. Second, Rawls notes that an ideal market process achieves efficiency even if all participants in the process merely pursue their own advantage. In fact, Rawls notes, efficiency theory assumes economic agents normally behave in such a manner. In participating in the market, agents do not attempt to form judgments about what transactions or behavior will best realize social efficiency; they simply advance their own ends. A just constitution, however, "must rely to some extent on citizens and legislators adopting a wider view and exercising good judgment in applying the principles of justice" (*TJ*, 317). If all citizens "take a narrow or group-interested standpoint," the process will not produce a just outcome (*TJ*, 317). Thus, Rawls concludes, there are "grave limitations" to any attempt to achieve justice by applying economic theory to the constitutional process. This conclusion, moreover, underlines the contrast between justice as fairness and social choice theory. Social choice theory aims for an optimal approach to satisfying the preferences of persons who merely pursue their own advantage, while justice as fairness relies upon citizens to form judgments about what policies will best realize justice.

Unlike the participants in an ideal market, then, the choosers of a just constitution in the second stage of the original position deliberations know the standard that they wish to realize but must employ an imperfect procedure to realize that standard. Consent to a form of constitution by the choosers in the original position therefore constitutes an instance of imperfect procedural justice. However, while any feasible constitution will therefore realize justice imperfectly, Rawls argues that consent to one of these forms of constitution "is surely preferable to no agreement at all" (*TJ*, 311). The choosers in the second stage of the original position would therefore consent both to the principle of majority rule and to accept the authority of legislation enacted under that principle that they view as unjust.

This consent to the authority of unjust laws is, however, limited by certain conditions. First, the burdens produced by unjust legislation should be "more or less evenly" distributed over individuals and groups, and hardships produced by unjust policies "should not weigh too heavily in any particular case" (*TJ*, 312). Second, no citizen should be required to accept invasions of his or her basic liberties. Generally, Rawls concludes, the duty to comply with unjust laws holds only as long as those laws "do not exceed certain bounds of injustice" (*TJ*, 312).

## 2. A Just Constitutional Regime

Citizens have a duty to obey law and to respect the authority of existing institutions that are established by a (for the most part) just constitution. Such a just constitution must satisfy the requirements of equal liberty and must be the feasible just arrangement most likely to result in a just and effective system of legislation. A just constitutional regime, Rawls notes, consists of a number of basic elements. First, the authority to legislate is assigned to a representative legislature that is accountable to the electorate. Second, firm constitutional protections are provided for certain liberties, in particular freedom of speech and assembly, and the liberty to form political associations.

The principle of equal liberty, when applied to constitutional design, requires that all citizens must be assured "an equal right to take part in, and to determine the outcome of, the constitutional process that establishes the laws with which they are to comply" (*TJ*, 194). Rawls refers to the liberty principle, as applied at the constitutional level, as the equal participation principle. This principle, Rawls states, transfers the notion of fair representation from the original position to the constitution.

Rawls emphasizes three requirements that the equal participation principle imposes on constitutional regimes. First, each vote should have approximately the same weight in determining the outcomes of elections. Interpreted strictly, this requirement would mandate that each member of the legislature should represent the same number of constituents and that legislative districts are drawn up under the guidance of standards designed to prevent gerrymandering. Rawls concedes, however, that it may be necessary to introduce some "random elements" in the process of designing districts since "the criteria for designing constituencies are no doubt to some extent arbitrary" (*TJ*, 196). In addition, citizens must have equal access to public office – that is, each must be eligible to join political parties, to run for office, and to hold political offices.

Second, the principle of equal participation requires that significant political decisions must be decided by the bare majority rule, as long as those decisions do not involve issues on which the constitution limits the scope of majority power. Employment of the bare majority rule is intended to implement the requirement that all citizens must be assured an equal right to determine the outcome of the process that establishes the laws. The restriction on the scope of majority power simply acknowledges that equal political liberty is only one of the basic political liberties and that respect for the will of the majority cannot justify institutional arrangements that violate fundamental interests protected by the other basic liberties. Rawls notes several traditional constitutional devices that are designed to limit the scope of the majority's political authority: bicameral legislatures, separation of powers, checks and balances, a bill of rights, and judicial review. These arrangements, Rawls notes, are consistent with equal political liberty as long as similar constraints apply to everyone and the effects of those constraints "fall evenly upon all sectors of society" (*TJ*, 197). As discussed below, Rawls will also argue that many of these constraints are necessary in order to ensure essential aspects of political liberty.

Third, the constitution must contain elements that secure the worth of political liberty. In particular, the constitution must underwrite fair opportunity for citizens to participate in the political process. Freedom of speech and assembly and liberty of thought and conscience, which are protected under the first principle, are essential to ensuring the worth of political liberty. In addition, all citizens should have the means to be informed about political issues and should have a fair opportunity to affect the political agenda. Moreover, Rawls notes, liberties protected by the equal liberty principle will lose much of their value if those with greater private means are permitted to exploit their advantages to dominate public debate. A just arrangement must therefore take steps to preserve for all fair value of their equal political liberties. These steps may include the provision of funds to encourage free public discussion, public financing of political campaigns, and government efforts to avoid extreme concentration of wealth. In addition, just arrangements must secure the worth of liberty by ensuring that constraints such as poverty, ignorance, or lack of means generally do not deprive persons of their capacity to take advantage of their rights.

While a just constitutional order must satisfy the equal participation principle, however, Rawls notes that such a just social arrangement will nevertheless need to regulate or restrict certain aspects of political liberty. Following Kant, Rawls argues that a basic liberty may be limited "only for the sake of liberty itself" (*TJ*, 179) – that is, only to ensure that that liberty or some other basic liberty is properly protected. The basic liberties, Rawls argues, are to be assessed as a whole – that is, as a single system (*TJ*, 178). Each liberty is to be defined so that the central applications of each can be simultaneously secured. In order to ensure that the system of liberties as a whole effectively secures the core applications of each basic liberty, the scheme is to be assessed from the standpoint of the representative equal citizen, and the various liberties are to be broadened or narrowed to reflect the ways in which they affect one another.

Rawls notes that liberties may be limited in three ways: (i) the constitution may define freedom of participation more or less extensively; (ii) the constitution may allow inequalities in political liberties; and (iii) larger or smaller amounts of social resources may be devoted to ensuring the worth of freedom. The *extent* of the principle of participation is determined by the extent to which the constitution restricts the application of the bare majority rule. A bill of rights generally removes certain liberties from majority regulation altogether, and separation of powers and judicial review also restrict the power of the legislature. These and other permissible restrictions on the extent of the principle of participation must bear equally on all persons. These restrictions are justified because they protect the other freedoms. Thus, restrictions on majority rule in a constitution are justified to the extent that the arrangements structured by the constitution further the ends of liberty, in particular, by mitigating the defects of the majority principle (*TJ*, 201).

*Inequalities in political liberty* must be justified, Rawls argues, in the same way. Such inequality is justified, Rawls argues, if – when viewed from the point of view of a representative citizen assessing the total system of freedom – the inequality would be acceptable, on due reflection, to the persons who are to suffer the lesser liberty because of the greater protection of their other liberties that results from the restriction (*TJ*, 203). The most obvious political inequality, Rawls states, is the failure to implement the precept of one person/one vote. John Stuart Mill, Rawls notes, was willing to argue for the violation of this precept on the grounds that political inequality would benefit those with lesser liberty. In particular, Mill argued that persons with greater education and intelligence should have extra votes. Such an arrangement, Mill argued, is in the interest of each because assigning more influence to better-informed voters was likely to increase the justice of legislation. For this argument to be successful, Rawls asserts, Mill would have to argue persuasively that this arrangement would in fact be acceptable to those persons whose franchise was restricted because the arrangement improved the security of other more fundamental liberties.[3]

# 3. Justifiable Noncompliance: Civil Disobedience and Conscientious Refusal

If social institutions are for the most part just, what should a citizen with a sense of justice do when confronted with an unjust law? While citizens have a general duty to obey unjust laws, Rawls discusses two instances in which certain forms of resistance are justifiable: (1) civil disobedience; and (2) conscientious refusal.

## 3.1 Civil Disobedience

Rawls's account of civil disobedience is designed to illustrate his account of the principles of natural duty and obligation by determining the point at which the duty to comply with laws enacted by the legislature of a nearly just democracy ceases to be binding. A constitutional theory of disobedience, Rawls notes, has three parts. It must define civil disobedience by specifying the kind of dissent that distinguishes it from other forms of opposition to political authority; it must set out the grounds that justify disobedience and the conditions under which such action is justified; and it must explain the role of civil disobedience in a nearly just constitutional system.

*Kind of dissent*  Rawls defines civil disobedience as a public, nonviolent political act contrary to law that is done with the aim of bringing about a change in law or policy. Civil disobedience specifically addresses the sense of justice of the majority and declares that the principles of justice that the majority accepts are not being respected. Civil disobedience, then, challenges the majority to live up to its own principles. Rawls immediately offers two glosses on this definition. First, he notes that the civilly disobedient act need not violate the particular act that is being protested. Often there are strong reasons, Rawls notes, for not violating a particular unjust law. For example, if the government enacts a vague or unacceptably harsh law against treason, civil disobedience in protest of that law need not – in fact, should not – take the form of committing treason. Rather, the protestor may present her case by violating traffic ordinances or laws of trespass. In other cases, such as laws affecting foreign affairs or another part of the country, there may be no way for an individual to violate the law directly. Second, Rawls notes that a civilly disobedient act must in fact be contrary to law, in the sense that the protestors are not merely raising a test case to be resolved in the courts. Rather, they must be prepared to continue violating the statute even if it is upheld and to accept the legal consequences.

A civilly disobedient act is essentially political in nature, both because it is addressed to the majority, and because the act is "guided and justified by political principles" (*TJ*, 321). That is, in civil disobedience, the protestor does not appeal to her personal moral or religious views or principles. Rather, she appeals only to a conception of justice that is commonly shared. The majority's deliberate and persistent violation of the principles of that conception, in particular the violation of basic liberties, invites submission but justifies resistance. Civil disobedience, Rawls notes, "forces the majority to consider whether it wishes to have its actions construed in this way" (*TJ*, 321) or whether it wishes, instead, to conform to its own conception of justice. Civil disobedience, then, is designed to call attention to an inconsistency between the conception of justice that the majority affirms and its policies.

A related point, Rawls notes, is that civil disobedience is public. The protestor does not merely violate an unjust law; her action, rather, is the public expression of her case against the law. One may, Rawls suggests, compare it to public speech – it is a form of address, an expression of conscientious political conviction. It tries to avoid the use of violence, not because of personal or principled abhorrence of the use of violence, but because violent acts are likely to undermine the case that the protestor is attempting to present to the majority. Interference with the civil liberties of others, Rawls asserts, in fact "tends to obscure the civilly disobedient quality of one's act" (*TJ*, 321).

The avoidance of violence is also appropriate for civilly disobedient resistance because civil disobedience has the curious quality of expressing disobedience to the law within the limits of fidelity to the law. Fidelity to the law is expressed by the public and nonviolent nature of the act, and by the actor's willingness to accept the legal consequences of her conduct. This quality, Rawls notes, distinguishes civil disobedience from militant resistance to the state. Militant resistance, Rawls notes, is much more profoundly opposed to the existing political arrangements. The militant does not view those arrangements as nearly just; rather, he views them as committed to a mistaken conception of justice or one that departs significantly from its fundamental principles. The militant, then, does not appeal to the majority's sense of justice; rather, he seeks to disrupt and replace what he views as an unacceptable public conception of justice. The contrast with militant resistance, then, illustrates the sense in which civil disobedience is informed by the quality of fidelity to the law. While militant resistance is profoundly opposed to the public's understanding of justice and existing political arrangements, civil disobedience is designed to restore the justice of law or policy within existing institutional arrangements.

*Grounds justifying civil disobedience*  Civil disobedience is justified, Rawls argues, only under a limited number of circumstances. First, civil disobedience is justifiable as a response only to instances of substantial and clear injustice. Thus, Rawls suggests that there must be a presumption that civil disobedience is justified only in circumstances involving serious infringements of the first principle of justice or blatant denials of equal opportunity under the principle of fair equality of opportunity. When, for example, certain minorities are denied the right to participate in the process of democratic self-government or to own property, the infringement of basic rights is sufficiently serious to justify civil disobedience. In contrast, Rawls suggests, since it is generally more difficult to establish definitively that the difference principle has been violated, violations of that principle provide a less acceptable justification for civil disobedience. Second, civil disobedience is appropriate only after the normal forms of appeal to the political majority have been made and have failed. For example, attempts to repeal unjust laws have failed, and legal protests have had no success. Third, it must not be the case that the civil disobedience threatens to cause disorder so serious that the existing and generally just constitution could no longer be effective.

Each individual must judge for herself the precise point at which these conditions are satisfied and the prima facie duty to obey the law ceases to be binding. Whether existing circumstances justify civil disobedience is therefore a question that is likely to generate reasonable disagreement.

*Role of civil disobedience*  In engaging in civil disobedience, Rawls asserts, citizens serve notice on the majority that the conditions of fair cooperation are being violated. As long as society is understood as a scheme of cooperation among equals, civil disobedience can be understood to be a stabilizing (if illegal) device of a constitutional system. As long as it is employed with restraint, Rawls suggests, civil disobedience can be seen to operate in a manner similar to regular elections and judicial review – that is, as a device that helps to maintain the justice of institutions. Moreover, Rawls suggests, the theory of civil disobedience can be seen as supplementing the theory of constitutional government. This role can be illustrated by contrasting medieval and modern constitutionalism. In medieval constitutionalism, Rawls notes, the supremacy of law was not secured by institutional mechanisms. If a ruler acted unjustly, his unjust acts could be restrained only by the resistance of the whole society (or a significant part of that society). Thus, Rawls notes, medieval political theory lacked the idea of a sovereign people to whom the government is accountable. In the same way that the modern conception of constitutional government supplements the medieval conception, Rawls suggests, the theory of civil disobedience supplements the modern conception of constitutional democracy by attempting to formulate the grounds upon which justifiable dissent to legitimate democratic authority may be based.

## 3.2 Conscientious Refusal

Rawls contrasts civil disobedience with conscientious refusal in order to define the character of civil disobedience more precisely and to provide an account of justifiable nonpolitical resistance to unjust law in nearly just conditions. Like his theory of disobedience, Rawls's account of conscientious refusal has three parts. It first specifies the kind of dissent that distinguishes conscientious refusal from other forms of opposition to political authority; it sets out the conditions under which conscientious refusal is justified; and it explains the role of civil disobedience in a nearly just constitutional system.

*Kind of dissent*    Rawls defines conscientious refusal as noncompliance with a legal injunction or administrative order. The order is addressed to the dissenter, and the authorities are aware of her noncompliance. Rawls cites as examples the refusal of early Christians to participate in rites prescribed by pagan states, the refusal of pacifists to serve in the armed forces, and the refusal of a soldier to obey a manifestly unjust order.

Conscientious refusal is not political in nature, since acts of conscientious refusal are not designed to appeal to the majority's sense of justice. While such acts are not covert, they do not constitute efforts to address the majority. Rather, the dissenter simply refuses to obey a command or legal injunction. The dissenter does not, then, justify his act by appealing to the community's conception of justice or political principles. Thus, unlike civil disobedience, conscientious refusal – while not covert – is not public. The dissenter recognizes that he may not be able to justify his actions to other members of the community because he judges that the majority's conception of justice is flawed. Thus, the conscientious refuser is less optimistic than those undertaking civil disobedience, since the conscientious refuser does not hope or expect to change law or policy. Rather than seeking out occasions to act as an expression of his views, then, the conscientious refuser "bide[s] [his] time hoping the necessity to disobey will not arise" (*TJ*, 324).

Unlike civil disobedience, conscientious refusal is not necessarily motivated by political principle. It may, rather, be based on religious or other principles. For example, Rawls notes, if the early Christians justified their refusal to participate in pagan rites on the basis of religious convictions rather than on the basis of reasons of justice, their resistance would not be political. However, conscientious refusal may be motivated by political principles. A dissenter might, for example, refuse on the basis of considerations of justice to assist in a policy of enslaving members of a racial minority.

Rawls notes that particular problems are raised by the case in which principles of justice require that persons act in ways that violate their religious principles – for example requiring a pacifist to serve in a just war. It is tempting, Rawls notes, to say that the law must always respect principled judgments of conscience. He concludes, however, that such a view cannot be right. In the case of the intolerant, for example, the pursuit of religious principle must be regulated by the law in order to secure equal liberty. Religious or moral principles cannot be allowed their full expression, then, if the result would violate the equal liberty of others. Thus, the law may treat pacifism with respect, not because the law must always respect principled judgments of conscience, but rather because pacifism is reasonably consistent with principles of political justice. In fact, the foundations of a just community's conception of justice are grounded in considered judgments shared by the pacifist – the view of men and women as equal moral persons and the abhorrence of war are common foundations for both views.

*Grounds justifying conscientious refusal*    In examining the grounds justifying conscientious refusal, Rawls extends the discussion beyond the range of domestic affairs to a consideration of the law of nations. His first concern, in discussing this topic, is to explain how the analytic approach that he employs in *TJ* may be extended to issues relating to the law of nations. In order to form reliable judgments relating to these issues, Rawls suggests, a person must view those issues from a standpoint reflecting an extended interpretation of the original position. In this interpretation, the parties are viewed as representatives of different nations who must choose fundamental principles to regulate conflicting claims among states. The parties know that they represent different nations with populations living under the ordinary circumstances of human life, but they know nothing about the particular circumstances of their societies. The parties are permitted only enough knowledge to form rational choices protecting the interests of their societies. Thus, as in the case of the domestic original position, this extended interpretation of the original position is designed to neutralize the influence of considerations that are arbitrary from the moral point of view – such as contingencies of historical fate or endowment of natural resources – over the choice of principles.

This extended interpretation of the original position thus clearly anticipates the notion of a second original position that Rawls develops in *The Law of Peoples*. In fact, the features of this extended interpretation of the original position are in many ways similar to the features of the second original position. In both decision procedures, the parties in the decision procedure represent groups rather than representative individuals – although in *LP* they represent *peoples*, while in *TJ* they represent *nations*. In both cases, the parties are situated equally. Each representative of a nation or people participates as a fully free and equal participant in the process of selecting principles. In both cases, the parties are "moved by appropriate reasons" (*LP*, 63). This feature of both the extended interpretation of the original position and the second original position is secured by a veil of ignorance. And in both cases, the choosers are characterized as rational.[4] Unlike the representatives of nations in *TJ*, however, the representatives of liberal peoples "know that reasonably favorable conditions obtain that make constitutional democracy possible" (*LP*, 33).[5]

The extended interpretation of the original position, Rawls argues, provides a basis for the judgment that representatives of free and equal nations would choose a set of principles including the principles of the equality of nations, the right to self-determination, the right to self-defense, and respect for treaties. In addition to these principles defining the circumstances in which a nation has a just cause in war, Rawls argues, the parties would select principles regulating the conduct of war. These principles would forbid the use of means of warfare that destroyed the possibility of peace or encouraged contempt for human life. Under these principles, Rawls argues, a soldier may conscientiously refuse to obey certain orders if he reasonably judges that the conduct involved would plainly violate the principles of justice regulating the conduct of war. As Rawls notes, such a case would involve conscientious refusal grounded in principles of *justice*, since reflection in the extended interpretation of the original position grounds the selection of principles of justice for nations.

*Role of conscientious refusal*    Rawls declines to provide an explicit account of the justifying conditions of conscientious refusal,[6] but his discussion of both the definition of and grounds justifying conscientious refusal offers some indication of his views regarding its role. In discussing pacifism as a justified form of conscientious refusal, for example, Rawls suggests that respect accorded to pacifism may alert citizens to the wrongs that may be committed by the state. Even if the views of the pacifist are not completely sound, Rawls asserts, the pacifist's warnings "may have the result that on balance the principles of justice are more rather than less secure" (*TJ*, 325). Conscientious refusal based upon the principles of justice between peoples may also, Rawls suggests, restrain governments from unjust acts: "such refusal is an affront to the government's pretensions, and when it becomes widespread, the continuation of an unjust war may prove impossible" (*TJ*, 335). Conscientious refusal may, then, function both to enlighten the views of fellow citizens and restrain unjust governments.

Rawls's accounts of civil disobedience and conscientious refusal thus supplement his account of the principles of natural duty and obligation by determining the point at which the duty to comply with laws enacted by the legislature of a nearly just democracy ceases to be binding.

## 4. Revolution

Rawls does not discuss revolution explicitly in *TJ*. Rather, he notes that because of his choice to focus upon issues in ideal theory, he will not address a number of important issues in partial compliance theory, such as "the justification of the various ways of opposing unjust regimes" (*TJ*, 8). Rawls does, nevertheless, provide a sketch of the conditions under which the policies of a regime diverge from legitimacy and justice sufficiently so that obedience to the law is no longer required by the natural duty of justice. Once social institutions fail to satisfy these minimum conditions, the duty to obey just institutions fails – since institutions are no longer just – and members of society are no longer obligated to obey existing law or to respect the authority of existing institutions.

In Chapter VI of *TJ*, Rawls sets out a standard of legitimacy for legislation: unless "the law actually voted is, so far as one can ascertain, within the range of those that could reasonably be favored by rational legislators conscientiously trying to follow the principles of justice," the decision of the majority is not "practically authoritative" (*TJ*, 318). A regime that systematically enacts legislation that violates principles of justice, then, forfeits its legitimacy. In particular, the state's "persistent and deliberate violation of the basic principles" of justice "especially the infringement of the fundamental equal liberties," Rawls asserts, justifies resistance (*TJ*, 321). Thus, a regime that fails to respect citizens' fundamental liberty interests lacks legitimate authority. A systematic pattern of disregard for fundamental liberty interests or other basic principles of justice, then, justifies organized resistance to the state.

The account of the limits of legitimate political power that Rawls attributes to John Locke in his *Lectures on the History of Political Philosophy* contains elements that can plausibly be employed to supplement Rawls's comments on failure of legitimacy in *TJ*. Locke, Rawls notes, both (i) provides a criterion of political legitimacy, and (ii) links that criterion to an account of the conditions under which citizens must recognize political obligation to a regime. Locke's criterion of legitimacy requires that a legitimate regime is a regime that "could have been contracted into during a rightly-conducted process of historical change, a process that began with the state of nature as a state of perfect freedom and equality" *LHPP*, 128–129). The notion of a "rightly conducted" process involves two requirements. First, the participants in that process must have acted rationally to pursue their legitimate interests – that is, their interests that are consistent with the law of nature, including respect for life, liberty, and estate. Second, the participants must have acted reasonably in respecting their duties and obligations under the law of nature. If participants, respecting these requirements of rationality and reasonableness, could have contracted into a particular regime, then the regime satisfies Locke's criterion. Regimes that could not satisfy the Lockean criterion include

(i) absolute tyrannies, (ii) regimes that fail to administer the law justly, and (iii) regimes that are "clearly unjust and violent" (*LHPP*, 134).

The fact that citizens have no obligation to obey a regime that falls into one of these categories does not, however, establish that they are not bound to obey the laws of such a regime. Rather, citizens may continue to be subject to a duty to obey the laws of the regime if resistance would not be effective – in particular, if resistance might simply cause the regime to become more repressive. A Lockean right to resist, then, exists when the regime is clearly unjust (either a tyranny or a state that is unjust in administration of the law or unjust in its employment of coercive force), and the likelihood is good that resistance will lead to the replacement of the current government with a just regime. How unjust must a regime be to fail Locke's criterion; and how likely must successful replacement of the regime be before citizens have a clear right to resist? These questions, Rawls asserts, depend upon judgment, which political philosophy cannot preempt. Locke's theory, then, provides a framework for judgment that each citizen must employ in due reflection.

As in Rawls's account, then, Locke's criterion of legitimacy tests legitimacy by asking whether the institution in question could be the product of consent among reasonable and rational deliberators. The conditions under which legitimacy fails in the Lockean account – unjust tyranny, arbitrary application of the law, or abuse of the state's coercive power – also seem reasonably similar to Rawls's view that a state that engages in "persistent and deliberate violation of the basic principles" (*TJ*, 321) forfeits legitimacy. The Lockean account supplements Rawls by linking observations regarding legitimacy to an account of the consequences if a government fails to satisfy the criterion of legitimacy. Such a failure justifies resistance, according to the Lockean argument, if a reasonable and rational person would on due reflection judge that (i) the degree of injustice justifies resistance; and (ii) there is sufficient likelihood that resistance may result in the restoration of a just and legitimate regime. The concern in this account regarding the practical consequences of resistance corresponds to Rawls's concern – in his account of civil disobedience – that citizens might have a duty to refrain from otherwise justified civil disobedience if such action would lead to "a breakdown in the respect for law" (*TJ*, 328).

Rawls's comments in *TJ* thus suggest at least the foundational principle for an account of revolution and justified resistance: "persistent and deliberate violation of the basic principles" of justice "especially the infringement of the fundamental equal liberties," Rawls asserts, justifies resistance (*TJ*, 321). Such disregard for the basic requirements of justice would also clearly violate the liberal principle of legitimacy, since laws violating basic liberties could not be the product of a process of historical change that evolved among reasonable and rational persons deliberating under fair conditions. Rawls's discussion of Locke supplements this view by elaborating the account of unjust behavior that may justify resistance and discussing the degree to which and the conditions under which a failure of legitimacy establishes that citizens have no obligation to respect the authority of a regime.

## 5. Conclusion

Rawls develops his account of authority in *TJ* from an examination of the appropriate relation between citizens and just political institutions, while he develops the account of legitimacy in *PL* from an examination of the bases upon which the exercise of coercive political power may be justified to citizens who may affirm inconsistent or conflicting comprehensive doctrines. Despite the more self-conscious focus in *PL* on issues raised by the fact of reasonable pluralism, the two accounts both reflect similar concerns regarding political justification. The concern to identify principles that could constitute the focus of an overlapping consensus leads Rawls to alter his standard from the criterion in *TJ* – legitimate laws must fall within "the range of those that could reasonably be favored by rational legislators conscientiously trying to follow the principles of justice" (*TJ*, 318) – to the standard embodied in the principle of liberal legitimacy – the exercise of political power is legitimate "only when it is exercised in accordance with a constitution the essentials of which all citizens may reasonably be expected to endorse in light of principles and ideals acceptable to them as reasonable and rational" (*PL*, 217). The later focus on the judgments of citizens that are informed by principles acceptable to them as reasonable and rational, rather than on the views of rational legislators trying to follow the principles of justice as fairness, reflects Rawls's aspiration to generate conclusions that can be justified in the context of reasonable pluralism, but Rawls's account continues to be oriented by the underlying notion that the legitimate exercise of coercive political power must be justifiable on terms that persons subject to that power can affirm on due reflection.

## Notes

1   In his earlier article, "Legal Obligation and the Duty of Fair Play," Rawls fails to make such a clear distinction between duty and obligation and, in fact, argues that the obligation to obey the law "is a case of the duty of fair play" (*CP*, 122).

2   Questions regarding the scope of Rawls's notion of legitimacy continue to stimulate controversy. Paul Weithman, for example, persuasively rebuts the suggestion, which he attributes to Charles Larmore, that Rawls views the liberal principle of legitimacy as imposing a necessary condition upon the choice of the principles of justice, themselves (see Weithman 2010, 350–352).

3   Mill's argument is interesting, Rawls suggests, because it enables one to see why political equality has sometimes been regarded as less essential than equal liberty of conscience or liberty of the person. To the extent that one assumes that it is the sole purpose of government to secure the common good, one may be persuaded that government by the more educated or intelligent is acceptable if that arrangement most effectively realizes the common good. However, if one does not view the purposes of government as entirely instrumental, Rawls suggests, this conclusion may seem less justifiable.

4   "The rational representatives of liberal peoples are to specify the Law of Peoples" (*LP*, 32). The rationality of the parties in the second original position is clearly of great importance to Rawls, and he is careful to emphasize, when he extends the second original position to justify the choice of principles for decent hierarchical peoples, that this aspect of the decision procedure remains unchanged: "the parties representing these decent hierarchical peoples are fairly situated, *rational*, and moved by appropriate reasons" (*LP*, 63, emphasis added).

5   Rawls also discusses a second set of deliberations in the second original position that include representatives of nonliberal "decent" peoples. In these deliberations, the representatives clearly do not know that conditions obtain that are favorable to constitutional democracy.

6   "In a fuller account the same kind of explanation could presumably be given for the justifying conditions of conscientious refusal . . . I shall not, however, discuss these conditions here" (*TJ*, 337).

## Works by Rawls, with Abbreviations

*Collected Papers* (CP), ed. Samuel Freeman. Cambridge, MA: Harvard University Press, 1999.

*The Law of Peoples, with "The Idea of Public Reason Revisited"* (LP). Cambridge, MA: Harvard University Press, 1999.

*Lectures on the History of Political Philosophy* (LHPP), ed. Samuel Freeman. Cambridge, MA: Harvard University Press, 2007.

"Legal Obligation and the Duty of Fair Play," in S. Hook (ed.), *Law and Philosophy: A Symposium* (3–18). New York: New York University Press, 1964. Also in *Collected Papers* (117–129).

*Political Liberalism* (PL) (1993, 1996), expanded edn. New York: Columbia University Press, 2005.

"Reply to Habermas" (1995), in *Political Liberalism* (372–434).

*A Theory of Justice* (TJ) (1971), rev. edn. Cambridge, MA: Harvard University Press, 1999.

## Other References

Freeman, Samuel (2007) *Rawls*. London: Routledge.

Maffettone, Sebastiano (2010) *Rawls: An Introduction*. Cambridge: Polity.

Weithman, Paul (2010) *Why Political Liberalism? On John Rawls's Political Turn*. Oxford: Oxford University Press.

# Part IV

# A Political Conception

13

# The Turn to a Political Liberalism

## GERALD GAUS

In the preface to *Political Liberalism* Rawls tells us that "to understand the nature and extent of" the differences between *Political Liberalism* and *A Theory of Justice* "one must see them as arising from trying to resolve a serious problem internal to justice as fairness, namely from the fact that the account of stability in part III of *TJ* is not consistent with the view as a whole" (*PL*, xv–xvii). Rawls goes on to tell us that the problem of the third part of *TJ* was its claim that a well-ordered society would come to embrace justice as fairness as a "comprehensive philosophical doctrine," but "the fact of reasonable pluralism" shows this to be unrealistic. Recasting justice as fairness to avoid this problem, he tells us, surprisingly "forces many other changes and calls for a family of ideas not needed before" (*PL*, xvii). So much is commonplace. There is, however, considerable dispute about almost every aspect of Rawls's "political turn," including whether it was well- or ill-advised (compare Weithman 2010 and Barry 1995). There is dispute about what Rawls meant by "stability" and whether it is primarily a sociological or a normative-justificatory idea (see Krasnoff 1998). Some pinpoint Chapter IX of *TJ*, "The Good of Justice," as the real source of Rawls's worry (Barry 1995, 915; Freeman 2003), while others (Weithman 2010) stress the close interconnections between all the main elements of Part Three (Chapters VI–IX). And there is extensive dispute about the details of the analysis of Part Three of *TJ*, what precisely were the problems, and in just what way *PL* sought to overcome them. Rawls apparently thought that almost all the main ideas of political liberalism were the result of fixing *TJ*'s account of stability. While it is manifest that the idea of overlapping consensus is a crucial part of *PL*'s response, many also stress the fundamental role of the idea of public reason (Freeman 2007), while others emphasize the way in which a concern for legitimacy rather than an account of justice becomes the focus in *PL* (Dreben 2003).

In this chapter I cannot hope to critically survey these debates. Simply to analyze Paul Weithman's (2010) deep and comprehensive recent study of Rawls's political turn would itself require a chapter. Instead, I shall sketch a reading that confirms Rawls's view that the stability argument of Part Three of *TJ* was crucial for the success of *TJ* as a whole, that it was

*A Companion to Rawls*, First Edition. Edited by Jon Mandle and David A. Reidy.
© 2014 John Wiley & Sons, Inc. Published 2016 by John Wiley & Sons, Inc.

indeed flawed, and that fundamental ideas of *PL* can be traced to the wide-ranging consequences of recognizing the flaw in that argument. The crux of this reading is in line with the main thrust of the fine work of Weithman (2010) and Freeman (2003, 2007), though I do not follow their accounts in all details (which is just as well, since they disagree; Weithman 2010, 128–129). I then argue, more controversially, that we can find in Rawls's political liberalism at least two (perhaps three) different accounts of the way in which stability considerations enter into justificatory arguments – one repairs the account in *TJ* and is similarly structured, while another pushes political liberalism in a more radical direction. The legacy of the Rawlsian project, I argue, is in developing this latter insight.

# 1. The Original Position and Stability in *Theory*: The Argumentative Structure

## 1.1 The First Two-Stage Argument: The Justificatory Role of Stability

The first step in understanding Rawls's political turn is to appreciate that the concern with stability as a basic justificatory consideration was by no means an innovation of political liberalism: it was fundamental to the argument of *TJ*. Rawls explicitly divided "the argument for the principles of justice into two parts" (*TJ*, 124, 465). The first part is the famous derivation of the two principles of justice via the argument from rational choice in the original position; this derivation requires that part of the "thin theory of the good" which allows us to identify "primary goods." As is well known, the parties in the original position choose the two principles of justice behind a "veil of ignorance" – a range of information that is specific to their own and their society's identity is excluded from the choice situation. Requiring the parties to choose under such conditions helps ensure that their choice will be reasonable and not moved by bias (*TJ*, 392). The problem is that without information about what they consider good and their particular plans of life, they do not have a clear basis of choice. Rawls requires that the parties have knowledge of some universal features of good lives, so they know what to aim at (*TJ*, 348–350). The point of Part Three of *Theory* is to explicate both structural and substantive features of all rational and good plans of life. At this first stage of the derivation, however, all that is required is, as it were, a part of the thin theory: that which specifies certain primary goods – things that rational individuals, "whatever else they want, desire as prerequisites for carrying out their plans of life" (*TJ*, 348). These are liberties, opportunity, wealth, income and the social bases of self-respect (*TJ*, 54). This part of the derivation aims to show that the parties to the original position, exercising their rationality to maximize an index of primary goods, will select the two principles of justice.

Now it is often supposed that this *is* the entire argument from the original position, and once the parties have made their choice their work is done and they can, as it were, fold up shop. Not so (see the 1989 essay "Domain of the Political and Overlapping Consensus"). "Persons in the original position," Rawls tells us, must consider whether a well-ordered society founded on justice as fairness will be more stable than alternative conceptions considered in the original position (*TJ*, 398). "Other things equal, persons in the original position will adopt the most stable scheme of principles" (*TJ*, 398). Although the "criterion of stability is not decisive" (*TJ*, 399), if the parties find that a conception is unworkable, this would force a reconsideration of their initial choice (*TJ*, 472, 505).

An ambiguity in Rawls's account of the justificatory role of stability must be noted. The official argument seems to be that of *relative stability*:

> There seems to be no doubt that justice as fairness is a reasonably stable conception of justice. But a decision in the original position depends on a comparison: other things equal, the preferred conception is the most stable one. Ideally we should like to compare justice as fairness with all its rivals in this respect, but as so often I shall only consider the principle of utility. (*TJ*, 436)

Somewhat puzzlingly, although Rawls asserts here that there can be "no doubt" that justice as fairness is reasonably stable, and that the hard question is one of relative stability, most of the argument in Part Three of *TJ* (the crucial chapter on the "congruence" argument has yet to come) aims to show that justice as fairness is feasibly stable. A few pages after the above quotation he writes:

> These remarks are not intended as justifying reasons for the contract view. The main grounds for the principles of justice have already been presented. At this point we are simply checking whether the conception already adopted is a feasible one and not so unstable that some other choice might have been better. We are in the second part of the argument in which we ask if the acknowledgment previously made should be reconsidered (§25). I do not contend that justice as fairness is the most stable conception of justice. The understanding to answer this question is far beyond the primitive theory I have sketched. The conception agreed to need only be stable enough. (*TJ*, 441)

Near the close of *TJ* Rawls claims in the same paragraph that it has been shown that with respect to stability "the contract doctrine is superior to its rivals" and that the result of Part Three has been to "justify a conception of justice" by showing that it is "sufficiently stable" (*TJ*, 504–505) – something Rawls had earlier claimed could not be doubted. Most commentators pay little attention to relative stability; I shall follow the general view of interpreting the main argument for stability in noncomparative terms, understanding it as a "test" that must be passed (Freeman 2003, 279).

In any event, in *TJ* the stability test is best understood as what we might call *population stability*. As Weithman (2010, 58, 66) notes, the aim is not to show that the stability test is passed by each and every person – that each and every person will have a stable disposition to act on justice as fairness – but that a well-ordered society has such a general disposition. To be sure, once again Rawls's text is not pellucid; in some passages he rather suggests that the parties, who choose under limited information, would make the same choice when acting on principles of rational choice with full information about their good (*TJ*, 451). The argument for stability can be read as applying to each and every member of a well-ordered society (as does Barry 1995, 885). However, Rawls acknowledges that even if it is successfully shown that justice as fairness is reasonably stable in a well-ordered society, there may be some citizens "who find that being disposed to act justly is not a good . . . in their case just institutions cannot fully answer to their nature" (*TJ*, 504). This is important. In this second stage of the argument from the original position parties are not asking whether they (or those whom they represent) will develop the appropriate dispositions, but whether a well-ordered society based on justice as fairness will do so. The parties thus switch from the perspectives of rational self-interested choosers to making a population-level judgment.

### 1.2 The Second Two-Staged Argument: The Two Elements of Stability

Rawls's analysis of the stability of a conception of justice in *Theory* has two parts (*TJ*, 397). The first issue is whether citizens living under that conception will develop a sense of justice to act on it: whether they will develop desires to act on the principles, and experience the appropriate moral sentiments and natural attitudes regarding them. Rawls thus sketches a moral psychology (*TJ*, §§71–75) that explains how citizens living in a well-ordered society regulated by justice as fairness will develop an effective desire to act on the principles. Now we might suppose that if we accept this moral psychology the argument for stability has been completed. A society that starts out well-ordered – each accepts justice as fairness and knows that others do and understand its bases – will tend to develop a reinforcing sense of justice in which people come to have an effective desire to act on that conception. What more can be required? As Weithman (2010, 46) shows, Rawls believes that fundamental problems remain. When individuals reason from the "self-interested" view, or the point of view of their own good narrowly defined, they may come to see that acting on their sense of justice is very costly, and so may resent their sense of justice and experience alienation (*TJ*, 295; Weithman 2010, 53). Thus, considering their good narrowly defined (leaving out the good of acting justly), they may be tempted to injustice. This confronts a well-ordered society with what Rawls called the "hazards of the generalized prisoner's dilemma" – each sees the collective rationality of acting on the principles but is tempted to defect in her own case when recommended by her self-interested point of view (*TJ*, 505, 435, 296; Weithman 2010, 48). To overcome this hazard, Weithman argues, Rawls sought to show in *TJ* that in a well-ordered society justice as fairness constitutes a Nash equilibrium: "Each member of the W[ell] O[rdered] S[ociety] judges, from within the thin theory of the good, that her balance of reasons tilts in favor of maintaining her desire to act from the principles of justice as a highest-order regulative desire in her rational plans, *when the plans of others are similarly regulated*" (Weithman 2010, 64, emphasis in original). Acting justly would then be the best reply to others acting justly.[1]

Rawls's stability argument thus has a second stage: having shown that a sense of justice would tend to arise in a well-ordered society regulated by justice as fairness, it must also be shown that the conceptions of the rational good in such a society would be such that people typically are not alienated from their sense of justice. The best life for a typical member of a well-ordered society based on justice as fairness would include a devotion to, and acting upon, the principles of justice when others do so as well (*TJ*, 382–383). If a society (1) does not encourage a strong sense of justice or (2) encourages conceptions of the good that tempt people away from their sense of justice, the society will fail the stability test as viewed from the original position (*TJ*, 398).

## 2. Stability in *Theory*: The Substantive Appeal to the Thin Theory

### 2.1 The Thin and Full Theories Related to the Question of Stability

Part Three of *Theory* develops both the "thin" and "full" theories of the good. The thin theory concerns core features of the structure and content of all rational notions of the good life, excluding aspects of the good that appeal to the principles of right or justice. The full theory concerns the good as applied to persons and actions in light of the principles of right (*TJ*, 355, 380ff.). As Rawls puts it, the original position can be viewed as a device for developing the thin theory into the full theory by employing the thin theory as the basis for identifying the principles of justice (*TJ*, 382). Once we have knowledge of the principles of right, this constrains and regulates our understanding of what is good (*TJ*, 494–495). In light of the full theory, a life of injustice could not possibly be good, whatever other advantages it may possess. Given this, from the perspective of the full theory, Rawls notes that it is trivially true that maintaining a sense of justice is good for a person, since the full theory is constrained by justice (*TJ*, 498). "Thus what is to be established is that it is rational (as defined by the thin theory of the good) for those in a well-ordered society to affirm their sense of justice as regulative of their plan of life" (*TJ*, 497, 350). Without appealing to the principles of right or justice, and so relying only on general structural and substantive nonmoral features of the good life, Rawls seeks to show that individuals would have strong reasons to affirm their sense of justice under justice as fairness.

## 2.2 The Elements of the Thin Theory of the Good

Before trying to sketch how the thin theory of the good is employed in Rawls's stability analysis, it will be useful to identify its main elements. It goes far beyond the theory of primary goods employed in the first stage of the argument from the original position (*TJ*, 347). The thin theory involves at least six elements.

a. *The good as plans of life with a certain structure*   The thin theory of the good contains an account of personhood according to which "a person may be regarded as a human life lived according to a plan" (*TJ*, 358). Rawls holds that certain formal principles of rational choice allow a person to identify a "maximal class" of rational plans for her, in which each member is superior to those outside the class but she cannot employ the formal criteria of rational choice to rank the elements within the set (*TJ*, 359, 365). At this point she must employ "deliberative rationality" – a "highly complex [idea], containing many elements" that Rawls does not fully enumerate (*TJ*, 367) – to choose a specific plan. A plan of life consistent with the principles of rational choice and deliberative rationality is a rational plan, and so the person's conception of the good is itself rational (*TJ*, 358–359). A rational interest is one encouraged and provided for by a rational plan (*TJ*, 359); it is from this idea that the account of primary goods is derived (*TJ*, 361). Note that the account of primary goods in *TJ* is thus derived from a conception of the person and the good life.

b. *Our social nature*   Rawls stresses that "the sociability of humans must not be understood in a trivial fashion" (*TJ*, 458). The account of "goodness as rationality" shows us that there is a maximal class of plans that is rational for us to adopt; we must employ our deliberative rationality to choose one of them. Because "one basic characteristic of humans is that no person can do everything he might do" and so we must choose what abilities to cultivate, the life of each falls short of his full potential (*TJ*, 458–459). In social life we help complete each other's nature; in a community the members "recognize the good of each as an element in the complete activity the whole of which is intended to give pleasure to all" (*TJ*, 459). Rawls thus affirms the doctrine of our natural "social interest" in the lives of others (Gaus 1983, ch. 2). It is a consequence of this that the diversity of others' life plans is itself valued in rational plans.

c.   *Love and friendship*   Agreeing with J.S. Mill, Rawls argues that we possess "natural sentiments of unity and fellow feeling" (*TJ*, 439; Gaus 1983, 91). As Weithman (2010, 109ff.) shows, the thin theory of the good supposes that all members of a well-ordered society seek ties of friendship; we seek relations that can express our attitude of desiring unity with others. This leads members of a well-ordered society with a rational plan of life to participate in associations that promote and express these ties. More deeply, humans experience the natural attitude of love, which is an element of all good lives.

d.   *Sincerity*   It would seem that, as a corollary of our natural desire to live in friendship, we aim at a sort of sincerity in our relations with others (*TJ*, 499–500). Ties of friendship and fellow feeling render hypocrisy and deception about our actions and motives significant costs (Weithman 2010, 109).

e.   *The Aristotelian Principle and its companion effect*   The above sentiments are at least partly based on the core principle of Part Three of *TJ*, the Aristotelian Principle, according to which "other things equal, humans enjoy the exercise of their realized capacities (their innate or trained abilities) and this enjoyment increases the more the capacity is realized, or the greater its complexity" (*TJ*, 374). The "exercise of our natural powers," Rawls explains, "is a leading human good" (*TJ*, 374n); this is a "natural fact" (*TJ*, 376). Rational plans of life thus must take account of this fact which, as Rawls notes, leads to a view of the good that has affinities with the idealist notion of self-realization (*TJ*, 378; Gaus 1983, 26ff.). Failure to develop excellences induces shame (*TJ*, 389). Rawls adds a "companion effect": "As we witness the exercise of well-trained abilities by others, these displays are enjoyed by us and arouse a desire that we should be able to do the same thing ourselves. We want to be like those persons who can exercise the abilities we find latent in our nature" (*TJ*, 376).

f.   *The desire to express our nature as free and equal*   "Human beings," Rawls tells us, "have a desire to express their nature as free and equal moral persons" (*TJ*, 462). And, he adds, according to the Aristotelian Principle, "this expression of their nature is a fundamental human good" (*TJ*, 390). Again, humans tend to feel shame when they fail to live up to their nature.

## 2.3  The Thin Theory and the Development of Our Sense of Justice

As noted in section 1.2, the first stage of the argument for stability is that individuals in a well-ordered society regulated by justice as fairness will develop an effective sense of justice – a desire to live up to the principles of justice. Rawls sketches an account of moral development that proceeds through three stages. It is important to realize that this moral psychology is drawn upon by the parties in the original position and affects the choice of principles in the second stage of justification (*TJ*, 405).

In the *Morality of Authority* a child is disposed to act on moral precepts without fear of punishment because of their source in parental authority (or, more generally powerful persons); the precepts are not generally followed because they appeal to the child's inclinations or reason (*TJ*, 408). This first stage presupposes the natural attitude of *love*, for it is the love of, and trust in, the parental authority figures that induces the disposition to act on their precepts. Although he does not explicitly appeal to it, something along the lines of the

240

companion effect to the Aristotelian Principle holds, since the child wishes to become the sort of person her parents are (*TJ*, 408). The next stage is the *Morality of Association*, which arises when the child participates in various associations. Here attitudes relating to *fellow feeling* and *friendship* come into play: "once a person's capacity for fellow feeling has been realized in accordance with the first psychological law, then as his associates with evident intention live up to their duties and obligations, he develops friendly feelings toward them . . ." and this leads to a desire to live up to "the ideals of his station" (*TJ*, 411–412). The companion effect to the Aristotelian Principle is explicitly drawn upon here: witnessing the skills and abilities of others as they do their part, we wish to emulate them (*TJ*, 413). In the *Morality of Principles* ties of friendship still play a role, but rather than wishing to be simply "a good sport" one comes to be devoted to principles that regulate practices beneficial to oneself and those one cares about (*TJ*, 414). The moral sentiments, focusing on principles of justice thus become independent of particular friendships, though Rawls insists that "the sense of justice is continuous with the love of mankind" (*TJ*, 417). Perhaps more importantly, acting on Rawls's two principles of justice *expresses our nature as a free and equal rational being*; such expression is an important element of our good (*TJ*, 417). Thus we see that in each stage of the development of the sense of justice critical elements of the thin theory of the good are employed, including the controversial Aristotelian Principle.

## 2.4  The Congruence of the Good with Justice

The first step in *TJ*'s argument for the stability of a society well-ordered by the principles of justice as fairness is thus to employ the thin theory to show how an effective sense of justice would arise in such a society. But, we have seen, Rawls does not think this is sufficient: if citizens' rational good regularly runs counter to the demands of justice, people may be tempted to turn their backs on their own sense of justice. To assuage this worry Rawls advances a series of arguments seeking to show how a rational plan of life characterized by the thin theory leads a typical member of the well-ordered society to affirm her sense of justice. As Rawls points out, the "argument is cumulative" and depends on marshaling a variety of considerations; collectively these constitute the overall congruence claim. There is certainly not space here to detail these arguments; Weithman's admirable book painstakingly reconstructs the core arguments, and should be consulted by those wishing to pursue the details. In my view there are four fundamental arguments that comprise the overall congruence claim: (i) the argument from the good community, (ii) the argument from justice and friendship, (iii) the Kantian congruence argument, and (iv) the argument from the unity of self.

"It is," says Rawls, "natural to conjecture that that the congruence of the right and the good depends in large part upon whether a well-ordered society achieves the good of community" (*TJ*, 456). The *argument from the good of community* draws on elements *b* and *e* of the thin theory of the good (section 2.2 above). Because we value social life (element *b*), and see the lives of others drawing forth and completing our nature (element *e*), it is part of our good to participate in a society in which others have the freedom and opportunity to flourish (*TJ*, 463). Our participation in a social life with shared ends – a "social union" – is itself a good; a just society itself constitutes a form of social union, "a social union of social unions" (*TJ*, 462). A society regulated by the two principles encourages a diversity of ways of life, and we saw (point *b*) that living in a society characterized by such diversity is part of the rational good. Justice as fairness thus structures a political community in which the excellences of each are brought out by, and complement, one another. "It follows that the collective activity of justice is the preeminent form of human flourishing" (*TJ*, 463), and thus the pursuit of justice constitutes a shared end of the community. The *argument from justice and friendship* also focuses on our social nature. Recall (point *c*) that we have natural fellow feeling; each is united by ties of friendship with many others in a well-ordered society (*TJ*, 499–500) and so just conduct benefits our friends and loved ones. We have seen that the sense of justice grows out of such love and, indeed constitutes a sort of love of mankind. We want to give justice to those we care about, and we have great difficulty targeting the victims of our injustice (*TJ*, 500); deceiving our friends and fellows in order to gain through injustice by ignoring our sense of justice is especially painful (point *d*).

As Weithman (2010, 182) points out, however, even if successful, these arguments do not show that we desire to act justly for its own sake; we know that in many cases unjust action will set back our good, but we do not know whether just action *as such* is congruent with our good: we do not know whether it is good for us to be "persons who act from the principles of right" (Weithman 2010, 190). *The Kantian congruence argument* seeks to overcome this weakness by appealing to a "special feature of our desire to express ourselves as moral persons" identified in point *f* (*TJ*, 503; Weithman 2010, 190). The desire to express our nature as free moral persons, Rawls argues, simply is (under another description) the desire to act justly (*TJ*, 501; Weithman 2010, 191). The good of expressing our nature is thus equivalent to a desire to treat our sense of justice as supremely regulative in our life; only a self whose rational plan of life is structured by her sense of justice accommodates this fundamental desire (see also Freeman 2003, 290ff.). Lastly, drawing on his conception of the self as one with a unified plan (element *a*), the argument from a unified self maintains that only a plan of life that accords our sense of justice a regulative role can provide the basis of a unified self. Recall that rational plans have a certain structure and a person is defined as one who lives according to a plan (element *a*). A plan that conforms to the *full* theory of the good (taking the principles of justice as regulative) assures the coherence of the self; it provides an area for our deliberative rationality to exercise itself that accounts for the main elements of the human good. The self is unified not through subservience to a single dominant end such as the pursuit of happiness but through a rationally coherent plan, fashioned by the deliberative rationality of each in accordance with the principles of right (*TJ*, §85; Freeman 2003, 295).

## 3. "The Fact of Reasonable Pluralism"

We have seen that both stages of *TJ*'s stability analysis are based on the thin theory of the good, which is not really all that thin (it might be better characterized as the nonmoral theory of the good, but cf. Barry 1995, 885ff.). Rawls commences the 1996 preface to *PL*[2] by proclaiming that its aim is to adjust *TJ*'s presentation of justice as fairness to "the fact of reasonable pluralism" (*PL*, xxxvi–xxxvii). What Weithman (2010, ch. 8) has called "the great unraveling" of *TJ*'s complex argument for stability has its roots in Rawls's conviction that a diversity of reasonable comprehensive conceptions of the good is "the inevitable long-run result of the powers of human reason at work within the background of enduring free institutions" (*PL*, 4). For *TJ*'s stability argument to succeed a free and well-ordered society would have to maintain a consensus (not complete, but overwhelming) on the full theory of the good, which includes justice as fairness as a theory of the right.[3] However, the long-term result of the exercise of reason under free institutions is to induce disagreement on fundamental questions of the good, the nature of the person (Weithman 2010, 258–259), and our moral natures (whether, for example, the aim of expressing our nature as an autonomous free and equal person is fundamental to our good). The doctrine of the "burdens of judgment" is of decisive importance in the evolution of Rawls's view, for it explains why disagreement about these matters is an enduring feature of a free society. We disagree on these matters because the evidence is often conflicting and difficult to evaluate and even when we agree on the relevant considerations, we often weigh them differently; because our concepts are vague we must rely on interpretations that are often controversial; the manner in which we evaluate evidence and rank considerations seems to some extent the function of our total life experiences, which of course differ; because different sides of an issue rely on different types of normative considerations, it is often hard to assess their relative merits; in conflicts between values, there often seems to be no uniquely correct answer (PL, 56–57). Recognizing the burdens of judgment is constitutive of being reasonable (PL, 88–89).

The differences that result are both reasonable and deep. It is not "the fact of pluralism" but the "fact of reasonable pluralism" that motivates Rawls's political turn; reasonable pluralism is the result of our best exercise of free practical reason (PL, 36–37). In stark contrast to differences in rational plans of life in TJ, the fact of reasonable pluralism does not suppose the Aristotelian's Principle's implication that our differences are ultimately complementary, or that we appreciate each other's comprehensive doctrines (Weithman 2010, 262, 265; but cf. PL, 323). We are faced with "intractable struggles" and "irreconcilable. . . conflict" (PL, 4, xxvi) of "absolute depth" (PL, xxvi).

# 4. Shallow Political Liberalism:
## Reasonable Pluralism of the Good

*Political Liberalism* is a difficult book to explicate. Although much of what Brian Barry claims in his extended review essay is dubious, he seems correct that within the pages of the 1993 hardback edition (and especially within the 1996 paperback edition, which contains a new extended preface and an additional essay – more on that anon), we find inconsistent views; the essays on which *PL* is based were written over a number of years, and superseded thoughts appear to be retained along with later ideas (Barry 1995, 891ff.; see also Dreben 2003, 320). I shall sketch two versions of political liberalism, the "Shallow" and "Deep" Versions (and within the Shallow Version itself I distinguish two formulations). Both can be found in the 1993 text, but I believe that the emphasis in the 1996 paperback is more clearly on the Deep Version. In any event, to separately explicate the two versions enhances our understanding of the logic of political liberalism.

## 4.1 *Overlapping Consensus and Stability I: Continuity with* Theory

The (first formulation of the) Shallow Version informs much of the original 1993 text of *PL*, as well as the proto-version of political liberalism we find in *Justice as Fairness: a Restatement*. In the Shallow Version Rawls carries over the two-staged derivation of the principles that we examined in *TJ* (section 1 above). First, parties in the original position derive the principles of justice under the veil of ignorance using the theory of primary goods, and then the parties check for the stability of the principles by determining whether they can be the focus of a reasonable overlapping consensus (*PL*, 78; *JF*, 88, 181). If not, then "justice as fairness . . . is in difficulty" – we must go back and see whether the principles can be revised (*PL*, 65–66, 141). However, the parties cannot go through the reasoning supporting an overlapping consensus; unlike in *TJ* where the theory of the good provides a common basis for checking the stability of the principles that the parties can undertake, overlapping consensus involves different reasons based on different comprehensive doctrines. The parties' task is to determine whether in a well-ordered society of diverse reasonable doctrines there is reason to believe that that the principles can either be derived from diverse comprehensive doctrines, be congruent with them, or at least not conflict with – or at a minimum not conflict "too sharply with" – them (*PL*, 11, 40, 140). Thus, in contrast to *TJ*, rather than demonstrating that the principles *will* be stable, Rawls does not show that an overlapping consensus will occur, but that the freestanding argument allows for it (*PL*, xlv–xlvi). Although Weithman (2010, ch. 9) makes out a strong case that, like *TJ*, *PL* is concerned with showing that justice as fairness can overcome the "hazards of the generalized prisoner's dilemma," it is perhaps more helpful to stress that Rawls's stability concern in his political liberalism is to show how it is possible for citizens with deeply conflicting comprehensive views to be "wholeheartedly" devoted to a liberal political order (*PL*, xxxviii).

As in *TJ*, the parties are seeking to make a population-level judgment; the overlapping consensus on the political conception should include "all the reasonable opposing religious, philosophical, and moral doctrines likely to persist over generations and to gain a sizable body of adherents" (*PL*, 15); at least a "substantial majority" of the "politically active citizens" must freely endorse the conception of justice from within their own comprehensive frameworks (*PL*, 38). If, as in *TJ*, the parties are concerned with a population-level stability question, it is not required that each and every reasonable comprehensive doctrine participates in the overlapping consensus; stability requires "sufficiently wide" support (*PL*, 39).

## 4.2 The Two Sets Model

Thus far the general model of the stability argument in *TJ* carries over into the Shallow Version. Recall that in *TJ*, the case for stability consisted of two stages: first, showing how a sense of justice would develop, and then showing how the thin theory of the good endorses the sense of justice. At one point Rawls affirms that *PL* has the same structure, except of course that the last step is to show that an overlapping consensus can support the sense of justice (*PL*, 140–141n). This no doubt leads some to conclude that the only problem with Part Three of *TJ* was the congruence argument in Chapter IX, not with the analysis of the sense of justice. But we have seen that the analysis of the sense of justice appealed to most of the now-abandoned thin theory, including the Aristotelian Principle and the good of expressing our natures as free and equal, so the story cannot be as simple as it seems. As we shall see presently, the sense of justice undergoes an important transformation in *PL*.

The core stability analysis of Rawls's political liberalisms (Shallow and Deep) proceeds by comparing two sets of values. As Rawls puts it, he supposes that citizens' "overall views have two parts: one part can be seen to be, or coincide with, the political conception of justice; the other part is a (fully or partially) comprehensive doctrine to which the political conception is in some manner related (*PL*, 38, xix; *JF*, 187; Weithman 2010, 33; Gaus 2011). The stability argument is that the values of these two parts *taken together* – the values of the political conception of justice conjoined with the large majority of reasonable comprehensive doctrines – endorse conformity to liberal principles and institutions, and so a well-ordered society based on justice as fairness can be stable (*JF*, 187).

## 4.3 The Political Set as Freestanding

It is essential to realize that in *TJ* the thin theory of the good was not simply employed in the second stage of the argument from the original position (stability checking), but was employed in the derivation of the two principles of justice in the first stage (section 1.1 above). The account of primary goods was part of the thin theory and, particularly the account of a good life and its structure (element *a*, section 2.2 above). If the fact of reasonable pluralism renders the thin theory of the good unsuitable as the grounds of stability, it certainly renders it unavailable as a supposition in the derivation of the political conception itself. A fundamental aspiration of political liberalism is to free the derivation of justice as fairness from any controversial comprehensive conception by showing that it is freestanding (*PL*, 40, 140). Because justice as fairness can no longer be built up from the reasonably disputable thin theory of the good, it must be built up from fundamental ideas that "are present in the public culture, or at least in the history of its main institutions and the traditions of their interpretations" (*PL*, 78, 8–9). By commencing with a shared public culture Rawls seeks to assemble the fundamental ideas to be employed in justifying the political set of values and ideas (*JF*, Part I), without grounding in comprehensive doctrines. We can thus appreciate how Rawls's move to a political constructivism, which seeks to construct the set of political values and ideas from the widely shared political culture (*PL*, Lecture III), and so provides the basis of a freestanding set of political values that is autonomous of comprehensive doctrines (*PL*, 98), is a consequence of his recognition of the fact of reasonable pluralism (*PL*, 38).

## 4.4 Migrations to the Political and Decreasing the Supporting Role of the Good

Freeman (2007, 195) notes that ideas associated with the thin theory of the good, which Rawls seems to take away with one hand in *PL*, he then gives back with another. One cannot understand the argumentative structure of *PL* without tracking the migration (and consequent reinterpretation) of values and ideas that in *TJ* were in the "comprehensive good" set of values into the "political" set of values in *PL*. The unifying idea behind this migration is the conception of citizens on which the freestanding, political set, of reasons is based. Rawls's fundamental claim is that implicit in our democratic culture is a conception of citizens who conceive of themselves as free and equal in three senses. First, they understand themselves to possess a moral power to have and revise a conception of the good (*PL*, 30). In explicating this moral power Rawls thus reintroduces a version of goodness as rationality and rational plans of life, but now understood as political ideas (*PL*, 176). Thus, for example, the idea that it is a power of citizens to change their plan of life does not imply that within any comprehensive doctrine such freedom is valued; rather the crucial idea is that our concept of a citizen is such that one's political identity does not change as one's plan does (*PL*, 30). The second sense in which citizens see themselves as free and equal is that they view themselves as possessing valid claims against others, and the third is that they take responsibility for their ends and regulate them according to political justice (*PL*, 32–35). This last clearly concerns a sense of justice, part of the moral powers of citizens (*PL*, 19) – understood now as part of the freestanding set of political values. All this allows Rawls to reintroduce the idea of primary goods, now as derived from our conception of citizens (*PL*, 178–190). Rawls also reintroduces (now as political values) the social union of social unions (*PL*, 320) and the (political) good of community (*PL*, 201–206).

Two implications of this migration of ideas and values from the conception of the good to the freestanding set of political values should be stressed. First, in evaluating stability, although parties to the original position cannot consider how different comprehensive conceptions support the political conception (since there are many such conceptions), many of the matters that previously were part of the nonpolitical good are available to them as elements of the freestanding political conception. So the parties do have quite a lot of common values to appeal to when thinking about stability. Secondly, in the "two sets" analysis of stability, a number of weighty values are included in the political set (*PL*, 139). Now because stability is, as it were, the net effect of the political and the nonpolitical sets of citizens, and because weighty values are included in the political set, it is not crucial to show anything like the strong congruence claim of *TJ*. This is why Rawls can correctly say what may at first seem so puzzling, viz. as long as the conflict of the political set with the comprehensive conception *is not too sharp* stability can be achieved (*PL*, 40). Because the political set is weighty, it can bear most of the weight of demonstrating stability so long as there is not a radical conflict with comprehensive conceptions. This feature of political liberalism has, I think, been overlooked: it is not just the case that overlapping consensus replaces the congruence argument – overlapping consensus has a more modest role to play in establishing stability than did the arguments of Part Three of *TJ*.

## 4.5 Overlapping Consensus and Stability II: The Individualized Version

In the "Reply to Habermas," added to the 1996 paperback edition, Rawls provides an extended analysis of the relation of justification of the principles of justice to stability, which presents an individualized account of overlapping consensus.[4] While elements of this account were in the 1993 text (e.g., *PL*, 143), the "Reply" clearly sets out an individualized, rather than a population-focused, analysis of overlapping consensus on a shared conception of justice. Here justification occurs in three stages. The first stage is the freestanding argument from the original position, the argument from the political set. This justification, says Rawls, is only a "*pro tanto*" ("as far as it goes") justification, as it is based only on the freestanding political set (*PL*, 386). The next stage is that of "full justification," which is carried out by individual citizens on the basis of their nonpolitical set of values (their comprehensive conceptions). Here they consider the relation between the implications of the political set and their nonpolitical set; at this stage the justification of the principles of justice "may be overridden once *all* values are tallied up" (*PL*, 386, emphasis added). Note that the justificatory role of overlapping consensus is no longer focused on population-level questions, but concerns each and every reasonable citizen. Unless reasonable citizen Alf affirms the principles on the basis of both sets, the principles are not justified to him. Because the full justification of the principles of justice to Alf depends on the implications of his personal nonpolitical set, it thus is impossible to say whether the principles of justice are fully justified simply by appeal to the argument of the original position.

The last stage of justification is "public justification," "a basic idea of political liberalism" (*PL*, 387). Public justification happens when *all* the reasonable members of political society carry out the justification of the *shared* political conception by embedding it their several comprehensive views" (*PL*, 387, emphasis added). Once public justification occurs there is a common knowledge that each citizen, consulting her own deepest normative convictions, endorses the political conception. We might say all citizens appreciate that the deepest normative and religious convictions of all are reconciled to the public conception: it is public knowledge that the political conception is seen by all as fully justified. Out of public justification comes "stability for the right reasons" (*PL*, 388–389); if achieved, both sets of all citizens (the shared political set and the person's nonpolitical set) together endorse a shared political conception, the principles of justice. This is a demanding account of stability of a particular shared conception of justice: justification requires an overlapping consensus of *all* reasonable citizens, something that was not required of the population-focused account carried over from *TJ*. Remember, though, that the shared political set does the lion's share of the work, because it contains such weighty values.

## 5. Deep Political Liberalism: Reasonable Pluralism of the Right

### 5.1 The Double Role of Reasonable Pluralism

Dreben (2003) thought that the 1996 paperback edition should be considered a second edition of *PL*. On his reading the distinctive feature of political liberalism is its principle of legitimacy. On my reading the 1993 hardback edition of *PL* contains a second account of liberal stability, which becomes more pronounced in the paperback edition. We can understand this as an implication of a fuller recognition of the ideas that generated the entire political liberal project – the fact of reasonable pluralism and the burdens of judgment. In the introduction to the 1993 edition, Rawls's discussion of reasonable pluralism is focused on the diversity of comprehensive conceptions, but this does not seem to radically infect agreement on the political conception; "the political conception is shared by everyone while the reasonable doctrines are not" (*PL*, xix). However, in the preface to the paperback edition Rawls stresses that reasonable pluralism and the burdens of judgment apply to the political conception as well:

> In addition to conflicting comprehensive doctrines, PL does recognize that in any actual political society a number of differing liberal political conceptions of justice compete with one another in society's political debate . . . This leads to another aim of PL: saying how a well-ordered liberal society is to be formulated given not only reasonable pluralism [of comprehensive conceptions] but a family of reasonable liberal conceptions of justice. (*PL*, xlvi)

Rawls thus observes: "The burdens [of judgment] have a double role in PL: they are part of the basis for liberty of conscience and freedom of thought founded on the idea of the reasonable . . . And they lead us to recognize that there are different and incompatible liberal political conceptions" (*PL*, xlvii).

## 5.2  The Principle of Liberal Legitimacy and Public Reason

In the introduction to 1996 paperback edition, Rawls states the principle of liberal legitimacy in terms of a principle of reciprocity and justification: "our exercise of political power is proper only when we sincerely believe that the reason we offer for our political action may reasonably be accepted by other citizens as a justification of those actions" (PL, xliv). Now because the fact of reasonable pluralism infects the political set – as we have seen there are many values in the political set, and so the burdens of judgment apply to it – appeal to justice as fairness cannot be required to justify political actions (in matters of basic justice and constitutional essentials; PL, 219). It is not the definitively reasonable way to organize and weigh the political values. Consequently, as the implications of the fact of reasonable pluralism for the political set become our main concern, the principle of liberal legitimacy takes center stage. We need to justify our actions to others, and this justification must take into account the fact of reasonable pluralism as applied to the political set. The guidelines for this justification are given by the idea of public reason (PL, 225–226, 243). In justifying the coercive use of political power on matters of basic justice and constitutional essentials, citizens are to appeal only to conceptions of justice involving reasonable weightings of the political set, along with methods of inquiry which themselves are part of the public culture. Rawls is explicit that the content of public reason cannot be restricted to justice as fairness. "Rather, its content – the principles, ideals, and standards that may be appealed to – are those of a family of reasonable political conceptions of justice" (PL, l–li).

## 5.3  Overlapping Consensus and Stability III: Individualized Justification of Liberal Legitimacy

Note that in the above statement of the principle of liberal legitimacy it is depicted as inherently justificatory, and this justification is owed to other citizens as such.[5] Throughout PL Rawls argues that the principle of liberal legitimacy seeks to address each citizen's reasonable framework to show why they should, given both their value sets, endorse a class of political conceptions (PL, 137, 143, 224). What Rawls considers the "more realistic" account of an individualized overlapping consensus justification focuses on a "class of liberal conceptions" rather than "a specific conception of justice" (PL, 164). Even in the "Reply to Habermas," after applying the three-stage account of justification to a shared specific conception of justice, when Rawls considers whether such overlapping consensus is too "unrealistic to hope for," he moves to legitimacy (PL, 392–393). In the end, the individualized account of overlapping consensus most powerfully applies to the justification of a fairly wide set of liberal conceptions of justice and guidelines of public reason conjoined with fundamental aspects of democratic governance (PL, 421–433).

# 6.  Conclusion

TJ's wide-ranging use of a not-all-that-thin theory of the good to show the congruence of justice and the rational good of citizens supposed that a free liberal society would maintain a consensus on the structure and much of the substance of a good life. The first corrosive effect of Rawls's conviction that free institutions encourage the growth of reasonable plural-ism was to undermine this assumption of a shared liberal theory of the good, and this ushered in what I have called the Shallow Version of political liberalism. This much is clear. The puzzle is in seeing just how Rawls reassembled pieces (and what pieces) of *TJ*'s account to produce a "political conception," and to evaluate how much of what were perceived as claims about the good that were too controversial to ground a theory of justice are uncontroversial as part of the liberal political good, which now does the lion's share of the work in the stability argu-ment. And there is the question of whether overlapping consensus and the argument for stability should be seen, as it was in *TJ*, as a population-level, or as an individualized, analysis. As Rawls more fully appreciated how the fact of reasonable pluralism infects not simply ideas about the good, but conceptions of political justice too, political liberalism enters a deeper phase. The aim of treating all as free and equal persons to whom justification is owed is faced with the problem of the indeterminacy of the justification of any specific political conception. It is, I think, Rawls's legacy to present this deep problem to us and show how radically we must revise our political theorizing if we take it seriously. It falls to us to more adequately cope with it.

# Notes

1   This would not assure stability on justice, for it only shows that acting justly is a possible equilib-rium. Because of this we confront a sort of assurance game: we need to be assured that others will play the cooperative equilibrium (Weithman 2010, 49).
2   The 2005 expanded edition of *Political Liberalism* republishes the prefaces to both the 1993 and 1996 editions; the expanded 2005 edition contains the entire text of the 1996 paperback edition, plus "The Idea of Public Reason Revisited." All *PL* pages references are to the 2005 edition.
3   Rawls comes to believe that as a comprehensive doctrine, "the full theory is inadequate" (*PL*, 177n).
4   Weithman (2010, 335–339) argues for the continuity of the account in "Reply to Habermas" with the overall account in the 1993 version.
5   In earlier statements, Rawls wrote of what citizens could be expected to "endorse" (*PL*, 137).

# Works by Rawls, with Abbreviations

*Collected Papers* (CP), ed. Samuel Freeman. Cambridge, MA: Harvard University Press, 1999.
"Domain of the Political and Overlapping Consensus" (1989), in *Collected Papers* (473–496).
*Justice as Fairness: A Restatement* (JF), ed. Erin Kelly. Cambridge MA: Harvard University Press, 2001.
*Political Liberalism* (PL),expanded edn. New York: Columbia University Press, 2005.
"Reply to Habermas" (1995), in *Political Liberalism* (372–434).
*A Theory of Justice* (TJ), rev. edn. Cambridge, MA: Harvard University Press, 1999.

# Other References

Barry, Brian (1995) "John Rawls and the Search for Stability." *Ethics* 105 (July): 874–915.
Dreben, Burton (2003) "On Rawls on Political Liberalism." In Samuel Freeman (ed.), *The Cambridge Companion to Rawls* (316–346). Cambridge: Cambridge University Press.

Freeman, Samuel (2003) "Congruence and the Good of Justice." In Samuel Freeman (ed.), *The Cambridge Companion to Rawls* (277–315). Cambridge: Cambridge University Press.

Freeman, Samuel (2007) "Political Liberalism and the Possibility of a Just Democratic Constitution." In Freeman, *Justice and the Social Contract* (175–214). Oxford: Oxford University Press.

Gaus, Gerald F. (1983) *The Modern Liberal Theory of Man*. New York: St Martin's.

Gaus, Gerald F. (2011) "A Tale of Two Sets: Public Reason in Equilibrium." *Public Affairs Quarterly* 25 (Oct.): 305–325.

Krasnoff, Larry (1998) "Consensus, Stability, and Normativity in Rawls's Political Turn." *Journal of Philosophy* 95 (June): 269–292.

Weithman, Paul (2010) *Why Political Liberalism? On John Rawls's Political Turn*. New York: Oxford University Press.

# 14

# Political Constructivism

## AARON JAMES

Political constructivism is associated with John Rawls more than any other contemporary philosopher. But what, exactly, is Rawls's "political constructivism"? The answer is not obvious, even for those schooled in Rawls's work.

If pressed to answer, many philosophers would point to Rawls's broadly Kantian thesis that social justice just *is* what would be agreed to in his famous Original Position. That is, according to what might be called *metaethical constructivism*, the principles which members of a society would agree to, deciding self-interestedly and in ignorance of their actual social positions, *constitute* justice for their society, rather than somehow *tracking or representing* an independent set of facts about what justice requires, as according to realist or "rational intuitionist" views. If asked to elaborate, one might highlight further Kantian or Rousseauian themes. Social justice is not then a mere worthy ideal represented in an independent order of moral facts, let alone an imposition of outmoded tradition or divine law, but "autonomously" self-legislated. A society is itself the author of its basic moral law, by its own practical reason.

Although this answer is not wrong, it does not characterize the "political constructivism" which is most central to Rawls's work overall. Rawls did indeed affirm the stated metaethical constructivism in his most Kantian phase ("Kantian Constructivism in Moral Theory," the Dewey Lectures (KC, 350). He also later distanced himself from that thesis in the very name of "political constructivism"; the relevant idea of "autonomy," Rawls explained, is not "constitutive" but "doctrinal" (PL, 98, 99). This might seem to simply reflect his "political turn" away from "comprehensive" moral outlooks (including such Kantian metaethical views) and toward concerns of legitimacy and narrowly "political" values. This essay will suggest, however, that Rawls's political constructivism is better understood as a general method of justification which runs throughout his work as a whole, including his early work and *A Theory of Justice*.

Political constructivism, in this central and unifying sense, is a methodology of *substantive* justification. Its aim is not to characterize the metaethical status of justice but to justify

*A Companion to Rawls*, First Edition. Edited by Jon Mandle and David A. Reidy.
© 2014 John Wiley & Sons, Inc. Published 2016 by John Wiley & Sons, Inc.

specific principles as a reasonable basis for public agreement in particular areas of social life. Specifically, the aim is to do so, in those areas, in a way that makes their reasonableness manifest to all involved. The hope is to *show*, as though by something vaguely akin to mathematical demonstration, that proposed principles can be worked out, in steps which are themselves manifestly reasonable, from rudimentary and highly plausible ideas arising from within a society's own essentially social kind of practical reason.

The main elements of this general method of justification may be summarized as follows. (Each element is to be duly adjusted in light of the others until we reach a state of "reflective equilibrium.")

- *Social role*   Principles of social justice are to be justified for a certain governing role, namely, the role of providing a public basis of mutual justification within an independently identified social practice.
- *Sources*   Reasoning to such principles begins from an organized group's own common practical reason. A group's "common practical reason" includes generally (perhaps implicitly) affirmed "fundamental ideas," as they are interpreted and applied in practice, in light of shared general understandings of the kind of social practice being maintained (e.g., a society seen as a fair scheme of cooperation among equals over time), and despite larger differences in worldview.
- *Interpretive basis*   Reasoning from such sources is to proceed by elaborating a version of the common social practice that each involved can find reasonably acceptable, from their respective standpoints. The "elaboration" mixes moral judgment with what has come to be called "constructive interpretation" of assumed fundamental ideas.
- *Representation*   Where appropriate, such reasoning is as far as possible to represent all morally relevant criteria in the form of a procedure of judgment which clearly leads to particular principles. For example, an original position model, appropriately tailored to the social practice at hand, might clearly show that certain regulative principles would be selected over a familiar range of available alternatives (e.g., parties using the "maximin" rule for self-interested decision under uncertainty would insist upon the two principles instead of the principle of utility).
- *Conclusion*   Given such reasoning, we have sufficient reason to accept the selected principles, as requirements of social justice, for the specified public social role. We are so justified by virtue of the *sufficiency* of the represented grounds, when their combined force is laid out in a convincing way. (The correctness of the resulting principles may or may not *consist* in being so supported in any further sense.)

In short, principles of justice are justified *for* a social practice, *from* its common practical reason, and *by* moralized constructive interpretation – which may include original position reasoning that yields specific principles. The goal is not simply a sociological description of what is already assumed in a practice; it is also to constructively propose a version of the assumed practice that we as theorists can endorse as reasonable. But the goal is not simply to convince ourselves. The hope is to establish a public basis for governance – a basis for mutual justification – by presenting a version of the practice whose reasonableness can – and hopefully will – become plain to all involved (at least short of persistent ill-will, incompetence, insufficient attention, fundamentalist resistance, and so on).

Here it is apt to speak of "construction" even without invoking a metaethical relation of determination or constitution. It is enough that the proposed form of justification offers a kind of *demonstration* akin to mathematical proof (albeit without the force of logical necessity and from moral starting points). In a successful proof, a significant theorem is shown to follow, by incontrovertible inferential steps, from relatively weak axioms. The correctness of the theorem is then made *evident* to all competent mathematical reasoners who adequately attend to its reasoning. Rawls's political subject matter calls for interpretation and informal argument rather than formal analysis. Yet the aspiration is similar: to justify substantial principles, as reasonably acceptable to all, in a way that makes it plain to all (competent, well-motivated parties) that those principles are indeed the right ones for their intended public role. As Rawls famously puts the idea, the principles are to be made evident by a kind of "moral geometry" (*TJ*, 105) from "widely accepted but weak premises" (*TJ*, 16).

The following discussion further develops this general characterization of Rawls's political constructivism. Its main elements are taken in turn and developed with special attention to the two places where Rawls discusses the topic in depth – his Dewey Lectures (KC) and its substantially revised version called "Political Constructivism" (*PL*, Lecture III).

Rawls's revisions of the Dewey Lectures starkly exhibit his "political turn," as partly reflected in his move away from metaethical constructivism. Though Rawls's "political turn" cannot be adequately situated here within his work overall, the continuity of Rawls's thought will be highlighted, especially in his basic political constructivist project. In particular, it is suggested that Rawls's "political turn" marks not a major break from a generally Kantian body of work, but rather a phase in which Rawls came to see the limitations of Kantian ideas within his larger and largely continuous political constructivism.

## Practices and Publicity

The first main element of our characterization of political constructivism is "social role": principles of justice have a distinctive social role as a public standard of mutual justification within an independently identified social practice.

Rawls is in this sense not a traditional "state of nature" theorist. He simply assumes, almost by stipulation, that the idea of social justice is essentially concerned with the structure of an ongoing "social practice," marked by a system of rules which define rights and duties (see, e.g., "Justice as Fairness," *CP*, 47 n1). He pays little or no attention to how a social practice might be established for the first time; his principles apply *within* a specified practice, to its form of social organization, and have no clear direct application elsewhere, whether to practices of other kinds or to individual conduct (further principles which relate practices or action within a practice are required).

A game, ritual, or parliament thus qualifies as a social practice in Rawls's sense. By contrast, Hume's famous rowers, who *merely* coordinate as a jointly beneficial Nash equilibrium, would not be appropriately guided by a commonly accepted set of role-defining rules. Beyond examples and suggestive characterization, however, Rawls nowhere provides general necessary and sufficient conditions for a "social practice." He instead focuses on the especially important social structures of his concern (the basic institutions of a society or international law and practice), leaving the precise scope of the general idea open to elaboration as specific social contexts require. So insofar as a Rawlsian political constructivism seeks to go beyond Rawls's focal areas, whether in human rights practice (Beitz 2009) or in the global economy (James 2012b), it must supply its own characterization of why and in what sense a social practice is to be found.

When a social practice is indeed on hand, Rawls assumes that principles of social justice function not as a normatively neutral standard of evaluation, but in a guiding, "public" role. Although Rawls characterizes "publicity" in many ways as his context of interest requires, it exerts considerable force over the content of principles. For example, when Rawls calls capabilities and welfare "unworkable ideas" from the point of view of effective public governance, in contrast with openly observable "primary goods" (such as income and wealth), he takes this to exclude them, for that reason alone, from eligibility as "regulative principles" for society (LP, 13 n3).

In that case, the question becomes: Why publicity? Rawls offers various answers, but also seems to assume certain minimal requirements of publicity, understood as forms of socially established agreement. For one thing, the very idea of "cooperation" in a social practice already implies that agents accept "publicly recognized" rules as properly regulative of their conduct, in contrast with cases in which agents merely coordinate their behavior according to centralized orders (e.g., out of mere fear) (PL, 16). In addition, Rawls sees a good measure of agreement about *justice itself* as part of the publicly assumed backdrop which defines the essential role of particular principles in a practice. As Rawls explains in KC, this comes along with justice's basic concern with mutual social recognition: "The social role of a conception of justice is to enable all members of society to make mutually acceptable to one another their shared institutions and basic arrangements, by citing what are publicly recognized as sufficient reasons." This is the "social role" of principles in the sense that it picks out not simply a welcome ideal but the very task of justification. As Rawls explains, "whenever a sufficient basis for agreement is not presently known, or recognized," the task becomes that of providing one (KC, 305).

This can appear little more than a worthy and potentially unachievable ideal. And in the early pages of TJ (5–6), Rawls does indeed lay out an ideal societal type, the fully "well-ordered human association," in which there is known to be all-out agreement on the very same principles, along with known compliance in basic institutions. But in that same passage, just after he notes that "well-ordered" societies rarely if ever exist, he goes on to explain that the proper role of principles of justice in actual societies is nevertheless founded upon a good measure of actual presumed agreement about justice. A measure of agreement about justice, as he puts it, is a "prerequisite for a viable human community" and has "wider connections" with "coordination, efficiency, and stability," as, for instance, when people contain their specific disputes because they accept the legitimacy of the larger system. Principles of justice function within and against this thick social background of moral agreement and exert their force where the extent of actual agreement runs thin.

Rawls would later develop the theme of mutual social recognition in terms of a "duty of civility" within a democratic polity, to listen to others and stand ready to give them one's reasons for supporting a specific exercise of political power (e.g., for voting in a certain way) (PL, 217). Yet the idea of mutual justifiability, of being in a position to give and ask for reasons, seems more general. In the KC passages quoted just above (KC, 305), Rawls goes on to at least briefly suggest that the basic concern comes along with any form of "social cooperation." What then is this more general concern?

T.M. Scanlon (1998) famously characterizes the idea of justifiability to others in terms of what they could reasonably reject (when informed and well motivated). This is suggestive, but too general, by itself, to capture the intended essentially social form of mutual recognition. For Scanlon, questions of justifiability to another arise whether or not we interact in regularized ways, even in a "state of nature." But for Rawls, the essential concern is with how an established social practice treats all involved, in part by publicly recognizing the reasonable claims of each. (For related contrasts, see Freeman 2007.) Yet if we press further questions about when, exactly, this basic and essentially social concern with mutual recognition arises, Rawls offers limited general help. Much as with the idea of a "social practice," the political constructivist who wishes to move beyond Rawls's focal cases (e.g., to mutual recognition in global economic life) must therefore work out the framing concern afresh for the distinctive case at hand.

## Conceptions of Practical Reason

According to the second element of our general characterization of political constructivism – what we called "sources" – reasoning about what mutual recognition in a social practice requires is to begin from the organized group's own common practical reason, including generally (if implicitly) affirmed "fundamental ideas," and especially shared understandings of the nature of the practice at issue.

This is not especially clear in *TJ*. But Rawls's later presentation of *TJ*'s project, in KC, clearly presents its intended culturally embedded nature. Even in his most Kantian phase – where he specifically means to highlight the "Kantian roots" of justice as fairness – he emphasizes a quite un-Kantian cultural grounding: "On the Kantian view that I shall present, conditions for justifying a conception of justice hold only when a basis is established for political reasoning and understanding within a political culture" (KC, 305). In particular, justice as fairness is said to be historically situated within the tradition of *democratic* thought, and, indeed, a quite specific "impasse in our political culture" (in Benjamin Constant's terms, the conflict between the "liberties of the ancients," as emphasized by Locke, and the "liberties of the moderns," as emphasized by Rousseau) (KC, 305).

As Rawls would later elaborate, although widely held convictions are open to change over time (e.g., they gradually settle against slavery, or in favor of tolerance), a "public culture," or "shared fund of implicitly recognized basic ideas and principles," can nevertheless persistently remain of "two minds" (*PL*, 8–9). The aim of political philosophy, in that case, is to find a way of "continuing public discussion" through "the work of abstraction": when certain shared understandings break down, we seek a correspondingly more general standpoint which provides a more neutral, agreed upon basis for adjudicating the more specific areas of dispute (*PL*, 45). Because the impasses are presumed to be deep, Rawls reaches for what he calls the public culture's "fundamental ideas," and, in particular, a very general conception of what a society is, which he takes to be implicit in democratic culture: society is a publicly governed fair cooperation among equals over time (*PL*, 13–15). These fundamental ideas are then presented as working "models" or "model conceptions," of society (as a fair, publicly governed scheme of cooperation) and of persons (as equal citizens). These abstract characterizations are intended to shape further reasoning, by clarifying and enriching both the question of social justice and the available specific answers.

In particular, they support the original position's design and so what principles are ultimately chosen from it.

Crucially, the appeal to a shared conception of society is not an appeal to the authority of tradition or culture per se, but to a society's own practical reason. Indeed, Rawls calls the fundamental ideas of person and society "conceptions of practical reason" (*PL*, 107). He explains, following Kant: "practical reason is concerned with the production of objects according to a conception of those objects – for example, the conception of a just constitutional regime taken as the aim of political endeavor – while theoretical reason is concerned with knowledge of given objects" (*PL*, 93). Accordingly, "practical reason" can include a group's (perhaps implicitly) shared conception of its common practice, as well as proposals of what organizational forms would realize or "produce" that social object.

Of course, if such "conceptions of practical reason" are supposed to somehow support a case for specific regulative principles, it would seem that they, too, should be founded upon principle. Otherwise, would not the suggested starting point for justification itself need to be justified? Rawls does indeed allude to a distinct class of abstract "principles of practical reason," which shape the "general form" of "conceptions." But, perhaps in a Hegelian spirit, Rawls mainly emphasizes the inseparability of "principles" and "conceptions." He offers no clear example of what an independent "principle of practical reason" would be. (An example of a "principle" would perhaps be "persons are self-originating sources of valid claims," while the relevant "conception" would be "citizens are equals, in virtue of their two moral powers.") He instead strongly emphasizes their psychological role in guiding actual inference and reasoning, suggesting that their full meaning is only expressed by their real use and understanding in a social practice (which is not to preclude review and judgment by our own lights as theorists). He writes: "the principles of practical reason are expressed in the thought and judgment of reasonable and rational persons and applied by them in their social and political practice." They do not "apply themselves," but are "used by us." The role of "conceptions," then, is to characterize this practical understanding. Conceptions, Rawls says, "specify the context for the problems and questions to which principles of practical reason apply." Without this, Rawls says, "principles of practical reason have no point, use, or application" (*PL*, 107–108).

How then do we come by such conceptions? Rawls answers that we "reflect on how these ideas appear in our practical thought" (*PL*, 108). Since the meaning of a principle is partly given in practice, the "we" here presumably refers to citizens of a democracy (or at least those of use who fully understand what democracy involves). We presumably are not beholden to all or even much of the prevailing culture of thought, much of which may depend on sheer misunderstanding or deliberate manipulation for cynical ends, and in any case may conflict with general democratic ideals and their embodiment in institutions. So there may be considerable room for deep cultural critique.

Even so, the question presents itself: Why look to a political culture at all? Why not rely *solely* on our own best ideas as theorists? Rawls suggests that the public political culture of a society reflects its own collective practical reason – especially in a democracy marked by public debate. But why not just reason out basic questions of justice for oneself, propose a fresh conception of a just society, and, if need be, conclude that a given group's practical reason has gone completely wrong? Why should prevailing culture matter?

Rawls's answer refers back to the social role of principles as a public basis of mutual recognition. He writes:

Justice as fairness aims at uncovering a public basis of justification . . . *Since justification is addressed to others, it proceeds from what is, or can be, held in common*; and so we begin from shared fundamental ideas implicit in the public political culture in the hope of developing from these a political conception that can gain free and reasoned agreement in judgment. (*PL*, 100, emphasis added)

As suggested above, the social role of principles is to provide a basis for people to justify their common practice *to* one another on publicly recognizable grounds. That in turn assumes "what is, or can be, held in common," given a common political culture. In *PL*, this becomes a call for an "overlapping consensus" which is available from each of different reasonable "comprehensive doctrines," in part because of their common political culture. Yet the main idea appears well before Rawls's "political turn." It is at least mentioned in *TJ* when Rawls writes that justification is "designed to reconcile by reason" and "proceeds from what all parties to the discussion hold in common" (*TJ*, 508). And, as noted above, the idea of a public kind of mutual recognition founded upon a society's public culture is a major theme in KC, which reflects the height of Rawls's Kantianism and shows no stated concern for specifically "political" values (KC, 305–306).

## Constructive Interpretation

The third main element of political constructivism – "interpretive basis" – concerns what it would be to reason from or within a society's practical reason. We are to elaborate a version of the common social practice that each involved can find reasonably acceptable, from their respective standpoints, and we are to do this by mixing moral judgment of what is a morally relevant and constructive interpretation of assumed fundamental ideas.

To see this, we might ask: If one cannot simply make one's own best moral judgment, by one's own best sense of what reasoning about justice requires, how is one to go on? Rawls repeatedly says we look to ideas "implicit" in the political culture, which suggests a kind of social interpretation. Yet appropriate reasoning cannot be *pure* social interpretation. Rawls also sees interplay between what is already "embedded in common sense" and the possibility of something to which common sense might be drawn by a process of reasoning, supplied by political philosophy. As he puts it, we can hope to "originate and fashion starting points for common understanding by expressing in a new form the convictions found in the historical tradition by connecting them with a wide range of people's considered convictions: those which stand up to critical reflection" (KC, 306).

This may be explained by seeing Rawls as instead engaged in *constructive* social interpretation (James 2005, 18–28). This involves three main argumentative stages. (As with the main elements of political constructivism, the order of argument is irrelevant within a broader reflective equilibrium methodology.) The first is *individuation*: we single out an object of social interpretation and moral evaluation, at first in relatively uncontroversial terms, with reference to various interpretive "data points" or "source materials" that any further conception of the practice should take into account and explain (or "explain away"). Thus Rawls identifies "modern constitutional democracies" as his domestic target, and "international law and practice" on the global scene. The second stage is *framing characterization*: We work up a general characterization of the practice, in light of its distinctive structure and (presumed legitimate) purposes. Thus Rawls offers general conceptions of society and persons. Here an interpretive characterization can be moralized (a "fair" scheme of cooperation, or "equal" citizens) so long as this comports with familiar interpretive constraints of consistency, coherence, explanatory power, simplicity, and so on. The third and final stage is *substantive argument*: we engage in substantive moral reasoning about what the various relevant reasons in play support, as framed and guided by the specified framing conception. It is at this stage that Rawls offers the original position and its principles as an elaboration of the more basic conceptions of person and society (of which more momentarily).

We find Rawls engaged in such moralized constructive interpretation on both sides of his political turn, in both KC and *PL*, but with at least two related shifts of interpretive emphasis. The first concerns the "work of abstraction." KC suggests that we frame the question of justice as abstractly as possible (imposing a "thick" veil of ignorance, given abstract conceptions of person and society) consistent with ultimately finding a basis for public agreement (KC, 336). Rawls here followed *TJ*'s relatively sanguine attitude about the extent of disagreement in society. As Rawls begins to take the depth of disagreement more seriously in *PL*, he begins closer to the sorts of disagreement we find in real society. Having found *TJ* "unrealistic" about how much agreement could be assumed (*PL*, xvii) – especially in democratic societies marked by freedom and divergence of thought – he is increasingly concerned to plausibly identify, rather than merely assume, a shared basis for his overall argument within the democratic societies of his concern. Greater abstraction comes at the potential cost of outstripping the basis of agreement that is actually there. So Rawls begins from a richer conception of democratic practice and its cultural basis.

The second and related shift is in the methodology of constructive social interpretation. As Rawls is increasingly concerned with the possibility of deep but reasonable disagreement – especially given persistent and potentially fundamental differences in religious or philosophical outlooks – he is also increasingly concerned to make arguments about what is available from *within* specific points of view (rather than in some sense generally present in a public culture). Rawls thus seems to have shifted from a "protestant" to a more "catholic" social interpretive methodology (see Postema 1987, in response to Dworkin 1986). A "catholic" interpreter assigns special authority to how participants in a social practice *themselves interpret what they are doing together*, and so will be especially sensitive to both shared understandings and disagreement in participant interpretations. A "protestant" interpreter gives no special authority to participant interpretation. Each interpreter is beholden only to his or her own interpretation of the practice; how participants interpret their practice, and whether they agree or disagree, represents only so much initial data or source material from which the interpreter must construct his or her own best characterization of the practice overall (Dworkin 1986). In these terms, Rawls's writings in *TJ* and KC are "protestant": he simply works out his own proposed best understanding of domestic societal practice without great concern for people in the practice who might disagree. The later Rawls, in *PL* and *LP*, is more "catholic": he accepts a special burden to take disagreement into account and addresses it on its own terms. He thus offers not simply a constructive interpretation of overall public practice, but a constructive interpretation of what is available to its (reasonable, informed, educated) participants, given the implicit understandings they can be said to have by being so involved. Their own presumed understanding of their shared practice is thus an important source of argumentative pressure against potentially resistant elements of their broader moral or philosophical outlook.

# Modeling Convergence

This brings us to our fourth main element of political constructivism, what we called "representation": where appropriate, in considering what form of the assumed practice would be reasonably acceptable, we are as far as possible to represent all morally relevant criteria in the form of a procedure of judgment which clearly leads to particular principles. As we have already suggested, Rawls's favored "device of representation" (*PL*, 24–25) is an original position model, which leads us to his two principles by characterizing all and only the factors relevant to what principles apply.

Rawls does not assume that an original position will always be available, and so one could have a form of "political constructivism" which proceeds without one. His account of human rights, for example, is added to rather than derived from his international version of the original position (*LP*, 65–80; James 2005, 31). Still, at least in certain cases, Rawls's suggestion is that the thought experiment offers a valuable "means of public reflection and self-clarification," by helping us "work out what we now think, once we are able to take a clear uncluttered view" (*PL*, 26).

We may pass quickly over the familiar details of Rawls's favored model. Given uncertainty about their respective social positions (the "veil of ignorance"), self-interested parties rationally seek to maximize prospects for the worst situation (following the "maximin" decision rule). They converge upon the two principles (the principle of equal liberty and the difference principle) because the received alternative principles (e.g., utilitarianism) present uncertain chances that one's life prospects will go very badly or at least less well than under Rawls's two. In a context of uncertainty (in contrast with risks taken within known probabilities), one will not gamble when one's whole life is at stake.

Here there are familiar questions about why the model should be set up in Rawls's favored way. Why not imagine self-interested maximizers who have an equal chance of being anyone, who then choose average utilitarianism, à la John Harsanyi (1975)? (For Rawls's reply, see *JF*, 97 n19, 106ff.) More important for our purposes is the intended function of any such thought experiment within Rawls's larger political constructivism. Whatever the result, the goal is to make "perfectly evident which agreement would be made by the parties as citizens' representatives" (*PL*, 26). The goal is to clarify, for public reflection, that a society's practical reason favors a definite result (at least among the traditional menu of principles).

In particular, the goal is not simply to induce one psychologically into accepting certain conclusions, let alone to coerce thought. It is rather to show that they are supported by a free exercise of reason in way which *justifies* our resulting confidence. The aim is to "further [the] recognition" that we should accept certain principles, beyond considering the various underlying grounds of support directly and by themselves (*PL*, 45).

This works by both exclusion and ordered inclusion of potential considerations. We first exclude factors which are irrelevant to the question of what would be a justifiable practice. If you ask why it should be acceptable to you that I fare better than you, for example, it would not be relevant for me to cite the *mere* fact that I actually occupy a position of relative advantage. So insofar as we are modeling the set of *relevant* considerations, we may appropriately leave out facts about social position (e.g., by drawing a veil which blocks them from view). The same will go for the fact that I have a certain religious or philosophical outlook, or for my race, sex, gender, intelligence, or physical strength, not to mention factors such as my bare circumstantial bargaining advantage, or my threats of coercion, force, deception, and fraud (*PL*, 24–25). Removing these "arbitrary" or morally irrelevant factors will leave a range of relevant considerations, for instance, that citizens of a society are moral equals, with certain basic interests and claims in the society's cooperatively produced fruit. The modeling task is then to put these relevant factors in good order, to put them together in a way which leaves the "overall balance of reasons plainly favoring one conception over the rest" (*PL*, 26). Last and most important, the model is supposed to show how the proposed order would "plainly" support certain principles, much as with deductive argument. As Rawls explains:

> Deductive argument lays out the order of how statements can be connected; axioms, or basic principles, are illuminating in setting out these connections in a clear and perspicuous way. A conception such as that of the original position is illuminating in the same way and enables us to present justice as fairness as having a certain unity. (*PL*, 242 n31)

It is important here that the "illumination" in seeing a "certain unity" is not necessarily meant to closely track the strength of underlying relevant reasons. Rawls explicitly distinguishes what he calls "order of deduction" from "order of support": "If we rank principles and convictions according to how strongly they support the doctrine that leads to them," he explains, "then principles and convictions high in this order of support may be low in the order of deduction" (*PL*, 242 n31). Or as Rawls illustrates in a related connection, in geometry "we may accept the axioms as much because of the theorems they lead to as the other way around" (*PL*, 242).

In that case, however, we might ask why the proposed deduction should make any difference for what we should ultimately accept. Although we *might* be justified in accepting certain moral "theorems" because they follow from certain justified moral "axioms," we might equally be justified in rejecting certain axioms because we have reason to reject the theorems they support. Why favor Rawls's principles instead of simply rejecting one or more of the assumptions from which they are "deduced"?

While Rawls does seem to hold that displayed relations of deduction add something further to the argument, he clearly does not assume this is true in the absence of background reasons to accept his starting points. The original position model is not supposed to be self-evidently appropriate. It is appropriate in virtue of a set of more modest and relatively plausible claims about what is relevant to justificatory argument and what our culturally assumed "fundamental ideas" of person and society come to. The original position's chief function is to show – what would otherwise remain obscure – that these various "widely accepted but weak premises" add up to quite a lot. That is, we not only reaffirm views already widely held (e.g., in the equal liberty principle), but also extend or deepen commonsense understanding by affirming conclusions that would otherwise be controversial (e.g., the difference principle).

This is not yet to explain *why* exactly displayed relations of deduction would add something further to the argument. Rawls's answer is that they do add something, but not necessarily by adding further justificatory support beyond the underlying considerations. Their contribution instead flows from their potential power to convince through reason. In the passage from *TJ* quoted above, when Rawls says that justification is "designed to reconcile by reason" and "proceeds from what all parties to the discussion hold in common," he continues:

> Ideally, to justify a conception of justice to someone is to give him a proof of its principles from premises that we both accept, these principles in turn having consequences that match our

considered judgments. Thus mere proof is not justification. A proof simply displays logical rela-tions between propositions. But proofs become justification once the starting points are mutually recognized, or the conclusions so comprehensive and compelling as to persuade us of the sound-ness of the conception expressed by their principles.

It is perfectly proper, then, that the argument for the principles should proceed from some consensus. This is the nature of justification. (*TJ*, 508–509)

Or least this is the nature of justification-*to*, in a morally significant sense. If it is a kind of geometry, it is *moral* geometry.

## Justification Rather Than Determination

Our fifth and final element of political constructivism – "Conclusion" – tells us what to make of all this: given such reasoning, we have sufficient reason to accept the selected principles as *requirements of social justice*, for the specified public social role. We are so justified by virtue of the *sufficiency* of the represented grounds, when their combined force is laid out in a con-vincing way. This needn't be the only or even the strongest reasons to accept the favored principles; there may well be a separate argument for them. But so long as we have correctly worked through the steps of the reasoning – from starting points we accept, and reaffirm in our process of reflection – we are unjustified in refusing to accept the result. Or if we do reject it, we are required to find some error we have made along the way.

Rawls's argument succeeds to the extent that this requires us to reject an assumption or step in reasoning which is *more plausible* on its merits than the conclusion itself. Rawls will admit that plausibility is holistic; it is to be settled only in a larger reflective equilibrium of convictions, principles, and argument steps. Yet we will not be justified in rejecting an assumption *simply* because it leads to a conclusion we do not like or find hard to admit; adequate reasons will be required. And to the extent Rawls's argument assumes only "widely accepted but weak premises," such reasons are hard to come by, at least short of a radical – and, as Socrates might say, shameful – departure from reasoned common sense.

This does not necessarily assume metaethical constructivism. It is a further thesis to claim that the resulting principles count as correct requirements of social justice because social justice is nothing more, and nothing less, than the outcome of some such constructive reasoning, carried out in appropriate circumstances (see James 2012a). But even without this further claim, the resulting principles can count as correct requirements of social justice simply because there is a good argument for regarding them as such. A good argu-ment can suffice to justify us in accepting principles as correct requirements of social justice whether or not there is any deeper relationship between correctness and good justifying arguments.

Nor does it follow that political constructivism cannot then be "productive" of, as it were, something not already there. A metaethical constructivist will say that certain reasoning "produces" the truth about social justice from something else (from truth-independent requirements of practical reasoning). Whether or not this is also true, the political construc-tivist can say that a good argument is "productive" in the sense that someone who goes through it might be required to accept a conclusion he or she would not have otherwise reached, or at least now justified in having a greater degree of confidence he or she would not have otherwise had. As we have suggested, even a "device of representation" can be productive in this sense. It does not simply warm over grounds that are anyway there, but rather puts them together in a way that convinces one of their combined force.

The same will be true if, as Rawls suggests, the argument from the original position is an instance of "procedural justice" – if, that is, a result counts as just because it is reached by the right procedure (as with a fair lottery), instead of the other way around (as when the "I cut, you choose" rule reliably leads to an independently fair division of a cake) (*TJ*, 74). In the overall argument, the relevant "result" is our being justified in accepting certain principles as correct requirements of justice. But this result obtains in virtue of our having appreciated where the constructive argument leads by a process of thought. We aren't so justified by working through the argument merely because the principles it supports are independently justified. Our consideration of the argument adds something to our grounds for confidence. We are to be convinced by the principles in part because of our sense of how we have arrived at them, through our own free exercise of public practical reason.

## Rawls's Kantian Phase

If we have focused on the continuity between KC and *PL*, there is of course one major difference: in KC Rawls accepted metaethical constructivism (KC, 350, 354–356) and indeed says that he means to highlight the neglected "Kantian roots" of justice as fairness as previously articulated in *TJ* (KC, 303). It is therefore at least plausible to view metaethical constructivism as part and parcel of his general approach to justice, including his previous political constructivism. His later "political turn" in *PL*, in this case, would amount to a major break from his earlier generally Kantian approach. (See also Weithman, 2011.)

We suggest a different interpretation: Rawls's Kantian period, as chiefly represented by KC, is a mere phase. It helped Rawls clarify the general nature of the project he had undertaken from the start, but does not reflect a major break. On this reading, Rawls endorsed a Kantian metaethical constructivism in part because it offered a way of more deeply characterizing how his previous political constructivism (in our general, non-metaethical sense) could be a live and distinct possibility. Although metaethical constructivism is not affirmed in *TJ*, Rawls may even have accepted it all along and only gradually saw that it was not essential for his basic approach. His increasing concern for what forms of social agreement could be plausibly assumed, starting in *PL*, gave him reason to see, or at least newly emphasize, that his metaethical claims in KC are in fact responsive to a quite different and only indirectly related set of issues. Rawls's Kantian phase did not then reveal the true nature of justice as fairness as expressed in *TJ*. It merely unearthed some of its "roots," in a way which showed how political constructivism could be grounded in a familiar rationalist picture. While that development of Kantian themes helped him distinguish his rationalism from competing conceptions of justice and political authority, it equally helped him characterize how his own rationalism stands independent from those very Kantian ideas.

We find indirect support for this reading in a similar account of Rawls's move away from a different set of Kantian ideas, ideas which, unlike metaethical constructivism, were explicitly advanced in *TJ*. As with political constructivism, here the fact that Rawls shed Kantian ideas clarified the general nature of his project rather than marking a dramatic break from a previous generally Kantian approach.

An appeal to Kantian personal autonomy is especially central to Rawls's account of "stability" in Part Three of *TJ*. Rawls later says, in *PL*, that this created a "serious internal problem" in that book (*PL*, xv). It was "unrealistic," he says, to suppose that a just society could last (by reproducing itself across generations and recovering from external shocks) if this depended upon people reliably attaching special importance to their own personal Kantian autonomy, as realized in just social arrangements. In *PL*, he replaces this assumption with the more modest, more realistic conjecture that people can be brought to abide by and support fairness, in part because it is personally beneficial in various ways, and in part for its own sake. (See *PL*, 202–203 on the "two moral powers.")

The important point for our purposes is that Rawls's replacement of Kantian ideas in no way detracts from the significance he all along attached to realistic stability, even in *TJ*. Indeed, it arguably highlights it. While stability became a focal issue of Rawls's later work (in *PL*, and especially in *LP*), the concern is central to *TJ* (albeit often neglected). One guiding aim of *TJ* was to show, by a kind of demonstration, that a "well-ordered society" in which we all accept the same principles is a real possibility for us. And indeed, as we have seen, the demonstrative aim was precisely to draw us all into that very acceptance, through engagement in political philosophy. Agreement on the same regulative principles is then assumed to be really available to us, through pubic practical reason.

Rawls presumably had no illusions about actually getting to such agreement, or about preserving it if it could be achieved. Yet it is significant that the problem becomes one of understanding. The problem is one of moving beyond the ill-will and other impediments to reason that prevent us from seeing where reason in practice leads.

## Note

I am grateful to Samuel Freeman, Jon Mandle, Daniel Pilchman, David Reidy, and T.M. Scanlon for comments or relevant discussion.

## Works by Rawls, with Abbreviations

*Collected Papers* (CP), ed. Samuel Freeman. Cambridge, MA: Harvard University Press, 1999.
"Justice as Fairness" (1958), in *Collected Papers* (47–72).
*Justice as Fairness: A Restatement* (JF), ed. Erin Kelly. Cambridge, MA: Harvard University Press, 1999.
"Kantian Constructivism in Moral Theory" (KC) (1980), Dewey Lectures, in *Collected Papers* (303–358).
*The Law of Peoples, with "The Idea of Public Reason Revisited"* (LP). Cambridge, MA: Harvard University Press, 1999.
*Political Liberalism* (PL), expanded edn. New York: Columbia University Press, 2005.
*A Theory of Justice* (TJ), rev. edn. Cambridge, MA: Harvard University Press, 1999.

## Other References

Beitz, Charles (2009) *The Idea of Human Rights*. New York: Oxford University Press.
Dworkin, Ronald (1986) *Law's Empire*. Cambridge, MA: Harvard University Press.

Freeman, Samuel (2007) "The Burdens of Public Justification: Constructivism, Contractualism, and Publicity." *Politics, Philosophy and Economics* 6: 5–43.

Harsanyi, John (1975) "Can the Maximin Principle Serve as a Basis for Morality? A Critique of John Rawls's Theory." *American Political Science Review* 69: 594–606.

James, Aaron (2005) "Constructing Justice for Existing Practice: Rawls and the Status Quo." *Philosophy and Public Affairs* 33: 1–36.

James, Aaron (2012a) "Constructing Protagorean Objectivity." In James Lenman and Yonatan Shemmer (eds), *Constructivism in Practical Philosophy*. Oxford: Oxford University Press.

James, Aaron (2012b) *Fairness in Practice: A Social Contract for a Global Economy*. New York: Oxford University Press.

Postema, Gerald (1987) "'Protestant' Interpretation and Social Practices." *Law and Philosophy* 6: 283–319.

Scanlon, T.M. (1998) *What We Owe to Each Other*. Cambridge: Harvard University Press.

Weithman, Paul (2011) *Why Political Liberalism? On John Rawls's Political Turn*. New York: Oxford University Press.

# 15

# On the Idea of Public Reason

## JONATHAN QUONG

The idea of public reason is at the center of John Rawls's political philosophy. Although the mature statement of this idea is fully expressed only in the 1996 revised edition of *Political Liberalism* (see the expanded edition of 2005) and the 1997 *University of Chicago Law Review* essay "The Idea of Public Reason Revisited" (see *LP*), Rawls's contractualism is an expression of the same basic moral insight: our laws and political institutions must be justifiable to each of us by reference to some common point of view, despite our deep differences and disagreements. This commitment to the public justification of political power is at the heart of Rawls's vision of a just and stable society.

Public reason, however, is not only a standard by which we measure laws and political institutions. It is also a set of guidelines to regulate the behavior of legislators, judges, and ordinary citizens. Public reason requires a form of deliberative democracy, whereby citizens only support those fundamental laws and political institutions that they sincerely believe can be justified by appeal to political values that others could reasonably accept. In particular, public reason entails a moral *duty of civility* that requires us to explain to one another how our important political positions are justifiable by reference to a reasonable political conception of justice, and to refrain from supporting positions when we believe they can only be justified by appeal to a religious doctrine, or some other comprehensive doctrine that we cannot reasonably expect everyone to endorse (*PL*, 217; *LP*, 135). Acting in accordance with this duty would require radical changes to our existing political institutions and behavior. Currently, many political issues such as abortion, stem-cell research, gay marriage, prostitution, gambling, pornography, school curriculum and school prayer, foreign policy, and other constitutional essentials or matters of basic social justice are often debated and sometimes even decided by appeal to religious arguments or other controversial moral doctrines over which reasonable people disagree. The idea of public reason requires us to abandon this practice and reshape our behavior so that our most important political issues are decided by appeal to conceptions of justice that reflect only the shared political values implicit in the culture of a constitutional democracy.

*A Companion to Rawls*, First Edition. Edited by Jon Mandle and David A. Reidy.
© 2014 John Wiley & Sons, Inc. Published 2016 by John Wiley & Sons, Inc.

In this chapter I discuss the practice of public reason (section 1), the moral basis of public reason (section 2), and the challenge posed by religious critics of public reason (section 3).

# 1. The Practice of Public Reason

## 1.1 Subject

What is the subject matter of public reason? What are the topics to which public reason applies? At the most abstract level, the subject of public reason is the good of the public in a constitutional democracy (*PL*, 213). More specifically, public reason is the reason of equal citizens in a democracy when they collectively exercise final political and coercive power. This means that the primary subject matter of public reason is what Rawls calls the constitutional essentials and matters of basic justice (*PL*, 214). Constitutional essentials include (*PL*, 227):

a.  The principles that structure the government and political process (e.g. rules determining who may vote, and whether a system is parliamentary or presidential).
b.  The basic rights and liberties of citizens.

Matters of basic justice concern the principles that determine the distribution of important goods such as income, wealth, opportunities, and positions of power that are not already covered by the constitutional essentials (*PL*, 228–229). There are other political issues – for example, funding of the arts, or environment regulation – which, according to Rawls, are not constitutional essentials or matters of basic justice, and so do not form part of the subject matter of public reason (*PL*, 214). I will refer to these issues as matters of ordinary legislation. The scope of public reason is thus limited on Rawls's account to constitutional essentials and matters of basic justice, and excludes ordinary legislation.

Is the distinction between constitutional essentials and matters of basic justice, on the one hand, and matters of ordinary legislation, on the other, tenable? Surely almost everything that might be described as a matter of ordinary legislation has some bearing, however small, on more fundamental matters (Greenawalt 1994, 685–686)? For example, any resources spent on ordinary matters could always be reallocated to protecting basic rights and liberties. And even setting this worry aside, why focus on constitutional essentials and matters of basic justice? Rawls offers no definitive answer to this question, but he offers the following suggestion (*PL*, 230): provided constitutional essentials and matters of basic justice are settled by appeal to public reason, willing political and social cooperation between free and equal citizens will usually be possible. Perhaps social order could also be maintained by threatening or manipulating citizens, but under these conditions we could not say that citizens willingly cooperate with each other on terms that are acceptable to all.

Even if this provides a satisfactory answer to our second question – why focus on the constitutional essentials and matters of basic justice? – it doesn't provide a satisfactory answer to a third question: why exclude matters of ordinary legislation from the scope of public reason? Why not extend the scope of public reason to include all the political questions that citizens face in a democratic society? I have, elsewhere, expressed my doubts regarding Rawls's resistance to expanding the scope of public reason in this way, and so I will not pursue this question here (Quong 2011, 273–287).

## 1.2 Content and Structure

The content of public reason has two parts (*PL*, 224).[1] First, there is a political conception of justice that provides citizens with the substantive principles designed to regulate the basic structure of society. Rawls favors his conception of justice as fairness and its two main principles, but any political conception of justice can serve this role, provided it: (1) includes basic rights, liberties, and opportunities, (2) assigns this list a certain special priority compared to other goods, and (3) ensures citizens are provided with all-purpose means to make effective use of these freedoms (*LP*, 141). A conception of justice is suitably *political* when (a) its principles apply to the basic structure of society, (b) it can be presented independently of any comprehensive doctrine, and (c) it can be worked out from fundamental ideas implicit in the public political culture of a constitutional regime (*LP*, 143). The principles of such a political conception (or the family of liberal conceptions that have these features) provide the normative framework to which citizens can appeal when debating and voting on constitutional essentials or matters of basic justice. Second, the content of public reason contains guidelines of public inquiry, which include both "principles of reasoning and rules of evidence" as well as the virtues of reasonableness and civility that help make public discussion possible (*PL*, 224).

One important challenge regarding the content of public reason arises from Rawls's claim that public reason needs to be *complete* (*PL*, 225; *LP*, 144–146). The content of public reason must be sufficiently detailed and ordered in a way that will give at least one reasonable answer to all, or almost all, questions concerning constitutional essentials and matters of basic justice. If the content of public reason was not complete in this way – if it was indeterminate regarding many important political questions – it would not be able to perform its main function, namely, to provide a common framework for citizens to use as the basis for resolving fundamental political questions. A conception of justice – such as Rawls's justice as fairness – with very specific principles that are also ordered in a particular manner helps to ensure the completeness of public reason. But some critics argue that this concern for completeness merely creates a different problem. If the content of public reason must be sufficiently detailed and specific to be complete, it seems like all the important normative work is done by the philosopher who designs the political conception of justice, and not by the actual citizens who deliberate about political questions. To some, Rawls's account of the content of public reason thus wrongly prioritizes philosophically derived liberal principles over the democratic autonomy of actual citizens (Habermas 1995, 127–128).

I believe this objection is misguided. First, certain fundamental liberal rights and principles – for example, free speech and freedom of religion – are beyond reasonable dispute, and so incorporating such rights and principles into the content of public reason does nothing to unreasonably threaten democratic autonomy; a democracy that sought to deny such rights would be acting unjustly and illegitimately. Second, as Rawls has emphasized, the content of public reason is not fixed by one specific conception, but rather it can include any conception of justice within a broadly liberal family, and so there is ample scope for each citizen to exercise his or her democratic autonomy by advocating for the conception of justice he or she thinks best. Finally, even if the content of public reason is too abstract to provide a single determinate answer to any important political question we might face, this does not mean that public reason fails to be suitably complete. So long as the content of public reason alone provides enough normative material to arrive at one or more reasonable answers, this degree of completeness is all citizens require in order to be able to eschew nonpublic reasoning over essential matters (*PL*, 246). Rawls does not believe that citizens must all agree on the content of public reason – he does not suppose that a reason or argument fails to be suitably public unless it is in fact accepted by all citizens. Instead, public reason simply requires that we sincerely believe that the arguments we offer to others are drawn from a political conception of justice that others *could* reasonably endorse, even if they do not *in fact* endorse our preferred conception (*PL*, 241).

Let us turn to the structure of public reason. Rawls argues that certain core ideas that are implicit in the public political culture of a constitutional democracy – the idea of citizens as free and equal, or society as a fair system of social cooperation – provide the normative bases from which public reasoning must proceed. Public reasoning thus involves an appeal to *shared* democratic and liberal ideas, whereas nonpublic reasoning necessarily invokes values or modes of reasoning that are controversial and the subject of reasonable disagreement among citizens.

Some theorists of public justification, however, argue that public reason need not appeal to shared reasons, and can instead be achieved solely through a convergence of different individuals' non-shared reasons (Gaus 2011, 283–292; Gaus and Vallier 2009). Provided a law could be justified to each citizen by appealing to his or her own religious or otherwise comprehensive doctrine, then the law is publicly justified via a convergence of these different (and possibly conflicting) non-shared reasons. This alternative conception of the structure of public reason would have wide-reaching implications regarding the duty of civility and the evaluation of many laws and institutions. I believe, however, that there are sound reasons to reject this convergence view of public reason's structure. Most importantly, when a law is only supported by a convergence of different non-shared reasons it seems unlikely, given the fact of reasonable pluralism (*PL*, 54–66), that we could each sincerely regard the law in question as being genuinely justified to all reasonable citizens of different faiths and doctrines. It is more likely, under these conditions, that we would believe some of our fellow citizens of different faiths or doctrines simply lack sufficient reasons to endorse the law in question since they are not justified in endorsing the comprehensive doctrines to which they adhere (Quong 2011, 261–273).

## 1.3  Constituency, Site, and Civility

To whom do our fundamental principles and laws need to be justified? The short answer is, everyone – all those to whom the laws and principles apply. However, justifying a principle or law to a person does not require showing that the person can or would accept the law based on his or her current beliefs. Rather, it requires that we offer a justification that all persons could endorse in their idealized role as *reasonable citizens* (*PL*, 54–61).[2] Reasonable citizens accept the idea of society as a fair system of social cooperation for mutual benefit between free and equal citizens. They also accept what Rawls calls the burdens of judgment and the resulting fact of reasonable pluralism. Because reasonable citizens accept these two ideas, they accept the *liberal principle of legitimacy*: the exercise of political power is only legitimate when it can be justified in accordance with constitutional essentials and matters of basic justice that can be justified by appeal to values and principles acceptable to all reasonable and rational persons (*PL*, 217; *LP*, 136–137). Specifically excluded from the constituency of public reason are *unreasonable* citizens: those who reject one or more of the preceding ideas. This does not mean that unreasonable persons are excluded from the rights and benefits of citizenship, but it does mean that they are excluded from the constituency of persons to whom arguments about the rights and benefits of citizenship must be justifiable (Quong 2011, 290–314).

A different question is this: to whom do the requirements of public reason apply? That is, who must adhere to the moral duty of civility: the duty to support only policies and principles that are defensible by reference to suitably political values and political conceptions of justice, and to articulate those shared reasons when deliberating with others? In one sense, again, the answer is all of us: all citizens ought to respect the duty of civility when deliberating or voting on constitutional essentials and matters of basic justice (*PL*, 217–218). But the requirements of public reason impose more stringent duties on judges, as well as other elected officials or those running for office (*LP*, 133–135). This is because, in their role as state officials, these people operate at the main *site* of public reason, or what Rawls calls the public political forum. This forum has three parts: (1) the discourse of judges, (2) the discourse of government officials, and (3) the discourse of candidates for public office and their campaign managers (*LP*, 133–134). Ordinary citizens, however, are also expected to adhere to the duty of civility when they deliberate and vote on essential issues, thus doing what they can to hold government officials accountable to the standards of public reason. Rawls says that in these cases citizens ideally ought to think of themselves as if they were legislators (*LP*, 135–136). Rawls also says that the idea of public reason applies to the *discourse* of citizens when debating constitutional essentials and matters of basic justice (*PL*, 217–218).[3]

The duty of civility, however, only applies to individuals in their capacity as citizens, that is, when they enter the public political forum, and only when they support, or vote on, some constitutional essential or matter of basic justice. Citizens are not generally constrained by the duty of civility in their daily lives, for example, when they discuss issues with their family, or as members of religious groups or universities, or in their roles as members of any association in what Rawls calls the background culture of society (*LP*, 134). The duty of civility is also only a moral, and not a legal duty, and thus no one's speech could be legitimately restricted by appeal to this duty. For Rawls, the right to free speech is lexically prior to the duty of civility (*LP*, 136).

The duty of civility also does not preclude citizens from introducing their religious or otherwise comprehensive reasons into political debate provided these arguments are supplemented by sufficient public reasons in due course (*LP*, 152). This is what Rawls calls the "wide view," and the requirement that citizens who initially offer only nonpublic arguments must provide public reasons in due course is known as "the proviso." He emphasizes that under different types of political circumstances – particularly when a society is not justly arranged or when divisions in political society run deep – there may be substantial benefits to be had if citizens introduce their religious or comprehensive rationales into political debate to reassure other citizens of their sincere commitment to core political values and help bring about a more just society (he cites Martin Luther King's religious arguments in favor of civil rights as an exemplar). In these cases, the introduction of nonpublic reasons can ultimately strengthen the ideal public reason.

Some critics protest that the duty of civility is unrealistic, unreasonable, or counterproductive in the harsh world of contemporary democratic politics. Put crudely, in order to promote justice, one must wield some degree of power or influence, and so the main point of democratic politics is to use whatever legal means are available to win political power. Manipulative rhetoric, political bargaining, and any other legal means available can and should be used to win power and influence people. Since this is how one's political opponents will behave, it is naive and self-defeating to constrain one's pursuit of political justice by adhering to Rawls's duty of civility.

In one sense, this objection simply misunderstands Rawls's position. Rawls is careful to state that the idea of public reason and the duty of civility belong to an *ideal* of how things ought to be in a democratic society, assuming citizens as just and society as well-ordered according to a political conception of justice (*LP*, 131). This "describes what is possible and can be, yet may never be" (*PL*, 213). Pointing out that adhering to the duty of civility may be counterproductive under current conditions is thus no objection to the ideal, since current democratic societies are far from ideal or well-ordered. However, there is another sense in which the objection remains powerful and largely unaddressed. If Rawls's conception of public reason is only intended for an ideally just and well-ordered society, how should citizens behave in our imperfect and nonideal world? What, if anything, do public reason and the duty of civility entail in our current nonideal conditions? This is a hugely important question that has received insufficient attention.

## 2. The Basis of Public Reason

The idea of public reason, we have seen, is a view about what kinds of reasons citizens in a well-ordered democratic society ought to invoke when deciding important political questions. It asks us to refrain from appealing purely to religious or comprehensive doctrines over which reasonable people disagree, and instead to seek shared reasons acceptable to similarly motivated persons to justify political principles and laws. But why should we accept this idea? What is the moral basis for endorsing this particular conception of democratic politics? In this section I consider three possible answers. There is some textual support for each of these answers in Rawls's work, but I will argue that the third represents the best interpretation of Rawls's own view, and is also the best answer for those committed to a political liberalism.

### 2.1 Autonomy

On one view, we are not truly free unless we act in accordance with laws that we rationally give ourselves. To follow laws that are authored by others and not yourself is to be subject to the will of those others, and thus to be unfree. And even if you are not subject to the will of others, you can fail to act autonomously if your actions are capricious or influenced by transient desires, rather than being guided by your own rational choices. On a Kantian account, we express our nature as rational beings – and act autonomously – by acting in accordance with maxims that we could rationally will to be universal laws. On a view with Rousseauvian roots, democratic autonomy is realized when the laws governing our society are justified by appeal to the common good and thereby express the general will of all citizens.

There are elements of these ideas in Rawls's early work. Rawls famously offers a Kantian interpretation of his account of justice as fairness (*TJ*, 221–227). He suggests that the principles that the parties would accept in the original position are like categorical imperatives since they express our nature as free and equal rational beings – the principles are agreed to by parties without knowledge of any of the contingent features of our individual lives. This means that when we act in accordance with those principles, we act autonomously. Having explained how his own theory may be given this Kantian interpretation, Rawls then goes on to say that "Kant's main aim is to deepen and to justify Rousseau's idea that liberty is acting in accordance with a law that we give to ourselves" (*TJ*, 225). A commitment to public reason might thus be grounded in a Kantian or Rousseauvian claim regarding the preeminent value of a certain kind of autonomy.[4]

The main difficulty with such arguments is that they seem to presuppose a particular comprehensive doctrine. Rawls developed the idea of a political liberalism in part because his account of stability in *A Theory of Justice* was grounded in a Kantian view whereby the exercise of our rational agency is seen as the preeminent form of human flourishing (*PL*, xvi–xvii).[5] But if reasonable and rational people will always disagree about human flourishing under liberal conditions, then an internally consistent liberal theory must not assume that citizens endorse any particular view of human flourishing. Thus the later Rawls, and all those who share his assumption about the fact of reasonable pluralism, cannot ground a commitment to public reason in the role that autonomy plays in expressing our rational nature. It would not be unreasonable for some citizens to reject this account of autonomy, and thus this account of public reason's basis would be unstable in a well-ordered society (Weithman 2002, 188–191).

## 2.2 Coercion and Respect

A second view regarding the basis of public reason concerns how coercion can be made compatible with respect for persons as ends. Charles Larmore, for example, argues that "to respect another person as an end is to require that coercive or political principles be as justifiable to that person as they presumably are to us" (1999, 608). Conversely, "if we try to bring about conformity to a rule of conduct solely by the threat of force, we shall be treating persons merely as means, as objects of coercion, and not also as ends, engaging with their distinctive capacity as persons" (1999, 607). Similarly, Thomas Nagel says:

> if you force someone to serve an end that he cannot be given adequate reason to share, you are treating him as a mere means – even if the end is his own good, as you see it but he doesn't. In view of the coercive character of the state, the requirement [for unanimity, similar to the idea of public reason] becomes a condition of political legitimacy. (1991, 159)

Clearly this view also has Kantian roots, though the emphasis is different; the issue is whether those who are subject to coercion are treated with appropriate respect as ends-in-and-of-themselves, and not whether we act autonomously in following laws we can all rationally will.

Gerald Gaus also advances a view of public justification grounded in the importance of reconciling coercion with respect for persons:

> Because we recognize other moral persons as free and equal, having authority – perhaps we should say "moral sovereignty" – to interpret their own moral obligations for themselves, our claims to have standing to command that they comply with our view of the demands of morality appears to manifest disrespect for them as equal interpreters of morality. (2011, 17)

271

For Gaus we avoid manifesting this disrespect when our claims to moral authority can be justified to those against whom the demands are pressed. Like Larmore and Nagel, Gaus sometimes focuses on moral demands backed by threats of coercion. He argues that there is a *presumption in favor of liberty*, whereby there is no obligation to publicly justify our choices to others unless we are interfering with, blocking, or thwarting the agency (or negative liberty) of another person (2011, 341–346).

This thesis – that coercion can only show due respect for persons as ends (or as sovereign interpreters of morality's requirements) when it can be reasonably justified to those subject to the coercion – has a wide currency, and it is sometimes attributed to Rawls.[6] But I do not believe this is the best interpretation of Rawls's view. Though some of Rawls's remarks do point in this direction, he never explicitly formulates or develops his view in this way, and he rarely mentions coercion in his discussion of public reason.

Setting the exegetical issue aside, should we endorse this respect-based and coercion-centric account of public reason's moral basis? There are several reasons to be skeptical of this view. To begin, the conception of respect for persons to which Larmore and Nagel appeal remains vulnerable to the same objection pressed against the appeal to autonomy (I do not believe this objection applies to Gaus's different view of respect). That is, the Kantian idea of respecting persons as ends-in-themselves will be the subject of reasonable disagreement among citizens in a well-ordered society, and so grounding a commitment to public reason in this way is unstable. Larmore denies this charge (1999, 623–624), but I won't attempt to settle the dispute here. Let us instead consider the coercion-centric aspect of this view.

I think we should reject the view that the main purpose of public reason is to legitimate or render permissible coercion or threats of coercion against individuals. First, this view presupposes a noncoercive benchmark from which departures must be publicly justified in order to be legitimate. But there is no good reason to believe that coercive rules or actions always stand uniquely in need of justification when compared to noncoercive alternatives.

Second, consider the following example:[7]

> *State Religion*   Our country is deciding whether or not to make Catholicism the sole national religion. If implemented, this decision would involve the incorporation of religious references into official government documents, declaring certain important Catholic holidays to be national holidays when federal employees would not be required to work, and using state-run lottery funds to support Catholic charities and subsidize the Catholic Church in other ways.

It is implausible to suppose that the set of policies above are not the proper subject matter of public reason, but the coercion-centric view will have difficulty reaching this conclusion since none of the policies involve the coercive use of state power to interfere with citizens' liberty.

Finally, imagine a society where laws are debated and determined democratically, but laws are not coercively enforced because all citizens always internalize and voluntarily comply with the rules and requirements issued by the government even when they believe them to be deeply mistaken or lacking a coherent rationale. They do so because they believe they are required either as a matter of justice or legitimacy to comply with a democratic government's demands. Since these rules will be followed as a result of internalization rather than via the threat of coercion, the coercion-centric account of public reason cannot explain why the fundamental institutions, rights, and laws in this imagined society ought to be regulated by the idea of public reason. But this is a serious flaw. Public reason is always needed to assess our fundamental political principles and institutions even when, indeed perhaps *especially when*, citizens obey out of a sense of justice or civic obligation rather than out of fear of coercion.

## 2.3 Justice

I believe we do better to see public reason as grounded in the value of justice, more specifically the moral value of ensuring that the fundamental rules that regulate a constitutional democracy are fair, so that citizens can live with each other on just terms. Consider the question with which Rawls begins his political liberal project: "how is it possible for there to exist over time a just and stable society of free and equal citizens, who remain profoundly divided by reasonable religious, philosophical, and moral doctrines?" (*PL*, 4). Rawls believes this realistic utopia can only exist if we can find a shared basis for settling fundamental political questions:

> Justice as fairness tries to do this by using a fundamental organizing idea within which all ideas and principles can be systematically connected and related. This organizing idea is that of society as a fair system of social cooperation between free and equal persons viewed as fully cooperating members of a society over a complete life . . . this conception provides a publicly recognized point of view from which all citizens can examine before one another whether their political and social institutions are just. It enables them to do this by citing what are publicly recognized among them as valid and sufficient reasons singled out by that conception itself . . . the aim of justice as fairness, then, is practical: it presents itself as a conception of justice that may be shared by citizens as a basis of a reasoned, informed, and willing political agreement. It expresses their shared and public political reason. (*PL*, 9)

Adhering to the requirements of public reason is thus how we can each endeavor to treat each other justly. Of course there will be those who deny that a purely political conception of justice is valid, and insist that political decisions should be based on the whole truth as defined from within their comprehensive perspective. But such people are unreasonable in at least one of two ways. Either such people deny the fact of reasonable pluralism, or they deny that the fundamental principles of justice ought to be reasonably acceptable to other free and equal citizens. To deny the former is to deny something that proponents of public reason believe is a plain fact about the exercise of rationality under free conditions (*PL*, 4, 55–57). And to deny the latter is to deny the equal status of other citizens. As Rawls says,

> Since many doctrines are seen to be reasonable, those who insist, when fundamental political questions are stake, on what they take to be true but others do not, seem to others to simply insist on their own beliefs when they have the political power to do so. Of course, those who do insist on their beliefs also insist their beliefs alone are true: they impose their beliefs because, they say, their beliefs are true and not because they are their beliefs. But this is a claim that all equally could make. (*PL*, 61)

To insist that the principles of justice should be grounded in one's own comprehensive doctrine despite the fact this doctrine is reasonably rejected by one's fellow citizens assumes that one's own claims to have access to religious, moral, or philosophical truth carry greater weight than the claims of others; it denies that the relationship between citizens in a democratic society ought to be characterized by an ideal of equality (LP, 132–133).

Someone might reply by saying that she does not claim any greater access to truth than her fellow citizens, she only insists her comprehensive doctrine can ground political principles because there are *more* adherents of her doctrine in society than of other doctrines, and thus the appeal to her comprehensive doctrine is grounded only in a majoritarian interpretation of the principle of political equality. A full response to this claim is not possible here, but proponents of public reason should reject this argument by pointing out that purely majoritarian or procedural interpretations of political equality are untenable (Dworkin 2000, 184–210; PL, 429–431). Part of what political equality necessarily requires, proponents of public reason rightly insist, is that the substantive grounds supporting certain laws be reasonably acceptable to each person – to reject this idea risks reducing the democratic process to a competition for power, rather than a process of reasoning among equals about the fair terms of social cooperation.

Some may wonder: if the value of justice provides the normative basis for public reason, how can justice also be the subject matter of public reason? That is, how can citizens engage in public reasoning about what the principles of justice ought to be if justice is also meant to be the grounds for their adherence to the practice of public reasoning? This apparent puzzle dissolves once we distinguish the *concept* of justice from particular *conceptions* of justice (TJ, 4). It is the Rawlsian concept of justice – the ideal of a fair system of social cooperation between free and equal citizens – which provides the moral basis for public reason. Given this basis, citizens then engage in the practice of public reason with one another. Different conceptions of justice are proposed and debated, and the result, hopefully, is a political conception of justice (or a family of liberal conceptions) that can serve as the shared basis of political reasons.

This account of public reason's moral basis has important virtues. First, it illustrates the important role that public reason plays in securing what Rawls calls "stability for the right reasons" (PL, 390). A political conception of justice serves as a shared basis of reasons in debating and deciding constitutional essentials and other matters of basic justice. When citizens know that such a shared framework exists and is agreed upon by others, they can be assured that the political process is not a mere clash of competing interests, but is rather grounded in a freestanding conception of justice that all citizens can reasonably affirm.[8] Second, and relatedly, unlike accounts appealing to autonomy or respect, this view of the moral basis of public reason does not rest on a particular comprehensive doctrine or view of human flourishing. Justice is a central political value and is assumed by all who are sympathetic to the political liberal project to be exactly the sort of value whose moral importance can be affirmed by all reasonable citizens. Third, it is widely believed that considerations of justice ought to have great weight in our practical deliberations. Rawls famously declares that justice is the first virtue of social institutions (TJ, 3), and that the principles of justice define the limits on permissible conceptions of the good life (PL, 174). Thus, by grounding our commitment to public reason in the value of justice, we can more easily answer an important question, namely, if you are certain that your comprehensive doctrine is true, why give priority to reasonable public justification over truth? The answer, we can now see, is that this is what justice demands. To abandon the commitment to public reason in order to better conform with one's comprehensive doctrine is to abandon the aim of treating one's fellow citizens justly.

Some may protest that this simply pushes the problem back one step further. If justice is the moral basis of our commitment to public reason, then what is the basis of our commitment to justice? Why give justice priority over the demands of our comprehensive doctrines?

One reply to this worry is to point out that reasonable citizens can all converge on the moral importance of justice for their own different comprehensive reasons. There is thus *no need* for proponents of public reason to provide a single and ultimate account of the moral basis of public reason – it is enough to show that the commitment to public reason follows from the commitment to living with others on just terms. Second, a purely political liberalism *should not* aspire to answer the question of why justice ought to have priority over our other comprehensive values, since answering this question requires going beyond the boundaries of the political and explaining how the values of liberal justice fit or cohere with comprehensive commitments. In order to remain a political doctrine that all reasonable citizens can endorse, political liberalism must leave this task to citizens to work out for themselves (Quong 2011, 230–242).

This does not mean, however, that there is *nothing* we can say about the value and importance of liberal justice. On Rawls's view, liberal justice is organized around an attractive ideal of society as a fair system of social cooperation between free and equal persons. Persons are free in the sense that each possesses the two moral powers: (1) the capacity to form, revise, and rationally pursue a conception of the good life, and (2) the capacity to understand and act on a public conception of justice. Persons are equal in the sense that we assume they each possess these two moral powers to the requisite minimum level necessary to be fully participating members of society (*PL*, 19). In order for the terms regulating social cooperation between such persons to qualify as fair, they must be terms that could be reasonably acceptable to each person in light of their two moral powers. A form of democratic politics which allowed some people to exercise power over others by claiming to have privileged access to religious, philosophical or moral truth, or which was premised on the idea that some citizens were less able to rationally pursue their own conception of the good than others, would not be fair. Public reason and the duty of civility are thus grounded in the most fundamental values of a liberal democratic society: freedom, equality, and fairness. To reject the importance of public reason is to reject these values, or else to believe that fair cooperation between free and equal persons is somehow possible even when our fundamental political rules and institutions are not justifiable to some of the persons who will be governed by them.

## 3. Religion and Public Reason

One of the most persistent objections to Rawls's idea of public reason is that it makes demands on religious citizens that are unfair, disrespectful, or in some other way wrongful. Some complain that the idea of public reason prevents or discourages religious citizens from articulating their religious beliefs in the public political forum, or disenfranchises religious persons as fully participating members in democratic society (McConnell 2007). Others assert that public reason illicitly privileges secularism in politics (Smith 2010). These objections, however, depend on inaccurate or misleading interpretations of public reason. As we have already seen, the wide view of public reason permits citizens to introduce comprehensive reasons into political debate at any time, provided that public reasons are also offered in due course, and indeed Rawls argues it will sometimes be very valuable for citizens to do so. The duty of civility is also a moral and not a legal duty, and thus religious citizens are never prevented by state officials from expressing their religious beliefs. And Rawls is clear that many secular doctrines may be comprehensive (e.g., hedonistic utilitarianism), and are thus treated in the same way as religious views. The relevant distinction is between the political and the comprehensive, not between the secular and the religious.

There are, however, other objections along similar lines that merit more careful consideration. Some critics argue that citizens can and do reasonably disagree about the best conception of liberal democratic citizenship, and this includes reasonable disagreement as to whether Rawls's duty of civility is in fact a moral requirement that follows from our role as citizens in a constitutional democracy (Stout 2004, 70–71; Weithman 2002). Even if, as some of these critics concede, Rawls's conception of democratic citizenship is compelling, there are other reasonable ways of conceptualizing the duties of citizenship – other plausible ways to treat one's fellow citizens fairly as free and equal participants in a democratic society. In short, one can reasonably reject Rawls's specific conception of public reason and its duty of civility. Let's call this the *reasonable disagreement thesis*.

Notice that this thesis does not yet establish anything with regard to the use of religious reasons to settle fundamental political questions. Perhaps, for example, the range of reasonable conceptions of citizenship *all* place stringent restrictions on the use of religious reasons in political debate. If this were the case, then the reasonable disagreement thesis would not be of any help to those who want to establish that Rawls's view of public reason is too constraining with regard to religious citizens.

But these critics combine the reasonable disagreement thesis with a second claim. They argue that, at the very least, reasonable conceptions of liberal democratic citizenship can include views which, when fundamental political matters are stake, permit citizens to argue and vote for their favored political positions on the basis of religious or comprehensive reasons alone, even when they lack a sufficient public justification for their favored view. I will call this the *alternative civility thesis*. Different authors defend this thesis in different ways. Christopher Eberle argues that public justification is primarily grounded in a particular conception of respect for persons. This conception requires that citizens make good faith attempts to pursue public justifications for their preferred political views, but does not require that they succeed – citizens are morally permitted to rely only on religious reasons after having made a good faith effort to find public reasons (Eberle 2002, chs 4–5). Jeffrey Stout presents a pragmatist conception of democratic citizenship that places greater emphasis on the value of expression and dialectical engagement with one's fellow citizens, and does not require political debate to take any particular form with regard to content (2004, 67–85). And Paul Weithman argues that religious associations play an important and valuable role in liberal democratic societies, and this provides many citizens with an alternative conception of what it means to be a good citizen, one where religious reasons alone can form the basis of permissible advocacy and support for laws and policies (Weithman 2002). If these authors are correct, then religious citizens can reasonably reject Rawls's idea of public reason and its duty of civility in favor of a view that permits citizens to advocate and vote, when fundamental political matters are at stake, on the basis of religious reasons alone.

There are, however, several difficulties with this general line of argument. First, the critics who advance the reasonable disagreement thesis rely on what I will call an *epistemic adequacy account* of reasonable disagreement (Stout 2004, 71; Weithman 2002, 136–137). On this account, a disagreement is reasonable when the disputing parties each arrive at their differing positions in a manner that meets some threshold of epistemic adequacy. We decide whether this threshold has been met by asking certain questions, for example, whether the parties "had adequate evidence available to them, took adequate account of the evidence or whether their reasoning was in some way faulty or corrupted" (Weithman 2002, 136; also see Stout 2004, 71). If people can, as Stout and Weithman suggest, reject Rawls's idea of public reason and its duty of civility without making any obvious epistemic mistakes, then the disagreement over Rawls's view will qualify as reasonable.

But this account of reasonable disagreement differs in important respects from Rawls's own account. Rawls does not develop epistemic criteria to determine when a given disagreement qualifies as reasonable. Instead, he stipulates which ideas can and cannot be the subject of reasonable disagreement. On Rawls's account, reasonable people necessarily accept (1) the idea of society as a fair system of social cooperation between free and equal persons, (2) the burdens of judgment and the fact of reasonable pluralism, and therefore accept (3) the idea of public reason (PL, 54–62). Rawls also allows that comprehensive doctrines can qualify as reasonable even if they are not open to rational appraisal or evidentially supportable (LP, 152–153), provided the doctrines are consistent with the points listed above. Rawls's conception of reasonable disagreement is thus *normative or moralized*: it is grounded in Rawls's particular normative theory of democratic citizenship, and not an epistemic view of when disagreements are reasonable.

When Rawls's critics advance the reasonable disagreement thesis, they thus begin with a very different conception of reasonable disagreement. Of course this does not show that the critics' view is mistaken, only that their objection to Rawls is not an internal or immanent critique as it depends on assumptions he does not make. I also believe there are independent reasons why we ought to reject epistemic accounts of reasonable disagreement (Quong 2011, 248–249, 293–298), but this would take us too far afield, so we can focus instead on the alternative civility thesis.

I believe the plausibility of the alternative civility thesis depends heavily on whether public reason is *complete*, that is, whether the content of public reason can yield reasonable answers to all, or almost all, questions concerning constitutional essentials and matters of basic justice. *If* public reason were *not* complete – if there were important political questions to which no liberal conception of justice could give any reasonable answer – then *perhaps* there would be nothing disrespectful, unjust, or otherwise problematic in allowing citizens to rely on nonpublic reasons when debating and voting on certain political questions.[9]

But what if public reason *is* complete? What if a political liberal conception of justice grounded in the values of freedom, equality, and fairness can always yield at least one reasonable answer for each important political question that we face? Under these conditions, the alternative civility thesis is far less plausible. Imagine a citizen, Albert, who is opposed to legislation permitting same-sex marriage on religious grounds alone. Suppose Albert also knows that public reason is complete, and the answer it yields is one that requires permitting same-sex marriage. Albert tries to persuade his fellow citizen Betty of the correctness of his religious doctrine and its conclusion about same-sex marriage (as allowed by Rawls's duty of civility). He engages in a respectful and open-minded dialogue with Betty, but she is ultimately unconvinced by Albert's religious arguments and remains convinced by the available public justification permitting same-sex marriage. Now suppose Albert does what the alternative civility thesis permits, and he votes to oppose same-sex marriage for religious reasons alone when he knows there is a sufficient public reason to support same-sex marriage, and when he knows Betty cannot reasonably accept his religious reasons. How does Albert treat Betty? Does he treat her as someone with the capacity to reason effectively about the requirements of justice, and as someone who holds a reasonable comprehensive doctrine? If Albert agrees that Betty has a capacity for justice and a capacity to form a reasonable comprehensive doctrine, why does he persist in supporting a political position that Betty has decisive public reasons to reject? Under these conditions, I think Albert's behavior cannot be reconciled with a conception of Betty as free and equal, as possessing Rawls's two moral powers to the requisite minimum degree.

Proponents of the alternative civility thesis claim to believe in the importance of offering reasons to your fellow citizens in defense of your favored political positions, and in the value of treating your fellow citizens as capable of understanding and responding to reasons. But when we consider what the alternative civility thesis entails in practice, it is hard to understand how someone like Albert does manifest a commitment to these ideas. The alternative civility thesis allows Albert to ignore sufficient public justifications when they exist, and continue to support a political position for his own religious reasons even when he cannot convince his fellow citizens as to the soundness of those reasons. It effectively allows Albert to behave as if Betty and his fellow citizens are irrelevant – he can continue to support his preferred view regardless of what anyone else may be justified in believing, so long as he himself is sincerely convinced of the truth of his own doctrine.

This critique of the alternative civility thesis is not decisive. In particular, proponents of that thesis may protest that public reason is not complete – that it is radically indeterminate over a range of important issues – and thus in many cases a person, like Albert, who relies on religious reasons alone will not be overriding or ignoring any public justification.[10] This debate over the completeness of public reason is important. Those who challenge public reason's completeness must do more than merely assert that a political conception of justice cannot yield reasonable answers to important political questions – they are under an obligation to offer detailed analyses of specific issues in order to make good on this assertion. Conversely, defenders of public reason must do more to explain why public reason is complete – to show that it offers answers to controversial political questions. This debate will not be settled anytime soon, but in the meantime I think we ought to maintain a reasonable faith in the ideal of public reason; in a democratic society governed by principles of justice that each of us can accept in light of our shared political values such as freedom, equality, and fairness.

## Notes

I am very grateful to Rich Dagger, Andrew Lister, Jon Mandle, Tom Porter, David Reidy, Rebecca Reilly-Cooper, Micah Schwartzman, and Rebecca Stone for comments on earlier drafts.

1   Note that in the later essay "The Idea of Public Reason Revisited" Rawls does not mention the second part in his discussion of public reason's content. But Rawls does not disavow his discussion of the second part, and so it seems best to follow the original two-part presentation.
2   Rawls also lists two further characteristics of reasonable persons: (a) the desire to be recognized as a fully cooperating member of society, and (b) a reasonable moral psychology (PL, 81–82, 86).

3 Rawls does not include this latter claim about ordinary citizens in the later essay "The Idea of Public Reason Revisited." See Paul Weithman's instructive discussion of this puzzling omission (2002, 183–185).

4 Rawls says that "public reason with its duty of civility gives a view about voting on fundamental questions in some ways reminiscent of Rousseau's *Social Contract*" (PL, 219).

5 For Rawls's earlier stability argument, see *TJ*, 450–464, 496–505.

6 Larmore makes the case that this view is implicit in Rawls's work, and that Rawls's account requires it (1999; 2002).

7 A similar example has been independently developed by Colin Bird (2012) to make broadly the same point.

8 For a detailed argument about the relationship between public reason, mutual assurance, and stability, see Weithman 2011, 327–335.

9 I say "perhaps" since there are important arguments against relying on nonpublic reasons even under these conditions (see Schwartzman 2004; Williams 2000).

10 The earliest and most detailed challenge to the completeness of public reason is offered in Greenawalt 1988. Others who press this challenge include Horton 2003; de Marneffe 1994; Reidy 2000. For replies, see Schwartzman 2004; Williams 2000.

## Works by Rawls, with Abbreviations

*The Law of Peoples, with "The Idea of Public Reason Revisited" (LP)*. Cambridge, MA: Harvard University Press, 1999.

*Political Liberalism (PL)* (1993, 1996), expanded edn. New York: Columbia University Press, 2005.

*A Theory of Justice (TJ)*, rev. edn. Oxford: Oxford University Press, 1999.

## Other References

Bird, Colin (2012) "Coercion and Public Justification." Unpublished Paper, University of Virginia.

de Marneffe, Peter (1994) "Rawls's Idea of Public Reason." *Pacific Philosophical Quarterly* 75: 232–250.

Dworkin, Ronald (2000) *Sovereign Virtue: The Theory and Practice of Equality*. Cambridge, MA: Harvard University Press.

Eberle, Christopher J. (2002) *Religious Conviction in Liberal Politics*. Cambridge: Cambridge University Press.

Gaus, Gerald (2011) *The Order of Public Reason: A Theory of Freedom and Morality in a Diverse and Bounded World*. Cambridge: Cambridge University Press.

Gaus, Gerald and Vallier, Kevin (2009) "The Roles of Religious Conviction in a Publicly Justified Polity: The Implications of Convergence, Asymmetry, and Political Institutions." *Philosophy and Social Criticism* 35: 51–76.

Greenawalt, Kent (1988) *Religious Convictions and Political Choice*. New York: Oxford University Press.

Greenawalt, Kent (1994) "On Public Reason." *Chicago-Kent Law Review* 69: 669–689.

Habermas, Jürgen (1995) "Reconciliation through the Public Use of Reason." *Journal of Philosophy* 92: 109–131.

Horton, John (2003) "Rawls, Public Reason, and the Limits of Liberal Justification." *Contemporary Political Theory* 2: 5–23.

Larmore, Charles (1999) "The Moral Basis of Political Liberalism." *Journal of Philosophy* 96: 599–625.

Larmore, Charles (2002) "Public Reason." In Samuel Freeman (ed.), *The Cambridge Companion to Rawls* (368–393). Cambridge: Cambridge University Press.

McConnell, Michael W. (2007) "Secular Reason and the Misguided Attempt to Exclude Religious Argument from Democratic Deliberation." *Journal of Law, Philosophy and Culture* 1: 159–174.

Nagel, Thomas (1991) *Equality and Partiality*. New York: Oxford University Press.

Quong, Jonathan (2011) *Liberalism Without Perfection*. Oxford: Oxford University Press.

Reidy, David A. (2000) "Rawls's Wide View of Public Reason: Not Wide Enough." *Res Publica* 6: 49–72.

Schwartzman, Micah (2004) "The Completeness of Public Reason." *Politics, Philosophy, and Economics* 3: 191–220.

Smith, Steven D. (2010) *The Disenchantment of Secular Discourse*. Cambridge, MA: Harvard University Press.

Stout, Jeffrey (2004) *Democracy and Tradition*. Princeton: Princeton University Press.

Weithman, Paul (2002) *Religion and the Obligations of Citizenship*. Cambridge: Cambridge University Press.

Weithman, Paul (2011). *Why Political Liberalism?* New York: Oxford University Press.

Williams, Andrew (2000) "The Alleged Incompleteness of Public Reason." *Res Publica* 6: 199–211.

# 16

# Overlapping Consensus

## REX MARTIN

## 1. Introduction: Overlapping Consensus

In 1971 John Rawls published *A Theory of Justice*; in time, he appears to have become dissatisfied with the shape his theory had originally taken. Rawls traces the roots of this dissatisfaction to a paper he received from Samuel Scheffler in 1977 (published in 1979). Scheffler's paper argued that the account of stability developed in *A Theory of Justice* was in conflict with Rawls's "The Independence of Moral Theory," section III. Rawls says of Scheffler's paper that he remembered it as "the moment . . . when I started thinking whether and how far the view of *Theory* needed to be recast" (*PL*, xxxii–xxxiii).

The problem with *A Theory of Justice*, Rawls says, is that he had assumed that the two principles of justice as fairness (the principle of equal basic rights and liberties and the principle of fair equality of opportunity paired with mutual benefit in outcomes and, in the ideal case, the greatest benefit of the least well-off group) would become part of an overarching moral theory in any well-ordered society in which these principles were the public principles of justice. Such a society would be stable because everybody in it would continue to hold to the two principles in the light of this overarching moral theory, which contained those principles as an integral part. But such uniform acceptance, Rawls now says, is implausible. (For Rawls's own account of the problem, see *PL*, xv–xviii; also "Justice as Fairness: Political not Metaphysical," 414 n33.)[1]

In Rawls's writings in the 1980s (especially in "Justice as Fairness: Political not Metaphysical," "The Idea of an Overlapping Consensus" (IOC), and "The Domain of the Political and Overlapping Consensus"), he argues that there is going to be, in a continuing free and open society, an irreducible pluralism of reasonable comprehensive moral and religious and philosophical doctrines. This pluralism of principles is a permanent and ineradicable fact, now and for the foreseeable future. In his writings since 1985, Rawls seems especially concerned with the problem of assuring political stability in a pluralist or multicultural social environment. Rawls gives this preoccupation its most complete elaboration in *Political Liberalism*.

---

*A Companion to Rawls*, First Edition. Edited by Jon Mandle and David A. Reidy.

Rawls claims that his theory is specifically a *political* theory of justice, which is itself not a general or comprehensive critical moral theory. Rather, the most significant feature of Rawls's current, revised theory is that he takes the public political culture of a contemporary democratic society to be the deep background of the entire theory. For the leading ideas out of which the political conception of justice is to be constructed and by reference to which it is to be justified are said by Rawls to be implicit in that culture (*PL*, 13, 15, 175, 223).

Here political justification sets out from four "model conceptions" or "fundamental ideas" (*PL*, Lecture I). First is the idea of the person or citizen as free and equal and as having two distinctive capacities or moral powers and two corresponding "higher-order interests" in the realization of these capacities (*PL*, 74, 75). Thus, each person has, over that person's entire life, (i) an interest in being able to have, formulate, revise, promulgate, live according to, and advance one's particular determinate conception of the good, and (ii) an interest in exercising one's "sense of justice" and being motivated by it, providing others do so as well. To amplify point (ii), each person has an interest in living with fellow citizens on terms of mutual respect under a unified and stable scheme of basic political and economic institutions that has been organized by a shared set of principles of justice (*PL*, Lectures II and VIII). Next is the idea of fair cooperation by free and equal citizens for mutual (or, better, reciprocal) benefit. Third is the idea of the well-ordered society and its basic institutional structure, and last is the idea of a linking or mediating conception which lays out the standards for discussion and decision-making to which fellow citizens could be expected to adhere in reaching a decision respecting the governing principles of political justice (principles for the basic structure of their well-ordered society, in which they could expect to live their entire lives). This fourth idea is linked with what Rawls called "the original position" in his earlier book (*TJ*, ch. III). Herein would be included such ideas as sharply limited information (the so-called veil of ignorance), publicity, and unanimity. The function of this mediating conception is to help unify the other fundamental ideas into a single coherent whole from which one could then reason to certain principles and institutional arrangements.

Establishing terms for social cooperation for mutual benefit – principles for a fair distribution of certain primary goods (including such things as liberties, opportunities, social and economic positions, income and wealth) – continues to be the main object of Rawls's conception of justice. In the new account, though, the principles that emerge as preferred (from among a small set of historically available candidate principles) are the principles that are best supported by the background *democratic* ideas, from within the nexus formed by the four "model conceptions." The preferred principles are the principles most appropriate to these fundamental ideas, under the assumption that there is going to be, in a continuing free and open society, an irreducible and incommensurable pluralism of reasonable comprehensive moral and religious and philosophic doctrines.

Rawls thinks that those best-supported principles will be his own two principles of justice, understood now as *political* principles. (See *PL*, 5–6 for Rawls's current version of these principles.) Or, to be precise, he thinks the preferred set will actually be a "family" of principles, among which are included the two he emphasizes. (See *PL*, xxxvii, xlv, xlvi, l–li, 7, 164, 439; "The Idea of Public Reason Revisited" (IPRR), 581, 582, 584, 592, 594, 607, 611.)

This "family" is constituted by the set of "generic" liberal principles. Generic liberalism, as Rawls conceives it, has three main features: (1) certain familiar rights, liberties, opportunities are to be singled out and specified and maintained; (2) a certain priority is to be given to these rights, etc. over against "the claims of the general good and of perfectionist values"; (3)

measures to help citizens make effective use of these rights (etc.), by having an adequate base of income and wealth, are to be set in place. (See *PL*, 6; also xlvi, 156–157, 375; IPRR, 581–582; *LP*, 14, 49.) These generic liberal principles are well designed to specify an acceptable distribution of primary goods in the context of existing democratic "fundamental ideas."

The "political conception of justice," as Rawls calls it, is not limited to such principles alone. It also includes certain of the institutional arrangements that are required to put the principles into effect in a given society. These institutions – political, economic, social – are the sort of thing Rawls had in mind when he referred to the basic structure of a society. But he tends throughout to emphasize the basic political institutions.

Rawls's account of the political conception proceeds in two main stages (see *PL*, 64–65, 140–141, 385–388). The first stage is the one we have focused on up to now. The main project here is to settle on that principle or set of principles for distributing primary goods which is optimally appropriate, given the fundamental democratic ideas from which we started. This first line of justification (justification from democratic ideas in a democratic context) is said by Rawls to be "freestanding," in the sense that it draws only on these background democratic ideas (*PL*, xlii, 10, 12, 25 n27, 40, 140, 374–378). Such justification is independent (*PL*, 144), and does not draw, in an essential way, on the ideas or values of any comprehensive moral or religious doctrine.

What Rawls calls overlapping consensus is a second stage in which the antecedently established "freestanding" justification is endorsed from the respective points of view of a variety of comprehensive ethical doctrines (such as Kant's moral theory or Mill's utilitarianism) and religious doctrines (such as contemporary Catholic Christianity). On this view, the political conception is a "module . . . that fits into and can be supported by various reasonable comprehensive doctrines that endure in the society regulated by it" (*PL*, 12; also 145, 387). But it need not be *presented* by reference to such support initially; rather it is established completely independently of direct consideration of any and all such doctrines (hence Rawls's description of it as "freestanding").

At this second stage, we contemplate the support provided the political conception from *within* the confines of a variety of comprehensive views. In some of these cases such endorsement will follow a pattern of derivation; in others it will be more like endorsement based on an instantiation model – here the political conception counts as a feasible real-world exemplification of the comprehensive view in question. And, for yet others, it will be endorsement only in a weak sense: the political conception is said merely to be compatible with – that is, not incompatible with – the comprehensive doctrine in question (*PL*, xix, 11, 140, 169–171, 242 n31; see also 158–164). In any event, where several different comprehensive doctrines, each for its own reasons, can converge on and support a single political conception (for example, the generic liberal conception outlined in *PL*, 6) in one of these ways, we say that there is an overlapping consensus among these comprehensive doctrines, all centering on this common focal point.

## 2. Constitutional Consensus

Rawls is concerned that the idea of overlapping consensus might seem utopian. He tries to suggest that it is not by locating the overlapping consensus within an undergirding substructure which he calls constitutional consensus.

Constitutional consensus is one of the important new ideas in *Political Liberalism*, and one of the least discussed (for instance, there is no mention of it in Brian Barry's critical review essay, 1995, or in Weithman 2010 – see 311 – and no index entry for it in the *Cambridge Companion to Rawls*, Freeman 2003a). Constitutional consensus is first introduced in Rawls's argument (in *PL*, Lecture IV, §6) where he attempts to deal with the charge of utopianism by showing how it is possible to move away from a mere political modus vivendi to a quite different sort of social order.

## 2.1 Main Themes of Constitutional Consensus

In a mere modus vivendi, certain principles and practices are accepted as a way for people to live together without constant fighting and disruption. Rawls's own example of accepting religious toleration (in a time of deep intolerance) is one important instance. Both Catholics and Protestants in the sixteenth and to some extent the seventeenth century "held that it was the duty of the ruler to uphold the true religion and to repress the spread of heresy and false doctrine; [here] the acceptance of the principle of toleration would indeed be a mere modus vivendi, because if either faith becomes dominant, the principle of toleration would no longer be followed" (*PL*, 148).

The agreement that exists in such a case is not wide (it covers only a fairly narrow range of rights – for example, the right of religious toleration – and institutions). It is not deep (in that the reasons offered for the desirability of these accepted arrangements do not go beyond the idea of establishing a modus vivendi). And it lacks a distinctive political focus: fellow co-inhabitants have no shared conception of a public political life – no animating reasons, widely accepted, that would take them beyond the status quo, beyond the modus vivendi itself; they have accepted that status quo simply out of fear of a worse alternative.

There is nothing in a mere modus vivendi that goes beyond the horizon set by the co-inhabitants' own morality or their own religion or their own philosophical view of the world (though such reasons are often coupled with considerations of prudence and of strategy). No constituency has been created for a shared public political conception and there is no principled commitment to it (*PL*, 392).

A constitutional consensus comes about, then, as the agreed-upon area of rights and practices widens; it comes about as the ground under that area deepens (as convincing political reasons for having such arrangements, reasons that go beyond the mere utility of a modus vivendi, gain acceptance and are taken on board). And it comes about as a conception of public principles of justice, with greater focus and definition, gains widespread support. These moves away from a mere modus vivendi allow a space to be created for citizenship. This new dimension creates the availability of a new role for political co-inhabitants, that of fellow citizens. (Rawls's main discussion of constitutional consensus is found in *PL*, Lecture IV, §§3, 5–7.)

The story told in *Political Liberalism* (respecting constitutional consensus) largely emphasizes a vigorous version of generic liberalism (as found in *PL*, Lecture VI, §5). It is, presumably, where democratic political culture is at today. (i) Here the consensus has become *wide* enough to embrace most of the well-known constitutional rights, liberties, and opportunities and to cover the main contemporary democratic political institutions – universal franchise, contested voting, and majority rule decision making. And it is wide enough to embrace such further basic structure institutions as an open and competitive market (but ultimately subject to political overview) and a system of free state-supported schooling. (ii) And the consensus has become *deep* enough to draw, as background, on a well-established, viable democratic political culture and to draw on the "model conceptions" latent there as the ultimate ground of justification of a "freestanding" political conception of justice. (iii) This political conception has gained increasing focus and detail. It embraces the main features of the "family" of liberal conceptions and accepts the idea, expressed there, that "these elements can be understood in different ways, so there are many variant liberalisms," including Rawls's two principles of justice as fairness as one of the options (*PL*, 6, 164, 223; IPRR, 581–582).

Rawls takes the term "constitutional consensus" from Kurt Baier, but Rawls means by it something very different. For Baier, in the paradigm case, a constitutional consensus is procedural in character – a mere "agreement on the process of adjudication," as he puts it – and would lack, essentially lack, agreement on a conception of justice; in particular, it would exhibit no convergence on such things as the principles of generic liberalism or Rawls's own two principles of justice. (See Baier 1989, 775, 776, 789.) For Rawls, a constitutional consensus is never simply an institutional matter, never simply an agreement on political procedures (*PL*, 149, 164), and it is open to the possibility of agreement on political principles of justice, certainly to agreement about some version of generic liberalism.

## 2.2 Temporal Development and Orderly Contestation

One important idea in constitutional consensus is that it involves change over time. Rawls presents the generic liberal constitutional consensus, just described, as itself based on successive and agreed-upon moves away from acceptance of a mere political modus vivendi (*PL*, xxxix, 159, 208).

At the stage currently reached (in a vigorous version of generic liberalism), the set of generic principles and the practices that apply them are in place *because* they constitute, on the balance of reasons, a sound interpretation and application of the "model conceptions" in the background democratic political culture. These principles and practices reflect the institutional history embedded in that particular culture and the profile of existing basic structure institutions that this history has currently given rise to.

This process of change can be presumed to continue over time. Such change could involve the fundamental ideas themselves, or the constitutional and other institutional essentials, or the liberal principles themselves and the "family" they constitute (*PL*, li; IPRR, 583). But there is a deeper background change that should be noted here. In the late seventeenth and in the eighteenth century, as the idea of constitutional government took hold, parliamentary or republican models competed with theories of royal absolutism and became in time the main options. The ideas of electoral democracy and representative government began to grow in prominence in the nineteenth century and became, in the twentieth century, the preferred view in liberal democratic societies.

We need to take account of this particular shift to egalitarian democracy as we consider Rawls's own ideas. In *Political Liberalism*, Rawls modified the statement, the actual formulation, of his first principle (the principle of equal basic rights and liberties) to give special place to the political participation liberties. He added there that "the equal political liberties, and only those liberties, are to be guaranteed their fair value" (*PL*, 5). By "fair value" Rawls means that steps are taken to make people substantively equal (or more nearly equal) in their exercise of these liberties, in voting and in campaigning (*LP*, 197–199; *JF*, 148–152). Among the steps designed to do this are such things as public funding of elections (*JF*, 131, 149).

I have, up to now, emphasized change as one of the main motifs in Rawls's theory of constitutional consensus. But there's *one* change he doesn't contemplate; he doesn't really consider a change that takes us beyond the family of liberal principles in the direction of one single agreed-upon liberal principle or set of principles. At one time, I thought that Rawls believed that, eventually, constitutional consensus would single out justice as fairness and its two principles as the overall preferred liberal theory (Martin 2001, 86–87). I now believe that this view was a mistake.

It isn't borne out by a careful reading of Rawls's post-1993 texts. But there's an even stronger reason for rejecting my earlier reading. If we look at the history of democratic liberal societies from its beginning point in the nineteenth century, we note that democratic liberal societies are all characterized by the fact of having two- or three-party political systems (or, in some cases, multiparty systems) that controlled contestation at the electoral level and at the parliamentary one. In each case the number of viable liberal theories probably exceeded the number of political parties, certainly in the two- or three-party systems. Political systems that had only one-party governments were characteristically autocratic and antidemocratic/antiliberal in character.

The rise of egalitarian democracy has changed and added to the public political culture of liberal societies. And, just as significantly, it has altered the shape of liberal theories, moving them away from the ideal of a single agreed-upon principle or closely integrated set of principles toward a family of rather variegated liberal principles – a family of principles having certain generic features in common and offering varying and even competing interpretations not merely of policy issues but also of the constitutional and institutional essentials in the various liberal polities and even of the fundamental ideas of a democratic public political culture as such (see IPRR, 585–586 n35).

The idea of a family of liberal theories accords nicely with fundamental democratic thinking and practice; the ideal of a *single* liberal principle, agreed upon by all, does not (see Dreben 2003, 322, 338). One might wonder, then, what is the place of justice as fairness and its two principles in constitutional consensus, as Rawls sees that consensus.

Rawls thinks that justice as fairness would continue to be *one* of the primary contending perspectives on political justice within the family of liberal conceptions. Indeed, it would be at the "center of the focal class" there because, in his view, it fits in well with the fundamental democratic ideas and is compatible with the developing pattern of democratic institutions. And Rawls, personally, regards justice as fairness as the "most reasonable" member of this family. (For the quoted phrases, see *PL*, 168, xlvi–xlvii; also 164, 167 and IPRR, 582 n27.)

What we can reasonably expect is that the process of broadening, of deepening, and of gaining greater specificity and focus in the family of liberal principles will go on for the foreseeable future. Justice as fairness can be expected to continue to be among the viable principles in that family. And political debate will be framed by the interpretations that the principles (in this family of generic liberalism) take from the public political culture, with its ingredient fundamental ideas, and apply to the constitutional and institutional essentials and to debates and decisions about matters of policy, insofar as such essentials bear on these matters.

There is no teleology in Rawls's theory beyond what I've just described, no ultimate goal picked out by history or by philosophical reason (be that goal justice as fairness per se or any one of the other liberal principles, within generic liberalism, that contend with it). Rawls says:

> It is inevitable and often desirable that citizens have different views as to the most appropriate political conception; for the public political culture is bound to contain different fundamental ideas that can be developed in different ways. An orderly contest between them over time is a reliable way to find which one, if any, is most reasonable. (PL, 227)

A mere modus vivendi is not a political conception of justice; it lacks the dimension of depth altogether. But all the liberal political conceptions of justice have this dimension (sufficient to count as freestanding). The liberal conceptions have one other feature in common, besides the dimension of depth.

They all have a fairly high degree of consensual acceptance and support by their citizens. (1) The specific rights and practices the conceptions range over (dimension of breadth) are widely accepted. (2) The various articulated liberal conceptions of justice (within the family of generic liberalism) can be supported, to an appreciable degree, by sound arguments. Citizens may differ in that some think one conception is the best supported, and others others; but they agree in believing that a certain threshold of argumentative adequacy has been passed by them all – or at least this is the (rebuttable) presumption (PL, xxxvi, xlvi–xlviii, 223, 226–227, 241; IPRR, 578, 581–583). Here a pattern of support (or justification) by reference to the fundamental political ideas is in place for the various principles within that family; these principles allow cooperation on the basis of "political terms that everyone can accept" (PL, 163). (3) Finally, there is consensus over "the general structure of political authority" (PL, 393), that is, consensus over the legitimacy of a fairly detailed set of constitutional essentials, the features of which "all citizens may reasonably be expected to endorse" (PL, Lecture VI, §§5–6; see 217 for the quotation; see also xlviii, 137, 226, 241, 393, and IPRR, 578–579, 594). This consensual element, as identified in these three points, is a large part of what Rawls intends when he says a given liberal political society is well-ordered (see PL, Lecture I, §6).

It seems, then, if we find a sizable degree of citizen support at these three points, an important degree of stability is built into the public political conception of justice (of the sort formed by the family of liberal principles with certain generic features in common). A vigorous version of constitutional consensus (focused on the family of liberal political conceptions) would represent a high level of development – in the dimensions of breadth, depth, and focus – and would enjoy considerable consensual support. The degree of internal stability of any such family of liberal conceptions would, arguably, be considerable; such an order would be less likely to be overturned by divisive issues (see PL, 161–164, Lecture IV, §7). The political consensus here covers more important areas, for deeper and better reasons. And the public has come to recognize the "great values of the political virtues" – the virtues of tolerance, civic peace and order, civility, cooperation and trust – embodied in such a political consensus (PL, 157, 171).

A constitutional consensus robust enough to attract and to support overlapping consensus would itself go a long way toward solving the problem of stability on its own. Thus, the same measure – that is, constitutional consensus – which solves the utopianism problem for Rawls also appears to undercut and perhaps even remove much of the *raison d'être* he had offered, in the first place, for overlapping consensus.

## 3. Overlapping Consensus: Stability or Public Political Justification

This raises the question, much disputed in contemporary Rawls scholarship, of what the main point of overlapping consensus is: is it stability (as Rawls initially had suggested) or is it justification? Some – Charles Larmore (2003, 377), Thomas Scanlon (2003, 159–160), and Charles Beitz (2009, 76–77) – have put the emphasis on stability, to the exclusion of justification; others – Samuel Freeman (2003b, 36–37) – have made justification the main concern.

Paul Weithman's recent account falls somewhere in between. He sees stability (an idea which he develops in a very complex and nuanced way) as the principal object of overlapping consensus. But he also sees that drawing on comprehensive moral and religious doctrines, as found in an overlapping consensus, will provide a distinctive sort of background support for political stability. However, he does not see overlapping consensus as providing justification per se for the political conception; instead his discussion of any such support is always deflected back onto the issue of stability (Weithman 2010, ch. 10, §§6–8). Weithman's middle ground is closer to the stability pole than to the justification pole.

These two emphases (on *stability* and on *justification*) can be contrasted. Stability is basically a matter of fact (of likelihood). In Rawls's view a political system tends to be stable (i) when, drawing on its own resources, it is able to generate from one generation to the next widespread support for itself (adequate to satisfy the citizens' sense of justice), and (ii) when there is congruence over time, for most citizens, between a conception of their own good (as informed, in the typical case, by one comprehensive doctrine or another) and the operating principles of justice in their society. In a situation of longstanding and irreducible pluralism of reasonable comprehensive moral and religious and philosophical doctrines, overlapping consensus would contribute to stability so understood.

Justification is a normative issue. Overlapping consensus – in deploying several *different* comprehensive doctrines that converge, each for its own reasons, on a single political conception – plays a normative role (alongside freestanding justification) by providing a distinctive form (moral in character) of public justification for the principles of a liberal political order.

Granted, one can *distinguish* these two emphases (on stability and on justification); but there's no need to separate them. They can have complementary and mutually supporting roles in Rawls's account. The second of these emphases has received less attention. I want in this section to develop a view which stresses the justificatory character of overlapping consensus.

Rawls thinks that an overlapping consensus presupposes and arises in concert with constitutional consensus. In the case envisioned, there is already an independent, widespread, and long-lived support by citizens for the public political conception – that is, for a family of liberal principles. (See *PL*, 164, 168.) An overlapping consensus would arise, then, where the great bulk of citizens could also affirm, upon reflection and given experience, that the fundamental ideas and the governing principles and institutional essentials of the public political conception were compatible (or could be made so), in each of their respective cases, with the various comprehensive moral and religious and philosophical doctrines that they individually held. (See *PL*, 140, 160, 187–188, 210, 386.)

The general run of citizens in that society don't regard the perspectives they individually have as *in*compatible, in general or in principle, with the overall public political conception there. If a sizable number of the citizens actually are as reflective as ordinary people can be expected to be, then it follows, for the variety of diverse perspectives that happen to be held by these citizens en masse, that these diverse views constitute (or can be regarded as constituting) an overlapping consensus on a family of liberal principles and on a given set of institutional essentials. Rawls describes this as a "concordant fit between the political conception and the comprehensive views together with the public recognition of the great values of the political virtues" (*PL*, 171; see also 158).

Here it is not so much that various comprehensive doctrines (understood as "isms") converge on a single public political conception of justice; rather, it is that a considerable bulk of citizens, coming from diverse perspectives, do. In the end it is the citizens themselves – "a substantial majority of . . . politically active citizens," as Rawls puts it – who decide (*PL*, 38). This is consistent with his claim that here there are no "experts," no philosopher kings (*PL*, xxvi–xxvii, 383, 426–427; also Scheffler 1994, 11–12).

An overlapping consensus, like the public political conception on which it focuses, is directed to the basic framework, to the institutional essentials themselves; it does not require or imply an agreement on all matters of policy. Indeed, it is compatible with disagreement, even considerable disagreement, on such matters – on detailed pieces of legislation, say (see IPRR, 604–607).

Such an overlapping consensus would, arguably, be stronger and more enduring were it to attach itself to a suitably broad, deep, focused public political conception, for example, to a family of liberal political conceptions (with justice as fairness among its members). An overlapping consensus of this sort would, of course, occur gradually; it would take time to gel. (See *PL*, 160 n25.) None of this shows, of course that an overlapping consensus *will* occur: nothing is guaranteed. It shows merely that such a consensus plausibly could occur, in the way Rawls envisioned. (See *PL*, xlv–xlvi.) Its occurring in that way is not utopian.

What would overlapping consensus add here? What overlapping consensus provides is not political stability per se, but rather "stability for the right reasons" (*PL*, xxxvii, xli, 388 n21, 390, 391, 394; IPRR, 589).

A political conception, simply on its own, is always a consensus within and from public political reasons; in the case at hand, the reasons appropriate to a liberal democratic society. As such it lacks a certain dimension: it lacks moral credentials of the sort afforded by a comprehensive critical moral theory. Several different critical moral and religious doctrines can be drawn on, at a given time, in a liberal society. Each of them is controversial; no one of them is accepted by everybody. Insofar as we are concerned, then, with anything like a full *public* justification of the political conception, using accredited critical moral doctrines, we must accept that the doctrines there admissible as premises in *that* form of justification, doctrines such as the utilitarian general happiness principle and Catholic natural law, are clearly *not* acceptable to all reasonable citizens. The only form a full public justification could take in a morally and religiously pluralistic society and still have authority outside a narrow circle of partisan sentiment would be as an overlapping consensus – with the public political conception as focal – of these various doctrines.

Citizens in general could not participate as adherents in *each* of these lines of moral or religious justification. What they could do, as adherents of one such line (or even of none), is to note and register the fact of overlapping consensus. This fact is a *public* fact and general acknowledgment – common knowledge – of this fact is the form that overlapping consensus would take insofar as it was itself a matter of full public justification of the political conception. (For discussion of what Rawls calls a "full justification" and of "public justification of the political conception by political society," as both of them aspects of overlapping consensus, see *PL*, 385–394, also 67.)

If it could be established as a matter of public fact (based on settled judgments of compatibility by the great bulk of citizens) that various of the main present-day comprehensive moral doctrines and religious faiths could converge – each for its own reasons (*PL*, 134) – on one and the same public political conception of justice, as a common focal point, then that particular conception would be fully and publicly accredited by the standards of these various comprehensive doctrines. And this means that each citizen can affirm that the political conception is a reasonable one; it can be regarded as mutually intelligible among them and as justifiable, under one or another of the constituent doctrines in the overlapping consensus, on normative grounds that all (taken severally) can endorse. In an overlapping consensus, the political conception is "affirmed on moral grounds" (*PL*, 147; see also "Justice as Fairness: Political not Metaphysical," 410–411; IOC, 422, 432; "The Priority of Right and Ideas of the Good," 470–471; *PL*, Lecture IV, §3, and xli, 126, 150–151, 168–169, 208, 211 n42).

Thus, even in the face of a continuing and very likely ineradicable pluralism, we would have achieved stability (as provided by a public political conception embedded in a constitutional consensus) *and* for the right reasons (as provided by an overlapping consensus, and not a mere compromise, among the various relevant critical moral and religious doctrines). A mere compromise would be a tenuous solution, continually subject to renegotiation as the balance of powers and interests shifts (*PL*, 148, 161). By avoiding such constant renegotiation, or the continuing threat of defection, overlapping consensus reinforces the existing stability of a suitably broad, deep, and focused public political conception; and this is the contribution it makes to the stability of such a regime.

Rawls had assumed in *A Theory of Justice* that, since his preferred principles of justice came out on top in the contest with utilitarianism and with perfectionist values such as Platonic aristocracy or Nietzschean elitism, these principles would in effect be endorsed by everybody, and for the *same* reasons. Thus these principles would become the moral theory or part of the moral theory of any well-ordered society whose principles of justice were constructed in the original position behind the veil of ignorance, subject to the constraints of publicity and unanimity. Such a society would be stable, in short, because *everybody* in it would adopt the two principles as among their moral principles. In fact, there would likely be (given the argumentation of *A Theory of Justice*) a high level of consensus, amounting to virtual unanimity, in favor of *one* comprehensive moral doctrine in particular; and that one moral doctrine would be a version of contractualism. Ultimately, then, it is this almost universal convergence upon a single justifying moral theory that underwrites Rawls's account of stability in *A Theory of Justice*.

Rawls makes the point here, that his "premiss" in *A Theory of Justice* was that there would be an almost universal convergence on a single comprehensive moral doctrine, quite explicit in his later writings. (See *PL*, xv–xviii, xl, 388 n21; IPRR, 614; see "*Commonweal* Interview with John Rawls," 617, for the point about contractualism.) Such uniform acceptance, Rawls now says, is inconsistent with the idea that a pluralism of reasonable comprehensive moral and religious doctrines is here to stay, at least in any modern political society committed to free and open discussion. (See *PL*, xv–xviii, xxiv, xl, 4, 36–37, 129, 144.)

It was this problem, of moral justification under conditions of pluralism, which *A Theory of Justice* had conspicuously failed to solve. And overlapping consensus, one of Rawls's new ideas in *Political Liberalism*, was called upon to address this self-professed defect.

In *Political Liberalism* the problem of political stability, in a world of moral pluralism, was tackled first and on its own, using political devices: constitutional consensus and the attendant idea of institutional essentials that all citizens "may reasonably be expected to endorse." The solution to the next problem, that of critical moral justification, was first tailored to confront the fact of a presumably permanent and unresolvable pluralism of moral and religious doctrines and was then brought to bear, in the idea of overlapping consensus, on a "freestanding" political conception of justice and on a preexisting political solution to the problem of internal stability. The job of overlapping consensus is to provide an *independent* critical moral grounding for each, for the public political conception itself and for the inbuilt stability afforded by that conception. Overlapping consensus is directed at the issue of stability for the right reasons. The argument I have sketched here suggests that a pluralistic society, given freestanding justification and overlapping consensus, could be well-ordered and stable.

## 4. Utilitarianism and Overlapping Consensus

There remains an important concern with overlapping consensus. Can it actually draw on most, if not all, of the major comprehensive moral and religious doctrines that are prominent in the societies that call themselves liberal? In particular, the question is whether traditional utilitarianism could be a contributor to and supporter of an overlapping consensus that does not assign priority to the general good or to the greatest happiness.

Contrary to what he says elsewhere, in *Political Liberalism* Rawls suggests that utilitarianism could support not only equal "rights, liberties, and opportunities" but also their priority over "claims of the general good," as he puts the matter in his discussion of generic liberalism (*PL*, 6). At one time, I thought Rawls's latter claim, concerning priority, was simply wrong (see Martin 1994, 757–761). The problem was that utilitarianism, where we stick with the prevailing interpretation of it, cannot allow for moral or constitutional rights that have a built-in, standing priority over considerations of general (or common) good, understood as *maximized* aggregate welfare.

In an effort to deal with this problem, significant attempts have been made within utilitarianism (under the name of "rule" utilitarianism) to address and perhaps resolve it. The theorists of rule utilitarianism assert that direct appeals to the greatest welfare are self-defeating, all things considered, and that putting standing constraints on the basic utilitarian principle – such as a system of moral rules or a coherent set of civil or constitutional rights justifiable by the utilitarian standard – in fact produces the greater well-being.

Rule utilitarians do not, however, assert that moral rules should never be overridden nor individual rights ever broached. Rather, on their view, where rules conflict or rights do, some sort of appeal to the greatest happiness is in order. Here is where the notion of *indirect* utilitarianism – as developed by John Gray (1996), David Lyons (1994, chs 2–5), and others – comes crucially into play. Its advocates argue that the happiness principle should *not* directly determine what is to be done even here. Rather, the principle operates only indirectly in all such cases. Here the general welfare principle is used merely to help contribute, in a continu-ing way, to an *ongoing* cumulative ranking of "the opposing obligations" so as to achieve a refined and resultant clear ranking of those obligations, for use on particular occasions of conflict. (See Lyons 1994, 61.) In indirect utilitarianism there is never a *direct* and determin-ing appeal to the general happiness principle as to what to do, what act to perform or what rule to follow, *on a particular and given occasion.*

On the indirect utilitarian account, it is possible to have policies for action (to have both moral rules and rights) that are justifiable by the standard of general happiness and at the same time to shield these policies from direct confrontation with (and possible overthrow by) the happiness principle on individual occasions. And it is possible to do so while still allowing these policies to remain sensitive to what produces the greater or more general benefit – a sensitivity that is registered in the differential weights assigned the various rights and policies, an assignment that occurs gradually (over time and with experience) and cumulatively. Utili-tarianism casts a wide net. Jeremy Bentham famously claimed the "greatest happiness of the greatest number" to be the master principle of utilitarianism. This well-known formula can be and has been read in two distinct ways: as enjoining the greatest *aggregate* amount of happiness (of net well-being) or, alternatively, as setting as the goal the *general* happiness (the happiness of the greatest number of persons).

We need to refine our view of utilitarianism. With Bentham's formula as background, we can distinguish and develop two issues: (a) the utilitarian standard of right, and (b) how that standard figures in deliberation and in actual attempts to realize or approximate the standard, in general and on particular occasions. Two of the utilitarian theories we have considered follow the "greatest happiness" part of Bentham's formula.

The classical or orthodox strand singles out that action whose total consequences will have the greatest aggregate benefit; that particular *act token* is the right-making standard. And agents determine what in particular is to be done on given occasions by appealing directly to this standard, making careful estimates of consequences, in the factual setting they currently occupy.

The other main strand (traditional rule utilitarianism) identifies, as the right-making standard, an ideal rule or set of *rules specifying types of action* that, if generally accepted and generally conformed to, would have a higher expectable benefit than would alternatives (such as having no rules at all or having simpler rules that excluded explicit and well-grounded exceptions). Acting according to these ideal rules would approximate, as closely as is humanly possible, the overall goal of achieving the greatest happiness. Here agents are concerned with installing and abiding by that set of rules which optimally conforms to the right-making standard. On given occasions, rules within that set might conflict; here agents would attempt to determine which of the constituent rules would probably give the best result if consistently followed in similar cases of conflict.

The third type of theory we looked at, so-called indirect utilitarianism, doesn't emphasize the greatest *aggregate* amount of happiness but, rather, (following John Stuart Mill) adheres to a more distributive view – to the improvement of the *general* happiness. For indirect utili-tarians the right-making standard is conduct (*act types*) which has a pronounced tendency toward the goal of achieving the happiness, at an acceptable level, of the greatest number of persons, ideally, of each and all.

Indirect utilitarians don't *begin* by trying directly to ascertain what the general happiness principle might require and then reasoning directly from that to precepts, as would ideal-rules utilitarians; instead, indirect utilitarians first make a decision about exceptions or conflicts by reasoning from existing tried-and-true precepts which embody right-tending conduct (taking account, in so doing, of reasons for the success of these precepts, making judgments of fairness and appropriateness, factoring in maxims and paradigm cases, and so forth). For indirect utilitarians an appeal to the principle of utility doesn't involve going outside the rules so much as it involves building upon them.

The version of indirect utilitarianism I'm stressing, as developed by Gray and Lyons, is not merely a decision procedure. It has a distinctive right-making standard (founded on the notion of the *general* happiness) and is thereby quite different from either orthodox utilitarianism or from ideal-rules utilitarianism. Of course, there are some who describe themselves (or are described) as indirect utilitarians and who adopt a hybrid approach. They combine an act-token standard of maximizing general happiness with indirect utilitarianism simply as a strategy, a decision procedure, in which one uses a rule or precept to decide how to act on all given occasions, regarding it as a more reliable procedure to follow than consistently going directly to the principle of general happiness to so decide (for example Sumner 1987, 180–198).

Indeed, we'll find that for each of the main utilitarian theories examined here, there are existing or imaginable alternative or variant (often hybrid) versions, sometimes more than one. Bentham's master principle, the "greatest happiness of the greatest number," does not reduce to any one of these theories; it can embrace them all. As internal debates within utilitarianism make clear, there are multiple perspectives for assessment within utilitarianism, all of them presumably legitimate by the lights of that theory. (See Lyons 2000.)

In an overlapping consensus involving various comprehensive moral and religious doctrines that exist in the Western world today, orthodox utilitarianism is prominently mentioned by Rawls as one of the doctrines that would support and endorse the family of liberal principles and the basic structure institutions involved with that family. (See *PL*, 169–170.)

But it is doubtful, in my view, that the utilitarian principle of *greatest* happiness, as an aggregative and maximizing one, could join any such consensus. That principle could not support the sort of radically distributive program we associate with rights – could not support the assignment of constitutionally guaranteed benefits and protections, to each and every individual person in advance, so to speak, and across the board. I don't believe then, contrary to Rawls's claim, that the utilitarian theories of Bentham and Sidgwick could accept the idea that the rights and liberties appropriate to the family of generic liberal principles could have a standing priority over policies favoring the general good (understood as a form of aggregative and maximizing well-being). The aggregative/maximizing version of philosophical utilitarianism is simply incompatible with the notion of basic rights and their priority developed by Rawls, and others. (See also Scheffler 2003, 451–453.)

But indirect utilitarianism (if all its arguments and presumptions are allowed) seemingly establishes that utilitarianism is compatible with human rights or basic constitutional rights and with the priority of such rights – at least in the case of those rights that are themselves justifiable in accordance with the general happiness principle. Certainly, it preserves the priority of such rights over against considerations of general good or corporate good that mark but a marginal increase in aggregate welfare. In any event, the point of indirect utilitarianism is not to maximize aggregate welfare but, rather, to improve the *general* happiness – the happiness, at an acceptable level, of the greatest number of persons, ideally, of each and all.

For these reasons indirect utilitarians can plausibly be counted as joining into an overlapping consensus that has generic liberalism and its institutions as a focus.

I have argued elsewhere (Martin 2008 and 2011) that Millian utilitarianism has several essential points in common with indirect utilitarianism. Rawls thought that Mill's view (as interpreted by John Gray) exemplified a form of indirect utilitarianism (IOC, 433–434, esp. n20). In his view, Mill's theory, like contemporary indirect utilitarianism, was compatible with a constitutional regime that included both rights and liberties and their priority over the general good (understood aggregatively).

Establishing this point is important. If some versions of utilitarianism, including some historic or classical utilitarians, can be included in such an overlapping consensus, then that fact would, I think, make Rawls's idea of such a consensus plausible, both philosophically and practically.

## 5. Concluding Thoughts

In this chapter I have attempted principally to do three things. I wanted first to bring overlapping consensus and its relation to constitutional consensus together, center stage. The idea of constitutional consensus is significant primarily because – when it is exemplified in what I called a "vigorous version of generic liberalism" – it fleshes out the notion of what the political conception of justice, as supported by freestanding justification (that is, political justification from democratic ideals embedded in a democratic political culture), ultimately amounts to.

Since constitutional consensus on its own goes a considerable distance toward providing political stability, it then became necessary to show how *overlapping consensus* goes beyond constitutional consensus. This was the second main object of the present chapter. What overlapping consensus supplies, which freestanding justification and constitutional consensus can't, is a distinctive set of comprehensive moral and religious reasons endorsing and thereby justifying, each for its own reasons, the liberal order. Overlapping consensus provides, not simply stability, but stability "for the right reasons" (the right moral reasons). Overlapping consensus addresses the questions of political stability and of normative justification in the context of a continuing pluralist or multicultural social environment.

Once overlapping consensus was fully displayed, I turned to the final main object of the chapter – by taking up the difficult question whether traditional utilitarianism could figure in an overlapping consensus that assigns priority to the "rights, liberties, and opportunities" characteristic of liberalism over the "claims of the general good." I attempted to provide an argument for saying that a well-known version of utilitarianism (called "indirect" utilitarianism) could in fact be part of an overlapping consensus so conceived.

## Note

This chapter draws on my work published in "Conceptions of Rights in Recent Anglo-American Philosophy," *IVR Encyclopedia of Jurisprudence, Legal Theory, and Philosophy of Law,* 2007, at http://ivr-enc .info/index.php?title=Conceptions_of_Rights_in_Recent_Anglo-american_Philosophy (accessed May

2013); and "Rawls," in David Boucher and Paul Kelly (eds), *Political Thinkers: From Socrates to the Present* (554–574), 2nd edn (Oxford: Oxford University Press, 2009).

1   Page numbers for Rawls's works included in *Collected Papers* refer to that collection.

## Works by Rawls, with Abbreviations

*Collected Papers* (CP), ed. Samuel Freeman. Cambridge, MA: Harvard University Press, 1999.
"*Commonweal* Interview with John Rawls" (1998), in *Collected Papers* (616–622).
"The Domain of the Political and Overlapping Consensus" (1989), in *Collected Papers* (473–496).
"The Idea of an Overlapping Consensus" (IOC) (1987), in *Collected Papers* (421–448).
"The Idea of Public Reason Revisited" (IPRR) (1997), in *Collected Papers* (573–615).
"The Independence of Moral Theory" (1975), in *Collected Papers* (286–302).
"Justice as Fairness: Political not Metaphysical" (1985), in *Collected Papers* (388–414).
*Justice as Fairness: A Restatement* (JF), ed. Erin Kelly. Cambridge, MA: Harvard University Press, 2001.
*The Law of Peoples, with "The Idea of Public Reason Revisited"* (LP). Cambridge, MA: Harvard University Press, 1999.
*Political Liberalism* (PL), expanded edn. New York: Columbia University Press, 2005.
"The Priority of Right and Ideas of the Good" (1988), in *Collected Papers* (449–472).
*A Theory of Justice* (TJ), rev. edn. Cambridge, MA: Harvard University Press, 1999.

## Other References

Baier, Kurt (1989) "Justice and the Aims of Political Philosophy." *Ethics* 99: 771–790.
Barry, Brian (1995) "John Rawls and the Search for Stability." *Ethics* 105: 874–915.
Beitz, Charles (2009) *The Idea of Human Rights*. Oxford: Oxford University Press.
Dreben, Burton (2003) "On Rawls and Political Liberalism." In Samuel Freeman (ed.), *The Cambridge Companion to Rawls*. Cambridge: Cambridge University Press.
Freeman, Samuel (ed.) (2003a) *The Cambridge Companion to Rawls*. Cambridge: Cambridge University Press.
Freeman, Samuel (2003b) "Introduction: John Rawls – An Overview." In Samuel Freeman (ed.), *The Cambridge Companion to Rawls*. Cambridge: Cambridge University Press.
Gray, John (1996) *Mill on Liberty: A Defence*. 2nd edn. London: Routledge.
Larmore, Charles (2003) "Public Reason." In Samuel Freeman (ed.), *The Cambridge Companion to Rawls*. Cambridge: Cambridge University Press.
Lyons, David (1994) *Rights, Welfare, and Mill's Moral Theory*. New York: Oxford University Press.
Lyons, David (2000) "The Moral Opacity of Utilitarianism." In Brad Hooker, Elinor Mason, and Dale E. Miller (eds), *Morality, Rules, and Consequences*. Edinburgh: Edinburgh University Press.
Martin, Rex (1994) "Rawls's New Theory of Justice." *Chicago-Kent Law Review* 69: 737–761.
Martin, Rex (2001) "Rawls on Constitutional Consensus and the Problem of Stability." In David Rasmussen (ed.), *Social and Political Philosophy*, vol. 11 of *Proceedings of the Twentieth World Congress of Philosophy* (81–95). Bowling Green, OH: Philosophy Documentation Center.
Martin, Rex (2008) "Two Concepts of Rule Utilitarianism." *Journal of Moral Philosophy* 5: 227–255.
Martin, Rex (2011) "Mill's Rule Utilitarianism in Context." In Ben Eggleston, Dale Miller, and David Weinstein (eds), *John Stuart Mill and the Art of Life*. New York: Oxford University Press.

Scanlon, Thomas (2003) "Rawls on Justification." In Samuel Freeman (ed.), *The Cambridge Companion to Rawls*. Cambridge: Cambridge University Press.

Scheffler, Samuel (1979) "Moral Independence and the Original Position." *Philosophical Studies* 35: 397–403.

Scheffler, Samuel (1994) "The Appeal of Political Liberalism." *Ethics* 105: 4–22.

Scheffler, Samuel (2003) "Rawls and Utilitarianism." In Samuel Freeman (ed.), *The Cambridge Companion to Rawls*. Cambridge: Cambridge University Press.

Sumner, L.W. (1987) *The Moral Foundation of Rights*. Oxford: Clarendon Press.

Weithman, Paul (2010) *Why Political Liberalism? On John Rawls's Political Turn*. New York: Oxford University Press.

# 17

# Citizenship as Fairness

## John Rawls's Conception of Civic Virtue

### RICHARD DAGGER

Of all the topics surveyed in this volume, none is likely to seem more remote from the central concerns of John Rawls's political philosophy than civic virtue. The term itself does not even appear in the indexes of Rawls's books. Related terms do appear there, such as "the duty of civility," "political virtues," and "civic friendship," but none of them has gained the currency of such distinctively Rawlsian phrases as "the veil of ignorance," "reflective equilibrium," "the difference principle," or "public reason." If Rawls has anything of interest to say about civic virtue, it seems, it must only be in passing or as a largely unexamined implication of one or more of his central arguments.

To accept this judgment, however, is to do an injustice to Rawls. So, at least, I shall try to demonstrate in this essay. My claim is not that Rawls set out to devise or elaborate what is first and foremost a theory of civic virtue. If that had been his intention, his books and articles would bear titles quite different from the ones he gave them. Nevertheless, one need not look far beyond the titles and distinctive phrases to find a deep and abiding concern for civic virtue in Rawls's writings. That concern is most evident in his recurrent references to *citizens*, especially in *Political Liberalism* and later works. Indeed, civic virtue proves to be not only a recurring but a unifying theme in his political philosophy. My claim, then, is that we cannot fully appreciate Rawls's theory of justice as fairness unless we appreciate the part that civic virtue plays in that theory.

There is, of course, the further question of the adequacy or value of what Rawls has to say about civic virtue. I respond to this question below, but only after providing the necessary account of civic virtue and Rawls's conception of it. In doing so, I shall rely most heavily on Rawls's last book, *Justice as Fairness: A Restatement*. What he says about citizenship and civility in that book is consistent with what he says in *A Theory of Justice* and *Political Liberalism*, but the importance of these concepts is more evident in *Justice as Fairness*, perhaps because it both elaborates and compresses themes from the earlier, longer books.

*A Companion to Rawls*, First Edition. Edited by Jon Mandle and David A. Reidy.
© 2014 John Wiley & Sons, Inc. Published 2016 by John Wiley & Sons, Inc.

# Rawls and Republicanism

Civic virtue is a concept more often associated with the tradition of classical republicanism than with the liberalism that Rawls professed. Within the republican tradition, such legendary heroes as Lucius Junius Brutus (sixth century BCE) and Lucius Quinctius Cincinnatus (fifth century BCE) have served as the paragons of civic virtue. Not only did Brutus lead the uprising that drove the last king out of Rome, thereby establishing the Roman republic, but he also executed his own sons when he found them plotting against the republic. For his part, Cincinnatus became a paragon of civic virtue because he left his plow to lead an army in defense of Rome, then promptly relinquished power and returned to his humble farm when victory was won – an example of which George Washington was mindful as the Revolutionary War in America drew to a close (Wills 1984, 23 and passim). Such examples of disinterested devotion to one's country are admittedly extraordinary, even by republican standards, but they emphatically convey the classical ideal of civic virtue as the disposition to place the good of one's country above one's personal interests and inclinations. As the stories of Brutus and Cincinnatus illustrate, moreover, this is the virtue not simply of the patriot but of the *citizen* – of someone who is neither ruler nor ruled but, as Aristotle said, both in turn: a self-governing member of a self-governing polity (*Politics*, 1283b42–1284a3).[1]

Neither Brutus nor Cincinnatus nor other striking exemplars of civic virtue appear in Rawls's published works. To be sure, he does invoke Washington and Abraham Lincoln when he draws a distinction between statesmen and politicians, with both presidents placed in the former category; and he offers a rare laudatory comment when he says that a "remarkable aspect of Lincoln is his selflessness as a statesman" (*LP*, 97, 98 n13). In fact, the closest one can come to a civic or political hero in Rawls's writings is Lincoln, who receives five mentions in *Political Liberalism*, four in *The Law of Peoples*, two in *Justice as Fairness: A Restatement*, and one in *Lectures on the History of Political Philosophy*.[2] With the exception of the "remarkable aspect" comment, however, these references do not serve so much to praise or illustrate Lincoln's character as to illuminate a theoretical point about what counts as a "considered judgment" (*JF*, 29) or what kinds of considerations are admissible within "public reason" (*PL*, 254; *LP*, 174). Lincoln may be Rawls's model of a virtuous statesman, but he is not a model that Rawls urges upon his readers.

Nor does Rawls exhort citizens to devote themselves body and soul to their country, or even to bestir themselves to vote in its elections. He does allow that a just society may require serious sacrifices of its citizens – hence his conclusion that conscription is "permissible . . . if it is demanded for the defense of liberty itself" (*TJ*, 334; cf. *LP*, 91, and *JF*, 47). He also holds that citizens must display some degree of political awareness and activity if their society is to be well-ordered, and in one essay he maintains that they have an obligation to vote (*CP*, 127). But he is careful to distinguish his position, which he takes to be consistent with *classical republicanism*, from what he calls *civic humanism*.[3] Rawls regards the latter as "a form of Aristotelianism . . . that holds that we are social, even political, beings whose essential nature is most fully achieved in a democratic society in which there is widespread and active participation in political life" (*JF*, 142). He is willing to agree that "one of the great goods of human life is that achieved by citizens through engaging in political life" (*JF*, 143–144), but not that it is the greatest of all goods or an expression of our essential nature.[4] On that point he parts company with civic humanism and allies himself with classical republicanism, which he understands as the belief that "the safety of democratic liberties, including the liberties of nonpolitical life . . . requires the active participation of citizens who have the political virtues needed to sustain a constitutional regime" (*JF*, 144). "If we are to remain free and equal citizens," he goes on to say, "we cannot afford a general retreat into private life" (*JF*, 144).

Beyond this gentle encouragement of civic engagement, Rawls's "political liberalism" has other points of contact with the republican tradition – points that Rawls does not note.[5] One arises in connection with his defense of the difference principle, according to which social and economic inequalities must "be to the greatest benefit of the least-advantaged members of society" (*JF*, 42–43). The defense that Rawls marshals in *Justice as Fairness* shares with Cass Sunstein (1988) and other recent republican theorists the desire to move beyond the give-and-take, deal-brokering attitudes of interest-group pluralism to "an appropriate idea of reciprocity" (*JF*, 126) that will bind citizens together in a common enterprise. By affirming the difference principle when they could resist or attack it, Rawls writes, the most-advantaged members of a just society would demonstrate their commitment to a "public culture . . . that inhibits the wastes of endless self- and group-interested bargaining and offers some hope of realizing social concord and civic friendship" (*JF*, 126).

Another point of contact with republicanism occurs when Rawls indicates the importance to a well-ordered society of *civic education*.[6] In this regard, as when he distinguishes classical republicanism from civic humanism, Rawls is careful to separate the educational implications of his political liberalism from those of the comprehensive form of liberalism he associates with Immanuel Kant and J.S. Mill. The difference, according to Rawls, is that Kant and Mill believe, in keeping with their conceptions of the good life, that the education of children should aim at cultivating autonomy and individuality, whereas political liberalism has less demanding and less controversial aspirations. On this view, the fundamental purpose of education is to prepare children to be self-supporting and fully cooperating members of society; but education, Rawls adds, "should also encourage the political virtues so that they want to honor the fair terms of social cooperation in their relations with the rest of society" (*JF*, 156).

This statement about education tells us something important about both the content and the place of civic virtue in Rawls's political philosophy. It tells us, first, that "the political virtues" are in large part matters of fair play – that is, of doing one's part in a cooperative activity or enterprise. By invoking fairness and cooperation here, moreover, Rawls is also drawing a connection between the cultivation of the political virtues and what he calls "the fundamental organizing idea" of his theory of justice as fairness – that is, the idea "of society as a fair system of cooperation over time, from one generation to the next" (*PL*, 15; *JF*, 5). For Rawls, then, civic virtue is the virtue appropriate to this conception of society; it is the disposition that citizens must display if their society is truly to be a fair system of cooperation that will endure over time, "from one generation to the next." No political society can be a fair system of cooperation over time unless its members, as a rule, do in fact treat one another fairly and cooperate to advance their shared good as a society. When the disposition to act fairly and cooperatively is widespread, then there is "some hope of realizing social concord and civic friendship" (*JF*, 126). Civic virtue is thus intimately connected to Rawls's fundamental idea of political society as a fair system of cooperation over time from one generation to the next, where those engaged in cooperation are viewed as free and equal citizens and normal cooperating members of society over a complete life (*JF*, 4).

# Rawlsian Civic Virtue

Despite the absence of exemplary heroes and civic exhortations from his writings, there is ample evidence that Rawls's political philosophy is imbued with a concern for civic virtue. That much I take to be established at this point. Rawls's republicanism may be of a modest or chastened sort, but his political liberalism clearly has an affinity with the republican ideal of citizenship. To grasp how deeply civic virtue is involved with Rawls's conception of justice as fairness, however, and to form a clearer picture of what he means by "the political virtues," requires a closer examination of several of Rawls's key terms, among them *political society*, *citizen*, *the reasonable* and *the rational*, *public reason*, and even *public* and *political* themselves.

## Political Society

A *society*, Rawls insists, is neither an *association* nor a *community* (JF, 3–4; PL, 40–43). Associations are groups that people enter and exit voluntarily, such as clubs, churches, unions, and universities; but a political society, despite what some of Rawls's predecessors in the social contract tradition may have thought, is not voluntary in that way. "Rather," Rawls says, "we simply find ourselves in a particular political society at a certain moment of historical time" (JF, 4). But neither is a political society a community. For Rawls, the ties of political society are looser than those of community, taking a community to be "a body of persons united in affirming the same comprehensive, or partially comprehensive, doctrine" (JF, 3). That is, the members of a community share a set of beliefs about life and the good life that give them a sense of purpose and belonging that the members of a political society cannot – and in Rawls's view, should not – hope to achieve. That is because one of the distinctive characteristics of a society, or at least a democratic society with free institutions, is "the fact of reasonable pluralism" (JF, 3). The members of such societies may have much in common, in other words, but there will also be much that separates them from one another, including different views of what gives life its point and purpose.

To be sure, a member of a political society also may be a member of a community, just as she also may be a member of various associations that seem to suit her interests. Society, association, and community are not mutually exclusive categories. There is a sense, though, in which society is the most encompassing of the three, as the possibility – in fact, the frequency – of multiple memberships indicates. An association, we may say, brings together people on the basis of their self-interest, while the basis of community is a common bond. For the political society, the basis is the *public* interest – that is, an interest that all its members share as *citizens*, however much their interests may differ as members of communities and associations. Nor should we overlook another respect in which political society differs from, and is more encompassing than, either association or community: "only society with its political form of government and its laws exercises coercive power" (JF, 20).

## Citizen

The concept of citizenship, according to Andrés de Francisco, "is the center of gravity in Rawls' political philosophy" (2006, 271). That may seem to be an extraordinary claim about someone known principally for his theory of justice and advocacy of political liberalism, but the adjective "political" itself reveals something about the centrality of citizenship to Rawls's liberalism. If de Francisco's statement goes too far, it is only because citizenship is entangled with other concepts that are at least as central to Rawls's thought – notably *public* and *political*.

In Rawls's writings, all three of these concepts rest on the same side of a fundamental distinction between two aspects of our lives – that is, following Rawls, the lives of everyone whose "various native endowments such as strength and intelligence . . . [fall] within the normal range" (*JF*, 15). On the one hand, we are all persons, with a claim to being treated as free and equal in the use of our two moral powers: the capacities for a sense of justice and for a conception of the good (*PL*, 19; *JF*, 18–19). On the other hand, as members of political societies, we are *public* persons – that is, *citizens*. As persons, or private persons, we each have distinctive, individual identities shaped by different backgrounds, attributes, attachments, and inclinations; but as citizens of the same polity, we all share substantially the same public identity. Different as we are in other respects, as citizens, or public persons, we are equal and alike. Thinking solely as individual persons, we will want to take steps to advance our personal interests; but as citizens, we will be concerned to promote the public interest that we share as members of the public. The distinction is not absolute, of course. Neither personal nor civic life will be healthy if we are pulled apart by constant conflict between the person and the citizen, and in a well-ordered society the interests of the citizen and the person will often be identical. The knowledge that we all possess the two moral powers of persons should also help to strengthen the connection between the civic and personal aspects of our lives. But the tension between the two aspects will never vanish entirely, and the distinction between person and citizen will remain of fundamental importance.

In this respect Rawls's conception of citizenship has much in common with that of Jean-Jacques Rousseau. For both Rousseau and Rawls, the citizen is conceptually distinct from the *subject* and the *person* – or *man*, in Rousseau's terms – even though all three terms may apply to the same individual, as when we say that *X* is a person who is a citizen of a certain country and subject to its laws. One may be a person and a subject without being a citizen, however, as Rousseau observes in a long note on the meaning of "city" and "citizen" in his *Social Contract*: "I have not read that the title *cives* [citizen] has ever been given to the subjects of any prince . . ." (Rousseau 1978 [1762], 54). Only those who are fortunate enough to be members of a democratic society with a voice in the making of its laws will be citizens as well as persons and subjects. Yet these fortunate persons are likely to find themselves pulled in different directions by their different identities. As Rousseau puts the point,

> each individual can, as a man, have a private will contrary to or differing from the general will he has as a citizen. His private interest can speak to him quite differently from the common interest . . . And considering the moral person of the State as an imaginary being because it is not a man, he might wish to enjoy the rights of the citizen without wanting to fulfill the duties of a subject, an injustice whose spread would cause the ruin of the body politic. (1978 [1762], 55)

The distinction Rousseau draws here between the "private will" of the person and the "general will" of the citizen is not one that Rawls explicitly adopts. Given the complications and controversies surrounding Rousseau's references to the general will, it is easy to see why Rawls does not embrace the concept.[7] Still, the ideal of the citizen as someone who acts with the public interest in mind is as much a part of Rawls's political philosophy as it is of

Rousseau's. So, too, is a certain kind of reason or reasoning associated with the point of view of the citizen. Rawls makes the point himself in his *Lectures on the History of Political Philosophy*. There, in the second of three lectures on Rousseau, he observes that Rousseau's "general will is a form of deliberative reason that each citizen shares with all other citizens in virtue of their sharing a conception of their common good" (*LHPP*, 224). In the third lecture he adds that this "idea of deliberative reason . . . is framed to consider certain kinds of questions – those about which constitutional norms or basic laws best advance the common good – and it admits only certain kinds of reasons as having any weight." He immediately adds that "Rousseau's view contains an idea of what I have called public reason" (*LHPP*, 231).

For both Rousseau and Rawls, then, the citizen is someone who not only wants to act in the public interest but also believes that reasoning or deliberation about that common good should proceed in a certain way. That is to say, in Rawls's terms, that anyone who reasons *as a citizen* is engaged in *public reason*. To understand why he says this, however, we must first understand why he draws a distinction between "the reasonable" and "the rational."

## The Reasonable, the Rational, and the Citizen

In *A Theory of Justice*, Rawls remarks that the theory of justice is "a part, perhaps the most significant part, of the theory of rational choice" (*TJ*, 15). In subsequent writings, though, Rawls develops and defends justice as fairness as a form of *reasonable* rather than *rational* choice. In contrast to instrumental rationality, reasonableness has two basic aspects. The first is "the willingness to propose fair terms of cooperation and to abide by them provided others do"; and the second is "the willingness to recognize the burdens of judgment and to accept their consequences for the use of public reason in directing the legitimate exercise of political power in a constitutional regime" (*PL*, 54).

To be reasonable, then, is to be committed to fair cooperation. This is not a commitment to altruism but to reciprocity. As Rawls says,

> Reasonable persons . . . are not moved by the general good as such but desire for its own sake a social world in which they, as free and equal, can cooperate with others on terms all can accept. They insist that reciprocity should hold within that world so that each benefits with others. (*PL*, 50)[8]

So understood, the reasonable person and Rawls's citizen are one and the same. This citizen is not someone who dedicates herself entirely and selflessly to the good of others or to the general good of society; but neither is she someone who will exploit the cooperative efforts of others whenever she can advance her own interests by doing so. Instead, Rawls's citizen is someone who is willing to do her part in political society, understood as a fair system of cooperation over time, even when doing her part will involve significant sacrifice. What the citizen will insist on, though, is the assurance that the other persons involved in this society will also act as citizens by doing their part to maintain the cooperative enterprise. It may be reasonable, in other words, to act as a citizen rather than a free rider even when rationality prescribes the latter course of conduct; but reasonableness does not require one to sacrifice her personal interests when too many others are trying to advance theirs as free riders.

Civic virtue as Rawls understands it thus is largely a matter of being reasonable, and being reasonable is largely a matter of being willing to take on one's share of the burdens of social cooperation. Being reasonable also has its second aspect, however, according to which it is a matter of *reasoning* in the proper way about public matters. Rawls makes this point in his remarks on Rousseau's "idea of deliberative reason" (*LHPP*, 224, 231), as we have seen, and he makes it again, and at length, in developing his own idea of public reason.

## Public Reason

Rawls's appeal to public reason is one of the most important and controversial features of his political philosophy. The fact that he devoted a lecture to public reason in *Political Liberalism*, that he subsequently "revisited" the subject in "The Idea of Public Reason Revisited," and that he then appended this lengthy essay to both a new edition of *Political Liberalism* and to *The Law of Peoples*, attests to the importance of the idea and to the controversy it has aroused.[9] What has been largely overlooked, however, is the connection of public reason to Rawls's conception of civic virtue.

This connection is evident throughout Rawls's discussions of public reason. One example is the title of Lecture VI, §2, of *Political Liberalism*: "Public Reason and the Ideal of the Democratic Citizen" (*PL*, 216). Another is the opening paragraph of "The Idea of Public Reason Revisited," where Rawls proposes "that in public reason comprehensive doctrines of truth or right be replaced by an idea of the politically reasonable addressed *to citizens as citizens*" (*PL*, 441, emphasis added). As these and numerous other examples indicate, Rawls's conception of citizenship, like Rousseau's, is fundamentally ethical. Whether someone is or is not a citizen is in part a matter of legal status, of course, but what really matters for Rawls is that citizenship is an office or role, like that of judge and legislator, that carries with it both rights and duties (*TJ*, 413). In the plainest terms, each citizen has a right to be treated as a free and equal member of the body politic and a correlative duty to treat other citizens in the same way. Where reasoning is concerned, this means that each citizen should confine the arguments and evidence she advances in public discussions to those which she can expect other citizens, *qua* citizens, to find compelling. Jones, for example, may think that we can find the answer to all of life's problems by asking, "What would Jesus do?" When debating matters of public import with people who are not Christians, however, he will learn that they will not be persuaded by his appeal to Jesus' example, let alone his particular understanding of what Jesus prescribes. Jones's reasoning in this case is "nonpublic"; that is, it is "the reason appropriate to individuals and associations within society: it guides how they quite properly deliberate in making their personal and associational decisions" (*JF*, 92). But it is not the kind of reasoning that Jones should expect to move his fellow citizens *considered simply as citizens* – that is, as free and equal members of a fair system of cooperation over time. Nor is it the kind of reasoning that he and some of his fellow citizens, even a majority, should attempt to impose on their fellow citizens through the force of law. Given the reasonable pluralism of comprehensive doctrines that characterize modern societies, what Jones should do, as a citizen engaged in public discussions and debates, is to rely on arguments and evidence that he can expect all of his fellow citizens to find meaningful.[10]

For Rawls, then, public reason is an attempt to squeeze as much as possible out of the bare idea of citizenship. Thinking of oneself and others simply and strictly as citizens, in other words, what kinds of considerations are appropriate? The answer is given, in effect, by the process of elimination. Public reason is not the reason of individuals seeking to make rational choices, nor is it the reason of people within associations or communities, where rational advantage and "shared final ends" are appropriate considerations (*JF*, 93–94). Public reason is *public* because it is the form of reasoning appropriate to political society, the members of which regard one another as partners in a fair system of cooperation over time. One may think as a person, a sectarian, a member of a particular clan or tribe, or as someone with a comprehensive conception of the good life to advance; but one must also think of and argue for rules and policies that one believes will advance the interests of citizens – that is, of people in their strictly civic capacity. To reason in this way, according to Rawls, is to act in accordance with "an ideal of citizenship" that gives rise to "a duty of public civility" (*JF*, 92).

## The Duty of (Public) Civility

The duty of (public) civility[11] establishes a direct connection between Rawlsian public reason and civic virtue. The duty itself, however, first appears in *A Theory of Justice* in the course of a discussion of the duty to comply with an unjust law (*TJ*, §53). There Rawls says that "we have a natural duty of civility not to invoke the faults of social arrangements as a too ready excuse for not complying with them, nor to exploit inevitable loopholes in the rules to advance our interests" (*TJ*, 312). Rawls does not refer to public reason in this context – or, indeed, throughout *A Theory of Justice* – but his concern for what is *reasonable* is nevertheless evident. Here we have what is the first aspect of the duty of civility – to do one's part and not to look for excuses to do less than others. The second aspect is concerned with holding oneself and others to the standards of public reason.

In this case, the duty of civility takes different forms when applied to government officials and candidates for public office, on the one hand, and ordinary citizens, on the other. For officials and candidates, the duty of civility requires that they "act from and follow the idea of public reason and explain to other citizens their reasons for supporting fundamental political positions in terms of the political conception of justice they regard as the most reasonable" (*PL*, 444). When they do so, officials and candidates will realize "the *ideal* of public reason" (*PL*, 444, emphasis in original). As for ordinary citizens, Rawls says that they should "ideally" meet the same standard – that is, "to think of themselves *as if* they were legislators and ask themselves what statutes, supported by what reasons satisfying the criterion of reciprocity, they would think it most reasonable to enact" (*PL*, 444–445, emphasis in original). In a representative democracy, however, Rawls places the emphasis not on the readiness to explain one's position to others but on the citizen's duty to repudiate officials and candidates who violate public reason. "Thus," he declares, "citizens fulfill their duty of civility and support the idea of public reason by doing what they can to hold government officials to it" (*PL*, 445).

Being a citizen for Rawls, then, is a matter of doing one's duty as a cooperative and reasonable member of a political society. His language indicates, though, that Rawls has more than rigid adherence to duty in mind when he talks of citizenship, for he also refers to "disposition," "character," and "virtues" in this context. (See *JF*, 118, for character and virtue; *PL*, 445, for "disposition of citizens.") And he counts the willingness to "honor the duty of public civility" as one of the "cooperative political virtues," along with reasonableness, a sense of fairness, and a spirit of compromise (*JF*, 118).[12] Without ever explicitly drawing the distinction, Rawls alludes, here and elsewhere, to the difference between civic duty, which is to be expected of all citizens, and civic virtue, which is a disposition that some will display more fully than others. Citizenship is thus an "ideal" that includes, but is not exhausted by, the "duty of public civility" (*JF*, 92). But it is also an office that one holds, and offices, like positions in baseball or an orchestra, entail both minimum expectations and aspirational ideals. Someone who thinks and acts solely as a private person will not, for Rawls, be a citizen at all. Someone who discharges the duties of this office by exhibiting public civility, but grudgingly, will qualify as a citizen, but he will fall far short of the civic ideal. Those who do their duty willingly or cheerfully or without waiting to be called will approach more closely to the ideal, as will those who go well beyond the call of duty – those, for instance, who are models of reasonableness, fairness, and the spirit of compromise even at considerable cost to their personal lives. Indeed, for Rawls there is a direct connection between the realization of these virtues – of the ideal of citizenship – and a society that realizes justice as fairness (JF, 118).

## Virtue, Friendship, and Social Concord

"To be is to confront" (JF, 118). In that pithy sentence – a rarity in his writings – Rawls tries to capture an attitude toward politics that differs sharply from the civic disposition he hopes to foster. Rather than an activity in which reciprocity, the duty of public civility, and other "cooperative political virtues" are to be displayed, this attitude takes politics to be a contest in which the participants stake out unyielding positions and aim to subdue their opponents. In Rawls's words,

> much political debate betrays the marks of warfare. It consists in rallying the troops and intimidating the other side, which must now increase its efforts or back down. In all this one may find the thought that to have character is to have firm convictions and be ready to proclaim them defiantly to others. To be is to confront. (JF, 118)

So far as I am aware, Rawls never gives an equally pithy statement of his own view. If he had done so, I suspect he would have written, "To be is to cooperate." On Rawls's view, in other words, our lives must be lived in society if they are to go well, and a society must be grounded in cooperation if it is to endure confrontation. Moreover, a society can be a *well-ordered society* only when its people regard and treat one another as partners in a cooperative enterprise.

Rawls makes this point in both *A Theory of Justice* and *Justice as Fairness* by way of a contrast between a well-ordered society, which rests on the "social nature of mankind," and a "private society," which is held together not by "a public conviction that its basic arrangements are just and good in themselves, but by the *calculations* of everyone, or of sufficiently many to maintain the scheme" (TJ, 458, emphasis added; cf. TJ, 457, and JF, 199). In both books Rawls argues that a well-ordered society in which the cooperative political virtues are widely practiced will advance the good of its members in two ways. First, it enhances their lives individually. Rawls makes this point in different ways in *Theory* and in *Justice as Fairness*, with the emphasis in the former on how we rely on a division of labor with others to complete ourselves. Thus Rawls says in *Theory* that "a feature of human sociability is that we are by ourselves but parts of what we might be. We must look to others to attain the excellences that we must leave aside, or lack altogether" (TJ, 464).[13] In *Justice as Fairness*, though, the emphasis is on the ways in which "the well-ordered society of justice as fairness" encourages the exercise of the two moral powers and "guarantees persons public recognition of their status as free and equal" (JF, 200).

With regard to the second way in which a well-ordered political society will advance the good of its members, Rawls's position is fundamentally the same in *Theory* and in *Justice as Fairness*. In both cases the emphasis is on shared final ends and social goods, and in both cases Rawls takes examples from musical groups and team sports to support his claim that "whenever there is a shared final end, the achievement of which calls on the cooperation of many, the good realized is social" (*JF*, 201). This includes such political goods and historical achievements as establishing, maintaining, and reforming democratic institutions. To those who doubt that such goods truly exist, presumably because they believe that all goods are necessarily individual goods, Rawls says the following:

> That there should be such political and social goods is no more mysterious than that members of an orchestra, or players on a team, or even both teams in a game, should take pleasure and a certain (proper) pride in a good performance, or in a good play of the game, one they will want to remember. (*JF*, 201)

In the same way that the members of an orchestra or the players on a team, or even the opposing teams in a game, are cooperating to produce a social good – albeit a good that may consist not in a finished product but in the enjoyment of the activity itself – so citizens in a well-ordered political society are cooperating to produce a social, and specifically political, good. It is, in fact, a *meta*-good, in that it is a social good within which other social goods, such as playing in a game or an orchestra, may flourish. In Rawls's terms, it is a "social union of social unions" (*TJ*, 462; *PL*, 320–323; *JF*, 201).

In contrast to "private society," Rawls's well-ordered society of justice as fairness promises, as we have seen, a "public culture . . . that inhibits the wastes of endless self- and group-interested bargaining and offers some hope of realizing social concord and civic friendship" (*JF*, 126). But what exactly is civic friendship?[14] The term appears only once in Rawls's indexes, where it points to a passage in the "Introduction to the Paperback Edition" of *Political Liberalism*; there Rawls says that "the role of the criterion of reciprocity as expressed in public reason . . . is to specify the nature of the political relationship in a constitutional democratic regime as one of civic friendship" (*PL*, xlix). Rawls refers to civic friendship several times, however, and he does so as early as the first section of *Theory*: "Among individuals with disparate aims and purposes a shared conception of justice establishes the bonds of civic friendship" (*TJ*, 5; cf. 417, 454, 470). As these quotations indicate, Rawls's conception of civic friendship has two faces. First, it is *civic*. It grows out of the relations between citizens who treat one another *reasonably*, in keeping with the duty of (public) civility. That is why *reciprocity* is important to civic friendship: a virtuous citizen will only make demands on her fellow citizens that she is willing to have them make on her. Rawls calls attention to this face of civic friendship in "The Idea of Public Reason Revisited" by way of the example of "citizens of faith" who, moved to act by the parable of the Good Samaritan, "go on to give a public justification for this parable's conclusions in terms of political values. In this way citizens who hold different doctrines are reassured, and this strengthens the ties of civic friendship" (*PL*, 465).

The mention of "ties" in this last sentence points to the second face of civic friendship – that it is a matter of "ties" and "bonds," much as it is in personal friendship. The difference is that civic friendship is not a relationship that binds people as *persons* but as *citizens*. In political society we cannot expect everyone to be acquainted with all of his or her fellow citizens, let alone expect them all to be friends. Yet we can expect them to appreciate one another as citizens, at least when they conduct themselves as such. In other words, the fact that others are doing their part in our fair system of social cooperation over time should dispose us not only to do our part in turn, but to feel a kind of kinship with them. In this way civic friendship contributes to the stability of a well-ordered society. But because it is *civic* friendship, it is "stability for the right reasons" (*LP*, 12–13, esp. n2).

## Assessing Rawlsian Civic Virtue

This idea of "stability for the right reasons" is one that Rawls uses to distinguish a well-ordered political society grounded in justice and civic friendship from a modus vivendi, in which "society's stability depends on a balance of forces in contingent and possibly fluctuating circumstances" (*PL*, 392). Whether Rawlsian justice as fairness is capable of generating this "stability for the right reasons," or whether a modus vivendi is the best to be hoped for in a liberal society, is a much disputed question (e.g., Frohock 2006; Gray 2000; McCabe 2010; White 1997). What should be beyond question, though, is the importance of civic virtue to Rawls's theory. From stability to public reason to the difference principle and beyond, justice as fairness and political liberalism are informed by Rawls's concern for citizenship. In *The Law of Peoples*, he even distinguishes a "decent hierarchical society" from a liberal one by saying that, in the former, the "conception of the person . . . does not require acceptance of *the liberal idea that persons are citizens first*" (*LP*, 66, emphasis added).

What remains, then, is to assess, albeit briefly, Rawls's conception of civic virtue. There are several points of concern, some of which relate to the adequacy of Rawls's conception when viewed from outside his theory and others to tensions within the theory itself.

To begin with the latter category, we should acknowledge that Rawls was not as systematic or explicit in his treatment of civic virtue as he was in other topics. I suspect that he would have been had critics pressed him on these aspects of his theory as they did on others. That is not to say, however, that he was careless or loose in his terminology or arguments with regard to citizenship and the political virtues, despite occasional appearances to the contrary. For instance, my account of Rawls's conception of civic virtue may suggest a contradiction in his position on community and shared final ends. When distinguishing political society from association and community, as I have noted, Rawls holds that community, but not political society, involves "shared final ends" (*JF*, 94).[15] Subsequently, though, Rawls maintains that a well-ordered political society is a social good because it entails "a shared final end, the achievement of which calls on the cooperation of many" (*JF*, 201). Not only is there an apparent contradiction here, but it is one that threatens to undercut Rawls's fundamental distinction between political society and community. Yet Rawls is careful to specify that the final ends citizens share are not those of a comprehensive doctrine but ends that are strictly political. These include the "one basic political end" of "supporting just institutions and giving one another justice accordingly" together with "the other ends [citizens] must also share and realize through their political cooperation" (*JF*, 199). To those who would say that a political society, so defined, is indistinguishable from a community, Rawls replies that he is prepared to accept that term as long as we acknowledge that citizens must have "shared final ends of the requisite [i.e., political, not comprehensive] kind" (*JF*, 200).

A second problem his account of civic virtue poses for Rawls's political philosophy is not, I think, as easy to resolve. In this case there is no apparent contradiction, but there is reason to doubt that the distinction between political and comprehensive liberalism is as firm as Rawls wants it to be. In *Political Liberalism*, Rawls argues that both forms of liberalism rely on a conception of autonomy, but the "full autonomy of political life" differs from "the ethical values of autonomy and individuality, which may apply to the whole of life, both social and individual, as expressed by the comprehensive liberalisms of Kant and Mill" (*PL*, 78). When he turns to education, as we have seen, Rawls again sets political liberalism apart from the comprehensive liberalisms of Kant and Mill. But he also has to acknowledge that preparing children for citizenship may well be, "in effect, though not in intention, to educate them to a comprehensive liberal conception" (*PL*, 199). If his theory is to rely on the cultivation and practice of "the political virtues," in short, it is difficult to see how Rawls can maintain a sharp distinction between political and comprehensive liberalism (Dagger 1997, 189–191; Spragens 1999, 232–233; but cf. Davis and Neufeld 2007).

In addition to these possible problems within Rawls's political philosophy, there is also the question of whether his conception of civic virtue is adequate. That is, does Rawls give us a conception of civic virtue that is coherent and capable of doing what such a conception should do? Here there are at least three points of concern.

The first concern relates to Rawls's concentration on "ideal theory: the account of the well-ordered society of justice as fairness" (*JF*, 65). Rawls has plenty to say about civic virtue and civic friendship in such a society, but what of a society that falls well short of this ideal? Most of those who have been praised for their civic virtue, great heroes and humble citizens alike, have been people who have fought to preserve freedom and equality when their countries have been under threat. Can Rawls's conception of civic virtue be adequate if it does not speak to men and women in such circumstances?

A second and related worry is that Rawls invests too much in "citizens' allegiance to public reason and their honoring the duty of civility" (*PL*, 485), but too little in considerations such as patriotism, nationalism, or solidarity. Civic virtue is supposed to inspire people to put the public good ahead of their personal interests, but Rawls's conception seems too abstract and bloodless to provide such inspiration.

To these concerns, which raise the question of whether Rawls has strayed too far from traditional understandings of civic virtue, we should add the complaint that he has not ventured far enough. Here the concern is that Rawls's conception continues to reflect the masculine bias that has long defined civic virtue. For this reason, according to Sibyl Schwarzenbach, Rawls ignores the need to include the ethic of care in his conception of civic virtue, whereas he should allow "for the possibility that I, as a citizen, might actually in practice have to *care for others myself*" (Schwarzenbach 2009, 175).

These are, in my view, genuine reasons to worry about the adequacy of Rawls's account of civic virtue. There is reason, though, to believe that his account may contain the resources to meet these concerns. To be sure, Rawls intends his theory to apply to constitutional democracies, but there is no reason why his ideal of the well-ordered society cannot serve as an inspiration – a "realistically utopian" inspiration, in his terms (*JF*, 4) – to those living under regimes that are neither constitutional nor democratic. In this regard it is helpful to note Rawls's praise of the abolitionists' activities before the Civil War and of Martin Luther King, Jr, and other leaders of the civil rights movement (*PL*, 249–251). Neither the abolitionists nor the civil rights leaders confined themselves to arguing strictly in accordance with public reason, for they frequently appealed to comprehensive conceptions of the good, and to religious conceptions in particular. In doing so, however, "they could have seen their actions as the best way to bring about a well-ordered and just society in which the ideal of public reason could eventually be honored" (*PL*, 250). In this and other respects, they could be considered exemplars of Rawlsian civic virtue.

As for patriotism, nationalism, and solidarity, Rawls says that "peoples (as opposed to states) have a definite moral nature" and that a "proper patriotism" will allow them to "be proud of their history and achievements" (*LP*, 44; cf. 62, 111). Whether this concedes enough to patriotism will have to remain an open question. Still, it is clear that Rawls does not foreclose the possibility that the kind of civic virtue appropriate to justice as fairness may also speak to more traditional concerns. Nor does it foreclose the possibility of opening civic virtue in new directions, such as those suggested by feminist arguments for an ethic of care. Rawls's response in *Justice as Fairness* to Susan Moller Okin's criticisms gives some indication of how his conception of civic virtue might be made more congenial to feminist concerns (*JF*, 162–168; Okin 1989); and Schwarzenbach herself allows that "Rawls's difference principle genuinely embodies the first stages of caring for fellow citizens" (2009, 174).

There is, in sum, ample reason to believe that Rawls has an account of civic virtue that is worth assessing, even if we are not sure what the proper assessment is. Whatever conclusion one reaches on this point, it is clear that we cannot take justice as fairness seriously, or give Rawls his due, if we fail to appreciate the importance of his conception of civic virtue.

## Notes

I am grateful to Jonathan Quong and the editors for valuable comments on an earlier draft of this essay.

1   See Aristotle, *Politics*, trans. C.D.C. Reeve (Indianapolis: Hackett, 1998).
2   The five references to Lincoln in *Political Liberalism* do not include the reference in "The Idea of Public Reason Revisited," which appears in both the second edition of *Political Liberalism* and in *The Law of Peoples*. There is also a further reference to Lincoln in Rawls's "On My Religion," published posthumously with his undergraduate thesis, *A Brief Inquiry into the Meaning of Sin and Faith*. Rawls also refers to Martin Luther King, Jr, numerous times: once in *A Theory of Justice*, three times in *Political Liberalism*, and once in *The Law of Peoples* (again counting the reference in "The Idea of Public Reason Revisited" only in *LP*).
3   Rawls borrows this distinction from Taylor 1985, 334f. For further comments on Rawls's use of the distinction, see Dagger 1997, 186–188.
4   As Rawls says in his "Reply to Habermas," "to make the good of civil society subordinate to that of public life" is, from the perspective of justice as fairness, "mistaken" (*PL*, 420–421).
5   For further exploration of the republican aspects of Rawls's political philosophy, see de Francisco 2006.
6   So far as I am aware, Rawls never uses this term. For an indication of its appropriateness, see Davis and Neufeld 2007.
7   But note the following comment from one of Rawls's lectures on Rousseau: "While some references to the general will in the *Social Contract* are obscure, I believe the idea itself can be made clear, and the main things Rousseau says about it are consistent and make good sense" (*LHPP*, 228).

8  See also *JF*, 77, where Rawls says, "Reciprocity is a moral idea situated between impartiality, which is altruistic, on the one side and mutual advantage on the other."

9  For a valuable explication of Rawlsian public reason, see Jonathan Quong's chapter in this volume.

10  Strictly speaking, Rawls says that the strictures of public reason apply only "in cases raising fundamental political questions" (*JF*, 91). He also allows that we may "introduce into political discussion at any time our comprehensive doctrine, religious or nonreligious, provided that, in due course, we give properly public reasons to support the principles and policies our comprehensive doctrine is said to support" (*PL*, 453; cf. *JF*, 90).

11  I place "public" within parentheses here because Rawls sometimes refers to the "duty of civility" and sometimes to the "duty of public civility." So far as I am aware, he never distinguishes between the two locutions.

12  Elsewhere he refers to "the political virtues of mutual trust and cooperation" (*JF*, 133); "the cooperative virtues . . . of justice and fairness, fidelity and trust, integrity and impartiality" (*TJ*, 413); and "the necessary (political) virtues . . . such as a sense of fairness and tolerance and a willingness to meet others halfway" (*LP*, 15).

13  Note also what Rawls says in §79 of *TJ* (460 n4): "it is only in active cooperation with others that one's powers reach fruition. Only in a social union is the individual complete."

14  For helpful discussions of this concept, including Rawls's conception of it, see Schwarzenbach 2009, Spragens 1999, and Weithman 2010, who probably gives more weight to civic friendship than any other commentator on Rawls's political philosophy.

15  To be precise, Rawls says that political liberalism "insists on the distinction between a political society and an association. Associations within society *can be communities united on shared final ends*; indeed this is essential: were it not the case social life would lose its point" (*JF*, 94, emphasis added).

## Works by Rawls, with Abbreviations

*A Brief Inquiry into the Meaning of Sin and Faith, with "On My Religion"* (*BI*). Cambridge, MA: Harvard University Press, 2009.

*Collected Papers* (*CP*), ed. Samuel Freeman. Cambridge, MA: Harvard University Press, 1999.

*Justice as Fairness: A Restatement* (*JF*), ed. Erin Kelly. Cambridge, MA: Harvard University Press, 2001.

*The Law of Peoples, with "The Idea of Public Reason Revisited"* (*LP*). Cambridge, MA: Harvard University Press, 1999.

*Lectures on the History of Political Philosophy* (*LHPP*), ed. Samuel Freeman. Cambridge, MA: Harvard University Press, 2007.

*Political Liberalism* (*PL*), expanded edn. New York: Columbia University Press, 2005.

*A Theory of Justice* (*TJ*), rev. edn. Cambridge, MA: Harvard University Press, 1999.

## Other References

Dagger, Richard (1997) *Civic Virtues: Rights, Citizenship, and Republican Liberalism*. New York: Oxford University Press.

Davis, Gordon and Neufeld, Blain (2007) "Political Liberalism, Civic Education, and Educational Choice." *Social Theory and Practice* 33: 47–74.

de Francisco, Andrés (2006) "A Republican Interpretation of the Late Rawls." *Journal of Political Philosophy* 14: 270–288.

Frohock, Fred (2006) *Bounded Divinities: Sacred Discourses in Pluralist Democracies*. New York: Palgrave Macmillan.

Gray, John (2000) *Two Faces of Liberalism*. New York: New Press.

McCabe, David (2010) *Modus Vivendi Liberalism: Theory and Practice*. Cambridge: Cambridge University Press.

Okin, Susan Moller (1989) *Justice, Gender, and the Family*. New York: Basic Books.

Rousseau, Jean-Jacques (1978 [1762]) *On the Social Contract*, ed. Roger Masters, trans. Judith Masters. New York: St Martin's Press.

Schwarzenbach, Sibyl (2009) *On Civic Friendship: Including Women in the State*. New York: Columbia University Press.

Spragens, Thomas (1999) *Civic Liberalism: Reflections on Our Democratic Ideals*. Lanham, MD: Rowman & Littlefield.

Sunstein, Cass (1988) "Beyond the Republican Revival." *Yale Law Journal* 97: 1539–1590.

Taylor, Charles (1985) *Philosophical Papers*, vol. 2. Cambridge: Cambridge University Press.

Weithman, Paul (2010) *Why Political Liberalism? On John Rawls's Political Turn*. Oxford: Oxford University Press.

White, Michael (1997) *Partisan or Neutral: The Futility of Public Political Theory*. Lanham, MD: Rowman & Littlefield.

Wills, Garry (1984) *Cincinnatus: George Washington and the Enlightenment*. Garden City, NY: Doubleday.

# 18

# Inequality, Difference, and Prospects for Democracy

## ERIN I. KELLY

Rawls's signature and perhaps greatest innovation is the thought experiment he introduced to sort out the requirements of justice. Rawls proposed that in thinking about the requirements of justice, we are to imagine ourselves in an original position behind a veil of ignorance that obscures the details of our personal identity and social situation. We are to imagine that we do not know our own race, gender, social class, or religion. Furthermore, we are to suppose that we are ignorant of our particular talents and abilities, goals and ambitions, or any significant good or bad fortune that shapes our individual lives. We are to imagine choosing principles from behind this veil of ignorance in an effort to ensure that the principles we choose will not be biased to favor our particular social position, or personal attributes, ambitions, or values. Thus, Rawls conjectures, we will arrive at principles that are fair to all members of society.

Rawls argues that "justice as fairness" will be a form of political liberalism. Political liberalism is, first of all, a form of *liberalism*. Liberalism affirms that political institutions ought to specify and to assign high priority to certain basic rights, liberties, and opportunities for all citizens, and that inequalities in wealth and income ought substantially to be limited. Secondly, political liberalism is a *political* form of liberalism. Rawls claims, and rightly so, that under free institutions we should expect "profound and irreconcilable differences" in people's religious and philosophical worldviews, and in people's basic notions of what makes life worth living. These differences are to be expected even among people who are committed to cooperating with one another on fair terms. Since a social order under free, democratic institutions will not be one in which people accept the same religious and moral values, Rawls argues, justification in a free society will have to be based on a narrower set of values, including a commitment to fair cooperation, equal basic rights, the rule of law, and mutual toleration. He refers to these values as political values. These political values, and not the broader religious and moral philosophies in which they may variously be embedded, provide the terms of public justification. Rawls insists that the principles of justice should have a public justification in these terms.

*A Companion to Rawls*, First Edition. Edited by Jon Mandle and David A. Reidy.
© 2014 John Wiley & Sons, Inc. Published 2016 by John Wiley & Sons, Inc.

Some critics have been bothered by Rawls's political form of liberalism. They have argued that an abbreviated and "freestanding" set of political values is too thin a basis for generating the social solidarity needed to support and to stabilize just institutions. Instead, a more robust overlap of substantive values is required, values emphasizing shared history, language, religion, and other rich details of culture. What is needed is a shared form of identity, one that stands in some measure independently of political institutions. When collective identity is weak or absent, collective commitment to common political values will splinter and just institutions will lack adequate support and common direction, or so it is argued.

There are multiple versions of this criticism. Some emphasize the imperative of a unified conception of the good underwriting a shared national identity (see Taylor 2004; Miller 1995; MacIntyre 1984; Calhoun 2007). The aspiration is to build a shared national culture – to find unity in diversity. Others advocate a version of multiculturalism, arguing that taking equality seriously requires group rights that will enable the political and cultural affirmation of a plurality of ethnocultural identity groups – a politics of recognition (Tully 1995; Young 2000; Kymlicka 1995).[1] A common thread runs through this range of positions that endorse what I will refer to as broadly "communitarian" or "culture-based" criticisms of political liberalism. These critics, broadly speaking, emphasize the importance of organizing a conception of justice around cultural values and loyalties. The notion is that only by drawing upon cultural affinities will the obligations of justice take shape and attract support. The rights and liberties of citizenship must be adequately contextualized in history and culture, or so these critics maintain.

Communitarians rightly call attention to a stubborn obstacle to the realization of political liberalism: a lack of popular commitment to egalitarian principles of distributive justice. Clearly American society has experienced a collapse of commitment, if it ever had it, to any substantive ideal of equality. The income gap between rich and poor is large and has increased in the last 30 years, despite significant growth in the economy overall.[2] In this period the income share of the top 1 percent of the US population has doubled, and the share held by the top 0.1 percent has tripled.[3] At the same time, the real wages of the middle and lower income groups have declined. The wealth gap, which reflects the accumulation of inequality over time, is also stark and revealing.[4] The top 1 percent of the population now owns 40 percent of the country's wealth, while the bottom 40 percent of the population owns a mere 0.2 percent.[5]

There is little reason to think that efforts to forge a more robust common identity – with either nationalist or multiculturalist stripes – could counter this astounding and expansive inequality and lead Americans toward Rawlsian justice. A more inclusive social understanding of the meaning of citizenship has not in the past brought about greater socioeconomic equality. In fact, expanding the boundaries of citizenship has had just the opposite effect.

The rise in economic inequality in the last 40 years in the United States followed a marked change in social order brought about by the civil rights movements of the 1960s. American democracy became quite suddenly and strikingly more inclusive. This change was not an abstraction whose effects were confined to an impersonal reordering of legal principles and social institutions, detached from the social imagination and all that enlivens it. Rather, it reflected a serious social struggle by disempowered groups for recognition within American society and culture. Broad and deep social and cultural disruption put pressure on the public's conception of the benefits of citizenship and thus of the nation's self-conception. This struggle resulted in significant changes in the public conception of American citizenship, reflected in the Civil Rights Act of 1964, the Voting Rights Act of 1965, and the Fair Housing Act of 1968. The meaning of this new, broader notion of the citizenry was not easily absorbed and it remained a vexed matter of social and cultural concern. The public grappled – in the domains of art, music, religion, and social life, as well as politics and law – with the new meaning and value of a more inclusive democratic citizenry. It had to decide whether citizenship could be deep as well as inclusive.

As it has turned out, the civil rights struggle for greater inclusion was followed by a thinning of the socioeconomic benefits associated with citizenship. Increasing economic inequality across racial groups has been accompanied by persistent and, in some respects, growing racial inequality. In 2007, a Pew study found that 45 percent of black children whose parents belonged to the middle class in 1968 had fallen to the bottom fifth of the current income distribution (Pew 2007; see also discussion in McPherson 2007). Welfare and other social programs have been cut significantly, and this disproportionately affects African-Americans, especially black children, since relatively greater numbers of black children live in poverty (about three times more), compared with white children. Other social indicators also reflect racial disparity. De facto racial segregation in housing has persisted and, notably, is highest in metropolitan areas in the Northeast and Midwest where African-Americans have experienced the greatest gains in public life (Patterson 2009). Incarceration for nonviolent drug offenses, a mode of social and political exclusion, disproportionately affects the African-American population and has had staggering consequences.[6]

Racial inequalities in the education of children are also disturbing. In a crushing portrait of American education, Jonathan Kozol (2005) describes racial segregation and inequality so extreme he refers to it as "America's educational apartheid." In 2002–2003, public schools in the major American cities were between 75 and 95 percent black and Hispanic. In the poorest and most segregated neighborhoods of our cities, the numbers were even higher than that.[7] De facto racial segregation in education is paired with spending disparities.[8] The public and private schools attended by wealthier children have good facilities, pedagogically strong curricula and impressive records of feeding their graduates into elite universities, in contrast with curricula in poor inner city schools, which are not uncommonly designed around state exams and rudimentary preparation for low-paying vocations, such as hairdressing and sewing. In poor inner city schools it is common to find dilapidated buildings with overcrowded classrooms, no air conditioning, no playgrounds or gym, no libraries, no music or art programs, unclean and ill-equipped bathrooms, and inadequate medical staff and facilities for sick children. Not surprisingly, the high school dropout rate in these neighborhoods is very high.[9] Some of the children Kozol spoke with recognized the social and personal significance of these disparities. One girl explained to him her understanding of the racial segregation of her school and neighborhood. She said, "It's as if you have been put in a garage where, if they don't have room for something but aren't sure if they should throw it out, they put it there where they don't need to think of it again" (Kozol 2005, 43).

This racialized socioeconomic retraction of the benefits of citizenship in the post–civil rights era is part of a larger historical pattern. Inequality is no stranger to democracy. From the beginning, American democracy was rooted in inequality. The Founding Fathers' constitutional pact left almost 700,000 people in slavery, about 18 percent of the US population. Despite their affirmation of principles of liberty and equality, the founders were prepared to live with liberty for some and unfreedom for others. In fact, as sociologist Orlando Patterson tells us, subordination and social exclusion helped to give birth to the value of freedom

(Patterson 1991). From its origins in ancient Greece and extending to its conception in America, democracy was a system of exclusive inclusivity founded on the experience of slavery. Those treated unequally were outside of the democratic populace. This helped to give shape and meaning to the value of membership in the polis – the meaning and value of freedom and the benefits of citizenship.

As excluded segments of the population were incorporated, in stages, into the democratic citizenry, their inclusion brought with it resistance and revision of the social benefits of citizenship. Patterson describes a variegated process of extending citizenship and flattening its meaning that has been iterated at different points in our history, for example, in the aftermath of the American Revolution, and in the post–Civil War era. In these cases, forms of group identity – religious Puritanism in the North, white racial privilege in the South – gave way to and subsequently reacted against a more inclusive conception of citizenship (see Patterson 1999). The result was a winnowing of the egalitarian content of membership in the democratic polity, and the emergence of division, distrust, and a concerted effort by privileged individuals and groups to leverage their advantage through politics and other avenues of power in order to maintain their social and economic advantages. Beneath the surface of a more inclusive membership was a recalcitrant socioeconomic conflict of interests and the disturbing will of some groups to dominate others. This deeper truth about social division wears many disguises. Here is one: if we share a political identity – expressed in our common citizenship – and we fail to recognize egalitarian obligations, this must be because freedom is more important than equality.

Libertarians have picked up and exploited this theme. Policies aiming at economic redistribution or social entitlements are rejected as incompatible with the moral priority of property rights and freedom of contract – the heart of the libertarian conception of freedom. According to libertarians, the scope of equality should be limited to the equal liberty we each have to make choices in the pursuit of our interests and alliances and to acquire property that, in effect, expresses our choices. The state is restricted to a minimal function of securing our basic liberty, understood in this way. There are no requirements of justice to redistribute wealth. In fact, unchosen wealth-transfers violate liberty. Not surprisingly, inequalities in wealth can be expected to accumulate over time. There is no injustice in this, by libertarian principles. While we might admire a broader notion of equality, we cannot justly do much to bring it about.

In response, communitarians and some of their more egalitarian, liberal counterparts have insisted that mutual, ethically robust obligations of justice might be forged with the support of a stronger common identity. The extremes of socioeconomic inequality might at least be softened with the cultivation of sociocultural solidarity. But the notion that a common liberal identity could function to orient the obligations and substance of democratic justice is a nonstarter in the context of a deeper conflict of interests. A society cannot transform itself from radical socioeconomic inequality to a robust commitment to democratic values and the common good by inaugurating or amplifying a notion of collective solidarity. There is no reason to believe either that the obligations of justice have their source in mutual identity or that a common commitment to democratic values, however exactly they are to be understood, will arise through collective identity.

In Rawls's vision of democracy, the solidarity required to support common political values and egalitarian norms of distributive justice must be built through productive and fair social cooperation. There is no shortcut through shared identity, the affirmation of a common ideal of citizenship, or a nonpolitical public realm where this ideal is worked out. A free society rooted in the cooperation of its members depends on fair opportunity in politics, education, and employment. Social solidarity is indeed needed to support democratic equality, and Rawls's insight is that this solidarity must be built through the mutual production and reciprocal sharing of the fruits of social cooperation. An unfair division of social goods, by contrast, is a solidarity wrecker. When those who cooperate get less than a fair share, this produces mistrust, suspicion, insecurity, and hostility. Those who get less are bitter and resentful. Those who get more assume a right to rule and to enjoy superior social status that, naturally, makes them feel easily threatened. This is because their social position of advantage is not acceptable to the disadvantaged. Nor, increasingly, is it acceptable to the middle class, which is an unstable zone when there is no social commitment to fair opportunity and a robust social safety net. Inequality exacerbates social divisions.

Rawls describes two ways in which the least advantaged in an unequal society might react to their socially disadvantaged position. He writes,

> In the first way we become sullen and resentful, and we are ready as the occasion arises to take violent action in protest against our condition. In this case the least advantaged are bitter; they reject society's conception of justice and see themselves as oppressed. The second way is milder: we grow distant from political society and retreat into our social world. We feel left out; and, withdrawn and cynical, we cannot affirm the principles of justice in our thought and conduct over a complete life. Though we are not hostile or rebellious, those principles are not ours and fail to engage our moral sensibility. (JF, 128)

Rawls acknowledges that alleviating the first, more severe form of alienation might be achieved by ensuring a decent minimum standard of living for all citizens along with the equal protection of basic rights and fair opportunities for all. Avoiding the second form of instability, a milder form of alienation, Rawls argues, requires the "difference principle"; only when inequalities benefit the disadvantaged most will lower levels of alienation be eliminated.

One need not be as committed to egalitarian outcomes as Rawls is to recognize that social alienation is produced by the threat to equal social standing that comes from significant material inequality. We might also recognize that a materially and socially unequal state of affairs can produce the impression that self-interest and group loyalty are the only normative sources of concern and obligation, since a society marked by significant inequalities lacks the social bond produced by reciprocal gain. In other words, identity-based solidarity looks like the best hope for generating mutual obligations only when we take socioeconomic inequalities for granted. This suggests the possibility that underlying the communitarian focus on cultural recognition as a model of inclusion could be a rejection of egalitarian liberalism itself, however submerged this rejection might be in criticisms of Rawls's theoretical approach. Indeed, the weakness of the communitarians' theoretical criticisms leads one to suspect that there is a deeper preoccupation.

Communitarians have resisted Rawls's original position thought experiment precisely because it requires us to abstract from our personal and communal affinities in determining what justice requires. Some communitarians, Michael Sandel in particular, have argued that this is metaphysically impossible (Sandel 1982). Sandel thinks that we cannot abstract from these affinities because they make us who we are; apart from them we have no perspective. For example, it makes no sense for me to consider what principles I would choose were I not to know that I am a woman from a particular community with certain professional interests, family ties, and nonreligious values. I would have no basis for a meaningful choice.

This is a strong claim and it is not plausible. I see no reason why I could not imagine whether proposed social arrangements would be acceptable from social positions I do not actually occupy. Although I am not poor and do not face racial discrimination, I can understand that poverty and racial discrimination would pose difficulties that I would want to be free of, were I to face them. That is to say, I can understand that persons who face these difficulties would reasonably object to them. Although I am not a religious believer, I can understand that the freedom to worship is very important to someone who is. Rawls is right that our ability to consider what is fair to other people enables us to take up their perspective when evaluating institutions. We can perceive the importance of their interests and values to them even if we do not have the same interests and values. We can understand what matters to them and why by listening to what they tell us, noting their reasons, and considering their priorities.

The lucidity of this possibility suggests that some critics drawn to the communitarian position might have a deeper loyalty to the conviction that we will not agree on egalitarian standards of distributive justice and, morally speaking, we should not have to. A communitarian understanding of the importance of community to individual identity and well-being can be invoked to support a certain vision of both morality and politics. Loyalties and local alliances define the basic configuration of our moral obligations. As Michael Walzer describes it, morality expresses concentric circles of concern (1996, 126). At the core are loyalties to family and other loved ones. Circles of loyalty begin there and expand outward under pressure, weakening with their distance from the core. At the periphery are obligations to persons as such. Political compromise may lead us to the periphery, although it is also possible that we won't get there. Morality does not require us impartially to address the interests of people we do not care about. Morality does not demand equal consideration.

Politics, on this view, is a contest of self and group-interest, and legitimately so. Stakeholders in an identity group bargain in the public forum to affirm their shared interests as against the interests of other individuals and groups. Bargains and compromises are struck in this struggle for power and influence, that is, when the parties are rational. The outcomes of rational bargaining and compromise express the claims of justice. Rational bargains are just because they represent the advancement, by each party, of their most basic identity-based obligations without requiring, ethically speaking, that each impartially consider the claims advanced by other parties as if, to use Rawls's imagery, all bargainers were situated behind a veil of ignorance. This requirement of reciprocal consideration and concern would be, on this understanding, too demanding. Indeed, it could conflict with the substantial obligations we have to the individuals and groups of people with whom we bear the strongest affinities. Group loyalists might want a more civilized version of a bargaining model of politics, but it is not clear that they reject its ethical presumptions.

At the heart of this version of the communitarian position is the notion of an associative obligation. This type of obligation is distinguished from obligations that arise through contracts or promises in that it is nonvoluntaristic. Associative obligations are obligations, for example, to family members, colleagues, neighbors, and fellow citizens that we have not chosen. They arise directly from the nature and quality of the relationships – from the actions and attitudes of members toward one another (see Scheffler 2001, esp. 61–65). They are constitutive of these actions and attitudes, according to their defenders, and they produce the pleasures of friendship, the love of parents and children for one another, and the pride of patriots. Associative obligations express a notion of equality in this sense: they express reciprocal ties of equal concern between members of a self-identified group. They personally bind each member to every other member of the group, and they do not extend beyond the boundaries of the group (Dworkin 1986, 198).[10]

If we are to understand the benefits and burdens of citizenship in terms of associative obligations, as some communitarians suggest we should, then we must understand how associative obligations could be generated through the social practices, institutions, conventions, and attitudes that constitute political community. We need to understand how political community could be strong enough to support associative obligations, and how the associative obligations of political community could prevail in conflicts with other obligations – of friendship, family, and religious or ethnic community.[11]

The move intended to address these concerns is the assertion that political community cannot be "freestanding." The threat of conflict between competing spheres of obligation is reduced when areas of overlap are cultivated and expanded. As already discussed, both the nationalist and the multiculturalist versions of the communitarian ideal attempt to show that the political relation can be embedded in cultural meanings that are constitutive of individual and collective self-understanding and of mutual commitment. As David Miller describes the conversation about national identity,

> The conversation will usually be about specific issues: which language or languages should be given official status; which version of national history should be taught in schools; what changes, if any should be made to the constitutional arrangements; and so forth. But behind these lie the wider questions: what kind of people are we? What do we believe? How do we want to conduct ourselves in future? (1995, 137)

Crucial to this story is the idea that this enterprise of collective identity formation issues in political obligations that complement and express individual and group self-understandings because the content of associative obligations that ground the benefits and burdens of citizenship is prepolitical. On Taylor's nationalist and collectivist approach, a broader public sphere "enables a society to come to a common mind, without the mediation of the political sphere" (2004, 91; see also Miller 1995, 129). The public sphere is a sphere of social life, cultural values, and conversation. It is constituted through social practice, by common action and its history, what "we" do and have done together. Taylor maintains that when and only when the public sphere is (allegedly) independent of political power it can be normative for power (2004, 91). This relation of normative grounding is coherent because the public sphere that supports and directs political obligations is what those obligations are designed to protect.

The rhetoric of the multiculturalist story is surprisingly similar, even though the political substance of the view is typically, by contrast, quite liberal. Will Kymlicka writes:

> shared values are not sufficient for social unity . . . What more, or what else, is required for social unity? The missing ingredient seems to be the idea of a *shared identity*. A shared conception of

justice throughout a political community does not necessarily generate a shared identity, let alone a shared civic identity that will supersede rival national identities. People decide who they want to share a country with by asking who they identify with, who they feel solidarity with. What holds Americans together, despite their lack of common values, is the fact that they share an identity as Americans. Conversely, what keeps Swedes and Norwegians apart, despite the presence of shared values, is the lack of a shared identity . . . A fundamental challenge facing liberal theorists, therefore, is to identify the sources of unity in a democratic multination state. (1995, 188, 192)

Kymlicka resists nationalist aspirations by cultural minorities for statehood, although he thinks that secession should be a permissible option. His ideal is a form of multination federalism (Kymlicka 2004). He believes that social unity in a multicultural state can be achieved through a collective identification across ethnocultural groups with a thin liberal nationalism. Furthermore, Kymlicka argues, a thin liberal nationalism that emphasizes a nation's common history, language, and political forms should be supplemented by rights of self-government and territorial autonomy for national minorities, provided that the core liberal rights of individual members of national minority groups are guaranteed.

I am not skeptical of the value of these qualified group rights and I am sympathetic to several considerations Kymlicka stresses in their favor – particularly the concern to remediate historical injustice. My point is that a multiculturalist position is weak as an expression of the ideal of inclusion in a liberal democracy. A thin liberal nationalism that includes a shared recognition of the value of cultural self-determination might offer a broad basis for establishing the political loyalties of citizenship – but those loyalties will likely be too thin to support egalitarian norms of distributive justice.

From an ethical perspective that takes associative obligations as its starting point, it would not be surprising nor considered particularly disturbing that people would lack enthusiasm for the idea that they should be concerned to justify their political choices to others with whom they have weak, if any, ties of identity-based loyalty.[12] Nor should we be surprised or disconcerted, from this perspective, to find that without ties of loyalty people would lack motivation to secure for all citizens the basic rights and socioeconomic opportunities that are central to a liberal democracy. The loyalties on which identity is built fit uncomfortably with the egalitarian norms of distributive justice that an ideal of inclusive public justification would favor. As Walzer stresses, loyalties weaken as they are stretched. Both the nationalist and multiculturalist versions of the communitarian story are more compelling when the socioeconomic dimension of political justice is weak. In that event, the rights of the underprivileged can more plausibly be understood as rights of autonomy and self-representation or, alternately, as rights to secede.

Understanding politics as a terrain carved by allegiances of loyalty and contested by individuals and groups seeking to promote their differing interests gathers support, more generally, from political philosophies that deemphasize our positive obligations to other persons, even within identity groups. As we have seen, libertarians stress the negative nature of our duties to other people: we have duties not to violate their rights, but no positive duties to promote their good. A common thread in libertarian and some communitarian rejections of political liberalism could be this: persons who fundamentally disagree over morality, religion, and the meaning of life, or who do not freely choose to pursue joint projects that involve egalitarian commitments, should not have to reach political agreement to treat one another as equals, if that means to view one another as having a substantive claim on real opportunities, wealth, and other resources generated collectively through social cooperation. Rawls's criterion of strong reciprocity in the division of these goods is too demanding under conditions of liberty and difference.

Rawls cautions us that this ethical position has disastrous consequences for democracy. Socioeconomic inequality and the social alienation that accompanies it encourage a skeptical, even cynical, conception of politics. Politics as a matter of antagonistic if not outwardly hostile bargaining between conflicting interest groups is counter to the ideal of public reason, which insists that basic questions of justice should be resolved on the basis of principles that could secure reasonable agreement among all citizens, considered as equals. Unfortunately, a skeptical, even cynical, conception of politics is now widely accepted. Leveraging one's advantage is perceived to be legitimate and politically savvy. The result is an emphasis on private gain and the erosion of what we might think of as the public face of democracy – the protection of civil rights, access to education, free speech, and meaningful opportunities to participate in politics (see Patterson 2011).

Of course, communitarian skepticism about a just requirement of public justification – about the need to justify political institutions and policies outside of one's own group – can be encouraged by intractable disagreements between different individuals and groups about matters of morality and religion. When people disagree deeply about religion, morality, and other matters of personal value, this might aggravate their sense of alienation from one another. But this disagreement is not the deepest source of alienation nor is it an insurmountable obstacle to greater justice. Too often, in fact, it is exploited by powerful elites as a means of weakening a potential coalition of resistance by disadvantaged groups. A socioeconomically just democracy, by contrast, can support a broad conception of toleration. The retreat of some cultural-religious groups from public political life, for example, is tolerable and not destabilizing to just institutions (see Kelly and McPherson 2001). Justice might also support suitably qualified group rights. Territorial autonomy for national minorities whose inclusion was the result of conquest, for instance, might sometimes be required by justice, provided that their "autonomy" is not a form of political exclusion.

Constraining socioeconomic inequality is an essential aspect of a just scheme of social cooperation and a necessary basis for securing a mutual commitment to the rights, liberties, and opportunities that give democracy its substance and meaning. Were social cooperation stable enough to secure our equal basic rights, liberties, and fair opportunities, social alienation in its milder as well as its more severe forms would be greatly diminished. People might be prepared to accept some measure of socioeconomic inequality, provided that those who are willing to work could expect something like a decent middle-class wage. Stabilizing our democracy in this way would also put us in a better position to accept the social disunity produced by value pluralism and cultural differences. We might accept that a plurality of moral, religious, and philosophical worldviews is not an indicator of injustice or the limits of our mutual obligations, and it need not threaten the core values of a compelling vision of democratic justice.

If democratic rights and liberties are important to us, we should take care not to distract attention from the seriously unequal and alienating division of wealth that is the deeper threat to democracy. Rawls's concern to constrain inequality and to promote fair opportunity may be the best hope for achieving a stable social commitment to the basic rights, liberties, and opportunities that are the common currency of a reasonably just democratic society.

# Notes

For valuable comments and suggestions, I am indebted to Lionel McPherson, Jon Mandle, David Reidy, participants at a conference on the philosophy of John Rawls at the College of New Jersey (2010) and colleagues at the Center for Ethics and Global Politics at Libera Università Internazionale degli Studi Sociali (LUISS), Rome.

1   Kymlicka stresses the distinction between societal cultures and ethnic groups.
2   See Stiglitz 2012. Stiglitz predicts that the current income inequality will continue to grow.
3   According to the US Census Bureau, in 2011, the top 20% of the working population earned almost 50% of the nation's income, and the top 5% alone earned over 20%. This represents a substantial increase in the earning power of these segments of the population compared with what it was in 1973. The bottom 20% of American wage earners, by contrast, earned less than 4% of the aggregate income in 2011 – a small and decreasing portion of the pie. They earned about about 5.5% in 1973. In 2011 the official poverty rate was 15% compared with 11% in 1974. See http://www.census.gov/prod.2012pubs/p60-243.pdf (accessed August 2013).
4   According to analysis by sociologist Edward Wolff (2012), the top 20% of the population possesses 85% of the nation's wealth, and this group has absorbed the vast majority of new wealth generated by the US economy in the last three decades.
5   According to the Economic Policy Institute, the wealthiest 1% is 288 times wealthier than the median in the US, a gap that has more than doubled since the 1960s. See http://stateofworkingamerica.org/chart/swa-wealth-figure-6c-ratio-top-1-wealth/ (accessed June 2013).
6   For a compelling analysis of the criminal justice system as a system of racialized social control, see Alexander 2010.
7   For instance, at Adlai Stevenson High School in the Bronx, blacks and Hispanics made up 97% of the student body; less than 1% were white (Kozol 2005, 41–42).
8   $11,700 was spent per child in New York City in 2005, versus $22,000 in the wealthy suburban district of Manhasset, Long Island; the median teachers salaries were $53,000 and $87,000 respectively. Further, Kozol points out that affluent parents in New York City often "pay surprisingly large sums of money to enroll their youngsters, beginning at the age of two or three, in extraordinary early-education programs that give them social competence and rudimentary pedagogic skills unknown to children of the same age in the city's poorer neighborhoods" (2005, 46).
9   Kozol writes that in the United States from 1993 to 2002, "the number of high schools graduating less than half the ninth-grade class in four years has increased by 75 percent. In the . . . districts in New York State where white children make up the majority, nearly 80 percent of students graduate from high school in four years. In the . . . districts where black and Hispanic students make up the majority, only 40 percent do so" (2005, 54).
10  Equality of concern implies, Dworkin argues, that associative obligations arise in "communities of principle" – communities in which all members receive equal treatment, according to common principles. He believes that the legitimacy of government reflects and depends on the associative obligations of citizenship, and that if the relationship of citizenship lacks reciprocity, the coercive power of the state cannot be legitimized. I note that Dworkin's use of the notion of an associative obligation lacks the cultural emphasis characteristic of communitarian thought. He believes associative obligations can be grounded solely in the political relationship. In this sense, he is more accurately described as a liberal than a communitarian.
11  Dworkin argues that when the substantive requirements of institutional justice are not met, the political obligations of citizenship are difficult to reconcile with competing associative obligations – of family, for example, or community. Perhaps they cannot be reconciled at all and the lives of all individuals in an unjust society will inevitably be ethically impoverished (Dworkin 2000, 236).

12 To be clear, Kymlicka distances himself from the communitarian position that the scope of political obligation arises and is limited by ties of identity-based loyalty arising from a shared "way of life" or cultural tradition. He affirms multiculturalist ties of loyalty. See Kymlicka 2002, 257–261.

# Works by Rawls, with Abbreviations

*Justice as Fairness: A Restatement* (*JF*), ed. Erin Kelly. Cambridge, MA: Harvard University Press, 2001.
*Political Liberalism* (*PL*), expanded edn. New York: Columbia University Press, 2005.
*A Theory of Justice* (*TJ*), rev. edn. Cambridge, MA: Harvard University Press, 1999.

# Other References

Alexander, Michelle (2010) *The New Jim Crow: Mass Incarceration in the Age of Colorblindness*. New York: New Press.

Calhoun, Craig (2007) *Nations Matter: Culture, History, and the Cosmopolitan Dream*. New York: Routledge.

Dworkin, Ronald (1986) *Law's Empire*. Cambridge, MA: Harvard University Press.

Dworkin, Ronald (2000) *Sovereign Virtue: The Theory and Practice of Equality*. Cambridge, MA: Harvard University Press.

Kelly, Erin and McPherson, Lionel (2001) "On Tolerating the Unreasonable." *Journal of Political Philosophy* 9: 38–55.

Kozol, Jonathan (2005) "Still Separate, Still Unequal: America's Educational Apartheid." *Harper's Magazine*, Sept. 1.

Kymlicka, Will (1995) *Multicultural Citizenship: A Liberal Theory of Minority Rights*. Oxford: Clarendon Press.

Kymlicka, Will (2002) *Contemporary Political Philosophy: An Introduction*. Oxford: Oxford University Press.

Kymlicka, Will (2004) "Justice and Security in the Accommodation of Minority Nationalism." In Alain Dieckhoff (ed.), *The Politics of Belonging: Nationalism, Liberalism, and Pluralism*. Lanham, MD: Lexington Books.

MacIntyre, Alasdair (1984) *After Virtue: A Study in Moral Theory*. Notre Dame: University of Notre Dame Press.

McPherson, Lionel (2007) "The Hip Hop Generation in Decline." *Guardian*, Nov. 15. At http://www.guardian.co.uk/commentisfree/2007/nov/15/thehiphopgenerationindecline (accessed May 2013).

Miller, David (1995) *On Nationality*. Oxford: Oxford University Press.

Patterson, Orlando (1991) *Freedom*, vol. 1: *Freedom in the Making of Western Culture*. New York: Basic Books.

Patterson, Orlando (1999) "Liberty against the Democratic State: On the Historical and Contemporary Sources of American Distrust." In Mark Warren (ed.), *Democracy and Trust* (151–207). Cambridge: Cambridge University Press.

Patterson, Orlando (2009) "Equality." *Democracy: A Journal of Ideas* 11 (Winter).

Patterson, Orlando (2011) "Freedom and 9/11." *Democracy: A Journal of Ideas* 22 (Fall).

Pew (2007) "American Families' Ability to Climb the Economic Ladder Still Depends on Parents' Income." Press release, Nov. 13. At http://www.pewtrusts.org/news_room_detail.aspx?id=31110 (accessed May 2013).

Sandel, Michael J. (1982) *Liberalism and the Limits of Justice*. Cambridge: Cambridge University Press.

Scheffler, Samuel (2001) "Families, Nations, and Strangers." In Scheffler, *Boundaries and Allegiances: Problems of Justice and Responsibility in Liberal Thought*. Oxford: Oxford University Press.

Stiglitz, Joseph (2012) *The Price of Inequality: How Today's Divided Society Endangers our Future*. New York: Norton.

Taylor, Charles (2004) *Modern Social Imaginaries*. Durham, NC: Duke University Press.

Tully, James (1995) *Strange Multiplicity: Constitutionalism in an Age of Diversity*. Cambridge: Cambridge University Press.

Walzer, Michael (1996) "Spheres of Affection." In Martha C. Nussbaum, *For Love of Country*, ed. Joshua Cohen. Boston: Beacon Press.

Wolff, Edward N. (2012) "The Asset Price Meltdown and the Wealth of the Middle Class." At http://www.nber.org/papers/w18559 (accessed June 2013).

Young, Iris Marion (2000) *Inclusion and Democracy*. Oxford: Oxford University Press, 2000.

# Part V

# Extending Political Liberalism:
# International Relations

# 19

# The Law of Peoples

## HUW LLOYD WILLIAMS

Amartya Sen's recent critique provides a vivid illustration of a common disregard for the writings of John Rawls on the subject of international justice – in particular as they are presented in his most mature work, *The Law of Peoples*. One need only read a few pages into Sen's *The Idea of Justice* (2009) to gauge the latter's views: *LP* is an "emaciated" addition to Rawls's "justice as fairness"; the principles of international justice he presents are barely worthy of the name, applying as they do only to "matters of civility and humanity . . . very limited features of justice"; in fact, Sen tells us that Rawls "reduces many of the most relevant issues of justice into empty . . . rhetoric," presenting us with an uninspiring "minimal humanitarianism" (2009, 26).

Sen's sometimes pithy remarks are representative of an enduring response to *LP* in the fields of Political Theory and International Relations (IR), especially among cosmopolitan thinkers such as he. Taken together, their critique suggests it is not a book that merits much consideration: at best a flawed text, at worst an aberration in the oeuvre of Rawls to be ignored by Rawlsians and IR scholars alike. It seems the most useful purpose it serves, as evidenced in Sen's book, is to compound more general criticisms of Rawls's political theory and to persuade us that we must dispense with some of his most fundamental but ultimately limited ideas. This prevailing atmosphere of skepticism may in part be attributed to the desire of some contemporary Anglo-American philosophers to "go beyond" Rawls. In such a context it was perhaps inevitable that the perceived shortcomings of *LP* would be grist to the mill of those such as Sen who contend we should supersede Rawls's social contract theory.

This rather unsympathetic response from those more generally aligned with Rawls's philosophy has hardly paved the way for the text in the study of International Relations. Why, after all, should realist and more hard-nosed pluralist thinkers deploy their energies in engaging critically with *LP* if would-be advocates see little merit in the work? The ease with which it has been disregarded is reflected by how rare serious attempts are to engage critically with *LP* from the more traditional voices in the discipline. Given the wide-ranging and rather

*A Companion to Rawls*, First Edition. Edited by Jon Mandle and David A. Reidy.
© 2014 John Wiley & Sons, Inc. Published 2016 by John Wiley & Sons, Inc.

thorough nature of the cosmopolitan critique, it seems this was never a requirement (although Robert Jackson (2005) is one who at least deemed *LP* worthy of a response).

This rather stylized sketch of the "state of the art," adequate perhaps as a snapshot of the prevailing view in the academy, is mercifully misleading with regard to the debates of those who have engaged with *LP* on its own terms. Many such authors may have taken a critical view, but as the condemnation diminishes a great deal of lively debate has emerged, which points to the interest and potential contribution of *LP* to Rawlsian scholarship, as well as the study of world politics.

This chapter is a brief attempt to set out some of the most promising avenues of research. In particular, I will focus on how regarding *LP* as a key stage in the development of Rawls's thought might enrich Rawlsian scholarship and our understanding of his work. As a major, systematic thinker in political philosophy, it was to be expected that he would turn his attention to the international in order to complete his political theory. Regarded in this manner – and rather than as an afterthought addressed to his radical critics – *LP* can be seen to shed light on the other stages of his thinking, as well as answering some key questions in international theory. Further to suggesting the importance of this work in the broader context of his thought, I will engage with specific elements of world politics where Rawls's ideas provide promising alternatives – specifically on the question of the relations between liberal and nonliberal peoples. In conclusion I will look at how his realistic utopianism represents a form of theorizing that could constitute a genuine challenge to more traditional forms of thinking in IR. Before engaging in these arguments, however, I will set out some of the key ideas of Rawls's international theory through mapping the development of his thought, and indicate how critiques such as Sen's initially represented the predominant response.

## A Very Brief Intellectual History

Rawls first set out his perspective on international politics in his seminal work *A Theory of Justice*. Rather than a thoroughgoing international theory, this is a brief sketch of the law of nations, invoked as a means to discuss political duty and civil disobedience in the context of war. In so doing he describes principles of international justice, derived by using the same device he deploys for his "domestic" theory of justice. In this iteration, however, it is the representatives of states rather than individuals *qua* individuals behind the veil of ignorance, deciding on the appropriate principles for relations between states (*just* states, in the revised edition of *TJ*). They are denied knowledge of certain characteristics of their state that may bias their reasoning, and so the international original position represents fair conditions for specifying the basic terms of cooperation among states – or "the fundamental principles to adjudicate conflicting claims among states" (*TJ*, 331).

These principles are, of course, very different from those agreed upon within the domestic context, embodying the prevailing ideals of nonintervention and equality between states, as well as the principle that treaties and agreements are to be fully honored. Other essential principles are those to be applied to war, *jus ad bellum* and *jus in bello*. In this early formulation, however, there is no suggestion that principles of economic justice would have a role to play. In short, there is no attempt by Rawls to argue that the types of principles of justice applicable within a liberal democratic society might be writ large within a highly connected global society.

This rather brief sketch would represent the blueprint for Rawls's subsequent treatment of the subject – a treatment that from the very beginning put him on a collision course with many inspired by his work. In fact, the crux of what was to become the most prevalent response to his international theory was set out in Brian Barry's reply to *TJ* (Barry 1973, 129–132). Here he suggests that the stipulations of the original position are misconceived: rather than being applicable to discrete nation-states, it should rather be a universal original position that accounts for all humans. If a key intuition is that justice should address the contingencies that affect individuals' life chances, then given the extreme differences in the opportunities afforded in different countries, the most influential contingency to be mitigated should be the birthplace of the individual. The logical conclusion is that distributive justice should be global in scope, addressing the discrepancies between individuals not only within societies, but across societies.

This argument, suggested only briefly by Barry, was later taken up by Charles Beitz in his work on *Political Theory and International Relations* (1999, first published in 1979), which sought to emphasize the interdependence of global society and the necessity of thinking in terms of "global justice." Rejecting the prevailing traditions of IR theory, Beitz argues in effect that individual rights supersede sovereignty as the organizing principle for international politics. In setting out his cosmopolitan vision, Beitz deploys the idea of a global original position, with the attendant argument that those behind the veil of ignorance would demand that Rawls's two principles of justice, in theory, be applicable to all. This type of argument was to be taken up with great force a decade later by Rawls's former student Thomas Pogge, in his work *Realizing Rawls* (1989).

The stage was set, therefore, for Rawls's response to these cosmopolitan recapitulations of his theory. In a lecture published in 1993, he set out his "The Law of Peoples," which rejected their approach and remained faithful in the most basic sense to the vision he outlined in *TJ*. He did, of course, flesh out his ideal, but began on the same basic premise that the first original position in the global context would see the representatives of nation-states come together to discuss principles of international justice. As we will see, in the same ways as his original principles of justice articulate for Rawls the moral ideals and principles that provide the best support for liberal democratic institutions and practices, so too his approach to international politics seeks to articulate the ideals and principles that underlie progressively emergent international norms and practices – such as an international order organized around autonomous political communities. However, as much as his thinking might be described as a posteriori in this sense, his ideal theorizing generates certain concepts and injunctions that set out clear normative aims and aspirations. Two such developments in Rawls's position by 1993 (which would remain central to the completed *The Law of Peoples* in 1999) are especially noteworthy.

The first of these is the deployment of the term "peoples" which represents more than simply a semantic adjustment. Rather, this moniker for nation-states is symbolic of the normative approach that he takes: peoples represent a different type of entity to states, traditionally conceived. They embody collective moral agents, manifesting the emergent norms in international relations in the twentieth century – and providing an ideal type to aspire to. Rather than being able to declare war for their own self-interested, rational purposes, or treating their citizens with impunity, peoples are conceived as moral entities who recognize human rights, and cooperate on the basis of reciprocity and reasonableness in the name of the twin aims of the Society of Peoples: peace and justice. These aspirations are reflected in the seven principles they agree upon as normative guidelines for their cooperation, which not only embody the traditional ideas identified in *TJ*, but also identify a duty to uphold human rights. Although not listed in the initial charter at this stage, Rawls also identifies a duty of assistance to societies burdened by unfavorable conditions – but as will be discussed, he crucially stops short of advocating an ongoing distributive principle to address their difficulties.

Another key development in the 1993 article is Rawls's treatment of nonliberal, or what he calls "hierarchical" societies. These are societies that do not hold to a liberal political conception of justice. However, they are peaceful and subscribe to political principles that, although not impartial with regard to conceptions of the good, are sufficiently coherent and respectful of basic human rights that liberal societies can tolerate them and treat them as equals. Rawls's method is to envisage a first original position between the representatives of *liberal* peoples, where they agree upon the initial principles as normative benchmarks for their reciprocal relations. However, Rawls reasons that for them to represent a truly *liberal* set of values, these principles must be such that other reasonable, *nonliberal* societies can agree to and acknowledge them as representing their own interests. This would be proof of the impartiality required of a liberal political theory. Moreover, should others not advocate these principles they would fail to represent a sufficiently stable basis for an extended Society of Peoples seeking continually to increase its family of well-ordered societies. As with his domestic principles of justice, Rawls desires more than simply a modus vivendi between competing moral agents. Rather, he wishes for an overlapping consensus on principles that various reasonable peoples deem to represent their and others' interests fairly. For these reasons, a second original position including hierarchical peoples is convened to reflect on the principles agreed to by liberal peoples.

Rawls's second exposition of his international theory was greeted largely with disappointment. Those who responded, such as Pogge (1994), were mostly of cosmopolitan persuasion, and hoped that Rawls would reconsider his position in line with their aspirations. Kok-Chor Tan (2000) provides the most comprehensive and thoughtful reply, with the virtue that he tries to rationalize Rawls's position as a development in his thought from *TJ* to *Political Liberalism*. He characterizes Rawls's law of peoples as neutral, political liberalism writ large (however badly misconceived) against the more comprehensive liberalism of cosmopolitans such as himself. Rawls is guilty, it seems, of two particularly grievous errors: first the apparent indifference in the face of nonliberal societies' compromising of liberal individual rights, and second – even accepting his ideal of discrete peoples – his apparent disregard of the arguments in favor of far-reaching measures pursuing economic global justice.

Rawls's third and final rendition of his international theory was, in a sense, the last chance to redeem himself in the eyes of his admirers. If the 1993 "The Law of Peoples" was greeted with disappointment, then dismay seems to be the most appropriate word to describe the cosmopolitan response to his definitive monograph. Rawls's method essentially remained the same, and the full-length version presented largely similar principles, albeit with a far more lengthy treatment of the core issues and the formal addition of the duty of assistance as the eighth principle included in the charter. He elaborates extensively on this idea in an attempt to address previous reservations about his silence on the issue of material inequality. However, as the raft of critical articles would testify, Rawls was unable to convince his doubters either in regard to his rationale for tolerating nonliberal societies or to his duty of assistance, which was described by Pogge as "libertarian law-making" (2001, 250). In the words of Tan: "Rawls's hesitation to extend his principle of distributive justice to the global context in his earlier writings was largely seen as an oversight that is in principle remediable. It is thus disappointing that in his articulation of a law of peoples, Rawls affirms his rejection of an egalitarian international theory" (Tan 2001, 495).

How could a thinker, so original and radical in his demands for the basic liberties and egalitarianism within the nation-state, deem claims for individual liberal rights and greater material equality to be beyond the scope of principles of global justice? This was the great puzzle for the cosmopolitans who dominated the early responses to *LP*. The tone of their writings suggests that the most favored explanation was that Rawls simply misunderstood the implications of his own thought – that he had taken a wrong turn in advocating the status quo of a society of states, rather than a more radical cosmopolitan perspective more attuned to his original philosophical insights, and that, at worst, he was guilty of philosophical incoherence. No self-respecting liberal could tolerate nondemocratic societies or vast inequalities between states. Such was the tenor of the overwhelming number of initial responses to *LP*, authored by the likes of Beitz (2000), Buchanan (2000), Caney (2002) and Pogge, which to a great extent has come to define the popular response to the book. Rawls's greatest mistake, it might be suggested, is that he took a different view of the issues to these thinkers.

However, it is not an overly onerous task to construct an account of his international theory that reveals its rationale and provides the basis for engaging constructively with some of its core ideas. Crucial to this is beginning at the beginning, with an acknowledgment of the method deployed by Rawls. In his political theory, he seeks a reflective equilibrium on the principles of justice he articulates – a state of affairs where these principles are attuned to our considered judgments. In this sense Rawls believes any moral theory must begin with, or acknowledge, our position in the world. Finding such an equilibrium should allow us to articulate, reflect upon, and adjust either our judgments or our principles, or both, so that we may settle upon ideals that can help guide and regulate our behavior. This approach, appropriate to all moral theory, is clearly context dependent in that the emergent principles will depend to a large extent on the cumulative considered judgments in the relevant moral realm. In the liberal democratic state we should look to our public political culture, and analogously, in trying to articulate principles of justice appropriate to world politics, we should look to the international public political culture.

It seems these steps are sometimes lost sight of in the criticisms of Rawls, but as the likes of Wenar (2006, 102) and Lehning have argued (2009, 183), viewed from this perspective the principles Rawls articulates are entirely consistent with his philosophical thinking, taken as they are from "familiar and largely traditional principles . . . from the history and usages of international law and practice" (*LP*, 57). To engage in constructing a cosmopolitan theory such as those of Beitz and Pogge would be to leave aside this method and seek instead more utopian principles that are disconnected from the reality of how international politics is understood and practiced. Rawls's aim is rather to reconcile ourselves to our political and social condition while constructing principles that push the limits of practical political possibility (*LP*, 11).

Thankfully, there are many thinkers – those perhaps not disaffected by the development of Rawls's thought or preoccupied with superseding it – who have taken *LP* on its merits and have either taken for granted the fundamental consistency of Rawls's position or disregarded these more fundamental questions about his approach, thus engaging with *LP* on its own terms. The result has been a gradual proliferation of secondary literature that takes his work in interesting directions, revealing the potential of some of his key ideas – both for Rawlsian scholarship and thinking about world politics.

## *The Law of Peoples* in the Greater Scheme of Rawls's Work

Given that *LP* has been characterized as an unwelcome departure from his earlier publications, it is unsurprising that little consideration has been given to how it contributes to Rawls's body of work, and how we might reconsider his political philosophy in light of the monograph. This reluctance to consider *LP* as the completion of Rawls's political theory undermines both its value and status, and as more recent contributions by Percy Lehning (2009), and particularly Catherine Audard (2007), have demonstrated, denies us an additional and insightful layer of understanding in our appreciation of Rawls's oeuvre.

Lehning points out that Rawls recognized the fact that *TJ*, in dealing with a self-contained society, placed certain limits on his project – and thus deferred a methodical treatment of international politics. In a sense, Rawls can be seen to use a lexical ordering in his own theorizing, deciding that "in justice as fairness the question of justice between peoples is postponed until we have an account of political justice for a well-ordered democratic society" (*JF*, 13). Lehning thus views *LP* as completing the "justice as fairness" jigsaw. He claims it "fully extends [the] theory of justice to the international domain. With this study we have arrived at the third phase of Rawls's development of his theory of justice . . . [he] has constructed the final, 'missing' part" (2009, 174).

Audard's critical engagement with Rawls goes further in both accepting *LP* as a constitutive part of his theory of justice, and enrolling it to further prove her broader critical thesis: that there is an inherent, perhaps incurable tension between the primacy of moral individualism in his earlier work and the *social holism* – manifest in the constitutive importance assigned to social structures – he develops in his later work. Such arguments are important and to be further discussed, but initially what is most significant is the sense in which Audard chooses to use her interpretation of *LP* to buttress her argument, and add another level of complexity to her assessment of Rawls's position. It is thus an exemplar of the broader point here, which suggests that *LP* should be further deployed in analyses of Rawls's work, as part of a coherent whole. As Audard herself makes the point, *LP* is valuable "as an element of internal exegesis of Rawls's whole project" (2007, 230).

Audard's key argument is that what she describes as Rawls's holistic conception of justice leaves in jeopardy his emphasis upon moral individualism, to the extent that it may cause him to abandon it entirely. She implies it is by considering *LP* alongside his earlier work on political liberalism that she can construct her argument with the greatest authority. This is because the most explicit manifestation of Rawls's social holism is that peoples rather than persons are regarded as the primary referent with regard to international justice – it is the political communities that Rawls views as ensuring the rights and liberties of individuals that take moral precedence. She argues the attendant conception of the individual, not first and foremost as "person" but rather as "citizen," is indicative of the development in Rawls's thinking between *TJ* and *PL*, whereby a political conception of the person, constituted through their status as members of a political community, becomes his "individualism" of choice. As such, the nation-state, or in the lexicon of *LP*, a people, becomes constitutive of and crucial to the individual as a subject of justice. Just how important Rawls regards the political community, or put another way, just how communitarian his views are, only becomes entirely evident in light of his international theory.

The emphasis on peoples and the systemic features that facilitate the functioning of their institutions leads to Rawls advancing their ongoing integrity, even when they come into conflict with his individualism. This is manifest in the narrow set of human rights he identifies, which constitute a considerable compromise on the liberal rights of his domestic principles. Moreover, agreement on these norms cannot be arrived at purely through liberal justifications. If nonliberal peoples are to be respected as equals and dealt with on a reciprocal basis, these rights must be disconnected from liberalism and justifiable from the perspective of various political conceptions of justice. Audard feels that Rawls's social holism "may have gone too far" in this regard, to the extent that it is "upsetting and does not sit easily with his main thesis of the priority of justice and the inviolability of persons" (2007, 258). Most significantly, we cannot appreciate the nature or roots of this tension evident in *LP* without reference to the earlier development in Rawls's thought, while without *LP* we cannot appreciate the full "communitarian" implications of the development in his domestic political theory. Only by incorporating *LP* into the analysis can we grasp the wider picture.

A further point – on what may first appear to be a tangential theme – is the extent to which Immanuel Kant "is a source of inspiration" for Rawls (Lehning 2009, 174). The debt he owes to the Enlightenment philosopher is emphasized repeatedly in *LP*, and is perhaps at its most prominent in Rawls's rejection of the idea of a world state (*LP*, 36). The relationship between *LP* and "Perpetual Peace," or the extent to which they can be compared, has been disappointingly understudied. As Bernstein's article demonstrates (2009), this is somewhat surprising given the interesting and revealing discussion it can stimulate with regard to both texts. In the context of the current discussion, this omission bears further reflection.

"Perpetual Peace" is a text given a great deal of scholarly attention by political philosophers and IR theorists alike. This is not only because of the author's status, the myriad ideas of great importance it presents, and the extent to which it has inspired thinking in the realm of IR. It is also because it is generally regarded as a key part of Kant's political theory (although some Kantian scholars challenge the view that it is a major work and point instead to the primacy of *The Doctrine of Right*). Moreover, from the perspective of Kant's political theory, perpetual peace, in the most basic sense, is fundamental to the realization of individual right. The latter cannot be secured in a world of conflict and war. A similarly significant point can be made with regard to *LP*. The rights of individual citizens in liberal and decent societies, and the social institutions that underpin these rights, will always be subject to threat in an unjust, unstable and violent world. This is illustrated, for example, in the case of conscription in the face of an overwhelming threat to a people's way of life. As Audard recognizes, "Liberal democratic societies cannot survive in isolation, sheltered from the global threats of terror, famines and widespread injustices. They live in a dangerous and violent world, and have to protect themselves" (2007, 233). In the same way as the consolidation of international right requires perpetual peace, so the just and decent institutions of peoples and the principles they embody require international principles that can guide them in securing a peaceful world.

This is an obvious illustration of the claim that *LP* represents the final, missing part of Rawls's theory of justice. Furthermore, there are examples of ideas and motifs developed in this work that might shed new light or provide new perspectives on Rawls's understanding of politics more generally – the concepts of "proper patriotism" and "the statesman" being two of the more obvious candidates for consideration. However, given the less than favorable reception of the book, there is a tendency even among some Rawlsian scholars to disregard it as a possible source of insight and new material. Were *LP* to be more widely recognized as being as important to Rawls's oeuvre as (generally speaking) "Perpetual Peace" is to Kant's political theory, not only could it lead to more insightful work following Bernstein's lead; it would also endow *LP* with its rightful status, further encouraging its closer study both in relation to Rawls's political theory and international politics more broadly.

## *LP* and World Politics

If *LP* is to be recognized as a work of status and significance, it follows that some of its key ideas should be considered seriously with regard to the here and now of international politics – especially so given Rawls's key aim of setting out "the ideals and principles of the *foreign policy* of a reasonably just *liberal* people" (*LP*, 10, emphasis in original). Moreover, an inherent aspect of the liberal conception of justice is that it provides principles appropriate for those societies that are decent and reasonable. They should therefore be capacious and impartial enough to embody suitable foreign policy goals for *all* well-ordered societies.

Despite the cynicism of some commentators, others have accepted Rawls's vision of international politics on its own terms – at least to the extent that it has allowed them to discuss and analyze some of his ideas in a productive manner and to speculate as to what they might bring to our understanding of various aspects of world politics. There were early examples of such writings (Brown 2002; Wenar 2001), but somewhat of a sea change was signaled with the publication of Rex Martin and David Reidy's volume (2006), which included a series of prominent and thoughtful contributions. It was an important demonstration that *LP* is a serious work with much to offer. More recent publications on a range of issues suggest the book is increasingly recognized as one of Rawls's key texts, exemplified by critical discussions of *LP* with regard to the World Trade Organization (Maffettone 2009), human security (Agafonow 2011) and climate change (Gardiner 2011). I will focus here, however, on two themes of world politics that are directly linked to the two key strands of the cosmopolitan critique: the supposedly excessive toleration of nonliberal societies, and the lack of substantial measures to address global poverty. This is in part because a reposte to these criticisms does much to blunt this critique and thereby assert the relevance of *LP*, but more importantly because Rawls has something original and thought-provoking to say on both matters.

A great deal has been written on how misconceived the omission of a global distributive principle is on Rawls's part. There is no need to recapitulate here the many versions of this argument, but the most forceful of these is the claim that even accepting Rawls's social holism and the framework of a society of peoples, there should still by his own standards be an international distributive principle, given the need to mitigate the influence of economic inequalities on weak states' development.[1] Rawlsians such as Freeman (2007) have pointed out that the circumstances of justice in the global arena are different, and that the level of social cooperation for mutual advantage of a nation-state does not exist at the global level. Lehning (2009, 183–184) asserts this point with reference to Rawls's philosophical method and the requirements of reflective equilibrium. In essence, given the less pronounced cooperation between states there is no common considered judgment in favor of such a far-reaching measure, which would effectively constitute a global taxation regime.

These arguments are certainly relevant, but there are other interesting reasons for Rawls's position – which also explain the kind of approach he *does* prescribe as part of an apparently toothless duty of assistance. A key premise for Rawls is that the transfer of wealth will do very little in itself for burdened societies, as what characterizes these societies is the lack of institutional capability to make use of their resources. The effective solution for these societies is not, as the cosmopolitans have tended to argue, to focus first on the redistribution of wealth, or even the reform of the global economy, but to begin with the importance of domestic institutional reform. It is interesting but predictable – in view of his social holism – that Rawls should take such an "institutional" perspective on development; if one looks at Rawls's oeuvre as a whole (the approach argued for here), then one can explain his focus on institutions not only as a critique of the cosmopolitans and rejection of redistribution, but first and foremost as a natural extension into his international theory of the fundamental importance assigned to social structures. Risse (2005) has pointed out that this perspective is actually more in keeping with recent trends within the field of development, where the mantra of "institutions matter" has dominated for some time – to the detriment of other developmental narratives.

It must also be appreciated that whereas these ideas have been promoted as the most effective means to economic prosperity in the field of development, Rawls has a different, more fundamental aim in mind. He is not interested in economic development per se, and the utility of institutions for achieving growth. Instead, he is concerned with the development of these institutions as the structural foundation for well-ordered, decent or liberal societies. The international minimum he prescribes as the target, or cut-off point for assistance, is not to be measured in terms of *economic* development, but rather by the extent to which societies are able to protect basic rights. The accumulation of wealth is of instrumental importance only, and is irrelevant to questions of international justice beyond the point that there are enough financial resources to ensure a sustainable basis for previously burdened societies. Naturally, ensuring such a basis may itself entail far-reaching economic policies, but it should be remembered that its ultimate aim is the provision of worthwhile lives and not increases in GDP.

Thus assistance is not to be defined in the first place by the aim of prosperity, but rather the building and development of decent or liberal institutions, which would encourage the kind of policy-making that addresses extreme injustice. Moving away from a focus on distributive measures can be seen in one sense as an antidote to cosmopolitan thinking, but as I have argued elsewhere (Williams 2011), it is not to say that the duty of assistance is incompatible with some of the policies they advise. Insofar as they are compatible with the idea that there is a cut-off point, then the entire range of measures applicable for increasing institutional capability should be administered as a matter of justice – including financial redistribution.

In this sense Rawls's approach also implies a more open-ended outlook on the question of development than typically seen in the differing literatures on the subject. One reading of the duty of assistance is to regard it as eschewing a one-size-fits-all model (the

Washington Consensus being an obvious example), instead taking societies as they are, appreciating their particular culture, structures and contemporary problems, thereby prescribing more appropriate means for each case. This moves us away from a tendency to focus on some policies rather than others as the silver bullet. Ideas about the remedies for global poverty tend to become polarized between, for example, those who regard global structural change as the defining factor, and explanatory nationalists who point to indigenous institutional weakness or political culture as the root of the problem – with a seemingly limited middle ground.

Rawls has been accused of the latter approach, but a more careful, sympathetic assessment reveals a perspective that goes beyond these ideological fissures and acknowledges a potentially broad range of obstacles to the freedom of peoples. In setting an international minimum, Rawls implies a duty of justice on behalf of the Society of Peoples to address all those relevant factors that can be construed as affecting the capability of burdened societies to meet this minimum. These can range over the type of broad structural policies typically associated with arguments for fair trade (presented by economists such as Joseph Stiglitz) to the sometimes more inscrutable factors identified in the state-building literature such as the need for "cultural change." Typically these are differing types of arguments made by analysts concerned with particular elements of development, very often ideologically opposed to each other. A Rawlsian framework, however, can be seen to gravitate away from such tendencies by focusing first on the society in question, rather than prescribing a particular policy approach. We are to look first to the circumstances of their institutional and structural weaknesses – whether its causes are located primarily in global economic structures, material and technological disadvantages, geographical circumstances, or cultural practices of a burdened society (or most likely a combination of these and other factors). As such, the attendant policies of the duty of assistance can be regarded as a potentially broad range of actions to be taken on the basis of the particular requirements of the society in question. These might include favorable adjustments of trade agreements, investment in infrastructure, through to micro-level policies designed to try and promote social capital at a community level.[2]

A further distinguishing aspect of Rawls's duty of assistance is the principle of toleration that remains at its core, signified by the injunction to avoid paternalism in relation to the affected burdened societies. Maintaining such a principle suggests that policies would have to be agreed upon through some form of dialogue, wherein the burdened society in question is be treated in the spirit of equality and reciprocity. Exactly what Rawls has in mind in practice is less than obvious, but beginning on this premise represents an important commitment that raises issues about the dynamic in the relationship between donor and recipient.

However, this commitment represents somewhat of a conceptual problem from the perspective of Rawls's theory. Burdened societies are excluded from participating in the original position, implying that they are not in fact equals, which in turn raises fundamental questions about the status of the duty of assistance. It is difficult to see at first glance why burdened societies should be treated in the spirit of equality, or how this principle can be conceived as a strong duty of justice rather than a weaker, humanitarian duty, when duties of justice are grounded in the equality of agents cooperating for mutual advantage. In trying to square this circle, one possible line is to take the more cosmopolitan route of suggesting that a natural duty of justice pertains to the reasonable and rational individuals that constitute these societies – and as moral agents demand assistance and respect as equals.

There is also scope to present an argument that maintains a less cosmopolitan line (but one that may ultimately be regarded as complementary). Such a perspective regards burdened societies as future members of the Society of Peoples. Therefore, despite being absent from the initial decision-making procedure, their interests are represented equally because of their potential moral status as future members of the Society of Peoples. In this way, their initial absence is not regarded as undermining their moral status: despite lacking actual equality of status, they can still be treated in the spirit of equality, while commitments toward them can still be formulated as duties of justice.[3]

Perhaps the most controversial implication of the duty is the conviction that assistance should not *necessarily* include the democratization of these societies. Given Rawls's toleration of nonliberal societies and the injunction against paternalism, then those carrying out the duty may not insist on far-reaching democratic restructuring (although the spirit of the duty implies that reforms will have to move toward greater representation and basic equality). Although contentious, such a perspective represents an alternative, potentially exciting view of development that offers a different liberal perspective to that of the hegemonic democracy promotion agenda. It allows for the possibility that burdened societies may be able to develop in ways that are tolerable to others in international society and sympathetic to their own cultures and traditions and that do not require the full-scale imposition of alien customs, practices and institutions.

Here, however, there is an implicit tension that Rawls does not work through. Despite opening up the conceptual ground for a less prescriptive approach to development, which might imagine different destinations, his own arguments are grounded explicitly in the work of Amartya Sen – arguments that propose a deep and unique connection between democracy and development. Rawls clearly couches his arguments in less explicit language, but ultimately his view that the promotion of human rights is essential to burdened societies' future is grounded on a body of scholarly work that has no room for any system other than democracy. (Admittedly, Rawls would be hard-pressed to find any body of research on institution and state-building that would support his normative outlook, such is the presumption that all roads must "lead to Denmark.") However, despite this weakness in Rawls's argumentation, it would be premature to cast aside his core ideals. Given the problems associated with the democracy promotion agenda, there is a strong case to be made for articulating an alternative liberal discourse on development, one that is capacious enough to accept other forms of government that are more attuned to the ongoing practices and institutions of a society and focused less myopically on the importance of voting and elections. One might think of Rawls as providing the moral groundwork for taking an alternative approach to state-building, one which does not begin with the presumption of a narrowly conceived liberal democratic state as the end goal.

This leads us to the second major criticism aimed at *LP*, concerning the toleration of other, nonliberal forms of government. Many critics ask of Rawls why it is he can argue so persuasively and forcefully in *TJ* and *PL* for far-reaching individual democratic rights, only to condone the idea of nonliberal societies that violate those very rights that he regards as fundamental to his chosen conception of domestic justice. The general tenor of their argument is that a liberal who is consistent should regard a threat to the primary rights of any individual as a moral affront – even if opposition to such practices is possible only in principle. Far from extending his championing of liberal rights into the international realm, Rawls argues in favor of reciprocal relations, toleration and the embracing of nonliberal societies as equals.

There are limits to the toleration, however, and he sets out in great detail an archetypal "decent hierarchical people" which helps to illustrate the requirements for a tolerable society from the liberal perspective. Jon Mandle (2005) identifies four criteria that Rawls prescribes for such societies, the first of these being that they are peaceable and without aggressive aims. The following three criteria are explicitly identified by Rawls (*LP*, 65–67): the protection of a minimal number of human rights; the system of law imposes bona fide moral duties; and the law is in the spirit of a "common good idea of justice." With regard to human rights, the package Rawls views as essential is in fact very limited compared to, for example, the Universal Declaration of Human Rights, protecting basic liberties and basic equality but with little to say on more substantive issues such as social justice.[4] Perhaps most significant in terms of characterizing decent societies is the claim that the right to democratic government should not be regarded as fundamental. As Mandle (2005, 223–227) explains, there is a close association here between Rawls's argument on the right to democracy and his understanding of decent societies as maintaining legitimate legal systems that issue bona fide duties and obligations, in the spirit of a common good idea of justice. For such systems to be maintained it is not necessary for every individual to have the right to vote, but it must be the case that the law is considered to take into account the good of each citizen. For this to be the case there must be freedom of conscience, and to further guarantee that it is a system of legitimate law there must be appropriate channels through which individuals can challenge or attempt to change this conception of the common good. Therefore although Rawls is of the view that nondemocratic states can be tolerated, and that a right to democracy is not a necessary element of an international overlapping consensus, he does make some very particular assumptions about how such a society should function in practice. These types of societies are far removed from Rawls's account of justice as fairness, or even his broader idea of politically liberal conceptions of justice, but they constitute legitimate forms of government and represent collective moral agents worthy of respect.

Although Rawls presents an unusually high level of specificity with regard to the kind of society he believes demands liberal toleration and recognition, there is more controversy over what this means in practice. Mandle, for example, considers toleration first and foremost in contrast to the use of force against decent societies, and as he explains it foreign intervention is very clearly unacceptable if the members of decent societies themselves "ought not use force to change its laws" (2005, 230). However, there is less clarity when we enter the conversation on what other types of policies might apply beyond force. Mandle is of the opinion that Rawls leaves room for liberal peoples to try and persuade decent societies to change their policies and become more democratic. This is less than clear, however, and as Mandle points out, Rawls prohibits the idea of democratic societies offering funds to encourage such reform (*LP*, 85).

In such passages it is possible to read Rawls as extolling a particularly hard line on liberal interventionism, dismissing even soft diplomacy as an affront to decent peoples, demonstrating a lack of respect, which in turn is likely to stymie rather than promote reform. Reidy (2013) suggests two different elements of Rawls's stance, one grounded in respect for persons, the other in respect for peoples. If decent hierarchical societies are deemed to be legitimate, with mechanisms that allow individuals to press for reform through their political structures, then to attempt to force change fails to respect both ordinary members and leaders of these societies as reasonable and rational persons capable of making their own free decisions. Moreover, such moves to influence how decent peoples conceive of the good undercut their status as moral agents and the reciprocity that should define their relationship with liberal peoples. If they are assumed to have a legitimate legal system and the capacity for reform, then there must be a sense in which the analogy applies that peoples, as with persons, cannot be forced to be free, and it is not the role of liberal powers that regard themselves as recognizing the truth to try to force them to be otherwise. As Reidy points out, liberal peoples themselves came to their own systems often through centuries of struggle, and it would be presumptuous of them to assume that other societies do not have the capability of making these leaps by themselves. From this perspective, even trying to induce them to change their conception of the common good has to be considered inappropriate.

As a normative, liberal perspective on international relations, the significance of what Rawls prescribes should not to be underestimated. He presents a welcome alternative, which is at present underappreciated and misunderstood, to a more aggressive cosmopolitanism. As illustrated with regard to development, Rawls's international theory demands consideration simply because it offers a different liberal approach, and an alternative vocabulary to the value-laden rhetoric of many Western states. It is a reasonable suggestion that more thoroughgoing, extended articulations of a Rawlsian foreign policy could present us with effective and attractive liberal alternatives at the present time. Given the huge costs of recent Western adventurism and the subsequent blow to the democracy promotion agenda, there is surely a need to reconsider how relations between the West and the rest are conceived. Rawls's recognition that there are conceivably other forms of government that can emerge which are capable of protecting the basic rights of people – and that it is a liberal duty to tolerate such societies – is significant. Just as the burdens of judgment tell us that there are many ways for individuals to conceive of reasonable conceptions of the good, so we should be open to the possibility that there are many possible forms of decent government. Indicative of this stance is a refusal to fall into liberal democratic hubris, represented by the end of history thesis, and a recognition that other peoples have the right to develop in their own ways and at their own speed – insofar as they are reasonable and decent. This extends to the prohibition of any action taken to influence decent societies to reform.

In one sense, this is a deontological stance, in that Rawls regards it as morally wrong to try and pressure other societies that represent reasonable, collective moral agents – in the same way as it would be wrong to interfere with the reasonable beliefs and practices of the individual. There is, however, a consequentialist aspect to his argument, in the sense that Rawls believes that the most effective way to ensure that nonliberal societies come to appreciate liberal values and reform internally is by allowing them to develop in their own time and manner. This is a better guarantee of a more liberal world than falling into the trap of arrogance and a presumptuous foreign policy that attempts to reform others against their own judgment. There is even a sense in which Rawls suggests the potential for cultural and ideational exchange. It is certainly self-evident that if the relations between peoples are grounded in equality and reciprocity, there are the foundations for multilateral relations where there is at least the potential for Western states to consider that governments in the developing world (democratic or otherwise decent) may have useful and worthwhile ideas to share, for example, in regard to our relationship with the natural environment.

It seems to me, therefore, that it is a sense of a humility, and even a degree of skepticism, that infuses a Rawlsian view of world politics – the knowledge and recognition that liberal societies do not have a monopoly on the truth, that there may be other ways of organizing political communities, and that we certainly do not have the capability of bringing others around to our own worldview through power alone. Equally, Rawls remains steadfast in his belief that justice as fairness represents the *most* just way of organizing a society, but through his political liberalism, his belief in the importance of toleration, his philosophical skepticism, and an adherence to a reflective equilibrium that ties his moral theory to the limits of the here and now, he is able to articulate the moral basis for a foreign policy that rightly restricts liberal individualist ambitions. A perspective informed by Rawls's philosophy deserves and requires further substantiation and could provide helpful ideas and guidance in negotiating the challenges and crises of international politics, such as the Arab Spring – and the myriad forms of government that may emerge from these events. Indeed, the multilateralism, caution and early attempts to embrace the Muslim world of the Obama administration might lead the more whimsical among us to ask whether, to some extent, it already does so.

## *LP* and IR

In light of these claims about the possible contribution of *LP* and the insights its further study could provide, it is a natural step to reflect on its broader impact with regard to the field of IR. This is a question Chris Brown addressed shortly after the publication of the monograph, in an article that he himself noted constitutes a "qualified defence" of the work, in the face of early cosmopolitan criticism (2002, 6). Brown, as with Audard and Lehning, notes how the text can be regarded as the completion of Rawls's project and that it should be analyzed in the context of his broader set of works – drawing an appropriate analogy with Kant's "Perpetual Peace." The dearth of subsequent attempts to situate or analyze *LP* from the perspective of IR theory says much about its impact, or lack thereof, and the extent to which IR scholars regard Rawls to be a relevant thinker.

This may in part be explained with reference to a point elucidated by Brown: Rawls seems to have very little interest in IR theory as a discipline and makes limited reference to it. Brown, it should be noted, is keen to add that this in some sense makes Rawls's work more thought-provoking and original, as he problematizes the field and looks at the subject "with the mind of an outsider" (Brown 2002, 17). Rawls does not set up *LP* as a reply to "rival" theories in the manner of *TJ*, but as Audard notes, the underlying agenda is that "he is searching for an alternative to two prominent albeit disappointing normative theories of global relations: so-called 'realism' and 'cosmopolitan' liberalism" (2007, 231).

Audard, despite being critical of many aspects of Rawls's theory, emphasizes the value of his approach, arguing that it "offers a truly 'critical' theory of international justice . . . avoid[ing] both the dogmatism of cosmopolitans and the skepticism of both 'realists' and cultural relativism. This is a difficult and courageous position" (2007, 273). It is therefore slightly disappointing that Rawls's realistic utopianism has not been regarded as more of a challenge to realism, or at the very least, that this form of theorizing has not been more readily pursued by others (David Miller being a prominent and persuasive exception (2007)).

It is the *kind* of theorizing Rawls represented with his political philosophy that is most significant, in the alternative it offers to what might be described as the comfort of realist thought. He seeks to set out principles of justice that represent normative guidelines for the relations between states, and such a position relies on a basic assumption that cuts against the grain of realist theory: that the nature of humanity, and the political and social institutions we live in, even at a global level, are malleable and mutable. His explicitly normative approach is perhaps best represented in what Brown identifies as the move from rationality to reasonableness, as manifest in the move from states to peoples. Rationality represents the kind of self-interested, instrumental thinking that states deploy in pursuit of their own interests. Rawls does not dispute their right to do this, but the difference with peoples is that they also deploy reasonableness – which includes a willingness to cooperate and recognize the interest of others. Brown believes that Rawls is correct in thinking that states, as depicted by the majority of IR theorizing, promote rationality at the expense of reasonableness in a world of interstate politics typified by purely prudential thinking. What Rawls offers, to Brown's mind, is something closer to the idea of the ethical state in the continental tradition and "a recovery of what the state could be under ideal conditions" (2002, 19). More broadly, and importantly, his type of ideal theorizing tells us that we don't have to be satisfied with the status quo.

By setting out such normative aims, Rawls also avoids falling into the trap of dangerous idealism, as his vision does not require that "we remake ourselves as human beings" (Brown 2002, 20). We can set out a vision of what we think the world ought to look like, which does not fall foul of a lack of imagination or hope, but at the same time remains grounded in the best considered judgments we have of our world. Most importantly, "[r]ejecting the idea of a just and well-ordered Society of Peoples as impossible will affect the quality and tone of those attitudes and will determine our politics in a significant way" (Brown 2002: 20).

Although Brown regards this sort of ideal theorizing as vital in analyzing and clarifying where we want to go and what kind of world we should aim for, he does question the extent to which it can provide answers on a more practical level. He notes that Rawls's contributions to nonideal theory with regard to just war and burdened societies are more limited and this, to his mind, may be illustrative of the unwillingness of Rawls to grapple with the prospect that in the real world principles of justice cannot always put limits on the exercise of power, but must sometimes – as E.H. Carr argued – be subject to compromise. This is a question ripe for further discussion, and may go to the heart of how persuasive Rawls's realistic utopianism is as a paradigm for addressing world politics.

Brown's point in some senses undercuts the potential contribution of Rawls's theorizing – if his is a sound claim that power inevitably trumps principles in the face of the realities of war and poverty. I would be less prepared than Brown to concede this point, however, because nonideal theory as conceived by Rawls does not on the face of it involve compromising on ideal principles; rather it is about looking "for policies and courses of action that are morally permissible and politically possible as well as likely to be effective" (*LP*, 89). Simply because the realities of world politics present certain limits and barriers in terms of taking the most straightforward moral decisions, and inevitably compromise agents' abilities *to achieve the most direct route to their normative goals*, this does not mean that the *principles themselves* should be compromised.

The general, long-term goals of peace and justice remain the same, through bringing "all societies eventually to honor the Law of Peoples and to become full members in good standing of the society of well-ordered peoples" (*LP*, 93). Rawls admits, however, that in this regard, "[h]ow to bring all societies to this goal is a question of foreign policy; it calls for political wisdom, and success depends in part on luck. These are not matters to which political philosophy has much to add" (*LP*, 93). Rawls in fact puts a great emphasis on the role of the statesman in negotiating and overcoming the emotions, anxieties and social distance that often hinder progress (*LP*, 126).

Whatever difficulties and obstacles they might face, however, they should endeavor never to compromise on their principles, instead using all of their skill in identifying the most effective course of action toward these goals. Sometimes, inevitably, they may have to acknowledge when consequentialist reasoning must trump deontological principles in pursuit of long-terms goals. There may, unfortunately, be occasions where they will have to compromise a principle in pursuit of the broader aims of the Society of Peoples (such as the supreme emergency exemption). Such exceptions are rare, however, and it is the statesman's task to ensure that moral integrity is maintained as far as possible, and that actions are not influenced by the emotions of anger and passion.

The extent to which Rawls's nonideal theory is equipped for the real-world problems of international politics is a matter for some debate, in particular because it might appear that it presupposes the realistic utopia of a well-ordered Society of Peoples, which we are clearly some way from achieving. However, the fact that it represents a perspective that rejects the deterministic tendencies of realism, while remaining rooted in the values and norms of international society, in itself merits consideration. The realist response would be to argue that moral actions are a chimera in the world of international relations, and that norms are always an expression of the self-interest of the powerful. However, Rawls is more than happy to acknowledge the driving force, and utility, of self-interest. He argues, for instance, that the duty of assistance will in the first place need to appeal to the members of the Society of Peoples in this regard – as the necessary mutual affinity has yet to develop between peoples to ensure it is enacted on the basis of principle alone. The threat of instability and disorder in these societies may be the necessary trigger for action in the first instance. Then, over time, through the development of ties and a process of moral learning, such actions will also become the result of moral compulsion, but for Rawls, to deny the role of self-interest would be as foolish as to deny the possibility of moral action.

And here a broader point emerges: principled cooperation among reasonable peoples in pursuit of peace and justice may appear to be a pipe dream for some, as the self-interested rationality of states is perceived to be the immutable condition of international relations. However, with the increasing interdependence of our contemporary world, the threats of economic crises and climate change, and the shifting balance of power, the most promising rational, self-interested course of action may yet emerge as self-limiting cooperation, based on reciprocity and reasonableness.

## Conclusion

To end at the beginning, as it were. As is evidenced by Sen's views, there is still a tendency for *LP* to be regarded as a text that can be largely disregarded, either in terms of the study of Rawls's oeuvre or as a work of international theory in its own right. I hope, however, to have established that Sen's dismissal of the monograph is misplaced. The secondary literature has increasingly looked beyond the type of cosmopolitan critique his perspective represents, engaging with Rawls's work on its own terms in reference to some of the key themes of his international theory.

As I have argued, *LP* has a great deal to offer in at least three different respects: as the completion of Rawls's philosophical project, as a guide to foreign policy, and as a different way of understanding international relations. This chapter has outlined arguments put forward in respect to these three themes, demonstrating that they represent promising avenues for further debate, while pointing to *LP's* broader value and merit. To some extent they are interconnected, in the sense that the serious study of *LP* as part of Rawls's oeuvre is likely to encourage those who are not Rawlsian scholars to explore the insights of his work for foreign policy. Furthermore, it is only by demonstrating that his ideas provide new and valuable insights into the practice of foreign policy that Rawls's theoretical approach will be taken more seriously in the field of IR.

If approaches such as Rawls's realistic utopianism are unable to challenge the presumptions of realist thought, this is not only restrictive for the study of international politics; it has broader implications as to how we understand ourselves and our future as human beings in an interconnected world. For if we are unable even to entertain the possibility of states regulating self-interested rationalism through reasonable cooperation, then we are bound to ask Rawls (and Kant's) closing question: "whether it is worthwhile for human beings to live on the earth" (*LP*, 128). Given the global economic, environmental and political challenges we face, a foreign policy influenced by Rawls's realistic utopianism would seem to offer better prospects for ourselves, and our children.

# Notes

1  Allen Buchanan's arguments provide the most persuasive and challenging version of this argument (2000).

2  See Williams (2011, ch. 6) for a more extensive summary of the types of policies that might be included under the auspices of the duty of assistance.

3  In keeping with the theme of treating Rawls's writings as a coherent whole, this reasoning can be presented as *conceptually* analogous to his treatment of children as future citizens in *TJ*, who enjoy "the full protection of the principles of justice" (*TJ*, 445–446), with the caveat – given obvious sensitivities about such comparisons – that the analogy applies strictly in terms of the *logic* of the argument, and is not intended in any way as a characterization of burdened societies.

4  "Among the human rights are the right to life (to the means of subsistence and security); to liberty (to freedom from slavery, serfdom, and forced occupation, and to a sufficient measure of liberty of conscience to ensure freedom of religion and thought); to property (personal property); and to formal equality as expressed by the rules of natural justice (that is, that similar cases be treated similarly)" (*LP*, 65).

# Works by Rawls, with Abbreviations

*Justice as Fairness* (*JF*), ed. Erin Kelly. Cambridge, MA: Harvard University Press, 2001.

"The Law of Peoples," in *On Human Rights: The Oxford Amnesty Lectures*, ed. Stephen Shute and Susan Hurley. New York: Basic Books, 1993.

The Law of Peoples, with "The Idea of Public Reason Revisited" (LP). Cambridge, MA: Harvard University Press, 1999.

Political Liberalism (PL), expanded edn. New York: Columbia University Press, 2005.

A Theory of Justice (TJ), rev. edn. Oxford: Oxford University Press, 1999.

# Other References

Agafonow, Alejandro (2011) "Rawlsian Compromises in Peacebuilding: A Rejoinder to Begby." Public Reason 3(1): 98–102.

Audard, Catherine (2007) John Rawls. Stocksfield, UK: Acumen.

Barry, Brian (1973) The Liberal Theory of Justice: A Critical Examination of the Principal Doctrines of A Theory of Justice by John Rawls. Oxford: Clarendon Press.

Beitz, Charles (1999) Political Theory and International Relations. 2nd edn. Princeton: Princeton University Press.

Beitz, Charles (2000) "Rawls's Law of Peoples." Ethics 110: 669–696.

Bernstein, Alyssa (2009) "Kant, Rawls, and Cosmopolitanism: Toward Perpetual Peace and The Law of Peoples." In Jahrbuch für Recht und Ethik/Annual Review of Law and Ethics, vol. 17. Berlin: Duncker & Humblot.

Brown, Chris (2002) "The Construction of a 'Realistic Utopia': John Rawls and International Political Theory." Review of International Studies 28: 5–21.

Buchanan, Allen (2000) "Rawls's Law of Peoples: Rules for a Vanished Westphalian World." Ethics 110: 697–721.

Caney, Simon (2002) "Survey Article: Cosmopolitanism and the Law of Peoples." Journal of Political Philosophy 10: 95–123.

Freeman, Samuel (2007) "Distributive Justice and the Law of Peoples." In Freeman, Justice and the Social Contract: Essays on Rawlsian Political Philosophy. Oxford: Oxford University Press.

Gardiner, Stephen (2011) "Rawls and Climate Change: Does Rawlsian Political Philosophy Pass the Global Test?" Critical Review of International Social and Political Philosophy 14: 125–151.

Jackson, Robert (2005) Classical and Modern Thought on International Relations: From Anarchy to Cosmopolis. New York: Palgrave Macmillan.

Lehning, Percy (2009) John Rawls: An Introduction. Cambridge: Cambridge University Press.

Maffettone, Pietro (2009) "The WTO and the Limits of Distributive Justice." Philosophy and Social Criticism 35: 243–267.

Mandle, Jon (2005) "Tolerating Injustice." In Gillian Brock and Brighouse (eds), The Political Philosophy of Cosmopolitanism. Cambridge: Cambridge University Press.

Martin, Rex and Reidy, David A. (eds) (2006) Rawls's Law of Peoples: A Realistic Utopia? Oxford: Blackwell.

Miller, David (2007) Global Justice and National Responsibility. Oxford: Oxford University Press.

Pogge, Thomas (1989) Realizing Rawls. Ithaca: Cornell University Press.

Pogge, Thomas (1994) "An Egalitarian Law of Peoples." Philosophy and Public Affairs 23: 195–224.

Pogge, Thomas (2001) "Critical Study: Rawls on International Justice." Philosophical Quarterly 51: 246–253.

Reidy, David (2013) "Cosmopolitanism: Liberal and Otherwise." In Gillian Brock (ed.), Cosmopolitanism versus Non-Cosmopolitanism: Critiques, Defenses, Reconceptualizations. Oxford: Oxford University Press.

Risse, Matthias (2005) "What We Owe to the Global Poor." Journal of Ethics 9: 81–117.

Sen, Amartya (2009) The Idea of Justice. London: Allen Lane.

Tan, Kok-Chor (2000) Toleration, Diversity and Global Justice. University Park: Pennsylvania State University Press.

Tan, Kok-Chor (2001) "Reasonable Disagreement and Distributive Justice." *Journal of Value Inquiry* 35: 493–507.

Wenar, Leif (2001) "Contractualism and Global Economic Justice." In Thomas Pogge (ed.), *Global Justice*. Oxford: Blackwell.

Wenar, Leif (2006) "Why Rawls Is Not a Cosmopolitan Utilitarian." In Rex Martin and David A. Reidy (eds), *Rawls's Law of Peoples: A Realistic Utopia?* (95–114). Oxford: Blackwell.

Williams, Huw L. (2011) *On Rawls, Development and Global Justice: The Freedom of Peoples*. Basingstoke: Palgrave Macmillan.

# 20

# Human Rights

## GILLIAN BROCK

## 1. Introduction

John Rawls's most influential work on human rights appears in his book *The Law of Peoples*. There is a lively debate between critics and advocates of Rawls's approach about a number of issues, including whether Rawls endorses a particularly concise list of human rights as establishing important ground rules in international affairs, whether he should endorse further or different candidates as belonging to the list of human rights deserving respect, whether his conception of how human rights should function in the global domain is normatively desirable or accurate, and how liberals should reconcile appropriate toleration for diversity with respect for human rights.[1] In this chapter these debates are covered. In the next section I offer some relevant background important to orient the focused discussion on human rights in section 3. Section 4 covers a general overview of common critical responses to Rawls's position on human rights and influential responses to these. Section 5 deepens the analysis with a more detailed treatment of the function of human rights and the list question. In section 6 I identify some areas for further reflection related to these important debates.

## 2. Rawls's *Law of Peoples*: Some Essential Orienting Background

The notion of human rights plays an important role in Rawls's *Law of Peoples*. Respecting human rights is not only a core principle of political justice and legitimacy, it also assists in determining which people are well-ordered and when military intervention might be permissible. To orient our discussion about human rights, we need to cover some background, albeit very briefly. Rawls argues that "well-ordered peoples" (for now, roughly but importantly,

*A Companion to Rawls*, First Edition. Edited by Jon Mandle and David A. Reidy.
© 2014 John Wiley & Sons, Inc. Published 2016 by John Wiley & Sons, Inc.

those that have institutions of self-governance or of consultation in their internal setup among other features to be discussed below) should be governed by eight principles, which constitute his Law of Peoples. These are principles acknowledging peoples' independence, their equality, that they have a right to self-defense, and that they have duties of nonintervention, to observe treaties, to honor a particular set of human rights, to conduct themselves appropriately in war, and to assist other peoples living in unfavorable conditions. These principles do not include distinctively liberal rights, fair equality of opportunity, or egalitarian distributive principles. In order to understand Rawls's reasoning for this position (which is also key to his account of human rights), it is necessary to attend briefly to what Rawls is trying to achieve in *The Law of Peoples*. Rawls aims to derive the laws to which well-ordered peoples should be able to agree (Griffin 2008, 22). Rawls argues that the Law of Peoples he endorses is a realistic utopia. It is realistic because it takes account of many real conditions, by (for instance) assuming a fair amount of diversity exists in the world; not all peoples of the world do or can reasonably be made to endorse liberal principles. It is also realistic because it takes people as they actually are, and "its first principles and precepts" must be "workable and applicable to ongoing political and social arrangements" (*LP*, 13).

What exactly is the question that Rawls tries to answer in *Law of Peoples*? The text provides at least two plausible answers (*LP*, 10, 5–6). First, what should the foreign policy of liberal peoples be? Second, is a realistic utopia possible and what conditions would define it? These two questions might send us off in different directions (that will also have a bearing on the set of human rights we should endorse). An answer to the question about foreign policy is more likely to focus on issues such as the limits of liberal tolerance. By contrast, the second question suggests that what Rawls offers is a visionary theory of global justice, one we can recognize as having some normative claim on us, albeit one we can realistically achieve. An account of a realistic utopia might indeed take a broader view of what kinds of changes should be made to realize something that could still legitimately lay claim to the title of a utopia of sorts. As the text provides both answers, one may interpret Rawls's project in two different ways and this is at the root of some common criticisms often made concerning Rawls's account of human rights.

Rawls's derivation occurs in several stages. Rawls argues first that liberal peoples would select the eight principles outlined above before considering the case of decent peoples and the principles they would endorse. Rawls specifies that for a people to count as a decent one, at least four *central* conditions must be met. First, the society must conduct its affairs in ways that are peaceful and respectful of other societies. Second, the system of law and its idea of justice must secure basic human rights for all members of the people. *At this stage in the argument*, the list of particular rights that Rawls presents appears to be very short (but as we come to understand, this appearance is misleading) (*LP*, 65). The third condition a decent people must satisfy is that judges and others who administer the legal system must believe that the law incorporates an idea of justice according to which there is a common good. Fourth, a decent people must have a decent consultation mechanism, whereby constituent groups are consulted in an attempt to reflect all groups' significant interests. After having offered an account of decent peoples, Rawls's derivation of his Law of Peoples continues with another international original position reserved only for decent nonliberal and/or nondemocratic peoples that parallels the international original position for liberal societies. Rawls briefly (perhaps too briefly) argues that a decent people would accept the Law of Peoples he earlier derived.

Rawls describes a case of a hypothetical decent people, Kazanistan, that he believes fulfills his requirements for qualification as a decent people. Kazanistan is an idealized Islamic people in which only Muslims are eligible for positions of political authority and have influence in important political matters, though other religions are otherwise tolerated and encouraged to pursue a flourishing cultural life. So the right to political participation, to be enjoyed on an equal basis with others, is not upheld in Kazanistan (*LP*, 76). Rawls believes Kazanistan can be admitted to the society of well-ordered peoples. Liberal societies should tolerate states such as Kazanistan. For those who have trouble with the idea that such a society should be considered as a member of the Society of Peoples (as many do),[2] Rawls believes that "something like Kazanistan is the best we can realistically – and coherently – hope for" (*LP*, 78). Moreover, he thinks that liberal peoples should "try to encourage decent peoples and not frustrate their vitality by coercively insisting that all societies be liberal" (*LP*, 62). Rawls also argues that it is crucial that we maintain "mutual respect among peoples." Indeed, failure to recognize such peoples might well lead to a more uncooperative and aggressive stance in the international realm, which would be unhelpful in sustaining a peaceful world order, which should be our first priority.

According to Rawls, some societies "lack the political and cultural traditions, the human capital and know-how, and, often, the material and technological resources needed to be well-ordered" (*LP*, 106). Well-ordered peoples have a duty to assist such societies to become part of the society of well-ordered peoples. The aim of assistance is to help such burdened societies to manage their own affairs and eventually to become members of the society of well-ordered peoples. The aim is to realize and preserve just (or decent) institutions that are self-sustaining. Importantly, this means that well-ordered societies have duties to offer assistance to develop institutions that can respect, protect and promote human rights. Our duties of assistance have important implications for human rights support.

## 3. Rawls on Human Rights: Some Exposition and Discussion of Key Passages

We start our more focused analysis of Rawls's position on human rights by considering what Rawls says about them in *Law of Peoples*. The order in which Rawls presents his ideas is not necessarily the most helpful one and probably contributes to some widespread misunderstandings about his views. I therefore present the ideas in a different and hopefully more helpful order, which I think will assist in clarifying some of the misunderstandings. I start with his exposition in §10, "Human Rights" (*LP*, 78–81). In §10.2 Rawls outlines what he takes to be the role human rights play in the Law of Peoples. He says:

> Human rights are a class of rights that play a special role in a reasonable Law of Peoples: they restrict the justifying reasons for war and its conduct, and they specify limits to a regime's internal autonomy. In this way they reflect the two basic and historically profound changes in how the powers of sovereignty have been conceived since World War II. First, war is no longer an admissible means of government policy and is justified only in self-defense, or in grave cases of intervention to protect human rights. And second, a government's internal autonomy is now limited. (*LP*, 79)

As he continues: "Human rights set a necessary, though not sufficient standard for the decency of domestic political and social institutions. In doing so they limit admissible domestic law of societies in good standing in a reasonably just Society of Peoples" (*LP*, 80). He then identifies three specific roles that human rights should play:

1 Their fulfillment is a necessary condition of the decency of a society's political institutions and of its legal order (§§8–9).
2 Their fulfillment is sufficient to exclude justified and forceful intervention by other peoples, for example by diplomatic and economic sanctions, or in grave cases by military force.
3 They set a limit to the pluralism among peoples. (*LP*, 80)

In an important footnote to this section, note 23, which elaborates on the role human rights play in restricting admissible domestic law, he distinguishes among the rights

> that have been listed as human rights in various international declarations. Consider the Universal Declaration of Human Rights of 1948. First *there are human rights proper*, illustrated by Article 3: "Everyone has a right to life, liberty and security of person"; and by Article 5: "No one shall be subjected to torture or to cruel, degrading treatment or punishment." *Articles 3 to 18 may all be put under this heading of human rights proper*, pending certain questions of interpretation. Second, *there are human rights that are obvious implications of the first class of rights*. The second class of rights covers the extreme cases described by the special conventions on genocide (1948) and on apartheid (1973). These two classes comprise the human rights connected with the common good, as explained in the text above.
>
> Of the other declarations, some seem more aptly described as stating liberal aspirations such as Article 1 of the Universal Declaration of Human Rights of 1948: "All human beings are born free and equal in dignity and rights. They are endowed with reason and conscience and should act towards one another in a spirit of brotherhood." Others appear to presuppose specific kinds of institutions, such as the right to social security, in Article 22, and the right to equal pay for equal work in Article 23. (*LP*, 80 n23, emphasis added)

Human rights, as Rawls understands them, are "universal" in that they apply to all societies, whether or not these societies recognize them. In §10.3 he confirms that liberal states do not have to tolerate those states that do not recognize human rights, namely outlaw states. And they have good reason to put limits on toleration here – "outlaw states are aggressive and dangerous; all peoples are safer and more secure if such states change, or are forced to change, their ways. Otherwise, they deeply affect the international climate of power and violence" (*LP*, 81). Indeed, so dangerous are outlaw states that the Society of Peoples must "develop new institutions and practices under the Law of Peoples to constrain outlaw states when they appear. *Among these new practices should be the promotion of human rights: it should be a fixed concern of the foreign policy of all just and decent regimes*" (*LP*, 48, emphasis added). So here he seems to admit that promoting human rights is very much to be encouraged and promoted. In a world filled with much diversity, outlaw states pose a grave threat which we should seek to contain. If this is indeed a central threat that needs to be managed we will need to enlist as many allies as possible, and this might partially explain why decent peoples, who are by definition peaceful and recognize human rights, are to be especially welcomed as partners in this most important pursuit – the containment of outlaw states.

The other sustained area in which discussion of human rights takes place is in covering the criteria for which peoples count as decent (especially §8.2). Here the discussion appears more measured than that found in §10. Decent peoples must meet various criteria to qualify as decent, such as having mechanisms for consultation and, most importantly, not having aggressive aims. The second criterion for eligibility involves a commitment to human rights. Rawls says that a decent peoples's system of law

> in accordance with its common good idea of justice . . . secures for all members of the people what have come to be called human rights. *A social system that violates these rights cannot specify a decent scheme of political and social cooperation.* A slave society lacks a decent system of law, as its slave economy is driven by a scheme of commands imposed by force. It lacks the idea of social cooperation. . . .
>
> Among the human rights are the right to life (to the means of subsistence and security); to liberty (to freedom from slavery, serfdom, and forced occupation, and to a sufficient measure of liberty of conscience to ensure freedom of religion and thought); to property (personal property); and to formal equality as expressed by the rules of natural justice (that is, that similar cases be treated similarly). Human rights, as thus understood, cannot be rejected as peculiarly liberal or special to the Western tradition. They are not politically parochial. (*LP*, 65)

Notice that Rawls begins his set of illustrations of the rights that must be satisfied with the phrase "Among the human rights are . . ." which indicates that this is intended to be a nonexhaustive list. It is important to draw attention to the fact that Rawls here offers only a partial list, as many commentators take him to be offering an exhaustive treatment of the human rights that are to be honored. But this is not the case. Even at this phase in the exposition, in the footnotes he also offers some important qualifications to the picture presented so far. For instance, he says that subsistence rights include economic security, since the "sensible and rational exercise of all liberties, of whatever kind, as well as the intelligent use of property, always implies having general all-purpose economic means" (*LP*, 65). Another important claim made in this section occurs when he says: "What have come to be called human rights are recognized as necessary conditions of any system of social cooperation. When they are regularly violated, we have command by force, a slave system, and no cooperation of any kind" (*LP*, 68).

A more neglected aspect of Rawls's argument seems to be his idea that liberal and decent peoples have a "duty of civility to offer other peoples public reasons appropriate to the Society of Peoples for their actions," especially for interventive actions or actions concerning recognition, toleration, and the like (*LP*, 59). So in this way the idea of public reason plays an important part in the argument offered for the Law of Peoples. These public reasons must refer to shared principles, norms, and the like. This shared set of norms and principles helps stabilize a mutually respectful peace. Appealing to human rights constitutes one such relevant shared norm.[3] Indeed, part of our shared norms are that human rights are "a special class of urgent rights" whose violation is condemned by both reasonable liberal peoples and decent peoples. This class of urgent rights would include those necessary for any "common good idea of justice" and therefore this makes them not "peculiarly liberal or special to the Western tradition." Liberal and decent peoples can agree to this set of human rights each for their own reasons.

## 4. Some Critical Responses to Rawls's Conception of Human Rights and Notable Defenses: A General Overview

Often drawing on the text at §8.2, there is a widespread perception among critics that Rawls endorses only a quite limited set of human rights as requiring respect. Some, such as James Nickel, characterize Rawls's position on human rights as "ultraminimalist" (2007). Indeed, this may be one of the most common complaints concerning Rawls's account of human rights.[4]

Another common criticism is that Rawls provides little argument for why decent societies would endorse even the limited set of human rights that Rawls offers initially (Pogge 1994, 214–215). Liberal societies, by contrast, may want to add more to the list of human rights; for instance, freedom of speech, democratic political rights, and equal liberty of conscience. In neither the case of decent peoples nor that of liberal ones would the precise list Rawls appears to offer be chosen in his original positions constructed for the international case, and moreover it is noted that the attempt to find a politically neutral law of peoples acceptable to both peoples is not promising, or so critics maintain (Pogge, 215).

Some critics charge that Rawls's failure to include democratic rights is quite mistaken (Kuper 2000). Amartya Sen, for instance, provides extensive evidence to support the claim that nondemocratic regimes have severely adverse consequences for the well-being and human rights of those over whom they rule (1999, 147–148, 154–155). Sen also argues that respect for human rights and ideas of democracy are not simply Western values, but rather that substantial elements of these ideas can be found in all major cultures, religions, and traditions.

Critics claim that in failing to provide a sufficiently robust list of human rights, Rawls includes too many societies as well-ordered. Critics charge that this is a grave mistake. A common view is that Rawls has offered us nothing more than a modus vivendi with oppressive states (such as "Kazanistan"), taking cultural pluralism perhaps too seriously at the expense of the individual persons who must sometimes suffer in their nonliberal states. States such as Kazanistan should not be considered well-ordered, these critics maintain, and liberals betray their fundamental commitment to honoring liberty if they do so.[5]

Having presented an overview of some common criticisms, I leave for separate, more extended analysis in later sections further criticisms, such as the claim that Rawls's view of the function of human rights is too limited. In the rest of this section I canvass some of the more influential defenses offered to rebut these common charges.

Many philosophers have tried to defend Rawls against these criticisms, especially against the most common complaints.[6] Several lines of defense have been attempted. It is often pointed out that critics have failed to appreciate some salient issues that orient *Law of Peoples*. As Samuel Freeman emphasizes, *Law of Peoples* is commonly misunderstood to be asking questions such as what is the nature of global justice or what would a globally just world order look like? According to Freeman, Rawls's Law of Peoples addresses a less ambitious question, namely: What should the foreign policy of liberal peoples be? In particular, how should liberal peoples relate to nonliberal peoples? Should they tolerate and cooperate with nonliberal peoples, or should they try to convert nonliberal peoples to liberal ones? What are the limits of what liberal peoples should tolerate with respect to nonliberal peoples? To address these less ambitious questions, Rawls needs to distinguish the concept of a decent society from a fully just one (in the liberal democratic sense), with the idea of a decent society playing the role of a theoretical construct. While liberal peoples should tolerate decent peoples, this is not the case with outlaw regimes. It is not reasonable to expect all decent societies to conform to all the norms of a constitutional democracy as a requirement of peacefully coexisting and cooperating with them (Freeman 2003, 46). If we reject Rawls's way of addressing the issues, it appears the only alternative is to intervene constantly in other states' affairs, which seems unattractive and destabilizing. According to Freeman, this stance does not entail that citizens of liberal states must refrain from criticizing illiberal societies. However, there is a key difference between liberal citizens engaging in criticism and their "government's hostile criticisms, sanctions, and other forms of coercive intervention. The Law of Peoples says that liberal peoples, *as peoples* represented by their governments, have a duty to cooperate with, and not seek to undermine, decent nonliberal societies" (Freeman 2003, 46–47).

While Rawls certainly does confirm that he is trying to work out what the foreign policy of a liberal peoples should be in *Law of Peoples* (e.g. §10), he also suggests that an alternative interpretation of his project is plausible when he constantly reiterates that his view offers a realistic utopia. The phrase suggests that he is trying to determine the conditions under which a utopian world order might be possible, although he constantly emphasizes that it must also be realistic (*LP*, 5–6). Here some defenders are quick to point out that on this interpretation of what Rawls's project is about, he aims to establish under what conditions we can secure a *peaceful and stable* world order, rather than one which is *just* (Audard 2006, 73). This is the proper ambition, it is maintained, because of the constraints provided by wide diversity, reasonable pluralism, and respect for peoples' self-determination. If securing a peaceful world order is our primary objective, we should sanction coercion only in the most essential cases. The notion of legitimacy plays a key role. Rawls's work is concerned with the legitimacy of global coercive political power, rather than with a range of other ideas that occupied him in earlier works (such as matters concerning a more robust conception of justice as fairness). Legitimacy is a more permissive standard than justice and this is the relevant issue in working out core matters related to a peaceful and stable world order.[7]

But even if we accept the significant role legitimacy plays, critics might argue that that would still not explain away other puzzling features of the Law of Peoples. One criterion by which we gauge legitimate governments is how well they respect human rights. Critics frequently remark that Rawls appears to endorse an overly concise list of human rights. Would his commitment to legitimacy not require him to embrace several of the rights he seems notably to exclude, such as freedom of expression, association, political participation, and nondiscrimination?

Much has been said in attempting to defend Rawls's abbreviated list of human rights. Two approaches are standardly used: one revolves around a concern with wide acceptability and the other draws attention to the way violations of human rights can function to legitimate coercion in Rawls's account.[8] I say more about these two strategies next.

According to the first line of defense, Rawls is concerned with how one might justify a generous list of human rights in the face of a wide range of views about conceptions of valuable lives in the international community. He wants to ensure his account is able to avoid the charge of parochialism. The idea is that a list of rights containing only the most essential of human entitlements would gain the relevant international consensus and therefore circumvent accusations that such a list could be endorsed by only a slim set of the world's nations.

According to the other common line of defense, attention is drawn to the status of violations of human rights in justifying coercion in the international order.[9] On this account, failure to comply with human rights on the concise list he offers would constitute legitimate grounds for considering the possibility of external intervention, including military intervention (Hinsch and Stepanians 2006, 126–127). It is this particular view of the function of human rights that accounts for the minimalist approach to human rights that Rawls adopts. Intervention in the affairs of a sovereign people being such a weighty matter, we should reserve space on the list of human rights for only those rights for which noncompliance could adequately justify considering the full force of international interventive measures. This might explain why certain rights, such as the right to belong to a trade union or free speech, are not included, it is thought.

A prominent defender of Rawls's views on human rights, David Reidy, argues that Rawls's endorsed list of human rights is much fuller than his critics seem to appreciate. In the commonly identified passages in which Rawls presents his list, Rawls offers only an incomplete sketch of what he has in mind. David Reidy notes that most readers think Rawls's list is excessively minimalist, but he draws attention to the fact that Rawls begins his list with the words "Among the human rights are . . ." and therefore leaves open the possibility that what he presents is not an exhaustive treatment (Reidy 2006a, 170). Indeed, as we see below, there is much textual evidence that he endorses a wider set of human rights than the set commonly attributed to him.

Still, even the most creative defenders of Rawls's work need to explain some notable omissions, such as a general right to nondiscrimination. Reidy suggests that the articles Rawls does affirm set important constraints on the kind of discrimination he permits. Furthermore, Rawls makes allowance for the fact that some nondiscrimination and democratic rights may be included in the list of basic rights if they turn out to be "empirically necessary" (Reidy 2006a, 173) to other basic rights. Note also that despite the short introductory list often invoked, in other sections of *Law of Peoples* Rawls lists apartheid and the mistreatment of women as human rights abuses, so there does seem to be some recognition of the impermissibility of some kinds of discrimination in Rawls's account of human rights (*LP*, 80 n23, 109–111).

Another noteworthy attempt to defend Rawls's more problematic omissions to the list of human rights is made by Samuel Freeman, who draws attention to Rawls's own arguments on this matter. Rawls says: "What have come to be called human rights are recognized as necessary conditions of any system of social cooperation. When they are regularly violated, we have command by force, a slave system, and no cooperation of any kind" (*LP*, 68). For Rawls, social cooperation involves reciprocity and an idea of fair terms of cooperation (Freeman 2006, 37). The minimum reasonable terms of cooperation are respect for those rights he includes on his basic list. Freeman points out that the "right to vote and the right to run for office, however central to democratic societies, are not necessary for social cooperation. Historically, most people in most societies have not enjoyed democratic rights, and even in societies where they do, these rights often willingly go unexercised" (2006, 37). Similarly, the minimal reasonable terms of cooperation need not include full liberal freedoms of speech or association, which might include "the right to defile or destroy national or sacred symbols, or enjoy pornography, or freedom of same-sex relations. To hold otherwise is not to take the idea of human rights seriously" (2006, 38).[10]

Is it still mysterious why decent societies must endorse even Rawls's truncated list of human rights? Given the arguments raised by Freeman (2006) and Reidy (2006b), this is no longer puzzling. Any decent political system must secure for its members certain minimum protections if it is to be a system of social cooperation. The minimum reasonable terms of cooperation include the items on the truncated list, though they would include others as well, including Articles 3–18 of the Universal Declaration of Human Rights (UDHR). Furthermore, when we consider the ways in which failure to respect central human rights might be grounds for coercive intervention, the firm limits placed on the core rights seem eminently reasonable. We turn next to consider in more detail what the appropriate functions of human rights are.

## 5. The Functions of Human Rights and the "List Question": A Deeper Analysis

It is often held that Rawls has a rather limited account of the function of human rights, namely, being able to command wide acceptance (while also setting a limit to permissible pluralism) and legitimating interventions. Critics challenge whether the roles Rawls picks out for human rights in regulating international relations (especially regulating and sanctioning interventions) are the only ones that can coherently be upheld.

James Nickel argues that human rights have multiple functions besides their role in legitimating intervention, and it is a mistake to rest too much on the one function for which he takes Rawls to be advocating. He notes that if we look at how human rights function within the Council of Europe, the Organization of American States, the African Union, and the United Nations, we see at least the following roles: first, "standards for education about good government"; second, "guides to suitable content for bills of rights at the national level"; "guides to domestic aspirations, reform, and criticism"; and he notes at least another 11 roles human rights commonly serve (2006, 270).

Nickel remarks that Rawls holds a nonstandard view of human rights, and he also usefully examines ways in which countries may influence each other that are not considered by Rawls. He calls criticism and condemnation of other countries that is not accompanied by significant threats "jawboning." Governments can express disapproval in a variety of ways including dissociation from diplomats; cancellation of cultural exchanges; calling home the ambassador for "consultation" or for an extended period; closing the embassy; and private criticism of an explicit sort (2006, 264, 271, 272). Many human rights treaties deal with human rights violators by gentle means, such as consciousness-raising, persuasion, criticism, mediation, and negotiation. Jawboning has done much to advance human rights, and he claims Rawls does not seem to appreciate adequately its potency.[11]

However, it is not clear that Nickel has been entirely fair to Rawls here, since Rawls appears to allow liberal societies to criticize decent ones. Rawls says, "Raising [critical] objections is the right of liberal peoples and is fully consistent with the liberties and integrity of decent hierarchical societies" (*LP*, 84). (Notably, here Rawls makes no distinction between individuals acting as citizens or in some official capacity.)

At any rate, it is not clear that Rawls has failed to appreciate the role criticism can play in advancing human rights, as Nickel claims. However, if Rawls intends to give us a practice-based conception of human rights, one which derives its standing from the international public culture, its norms, principles or operation, then as Nickel points out, human rights also offer standards for education about good government, guides to suitable content for bills of rights at the national level, guides to domestic reform, and the like. On this account, perhaps Rawls should have endorsed a more expansive list of human rights, at least when these alternative functions for human rights are in view.

We need to review the function of human rights in Rawls's account once more. In "Human Rights and Liberal Toleration" (2010), David Reidy suggests that, contrary to popular interpretations, Rawls might well have two different list questions in play in addressing two distinct ways in which we can respect human rights (or at any rate, there is no reason to think Rawls is hostile to such a view). One issue is: which human rights should be respected when deciding on international coercion? Another concerns which human rights must be respected to gain recognitional legitimacy or "status recognition" – which peoples deserve respect as a free and independent polity within the international order. These two questions get different answers. Reidy argues that well-ordered peoples and benevolent absolutisms are both entitled to noninterference. But only well-ordered peoples (liberal and decent peoples), should get status recognition. The key points in these arguments are summarized next.

What Rawls calls "human rights proper" concern and secure the common good of human persons, and they cover the material and social conditions necessary to human persons having a minimally decent life. These human rights proper are UDHR Articles 3–18 and whatever rights they obviously imply. Human rights proper can delimit permissible intervention. However, though respecting human rights proper is necessary, it is not sufficient for social cooperation among persons. Human rights proper can be secured through a benevolent system of coordination. However, as Reidy observes, social cooperation among persons

> requires some measure of reciprocity, not just in advantage but also in recognition and thus justification or reason-giving. That is, it requires that there be some reciprocal recognition and reason-giving between ruler and ruled so that authority arises constitutionally, from within the system of social co-operation, the cooperative relationship, and as a function of the public exercise of the shared reason of those persons cooperating. Thus, in addition to human rights proper, some minimal political participation rights are also essential to social cooperation between human persons. (2010, 293)

So even though Rawls does not view meaningful political participation rights as among human rights proper, he believes that they are "essential to social cooperation between persons or to well-ordered and decent political and social institutions" (Reidy 2010, 293). Importantly on Rawls's view, status recognition requires human rights proper plus meaningful political participation rights.

> Respect for persons as moral agents subject to the natural duty of justice, then, entails, first, a commitment to human rights proper as marking the principled conditions and limits of coercive international intervention, and second, a commitment to human rights proper conjoined with meaningful political participation rights as marking the principled conditions and limits of status recognition and respect between peoples within the international order. (Reidy 2010, 293)

As Reidy notes, there are at least two important senses of tolerance: tolerance as noninterference or tolerance as status recognition. Both are used throughout *Law of Peoples*. So in fact we have two lists associated with principle six, the requirement to respect human rights, each associated with a distinct conception of liberal toleration and therefore with a distinct function to be performed by human rights. Both forms of toleration arise from a liberal commitment to avoid coercion where possible and also to respect diverse values to the greatest extent.

## 6. Some Areas for Further Reflection

There are several areas which deserve more scrutiny in determining a cogent view of how human rights might operate in international affairs, and particularly, Rawls's conception of this.[12]

(1) How should we understand the ideal of toleration? One function of human rights is to specify the conditions and limits of morally required and acceptable toleration. But toleration is a complex idea. When the United States refuses to cooperate with Islamic states that fail to enfranchise women, this does not necessarily constitute a lack of respect for the Islamic states as free and independent members of the international order, or coercive interference with domestic affairs. Similarly, if European Union states refuse to cooperate with the US on extradition matters when the death penalty may apply to the person extradited, that does not constitute coercive interference with US domestic matters or an important failure of toleration. What kinds of actions then are clearly inconsistent with required toleration?

(2) There is a cluster of issues around legitimacy. For instance, how should we understand legitimate coercion? What constitutes legitimacy and how does it block coercion? What is the relationship between justice and legitimacy? Sometimes justice considerations can make illegitimate coercion defensible, and sometimes considerations of legitimacy can block intervention and prove sufficient to justify living with injustice. The relationship between justice and legitimacy is complex and deserving of sustained analysis.

(3) Third, what is the content of the natural duty of justice: is it to form a well-ordered society or to try to improve it in the direction of justice, toward more perfectly just institutions?

(4) Fourth, how should we understand the nature of human rights within international political morality? There are at least two ways to theorize human rights. First, we could see them as moral rights from a point of view external to practices and institutions, with the aim of arriving at one true universal theory.[13] Alternatively, we could hold a practice-based conception, according to which we look at how human rights function in practices and institutions and work out what they should be and how they should function from making sense of our practices around human rights.[14] A practice-based view is at least implicit in Rawls's view.[15]

(5) We need more analysis of several questions, such as: What are "human rights proper"? Why exactly is UDHR Article 19 about freedom of expression (for instance) not included? Further thought could also examine what additional rights are "obvious implications" of the set of rights that Rawls declares as "human rights proper." Reidy argues that they include these: economic rights to buy, sell, trade, invest (Articles 23, 25, 27); rights to peaceful assembly and association; freedom of movement and residence (Article 17); rights to manifest religious belief publicly and in community with others (Article 18); some freedom of

opinion, expression, and the press; some right to privacy (e.g., freedom from arbitrary interference with correspondence); rights to property; rights to freedom of thought, conscience and religion (Article 18). Might there be others that are also "obvious implications"?

(6) What kinds of human rights are necessary for a scheme of political and social cooperation to be *decent*? Are unequal liberty of conscience and unequal rights to political participation really consistent with a scheme being decent? One might wonder whether *equal* liberty of conscience or political participation are needed for a decent scheme of social and political cooperation.

(7) What are permissible ways to promote human rights? Rawls says he is against liberal governments offering incentives to promote human rights beyond human rights proper (*LP*, §11.3). Though it is not reasonable for a liberal people's government to offer subsidies for liberalization as part of its foreign policy, it may be perfectly reasonable for liberal citizens to raise funds for such a purpose. In defense of this he says that it is "more important that a liberal democratic government consider what its duty of assistance is to peoples burdened by unfavorable conditions" (*LP*, 85). But he also says in several places that we have duties to promote human rights so we do need to know more clearly how to fulfill this duty (*LP*, 48, 85).

(8) Current discussion of responsibilities with respect to human rights includes analysis of the responsibilities of different duty bearers (Barry and Pogge 2005; Kuper 2005; O'Neill 2000; Pogge 2002). There are plenty of other actors in the international arena besides states and peoples. Respecting human rights also has multiple dimensions, as Henry Shue (1980) has powerfully argued. The duties of nonstate actors in relation to respecting human rights are also important. Though working out the duties of nonstate actors was not a primary concern for Rawls, who was concerned primarily with foreign policy issues, we might extend the project to embrace such concerns, as many do (Barry and Pogge 2005; Kuper 2005; O'Neill 2000; Pogge 2002).

(9) It is hard to get away from the fact that one of the ways in which human rights function in our international practices is to reform existing institutions by drawing attention to failures to provide for those rights specified by the UDHR. In short, human rights can also function as legitimate aspirations – they have an important aspirational character. We often cite our human rights, what we are owed as human beings, when we want to draw attention to lacks and failures to accord what is perceived as a basic entitlement in virtue of our humanity. So-called "manifesto rights" are part of our practice, part of our well-established international public culture, and play an important role in the public reasons we offer in this realm. Though Rawls does not explicitly endorse this aspect of human rights practice – indeed, he rather distances himself from it, failing to count such articles and elements as human rights proper – it is hard for a practice-based conception of human rights to do so entirely.

How should we accommodate this aspect of human rights in a practice-based conception? Perhaps a more hierarchical view of the functions of human rights could allow for this aspect without it affecting some of the other core functions human rights should play, especially concerning coercion. So, instead of just the two central functions that Rawls identifies, there may be something like a hierarchy of functions that human rights can play. Failure to meet the first set of human rights can be grounds for coercion (and this should relate only to grave violations of core rights). Failure to respect the second set can be grounds for withholding status recognition of the sort that would allow that one is a well-ordered people entitled to be treated as a free, equal and independent member in good standing in the Society of Peoples. And a third function of human rights is salient when the first two functions are secured, namely a duty to improve institutions in the direction of better instantiations of justice. I believe this is consistent with Rawls's position: we have a general duty to promote human rights; indeed Rawls says it should be a fixed concern of all decent and just peoples' foreign policy. Allowance would thereby be made for further concern with a longer list of human rights in propitious circumstances, should they arise. At any rate, perhaps it would be worthwhile to reflect further on the different functions human rights can and should play, and the lists that might correspond to these different functions, noting their clear and important prioritization.

# Notes

1　For some of this debate see Martin and Reidy 2006; Pogge 1994 and 2002; Kuper 2000; Mandle 2005; Tan 2000; Freeman 2006; Reidy 2004; Freeman 2003; Moellendorf 2002; Ackerman 1994; Tasioulas 2002.

2　By "Society of Peoples" Rawls means all those peoples who follow the principles of the Law of Peoples in their relations.

3　In embracing the idea that human rights are elements of the public reason of the Society of Peoples, Rawls offers a contrast with naturalistic or agreement conceptions.

4　Many comment on the mistakes Rawls has made in endorsing a too concise or idiosyncratic list of human rights. These include Pogge 1994; Moellendorf 2002; Macleod 2006; and Buchanan 2006, e.g. 167.

5　The case of Kazanistan is puzzling. Note on LP, 77 that further requirements are specified, including that "each group must be represented by a body that contains at least some of the group's own members who know and share the fundamental interests of the group." So it sounds as if there must be something like guaranteed seats in a legislature for minorities. But if this is the case then rather than being excluded from political decision-making, members of non-Muslim groups are guaranteed a voice in such processes. Though they have no right to stand for some offices, their group has a right to special representation in political decision-making bodies.

6　For some notable attempts see, for instance, Freeman 2006; Heath 2005; Reidy 2004; Mandle 2005.

7　For an important defense of the role of legitimacy in Rawls's account see Mandle 2005.

8　Indeed, Rawls says as much in Law of Peoples at LP, 65, 80, and, more generally, §10.

9　Rawls says this in Law of Peoples at LP, 80. See also Tasioulas 2002; Hinsch and Stepanians 2006, 126–127.

10　For another excellent attempt to show why the short list is robust and why decent societies are committed to it, see Reidy 2006b.

11　For more on alternative forms of having influence with nonliberal peoples that do not involve military interventions, see Follesdal 2006, 306.

12　David Reidy identifies four fault lines underlying much contemporary discussion of human rights and I begin by outlining those before discussing at least five others. So the first four points are all ones raised in Reidy 2010.

13　For an excellent example of this approach see Talbott 2005.

14　For an excellent practical (or practice-based) account of human rights which draws initially on Rawls's work in The Law of Peoples, see Beitz 2009.

15　For discussion of the merits and disadvantages of these approaches see for instance, Beitz 2009; Griffin 2008; Talbott 2005 and 2010).

# Works by Rawls, with Abbreviations

*The Law of Peoples, with "The Idea of Public Reason Revisited"* (LP). Cambridge, MA: Harvard University Press, 1999.

# Other References

Ackerman, Bruce (1994) "Political Liberalisms." *Journal of Philosophy* 91: 364–386.

Audard, Catherine (2006) "Cultural Imperialism and 'Democratic Peace.' " In Rex Martin and David Reidy (eds), *Rawls's Law of Peoples* (59–75). Oxford: Blackwell.

Barry, Christian and Pogge, Thomas (eds) (2005) *Global Institutions and Responsibilities: Achieving Global Justice*. Oxford: Blackwell.

Beitz, Charles (2009) *The Idea of Human Rights*. Oxford: Oxford University Press.

Buchanan, Allen (2006) "Taking the Human Out of Human Rights." In Rex Martin and David Reidy (eds), *Rawls's Law of Peoples* (150–168). Oxford: Blackwell.

Follesdal, Andreas (2006) "Justice, Stability, and Toleration in a Federation of Well-Ordered Peoples." In Rex Martin and David Reidy (eds), *Rawls's Law of Peoples* (299–317). Oxford: Blackwell.

Freeman, Samuel (2003) "Introduction: John Rawls – An Overview." In Freeman (ed.), *The Cambridge Companion to Rawls* (1–61). Cambridge: Cambridge University Press.

Freeman, Samuel (2006) "The Law of Peoples, Social Cooperation, Human Rights, and Distributive Justice." *Social Philosophy and Policy* 23(1): 29–68.

Griffin, James (2008) *On Human Rights*. Oxford: Oxford University Press.

Heath, Joseph (2005) "Rawls on Global Distributive Justice: A Defence." *Canadian Journal of Philosophy* (suppl. vol.) 31: 193–226.

Hinsch, Wilfried and Stepanians, Markus (2006) "Human Rights as Moral Claims." In Rex Martin and David Reidy (eds), *Rawls's Law of Peoples* (117–133). Oxford: Blackwell.

Kuper, Andrew (2000) "Rawlsian Global Justice: Beyond the *Law of Peoples* to a Cosmopolitan Law of Persons." *Political Theory* 28: 640–674.

Kuper, Andrew (ed.) (2005) *Global Responsibilities: Who Must Deliver on Human Rights?* New York: Routledge.

Macleod, Alistair (2006) "Rawls's Narrow Doctrine of Human Rights." In Rex Martin and David Reidy (eds), *Rawls's Law of Peoples* (134–149). Oxford: Blackwell.

Mandle, Jon (2005) "Tolerating Injustice." In Gillian Brock and Harry Brighouse (eds), *The Political Philosophy of Cosmopolitanism* (219–233). Cambridge: Cambridge University Press.

Martin, Rex and Reidy, David (eds) (2006) *Rawls's Law of Peoples: A Realistic Utopia?* Oxford: Blackwell.

Moellendorf, Darrel (2002) *Cosmopolitan Justice*. Boulder, CO: Westview Press.

Nickel, James (2006) "Are Human Rights Mainly Implemented by Intervention?" In Rex Martin and David Reidy (eds), *Rawls's Law of Peoples* (264–277). Oxford: Blackwell.

Nickel, James (2007) *Making Sense of Human Rights*. 2nd edn. Oxford: Blackwell.

O'Neill, Onora (2000) *Bounds of Justice*. Cambridge: Cambridge University Press.

Pogge, Thomas (1994) "An Egalitarian Law of Peoples." *Philosophy and Public Affairs* 23: 195–224.

Pogge, Thomas (2002) *World Poverty and Human Rights*. Cambridge: Polity.

Reidy, David (2004) "Rawls on International Justice: A Defense." *Political Theory* 32: 291–319.

Reidy, David (2006a) "Political Authority and Human Rights." In Rex Martin and David Reidy (eds), *Rawls's Law of Peoples* (169–188). Oxford: Blackwell.

Reidy, David (2006b) "Three Human Rights Agendas." *Canadian Journal of Law and Jurisprudence* 19: 237–254.

Reidy, David (2010) "Human Rights and Liberal Toleration." *Canadian Journal of Law and Jurisprudence* 23(2): 287–317.

Sen, Amartya (1999) *Development as Freedom*. Oxford: Oxford University Press.

Shue, Henry (1980) *Basic Rights: Subsistence, Affluence, and US Foreign Policy*. Princeton: Princeton University Press.

Talbott, William (2005) *Which Rights Should Be Universal?* Oxford: Oxford University Press.

Talbott, William (2010) *Human Rights and Human Well-Being*. Oxford: Oxford University Press.

Tan, Kok-Chor (2000) *Tolerance, Diversity, and Global Justice*. University Park: Pennsylvania State University Press.

Tasioulas, John (2002) "From Utopia to Kazanistan: John Rawls and the Law of Peoples." *Oxford Journal of Legal Studies* 22: 367–393.

# 21

# Global Poverty and Global Inequality

## RICHARD W. MILLER

In *A Theory of Justice*, apart from a very brief discussion of international justice in a section on conscientious refusal to engage in acts of war, Rawls adopts the simplifying assumption that fellow citizens spend their whole lives in a "self-contained national community," "a closed system isolated from other societies" (*TJ*, 401, 7). Once this assumed national isolation is removed, the egalitarian principles of justice that Rawls defends as fair terms of cooperation within a closed society might seem to extrapolate to the world at large, justified by a globalization of his argument that fellow citizens would choose them if they pursued their fundamental interests in ignorance of their advantages and disadvantages. After all, in the world at large, inequalities of opportunity and expectations are steep, birth in one country or another correlates with huge differences in advantage, and people cooperate via global commerce. But this was never Rawls's own conclusion. The different tenor of the brief discussion of international justice in *A Theory of Justice* could be dismissed as a consequence of the book's domestic focus. But when Rawls finally presented a detailed conception of justice in international relations in his last book, *The Law of Peoples* (1999), and an essay with that title six years before, the contrast between the global and the domestic was stark. Rawls emphatically denied that the egalitarian principles that ought to guide fellow citizens in shaping their shared basic structure determine global economic justice, and used a new version of the original position, in which representatives of entire peoples, some quite nonegalitarian, advance interests in collective self-determination, as a device for identifying the right norms.

Was Rawls's refusal to embrace a cosmopolitanism of equality in which global principles of economic justice resembling his domestic ones are based on a global original position of individual people an apt acknowledgment of relevant differences or a failure of nerve? The assessment of this controversy is extremely difficult. In part, the difficulty reflects limitations of Rawls's terse, fragmentary arguments against this global extrapolation, written under increasing burdens of illness. Much more important, the difficulty of judging Rawls's refusal to extrapolate reflects the need to clarify what might have been extrapolated, Rawls's account of justice within borders.

*A Companion to Rawls*, First Edition. Edited by Jon Mandle and David A. Reidy.
© 2014 John Wiley & Sons, Inc. Published 2016 by John Wiley & Sons, Inc.

In an attempt to cope with these difficulties, I will discuss, in turn, Rawls's own defenses of his refusal to extrapolate, a better defense reflecting the nature of the fundamental interests impartially represented in the domestic original position, and the prospects of reconciliation between Rawls's theory of international justice and a more moderate cosmopolitanism concerned, not with equality, but with basic needs. Here are my main conclusions.

First, Rawls's own quick arguments against the cosmopolitanism of equality are unfair. The claims that he ascribes to the rival view are too rigid and demanding, producing more stringent tests of adequacy than he employs in his own case.

Second, the cosmopolitans of equality are wrong to suppose that the global extrapolation of the original position for individual people would yield egalitarian principles of global justice. The fundamental interests in self-reliance and association that play a central role in Rawls's theory of justice within borders block the extrapolation of principles when the original position for individuals is extended worldwide. (In the rest of this essay, when "the original position" is used without qualification, it will refer to the device used in *A Theory of Justice*, involving individual fellow members of a society choosing behind a veil of ignorance.)

Third, if this extrapolation of the original position is used to determine duties to advance global justice, a duty to support potentially demanding measures to relieve global poverty results. The demands that might be placed on those who are not poor to relieve global poverty are much heavier than those potentially imposed by Rawls's own transnational duty of assistance. So, a defense of the coherence of Rawls's whole theory requires a rationale for applying the original position domestically but not globally. This justification will turn out to rest on distinctive features of the modern state that Rawls did not emphasize and on a moral prerogative to exclude the needy from sharing in one's attainments that is stronger than any that Rawls affirmed. Rawls's moderation about global economic justice is consistent with his egalitarianism within borders, but it restricts the range of societies to which his egalitarianism applies and reduces its distance from libertarian perspectives.

## A Global Political Conception

At the start of *The Law of Peoples*, Rawls says that he means to defend "a particular political conception of right and justice that applies to the principles and norms of international law and practice" (*LP*, 3). The conception specifies an ideal of well-ordered relations among governments that ought to regulate the foreign policy of a liberal government (and, hence, of any government that is internally just). This ideal of global order is a political conception in four important ways. It regulates proper conduct among governments. It provides the rationale for transnational political coercion – in a broad sense including mere diplomatic pressure and conditioned loans – as a means of promoting conduct that adheres to its norms. Its norms must, therefore, have a political justification that makes coercion compatible with due respect for reasonable differences, as opposed, for example, to one depending on a comprehensive doctrine, which will inevitably conflict with other doctrines central to the outlooks and identities of reasonable people. Finally, even if these norms could not now serve as a secure basis for international cooperation, such cooperation must be a realistic eventual goal, a "realistic utopia," as Rawls puts it, made feasible by sentiments and dispositions that people might actually develop. In this feasible ideal, international political life is reliably shaped by willing support for the norms on the part of all liberal peoples and all others to whom they accord full and equal standing.

Rawls first offers a list of norms by which liberal peoples would regulate interaction with one another and then argues that liberal peoples would willingly interact on the same, reciprocated basis with a certain narrow category of "decent" nonliberal peoples, who are committed to a political order seeking the common good on the basis of responsive though nondemocratic political consultation. In contrast to Rawls's conception of domestic justice, this list of international norms is familiar and uncontroversial. Liberal peoples (and, it turns out, decent peoples) are to respect one another's freedom and independence, observe treaties and the like. Rawls also lists certain principles that are "superfluous" within a society of well-ordered (i.e., liberal and decent) peoples, but needed to govern their relations with outsiders: requirements to honor human rights and "assist other peoples living under unfavorable conditions that prevent their having a just or decent political and social regime" (*LP*, 37). But a commitment to reduce inequalities of economic opportunity or lifetime economic expectations is missing from the list, a silence converted to emphatic rejection toward the end of the book (*LP*, 119f.). That the international norms are fair terms of cooperation is supposed to be confirmed by their choice in a distinctive, international original position. In this device, representatives of well-ordered peoples pursue their peoples' interests in the independent, collectively self-determined continuance of a social life regulated by their internal conception of justice, an achievement upheld with pride and to be respected by others (*LP*, 34f.). While differences in economic advantage are put behind a veil of ignorance, this produces no transnational obligation to reduce inequality since the representatives of peoples are not concerned with the further, individual interests of people.

## Rawls's Grounds for Nonextrapolation

How could a political conception of justice suitable to a well-ordered society of peoples be so different from the political conception that Rawls always advanced as the most reasonable basis for political choices among people sharing a political society? In *The Law of Peoples*, Rawls's most detailed effort to justify the difference involves examples meant to show that the transnational extrapolation would misallocate responsibilities. If one well-ordered people freely, responsibly, democratically chooses economic policies allowing more leisure and producing less growth than another, it "seems unacceptable" to require the people who work harder and save more to make up for the consequent gap in wealth some decades later (*LP*, 117). But this example (like Rawls's other one) needs further specification to present the sort of "deep inequalities . . . affect[ing] men's initial chances in life" that troubled Rawls in *A Theory of Justice* (*TJ*, 7). If basic needs are met – as they are in a well-ordered society – fewer possessions combined with more leisure need not make for a worse life. Moreover, people in a well-ordered society may be able to monitor and reverse the consequences of economic policies over the course of decades. Suppose, in contrast, that the worst-off people in the whole Society of Well-Ordered Peoples have substantially worse life chances than the people living in the best-off societies, and that this will continue to be their situation on account of disadvantages inherited from past generations if they are not helped by better-off foreigners acting through their governments. It might still be said that they have no claim on better-off foreigners. But it is by no means clear how this can coherently be said by someone like John

Rawls who takes inferior opportunities and lifetime expectations to create claims for help from better-off fellow citizens.

Another response, implicit in *The Law of Peoples* and explicit in the preceding essay, appeals to the central role of toleration in political liberalism. The egalitarian liberalism of *A Theory of Justice* is just one of a variety of reasonable liberal conceptions. It is even farther removed from the common-good conceptions of decent nonliberal societies. So egalitarian principles would be intolerant impositions in norms proposed for a Society of Well-Ordered Peoples.[1]

Since the list of norms whose narrowness is in dispute is offered as part of an ideal, this appeal to pluralism must be reconciled with Rawls's view that egalitarian liberalism is the most reasonable interpretation of values that must be upheld in a fully just society. Living in a society very far from this conception, Rawls tried to persuade his fellow citizens to adopt it and thought it was a realistic hope that it would be generally shared some day. At that point, he certainly believed, it could be legitimate for the egalitarian liberal majority to support coercively enforced laws required to realize this standard of justice. If this was a realistic hope, a global society in which all peoples are liberal egalitarian would seem to be a realistic utopia, as well. So the global ideal that Rawls is concerned to specify could be governed by egalitarian norms without intolerant disrespect.

Finally, a more plausible distinction between domestic and global possibilities provides one further, nearly explicit argument against an egalitarian specification of the norms of Rawls's global realistic utopia. To be part of a realistic utopia, a political conception of justice must be an ultimately realistic basis for stable regulation of the choices in its domain, resting on willing adherence of those who make these choices. In connection with the duty of assistance, Rawls notes that the affinities of members of different peoples are "naturally weaker (as a matter of human psychology)" than the affinities of people who share a common government, political culture and social institutions, and adds, "In a realistic utopia, this psychological principle sets limits to what can sensibly be proposed as the content of the Law of Peoples" (*LP*, 112). A psychological limit that seriously weakens responsiveness to the plight of the global poor – the topic of this passage – would even more severely constrain responsiveness to the situation of foreigners who are merely worse off.

If a strong enough national limit to sympathy is sufficiently enduring, then global egalitarianism would not sustain the sort of political order that political liberalism seeks: stability based on willing adherence of the vast majority, in which governmental coercion is grounded on a principled consensus among the politically reasonable people who are subject to its imposition. But it is not clear whether acceptance of such an enduring limit would settle the dispute over the cosmopolitanism of equality, or even whether such an enduring limit to sympathy should be accepted by someone who shares Rawls's hopes for domestic egalitarianism.

In both *A Theory of Justice* and *Political Liberalism*, Rawls takes most of the considerations that justify his liberal egalitarianism to be independent of considerations of stability. (See *TJ*, 398f., 441, and *PL*, 65f., 252.) While the failure to persuade the majority of one's fellow citizens that a favored interpretation of liberal values is most reasonable is a reason not to seek to impose this conception, one ought to keep trying to persuade them, as Rawls did throughout his life. While Rawls hoped that such arguments would eventually produce a society uniting political virtues of fairness and autonomy, properly interpreted, with the virtue of consensus characteristic of political liberalism, this was a tenuous hope, a "conjecture" concerning "highly speculative matters" (*PL*, 167). He never claims that someone who despairs of this eventual unity among political virtues should stop making arguments for laws realizing her favored interpretation of the virtues other than consensus. In a global economy of well-ordered people in which international inequalities in opportunities and life chances are serious, such abstinence from arguments supporting the cosmopolitanism of equality seems morally unbalanced consensus-worship. Departures from a background consensus on general principles in order to help the worst off on grounds of fairness and autonomy could make global political life more just, even if it makes global political life less neat.

Cosmopolitans of equality who share Rawls's view of the limitations of human sympathies among the vast majority (the most that he could plausibly claim) make their arguments in just this spirit. They regard the Rawlsian limit as a moral limitation, like the limit in sympathy which, Rawls admits, might make it desirable but unjust to permit enslavement of war captives in a society in which they would otherwise be killed (*TJ*, 218).

In any case, it is not clear that global egalitarianism could not be the basis for a stable political order in a realistic utopia. Rawls offers his domestic standard of justice as the shared commitment of a well-ordered society in "favorable conditions," including historical and social contingencies arising in the course of economic development. In contrast, he thinks that Burke's arguments from class-based limits of political competence might have justified a limited franchise, departing from Rawls's first principle of justice, in Burke's unfavorable conditions (*TJ*, 215–217). In a global extension of this envisioning of eventual favorable conditions, suppose that economies will one day converge enough to make the transnational demands of improvement of the worst off much lighter than they are now, without abolishing serious inferiorities. And suppose that practices of international cooperation in global institutions will become increasingly important, as Rawls himself expects. The thought that an extrapolation of Rawls's domestic egalitarianism could be the focus of a stable global consensus in these favorable conditions is very far from being the psychological fantasy that the appeal to human nature suggests.

## The Cosmopolitanism of Equality and the Original Position

Those whom I have called "the cosmopolitans of equality" – for example, Charles Beitz, Darrel Moellendorf, and (at least in his first book) Thomas Pogge – extrapolate Rawls's theory of justice within borders at two levels. They extend the principle of fair equality of opportunity and the difference principle worldwide, and they do so on the basis of a global extension of the domestic original position in which the participants, united by global commerce, are ignorant of where in the world they live.[2] In addition to accepting the validity of Rawls's domestic theory, they join with him in ignoring certain sad features of current global political life as irrelevant to the justification of their global principles. Like him, they do not base their view of the extent of transnational duties to help on the need to repair or justify the effects of domineering influence over foreign people. They describe transnational duties of economic concern that would exist even if no facts of transnational interaction were relevant beyond the mere fact of global economic interdependence based on commerce. I will call this global situation, much simpler and nicer than our own, the Standard Case. Their global extrapolations of Rawlsian domestic justice as holding in the Standard Case have survived Rawls's own criticisms. But further specification of Rawls's domestic theory of justice provides further resources for resisting their two-level globalization.

Since the global extension of the original position is an appealing way of expressing full and equal respect for persons, while the global principles initially seem to impose extreme demands, one might begin assessing the cosmopolitanism of equality by asking whether its principles would in fact be chosen by individual participants (or their representatives) when Rawls's device is extended to people throughout the world. An accurate understanding of the fundamental interests to which Rawls appeals in his domestic argument casts doubt on this derivation.

Rawls insisted, with increasing emphasis over the years, that a device of impartial choice that justifies moral principles had better involve pursuit of the right kinds of interests, graded according to their moral importance. The fundamental interests, that is, the interests that have standing in this choice, are the interests that each must treat as important (and equally so) for all in deliberations over relevant principles of choice that express full and equal respect for herself and others. Determining what these interests are requires moral reflection, taking relatively secure specific moral judgments as its raw material.[3]

Rawls emphasizes interests that set no significant constraint on the reduction of economic inequality, for example, interests in the free expression of one's religious outlook and in political autonomy in forming and revising final ends. But he also posits fundamental interests that set limits to equality, as he, more quietly, admits. As much as Robert Nozick, he insists that a just society must guarantee secure principles of entitlement, extending at least as far as guarantees of personal property. In the original position, the choice of this guarantee reflects a fundamental interest in advancing the life goals and relationships that one values through one's own efforts. People want to get ahead on their own steam, shaping the contours of their own lives along the lines of what they care about. Those with no such interest in self-reliance lack self-respect, the attitude whose social underpinning is a hallmark of basic liberties for Rawls. In *Justice as Fairness*, Rawls takes the ultimate goal of economic justice to be "to put all citizens in a position to manage their own affairs on a footing of a suitable degree of social and economic equality" and bases rights to personal property on "fundamental interests," including the interest in "a sufficient material basis for personal independence and a sense of self-respect" (*JF*, 139, 144). The Preface to the Revised Edition of *A Theory of Justice* concludes with acknowledgment of "a right to personal property as necessary for citizens' independence and integrity" (*TJ*, xvi). Because the interest in self-reliance concerns the goals that determine the contours of a life, not just desires for current enjoyments, its great importance gives strong priority to a system of secure entitlement, through which people are assured that their efforts to acquire material means to their own ends will not be deprived of point and value. Securing gains due to lucky breaks is an inevitable result of such a system, and a price that must be paid to honor those values of self-reliance.

A second fundamental interest that limits the pursuit of greater equality underlies Rawls's insistence on freedom of association. This is the interest in effective engagement in valued relationships, with mutual caring among intimates as its core. Within valued relationships, people committed to self-reliance willingly receive help, but there is no real contradiction here, since they are committed to ultimate reciprocity. To insist that laws and institutions should thwart core interests in mutual caring among intimates in order to promote equal opportunity or material expectations for the worst off would be perverse: a violation of what people rightly want to protect, in the name of advancement of their interests. Avoiding this perversion, Rawls insists on protection of nurturance within families (and, implicitly, mutual care among friends), despite the inevitable widening of inequality of opportunity.

If the original position is extended worldwide, the construal of the interests in self-reliance and association should be extended to embrace distinctive relations to one's political society. This extension of relevant interests would block the global extrapolation of Rawls's liberal egalitarianism.

Fellow members of sovereign citizenries typically devote energy and attention, take risks and make sacrifices in a collective project of advancing prosperity and justice in their territory. The fundamental interest in self-reliance ought to be extended to include an interest in collective self-reliance in these endeavors. Not to want prospects of self-advancement among those with whom one is engaged in the civic endeavor to reflect sacrifices, risks, and choices in this endeavor, as opposed to outside aid, shows a lack of self-respect. In the sparse list of fundamental interests that Rawls takes to be relevant to global justice, this would violate "proper patriotism," pride in one's people's accomplishments, whose expression is a fundamental interest because of its role in "proper self-respect" (*LP*, 44, 34f.).

The fundamental interest in mutual concern in valued relationships also affects transnational commitments to help the disadvantaged that emerge from a global original position. Engagement with fellow citizens in shaping beneficial lifelong terms of self-advancement, in a process requiring sacrifice and trust, properly gives rise to special mutual concern. Rawls speaks of the mutual concern appropriate to civic association as "civic friendship," going so far as to say that the right explication of political justification would "specify the nature of the political relation in a constitutional democratic regime as one of civic friendship."[4] A fundamental interest in friendship is not properly expressed in a policy of leaving a friend in the lurch whenever enticed by the opportunity to help more disadvantaged strangers.

The concentration of concern on disadvantaged compatriots, not the disadvantaged of the world at large, is one reason why the global extrapolation of Rawls's egalitarian principles would be rejected, if the original position is extrapolated worldwide with proper attention to fundamental interests. In addition, differences between global and local interactions in the Standard Case provide further reasons to reject globalized versions of the specific domestic egalitarian principles that are the common ground of Rawls and the cosmopolitans of equality.

For one thing, the political goal of fair equality of opportunities to succeed would be domestic because of the relevant grounds for assessing greater or lesser success. In a theory of justice, such comparisons should not be matters of lesser or greater frustration, determined by intensity of desire. Someone's intense desire to write avant-garde poetry full-time ought to be his own responsibility, as the proper valuing of self-reliance requires. In a political choice to devote resources to helping people to get ahead, certain scales of attainment are properly singled out as the politically relevant measures of advancement. The fundamental interests in self-reliance and civic friendship would single out responsibility and authority, interesting work and "a skillful and devoted exercise of social duties" (*TJ*, 73) as the primary standards of success in the politically relevant hierarchy. This fits Rawls's emphasis on "offices" and "positions," not incomes, as the primary topic, at the start of the section on fair equality of opportunity in *A Theory of Justice* (*TJ*, 73; see also *JF*, 43).[5]

The task of reducing inequalities in opportunity assessed by these criteria, among those with equal aptitude and interest, is local, at least in the Standard Case and among societies in which basic needs are met. Members of such societies can achieve fair equality of opportunity to reach positions within their relevant hierarchies through domestic political initiatives and will want to do so in order to show respect for their fellow citizens and to honor values of collective self-reliance. In contrast, international transfers to reduce additional international inequalities in opportunities (for example, additional international inequalities in opportunities to be an investment banker or to be rich) would have to cope with barriers of geography, society and culture that are extremely costly to overcome in order to achieve politically unimportant gains in opportunity in ways that infringe on collective self-reliance and civic friendship.[6] Behind a global veil of ignorance, people advancing relevant interests will see no reason to take on the risk of bearing these extra burdens in order to eliminate those inequalities of opportunity.

Finally, the global context blocks needed responses to two important objections to the difference principle. According to one, the difference principle ought to be rejected in the original position as ruling out very large improvements in the wealth and income of those who are not worst off when small gains for the worst off will be foregone. In response, rather than dismissing the objection as fundamentally misguided, Rawls appealed to the workings of the prior principles of unrestricted access to occupations and fair equality of opportunity. He argued that very large gains in lifetime expectations for the better off will not coexist with small losses for the worst off since a free labor market and fair equality of opportunity will eliminate such gains by attracting hordes to compete for the better-off positions (*TJ*, 136f.). In the global economy, in contrast, local ties and the difficulties of acquiring skills, linguistic, cultural and economic, needed for success abroad make economic fates much less close-knitted. So, a global difference principle would be rejected as too restrictive of improvements for the non-worst-off, when economic commitments are made behind the global veil of ignorance.

The second objection is even more fundamental. After guaranteeing equal civil and political liberties and protecting against unfair inequalities of opportunity, why would someone with appropriately strong fundamental interests in self-reliance and in special concern within limited associations insist on political measures to reduce inequality in lifetime economic expectations? In defending his liberal egalitarianism, Rawls responded to this question with reasons for political concern about unequal outcomes that became increasingly specific and diverse over the decades. The lists of reasons for "being concerned about inequality in domestic society" (*LP*, 114) in both *The Law of Peoples* (*LP*, 114f.) and *Justice as Fairness* (*JF*, 130-32) begin by noting the duty to meet "basic needs" (*JF*, 130), relieving "the suffering and hardship of the poor" (*LP*, 114), *and* by noting that this is not, in fact, a concern to reduce inequality, as such. The lists go on to note that when inequalities of income and wealth become too great they contribute to political domination by corrupting democratic governance and encourage attitudes of servility, deference and arrogance. Here, the interest in self-reliance is well served, since it includes concerns to avoid subordination and not to live off of benefits of domination. Finally, Rawls notes that "a certain equality, or well-moderated inequality" is needed to ensure that "society makes use of fair procedures" (*JF*, 131). His examples are the needs to break up monopolies that interfere with "fair, that is open and workably competitive markets," to eliminate unfair influence of "a wealthy few" in political elections (*JF*, 131) and to promote fair equality of opportunity. Elsewhere, developing the strains-of-commitment argument in *A Theory of Justice*, Rawls proposes that a shared public commitment to the difference principle is a prerequisite for active allegiance to the shared political order on the part of all citizens, advantaged and disadvantaged (*JF*, 128–130, 133). Taken together and appropriately connected with fundamental interests, these considerations would support a commitment to maximize (within broad limits, as required by further principles and fundamental interests) the expectations of the "worst-off representative individual." These might, Rawls speculates, be identified, on further reflection, with the expectations typical of those who can expect no more than unskilled workers, or with the expectations of those with less than half of median income and wealth (*TJ*, 84). Some such broad standard of primary concern would be chosen as a shared public means of monitoring the vast package of relevant laws and policies to prevent violation of the various specific interests in equality.

Such reasoning reconciles concerns to reduce inequality of outcome with interests in self-reliance and association. But the concerns are specific to the shared social life of compatriots. Of course, in the real world, excessive international economic inequalities give rise to domination of international organizations by "a wealthy few," promote arrogance and guarantee that multinational deliberations will be unfair. But the Standard Case, in which the only relevant international fact is the mere fact of commerce, excludes these further considerations.[7]

In sum, if the original position is extrapolated worldwide, the cosmopolitanism of equality ought to be rejected as inappropriate in the Standard Case. In contrast, a transnational demand for relief of abject poverty *would* be appropriate. The interest in shaping the contours of one's own life that requires protection of achievements also requires protection against a situation in which one's life is dominated by a struggle for survival, rather than advancement of one's distinctive life goals. The interest in mutual concern in valued relationships requires protection of one's efforts to take care of others, but if a dependent could not thrive on the basis of one's own efforts, the same interest calls for help in nurturance. Sovereign self-reliance and civic friendship may make compatriots the first resort in rising above these thresholds. But it would show a lack of self-respect, an obsessive pursuit of independence detached from the sources of its value, not to seek outside help as a last resort.

This cosmopolitanism of need, basing a global political duty to relieve abject poverty on a global original position of individuals, accommodates all of the specifications by Rawls of domestic and global justice that I have described so far. Although he relied on a global original position of peoples, not people, he was explicitly open to the possibility that a global original position of individuals might confirm the global norms that he proposed (see "The Law of Peoples," in *CP*, 549f.). The attitudes that he ascribes to peoples – patriotic pride, common sympathies and the like – parallel the attitudes of individual people that result from addressing fundamental interests in the domestic original position to global circumstances. However, there is one further element that resists accommodation, the limited duty of assistance that is Rawls's actual demand for relief of foreign poverty.[8]

## Goals and Burdens of Assistance

The two crucial questions about any duty of assistance are the nature of its target and the extent of its demands. Rawls's answer to the second question seems less demanding than what would be upheld in the global original position of the cosmopolitanism of need.

The target of the duty that Rawls posits in *The Law of Peoples* is the removal of burdens that bar the way to a society's becoming well-ordered, that is, liberal or decent (*LP*, 37, 106). Such a society need not be wealthy. Indeed, Rawls says it might be "relatively poor" (*LP*, 111). But the goal requires the elimination of at least some of the deprivations constituting poverty. Rawls insists that any liberal regime (not simply the sort specified by his favored interpretation of liberal values) must assure "to all citizens the requisite primary goods to . . . make intelligent and effective use of their freedoms" (*LP*, 14). While decent nonliberal societies are not committed to the neutrality evoked by concentration on primary goods and do not give priority to liberal freedoms, they, too, must, evidently, guarantee the substantive value to their subjects of their characteristic rights and prerogatives. For all well-ordered regimes must "secure a social world that makes possible a worthwhile life for all" (*LP*, 107).

At one point, Rawls presents a more specific account of what a liberal society must provide, in which it must be the "employer of last resort" and must assure "basic health care . . . for all citizens" (*LP*, 50). If this is a liberal prerequisite, it would also seem to be a prerequisite for a decent society in modern circumstances. If these guarantees must assure a costly but nonexorbitant cure for a painful but nondebilitating illness and protect against recurrent, involuntary but temporary unemployment, then Rawls's target would seem to be the same as that of a cosmopolitanism of need based on the original position I described. The question would be whether these compassionate guarantees can, in fact, be derived from Rawls's fundamental standards of political good order, involving "effective and intelligent use of freedoms" and "a worthwhile life." People who bear those physical and economic burdens can make intelligent and effective use of civil and political liberties. To deny that they can live worthwhile lives is a misguided insult to many millions of people. Yet these and other lacks that seem compatible with Rawls's fundamental standards of good political order are ingredients of poverty that people behind a global veil of ignorance would be concerned to prevent.

Still, Rawls's specific remarks about employment and health care suggest that his goal in international assistance may not have differed much, if at all, from the goal of the cosmopolitanism of need. The same cannot be said of the demandingness of the two perspectives. Rawls's discussion of the commitment on the part of the better off that his global duty of assistance requires does not impose anything like the potential demands of the cosmopolitanism of need.

In justifying his duty of assistance, Rawls asks us simply to "take as a basic characteristic of well-ordered peoples that they wish to live in a world" in which all peoples are well-ordered (*LP*, 89; see also 104f.). It makes sense that proper patriotic pride in the moral accomplishments of one's well-ordered people would be accompanied by this wish. But a sincere wish that all societies will someday be well-ordered would not seem to dictate any significant sacrifice now, even if significant sacrifice on the part of much better-off peoples would substantially help. In contrast, individuals behind a global veil of ignorance would, presumably, choose a principle demanding significant sacrifices by the better off if this would significantly relieve the suffering of much needier foreigners in countries powerless to relieve their burdens independently. Even if development relying on local resources would be a sufficient basis for relief of severe neediness in these countries some day, people behind the veil would be moved by the thought that this day might come long after they are dead.

Rawls's brief discussion of the process of help suggests that no significant sacrifice is needed: merely "throwing funds at [a burdened society] is usually undesirable" (*LP*, 110) and Amartya Sen, Jean Drèze, Partha Dasgupta, and David Landes offer evidence of the importance of the local political culture. But he accepts that "money is often essential" (*LP*, 109f.) and provides no sufficiently compelling argument that developed countries could not significantly quicken the pace of global poverty relief through aid, trade or other policies through which their citizens give up significant wealth, income, luxuries or even comforts. Certainly, the somewhat selective use of a few recent writings does not appeal to the secure common knowledge which ought to be the basis for specifying a basic political duty. In general, Rawls provides no reason to reject criticism of the status quo based on a potentially demanding political duty to relieve global poverty. But neither does he endorse this moral practice, in his anodyne "principle of *transition*" (*LP*, 118).

Of course, silence does not entail rejection. Perhaps Rawls thought, but did not say, that people in developed countries would be wrong not to support demanding measures, requiring substantial sacrifices of advantage, to alleviate global poverty. However, such reticence would be very hard to justify in a chapter on "Nonideal Theory" in a book on global justice in a world that was as nonideal as Rawls's. When *The Law of Peoples* appeared in 1999, about 1.7 billion people lived on less than $1.25 a day. In low income countries where 40 percent of the world's people lived, the chance of death before the age of five was greater than one in ten.[9] In these surroundings of destitution, Rawls's nonassertion of a potentially demanding duty of assistance would be hard to justify if he actually believed what he did not assert. But if he accepted no such duty and it results from a global original position faithful to the fundamental interests he posited, then his actual moderation is in need of support. In particular, there is a need to justify reliance on the original position in matters of domestic justice, but not when principles of transnational assistance are established.

## What Is It about Government?

The contours of public opinion are not a sufficient basis for this distinction of spheres. Granted, people do not commonly extend their political demand for fair terms of cooperation to the global economy as a whole, or, in any case, would not commonly accept a global original position as the most reasonable interpretation of this global value. But this refusal stands out as a prejudice, expressing inadequate respect for people abroad, unless a further justification is available.

In *The Law of Peoples*, Rawls's argument against extrapolating worldwide the original position of *A Theory of Justice* appeals to the need for tolerance toward decent but nonliberal peoples. Insufficient respect would be shown in imposing sanctions on, or forcibly interfering with a decent nonliberal people, their institutions or their political culture on the basis of this alien individualist perspective (*LP*, 82f.). But help for desperate neediness abroad does not entail foreign coercion. Moreover, a decent, nonliberal people is as committed to the relief of dire poverty within its borders as a liberal people. If toleration is the only reason to refuse to extrapolate the domestic original position worldwide, a variant of Rawls's actual global device will produce the strong demand to relieve global poverty. Including representatives of peoples burdened by destitution, to express respect for their needs, will produce a duty of assistance more demanding than Rawls's, which would reflect any well-ordered people's values.

It might seem that global fair terms of cooperation should not give so much scope to demands of need because of the typical structure of global economic life: commerce crossing the national borders typically contributes much less to well-being than commerce within the borders. However, the correlation of burdens of assistance with reliance on trade would produce an implausible allocation of demands for help to the global poor – much greater for citizens of Singapore, say, than for citizens of the United States. And, more fundamentally, the requirement that duties of aid reflect net gain from interactions with the relevant recipients does not fit Rawls's domestic practice. Egalitarian duties are generated by an original position including disadvantaged fellow citizens, even if the duties impose costs of helping that they do not pay back.

These failures to fend off the cosmopolitanism of need by appeals to common opinion, toleration or the structure of commerce make it all the more appealing to base the use of the original position to determine justice among compatriots, but not worldwide, on some aspect of the specifically political interactions that bind compatriots with one another, but not with foreigners. This general strategy is typical of those who are broadly sympathetic to Rawls's egalitarianism within borders, but resist its extrapolation.[10] However, in specifying this confined basis, no narrow set of political interactions will do. The aim of monopolizing permission to use force throughout a territory is not enough. If households farming an as yet ungoverned territory decided to set up such a monopoly to prevent murder and rape, the better-off farmers would not take on a duty impartially to promote the fundamental interests of everyone in their territory.[11] Even protection against theft works no such moral magic in itself. One might as well claim that a farmer acquires a duty to help the needy even to the serious disadvantage of his household by putting a lock on his granary.[12] Nor would an isolated step beyond protection against unilateral interference be enough. If a community of farmers are politically united by a public irrigation authority, they need not govern themselves by principles concerning whole life-prospects that would be chosen behind a veil of ignorance of all advantages and disadvantages.

What might sustain the moral authority of the original position on a basis that does not globalize is the breadth, depth and constant change of protection and provision on the part of any modern government, the sort of government that is the shared concern of Rawls and his cosmopolitan critics. In modern circumstances, governments properly aim to promote the interests of people in their territory through diverse, shifting, wide-ranging legislation of rights and responsibilities, coordination, maintenance and start-up of all sorts of facilities for transportation, communication, education, research, protection and insurance, and fiscal and monetary policies. A government with this broad authority is in the interest of all. But the particular ways in which this broad authority is exercised can benefit some much more than others. Indeed, while it is in the interest of all to grant their government authority to advance the interests of its citizens, some will lose out in nearly every particular exercise of this authority, because their skills, location, needs or the goals with which they identify are less well-suited to the generally progressive alternative than to the situation that was changed.

The broad scope of a modern government's proper authority creates a correspondingly broad requirement of fairness that makes the original position, fair equality of opportunity and the difference principle parts of justice. The imposition of political authority is subordination if the imposed arrangements are unfair. If the government confined itself to imposition of obligations needed to sustain one specific public project, then fairness would only require impartial selection among alternative packages of burdens and benefits of the project. But acceptance of an indefinitely extensive authority to advance interests among those who can only leave at great cost, by imposing measures that often burden some without commensurate benefits, requires a correspondingly extensive assurance of impartiality.[13]

One cannot achieve fairness in the general project of betterment through a rule that each contribute in proportion to what she receives. For this would beg the question of the fairness of the public enterprise as a whole. As Rawls insists in response to Gauthier's equation of social fairness with mutual benefit, abilities to contribute and needs and desires determining what counts as contribution and benefit are themselves importantly determined by the selection among opportunities, rights and responsibilities in the exercise of authority whose fairness is being judged (see "The Basic Structure as Subject," *PL*, 269f., 277–279).

While modern governments actually commit themselves to promoting the common good, one would not want to make this commitment a prerequisite for a duty to govern fairly. A tyrant who frankly proclaims that he will use his power to enrich himself wrongs his subjects through unfairness, even if he does not insult them through hypocrisy.[14] Breadth of imposition is what counts, independent of the intentions that accompany it. While the imposition of a broad and important framework for self-advancement throughout a territory is always in fact backed up by coercion, this is not essential to the grounding of the original position. If the terms of self-advancement were to be sustained solely by everyone's commitment to a sufficiently extensive lifelong covenant, in which each gives up legitimate prerogatives of self-government on condition that others do the same, an unfair covenant would still generate injustice, and impartial reflection on lifelong prospects, guided by appropriate fundamental interests, would be the appropriate test of fairness.[15]

This basis for reliance on the original position of *A Theory of Justice* interprets and elaborates Rawls's description of its topic as "a system of cooperation designed to advance the good of those taking part in it" (*TJ*, 4). The argument against the cosmopolitanism of need might, then, appeal to the absence, in the Standard Case, of the transnational imposition of protections and facilities with such broad, deep impact. For this argument to succeed, two alternative bases for the global extrapolation will have to be refuted – leading to substantial changes in what once seemed to be the basis for the egalitarianism of *A Theory of Justice*.

First, the Kantian Interpretation must be abandoned. It can no longer be said that moral criticism guiding political reform should ultimately express the aspiration to the "purity of heart . . . grace and self-command" celebrated in the peroration of Rawls's first book (*TJ*, 514), a commitment to guidance by rules one would choose pursuing one's rational good without relying on knowledge of morally arbitrary facts affecting one's prospects. Moreover, abandonment of the full doctrine that Rawls once preached, as too comprehensive, will not be enough. Rejection of the cosmopolitanism of need depends on an adequate response to a limited, plausible position, the condemnation, as unfair, of benefits from engagement in economically interdependent self-advancement that depend on undeserved initial advantages. Such a rebuttal might note that undeserved initial advantages, say, from especially beneficial upbringing or early environment, are not, just by that token, illegitimately provided. People can rightly refuse to give up benefits from their making good use of undeserved advantages that did not result from unfair impositions.

The principled rejection of the cosmopolitanism of need by someone who relies on Rawls's domestic original position also seems to require acceptance of a natural right to resist interference that Rawls never explicitly endorsed. As Henry Shue emphasizes in *Basic Rights*, commerce entails exclusive property rights, coercively enforced against all potential takers. In the Standard Case, foreigners are prevented from coming and taking. If all coercive protection must be justified by rules to which all affected would agree if they pursued their interests behind a veil of ignorance, the cosmopolitanism of need results. Indeed, even apart from the device of the original position, relief of severe deprivation among economic associates might seem to be a dictate of reasonableness in property rights. Insistence that the desperately poor prohibit themselves from taking to relieve their burdens seems unreasonable. If so, the protection of property when severe poverty might be relieved is wrong, if the justifiability of protection depends on reasonable acceptability to all. (See Shue 1996.)

An adequate anticosmopolitan response would seem to depend on a natural right such as this: in the absence of relevant shared provision, people may prevent others from unilaterally interfering with their going about their business in pursuit of legitimate interests, even if they do not offer the others an arrangement that they could willingly support. This prerogative might be qualified by a requirement of aid. But a limited requirement, such as Rawls seems to endorse, might well be insufficient for reconciliation of haves and have-nots. In the past, poor pastoralists have sometimes raided better-off agricultural communities to relieve dire poverty in times of famine. Perhaps the farmers could not provide a safety net that the herders have adequate reason to accept as good enough without significant loss to their more comfortable standard of living. One might say, then, that the farmers are not wrong to seek to preserve their standard of living by resisting the herders' attempts to take, even if the herders' raids are not wrong, either.

Rawls never went this far in affirming a natural right to resist interference. But if his theory of justice within borders is to be combined with a mild duty of transitional poverty-relief, it seems that this step must be taken. This delineation of natural rights, like the emphasis on fundamental interests in self-reliance and association, makes the Rawlsian picture of justice look more like the libertarian picture than most suppose. By the same token, it may make his political conclusions more plausible to those who are drawn to libertarianism.

## Beyond the Standard Case

In the Standard Case that Rawls and his cosmopolitan critics investigate, mildness in duties to relieve foreign neediness may be defensible. But the nice features of the Standard Case make it a fantasy. Even transnational buying and selling can have further features requiring correction to establish cooperation on fair terms. Arguably, transnational manufacturing is often a vehicle of domination in which employers take unfair advantage of urgent needs of the desperately poor that weaken their bargaining power. In addition, setting the framework for commerce and much else besides, a coalition of developed countries led by the United States has, arguably, used developing countries' desperate needs for loans and markets to steer their course of development, without due regard for the interests affected by this domination. Directly and by sponsorship, the United States has in recent decades engaged in violence that has killed millions and wrecked the lives of millions more without the informed consent of innocent victims of this destruction and, arguably, without a morally adequate effort to make good the damage. People in developed countries, especially the United States, continue to be the per capita leaders in the spewing of greenhouse gases, arguably evading their fair share of burdens of cooperation in reducing the global harm. Even though the arguable abuses of power would not sustain the demands of global egalitarianism, they would establish a vast, demanding unmet duty of people in developed countries to help needy people in developing countries.

Perhaps the most serious limitation of *The Law of Peoples* is the absence of detailed inquiry into routine transnational abuses of power. This is an understandable limit in a short book written in the frail old age of a great philosopher mainly concerned with the description of well-ordered institutions and mainly drawn to international questions by horror at the ravages of war and atrocity, rooted in both the depth of these stains on humanity and the anguish of his own experiences during and right after World War II. However, Rawls presents this work as a bare beginning and shows bitter awareness of international disorders caused by "the great shortcomings of actual, allegedly constitutional democratic regimes," including the United States.[16] His core commitment, opposition to injustice, suggests the need to move beyond the limit he observed, to systematic inquiry, using his great insights, into current global abuses of power.

# Notes

1  See "The Law of Peoples" in *CP*, 558. In *The Law of Peoples*, this requirement of tolerant pluralism is, explicitly, Rawls's reason for rejecting the global extrapolation of the original position of *A Theory of Justice* as insufficiently accommodating the political culture of decent nonliberal societies (*LP*, 82f.).

2  See Beitz 1975 and 1999 (originally 1979), esp. Part III; Pogge 1989, esp. Part III; Moellendorf 2002, esp. chs 3 and 4.

3  In explaining the central role of fundamental interests, as opposed to actual desires and inclinations, Rawls notes, "Remember it is up to us, you and me, who are setting up justice as fairness, to describe the parties (as artificial persons in our device of representation) as best suits our aims in developing a political conception of justice" (*JF*, 87; cf. 85, 107, 141).

4  "The Idea of Public Reason Revisited" (originally 1997), *CP*, 579. In the first section of *A Theory of Justice*, Rawls notes that "a shared conception of justice establishes the bonds of civic friendship" (*TJ*, 5).

5  In his reflections on fair equality of opportunity within a society, Rawls assumes that "levels of income and wealth . . . are sufficiently correlated with differences in authority and responsibility" (*TJ*, 83). But this sensible assumption about correlation within a modern capitalist society is absurd when the net is cast worldwide. Typically, business executives in Germany, much less Mali, do not reach the level of income and wealth of business executives in the United States.

6  The difficulties of framing a morally compelling transnational principle of equal opportunity are trenchantly explored, from a different but complementary perspective, in D. Miller 2005.

7  Admittedly, the presence of international cooperative organizations in Rawls's well-ordered society of peoples would import some of his reasons for guarding against excessive inequalities of outcomes. In a footnote to his brief discussion of cooperative organizations in *The Law of Peoples*, Rawls notes that background global inequalities can make "market transactions" unfair and create "unjustified inequalities" among peoples, adding that "they have a role analogous to that of the basic structure in domestic society" (*LP*, 42). It is a substantial defect in Rawls's book that the explicit survey of considerations favoring domestic equality and their international analogues (*LP*, 114f.) obscures these parallel reasons for concern with excessive power. Still, the analogous global considerations are an inadequate basis for a global difference principle. The distorting pressures are primarily pressures of need, due to local poverty and distress, not to mere economic inequality.

8  In *Global Justice*, Gillian Brock defends the cosmopolitanism of need, arguing that a global original position would not, in contrast, support egalitarian demands (2009, ch. 3). Rather than appealing to relevant fundamental interests, she bases her anti-egalitarian argument on an empirical finding about the principles people typically favor when instructed to deliberate impartially over principles of justice. This innovative use of empirical psychology has substantial liabilities: it is unclear whether the responses of the experimental subjects can survive moral scrutiny or how their

conclusions could be the outcome of the distinctive process of impartial choice that Rawls prescribes.

9   See World Bank 2001, Tables 1.1, 2.19; and 2011, 66. The World Bank's $1.25 a day poverty line, the average poverty line of the 15 poorest countries, is, more precisely, $1.25 at 2005 purchasing power parity. About 1.3 billion people still lived below that poverty threshold in 2008, while the 2009 below-five death rate was still greater than one in ten among the countries, including one-eighth of the world's people, that were classified as "low income" by the Bank. See World Bank 2011, 66, Tables 1.1, 2.22; Chen and Ravallion 2012, 2.

10  See, for example, Blake 2002; R. Miller 1998 and 2010, ch. 2; Nagel 2005; Sangiovanni (20079. All of these writers posit some political duty of beneficence, responsive to neediness as such. Blake and Sangiovanni seem to have in mind a demanding duty to do what can be done to raise all above a threshold of destitution (see Blake 2002, 259; Sangiovanni 2007, 4). But neither provides a detailed argument for such a duty. In contrast, Nagel and I posit undemanding duties, in line with Rawls's duty of assistance.

11  Cf. Blake's thesis that political coercion is a sufficient (and necessary) basis for egalitarian demands of a broadly Rawlsian sort (2002, 281–284).

12  Cf. Sangiovanni's claim that "the state's capacity to provide the basic goods necessary to protect us from physical attack and to maintain and reproduce a stable system of property rights and justice" is sufficient to make economic equality a demand of justice (2007, 19).

13  Perhaps some aspects of the whole system are especially important in arguing for local, but not global egalitarian justice. Samuel Freeman, for example, emphasizes the national legislative specification of economic rights and liabilities (2006, 245–247).

14  Cf. Nagel's attempt to limit obligations of distributive justice to situations in which a government claims to rule in the name of its subjects (2005, 128f.).

15  So coercion is not a necessary basis for Rawlsian justice, as Blake proposes. Arrangements depending on enduring collective self-imposition of constraints count as imposed, a source of self-inflicted domination, like a contract to enter into slavery, if they are unfair.

16  See *LP*, 53, where US interventions in Chile, Guatemala and Nicaragua are attributed to these shortcomings.

## Works by Rawls, with Abbreviations

The Basic Structure as Subject" (1977), in *Political Liberalism*, Lecture VII.

*Collected Papers* (*CP*), ed. Samuel Freeman. Cambridge, MA: Harvard University Press, 1999.

"The Idea of Public Reason Revisited" (IPRR) (1997), in *Collected Papers* (573–615).

*Justice as Fairness: A Restatement* (*JF*), ed. Erin Kelly. Cambridge, MA: Harvard University Press, 2001.

"The Law of Peoples" (1993), in *Collected Papers* (529–564).

*The Law of Peoples, with "The Idea of Public Reason Revisited"* (*LP*). Cambridge, MA: Harvard University Press, 1999.

*Political Liberalism* (*PL*), expanded edn. New York: Columbia University Press, 2005.

*A Theory of Justice* (*TJ*), rev. edn. Cambridge, MA: Harvard University Press, 1999.

## Other References

Beitz, Charles (1975) "Justice and International Relations." *Philosophy and Public Affairs* 4: 360–389.

Beitz Charles (1999) *Political Theory and International Relations* (*1979*). Princeton: Princeton University Press.

Blake, Michael (2002) "Distributive Justice, Coercion and Autonomy." *Philosophy and Public Affairs* 30: 257–296.

Brock, Gillian (2009) *Global Justice: A Cosmopolitan Account*. Oxford: Oxford University Press.

Chen, Shaohua and Ravallion, Martin (2012) "An Update to the World Bank's Estimate of Consumption Poverty in the Developing World." Feb. 29. At http://siteresources.worldbank.org/INTPOVCALNET/Resources/Global_Poverty_Update_2012_02-29-12.pdf (accessed May 2013).

Freeman, Samuel (2006) "Distributive Justice and *The Law of Peoples*." In Rex Martin and David Reidy (eds), *Rawls's Law of Peoples: A Realistic Utopia?* Oxford: Blackwell.

Miller, David (2005) "Against Global Egalitarianism." *Journal of Ethics* 9: 58–64.

Miller, Richard (1998) "Cosmopolitan Respect and Patriotic Concern." *Philosophy and Public Affairs* 27: 202–224.

Miller, Richard (2010) *Globalizing Justice: The Ethics of Poverty and Power*. Oxford: Oxford University Press.

Moellendorf, Darrel (2002) *Cosmopolitan Justice*. Boulder, CO: Westview Press.

Nagel, Thomas (2005) "The Problem of Global Justice." *Philosophy and Public Affairs* 33: 113–147.

Pogge, Thomas (1989) *Realizing Rawls*. Ithaca: Cornell University Press.

Sangiovanni, Andrea (2007) "Global Justice, Reciprocity and the State." *Philosophy and Public Affairs* 35: 3–39.

Shue, Henry (1996) *Basic Rights* (*1980*). Princeton: Princeton University Press.

World Bank (2001) *World Development Indicators 2001*. Washington, DC: World Bank.

World Bank (2011) *World Development Indicators 2011*. Washington, DC: World Bank.

# 22

# Just War

## DARREL MOELLENDORF

John Rawls discusses just war doctrines in four of his works. The earliest place is in a few paragraphs in *TJ* (§58). The other three places are in the articles "The Law of Peoples" and "Fifty Years after Hiroshima" and in the book *The Law of Peoples*. But the discussions of the doctrines of just war in the two articles are mostly incorporated into his discussions in *LP*. There are certain recurring themes in Rawls's discussion of the doctrines of just war. From his early discussion in *TJ* onward, Rawls holds the view that the doctrines of just war are part of a larger account of international justice. And the discussions in the later three works stress the importance of human rights to the doctrines of just war. Although in *TJ* considerations of just war are tangential to Rawls's focus, by *LP* they are an important element in his non-ideal theory of international justice and are directly related to a central question of that work, namely what the proper scope of toleration is in the foreign policy of liberal peoples.

After briefly discussing aspects of the tradition of just war theory, I turn to Rawls's comments in *TJ*. Then I move directly to Rawls's best developed discussions of the doctrines of just war and related ideas in *LP* where I discuss the place of these doctrines in Rawls's account of the law of peoples, the importance of human rights to the accounts, and Rawls's account of the conditions in which the hope for peace is reasonable. Where there are relevant differences between the account in *LP* and the two articles I note them.

## 1. The Just War Tradition

Just war theorizing in Western moral and political thinking occupies the middle ground between two views. One view is attributed to Athens in Thucydides' Melian Dialogue during the Peloponnesian war, namely that there is no moral standard that properly constrains the use of force in times of war. "[I]n human disputation justice is then only agreed on when the necessity is equal; whereas they that have odds of power exact as much as they can, and the weak yield to such conditions as they can get" (1839–1845 [431 BCE], vol. 9, para.

*A Companion to Rawls*, First Edition. Edited by Jon Mandle and David A. Reidy.
© 2014 John Wiley & Sons, Inc. Published 2016 by John Wiley & Sons, Inc.

89). Views similar to this in contemporary times are referred to as "political realism" or "international relations realism." The other view is pacifism. Historically, the early Christian church interpreted several New Testament passages as requiring pacifism. For example, in the Beatitudes Jesus proclaims "blessed are the peacemakers" (Matt. 5:9). And in the Sermon on the Mount, says "if any one strikes you on the right cheek, turn to him the other also" (Matt. 5:39).

The Christian view regarding war eventually changed. And it provided the intellectual basis for the contemporary doctrines of just war, which take wars to be morally permissible only if they satisfy moral criteria concerning (at least) the conditions under which a war may be initiated – *jus ad bellum* – and the means that may be used in prosecuting a war – *jus in bello*. St Augustine is perhaps the first Christian theologian receptive to the idea that wrong-doing may justify war, although he believes that everyone should be greatly pained by the circumstances that would provide the justification:

> For it is the wrongdoing of the opposing party which compels the wise man to wage just wars; and this wrong-doing, even though it gave rise to no war, would still be matter of grief to man because it is man's wrongdoing. Let everyone, then, who thinks with pain on all these great evils, so horrible, so ruthless, acknowledge that this is misery. And if any one either endures or thinks of them without mental pain, this is a more miserable plight still, for he thinks himself happy because he has lost human feeling. (1887 [426 CE], Book 19, ch. 7)

This is nothing like a theory of the justice of war, but it captures the basic attitude of the tradition. War is a regrettable evil, but one that can sometimes be justified.

The conditions justifying war get refined and developed by St Thomas Aquinas, who argues that a just war must satisfy three conditions. It must be prosecuted by sovereign political authority, not by individuals. It must have a just cause, involving a fault by those who are attacked. And the intention of those prosecuting must be right; they must seek to advance the good or at least avoid evil (1920 [1265–1274]). The first Western philosopher to seek an account of just war wholly on the secular grounds of natural law is Hugo Grotius. Grotius argues that humans naturally seek the society of others and that natural reason recommends that we do that which conduces to living in society (2005 [1625], Book 1, ch. 1). Natural reason finds war abhorrent to human society although possibly justified to preserve self or society (ch. 2). The secular natural law tradition of theorizing about the just war is carried on further by other writers in the modern tradition, including Samuel Pufendorf (1991 [1673]) and Emmerich de Vattel (2008 [1797]). Although Rawls's account of justice is not based on natural law, as an heir to the modern tradition of social contract theory, he follows broadly in the footsteps of these just war theorists.

## 2. A Theory of Justice

The discussion of the just war doctrines in *TJ* is brief and entirely in the service of an account of conscientious refusal to fight in war. Rawls is not interested in making a new contribution to just war theory. Rather, his concern is to account for the conditions in which conscientious refusal to fight in war might be justified. These include when just cause for the war does not exist and when "the moral law of war is being regularly violated" (*TJ*, 334). Just cause is a requirement of *jus ad bellum*; and "the moral law of war" refers to the principles of *jus in bello*. He also suggests that if these moral conditions are violated to a sufficiently strong degree, "one may have duty and not only a right to refuse" to participate in a war (*TJ*, 335).

Rawls understands the doctrines of just war theory in light of an extension of the original position in which parties represent "different nations who must choose together the fundamental principles to adjudicate conflicting claims among states" (*TJ*, 331). In this extension of the original position the parties "know that they represent different nations each living under the normal circumstance of human life," but "they know nothing about the particular circumstances of their own society, its power and strength in comparison with other nations, nor do they know their place in their own society" (*TJ*, 331–332). This is an underdescribed version of a second original position. Not enough is known about the motivations of the parties, the interests of states, and the content of sets of principle to deduce the choice of such parties. Rawls offers only a general description that the "representatives of states are allowed only enough knowledge to make a rational choice to protect their interests but not so much that the more fortunate among them can take advantage of their special situation" (*TJ*, 332).

## 2.1 Jus ad Bellum

The result of the extension of the original position is a set of four principles for justice between states (*TJ*, 332):

1  The principle of equality of states: States have equal fundamental rights.
2  The principle of self-determination: The right of states to settle their own affairs without foreign intervention.
3  The right of self-defense against attack, including the right to form defensive alliances.
4  The duty to keep treaties, which are consistent with the other three principles.

Rawls claims that principle (1) is analogous to the equal rights of citizens in domestic justice. Both the extension of the original position to the justification of the principles of international justice and the analogy between the content of the two sets principle stand in the tradition of Vattel's argument that the natural law of nations bears analogy to the natural law between persons.[1]

Principles (2) and (3) concern matters of *jus ad bellum*. Principle (2) prohibits all wars that are contrary to the self-determination of states. Hence, a war of conquest that advances the interests of a state is unjust. This appears to give tremendous license to states to do as they please within their borders and to their populations. The license is not as great as it appears, however, since the extension of the original position that produces this principle is based on the assumption that "we have already derived the principles of justice as these apply to societies as units and to the basic structure" (*TJ*, 331). Principle (2) then assumes compliance with the two principles of domestic justice. Principle (3) licenses wars of direct self-defense and of aid to those who are defending themselves against a state or an alliance of states that is unjustly intervening. Taken together, principles (2) and (3) establish a version of the traditional *jus ad bellum* criterion of just cause (*TJ*, 332). A cause of war is just if and only if the war is one of self-defense, or of assistance in the self-defense, of a just state that has suffered aggression.

## 2.2 Jus in Bello

Rawls also notes the importance of considerations of *jus in bello*, and he departs from some traditional versions of just war theory by asserting that what is permissible *in bello* varies with the justice of the cause: "where a country's right to war is questionable and uncertain, the constraints on the means it can use are all the more severe. Acts permissible in a war of legitimate self-defense, when these are necessary, may be flatly excluded in a more doubtful situation" (*TJ*, 332). He does not, however, elaborate on which *jus in bello* constraints he takes to be more severe in doubtful wars. Perhaps he has in mind the principle of noncombatant immunity, which in *LP* he takes to be defeasible in cases of supreme emergency.[2] Presumably, a war in pursuit of an unjust cause could never satisfy the requirements of a supreme emergency; and therefore intentionally targeting noncombatants would be "flatly excluded" when the cause is unjust.

Rawls does not explicitly state the principles comprising the doctrine of *jus in bello*. One thought for why this is the case is that the four principles of justice are to be taken as the ideal theory of international conduct, and principles of *jus in bello* need not be stated on the assumption of strict compliance since then there is no war. This assumption, however, seems contradicted by (3), the principle of self-defense against attack, which need not be stated if (2), the principle of self-determination, enjoys strict compliance. Thus, the assumption of strict compliance cannot explain why Rawls fails to lay out the principles of *jus in bello*.

Another interpretation is that Rawls does not take the principles of *jus in bello* to be principles of justice between states at all, but to be natural duties, which govern relations between persons but which "have no necessary connection with institutions or social practices" (*TJ*, 98). Rawls claims that the principles of *jus in bello* follow from taking the justified interests of states to be best served by the observance of the natural duties in times of war:

> The representatives of states would recognize that their national interest, as seen from the original position, is best served by acknowledging these limits on the means of war . . . Granting these presumptions, then, it seems reasonable to suppose that the traditional prohibitions incorporating the natural duties that protect human life would be chosen. (*TJ*, 332–333)

Non-combatant immunity then seems to be an expression of the natural duties not to harm or to injure and not to cause unnecessary suffering (*TJ*, 98). The absence of *jus in bello* principles in the principles of justice between states would be explained by the architectonic of Rawls's grander account that places the natural duties and the law of nations in different parts of the concept of right (*TJ*, 94).

The interpretation of the previous paragraph, however, is also problematic. For the quotation cited above has the principles of *jus in bello* chosen in the extension of the original position that sets out principles of justice between states. They would seem then to be part of the doctrine of justice between states, but a part that Rawls does not express. This is consistent with his introduction of the four principles with the claim that they are "only an indication of the principles that would be acknowledged" (*TJ*, 332).

Another problem is to understand the reasoning that leads to the principles of *jus in bello* in the original position. One possibility is that Rawls has them chosen by means of the following inference: The only reason to choose principles that would require violating natural duties would be their service in prosecuting a war of aggression, but prior principles have already ruled out such wars. Hence, principles for the conduct of war should express natural duties. This seems faithful to the text of the quotation above, but it is dubious because the first premise is implausible. It might be very effective to fight a war of self-defense by targeting the civilian citizens of an aggressive state, as both the United States and Britain did during several bombing campaigns in World War II. Another possibility is that Rawls is asserting that the same kind of moral constraints that rule out wars of aggression also rule out violations of principles of *jus in bello*. Such an interpretation, however, requires taking violations of the principle of self-determination to involve violations of natural duties (since the *jus in bello* principles express natural duties). It is not clear how Rawls might maintain that, given the architectonic, which places the law of nations and the natural duties in different parts of the concept of right (*TJ*, 94). There may be no satisfactory interpretation of Rawls's reasoning leading to the choice of the principles of *jus in bello* in the extension of the original position. This is somewhat mitigated by a recognition that his purpose is to develop an account of conscientious objection, not a doctrine of just war. But insofar as the conditions of justified conscientious objection include violations of the principles of *jus in bello*, a better developed account of the reasons supporting the latter would better support his purpose.

### 2.3 Contingent Pacifism

Although Rawls affirms that in principle wars may be just when satisfying the conditions of *jus ad bellum* and *jus in bello*, he also expresses support for a policy of general and radical skepticism that this is usually the case: "Given the often predatory aims of state power, and the tendency of men to defer to their government's decisions to wage war, a general willingness to resist the state's claims is all the more necessary" (*TJ*, 335). He argues that conscientious refusal is justified when a war is unjust for reasons either of *jus ad bellum* or *jus in bello*. The unlikelihood of satisfying the demanding conditions of these doctrines lends support to the position of contingent pacifism.

> [T]he conduct and aims of states in waging war, especially large and powerful ones, are in some circumstances so likely to be unjust that one is forced to conclude that in the foreseeable future one must abjure military service altogether. So understood a form of contingent pacifism may be a perfectly reasonable position: the possibility of just war is conceded but not under present circumstances. (*TJ*, 335)

## 3. The Law of Peoples

Rawls's first clarification that considerations of just war are part of the nonideal theory of international justice comes in "The Law of Peoples," where he claims: "the only legitimate grounds of the right to war against outlaw regimes is defense of the society of well-ordered peoples and, in grave cases of innocent persons subject to outlaw regimes and the protection of their human rights" (*CP*, 556). And in *LP* Rawls explicitly takes the right to war to be a matter of international justice. "Although domestic principles of justice are consistent with a qualified right to war they do not of themselves establish the right. The basis of that right depends on the Law of Peoples . . ." (*LP*, 26). Since the Law of Peoples involves a commitment to a set of human rights and is developed as a guide for extending the liberal idea of toleration to foreign policy, Rawls's account of just war theory, unlike some traditional accounts, is enmeshed in a rich set of practical commitments for international relations.

## 3.1 The Law of Peoples

As in *TJ* Rawls takes the justification of the principles of international justice to follow from a choice of parties in a second original position. In *LP* this is a two-step process. In the first step representatives of liberal peoples choose principles. In the second step representatives of decent hierarchical societies (or decent consultation hierarchies)[3] affirm the same set of principles. The principles are the following (*LP*, 37):

1 Peoples are free and independent, and their freedom and independence are to be respected by other peoples.
2 Peoples are to observe treaties and undertakings.
3 Peoples are equal parties to the agreements that bind them.
4 Peoples are to observe a duty of nonintervention.
5 Peoples have the right of self-defense but no right to instigate war for reasons other than self-defense.
6 Peoples are to honor human rights.
7 Peoples are to observe certain specified restrictions in the conduct of war.
8 Peoples have a duty to assist other peoples living under unfavorable conditions that prevent their having a just or decent political regime.[4]

With some differences in order these eight principles seem to include the four from *TJ*, with the possible exception of the first. The first principle of the *LP* – *LP* (1) – however might play the same functional role in the overall account as the first principle in *TJ* – *Theory* (1) – namely, the principle of equality. *LP* (2) is equivalent to *Theory* (4); *LP* (4), which states a duty of nonintervention, is the correlate of the right to self-determination stated in *Theory* (3); and *LP* (5) includes *Theory* (3), licensing wars of self-defense but also adding the prohibition of other grounds for war.

Rawls notices in *LP* that some principles are superfluous in the doctrine of the ideal theory of the Law of Peoples; among these he lists (7), which seems to stipulate observance of traditional principles of *jus in bello*, and (6), which requires respect for human rights (*LP*, 37). Principle (7) is not needed because given strict compliance to (4) there is no war. Principle (6) is redundant because liberal societies are committed to human rights along with other rights to liberal and democratic governance, of which human rights are an especially urgent subset (*LP*, 78–79). It is not clear at this point why (since the apparently superfluous reference to human rights is included) the complete package of rights to liberal and democratic governance is also not included. Presumably (6) is affirmed because parties have an interest in protecting their liberal conceptions of justice, and human rights are a piece of that conception. But that same interest would lead parties to include the full package of rights to liberal and democratic governance. Moreover, the representatives of egalitarian liberal societies would on the same grounds seek agreement on a principle affirming the importance of egalitarian distributive requirements.

The considerations of the previous paragraph have direct importance to Rawls's account of *jus ad bellum* because he takes both the duty to respect the external sovereignty of states expressed in (4) and the right to exercise internal sovereignty, which seems entailed by (1), to be qualified by (6), requiring the observance of human rights (*LP*, 37–38). The argument in defense of these two claims would seem to be that because the parties have interests in the protection of their liberal conceptions of justice, they agree that intervention may be justified to protect human rights. But the same premise would also allow for the possibility of inter-vention to protect the broader set of liberal and democratic rights. And if the parties were only representatives of egalitarian liberal peoples, that premise would accept interventions to protect egalitarian institutions. Now, if Rawls had endowed the parties with especially great concern for a smaller set of urgent rights, there would be grounds for limiting the qualifications of (4) and (1) to observance of such rights. In the absence of such concern there are no grounds for limiting the qualifications of (4) and (1), as long as the parties rep-resent only liberal societies.[5] Hence, the inclusion of principle (6) begs the question of why both other rights to liberal and democratic governance and a principle of distributive egali-tarianism are not also agreed upon.

## 3.2 Jus ad Bellum

The incorporation of the requirement that peoples observe human rights and the constraints that this places on invoking (1) and (4) entails a principle of just cause that is more complex than that contained in *TJ* (but recall in *TJ* the assumption is that states adhere to justice as fairness). A cause of war is just if the war is one of self-defense, or of assistance in the self-defense, of a state that has suffered aggression and the state observes human rights; just cause may exist even if the war is neither one of self-defense nor of assistance in self-defense, if the intervention responds to human rights violations that are sufficiently grave (*LP*, 38, 78, 80). Rawls leaves the notion of the gravity of the violation of human rights vague, but the one example he imagines (*LP*, 94 n6) of a society containing slavery and human sacrifice seems to fall short of genocide, which is on some accounts is the only humanitarian ground for intervention (see Walzer 2006, 108). There is in any case never just cause for war against a society that does not threaten the self-determination of another state and that honors human rights (*LP*, 92).

Human rights then play an especially important role in the account of *jus ad bellum*. Their observance is sufficient to make intervention unjust. And a failure to observe them, if suffi-ciently grave, may license intervention. There is a small set of rights that Rawls has in mind for this special role: life (including subsistence and security), liberty (including freedom from servitude and liberty – albeit not equal liberty – of conscience), personal property, and formal equality under the law (*LP*, 65).

Unlike the account of justice between states in *TJ*, which envisions only an international society of states adhering to justice as fairness, *LP* explicitly includes a class of nonliberal societies as full members of international society. These are decent hierarchical societies or decent consultation hierarchies. An explicit aim of *LP* is to work out how far a principle of toleration in international affairs may be extended beyond liberal societies. Since decent societies are imagined to be nonaggressive and to affirm the list of human rights stated above, they may not be attacked. Rawls also imagines another class of societies, benevolent absolut-isms, which because they are nonaggressive and honor human rights may not be attacked (*LP*, 92). The existence of the latter is tolerated, but they are not full members of international society.

Decent societies are (i) non-aggressive, (ii) respectful of human rights, (iii) sufficiently legitimate to impose real legal obligations on their citizens, (iv) adherents to a common good idea of justice that takes into consideration what the conception of justice counts as the interests of everyone, and (v) in possession of a judiciary that has a sincere and not unreasonable belief that the law is guided by a common-good idea of justice. Because of these features they are respected as full members of international society (*LP*, 67). Additionally, Rawls holds that the condition that the judiciary possesses a sincere and not unreasonable belief that the law is guided by the common-good idea of justice requires that decent societies include institutions of group consultation (*LP*, 72–73). Because of their respect for human rights and their various legitimate institutions, such societies are worthy of the full respect of liberal societies, even though they are not just (*LP*, 84). This moral judgment, and not the interests and motivations of the parties in the original position, best explains the logically problematic inclusion of the set of human rights – an inclusion which begs the question of the absence of other rights of liberal and democratic governance – in the first step of the original position. Rawls seeks to extend the liberal idea of toleration to the relations between liberal and decent peoples.

In contrast to benevolent absolutisms and decent hierarchical societies, outlaw states fail to comply with the Law of Peoples. Recalling the Athenian argument, such regimes hold that "a sufficient reason to engage in war is that it advances, or might advance, the regime's rational (not reasonable) interests" (*LP*, 90). They therefore fail to uphold principle (4), the duty of nonintervention; and they may also be oppressive regimes with internally "unjust and cruel" institutions (*LP*, 93). Unlike the existence of benevolent absolutisms and decent hierarchies, the existence of outlaw states poses a danger; and "all peoples are safer and more secure if such states change, or are forced to change their ways" (*LP*, 81). The last clause suggests that Rawls is open under the appropriate conditions to wars of regime change. Although peoples have the right of self-defense under principle (5), the long-term objective of policy toward outlaw states is to bring them into compliance with principle (1), which entails self-determination, and principle (4), which requires nonintervention, and when necessary also to force them to respect the human rights covered under principle (6).

In *LP*, as in *TJ*, Rawls does not discuss any other criteria for *jus ad bellum*. But his example of intervention to defend the human rights of slaves and the victims of human sacrifice only after the society has failed to respond to sanctions suggests a commitment to a version of the criterion of necessity. Furthermore, he might be interpreted as allowing preemptive wars in the case of sincere and reasonable belief of attack. For he says, "Well-ordered peoples, both liberal and decent, do not initiate war against one another; they go to war only when they sincerely and reasonably believe that their safety and security are seriously endangered by the expansionist policies of outlaw states" (*LP*, 90–91). If there could be such reasonable belief before an actual attack, then wars of preemption in those cases would be justified.

## 3.3 Jus in Bello

The human rights principle in *LP* avoids the puzzle in *TJ* regarding the justification of the principles of *jus in bello*. In *TJ* Rawls holds that there is some sort of connection between the commitment not to engage in wars of aggression and the affirmation of the principles of *jus in bello*. But the connection is obscure. In *LP* we have more to work with. If the principles of *jus in bello* are justified by a commitment to human rights, as one influential account argues (Walzer 2006, 137), then the commitment to human rights in principle (6) secures the commitment to the principles of *jus in bello* in principle (7).

Despite the inclusion of (7) in the Law of Peoples, Rawls takes the principles of *jus in bello* to be primarily principles of nonideal theory (*LP*, 94). This is a plausible approach since if principles (4) and (5) were strictly complied with there would be no wars of defense against aggression, and if principle (6) were complied with there would be no wars to defend the human rights of citizens oppressed by their governments. Nonideal theory offers guidance in bringing about the long-term goals of ideal theory. Taking principles of *jus in bello* as principles of nonideal theory need not deny that they are also required by human rights or natural duties, but it is to emphasize their instrumental value in the long-term project of achieving international justice.

The instrumental value noted above helps to explain the six considerations that Rawls states regarding *jus in bello*. The first holds that the aim of a just war is a just and lasting peace, suggesting that wars are only ever justified as a matter of nonideal theory (*LP*, 94). The second holds that liberal and decent peoples only wage war against states with expansionist aims that threaten the security and institutions of liberal and decent peoples (*LP*, 94). Neither of these two consideration is strictly a principle of traditional *jus in bello* since both concern when it is just to resort to war. Considerations three through six are more in accordance with the traditional understanding of *jus in bello*.

Consideration three distinguishes between an outlaw state's leaders and officials, its soldiers, and its civilian population (*LP*, 94). Rawls's intention here is not made clear, but apparently the distinction serves certain traditional claims of *jus in bello* that involve discriminating between targets within an enemy population. For example, Rawls argues that the leaders are responsible for the war and are therefore criminals (*LP*, 95). The distinction between leaders and soldiers seems to entail that only leaders are subject to prosecution. Assuming the combatants observe the laws of war, they are not then to be treated as criminals when captured. Rawls does not develop the idea further but he might be gesturing toward the traditional principle that combatants are subject to benevolent quarantine.[6] And because soldiers are not taken to be responsible for the war, attacking them is justified only on grounds of necessity (*LP*, 96).[7] The distinction between both leaders and soldiers on the one hand and civilians on the other hand would support the principle of noncombatant immunity, although once again Rawls does not explicitly state the principle. Noncombatant immunity entails that the killing of noncombatants cannot be justified on grounds of military necessity.

Consideration four makes explicit the dual value of principles of *jus in bello* as protectors of human rights and as instrumental to just ends:

> Well-ordered peoples must respect, so far as possible, the human rights of the members of the other side, both civilians and soldiers, for two reasons. One is simply that that the enemy, like all others, has these rights by the Law of Peoples. The other reason is to teach enemy soldiers and civilians the content of those rights by the example set in the treatment they receive. In this way the meaning and significance in of human rights are best brought home to them. (*LP*, 96)

Failures to comply with the principles of *jus in bello* are then wrong both because of the human rights violations that they constitute, but also because they frustrate the objectives of nonideal theory to propagate respect for human rights. Consideration five holds that the proclamations of the leaders of well-ordered peoples should also play a teaching role; they should foreshadow the aims of a just and equitable peace (*LP*, 96).

Consideration six expresses the limits of justifying actions on grounds of military necessity by asserting that "practical means-end reasoning must always have a restricted role in judging the appropriateness of an action or policy. This mode of thought . . . must always be framed within and strictly limited by the preceding principles and assumptions" (*LP*, 96). Hence, although military necessity may dictate a strategy designed to kill as many enemy combatants as possible, it could not normally be grounds for accepting a strategy that involves targeting civilians in contravention of the principle of noncombatant immunity. This approach to practical reasoning is characteristic of Rawls. In *LP* the defining property of peoples, as opposed to states, is that they accept that their sovereignty is constrained by the law of peoples (*LP*, 27). "A difference between liberal peoples and states is that just liberal peoples limit their basic interests as required by the reasonable" (*LP*, 29). The constraint, expressed in the sixth consideration, is simply the mark of moral and reasonable action, according to Rawls.

## 3.4 Supreme Emergency

One important feature of international society, according to Rawls, is that it might give rise to circumstances in which it is reasonable to suspend the otherwise reasonable constraints on rational action. Rawls follows Michael Walzer in referring to these circumstances as "supreme emergencies" and generally adopts Walzer's account of them (*LP*, 98–99).[8] In particular these are circumstances in which the principle of noncombatant immunity is suspended. As an example of this, Rawls follows Walzer in discussing the British bombing of German cities after the fall of France in June, 1940, until the Soviet Union had demonstrated its capacity to fend off the Nazi assault in the late summer and fall of 1941, and perhaps even through to the end of the defeat of Germany in the battle of Stalingrad in February of 1943.

To justify the application of the supreme emergency exemption during this period, Rawls makes two claims: "First, Nazism portended incalculable moral and political evil for civilized life everywhere. Second, the nature and history of constitutional democracy and its place in European history were at stake" (*LP*, 99). He echoes here the characterization that Walzer makes of a military leader wagering to suspend the principle of noncombatant immunity during in response to a supreme emergency: "But I dare to say that our history will be nullified and our future condemned unless I accept the burdens of criminality here and now" (Walzer 2006, 260). Elsewhere Rawls refers to Hitler's conception of the world and the Holocaust itself as "demonic" (*LP*, 20, 21).

Applying the supreme emergency exemption involves political judgment, which Rawls maintains might be disputed (*LP*, 99). Walzer argues that the bulk of the British terror bombing of German cities came too late to be justified by the exemption (2006, 261). Rawls rejects the fire-bombing of Japanese cities in the spring of 1945. And both philosophers strongly condemn the obliteration of Hiroshima and Nagasaki by atomic bombs (*LP*, 99–101).[9] Clearly, the exemption may not be casually invoked. It is never the product merely of military necessity or even of there being a just cause for war. Walzer is unremitting in seeing employment of the exemption as a kind of serious evil, albeit a lesser one, perpetrated against defenseless civilians:

> We can recognize their horror only when we have acknowledged the personality and value of the men and women we destroy in committing them. It is the acknowledgment of rights that puts a stop to such [utilitarian] calculations and forces us to realize that the destruction of the innocent, whatever its purposes, is a kind of blasphemy against our deepest moral commitments. (2006, 262)

The two justifying conditions that Rawls invokes for applying the supreme emergency condition to Britain's bombing of German cities are demanding. But they are also jointly insufficient since those conditions were in place later in the war as well. Rawls is implicitly relying on a third condition, a principle of a necessity.

The second of the two justifying conditions for applying the supreme emergency exemption to Britain's bombing of German civilian centers, that "the nature and history of constitutional democracy . . . were at stake," bears partial analogy to Rawls's priority rule for the equal basic liberties principle of justice as fairness:

> The first principles of justice are to be ranked in lexical order and therefore liberty can be restricted only for the sake of liberty: There are two cases: (a) a less extensive liberty must strengthen the total system of liberty shared by all, and (b) a less than equal liberty must be acceptable to those citizens with lesser liberty. (*TJ*, 220)

The analogy to the first of these two conditions is straightforward. The violation of the human rights of the German civilians that occurred when they were killed and injured and their homes were destroyed is permissible only if it is necessary for the survival of the society of liberal and decent peoples, who honor human rights. In the case of the second condition of the priority rule for liberty Rawls has in mind justified paternalism, which allows us "to argue that with the development of recovery of his rational powers the individual in question will accept our decision on his behalf and agree with us that we did the best thing for him" (*TJ*, 219). But Rawls does not also require of the application of the supreme emergency exemption that it be retrospectively justifiable to the people who suffered as a result.

Rawls's affirmation of the supreme emergency exemption, however, does not sit entirely comfortably with his aim of admitting decent societies into the Law of Peoples. To see why, we must appreciate that Rawls takes the Law of Peoples to be a political conception of justice (*LP*, 104). As such, presumably it is directed solely toward the institutions and practices of international society; it is freestanding with respect to comprehensive conceptions of the good; and it is expressed by means of ideas that are fundamental to an international society of liberal and decent peoples.[10] The content of the Law of Peoples also establishes the constraints on reasonable public criticism. "The Law of Peoples with its political concepts and principles, ideals and criteria, is the content" of the public reason in a society of liberal and decent peoples by means of which members debate "their mutual relations" (*LP*, 55). Rawls takes the constraints on debate to apply "whenever chief executives and legislators, and other government officials, as well as candidates for public office, act from and follow the principles of the Law of Peoples and explain to other peoples their reasons for pursuing or revising a people's foreign policy and affairs of state that involves other societies" (*LP*, 56). Moreover, the constraints on public reason apply to citizens considering such matters. "As for private citizens, we say, as before, that ideally citizens are to think of themselves *as if* they were legislators and ask themselves what foreign policy supported by what consideration they would think more reasonable to advance" (*LP*, 56–57). The tension arises because Rawls freely admits that the supreme emergency exemption – a doctrine in the domain of international public reason – explicitly contradicts the moral principles of certain comprehensive conceptions of the good, Catholicism in particular, which never permits intentionally killing noncombatants. Otherwise-decent hierarchical societies organized around religious conceptions that reject all intentional killing can affirm the Law of Peoples only if they reject certain tenets of their belief.[11]

The options available for responding to otherwise-decent societies religiously opposed to all intentional killing are not particularly satisfactory. Either they fall out of the Law of Peoples altogether, or the Law of Peoples is amended, or they have some sort of partial membership. Given that Rawls places so much emphasis on the disrespect that is expressed by nonadmittance as a member in good standing in the society of peoples (LP, 62), the first is not a happy option if the peoples on all other counts satisfy the conditions of membership. The second option is far from satisfactory if the arguments of Rawls and Walzer are correct regarding the importance of the supreme emergency exemption in certain limited circumstances. To prohibit the exemption is to allow the preventable triumph of demonic forces. Although according to some religious worldviews this may be an acceptable cost, to a great many other religious and secular people it is not. The third option comes at the cost of expressing a kind of disrespect. The reasons that otherwise-decent hierarchical societies employ to justify their objection will be considered outside the scope of public reason by other well-ordered societies. The objections will be judged unreasonable. This is especially important because in the circumstances envisaged by Rawls the stakes are very high indeed. Nonetheless the third option seems the best reconciliation.

Societies opposed to the extreme emergency exemption in international society might be treated on the analogy to treatment of Quakers in domestic society. Of the latter Rawls says that they

> can join an overlapping consensus on a constitutional regime, but they cannot always endorse a democracy's particular decisions – here to engage in a war of self-defense – even when those decisions are reasonable in the light of its political values. This indicates that they could not in good faith, in the absence of special circumstances, seek the highest offices in a liberal democratic regime. (LP, 105)

Otherwise-decent hierarchical societies, which abjure all intentional targeting of civilians, could presumably never have a role in the security council of an international society organized according to the Law of Peoples. Still the analogy to Quakers is imperfect since Quakers do not necessarily reject either of the two principles of justice as fairness, but otherwise-decent hierarchical societies that reject all intentional killing seem to reject a principle of international justice, or more precisely a clause in principle (7) once it is fully specified.

## 3.5  The Democratic Peace

Rawls takes Kant's *Perpetual Peace* as a guide for the development of his views in *LP* (LP, 10). But nothing could be further from Kant's concerns in *Perpetual Peace* than the interest that Rawls has in incorporating principles of just war into the Law of Peoples. Kant is openly hostile to just war principles and is scathing in his criticism of his predecessors who sought to develop the doctrines of just war.

> [I]t is astonishing that the word "right" has not yet been entirely banished from the politics of war as pedantic, and that no state has yet ventured to publicly advocate this point of view: For Hugo Grotius, Pufendorf, Vattel and others – Job's comforters, all of them – are always quoted in good faith to justify an attack, although their codes, whether couched in philosophical or diplomatic terms, have not – nor can have – the slightest legal force, because states, as such, are under no common external authority; and there is no instance of a state having ever been moved by argument to desist from its purpose, even when this was backed up by the testimony of such great men. (Kant 1917 [1795], 131–132)

According to Kant, war can never be stopped by a merely moral doctrine such as those concerning the justice of war.

Rather than comforting a sorrowful and suffering Job with a moral doctrine, intelligent institutional design is called for to guide the creation of a world without the sorrows and suffering caused by war. Although Kant takes war to be evidence of "the depravity of human nature" (1917, 131), he nonetheless sees reason for hope:

> This homage which every state renders – in words at least – to the idea of right, proves that, although it may be slumbering, there is, notwithstanding, to be found in man a still higher natural moral capacity by the aid of which he will in time gain the mastery over the evil principle in his nature, the existence of which he is unable to deny. (1917, 132)

In the domain of international affairs Kant sees our moral capacity as gaining mastery over the evil principle, not by limiting wars to just war principles, but by creating a *foedus pacificum* or covenant of peace among republican states that puts an end to war forever (1917, 134).

Republican states come together to form a peaceful international compact just as individuals come together to form a republican state. According to Kant the republican form of government alone is inclined to a peaceful compact because it is only in such a regime that the decision to go to war is in the hands of those who bear the costs of war.

> If, as must be so under this constitution, the consent of the subjects is required to determine whether there shall be war or not, nothing is more natural than that they should weigh the matter well, before undertaking such a bad business. For in decreeing war, they would of necessity be resolving to bring down the miseries of war upon their country. This implies they must fight themselves; they must hand over the costs of the war out of their own property; they must do their poor best to make good the devastation which it leaves behind; and finally, as a crowning ill, they have to accept a burden of debt which will embitter even peace itself, and which they can never pay off on account of the new wars which are always impending. (1917, 122–123)

So, the advent of republicanism creates the possibility of a peaceful international order because states are controlled by those who would bear the costs of war.

There are echoes of Kant's view in Rawls. "One does not find peace by declaring war irrational and or wasteful, though indeed it may be so, but by preparing the way for peoples to develop a basic structure that supports a reasonably just or decent regime and makes possible a reasonable Law of Peoples" (*LP*, 123). Despite the departure that Rawls makes from Kant by incorporating the principles of just war into the theory of international justice, Rawls's invocation of the democratic peace stands in the tradition of Kant's *foedus pacificum*. Rawls claims that history supports the empirical generalization that "major established democracies" do not go to war with each other (*LP*, 52). His explanation of these peaceful relations is not, however, the same as Kant's. Peace does not come merely by ensuring that the decision to go to war is in the hands of those who bear its costs. Instead, Rawls endorses a version of Raymond Aron's thesis of peace by satisfaction (1960). "There is true peace among them [peoples] because all societies are satisfied with the status quo for the right reasons" (*LP*, 47). Continuing on, "Domination and striving for glory, the excitement of conquest and the pleasure of exercising power over others, do not move them against other peoples. All being satisfied in this way, liberal peoples have nothing to go to war about" (*LP*, 47).

The domestic conditions that Rawls takes to be necessary to produce satisfaction for the right reasons are demandingly egalitarian. Rawls discusses the following five conditions: (a) fair equality of opportunity, especially in education and training; (b) a decent distribution of income and wealth, assuring all citizens the all-purpose means necessary for them to make intelligent and effective advantage of their basic freedoms; (c) society as the employer of last resort; (d) basic health care for all citizens; and (e) public financing of elections and making available public information on matters of policy (*LP*, 50). These conditions are sufficiently egalitarian to rule out libertarian societies from having stability for the right reasons (*LP*, 49–50). This is a remarkable claim, which Rawls makes only in passing. But the account of the conditions of satisfaction for the right reasons entails that libertarian peoples would not normally be sufficiently egalitarian to be satisfied in the relevant sense. To the extent that this is the case, libertarian societies will not be parties to the democratic peace, and thus not be members in good standing in The Law Peoples.

The robust social conditions that would produce satisfaction for the right reasons explain by their absence "the great shortcomings of actual, allegedly constitutional democratic regimes" (*LP*, 53) which have used war to oust democratically elected governments in countries where democracy is less well established. "[T]he United States overturned the democracies of Allende in Chile, Arbez in Guatemala, Mossadegh in Iran, and, some would add, the Sandinistas in Nicaragua" (*LP*, 53). Rawls's diagnosis of each of these crimes against democracy is roughly Leninist:[12] "Whatever the merits of these regimes, covert operations against them were carried out by a government prompted by monopolistic and oligarchic interests without the knowledge or criticism of the public" (*LP*, 53). Additionally, "Though democratic peoples are not expansionist, they do defend their security interest, and a democratic government can easily invoke this interest to support covert interventions, even when actually moved by economic interests behind the scenes" (*LP*, 53). Rawls's solution, of course, is not Lenin's prescription for socialist revolution. Rawls holds that a liberal society that satisfies the five conditions above is one that both insulates democratic institutions from economic power and through distributive institutions produces a population that would be unmoved by the pleasures of dominating others.

This account of peace by satisfaction creates a second obstacle to the aim of incorporating decent peoples into The Law of Peoples. As these peoples are imagined by Rawls they contain neither the institutional mechanisms that would insulate political power from capture by economic interests nor the distributive institutions that would prevent the population from becoming sufficiently dissatisfied so as to be susceptible to the desires for glory and domination. In the absence of these, the basis for Rawls's extension of the democratic peace to cover decent hierarchical societies is lacking. Rather, than developing that basis in detail he merely stipulates that such people are peaceful.

The stipulation that decent societies are peaceful might be defended as unproblematic since Rawls claims his "remarks about a decent hierarchical society are conceptual" (*LP*, 75

391

n16). Moreover, he does not even suppose that liberal peoples satisfying the conditions for a satisfied people exist. "In the case of democratic peoples, the most we can say is that some are closer than others to a reasonably just constitutional regime" (*LP*, 75). But there are three problems with such a defense of the stipulation. The first is that it is in tension with Rawls's reliance on the actual or alleged history of peace between major established democracies. If the concern is merely to develop the conceptual possibility of peace between states, then an appeal to history is superfluous. The second is that it is hard to understand why in the case of liberal societies Rawls would go to the effort of providing the institutional requisites for peace by means of satisfaction if nonbelligerence could simply be stipulated. Finally, and perhaps most importantly, the bare conceptual possibility of peaceful nonliberal peoples provides very weak grounds for a realistic hope for a peaceful world order comprising liberal and decent peoples (*LP*, 6).

The problem remains: if Rawls takes seriously the domestic institutional requirements necessary for peace by satisfaction, the hope for a peaceful order of liberal and decent peoples seems misplaced. Rawls maintains that it would be unrealistic to hope for an international society comprised entirely of liberal peoples (*LP*, 78). The account of peace by satisfaction suggests, however, that hope for a peaceful world order is perhaps best characterized as the hope for a world eventually constituted of egalitarian liberal peoples.

# Notes

1. "We must therefore apply to nations the rules of the law of nature, in order to discover what their obligations are, and what their rights: consequently the *law of nations* is originally no other than the *law of nature applied* to nations. But as the application of a rule cannot be just and reasonable unless it be made in a manner suitable to the subject, we are not to imagine that the law of nations is precisely and in every case the same as the law of nature, with the difference only of the subjects to which it is applied, so as to allow of our substituting nations for individuals" (Vattel 2008 [1797], Preliminaries §6, 31).

2. The supreme emergency exception is defended in Walzer 2006, 251–263. In his later work Rawls explicitly agrees with Walzer (*LP*, 98–103). So, it might be that Rawls has something like that in mind in *Theory* as well.

3. The term "decent" does not yet appear in "The Law of Peoples."

4. The first seven of these principles appeared first in "The Law of Peoples" (see *CP*, 540) in a different order.

5. This paragraph repeats an argument made in Moellendorf 1996 and in 2002, ch. 2.

6. For more on benevolent quarantine see Walzer 2006, 46.

7. See also Walzer 2006, 144–145 for the doctrine of military necessity applied to the justification for killing combatants.

8. For Walzer's account see Walzer 2006, 251–268.

9. See also Rawls, "Fifty Years after Hiroshima," and Walzer 2006, 263–268.

10. These three conditions are the approximate international analogues of the conditions for domestic society expressed in *PL*, 11–15.

11. A similar problem would apparently arise in societies affirming certain forms of Buddhism in which strictures on intentionally killing are even more severe. See Harvey 2000, ch. 6.

12. In *Imperialism: The Highest Stage of Capitalism* (1963 [1916]) Lenin argues that advanced capitalist societies are led to war to defend the economic interests that domestic capitalists have in foreign states, interests produced by the mechanism of monopoly capitalism domestically.

# Works by Rawls, with Abbreviations

*Collected Papers* (CP), ed. Samuel Freeman. Cambridge, MA: Harvard University Press, 1999.

"Fifty Years after Hiroshima," in *Collected Papers* (565–572).

"The Law of Peoples" (1993), in *Collected Papers* (529–564).

*The Law of Peoples, with "The Idea of Public Reason Revisited"* (LP). Cambridge, MA: Harvard University Press, 1999.

*Political Liberalism* (PL), expanded edn. New York: Columbia University Press, 2005.

*A Theory of Justice* (TJ), rev. edn. Cambridge, MA: Harvard University Press, 1999.

# Other References

Aron, Raymond (1960) *Peace and War*, trans. R. Howard and A.B. Fox. Garden City, NY: Doubleday.

Augustine, Saint (1887 [426 CE]) *The City of God*, Book 19. In *Nicene and Post-Nicene Fathers*, 1st series, vol. 2, ed. Philip Schaff, trans. Marcus Dods, rev. and ed. Kevin Knight. Buffalo, NY: Christian Literature. At http://www.newadvent.org/fathers/120119.htm (accessed May 2013).

Grotius, Hugo (2005 [1625]) *The Rights of War and Peace*, Book 1, ed. Richard Tuck. At http://files.libertyfund.org/files/1425/1032-01_LFeBk.pdf (accessed May 2013).

Harvey, Peter (2000) *An Introduction to Buddhist Ethics*. Cambridge: Cambridge University Press.

Kant, Immanuel (1917 [1795]) *Perpetual Peace*, trans. M. Campbell Smith. London: Allen & Unwin. At http://files.libertyfund.org/files/357/0075_Bk.pdf (accessed May 2013).

Lenin, V.I. (1963 [1916]) *Imperialism, The Highest Stage of Capitalism*. Moscow: Progress. At http://www.marxists.org/archive/lenin/works/1916/imp-hsc/ (accessed May 2013).

Moellendorf, Darrel (1996) "Constructing the Law of Peoples." *Pacific Philosophical Quarterly* 77: 132–154

Moellendorf, Darrel (2002) *Cosmopolitan Justice*. Boulder, CO: Westview Press.

Pufendorf, Samuel (1991 [1673]) *On the Duty of Man and Citizen according to Natural Law*, ed. James Tully, trans. Michael Silverthorne. Cambridge: Cambridge University Press.

Thomas Aquinas, Saint (1920 [1265–1274]) *Summa Theologica*, the Second Part of the Second Part, Question 40, trans. Fathers of the English Dominican Province. Rev. edn. At http://www.newadvent.org/summa/3040.htm (accessed May 2013).

Thucydides (1839–1845 [431 BCE]) *The History of the Peloponnesian War*, trans. Thomas Hobbes. In *The English Works of Thomas Hobbes*, vol. 9, ed. Sir William Molesworth. London: John Bohn. At http://files.libertyfund.org/files/772/Thucydides_0051-09_EBk_v6.0.pdf (accessed May 2013).

Vattel, Emer de (2008 [1797]) *The Law of Nations, Or, Principles of the Law of Nature, Applied to the Conduct and Affairs of Nations and Sovereigns, with Three Early Essays on the Origin and Nature of Natural Law and on Luxury*, ed. Béla Kapossy and Richard Whitmore At http://files.libertyfund.org/files/2246/Vattel_1519_EBk_v6.0.pdf (accessed May 2013).

Walzer, Michael (2006) *Just and Unjust Wars*. 4th edn. New York: Basic Books.

# Part VI

# Conversations with Other Perspectives

Conversations with Other Perspectives

# 23

# Rawls, Mill, and Utilitarianism

## JONATHAN RILEY

## 1. Rawls and Utilitarianism

John Rawls is an influential critic of standard utilitarianism, which he classifies as "teleological" in the sense that it specifies utility as the sole rational end independent of any moral concepts or principles and then maintains that morally right actions are those which maximize this independent good (*TJ*, 21–22). Like Isaiah Berlin, he dismisses as truly irrational any teleological doctrine that proposes to derive a best way of life including morality from but one end: "Although to subordinate all our aims to one end does not strictly speaking violate the principles of rational choice . . . it still strikes us as irrational, or more likely as mad" (*TJ*, 486).

Despite his firm rejection of teleological utilitarianism, Rawls is remarkably sympathetic to John Stuart Mill's unusual form of utilitarianism (*LHPP*, 249–316). In his view, Mill relies on a pluralistic conception of happiness together with certain fundamental principles of human psychology to construct an extraordinary utilitarianism that gives absolute priority to a liberal basic institutional structure similar to that of justice as fairness: "Mill's well-ordered society would have, I think, basic institutions quite similar to those of the well-ordered society of justice as fairness" (*LHPP*, 297). He seems to view Mill's doctrine as a deontological theory, although he is not explicit about this and even quotes Mill's reference to his utilitarianism in *A System of Logic* (Book VI xii.6–7) as "a doctrine of teleology" (*LHPP*, 313).[1] As defined by Rawls, a deontological theory "either does not specify the good independently from the right, or does not interpret the right as maximizing the good" (*TJ*, 26).

Rawls implies that Mill builds moral concepts and principles of equal justice into his notion of happiness, described in *On Liberty* i.11 as "utility in the largest sense, grounded on the permanent interests of man as a progressive being." As Rawls understands them, those permanent interests include, among others, an interest in institutions that guarantee the moral rights of justice (*LHPP*, 299–305). For him, then, Mill does not define the good independently from the right. Rawls also suggests that Mill does not view right actions as maximizing the

*A Companion to Rawls*, First Edition. Edited by Jon Mandle and David A. Reidy.
© 2014 John Wiley & Sons, Inc. Published 2016 by John Wiley & Sons, Inc.

good. One reason is that, according to Rawls, Mill subscribes to a rule utilitarianism that demands compliance with general rules of justice except in very unusual circumstances when "very great" utility gains can be expected from breaking the rules (*LHPP*, 275). The implication is that in ordinary circumstances the right action is to obey the rules, even though breaking the rules would maximize utility in some situations. While the loss of utility associated with following the rules in ordinary cases is never very great, such a rule utilitarianism is not standard utilitarianism: it assigns a value to obeying the rules which is distinct from utility. This plurality of basic values ties in with a second reason for concluding that Rawls's Mill does not regard right actions as maximizing the good, to wit, it seems pointless to speak in a monistic way of maximizing happiness in the context of a pluralistic conception of happiness.

At first glance, it may appear reasonable to say that right actions maximize the conception of happiness which Rawls attributes to Mill. In his more Kantian moments, however, Rawls insists that moral values are not like other kinds of values, that the good of equal justice cannot be balanced against competing goods, and that justice occupies a different dimension of value altogether from other values. He apparently believes that Mill's notion of happiness incorporates a rational hierarchy of plural distinct goods, with the good of justice sitting at the top of the hierarchy: the good of following the rules that distribute and sanction equal rights for all takes absolute priority over other goods, including mere enjoyment or pleasure. In that case, as Freeman points out, it "really adds nothing" to speak of maximizing the one good called happiness (2007, 53). Indeed, it is misleading to speak in this monistic fashion because no single good such as pleasure is being maximized. When we say that happiness in Mill's sense is maximized, we are saying that basic social institutions are designed to reflect the rational hierarchy of plural basic values so that, when people act in accord with the rules of the liberal basic institutions, they "maximize" his complex idea of utility merely by definition.

Rawls's evident fascination with Mill's deontological utilitarianism might well have softened his hostility toward utilitarianism broadly conceived, without softening it toward teleological utilitarianism. His contempt for the latter appears unabated in *Political Liberalism*, as when he says that "government can no more act to maximize the fulfillment of citizens' rational preferences, or wants (as in utilitarianism) . . . than it can act to advance Catholicism or Protestantism, or any other religion" (*PL*, 179–80, footnote omitted). If it were clear that his belated acceptance of the possibility of a coherent deontological utilitarianism had led him to reconsider his earlier sweeping opposition to utilitarianism, then it would be easier to understand his apparent change of heart after his political turn. Confusion has arisen, understandably, as a result of his suggestions that some forms of utilitarianism might serve as reasonable comprehensive doctrines of good and thus be included in the overlapping consensus of a liberal democratic society. It would be truly puzzling if the "irrational, even mad" teleological doctrines were now to count as reasonable, even allowing for Rawls's special political idea of public reason. But the puzzle evaporates if Rawls means to include only a deontological utilitarianism such as Mill's in the overlapping consensus. There is nothing problematic about including an extraordinary utilitarian doctrine that gives priority to a liberal basic structure.

Unfortunately, Rawls suggests more than once that even teleological doctrines such as classical utilitarianism or its close cousin, average utilitarianism, might serve as reasonable comprehensive doctrines.[2] As Samuel Scheffler remarks, "the suggestion that classical utilitarianism might participate in a consensus of this [overlapping] kind is startling" (2001, 170). In fact, it is quite impossible to see how a teleology in Rawls's sense can give priority to equal justice, even in a restricted public political domain, without compromising its own core commitment to maximize an independent good. Scheffler emphasizes that Rawls's desire to include some forms of standard utilitarianism as reasonable doctrines "no longer seems mysterious" once we consider Rawls's admiration for "utilitarianism's 'systematic' and 'constructive' character" (2001, 150, 172). And Freeman adds that Rawls can continue to personally oppose standard utilitarianism from within his own Kantian comprehensive doctrine while publicly tolerating it as a reasonable member of the overlapping consensus (2007, 189–191). But those arguments are beside the point. The point is that standard utilitarians are opposed in principle to a liberal basic structure whenever its priority conflicts with their maximizing criterion. If that means they cannot in principle be democratic citizens, then so be it: why pretend otherwise?[3]

It is best to admit that Rawls is mistaken when he suggests that one or another teleological utilitarianism can be a reasonable element of a democratic consensus. To restore consistency and give the best possible interpretation of his own doctrine, we should assume that he would, upon reflection, only include a deontological utilitarianism such as Mill's. Even if we make this assumption, however, Rawls's interpretation of Mill's utilitarianism cannot possibly be sustained. For there is no doubt that Mill's utilitarianism is a hedonistic doctrine. "By happiness is intended pleasure," Mill says, "and the absence of pain; by unhappiness, pain, and the privation of pleasure" (*Util.* ii.2). Admittedly, "supplementary explanations" are needed to clarify how his utilitarianism works: "in particular, what things it includes in the ideas of pain and pleasure; and to what extent this is left an open question." But "the theory of life" remains unaffected by these supplementary explanations. According to that theory, "pleasure, and freedom from pain, are the only things desirable as ends; and . . . all desirable things (which are as numerous in the utilitarian as in any other scheme) are desirable either for the pleasure inherent in themselves, or as means to the promotion of pleasure and the prevention of pain." For Mill, the standard of morality must be grounded on this hedonistic theory of life.

This is not the place to discuss my own interpretation of Mill's hedonistic utilitarianism.[4] In what follows, I shall ignore the fact that Mill is a hedonist. My main aim is to show that Rawls's interpretation is problematic even on its own terms. If we follow Rawls's line, Mill must be seen as a muddled utilitarian. A coherent Mill can be saved by suitably revising the special psychology ascribed to him by Rawls. But Mill is thereby transformed into a perfectionist who is fully prepared to use legal and social coercion to impose a comprehensive vision of human excellence. Nevertheless, even if Rawls's way of reading Mill must be abandoned, all is not lost. Rawls has opened up the possibility of deontological utilitarianisms which could serve as reasonable members of a democratic consensus. Indeed, perhaps Mill may still be properly interpreted as a deontological utilitarian, despite his avowed hedonism.

## 2. Mill's Utilitarianism: Rawls's Interpretation

Rawls offers "a psychological reading" of Mill's utilitarianism with the chief aim of clarifying how it works to give priority to a liberal basic structure with a firm guarantee of equal rights for all (*LHPP*, 300). In his view, Mill accepts the truth of a special psychology comprised of six fundamental principles, to wit, a principle of decided preference for higher pleasures, a principle of dignity, a principle of reciprocity, a principle of recognition of natural good, the Aristotelian principle, and a principle of individuality or moral autonomy. When combined with the notion of "utility in the largest sense" (*OL* i.11), this special psychology supposedly explains why rational people, once aware of their true human nature, "maximize" utility by choosing a liberal basic structure as essential to the promotion of their permanent interests. No values other than utility values need to be brought into the analysis. Rawls is skeptical of the special psychology and does not endorse it (*LHPP*, 269). Nevertheless, he concedes that it might be true, and so is willing to proceed with caution.

## 2.1 Higher Pleasures

Rawls insists that Mill, when speaking of one pleasure as higher in quality than another irrespective of quantity, is not saying that one kind of pleasant *feeling* is qualitatively superior to another kind of pleasant *feeling*. Rather, Mill is saying that humans decidedly prefer *activities* that exercise their higher faculties instead of *activities* that merely exercise their lower faculties (*LHPP*, 259). According to Rawls, "the higher faculties are those of intellect, of feeling and imagination, and of the moral sentiments" whereas "the lower faculties are those associated with our bodily needs and requirements, the exercise of which gives rise to pleasures of mere sensation" (*LHPP*, 259; cf. *Util.* ii.4).

For Rawls, then, higher and lower pleasures boil down to higher and lower activities. Higher activities are ones that exercise the mental faculties, and Rawls is emphatic that no further qualitative distinctions need be drawn within this broad class of higher activities, whereas lower activities are ones that merely involve physical drives and instincts. These two types of activities are different *sources* of pleasant feeling. Pleasant feelings are all homogeneous in quality. But there are distinct sources of this homogeneous feeling of enjoyment, and humans generally choose to get it from mental sources rather than merely physical ones. The decided preference for the higher source is revealed by people's choices: "All the distinctions that Mill makes, and needs to make, are reflected in our actual decisions and choices" (*LHPP*, 263).

As Rawls understands it, the higher pleasures doctrine implies that we choose to give "special priority" to higher activities in our way of life in the sense that at some point we refuse to sacrifice a higher activity for any amount of a lower activity which our nature is capable of (*LHPP*, 261). But, he says, there must also come a point at which we refuse to exchange a lower activity for any amount of a higher one: "The reason is that we must reserve a certain minimum of time and energy to keeping ourselves well and healthy, and in good spirits" (*LHPP*, 262). We need a certain amount of food, sleep, physical exercise, leisure and so forth to "carry out effectively our other activities, particularly the higher ones." It follows that there are different explanations for why the two rates of exchange become infinite in practice. We do not refuse to give up the lower activities because we think they are intrinsically more valuable than the higher ones. Rather, we are essentially forced to sacrifice the higher for the lower activities by physiological and psychological considerations beyond our control. In contrast, once we have secured "the necessary minimum [of lower pleasures] needed to keep us well and healthy, and in good spirits," we freely choose the higher activities because we think they are intrinsically more valuable than the lower ones. It is a rationally autonomous choice.

So, for Rawls, the higher pleasures doctrine says that, above a minimum of lower activities "required for normal health and vigor and psychological well-being," we freely choose to arrange our schedules so that higher activities "become the focus and center of our way of life" (*LHPP*, 262). A higher activity is any activity (including watching a baseball game) that exercises the mental faculties. People may choose to devote different amounts of time to different higher activities but everyone refuses to eliminate higher activities from their schedules. Marginal utility theory can represent how much time and energy an individual opts to spend on one higher activity rather than another: she reads poetry up to the point where its marginal utility (per unit of time) just equals the marginal utility (per unit of time) she gets from playing pushpin or from watching a baseball game.

Nevertheless, a key problem remains. As matters stand, no explanation has been given as to why people refuse to abandon higher activities for lower ones above the required minimum of lower activities, even though the pleasant feelings expected from lower activities may be more intense than the pleasant feelings expected from higher activities. After all, the feeling of enjoyment from both kinds of activities is homogeneous in quality. Why invariably prefer the higher source instead of the lower source of the same pleasant feeling? To deal with the problem, Rawls provides a nonhedonistic psychological principle, namely, a principle of dignity, to explain why people decidedly prefer higher activities over lower ones even when more enjoyment is expected from the lower activities.

## 2.2 Dignity and Happiness

Rawls points out that Mill explains the "unwillingness" of a person to resign higher for lower pleasures in terms of "a sense of dignity" (*LHPP*, 264; cf. *Util.* ii.6). According to Rawls, this notion of dignity adds a new element to the distinction between higher and lower activities: "The new element is this: not only do we have a decided preference for the higher over the lower pleasures, but we also have a higher-order desire to have desires cultivated by a way of life suitably focused on the higher activities and sufficient to sustain them" (*LHPP*, 265). The higher-order desire for dignity apparently overrides any desires to engage in lower activities even if they are expected to bring more intense feelings of pleasure than higher activities: "This higher-order desire is a desire, first, that as a human being with the higher faculties, these faculties be realized and cultivated; and second, that we have desires appropriate to set our higher faculties in motion and to enjoy their exercise, *and that we do not have desires interfering with this*" (*LHPP*, 265, emphasis added).

In short, our desire for dignity is "tied . . . to our recognition that some ways of life are admirable and worthy of our nature, while others are beneath us and unfitting." By introducing this sense of dignity, Mill injects perfectionist values into his conception of happiness: "He introduces, in effect, another form of value besides the enjoyable and the pleasing, namely, the admirable and the worthy along with their opposites, the degrading and the contemptible" (*LHPP*, 265). Rawls also notes that, because the test of qualitative superiority rules out choosing higher activities from a feeling of moral obligation, "the sense of dignity is not derived from a sense of moral obligation." Thus, the perfectionist values associated with the sense of dignity do not depend on morality but instead are "a different form of value" than that of justice and right.

## 2.3  Happiness and Equal Justice

When he turns to consider justice and right, Rawls wonders why Mill is so confident that equal rights for all can be identified and given priority without running into contradictions within his utilitarian framework. He agrees with H.L.A. Hart (1982) that Mill relies on a two-part criterion for identifying utilitarian rights but that the two parts may come into conflict: "My problem . . . and Hart's, is: we don't see how . . . we could know that in general, enforcing equal rights for all maximizes utility" (*LHPP*, 279). According to Rawls and Hart, one part of Mill's two-part criterion says to look to the basic needs of individuals, without reference to total utility: "we look to the essentials of human well-being, to the groundwork of our existence," Rawls says, and "these essentials and groundwork (apparently) justify moral rights apart from aggregative considerations" (*LHPP*, 278). The other part of the criterion says to look to those general rules which tend to maximize total utility when society employs sanctions to enforce them: "we look to those general rules the enforcement of which is especially productive of social utility in the aggregative sense, and hence tend to maximize that utility." Unlike the first part, which is concerned to identify vital personal interests shared by individuals, the second part is concerned to identify general rules which promote total utility despite the costs of inflicting some form of punishment on those who refuse to comply with the rules: the total disutility or harm to people's interests which is prevented by widespread compliance exceeds the total disutility of setting up and running legal and social institutions to enforce compliance, even though the refusal to allow deviations from the rules results in relatively minor losses of utility in some ordinary situations.[5]

"If Mill's account of rights is to avoid contradiction," Rawls emphasizes, "it must be the case that the two parts of Mill's criterion always happen to converge (barring freakish cases)" (*LHPP*, 278). But there is no reason to expect that the two parts of the criterion will always converge on the same equal rights for all: the individualistic part may contradict the rule utilitarian part. Indeed, Rawls poses the question which is invariably posed by critics: "Why can't it happen that greater social utility is achieved by denying a small minority certain of the equal rights?" It is remarkable that Mill fails to address this issue, Rawls admits. Like Hart, he goes so far as to suggest that Mill even seems unaware that there is a key difference between legal rights that recognize and reinforce preexisting moral rights, and legal rights that do not reflect anterior moral rights but instead are created entirely by the state and based merely on generally expedient policy considerations. Legal rights that are correlative with duties not to commit murder or other moral crimes are different in kind than legal rights that are correlative with duties not to import commodities at prices heavily subsidized by foreign governments, for instance.

Mill is only able to remove the possibility of contradiction between the two parts of his criterion for identifying moral rights, Rawls asserts, by relying on the special psychology, more specifically, the principles of reciprocity and of recognition of natural good. According to the reciprocity principle, also referred to as "the principle of living in unity with others," people have a deep desire to interact with one another as equals, that is, a desire to cooperate in accord with social rules of equal justice that distribute and sanction reciprocal moral rights (*LHPP*, 269, 282, 300). This desire for a united society of equals only becomes salient as it is given encouragement under modern social conditions of increasing interdependence, equality and democracy. But Mill insists that it is a natural desire which is "not undermined by analysis" (*LHPP*, 283). It is not an artificial desire which is manufactured by society and liable to melt away once its genesis is understood. Thus, Rawls ascribes to Mill yet another basic psychological principle depicted as "the recognition of our natural good," that is, "the capacity we have to recognize our natural good and to distinguish it from our apparent good as a mere artifact of social and associationist learning, often by some kind of reward and punishment" (*LHPP*, 300).

Rawls argues that "aside, then, from the principle of dignity," the reciprocity principle and the principle of recognition of natural good provide "the ultimate sanction of [Mill's] principle of utility with its concern for equal justice" (*LHPP*, 283). Humans in the modern age have allegedly become aware of their desire to live together in harmony in a well-ordered society whose institutions secure equal rights for all. The permanent interests referred to in Mill's conception of utility may be summarized as a permanent interest in achieving and maintaining such a well-ordered liberal democratic society, Rawls suggests (*LHPP*, 299–305). As depicted by Rawls, the well-ordered society is "the normal and natural state of society as one of full equality as described in *Utilitarianism* iii.10–11" (*LHPP*, 301). Not only is it "normal and natural" but it is also the best state of society of human beings: "So for Mill progress is an advance over time to, or in the direction of, the practically best, though normal and natural, state of society." Thus, the permanent interests are permanent in the sense that they are grounded in "human nature at its deepest level," and they are also tied to man as a progressive being in the sense that their full realization demands progress toward an ideal society in which all have equal rights.

Even so, this natural desire for a well-ordered liberal democratic society of equals is initially weak, only becoming noticeable under modern conditions. How does it become so powerful as to override competing desires and actually bring about a well-ordered society? Of crucial importance in this regard is Rawls's understanding of Mill's normative principle of liberty and its utilitarian justification in light of the Aristotelian principle and the principle of individuality.

## 2.4 The Liberty Principle

As Rawls interprets it, the liberty principle is "a principle of public reason in the coming democratic age: [Mill] views it as . . . a public political principle framed to regulate free public discussion concerning the appropriate adjustment between individual independence and social control" (*LHPP*, 286, 287). Rawls thinks of it as being akin to the liberal principle of legitimacy in his own political theory of justice as fairness.[6] He says it covers and gives "special protection" to "certain enumerated liberties . . . which are defined by certain legal and moral rights of justice" (*LHPP*, 288). More specifically, it gives special protection to three kinds of liberties, to wit: liberty of thought and opinion on all subjects, together with freedom of speech in so far as discussion is practically inseparable from thinking and forming opinions; liberty of tastes and pursuits as long as we do not violate the moral rights of others; and liberty of association for any purposes that do not violate others' rights. Rawls claims that the liberty principle gives special protection to these three kinds of liberties because that is the only way for a modern democratic society to make progress toward a well-ordered society of equals:

> Mill's idea is that only if a democratic society follows the Principle of Liberty in regulating its
> public discussion of the rules bearing on the relation of individuals and society, and only if it

adjusts its attitudes and laws accordingly, can its political and social institutions fulfill their role of shaping national character so that its citizens can realize the permanent interests of man as a progressive being. (*LHPP*, 289–290)

Rawls tries to make Mill's liberty principle thus interpreted more precise by formulating it in the form of three clauses. The first clause says that the sole justification for coercive interference with individual conduct is the prevention of harm to others, where harm means to "injure . . . legitimate interests, or . . . (moral) rights" (*LHPP*, 290). Although the idea of harm remains rather ambiguous, he also says that it means to "wrong or violate the legitimate interests of others, either in express legal provisions (assumed to be justified), or by tacit understanding ought to be considered as (moral) rights" (*LHPP*, 291). The idea of harm seems to boil down to violations of recognized rights, including legal rights expressed in laws and extralegal rights implicit in popular customs, assuming the laws and customary rules are justified. In short, "only reasons of right and wrong should be appealed to in public discussions" relating to legislation or to the guidance of coercive public opinion (*LHPP*, 290). Other kinds of reasons "count for zero" in Mill's idea of public reason (*LHPP*, 291).

Rawls proceeds to identify three kinds of reasons which are excluded by the liberty principle from the public discussions of how to employ legal and social coercion, namely: "paternalistic reasons," which appeal to some idea of a person's good at odds with the person's own idea; perfectionist reasons, which appeal to "ideals of excellence and perfection"; and "reasons of dislike or disgust, or of preference, where the disliking, disgust or preference cannot be supported by reasons of right and wrong, as defined in *Utilitarianism*, v.14–15" (*LHPP*, 290–291). As his reference to *Utilitarianism* shows, he implicitly interprets the last category of excluded reasons, those of mere dislike, disgust or preference, to cover appeals to prevent perceptible harms that are not violations of moral duties, and especially not violations of the perfect duties correlative with moral rights.

Unlike other revisionists who argue in favor of a first clause of this sort, Rawls at least acknowledges that Mill rejects it as a way to understand his liberty principle. Mill is explicit: "The acts of an individual may be hurtful to others, or wanting in due consideration for their welfare, without going the length of violating any of their constituted rights" (*OL* iv.3). Nevertheless, Rawls decides to override the text at this point. He defends his move by emphasizing Mill's remarks in *On Liberty* iii.9, which imply that society should permit the cultivation of individuality within the limits of rigid rules of justice that distribute equal rights, even though such social permission allows an individual to pursue a mode of living which harms others, annoys them and causes them pain, provided such harms and dislikes fall short of violating their constituted rights. As a result, Rawls interprets the liberty principle as a principle of public reason which gives special protection to the three kinds of enumerated liberties, and which rules out any coercive interference unless it can be justified to prevent violations of rights.

The second clause of the liberty principle as Rawls understands it says that if a type of conduct injures the rights of others, then public discussion may properly consider the question of whether to employ some form of coercion to prevent or punish the conduct: "The question may then be discussed on its merits, but of course excluding the three kinds of reasons noted above." He emphasizes that "because injury to the legitimate interests or moral rights of others (as currently understood, or specified) can alone justify the interference of law and moral opinion, it does not follow that it always does justify it" (*LHPP*, 292). The third clause then says that the question of coercive interference "must be settled" by public discussion of the merits of coercion, keeping in mind that prevention of rights-violations is the only admissible reason for coercion (*LHPP*, 293).

Rawls insists that "the substantive force of Mill's principle of liberty is given by the three reasons excluded by the first clause, with the last two clauses saying in effect that reasons of right and wrong . . . especially reasons of moral rights and justice, must settle the case" (*LHPP*, 293). But how precisely does the special psychology support the derivation of the liberty principle from the principle of utility, in his view? The answer is not easy to glean from his lectures on Mill. If I understand correctly, however, he inserts into his interpretation his Kantian argument for the congruence of the right and the good, originally made in the third part of *A Theory of Justice* but later abandoned (as a general stability argument) in *Political Liberalism*, because he assumes that Mill's comprehensive doctrine of the good, that is, of what it is rational for humans to desire, is like Kant's insofar as both give supreme importance to moral autonomy.

## 2.5 Congruence Arguments

The Kantian argument for congruence insists that humans are ultimately moral agents with a moral personality consisting of two moral capacities, to wit: the capacity to be rational, that is, form a coherent plan of life that is worthy of human nature; and the capacity to be reasonable, that is, develop a sense of justice that requires us to cooperate with one another as free and equal moral persons who recognize and respect equal rights for all. To achieve a good way of life, humans must express this moral personality by freely choosing activities that do not violate others' rights as distributed by general rules of their own making. But this is what it means to display moral autonomy. The ideal of a well-ordered democratic society, in which citizens comply with rules of justice that have been determined by themselves insofar as all have equal political rights as well as fair equality of opportunity to exercise their political rights, reflects this ultimate truth about human nature: our deepest, or highest-order, desire is to display moral autonomy. As Freeman suggests, this Kantian congruence argument purports to show that "under the circumstances of a well-ordered society, it is rational to be reasonable" because justice is a supreme intrinsic good: the desire for justice should regulate, or take absolute priority over, all competing desires because "by acting not simply in accordance with but also from a motive of justice, we realize our nature as free, equal, and rational beings, and are therefore morally autonomous" (2007, 182–183).

As applied to Mill, the Kantian congruence argument relies on the individuality principle, understood as a principle of moral autonomy, perhaps supplemented by the Aristotelian principle, to explain why any rational person chooses to strengthen her natural desire for a well-ordered society of equals, once she becomes aware of it, and so develops or educates herself into a moral agent who works to achieve, and flourishes in, such a well-ordered society. These psychological principles must help us to understand how people acquire under modern conditions an overriding desire to realize the well-ordered society, a highest-order desire that gives priority to liberal democratic institutions, including moral rights of justice and the three sorts of specific liberties covered by the liberty principle.

405

According to the Aristotelian principle, humans tend to get more enjoyment from exercising their abilities as they develop them, and they decidedly prefer higher activities that are more complex than others insofar as the more complex activity requires more highly developed mental faculties that are capable of "more intricate and subtle discriminations" than less developed faculties are capable of (*TJ*, 374). If the activities of justice and right are complex activities that call for the most extremely intricate and subtle discriminations of all, then the Aristotelian principle implies that people are naturally disposed to prefer this moral kind of higher activities above all else as they develop their higher faculties.

The individuality principle apparently says that the desire to display moral autonomy, once awakened, emerges as a highest-order desire that takes absolute priority over all other desires. It is something of a mystery why this desire to develop and exercise the two moral capacities has such priority. But Rawls seems to believe that the desire to act upon principles of justice carries within itself its own priority: "This sentiment [of justice] cannot be fulfilled if it is compromised and balanced against other ends as but one desire among the rest. It is a desire to conduct oneself in a certain way above all else, a striving that contains within itself its own priority" (*TJ*, 503). As a result, once triggered, the desire for moral autonomy takes over the process of self-development and determines its direction. In short, at some point in the process, people form a desire to act upon principles of justice, and this highest-order desire for justice then regulates all other desires so that the capacity for justice can be developed and progress toward a well-ordered society of equals can take place. People will freely choose to develop their faculties and dispositions in this direction, Rawls suggests, if the three kinds of specific liberties covered by the liberty principle are firmly guaranteed. The desire for moral autonomy will override competing desires during the transition to a well-ordered society; and it will continue unabated in the well-ordered society itself, so that people continue to exercise and maintain their moral powers in an ideal social context that reflects their ultimate nature as free and equal rational beings. Thus, the desire for individuality understood as moral autonomy underlies the great importance assigned to the liberty principle as a "mediate axiom" for the maximization of utility in the largest sense. In other words, the desire to develop one's faculties and character in the direction needed to realize the well-ordered society of equals, together with the prescription to "maximize" happiness as Mill understands it, explains why the liberty principle should be rigidly adhered to as a principle of public reason.[7]

## 2.6 Utility in the Largest Sense

Rawls also clarifies why he thinks that, for Mill, a liberal basic structure that reflects the principles of justice and liberty is "most effective in fulfilling our permanent interests" in light of the basic principles of psychology (*LHPP*, 305–306). According to him, the key consideration for Mill is that the decided preference criterion, which says that experienced people decidedly prefer a way of life in which higher activities are the central focus and concern, can only be "properly applied" in a well-ordered society of equals (*LHPP*, 304, 306). Rawls emphasizes the importance of this point: "it amounts to saying that only under conditions of free institutions can people acquire sufficient self-understanding to know, or make reasonable decisions about, what mode of life offers them the best chance of happiness (in Mill's sense)" (*LHPP*, 304). And he underscores "the striking consequence that in the absence of just and free arrangements, there is simply no way for society to acquire the specific knowledge and information it would need to maximize utility in Mill's sense" (*LHPP*, 306). "If society uses institutions other than these, hoping to maximize utility, it simply operates in the dark" (*LHPP*, 307).

Rawls offers two related reasons for his claim that people will have trouble figuring out which activities to decidedly prefer unless they live in a well-ordered democratic society "in which the equal rights of justice and liberty are firmly guaranteed." One reason is that just and free institutions are needed for individuals, "either singly or together with others," to develop their higher faculties "in ways that best suit their character and inclination" (*LHPP*, 306). So, in the absence of those institutions, we could not know which particular activities would be decidedly preferred by people as revealed by their choices. The second reason is that "there is no central agency in society . . . that could possess the information required to maximize utility" (*LHPP*, 306). The only way to gain access to the information about which particular activities are preferred is to guarantee the equal rights of justice and liberty so that individuals may freely reveal their decided preferences. Instead of trying to rely on a central planning board that must operate in the dark, society should endorse a liberal basic structure that permits individuals to freely provide the preference information needed to maximize utility in the largest sense.

As depicted by Rawls, Mill's utilitarianism is a doctrine that gives priority to liberal democratic institutions on the grounds that such institutions are indispensable if most individuals are to develop their faculties sufficiently to know which particular higher activities to choose as the central focus of their mode of life. Once they have developed the relevant higher faculties needed to realize a well-ordered society of equals, but only then, will people properly apply the decided preference criterion to correctly select the higher activities which are genuinely best suited to their own nature and character. Rawls insists that "Mill does not make a fine-grained distinction within the class of higher pleasures [activities]," which "means that Mill holds all normal persons to be equally capable of enjoying and exercising their higher faculties, even granting that some are more talented than others" (*LHPP*, 307). Moreover, Mill holds that, "given decent opportunities" provided by a liberal basic structure, normal people will actually make some higher activities the central focus of their life, "barring special explanations."

Indeed, Rawls goes so far as to suggest that there is no need to compare in value the different higher activities which different persons may choose in a well-ordered society: "All activities decidedly preferred by normal people, properly educated and living under just and free institutions, count the same" (*LHPP*, 307). Thus, there is no need in practice even to calculate a sum total of utility. Happiness in Mill's sense, both personal and collective, is "maximized" by leaving individuals alone in this ideal social context to freely pursue their ways of living in accord with their equal rights and liberties. When we refer to maximization of utility in the largest sense, then, we are merely saying that people comply with liberal basic institutions and rules and properly apply the decided preference criterion to select particular higher activities which are most suitable for them: there is no single independent good such as pleasure or desire-satisfaction which is being maximized.

## 2.7 Not Perfectionism

Rawls concludes that, despite the perfectionist elements in the pluralistic idea of happiness, Mill's doctrine remains utilitarian rather than fully perfectionist because Mill's principle of liberty excludes "perfectionist grounds for limiting individual liberty – these values cannot be imposed by the sanctions of law and common moral opinion as coercive social pressure" (*LHPP*, 312). As he sees it, because the liberty principle guarantees to individuals the kinds of specific liberties needed to freely settle for themselves in free association with like-minded others the extent to which ideals of human excellence and worth will be recognized in their modes of living, perfectionist values are not given any weight that forces people to modify or sacrifice the idea of happiness which they believe is best suited to their nature and character.

# 3. Against Rawls's Interpretation

I shall confine myself to a couple of objections against Rawls's interpretation. In addition to ignoring his brazen rejection of Mill's hedonism, I shall grant for the sake of argument other contestable aspects of his interpretation, including his understanding of Mill's liberty principle and equation of Mill's notion of individuality with moral autonomy, his neglect of Mill's fear that the desire for social unity may well turn out to be oppressive in the modern democratic age, and his failure to consider the extent to which Mill is prepared to bolster the influence of educated minorities as a check against ignorant or unjust majorities. Even so, Rawls's reading of Mill's utilitarianism is fatally flawed, or so I maintain.

## 3.1 Dignity and Individuality

In the psychology which Rawls attributes to Mill, the principle of dignity is in tension with the principle of individuality or moral autonomy and also with the Aristotelian principle. A problem arises because, according to Rawls, Mill does not draw any fine distinctions within the class of higher activities: any activity that exercises the mental faculties is a higher activity and all of these higher activities "count the same" if they even need to be compared in value at all (*LHPP*, 307). Dignity then seems compatible with a decided preference for immoral and illegal activities that engage the mental faculties. True, moral activities – the pleasures of "the moral sentiments" as Rawls understands them – are higher activities. But they apparently count the same as immoral activities that exercise the mental faculties because the class of higher activities is so broad and coarse-grained.

The dignity principle does not give priority to justice and right yet the individuality principle demands it. Given Rawls's insistence that such a broad range of higher activities count the same for a worthy way of life, the sense of dignity does not dictate the supreme importance that individuals must give to higher moral activities such as constructing and enforcing general rules of justice. Yet Rawls also admits that, for Mill, the perfectionist values associated with the sense of dignity are not derived from a sense of justice: the decided preference for higher activities is independent of moral obligation. So, not only does dignity not privilege justice, dignity also does not presuppose justice. Thus, it appears impossible to explain why individuals choose to give priority to equal rights and liberties on the basis of the psychology which Rawls attributes to Mill. Mill could not consistently maintain that a spontaneous rational will demands compliance with the moral law, for instance, a will that drives our higher-order desire for dignity and a worthy way of life. That would make the sense of dignity depend upon a sense of justice and moral duty but such a dependency is ruled out by Rawls's interpretation.

It is difficult to see any way to remedy the problem, in light of the constraints which Rawls has put on the psychology. A response that does not work, despite its superficial appeal, builds on a narrower definition of a higher activity. More specifically, Rawls might argue, after reflecting on Mill's reference to "the pleasures of the intellect, of the feelings and imagination, and of the moral sentiments" (*Util.* ii.4), that a higher activity must be all of these things at once, that is, any activity is higher if and only if it is simultaneously thoughtful, imaginative and morally permissible. That would exclude immoral activities but still permit a broad range of higher activities that count the same. And Rawls does appear to equate aesthetic standards of beauty and awe with anything that individuals care to think in the matter, as long as the rights of others are not violated: "The idea that the higher activities and faculties are exclusively intellectual, aesthetic, and academic is just rubbish" (*LHPP*, 307). Thus understood, a higher activity is any activity that exercises the mental faculties, including watching a baseball game or reading poetry, provided the activity does not violate the rights of others.

Even though it rules out immoral activities, this idea of a higher activity cannot repair the tension in the psychology which Rawls attributes to Mill. The class of higher activities counting the same is still too coarse-grained. There is a crucial difference between a higher activity that is morally permissible and one that is morally essential. A permissible activity such as watching a baseball game cannot count the same as a morally essential activity such as framing or enforcing the rules of justice. It cannot be a matter of indifference if, on the one hand, virtually everyone watches or plays baseball while the rest commit crimes, or, on the other hand, at least some people do the work required to construct and enforce a social code of equal rights and liberties. The higher activities needed to establish morality and law must be intrinsically more valuable than other higher activities that are permissible but not required for the implementation of equal justice. Thus, unless the idea of dignity is recast so that the desire for a worthy way of life implies a desire to give suitable priority to the morally essential type of higher activities over other types, the problem with the psychology remains.

It is puzzling that Rawls never notices the gap in the psychology. He almost seems to forget that somebody has to do the work to put the machinery of equal justice into place and run it. In the same spirit of generosity that he shows toward Mill, I shall override the text of his lectures on Mill and assume that he really intended for the sense of dignity to recognize and give priority to the sense of justice so that, when properly applying the decided preference criterion, experienced people decidedly prefer higher activities that engage their mental faculties but further, within this broad category of mental activities, they also decidedly prefer the morally essential activities as intrinsically more valuable than other types of higher activities. This is a marked departure from what Rawls actually writes about dignity and the doctrine of higher pleasures. But it seems the only way to repair the gap in the psychology which he foists on Mill.

In the amended psychology, the principle of dignity implies the principle of individuality as well as the Aristotelian principle. Although there are various ways of filling in the details, such an amended psychology might run along the following lines. Suppose that morality and dignity have separate origins. A spontaneous rational will prescribes general maxims of equal justice and urges us to respect the moral rights and legitimate interests of others. This autonomous moral will arises independently of any desire for dignity, and by itself does not dignify or lend any worth to humanity, even though it produces a desire for equal justice.

That desire for equal justice might not be good for us and might even be catastrophic as Nietzsche asserted. The separate sense of dignity must decide on the worth or otherwise of equal justice. This desire for an excellent way of life arises independently of the moral will. But it recognizes and affirms the overriding worth of the moral will and of the desire for equal justice. As a result, the desire for dignity gives suitable priority to the higher activities that are necessary to institutionalize and sanction the maxims of justice prescribed by the moral will. The supreme value of these morally essential activities for an excellent mode of life flows from the dignity principle. Thus, the desire for dignity is our highest-order desire but it affirms that our desire for equal justice ought to supremely regulate all of our other desires – apart from the desire for dignity itself – for a good, worthy and happy way of life. And so the decided preference criterion takes the more complicated form indicated above.

This amended psychology is incompatible with Rawls's Kantian account of the congruence of right and good, since on that account the desire for equal justice is our highest-order desire that carries its own normative priority with it. The Kantian account cannot be employed in the interpretation of Mill's psychology because, for Mill as Rawls reads him, the dignity principle drives the decided preference criterion: the sense of dignity determines our decided preference for higher activities, and does so independently of any feeling of moral obligation. Instead of the Kantian argument, an alternative Millian argument for congruence, which gives pride of place to the sense of dignity, is needed to make credible the claim that "normal" people will generally choose to prioritize the morally essential activities that underlie the institutions of equal justice.[8] Nevertheless, even with the amended psychology, serious problems remain for Rawls's interpretation.

## 3.2 Perfectionism

Unfortunately, with the amended psychology in place, Rawls's interpretation commits Mill to full-blown perfectionism. For now, legal and social coercion is legitimately employed to promote ideals of human excellence. True, the liberty principle as Rawls understands it continues to exclude from the public political discussion any reasons for coercion except the prevention of violations of rights. No direct appeal to perfectionist reasons is permissible to justify coercion. But the liberty principle, with its special protection for the three kinds of specific liberties, is now grounded on the dignity principle together with the prescription to maximize utility in the largest sense. The priority of equal rights of justice, including the rights that define the three sorts of liberties, is inseparable from the perfectionist ingredients of happiness in Mill's sense. As Rawls admits, Mill is clear that the promotion of happiness is the only reason to establish rights (*Util.* v.24–25). Thus, the liberty principle's ban on any appeal to perfectionist values comes too late. An appeal to ideals of excellence has already been made to identify the equal rights which are justified in terms of utility in the largest sense, and the liberty principle itself justifies the use of coercion to enforce those rights.

As I see it, this is the straw that breaks the back of Rawls's line of interpretation. He cannot repudiate the amended psychology, which is needed to remedy the conflict between individuality and dignity in the original psychology. If he accepts the amended psychology, however, then he must interpret Mill's doctrine as perfectionism rather than utilitarianism. Moreover, with the amended psychology, Mill's doctrine effectively becomes teleological in Rawls's sense. The idea of happiness with its perfectionist ingredients is defined independently of moral concepts and principles, and right actions are viewed as those which "maximize" this independent notion of happiness. Justice on its own does not have any worth: it is only made valuable because the sense of dignity confers value – indeed, supreme value – on it. True, the idea of happiness remains pluralistic in so far as it includes perfectionist values as well as pleasure and relief from pain. But the ideals of human dignity and worthiness, which now subsume justice and right, greatly predominate because higher activities that exercise the higher mental faculties are the central focus and concern of any rational person's way of life. If we are to avoid confusing it with a perfectionist teleology, another interpretation of Mill's extraordinary utilitarianism is required.

# Notes

1   I shall refer to chapters and paragraphs of Mill's texts rather than to pages of any particular edition. *Utilitarianism* will be denoted by *Util.* and *On Liberty* by *OL*. Thus, *Util.* ii.2 refers to *Utilitarianism*, chapter 2, paragraph 2.

2   Rawls suggests that classical utilitarianism might serve as a reasonable comprehensive doctrine (*PL*, 170–171). And he also presents an argument that average utilitarianism might be included in an overlapping consensus (*JF*, 107–109). Classical utilitarianism, which he labels BES utilitarianism after its main proponents Bentham, Edgeworth and Sidgwick, is that form of standard utilitarianism which defines utility as happiness in the sense of pleasure, including relief from pain (*LHPP*, 375–415). Whereas standard utilitarianism seeks to maximize the sum total of individual utilities, average utilitarianism seeks to maximize the average utility which individuals experience or expect to experience. They are equivalent doctrines in the context of a fixed population.

3   Even Freeman seems to concede as much, although he somehow manages to convince himself that standard utilitarians might nevertheless endorse something close to equal justice within a public political domain (2007, 170–172). Why would they do this, unless they are not really committed to maximizing their independent notion of utility?

4   For further discussion, see Riley 2009; 2010a; 2010b; 2012; 2013a; 2013b; 2013c; and additional references cited therein.

5   Rawls could maintain that, for Mill, compliance with the rules of justice is essential to a way of life which is worthy of human beings. The relatively minor losses of pleasure which flow from society's refusal to allow deviations from the rules in ordinary situations could then be outweighed by perfectionist values associated with the sense of dignity. But Rawls does not take this line of argument.

6   Rawls describes the liberal principle of legitimacy as "the principle that the collective political power of citizens on matters of constitutional essentials and basic questions of distributive justice should turn on the appeal to political values that all citizens may be reasonably expected to endorse, and so rest on a shared public understanding" (*LHPP*, 296). See, also, *JF*, 40–41, 90–91; and *PL*, 137, 217. For further discussion of Rawls's idea of public reason and the related idea of political legitimacy along with the duty of civility imposed on citizens by principle of legitimacy, see Freeman 2007, 196–256.

7   For further discussion of Rawls's Kantian congruence argument and of his reasons for abandoning it in political liberalism, see Freeman 2007, 143–256; and Weithman 2011.

8   Dworkin (2011) defends a moral and political theory in which the value of dignity underwrites our sense of justice and respect for the moral rights of others. In his view, value is "one big thing" whose various aspects fit together in harmony so that a truly flourishing life must simultaneously display personal dignity and moral virtue. Indeed, he argues that Kant is properly interpreted as insisting on a similar connection between dignity and morality: respect for our own humanity requires us to give equal concern and respect to the humanity of others.

# Works by Rawls, with Abbreviations

*Justice as Fairness: A Restatement* (*JF*), ed. Erin Kelly. Cambridge, MA: Harvard University Press, 2001.

*Lectures on the History of Political Philosophy* (*LHPP*), ed. Samuel Freeman. Cambridge, MA: Harvard University Press, 2007.

*Political Liberalism* (*PL*) (*1993, 1996*), expanded edn. New York: Columbia University Press, 2005.

*A Theory of Justice* (*TJ*) (*1971*), rev. edn. Cambridge, MA: Harvard University Press, 1999.

# Other References

Dworkin, Ronald (2011) *Justice for Hedgehogs*. Cambridge, MA: Harvard University Press.

Freeman, Samuel (2007) *Justice and the Social Contract: Essays on Rawlsian Political Philosophy*. Oxford: Oxford University Press.

Hart, H.L.A. (1982) "Natural Rights: Bentham and John Stuart Mill." In Hart, *Essays on Bentham* (79–104). Oxford: Clarendon Press.

Riley, Jonathan (2009) "The Interpretation of Maximizing Utilitarianism." *Social Philosophy and Policy* 26: 286–325.

Riley, Jonathan (2010a) "Justice as Higher Pleasure." In Paul J. Kelly and Geogios Varouxakis (eds), *J.S. Mill: Thought and Influence: The Saint of Rationalism* (99–129). London: Routledge.

Riley, Jonathan (2010b) "Mill's Extraordinary Utilitarian Moral Theory." *Politics, Philosophy and Economics* 9: 67–116.

Riley, Jonathan (2012) "Happiness and the Moral Sentiment of Justice." In Leonard Katz (ed.), *Mill on Justice* (158–183). London: Palgrave Macmillan.

Riley, Jonathan (2013a) *Mill on Liberty* (*1998*). 2nd edn. London: Routledge.

Riley, Jonathan (2013b) "Mill's Greek Ideal of Individuality." In Kyriakos N. Demetriou and Antis Loizides (eds), *John Stuart Mill: A British Socrates* (97–125). London: Palgrave Macmillan.

Riley, Jonathan (2013c) *Mill's Radical Liberalism*. London: Routledge.

Scheffler, Samuel (2001) "Rawls and Utilitarianism." In Scheffler, *Boundaries and Allegiances: Problems of Justice and Responsibility in Liberal Thought* (149–172). Oxford: Oxford University Press.

Weithman, Paul J. (2011) *Why Political Liberalism? On John Rawls's Political Turn*. Oxford: Oxford University Press.

# 24

# Perfectionist Justice and Rawlsian Legitimacy

## STEVEN WALL

Throughout his career, John Rawls rejected perfectionist state policies. Early on he insisted that state support for perfectionist goods, including relatively uncontroversial intrinsic goods such as art or knowledge, are not justified unless these goods, and the costs of supporting them, are agreed on by everyone "if not unanimously, then approximately so" (*TJ*, 250). He continued to reject perfectionism in his later work. Perfectionist views are classified as comprehensive doctrines – doctrines that, if enforced by the basic political institutions of a society, would contravene the requirements of political legitimacy (*PL*, 179–180). This chapter presents a critical assessment of Rawls's rejection of perfectionist politics. It advances both a negative and a constructive thesis. The negative thesis targets Rawls's account of political legitimacy. I argue that this account – on its standard interpretation – should be rejected, and so that even if perfectionist policies contravene the Rawlsian requirements of political legitimacy, this would not provide a compelling case for rejecting them. The constructive thesis picks up where the negative thesis leaves off. I contend that there are resources within Rawls's own theory of justice for vindicating state perfectionism. A key part of my brief for the constructive thesis appeals to what Rawls termed the "Aristotelian Principle." This principle, I argue, has important, and insufficiently appreciated, implications for Rawls's account of the human good and the state's role in promoting it in a well-ordered society.

## 1. Justice and Legitimacy

Since I shall be discussing both Rawlsian justice and Rawlsian legitimacy, I will begin by saying a few words about each. The terms "just" and "legitimate" are sometimes used synonymously; but for Rawls they refer to related, but distinct, ideas. Legitimacy refers to the morally permissible exercise of political power. A legitimate society is a society that satisfies a general test, one that is articulated by Rawls's *liberal principle of legitimacy*:

*A Companion to Rawls*, First Edition. Edited by Jon Mandle and David A. Reidy.
© 2014 John Wiley & Sons, Inc. Published 2016 by John Wiley & Sons, Inc.

LL: The exercise of political power is fully proper only when it is exercised in accordance with a constitution the essentials of which all citizens as free and equal may reasonably be expected to endorse in the light of principles and ideals acceptable to their common human reason. (*PL*, 137)

A plurality of rival conceptions of justice can satisfy LL. Rawls's own preferred conception, justice as fairness, is but one of these conceptions. So long as one agrees with Rawls that some of these conceptions are better than others, then one must allow that justice and legitimacy can come apart. A legitimate society can fail to be just, at least in some ways or to some degree. A more difficult question is whether the converse holds. Can a just Rawlsian society fail to be legitimate?

There is a strong case for answering the question affirmatively. To see why, consider the possibility that justice as fairness is realized fully in a society. Now imagine that in this society the arguments given in public to support the exercise of political power necessary to sustain this conception of justice are drawn from a comprehensive doctrine. Would not this establish that the exercise of political power in this imagined society is illegitimate under LL? If so, then a fully just Rawlsian society could be one that was not legitimate. It might be said that Rawlsian legitimacy requires only that it be possible for a given conception of justice to be justified in a way that satisfies LL. It is not necessary that the conception actually be so justified. But this view has the odd consequence that a society could be legitimate, even if no one knew that it was legitimate. A comprehensive conception of justice might be one that could, in principle, be justified in a way that satisfies LL, even though this fact about the conception was unknown.

Reflecting on the political activity of civil rights leaders like Martin Luther King, Jr, Rawls was led to modify his position. The introduction of reasonably rejectable doctrines into public political justification is legitimate "provided that in due course public reasons, given by a reasonable political conception, are presented sufficient to support whatever the comprehensive doctrines are introduced to support" (*PL*, xlix–l). This modification is puzzling. Does it mean that Dr King's political activity was illegitimate until the point in time at which it was justified by public reasons? Can illegitimate political activity be rendered legitimate ex post facto?

Perhaps the Rawlsian position should be construed as follows. If a conception of justice is defended in public by appeal to comprehensive doctrines, then the exercise of political power that it warrants may still pass the LL test providing that (i) it is possible for the conception to be adequately defended without appeal to comprehensive doctrines, and (ii) it is known at the time that this is true.[1] This construal avoids the problem that the legitimacy of a political society could be an unknown fact; but it still confronts a problem. Condition (ii) will be satisfied only in political societies in which Rawls's distinction between political and comprehensive conceptions has taken root. It is doubtful that Dr King, or others at that time, knew that his political activity could be justified by a political conception of justice, since the idea of a political conception of justice had not yet been articulated. The Rawlsian position, however, can be presented as one that is applicable once the key ideas of political liberalism have become part of the public culture of a modern society. So understood, a legitimate political society is one in which fundamental political matters are not only in principle justifiable by a political conception of justice, but known to be so.

Rawls evidently believed that justice as fairness could be adequately defended within the constraints imposed by LL. He probably would have accepted what I shall call the *no conflict thesis*. This thesis holds that the pursuit of Rawlsian legitimacy in no way impedes the pursuit of justice. Now it is an important question whether this thesis is true. Some critics have argued that the demands of LL obstruct the pursuit of Rawlsian justice by precluding its best defense in the kind of public debate that justifies the exercise of political power (Dworkin 2011; Taylor 2011). If these critics are right, then committed Rawlsians face a choice. They must decide whether to favor Rawlsian justice or Rawlsian legitimacy when the two values conflict.

The falsity of the no conflict thesis would bring into clear view the costs of accepting Rawls's account of political legitimacy. These potential costs are often not even considered, for it is tempting to think of Rawlsian legitimacy as establishing a threshold level of justice. Above the threshold, rival conceptions of justice compete to win allegiance among democratic citizens. But while it is true that there is an overlap between Rawlsian legitimacy and Rawlsian justice, the threshold picture is misleading. The strictures of Rawlsian legitimacy, including its doctrine of public reason, establish a public deliberative context in which conceptions of justice must be articulated. That context excludes some conceptions of justice, and it can make it more difficult for other conceptions to prevail in public debate. I have noted that is possible that even justice as fairness may not be fully defensible within this context. But when we turn from Rawlsian justice to comprehensive conceptions of justice, the costs of Rawlsian legitimacy become more apparent. Those who accept a comprehensive conception of justice likely will have good reason to reject the no conflict thesis. Perceiving a conflict between the pursuit of justice (as they see it) and the pursuit of Rawlsian legitimacy, they may conclude that they must reject the latter.

Rawls was not especially interested in responding to people who reject his account of political legitimacy. He often wrote as if he were merely describing how his own conception of justice could be understood to be a module that could fit into and be supported by a range of incompatible comprehensive doctrines (*PL*, 144–145). His hope was that Rawlsian justice could be reconciled with rival understandings of what is valuable in human life. Rawls's intentions aside, however, it remains important to ask whether the demands of a political conception of justice – demands expressed by LL and its associated doctrine of public reason – well serve the demands of justice. Proponents of perfectionist conceptions of justice often deny that this is so. To appreciate their view, we need to know more about what is and is not essential to perfectionist justice.

## 2. The Diversity of Perfectionist Justice

Perfectionism refers to a family of views in political philosophy.[2] The members of the family differ in content, but they all hold that a political order should aim to promote good human lives. Rawls presented his own characterization of this family of views. Perfectionism, he said, is a teleological theory that directs "society to arrange institutions and to define the duties and obligations of individuals so as to maximize the achievement of human excellence in art, science and culture" (*TJ*, 285–286). Rawls's characterization captures an important strand of thought within perfectionism, but it is not very good as a general statement of the view.

Not every perfectionist conception includes a maximizing injunction and not every perfectionist conception singles out art, science and culture as the preeminent areas of human excellence.

A failure to take account of the diversity of perfectionist views can lead one to reject the whole family after one has given reasons to reject only some of its members. This is illustrated by Rawls's own discussion. He claimed that perfectionism shares a defect with classical utilitarianism. Both theories fail to take the separateness of persons seriously in that they both countenance the sacrifice of some individuals for the sake of a greater sum total of good (*TJ*, 290). It is not necessary to pause to discuss the force of this objection. Even if it were sound, it would not apply to perfectionism as such, but only to some understandings of the view. It would not speak against egalitarian and deontological versions of perfectionism, for example.

To give perfectionism its due, we need to take account of its diversity. For present purposes, it will be useful to classify perfectionist conceptions along four main dimensions.

a.  Substance
b.  Controversiality
c.  Scope
d.  State-centeredness

The substance dimension picks out the goods that the conception identifies as worthy of promotion. For example, on a civic humanist view of perfection, a good human life is one that consists of active participation in politics. Only the good citizen can lead a fully good human life. The civic humanist conception is monistic. But perfectionist views also can be pluralistic in the sense that they recognize a range of good human lives consisting of incompatible pursuits, relationships and activities (Raz 1986). The controversiality dimension refers to how contentious the goods identified by the perfectionist conception are in the society in which it is advanced. The claim that a good human life must consist of some loving relationships with others is not especially controversial in modern societies, while the claim that a good human life must be one of religious devotion most certainly is. The scope dimension is highlighted by Rawls's discussion of comprehensive doctrines.

> A conception is said to be general when it applies to a wide range of subjects (in the limit to all subjects); it is comprehensive when it includes conceptions of what is of value in human life, as well as ideals of personal virtue and character, that are to inform much of our nonpolitical conduct (in the limit our life as a whole). (*PL*, 175)

As Rawls rightly noted, generality and comprehensiveness are matters of degree. The scope dimension expresses these variables. The civic humanist view mentioned above, for example, may not be very general or comprehensive. It may have nothing to say about the values and virtues of nonpolitical life. Finally, the state-centered dimension articulates the role the state should play in promoting the good (Chan 2000). At one extreme, a perfectionist view might hold that state promotion of the good is always self-defeating. At the other extreme, a perfectionist view might hold that all goods can and should be promoted aggressively by state action. Most perfectionist conceptions fall between these extremes, holding that some goods should be promoted by the state, but that the promotion of many others is best left to individuals, families and associations.

The state-centered dimension of perfectionist justice brings into view an often overlooked point. Critics of perfectionism frequently characterize the perfectionist state as one that imposes values on its citizens. There is some truth to this charge, but a perfectionist conception of justice can ground both reasons for the state to act and reasons for it not to act. The perfectionist ideal of individuality that Mill champions in *On Liberty*, to take one example, grounds reasons for the state to refrain from a range of actions that might be justified on antiperfectionist conceptions of justice.[3] In this kind of case, it is the antiperfectionist, not the perfectionist, who seeks to enlist the coercive power of the state in imposing justice.

The four dimensions of perfectionist justice reviewed here are by no means exhaustive. Other issues further distinguish perfectionist conceptions, but these four are sufficient to expose just how misleading Rawls's classification of perfectionism is as a comprehensive conception of justice. For Rawls generally described comprehensive conceptions of justice as ones that identify controversial goods, embrace a monistic conception of the good life, are wide in scope and are substantially state-centered. This led him to conclude that perfectionist conceptions of justice, as comprehensive doctrines, fail to accommodate the plurality of reasonable views about the human good and thereby justify state oppression.[4] But, as we have just seen, pluralistic versions of perfectionism with both wide and narrow scope are available; and some perfectionist conceptions identify goods that are not especially controversial, while others hold that the state has a diminished role in promoting the good.

Unlike Rawls's discussion, an adequate discussion of perfectionism must attend to the diversity of perfectionist conceptions of justice. This point should be borne in mind as we turn now to consider more directly the plausibility of Rawls's account of political legitimacy.

## 3. The Principle of Liberal Legitimacy

I have claimed that LL sets down a general test of political legitimacy. But LL speaks of the "fully proper" exercise of political power. To some ears, full propriety will suggest an aspirational ideal rather than a strict test for the morally permissible exercise of power. For consider, someone might accept LL and also accept a further principle, which I shall call the justice principle:

JP: The exercise of political power is fully proper only when it is exercised in accordance with a fully just constitution.

A person who accepts JP could hold that full justice is not a requirement of legitimacy. He could allow that unjust exercises of political power can be morally permissible, even if they are not fully proper. Might Rawls have thought something similar about LL; namely that it articulates an ideal or a desideratum, rather than a strict test of legitimate power? Rawls claimed that the values expressed by a political conception of justice "normally have sufficient weight to override all other values that may come into conflict with them" (*PL*, 138). What should we to think of those (nonnormal) cases in which the values of the political conception do not, in fact, override other values? Do they present instances of justified illegitimacy?

With such possibilities in mind, we might downgrade LL from a principle that articulates a strict test for political legitimacy to one that articulates a test that only normally must be

417

met for the exercise of political power to be morally permissible. Call this downgraded principle LL\*. Notice that if one embraces LL\* over LL, then one will need to think about the kinds of considerations that could properly override the requirements of liberal legitimacy? A plausible answer brings us back to the "no conflict thesis." A citizen who believed that in some circumstances the pursuit of justice can conflict with the demands of LL might be tempted to accept LL\* as the better construal of liberal legitimacy. But this maneuver looks contrived. The citizen simply would be adjusting the demands of liberal legitimacy to ensure that the no conflict thesis was true. It would be more perspicuous to claim that liberal legitimacy is correctly expressed by LL, but then allow that it can be overridden by justice.

I am not claiming that Rawls had these issues clearly in mind. My suspicion is that he implicitly accepted the no conflict thesis, and so he did not think carefully about the possibility that justice and legitimacy could conflict. But whatever Rawls may have thought on the matter, it is hard to believe that legitimacy (as expressed by LL) always takes precedence over justice. There are issues of justice, including those that touch on political fundamentals, that plausibly require appeal to comprehensive considerations for their resolution.[5] And if the pursuit of justice can sometimes trump legitimacy, then perfectionist justice can sometimes trump legitimacy – assuming, of course, that a perfectionist conception of justice could be sound.

To illustrate the point, consider what I shall term the *model case*. The model case assumes that there is a sound perfectionist conception of justice that applies to a modern society such that some reasonable citizens (as Rawls defines them) in the society reject it.[6] The conception, let us assume, identifies autonomy as a central human good. Proponents of this conception believe that the full range of rights and liberties necessary to promote autonomy cannot be justified without appeal to autonomy's perfectionist value. They conclude, at least with respect to certain political measures, that the constraints of LL are too restrictive and need to be set aside for the sake of justice. That is, they conclude that the perfectionist conception cannot be translated effectively into a political conception. Efforts to do so will look insincere, for the justificatory considerations that establish that autonomy is a central human good can be rejected by some reasonable citizens. Imagine, finally, that the proponents of this conception of justice win sufficient support for it such that they are able to enact it using the established democratic procedures in their society.

What should be said about the model case? If LL were accepted, and if it were construed as a strict requirement of political legitimacy, *and* if it were further held that considerations of legitimacy always trump considerations of justice, then it follows that it would be wrong for citizens in the model case to enforce their conception of justice. As a general conclusion, this is not very plausible. Liberal legitimacy may be important, but so is justice; and sometimes the latter ought to win out over the former.

These remarks cast doubt on LL when it is construed as articulating a necessary condition for the permissible exercise of political power. But if it is construed instead as expressing an ideal, then the model case need not speak against it. For then the exercise of political power, whether it was fully proper or not, could be justified even if it violated LL. More importantly, on this understanding of LL, proponents of perfectionist justice need not dispute that liberal legitimacy is important. They could acknowledge that it gives voice to a deep insight, perhaps best expressed by Rousseau, that an ideal society would be one that was not only regulated by just institutions, but also one that could win the allegiance of all who were subject to its institutions.

The dispute between the perfectionist and the Rawlsian now would turn on the weight that is assigned to this ideal. Here two points can be pressed. First, even if LL expresses an aspirational ideal, it might not express the best ideal of its kind. To explain: LL, on the present construal, is an antisubjugation ideal. It holds that there is a cost to imposing justice when some can reasonably reject it. But other antisubjugation ideals have also been advanced. Consider the consent principle:

CP: The exercise of political power is fully proper only when it is exercised in accordance with a constitution to the essentials of which all citizens have given their free and informed consent.

CP may be harder to achieve than LL, but this fact does not show that it is an inferior antisubjugation ideal. CP has the advantage that it gives voice to the interest in not being subjugated of all those who are not reasonable in the Rawlsian sense. This brings me to the second point. Like others, proponents of perfectionist justice can accept that in an ideal society just principles would not only be implemented but also be freely accepted by those bound by them. In such a society, justice would be done and be seen to be done by all. But under realistic circumstances, it is a mistake to tie the demands of political legitimacy too tightly to the fully proper exercise of political power. For a sound account of political legitimacy must take account of the imperfect circumstances to which it applies. Reaching agreement on justice in modern societies, whether among the reasonable or among all members of these societies, may be a valuable aspiration, but it should not lead citizens to exchange their considered views about what justice requires for views that might be more widely acceptable, but less sound. Nor should it lead them to hold that sound views of justice should not be enforced until these views can be reasonably accepted by all.

Taken in conjunction, the two points expose a tension in the Rawlsian account of political legitimacy. If the requirements of legitimacy and justice diverge too greatly, then the priority assigned to legitimacy becomes hard to sustain. However, if the requirements are brought closer together, then either citizens will be asked to adjust their conceptions of justice to fit what is reasonably acceptable to others or the demands of reasonable acceptability will need to be brought closer to the demands of justice, thereby dampening down the antisubjugation credentials of LL. This tension was not confronted by Rawls, for he proceeded as if the no conflict thesis were true. But once that thesis is questioned, and once LL is downgraded from a requirement of political legitimacy to an aspirational ideal, then the tension must be addressed. Perfectionist conceptions of justice, moreover, have the resources to address it. They can balance the demands of justice against the costs of subjugation by appealing to a more comprehensive account of political morality.

The main points of this section can be crisply summarized. Either LL is a condition of political legitimacy or it is not. If it is, then, on the assumption that the no-conflict thesis is false, it is implausible. But if LL does not condition political legitimacy, then it is best conceived of as an ideal of antisubjugation. Construed as such, it does not rule out perfectionist justice; but it does present a problem. The demands of justice must be weighed against the costs of subjugation. Here the perfectionist, in contrast to the Rawlsian, can appeal to a background comprehensive account of political morality to resolve the tension. Far from defeating comprehensive conceptions of justice, Rawlsian legitimacy, on this nonstandard construal, invites reliance on them.

419

# 4. A Brief Note on the Burdens of Judgment

The foregoing discussion casts doubt on the Rawlsian claim that a sound account of political legitimacy rules out perfectionist justice for modern societies. But nowhere in the discussion did I mention the so-called "burdens of judgment." Some readers may be inclined to concede that the no-conflict thesis is false. Some may even concede that a perfectionist conception of justice could be sound. But they will deny that anyone is in a position to know (with sufficient confidence to warrant its imposition) that a controversial perfectionist conception of justice is sound. Rawls's appeal to the burdens of judgment explains why this is the case.

Let's assume that the burdens of judgment do explain the possibility of reasonable disagreement. Suppose now that, on reflection, I affirm a particular perfectionist conception of justice. With the burdens of judgment in mind, I realize that others can reasonably reject this conception. How should I respond to this fact? Three responses need to be distinguished.

a. *Skepticism*  I should suspend judgment on the question of which conception of justice is correct.
b. *Fallibilism*  I should acknowledge that it is possible that I am mistaken about which conception of justice is correct.
c. *Discounting*  I should lower my degree of confidence in my belief that the conception of justice that I affirm is correct.

Response (a) is off the table. If the burdens of judgment imply skepticism, then the Rawlsian project itself is in trouble.[7] Response (b) is important, but harmless. Each of us should allow that we can be mistaken about justice. Fallibilism applies to most, if not all, topics of belief. Response (c) is the most interesting of the three. It raises a host of difficult issues that concern how one ought to update one's beliefs, and one's confidence levels in one's beliefs, in response to the recognition that others, some of whom may be one's equal in intelligence and virtue, disagree in good faith with one's judgment on the matter in question (Feldman and Warfield 2010). Fortunately, we need not tackle these issues to make the key point for present purposes.

The discounting response to reasonable disagreement, if accepted, applies across the board. To see this, suppose that I abandon my commitment to the perfectionist conception of justice I formerly accepted. Discounting considerations shake my confidence that it really is the correct conception. Unless I want to say that no conception of justice should be enforced, I must opt for some alternative conception. Suppose now that I opt for an antiperfectionist conception that satisfies LL. Then, if I am attentive, I should realize that this conception too confronts reasonable disagreement from others, and so I am back again with the problem with which I began. The discounting response, in short, would provide a case against perfectionist conceptions of justice only if the response did not apply with equal force to antiperfectionist conceptions of justice. But it plainly does apply to them. For even if a conception of justice passed the reasonable nonrejectability test articulated in LL, it does not follow that it would not be subject to reasonable disagreement in the epistemic sense. And it is reasonable epistemic disagreement that is the explanandum of the burdens of judgment.

The upshot is that the burdens of judgment do not call into question the conclusions reached above. Neither the perfectionist nor the antiperfectionist gains an advantage by the discounting response to reasonable disagreement. So long as one does not get tripped up by Rawls's use of "reasonable" as both an epistemic and a moral term, then one will see that a reasonable conception of justice (in Rawls's sense of the term) can be one that is subject to widespread reasonable disagreement. Indeed, this has been the fate of justice and fairness as well as all other conceptions of justice that have gained currency in modern societies.

# 5. Rawlsian Perfectionism

This completes my discussion of the negative thesis. I now turn to the promised constructive thesis. Putting Rawlsian legitimacy aside, is it possible that Rawls's own theory of justice provides resources for a successful defense of perfectionist politics? Despite Rawls's rejection of perfectionism, the answer may be yes. The key to understanding how requires us to attend carefully to Rawls's discussion of the Aristotelian Principle.[8]

## 5.1 Sidgwick and Beyond

First, however, a preliminary issue must be addressed. In *TJ*, Rawls defends an account of the good that borrows heavily from Sidgwick's account of a desirable life. For Sidgwick, the term "desirable" does not refer to "what a person ought to desire," but rather to "what a person *would* desire" if he had full information about the objects, and possible objects, of his desires (1907, 110–111). Building on this notion, Rawls introduced the idea of a "deliberatively rational plan of life." This is the plan of life that a person would choose under favorable circumstances if he had full information about all the possible plans of life that he could pursue. The details of Rawls's idea of deliberative rationality need not detain us. The crucial point is that, on Rawls's understanding, a person's good and the goods that contribute to the goodness of his life, are determined by what he would desire under conditions of full information.[9]

In fact, however, Rawls's discussion of the human good is more complex than this Sidgwickian picture suggests. For supplementing his formal definition of the human good, he propounds a basic principle of human motivation that he terms the Aristotelian Principle (AP). As we will see, this principle introduces an objective element into Rawls's account of the human good and provides a foundation for a type of perfectionist politics that runs counter to his explicit commitments.

## 5.2 The Aristotelian Principle

The AP gives voice both to Aristotle's claim that the exercise of our natural powers is a leading human good and to Mill's claim that the pleasures associated with the exercise of our higher faculties are more valuable than other kinds of pleasure (*TJ*, 374). It therefore looks like a perfectionist principle. But Rawls presents the AP not as an evaluative principle but rather as one that describes human motivation. It holds that: "other things equal, human beings enjoy the exercise of their realized capacities (their innate or trained abilities), and this enjoyment increases the more the capacity is realized, or the greater its complexity" (*TJ*, 374).

To illustrate the principle, Rawls refers to the game of chess. As people become more proficient at playing chess, they will tend to enjoy the game more. Further, playing chess well requires the exercise of a fuller range of human capacities than playing other less complex games such as checkers. For this reason, people who are capable of playing both games will tend to enjoy chess more than checkers. The AP thus explains why people are motivated to pursue more complex activities that require patience and costly training rather than sticking with simpler tasks that they have mastered. Without the increased enjoyment they expect to find in pursuits that draw on a greater realization of their capacities, they would not make the effort to develop these capacities.

The AP does not stipulate that any particular pursuits will be enjoyed by human beings generally. Different people will find enjoyment in the realization of different capacities. Still, the AP adds substance to the formal idea of a "deliberatively rational plan of life." If sound, it explains why rational human beings will prefer plans of life that enable them to develop their talents, realize their nature and pursue complex activities over simpler plans of life oriented toward the satisfaction of bodily needs (*TJ*, 376).

This conclusion sits well with perfectionist ideals. Perfectionist writers from Aristotle to Spinoza to Marx all have taken the development of human capacities and talents to be a central component of a good human life. Yet, since the AP merely describes a psychological fact about human beings, its acceptance is consistent with a fully subjectivist account of the human good. The good for a human being could still be fixed by what plan of life he would choose with full information, even if it were true that human beings generally and as a matter of contingent fact rationally would choose plans of life that enable them to develop substantially their capacities. The issues raised by the AP, however, are not simply descriptive issues. As Rawls allowed, even if the principle merely describes human nature, there is still the question of the extent to which the tendency it describes should be encouraged. Further, Rawls claimed that the "things that are commonly thought of as human goods should turn out to be the ends and activities that have a major place in rational plans. The [Aristotelian] principle is part of the background that regulates these judgments" (*TJ*, 379). Here Rawls moves beyond descriptive psychology and endorses the role that the AP plays in an account of the good for human beings.

The evaluative dimension of the AP can be challenged by considering Rawls' intriguing example of a man whose good is found in the pointless activity of counting blades of grass. The AP does not apply to such a man; but the subjectivist "definition of the good forces us to admit that the good for this man is indeed counting blades of grass" (*TJ*, 379).

A careful reading of Rawls's discussion of this example, however, reveals his own ambivalence on the matter, for he claims that "if we allow that [this man's] nature is to enjoy this activity and not to enjoy any other, *and that there is no feasible way to alter his condition*, then surely a rational plan for him will center around this activity" (*TJ*, 380, emphasis added). The italicized qualification strongly suggests that if it were feasible to alter his condition, then his good might lie with other pursuits. A more formidable challenge to subjectivism would imagine a man who *could* find enjoyment in worthwhile activities, but nonetheless preferred to engage in the pointless activity of counting blades of grass. I argue below that such a person would not realize the good of self-respect, for the realization of this good requires that one pursue a plan of life that satisfies the AP (*TJ*, 386).

Before turning to this matter, I need to mention one further aspect of Rawls's discussion of the AP, an aspect that will be important for the argument that ensues. The aspect in question concerns what Rawls terms the "companion effect" of the principle. As Rawls explains: "Human beings have various talents and abilities the totality of which is unrealizable by any one person or group." So when others develop their talents, it is as if they are "bringing forth a part of ourselves that we have not been able to cultivate" (*TJ*, 394). This fact explains why we tend to enjoy the self-development realized by others as well as that realized by ourselves.

## 5.3 Self-Respect

There is an important link between the AP and the social bases of self-respect that I now need to bring into view. Rawls claims that self-respect is a vital human good (*TJ*, 386). But he does not say much about the status of this good. On one view, self-respect is a good because human beings would rationally desire, under conditions of full information, to pursue a plan of life that would enable them to realize it. Thus self-respect would be a good in the same way that other things are good for human beings on the Sidgwickian view. By contrast, on a second view, the goodness of self-respect is presupposed in deliberation regarding the plan of life that it would be rational for a person to pursue. On this view, the fact that self-respect is good for a person is not determined by the fact that he would rationally favor a plan of life that included it. Rather, its goodness is presupposed in the choice of which plan of life it would be rational for him to make.

Rawls did not consider this distinction. However, as I now argue, Rawlsians should adopt the second view of the value of self-respect. Rawls claims that a person's good is determined by the plan of life that she would choose with deliberative rationality in light of all the relevant facts. Yet, in order for a choice to be deliberatively rational, it must be based on something. It must follow from the preferences, values, beliefs, etc. of the chooser. This means that deliberative rationality must presuppose criteria of evaluation.[10] The good of self-respect plausibly is among the criteria of evaluation. Self-respect, to quote Rawls, is "not so much a part of any rational plan of life as the sense that one's plan is worth carrying out" (*TJ*, 155). The person who is reflecting on the question "what plan of life would I choose under conditions of full information" is asking herself, in part, what plan of life do I believe is worth carrying out. And if she were to come to think that some particular plan of life would not allow her to realize the good of self-respect, then she would not rationally choose it as the plan of life that determines her good.

These remarks may suggest that self-respect is an idea without substantive content. If one pursues a plan of life that one believes is worth carrying out, then one will realize self-respect. But Rawls directly links the good of self-respect to the AP. The link occurs at two points. First, "when activities fail to satisfy the AP, they are likely to seem dull and flat, and to give us no feeling of competence or a sense that they are worth doing" (*TJ*, 386–387). Second, "the companion effect of the [AP] influences the extent to which others confirm and take pleasure in what we do." The companion effect, in turn, is vital to our self-respect; for, as Rawls claims, "unless our endeavors are appreciated by our associates it is impossible for us to maintain the conviction that they are worthwhile" (*TJ*, 387).

Bringing these points together, a rational plan of life for a person is one that determines that person's good; but such a plan must enable the person to realize the good of self-respect. Self-respect is an objective good that conditions the subjective choice of rational plans of life. But, importantly, to realize the good of self-respect, a plan of life must be one in which a person develops his talents to some substantial extent, for only then will others confirm to him the worth of his plan of life. The good of self-respect thus imparts an element of objectivity to the self-development that is enjoined by the AP. In this way, the Sidgwickian account of the good that Rawls embraced is supplemented by an account of objective goods.

## 5.4 State Promotion

Completing the case for Rawlsian perfectionism requires showing that the AP can ground a role for the state in promoting objective goods. Human beings, according to the principle, have a tendency to engage in activities that develop their nature. The tendency is "relatively strong and not easily counterbalanced" (TJ, 377). Yet elsewhere Rawls observes that as the costs of training increase for complex activities, human beings tend to lose the desire to engage in them. The point at issue is important; for, if the tendency were very strong, then there would be little need for the state to adopt measures to assist people in their efforts at self-development. But if the tendency were weak, then the state might have a role to play in this regard.

Consider the case of a talented artist. Suppose that, given his talents, he can best realize his nature if he devotes considerable time to his art. But now suppose that he will need to make substantial financial sacrifices to do so, and that this fact leads him to abandon a career in art for a more lucrative career in business. Cases of this kind are not uncommon in modern societies. They show that if the AP correctly describes a tendency of human nature, then this tendency is not so powerful that it is unnecessary to even consider the option of state measures to support it.

To be sure, in a well-ordered society there will exist a range of associations that support activities that give expression to people's talents. Rawls assumed that these associations, and the cultural marketplace more generally, will allow for the adequate development of the talents of all citizens, at least in a society regulated by his two principles of justice. There are reasons to doubt this assumption, however (Hurka 1995). *First*, some intrinsically valuable pursuits are costly to pursue. They are costly to pursue, in part, because their enjoyment depends on sensibilities that take training and effort to develop. For this reason, some – who otherwise would excel at them – will be discouraged from engaging in them, unless they receive support from others. But such pursuits may not receive the same level of support in civil society as other pursuits that are more widely appreciated. The state can play a role by providing subsidies that lower the costs of engagement with these pursuits, thereby making it more likely that people who would excel at them will take them up. *Second*, even in a well-ordered society, there is no reason to think that, absent state action, all citizens will be exposed to a sufficiently wide range of pursuits related to the development of their talents. The state can play a role in helping its citizens, particularly when they are young, discover valuable pursuits that they otherwise would not know.[11]

These two points are strengthened by a third reason to doubt Rawls's assumption. The AP, in conjunction with its companion effect, holds that people find enjoyment in the full and wide development of human powers. This fact about people helps to explain why the members of a well-ordered society will find their political association to be intrinsically valuable. By participating in the collective life of a well-ordered society, each member can "participate in the total sum of the realized natural assets of the others" (TJ, 459). From this it follows that each member of a well-ordered society has reason to prefer a society in which there is a wider and deeper development of human talents than one in which there is a narrower and less deep development. Following von Humboldt, Rawls sees in this thought an argument for an extensive freedom of association. But once the value of the breadth and depth of the development of human talents is recognized as an important societal good, then it becomes plausible to think that the state, under a range of circumstances, could have a more active role to play in ensuring that a wider range, and fuller development, of perfectionist activities and goods are realized.

These considerations in support of perfectionist state action rest on empirical claims. Their force will vary across societies. In some societies, the cultural marketplace left alone may do sufficiently well in eliciting the development of human talents and powers. The present argument is only that there is a presumptive Rawlsian case for state perfectionism.[12]

## 5.5  The Discrimination Objection

This presumptive case may be defeated by other considerations that are integral to Rawlsian justice. The main objection that Rawls presses against state perfectionism is that it would unfairly discriminate in favor of some citizens and against others.[13] There is, he claims, "no agreed upon criterion of perfection." Without a shared conception of the good by reference to which the perfectionist value of different pursuits could be assessed, state perfectionism runs the risk of arbitrarily privileging the values of some over others.

Against this objection, it can be said that the AP provides the common ground for state perfectionism. This principle is not a sectarian principle, but one that can be affirmed by persons with different conceptions of the good. However, it is true that the description of the AP is pitched at a fairly high level of abstraction. Citizens who accept it can disagree over which particular activities and pursuits warrant state support under it. As Rawls emphasized, the principle itself does not identify particular ends. The worry, then, is that if the AP is made the ground for perfectionist policies it will become, in practice, a sectarian principle. By necessity, the state will need to favor some activities that fall under the principle over others that also do so. This, in turn, will pose a threat to the self-respect of those citizens whose lives are bound up with activities that do not receive state support. This concern is presumably behind Rawls's claim that "democracy in judging each other's aims is the foundation of self-respect in a well-ordered society" (TJ, 388).

The first point to make in response to this objection is that the state perfectionism envisioned does not identify a small subset of activities and pursuits as deserving of support. The companion effect of the AP explains why. Citizens take pleasure in the self-development of their fellow citizens precisely because they can see in it the realization of talents that they value. State perfectionism grounded on the AP thus aims at the full development of human nature. The policies it recommends do not favor a few capacities – such as those involved in aesthetic or scientific pursuits – over all others. Instead, it supports policies that encourage a broad and deep development of human talents. Yet, while important, this point does not go to the heart of the objection. For not every activity that has perfectionist value (under the AP) can receive state support, even under the most accommodating set of policies. Just as states need to make decisions with regard to the public goods they provide, a perfectionist state would need to make decisions with regard to the perfectionist goods it supports. These decisions would reflect the character of the society over which the state governs. This raises the discrimination worry once again. In pursuing its aim of promoting a broad and deep development of human talents, the state may, in effect, if not by intention, favor some perfectionist pursuits over others that have an equal claim to state support under the AP. Proponents of the disfavored pursuits may justifiably feel that the state's action expresses the view that their pursuits and, by extension, their conception of the good is of less value than others. The absence of an agreed upon criterion of perfection, in this way, opens the door for discriminatory state action that can damage the self-respect of some citizens.[14]

The problem here is a general one. Not infrequently citizens share a commitment to an abstract aim, but disagree over how that aim is best pursued. One solution to the problem is to appeal to a decision procedure to determine how the aim should be pursued in practice. In the present case, I have been arguing that all citizens in a Rawlsian society share an interest in supporting the self-development that falls under the AP. They can agree on the abstract aim of state support for human perfection. Yet without an agreed upon criterion of perfection, they can be expected to disagree over how this aim is best pursued in practice. Nevertheless, it can be reasonable for them to accept the perfectionist policies that are selected by an established decision procedure, providing this procedure gives their favored options a fair chance of winning state support. And if it is reasonable for them to accept these policies on these grounds, then those whose favored activities fail to receive state support need not view this fact as one that expresses the view that their activities are of lesser value. Thus the state policies, controversial as they may be, need not threaten the self-respect of citizens.

## 5.6 The Political Liberal Turn

My argument has drawn on Rawls's discussion of the AP in *TJ*. As is well known, Rawls came to have reservations about some of the claims expressed in this work. It might be thought, then, that the case for Rawlsian perfectionism developed here must be abandoned once justice as fairness is presented as a political doctrine. Yet Rawls did not repudiate the AP in *PL*. While he said relatively little about it, he continued to invoke it to explain how a well-ordered society contributes to the good of its members (*PL*, 207). The reason for this must be that Rawls did not consider the AP to be a reasonably contestable principle. It states general facts about human beings that are consistent with a wide range of comprehensive doctrines. If so, then the public endorsement of the principle, and the perfectionist policies based on it, need not contravene the constraints imposed by political liberalism.

It also should be borne in mind that a political conception of justice applies to political fundamentals. With respect to much legislation, Rawls's view in *PL* is that it is appropriate, and perhaps even desirable, for citizens to appeal to their own comprehensive views to decide which legislation to support and defend in public (*PL*, 230). Many of the perfectionist policies I have been discussing fall into this category. Thus Rawlsian perfectionism is democratic perfectionism; and the constraints imposed by political liberalism, whether or not those constraints should be accepted, need not rule it out.

## 6. Conclusion

The relationship between perfectionism and Rawlsian political philosophy is a good deal more complex than is commonly recognized. On the standard view, Rawlsian justice is antiperfectionist and Rawlsian legitimacy rules out perfectionist justice. The standard view is sustained by the no conflict thesis. If that thesis were rejected, then it would become plausible to downgrade Rawlsian legitimacy from a constraint to an ideal. Doing so opens the door to perfectionist justice. Yet admitting perfectionist considerations into justice is not as alien to the Rawlsian project as it may appear at first. Rawls's rejection of perfectionist politics was not dogmatic. He noted that the exclusion of perfectionist considerations from justice might prove on reflection to be unacceptable (*TJ*, 291). In his late work, he allowed that perfectionist state measures could be legitimately pursued within a publicly justified constitutional framework. And his endorsement of the AP provides a footing for a form of state perfectionism that can strengthen the overall case for Rawlsian justice by enabling it to respond to the criticism that it is insufficiently responsive to the claims of human excellence.

# Notes

Thanks to David Reidy and Jon Mandle for valuable comments on an earlier draft.

1   Thus perfectionists who believe that, in due course, their political proposals could be adequately justified within the constraints of Rawlsian public reason, and that this fact could be publicly known, could happily sign on to LL. The view I term "Rawlsian Perfectionism," and discuss in section 5, may be a good example of such public-reason-compatible state perfectionism.
2   Perfectionism also refers to a range of views in ethics. But in this chapter I am concerned with perfectionist political philosophy.
3   The issue of education provides a good illustration. Mill argued that state-run education poses a threat to individuality. By contrast, many antiperfectionist conceptions of justice mandate state-run education as necessary to achieve fair equality of opportunity.
4   Note in particular that Rawls classifies the liberalism of Raz as belonging to the dominant tradition in holding "that there is but one reasonable and rational conception of the good" (*PL*, 134–135). My suspicion is that Rawls was confused here by his own classifications. Raz insists that there is a wide range of ways of leading a good human life. Yet since Raz reject Rawls's political conception of justice, Rawls groups him with the dominant antipluralist tradition.
5   The vexed issue of abortion can serve as an illustration. Rawls hoped that this issue could be resolved by appeal to political values only ("Public Reason Revisited"). In my judgment, the hope is difficult to sustain. The resolution of the abortion issue will require the state to take a stand on the moral status of the fetus; and doing so, in all likelihood, will require it to appeal to considerations that some can reasonably reject, given their comprehensive commitments. For related concerns about the completeness of Rawlsian public reason, as it pertains to a number of controversial political issues, see Reidy 2000.
6   Does the model case beg the question against Rawlsian legitimacy? It assumes that there could be a sound conception of justice that is not a political conception of justice, but this is impossible if a political conception of justice captures the truth about justice. The worry is misconceived, however. As we have seen, a conception of justice can be both correct and illegitimate (under LL). Rawls believed that the correct conception of justice could be presented in a way that enables it to satisfy the demands of LL. But this claim is one that the model case is designed to challenge, and it is a claim that will be rejected by anyone who does not accept the no conflict thesis.
7   This has sometimes been denied (Barry 1995, 168–173). But the standard Rawlsian view takes care to not endorse skepticism.
8   Parts of this section draw on the more detailed discussion in Wall (forthcoming).
9   Rawls may have misunderstood Sidgwick on this point. There is some evidence that Sidgwick rejected the full information account of the good that Rawls attributes to him (Shaver 1997). This interpretive issue need not detain us.

10  Some writers who have attempted to develop the Sidgwickian view have held that each person's personality – her values, preferences, etc. – provide the criteria of evaluation. But when a person is considering the plan of life that determines her good, she needs to adopt a standpoint that is independent from what she currently cares about. For discussion of the difficulties of characterizing such a standpoint see Rosati 1995. The present proposal partially avoids this difficulty by invoking substantive values, such as the good of self-respect, as criteria of evaluation.

11  In addition, the state could support economic arrangements designed to increase the leisure time of those who live in modern societies. Proposals for an unconditional basic income, for example, could be justified on the ground that citizens in these societies need sufficient time away from work to develop their talents as required by the AP.

12  The argument can be illuminated by considering the matter from the original position. The parties in the original position know general facts about human nature. They know that the AP, assuming it is a sound principle, accurately describes human motivation. They also know two further facts about the person whom they represent: (i) that person has an interest in pursuing a plan of life that satisfies the AP, and (ii) that person will tend to enjoy living in a society in which others develop talents and pursue activities that she is not able to realize herself. Both of these facts, in turn, are important to understanding the social conditions that are conducive to self-respect. For, as we saw above, to realize the good of self-respect, a person must pursue a plan of life that enables her to develop her talents to some substantial extent, for only then will others confirm to her the worth of her plan of life. The parties in the original position, accordingly, would want to make sure that those whom they represent live under social conditions that actively support the self-development of those that they represent.

13  Rawls also claimed that state perfectionism, in its strict maximizing form, is incompatible with respect for individual liberty. But more moderate forms of state perfectionism are available, and these forms need not conflict with his Principle of Equal Liberty. The state perfectionism in question here is of this moderate variety.

14  The objection discloses the complex relationship between the state perfectionism in question and the good of self-respect. On the one hand, perfectionist policies can be important for securing the good of self-respect. They can help to bring about social conditions that encourage the self-development of citizens, thereby promoting their self-respect. But, on the other hand, as the present objection brings out, they also can undermine the self-respect of citizens whose pursuits do not receive official state support. The objection then should be understood as holding that the latter negative effects outweigh the former positive effects.

# Works by Rawls, with Abbreviations

*Political Liberalism* (PL), expanded edn. New York: Columbia University Press, 2005.
"Public Reason Revisited," *University of Chicago Law Review* 64 (1997): 765–807.
*A Theory of Justice* (TJ), rev. edn. Cambridge, MA: Harvard University Press, 1999.

# Other References

Barry, Brian (1995) *Justice as Impartiality*. Oxford: Oxford University Press.
Chan, Joseph (2000) "Legitimacy, Unanimity and Perfectionism." *Philosophy and Public Affairs* 29: 5–42.
Dworkin, Ronald (2011) *Justice for Hedgehogs*. Cambridge, MA: Belknap Press.
Feldman, Richard and Warfield, Ted (eds) (2010) *Disagreement*. New York: Oxford University Press.

Hurka, Thomas (1995) "Indirect Perfectionism: Kymlicka on Liberal Neutrality." *Journal of Political Philosophy* 3(1): 36–57.

Rasmussen, Douglas and Den Uyl, Douglas (2005) *Norms of Liberty: A Perfectionist Basis for Non-Perfectionist Politics*. University Park: Penn State University Press.

Raz, Joseph (1986) *The Morality of Freedom*. Oxford: Clarendon Press.

Reidy, David (2000) "The Wide View of Public Reason: Not Wide Enough." *Res Publica* 6: 49–72.

Rosati, Connie (1995) "Persons, Perspectives, and Full Information Accounts of the Good." *Ethics* 105: 296–325.

Shaver, Robert (1997) "Sidgwick's False Friends." *Ethics* 107: 314–320.

Sidgwick, Henry (1907) *The Methods of Ethics*. 7th edn. Indianapolis: Hackett.

Taylor, Robert (2011) *Reconstructing Rawls: The Kantian Foundations of Justice as Fairness*. University Park: Penn State University Press.

Wall, Steven (forthcoming) "Rawlsian Perfectionism." *Journal of Moral Philosophy*.

# 25

# The Unwritten Theory of Justice

## Rawlsian Liberalism versus Libertarianism

### BARBARA H. FRIED

When *A Theory of Justice* was first published in 1971, utilitarianism was the game to beat in political philosophy, and Rawls made no bones about his intention to beat it. In his words, "Justice as fairness . . . offers, I believe, an alternative to the utilitarian view which has for so long held the preeminent place in our moral philosophy. I have tried to present the theory of justice as a viable systematic doctrine so that the idea of maximizing the good does not hold sway by default" (1999 rev. edn: *TJ*, 513). While other theories of justice – perfectionism, intuitionism and rational egoism – make cameo appearances in the book, Rawls's case for "justice as fairness" rests in significant part on its claimed superiority to utilitarianism, by virtue of its refusal to "justif[y] institutions on the grounds that the hardships of some are offset by the greater good of others" (*TJ* 1971, 15). The word "libertarianism" does not appear in the book (although Rawls likely had a Smithian version of libertarianism in mind in his brief discussion of "a system of natural liberty" (*TJ* 1971, 72–75)).

Three years later, Nozick published *Anarchy, State and Utopia* (*ASU*). Part II of *ASU*, which lays out Nozick's Lockean theory of the ideal libertarian state, is explicitly framed as a rejoinder to Rawls's *TJ*, and fully a third of its argument is given over to a close reading and critique of the book, in particular the difference principle. The publication of *ASU* singlehandedly made deontological libertarianism a political philosophy to be reckoned with in academic circles, at precisely the moment it was on the ascendency in political circles. For the general readership of *TJ*, it also singlehandedly enshrined libertarianism rather than utilitarianism as the chief rival to "justice as fairness," and put the difference principle at the center of Rawlsianism. Forty years later, to most nonspecialists "Rawlsianism" *is* the difference principle, and the most durable part of Nozick's argument has proved to be his critique of that principle. As mismatched as they are in aspirations and method, *ASU* and *TJ* have become the towering bookends of political theory, each the other's chief foil.

By the time that Rawls was working on the revised edition to *TJ*, libertarianism was well entrenched in the political scene. Rawls surely knew that to his general readership, "justice as fairness" and the many variants it spawned (equality of resources or assets, equal

*A Companion to Rawls*, First Edition. Edited by Jon Mandle and David A. Reidy.
© 2014 John Wiley & Sons, Inc. Published 2016 by John Wiley & Sons, Inc.

opportunity for welfare, equal access to advantage, democratic equality) were generally viewed as egalitarians' most cogent answers to libertarianism. Rawls, understandably, chose not to reformulate his argument to take cognizance of the changed political and philosophical landscape. As a result, the 1999 revised version of *TJ*, like the original one, is framed as a rejoinder to utilitarianism, making no mention of libertarianism or libertarian principles, beyond the same brief discussion of "systems of natural liberty" (*TJ*, 57–58, 62–64).

Thus it comes to be that Rawls's theory of justice has had two parallel lives in political theory. The first – the version Rawls wrote – is framed as an alternative to utilitarianism, and in particular utilitarianism's failure to take seriously the separateness of persons and each individual's right to pursue his or her own projects in life. The second – the version "received" by its general audience – is framed as an alternative to libertarianism, and in particular libertarianism's failure to take seriously our moral obligations to the well-being of our fellow citizens.

Notwithstanding the received view of *TJ* and *ASU* as the opposing poles of contemporary political philosophy, over the last 35 years a small cottage industry has emerged, dedicated to showing how little is required, logically speaking, to turn Rawls into Nozick and Nozick into Rawls (Lomasky 2005; Stick 1987; Buchanan and Lomasky 1984; Roemer 1988; Gibbard 2000). From one perspective, this development is hardly surprising, given the shared, foundational commitment of Rawlsianism and libertarianism to liberal individualism. As Loren Lomasky put it, "Is it possible to deny the fundamentally libertarian flavor of a theory in which [maximal liberty for all] enjoys lexical priority?" (2005, 180).

My aim here is to explore where and why, starting from that common commitment, Rawls's "justice as fairness" and libertarianism come apart. I focus on their respective treatments of the just distribution of wealth, as this is the point at which the two theories most clearly diverge. Among traditional (right) libertarians, I consider (in addition to *ASU*) the work of Loren Lomasky, Jan Narveson, Eric Mack, James Buchanan, Israel Kirzner, Richard Epstein, Gerald Gaus, Randy Barnett, John Simmons, David Schmidtz, John Hasnas and Murray Rothbard.[1] I also consider the arguments for "left libertarianism" offered by Michael Otsuka, Peter Vallentyne, Hillel Steiner and others. (Unless otherwise indicated, "libertarianism" refers to right libertarianism alone.)

In defending their respective theories of justice, both Rawls and libertarians (including self-identified deontologists like Nozick) move back and forth between prudential arguments – what will make people's lives go better overall/produce a stable society – and arguments from rights-based principles. I take up prudential arguments briefly at the end, but for the most part focus on the latter. The reason for this is simple. Disagreements about the instrumental value of a given arrangement of property rights or distribution of wealth rest principally on disagreements about the facts. That people's empirical assumptions tend to track their ideological predispositions is a significant (if slightly depressing) fact about human nature. But for my purposes, if that is all that separates, say, Rawls and Nozick, there is no mystery about how to bring them together: change one or both of their empirical assumptions. In contrast, turning Rawls into a principled libertarian or Nozick into a principled Rawlsian egalitarian requires us to understand where, starting from a shared commitment to liberal individualism, they faced the same choices and chose differently.

For the most part, we don't have to guess how libertarians would describe their points of divergence from Rawls. Much of the libertarian revival sparked by *ASU*, like *ASU* itself, is framed as a rejoinder to Rawls. From the perspective of libertarians, Rawls has assumed the rhetoric of liberal individualism, but at every juncture has proved himself (in Loren Lomasky's words) "more committed to his egalitarian redistributionist conclusions than he is to the [liberal individualist] premises that generate those results" (2005, 199). The net result, as far as libertarians are concerned, is that Rawls is a faux liberal individualist, and his disagreements with utilitarians are at most a friendly family squabble.

While Rawls did not address modern-day libertarianism in *TJ*, he did touch on the subject in other writings. But his comments are relatively brief, and focused exclusively on the Nozickean version, in particular Nozick's derivation of the minimal state. (See, e.g., *Political Liberalism*, *PL*, 262–265; *The Law of Peoples*, *LP*, 49–50.) As a result, for the most part, we have to infer how Rawls would have responded to the substantial libertarian critique of *TJ* that has amassed over the past four decades.

Finally, there is the question of method. In comparing Rawls to his libertarian counterparts, should we regard *TJ* as a procedural (constructivist) theory of justice or a substantive one? Rawls's answer was, both. The two principles are to be tested by "find[ing] the arguments in their favor that are decisive from the standpoint of the original position," from which vantage point there are "no given antecedent principles external to [the representative persons'] point of view to which they are bound." But they are also to be tested "by comparison with our considered judgments of justice," meaning our substantive ethical commitments (*TJ*, 132).

At this point, I would venture that most people are in agreement with Thomas Nagel's view, first expressed when the book came out, that the device of the original position offers no independent support for Rawls's substantive theory of justice. In Nagel's words, "The egalitarian liberalism which [Rawls] develops and the conception of the good on which it depends are extremely persuasive, but the original position serves to model rather than justify them" (1973, 233). At various points Rawls himself invites or offers the same assessment (*TJ* 1971, 141; *TJ*, 16; *PL*, 25–26). On the other hand, given the central rhetorical role that the heuristic of rational choice plays, both in unfolding "justice as fairness" and establishing Rawls's bona fides as a liberal individualist, one cannot ignore it. I will therefore consider both the procedural and substantive defenses Rawls offers for his theory of justice.

Libertarians have pursued both procedural and substantive derivations of the just state as well, although (with the notable exception of Nozick) generally not in the same work. Most, however, have focused on the latter. As John Simmons (2005) has observed, contemporary libertarian political philosophers have said relatively little about how a state gains political legitimacy, and with it the right to coerce its citizens. The omission is surprising, because libertarian principles hardly imply indifference to the process by which individuals come under the coercive authority of the state, and most versions of libertarianism (whether they start from self-ownership, autonomy/liberty, or concepts of mutual advantage) would seem to make individual consent a necessary precondition to legitimacy.

For anarcho-libertarians like Simmons (2005), Murray Rothbard (1977) and John Hasnas (2008), the explanation is straightforward. Believing that only explicit consent can justify subjecting an individual to the power of the state and that such consent cannot be obtained, they have concluded that the state cannot be justified.

The majority of libertarians, perhaps sharing anarcho-libertarians' skepticism about consent but unwilling to accept their conclusion, have, *sub silentio*, given up on consent. Instead, they have argued that the state is legitimized insofar as its political arrangements, however arrived at, are just. (As noted above, on one view of *TJ* – probably the predominant view at this point – this is precisely what Rawls has done.) But a small band of libertarians has pursued the classical liberal social contractarian tradition, deriving the legitimacy of the state from hypothetical consent to its arrangements pursuant to a properly moralized bargain. Notable among these are David Gauthier (1986), James Buchanan (1975, 1984), Jan Narveson (1988) and Loren Lomasky (1987).

Nozick is, perhaps ironically, the most famous expositor of *both* the second and third approach. Notwithstanding Nozick's waggish dismissal of the social contract as "not worth the paper on which it is not written," the Nozick of Part I of *ASU* pursues a procedural justification for the state that is essentially contractarian, although not labeled as such. The Nozick of Part II, abandoning procedural justifications for substantive ones, argues that the state is legitimate insofar as it conforms to just (Lockean) rights. In this respect at least, Rawls's and Nozick's projects parallel each other.

I start by comparing procedural derivations of the just state in Rawls's and libertarian accounts, and then turn to their respective substantive principles of justice.

## 1. Constructing the Choice Position

Rawls explains the motivation for the original position as follows:

> On the contract interpretation treating men as ends in themselves implies at the very least treating them in accordance with the principles to which they would consent in an original position of equality. For in this situation men have equal representation as moral persons who regard themselves as ends and the principles they accept will be rationally designed to protect the claims of their person. (*TJ*, 156–157)

Most contractarian libertarians would find little to quarrel with in this formulation. The disagreements all come from how Rawls on the one hand and libertarians on the other construct the choice situation into which such persons are put and the resulting knowledge imputed to them.

By "persons," Rawls insists he means "determinate-persons," each with his or her own "place in society, class position or social status . . . fortune in the distribution of natural assets and abilities, intelligence, strength and the like . . . psychological propensities . . . [and] conception of the good" (*TJ*, 11, 152, 464). This, more than any other feature of his contractualist thought experiment, was (in Rawls's view) what differentiated "justice as fairness" from Harsanyi-like contractualist arguments for average utilitarianism, and established its superiority. To quote Rawls, "the utilitarian argument assumes that the parties have no definite character or will, that they are not persons with determinate final interests, or a particular conception of their good, that they are concerned to protect." In short, "[t]hey are, as we might say, 'bare-persons,'" each with the same chance of "being any one of a number of persons complete with each individual's system of ends, abilities, and social position," expressed by the "same deep utility function" (*TJ*, 150, 152).

But having populated the original position with "determinate-persons" motivated by rational self-interest, Rawls famously puts them behind the veil of ignorance, which prevents them from knowing what those determinate traits are. Rawls argues that his "determinate-person" behind the veil differs from the utilitarians' "bare-person," by virtue of the fact that he knows he is different from other individuals, although he doesn't know how. As a consequence, while (contra utilitarianism) ethical considerations do not operate "in the characterization of the parties" in the Original Position, they operate in the characterization of the choice situation, by suppressing the information required for parties to favor their own interests over others' (*TJ*, 160, 166, 512). But to libertarians (and many others as well), this is a distinction without a difference. As Nozick famously argued, turning Rawls on himself, the choosing self behind the veil satisfies Rawls's ambition (contra utilitarianism) to "'take seriously the distinction between persons' . . . only if one presses *very* hard on the distinction between men and their talents, assets, abilities, and special traits" (*ASU*, 228).

The resulting "bare deontological ego" (Loren Lomasky's term) populating Rawls's original position may suffice to establish Rawls's credentials as a moral individualist in the limited sense that – unlike communitarian or other group-based accounts of justice – in evaluating institutional arrangements he counts only *individuals'* interests. But from the perspective of libertarians, the gulf between that "bare deontological ego" and the flesh-and-blood differentiated self at the heart of liberal individualism is vast – indeed, unbridgeable (*ASU*, 228; Narveson 1988, 132–133). As Lomasky put it: "Everything pertaining to persons except their personhood, whatever that could be when abstracted from ends, character, abilities, and relations to material possessions, is thoroughly socialized . . . The conclusion is thoroughly illiberal" (1987, 135, 138).

Rawls's motivations for imposing the veil are, in the view of most libertarians, thoroughly illiberal as well. Rawls defends the veil in (at least) two different ways in *TJ*. The first and most debated is that it prevents distributive shares from being "improperly influenced by . . . factors so arbitrary from a moral point of view," including natural and social endowments and an individual's choice of ends (*TJ* 1971, 59–60, 72). At this point, most libertarians conclude that "justice as fairness" is simply not a liberal individualist theory. Nozick, Lomasky and others have argued that Rawls here conflates two questions: whether people deserve their natural and social endowments, and whether they deserve to keep them and decide for themselves how to exercise them. Even if the answer to the first question is "no," because such endowments are what make individuals "determinate" people rather than "bare-persons," argues Lomasky, "[a] robust liberalism must . . . maintain that contingencies become imbued with moral weight once they are intimately attached to the lives that persons *actually* live" (Lomasky 1987, 136, 138; *ASU*, 216–227; Gauthier 1974 and 1986, 245–257).

Rawls's second justification is that without some sort of veil of ignorance, we cannot hope to reach agreement, because "we cannot reasonably expect our views to fall into line when they are affected by the contingencies of our different circumstances" (*TJ*, 453, 465, 267–268; *PL*, 53–54). The original position solves the problem by eliminating all such differences, thereby making "the deliberations of any one person . . . typical of all." Rawls makes clear that eliminating the potential for disagreement about moral principles is not just a happy byproduct of his having adopted the veil of ignorance for other reasons. It is, rather, one of the chief motives for adopting it: "Indeed, other things being equal, the preferred description of the initial situation is that which introduces the greatest convergence of opinion" (*TJ* 1971, 517).

At this point, libertarians (and others) have concluded that "justice as fairness" is not a contractualist theory either. Starting with the desideratum of unanimous agreement, Rawls, by his own acknowledgement, has reverse-engineered the original position to guarantee it. But surely, this puts the cart before the horse in any consent-driven theory of legitimation.

If determinate persons, each calculating their rational self-interest with full knowledge of their actual circumstances in life, cannot reach agreement on a just state, then – as the anarcho-libertarians have concluded – so much the worse for agreement.

Finally, the consequences of imposing the Rawlsian veil are, as far as libertarians are concerned, thoroughly illiberal as well. By making "the deliberations of any one person . . . typical of all," Rawls turns the problem of social choice into a problem of individual choice under conditions of uncertainty, endowing that one representative person with preferences that reflect the aggregated preferences of all. As a result, what is "rational" for the representative person to choose coincides with what an impartial observer, weighing every individual's preferences equally, would choose. What we are left with, in Eric Mack's words, is a vision of society that reflects collectivist, not individualist, values: "An abiding feature of liberal individualism – and more particularly moral individualism – is the deep-seated rejection of the idea of a shared substantive social end or hierarchy of ends to which all members of society are to be devoted" (2009, 133).

While it is difficult to turn Rawls's original position into a choice situation that would be congenial to libertarians, the reverse is not necessarily true. By insisting on determinate, situated persons who know who they are, libertarian contractarians face a host of difficult decisions in constructing the choice position that the Rawlsian veil allows Rawls to sidestep: What material goods, talents and social opportunities (including opportunities to exit the bargaining table) do we endow each of the hypothetical bargainers with? If we start from where people just happen to be as a matter of social fact, without regard to the justice of how they got there, why should their resulting hypothetical agreement carry any moral weight? And if we are going to construct a fictional set of goods, talents and social opportunities, where do we get them from? How do we deal with holdouts (strategic or otherwise)? What real-life constraints on bargaining should we build into the imagined bargain and what suppress?

Depending on how libertarians resolve each of these issues, it is a relatively simple matter, if not to turn libertarians into Rawlsians, at least to move them quite far in that direction. Consider the following two examples.

*Constructing the parties' threat point*    Whether a given agreement is to the mutual advantage of all parties depends on what the next best alternative is for each of them if they fail to reach agreement. The Rawlsian original position avoids the need to engage this question by eliminating any diversity of interests and hence any possibility of bargaining.[2] By contrast, social contractarians on the right have to answer it in order to derive any determinate conclusions. Doing so requires that they flesh out, in a variety of ways, the bargaining position each person finds himself or herself in. What is the value of each individual's endowments with and without social cooperation? Do we have to suppress social endowments that were not justly acquired? What alternative cooperative arrangements are available to the parties if they walk away from the bargaining table? How costly would it be to secure those alternatives, and should we take those costs into account in fixing the parties' threat point?

Depending on the answers to these and a host of other factors that (in the real world) determine individual bargainers' threat points, libertarians may find themselves legitimating wildly divergent political arrangements, from the fantasy Nozickean state in which everyone retains the full value of their marginal product, to the status quo (whatever it happens to be), to a highly redistributive state not that different from Rawls's (Fried 2003).

*The problem of holdouts*   In any realistic, large-number bargaining situation, no solution is likely to garner unanimous assent. Rawls dealt with that problem by eliminating all hetero-geneity among the parties, thereby guaranteeing unanimity. Social contractarians on the right, committed to making the parties to the bargain thick, determinate selves, cannot avail themselves of that solution. Instead, at crucial points they have dealt with the problem of holdouts by eliminating the requirement of unanimous consent.

Nozick's derivation of the minimal state in Part I of *ASU* is a case in point. Nozick famously sets out to demonstrate how the minimal state could arise from a nonpolitical Lockean state of nature without violating anyone's Lockean rights. This requires that any rearrange-ment of those rights be consented to by the rights-holder. But the moment Nozick confronts equal and incompatible rights claims – in this case, the rights of each person to an independ-ent protective agency of her choice – he gives up on consent, permitting the dominant protec-tive agency unilaterally to extinguish all other protective agencies by force (Fried 2011; Wolff 1991, 65–66). Nozick's motivation for doing so, it should be noted, is utilitarian: to achieve the social benefits of having one minimal state with coercive powers, rather than multiple warring proto-states. But if such welfarist considerations justify trampling on individual Lockean rights to create the minimal state, why not also to solve other collective action problems within the state, and with very different distributive consequences than libertarians may wish for?

## 2. The Content of Liberty

Rawls (*TJ*, 157) grounds his substantive case for the two principles of justice in the Kantian imperative to treat all individuals as ends in themselves, and not merely means, in keeping with their moral status as free and equal beings. Once again, most libertarians would find little to quarrel with in that formulation. From that shared sentiment, however, the two camps part company almost immediately over the content of liberty in the first principle and the meaning of equality in the second.

Consider the following quintessentially Rawlsian defense of the lexical priority of liberty:

> The moral adequacy of a society of project pursuers can be appraised by reference to the protec-tion it affords to individualism: this is almost a universal truth. It is difficult to imagine a civil order in which individualism thrives but liberty rights are not a prominent component of that society's moral grid.
>
> Therefore it will not oversimplify much to cast the fundamental moral imperative of a well-ordered society as:
>
>> Each person is to have an equal right to the most extensive basic liberty compatible with a similar liberty for others.

The author of this passage is not Rawls but Loren Lomasky (1987, 100), who, as if to under-score the common intellectual provenance of libertarianism and Rawlsianism (and, one suspects, to tweak Rawlsians), helps himself in conclusion to Rawls's first principle of justice.

In fleshing out the first principle, Rawls does achieve some common ground with libertar-ians (and also most clearly differentiates "justice as fairness" from utilitarianism). In the end, however, that common ground is (in the view of libertarians) severely limited by Rawls's construction of the "basic liberties."

## The Meaning of Liberty

The most expeditious way for Rawls to have packaged a social welfarist agenda in liberal individualist terms would have been to construe liberty as "positive liberty," in Isaiah Berlin's famous taxonomy. With the notable exception of political liberties, to which I return below, Rawls explicitly declined to do so (*TJ*, 179, 198, 291; *PL*, lv, 327; *LP*, 49; see also Brighouse 1997).[3] But having largely rejected substantive equality in favor of formal equality for purposes of the first principle, Rawls builds it into the second principle, via "equality of fair opportunity" and the difference principle. Thus, argues Rawls, does "the two-part basic structure allow[] a reconciliation of liberty and equality" (*TJ*, 179).

It is a nice question whether Rawls's division of labor between a largely negative conception of liberty and a positive conception of equality gets him to a significantly different conclusion than if he had simply given "liberty" a positive interpretation to begin with. But, as I discuss below, from the libertarian perspective the net result with respect to economic rights is the same: the positive conception of equality cedes whatever common ground Rawls might have been thought to establish with libertarians by adopting a negative conception of liberty in the first place.

## What Are the Basic Liberties?

Rawls's list of the "basic liberties" (*TJ*, 53), amended slightly from the original 1971 *TJ* to account for criticisms from H.L.A. Hart and others, includes:

> political liberty (the right to vote and be eligible for public office) and freedom of speech and assembly; liberty of conscience and freedom of thought; freedom of the person, which includes freedom from psychological oppression and physical assault and dismemberment (integrity of the person); the right to hold personal property and freedom from arbitrary arrest and seizure . . .

As Lomasky notes, "conspicuously absent from this catalogue are economic liberties, including freedom of contract to buy and sell, to employ and be employed, or to accumulate and invest" (2005, 180). Throughout his writings, Rawls remained agnostic about the choice between private and collective ownership of the means of production, arguing the question must be settled at the (later) constitutional or legislative stage, when the veil is partially lifted to allow knowledge of the "historical conditions and the traditions, institutions, and social forces of each country" (*TJ*, xv–xvi; *PL*, 298). But he expressly rejected the possibility that private property (other than personal property) was one of the basic liberties covered by his first principle of justice.

Whatever their other disagreements, all (right) libertarians are unified in their support of strong private property rights, although they get there by different routes. Lockean libertarians view private property rights (in one's self, in the external things one acquires through one's labor or other just means) as an extension of self-ownership and at least coequal in importance (*ASU*; Hospers 2003; Rothbard 1982, 113–119). Kantian and consequentialist libertarians, in contrast, support them because and only insofar as they are instrumental in

437

securing other desired ends (the ability to pursue one's projects in life, mutual advantage defined in more utilitarian terms).

Rawls (*PL*, 298; *LP*, 49–50) addressed his very brief remarks on libertarianism only to the former. But the latter group has always been a significant strain of libertarian thought, and among contemporary libertarians is arguably much more influential than the Lockean tradition represented by Nozick. In an earlier generation, one would have included among the defenders of private property rights on instrumentalist grounds von Mises, Hayek, Milton Friedman and sometimes Ayn Rand. More recent proponents include James Buchanan, Israel Kirzner, Richard Epstein, David Gauthier, Gerald Gaus, Chandran Kukathas, Jan Narveson, Randy Barnett, Eric Mack, and Loren Lomasky. The instrumentalist camp also stands in a more interesting relationship to Rawls, who purports to evaluate property rights – along with all other candidate primary goods – by the same instrumental criterion ("Social Unity and Primary Goods," 172–173; *PL*, 298): is it a good without which "persons cannot . . . achieve their essential aims"?

This raises the possibility that all that divides Rawls from most libertarians are their differing empirical assumptions about the instrumental value of property to liberty. If Rawls had been persuaded that a strong regime of private property rights was in fact essential to enable people to pursue their own projects in life, or libertarians were persuaded that it was not, would their disagreements vanish? One assumes not, but why, exactly?

The likely answer on Rawls's side is that, in the end, the priority he puts on political and civil liberties over and against economic liberties does not depend on the ends that persons in the original position would actually choose for themselves and the instrumental value of different liberties in the pursuit of those ends. Rather, it reflects Rawls's own conception of the good. In the text of *TJ* itself (*TJ*, 139), Rawls equivocates about whether his list of "basic liberties" and the lexical priority he assigns to them as a whole rest on the presumed desires of others or a perfectionist notion of what they ought to desire. In the years following the issue of the first edition, however, he unambiguously came down on the side of the latter (*TJ*, xiii; see also "Kantian Constructivism in Moral Theory," 525, 527, 547).

From the libertarian perspective, of course, this gives away the store. As Loren Lomasky (2005, 183–184) puts it, Rawls's willingness to give priority to his own "higher order" conception of the good cannot be squared with his ostensible commitment to respect equally the "different and indeed incommensurable and irreconcilable conceptions of the good" that individuals possess (*PL*, 303; "Social Unity and the Primary Goods"; *TJ* 1971). The latter would seem to require that we regard wealth accumulation, just as much as political participation, as a legitimate project in life if that is in fact what individuals want for themselves.

The opposite perfectionist notions are no doubt at work, *sub rosa*, in libertarians' ostensibly instrumental justifications for laissez-faire capitalism and strong private property rights. It is possible that a redistributive, social welfare state leads to worse outcomes than laissez-faire capitalism, *especially* for the least well off, as Loren Lomasky (2005, 191) and other libertarians have argued. But it is possible it does not, and I think it is a fair surmise that libertarians' empirical hunches here are following their political predilections and not the other way around.

## The Lexical Priority of Liberty

In his famous response to Rawls's first principle, H.L.A. Hart (1973) argued that Rawls's commitment to the "most extensive total system of liberty compatible with a similar liberty for others" ignores the reality that one person's exercise of her basic liberties may impinge on another's basic liberties. Rawls, responding to this objection in "The Basic Liberties and Their Priority" (*PL*, 291), revised the desideratum to a rhetorically more modest "fully adequate scheme" of liberties, and explicitly acknowledged that liberties must "be limited when they clash with one another," language that made its way into the 1999 revised edition of *TJ* (*TJ*, 54).

One could argue that both of these qualifications were implicit in Rawls's original formulation of the "most extensive total system of liberty *compatible with a similar liberty for others.*" The challenge for Rawls was not to acknowledge such clashes but to show they could be resolved by principles that sound in liberal individualism rather than utilitarianism. This problem is hardly unique to Rawls; it inheres in all deontological schemes (most definitely including libertarianism). Rawls (*PL*, 336) explicitly deferred the resolution to the constitutional stage, and de facto, most libertarians have deferred it as well. The omission matters for present purposes because, were both sides forced to explain how we should choose among plausible but incompatible liberty interests, both would likely be driven to some form of welfarist calculus, thereby bringing the two not only closer to utilitarianism but to each other as well.

The little that Rawls does say about reconciling clashing liberty interests supports that prediction. Rawls minimizes the problem by arguing that basic liberties are not "infringed when they are merely regulated, as they must be, in order to be combined into one scheme as well as adapted to certain social conditions necessary for their enduring exercise" (*PL*, 295). But the distinction between "infringing" liberties and "regulating" them is a verbal one only. And turning to the problem of regulating speech, Rawls's commonsense resolution of conflicting interests (*PL*, 335–336, 340–356) is not obviously distinct from what most people would intuit to be the optimal aggregative solution.

In the libertarian camp, Nozick's confused attempt in Part I of *ASU* to adjudicate between identical warring rights to self-protection in the state of nature provides its own cautionary tale. In the end, Nozick extricates himself by recourse to the decidedly nonlibertarian principle that might makes right, itself justified by the decidedly nonlibertarian desire to maximize social good by forcing warring factions into one minimal state (Fried 2011).

## 3. The Meaning of Equality

The obligation of a just society to lessen economic and social inequalities arises under three different requirements of "justice as fairness": the obligation under the first principle to equalize the fair value of political liberties, so that citizens have the same opportunities to hold office, influence elections, etc., irrespective of wealth or social class; the obligation under the second principle to assure fair equality of opportunity, meaning that citizens should have equal chances to acquire the skills on the basis of which merit is assessed; and the difference principle, which guarantees, *inter alia*, the "sufficient all-purpose means to enable all citizens to make intelligent and effective use of their freedoms."

As many have noted, guaranteeing the fair value of political liberties and fair equality of opportunity potentially entails redistribution as extensive as what is required by the difference principle. Given the lexical priority of the first two principles over the third, there may be little work left for the difference principle to do in the just Rawlsian state. Notwithstanding this possibility, disagreements among Rawlsians, utilitarians and libertarians about the just state's obligations to remedy social and economic inequalities have focused almost exclusively on the difference principle. Hence, I will do the same.

Rawls's difference principle has provoked more criticism than any other aspect of "justice as fairness." As many have noted, Rawls's maximin solution is rational only if we assume extreme (indeed, infinite) risk aversion. Rawls (*TJ*, 149, 512–513) repeatedly denies he is resting the case for the difference principle on that assumption. But it is difficult to see how else to interpret comments like "the two principles are those a person would choose for the design of a society in which his enemy is to assign him his place," or that the difference principle would be chosen by someone who "has a conception of the good such that he cares very little, if anything, for what he might gain above the minimum stipend that he can, in fact, be sure of by following the maximin rule" (*TJ*, 132–134). And it is difficult to see what, other than infinite risk aversion, *would* lead a self-interested person in the original position to select the difference principle rather than some less extreme version of sufficientarianism.

The maximin solution *is*, however, a rational choice from the perspective of those who find themselves *actually to be the worst off ex post*. Rawls's official position, of course, is that the choice of principles is to be made from an ex ante and not an ex post perspective (*TJ*, 124). But he frequently elides the two, and at least on occasion unambiguously adopts an ex post perspective, including in the passage that provoked a strong rejoinder from Nozick in *ASU*. Positing two individuals, A (the more favored) and B (the less favored), Rawls answers the hypothetical complaint of A that "he is required to have less than he might since his having more would result in some loss to B" by noting that A is still better off than he would have been under a system of noncooperation (*TJ* 1971, 103). Nozick famously responded that the same defense could be given for *any* scheme of cooperation, and that the question, left unanswered by Rawls, was why A wasn't justified in holding out for a scheme that gave him a larger share of the benefits than he would receive under the difference principle (*ASU*, 196).

But as Nozick (*ASU*, 196n) also noted in a lengthy footnote, there is a deeper, structural problem with Rawls's argument: how to make sense of it from the "perspective of the original position." In the original position, there would be no A and B; there would be only the representative person with some uncertain chance of being A and some uncertain chance of being B. If that representative person chose the difference principle, on balance, as the principle most advantageous to his future self given the possibilities of turning out to be A or B, to whom is he now complaining? And when is now? Nozick concluded (rightly in my view) that the only sensible way to construe A's and B's complaints, as Rawls presents them, is to imagine that A and B have stepped out of the original position and are viewing matters ex post, after the winners and losers are known. From that perspective, B, knowing he is the loser and A the winner, will understandably be unmoved by the statement that he should have less so that A might have more.

But if B's argument from the ex post perspective is decisive for Rawls, his contractualist thought experiment is not merely superfluous; it is misleading. For in that case, the notion of impartiality that motivates the difference principle is not that we should stand as equals in choosing the basic structure of society that will further each of our own interests, judged ex ante, but rather that we should stand as equals (at least as regards primary goods) at every moment of our lives. If it is a strain to fit the first notion of impartiality into the framework of mutually disinterested, rational choice, it is impossible to fit the second. The moral force of B's argument from the ex post position is that we must share what we have with the least among us, not because it is in our actual self-interest to do so and not because, from behind the veil, we would have calculated it to be in our self-interest as a form of insurance against the worst outcomes we might face, but because it is what we owe to others who are unambiguously *not* ourselves but whom we should nonetheless care about because they are less fortunate than we. Whether that duty is best realized through a maximin rule or instead by some other redistributive metric, it expresses a powerful moral perspective. But the perspective it expresses is not that of liberal individualism, conventionally construed. It is the perspective of those who (in Rawls's words) "agree to share one another's fate," as would members of a family who "commonly do not wish to gain unless they can do so in ways that further the interests of the rest" (*TJ* 1971, 102, 105).

Libertarians, not surprisingly, have pounced on that statement and similar ones in *TJ* as evidence that Rawls is a liberal individualist in self-description only. Judged by the commitments that actually motivate him, he reveals himself to be a communitarian, who conceives of society not (as libertarians would insist) as the mere aggregation of whatever individuals comprise it, with no identity or interests of its own, but instead as the highest organism, the "just social union of social unions," without which we are all "mere fragments" (*TJ*, 464).

Lomasky, assessing the resulting divide between libertarians and Rawls, concludes that the reason that Rawls does not end up a libertarian is "not because Rawls's theoretical underpinnings are fundamentally hostile to libertarian perspectives . . . [T]hey are in fact hardly more than a hair's breadth away from yielding a recognizably libertarian position." It is instead because Rawls

> is more committed to his egalitarian redistributionist conclusions than he is to the premises that generate those results. Whenever he enters into wide reflective equilibrium, opposition to libertarianism is one of those relatively fixed points unlikely to be dislodged . . . [H]is continued inability to come to terms successfully with libertarianism is due to an internal tension between his methodology and his convictions. One or the other has to give; invariably, it is former. (2005, 199)

But as John Stick notes, the same might be said of the other side as well: "The existence of these argumentative resources [to turn Rawls into Nozick and back again] suggests that the disagreements of Rawls and Nozick are founded upon the political content of their views, and not upon differences in method" (1987, 387).

# 4. And yet . . .

At this point, it is easy to see where Rawls and libertarians come apart and hard to see how to get them to agree on much of anything except by persuading one or the other to change their fundamental moral commitments. But a number of other considerations put that conclusion in doubt.

On Rawls's side, *TJ* makes two concessions that hold the real-world implications of "justice as fairness" hostage to human motivation and psychology.

The first is Rawls's concession to the "strains of commitment." Whatever principles we might otherwise regard as just, Rawls argues, must be tempered in light of the possibility that

441

they will have "consequences [the parties] cannot accept" or can do so "only with great difficulty" (*TJ*, 153). It is possible to understand this argument as addressed to the rational person choosing from the original position – that is, as arguing it would be rational for representative persons, *choosing principles ex ante*, to take into account people's likely ex post reactions to really bad outcomes. If so, the argument collapses into the argument for the ex ante rationality of extreme risk aversion, with all the problems that attend that argument. But the more likely concern behind the "strains of commitment" is that however rational it might be ex ante for people to take a given gamble, one cannot count on them to take their licks quietly ex post, when things in fact turn out very badly. Whatever the moral arguments for and against bailing people out of the adverse consequences of their informed choices, Rawls's "strains of commitment" sensibly suggests that we may want to do so as a matter of prudence, to maintain the stability of the social contract over time. Judged from this perspective, the difference principle dominates both average utilitarianism and libertarianism, because it protects would-be losers against the worst possible outcomes that the other two theories of justice would permit (*TJ* 1971, 176–178; *PL*, 17; *LP*, 49–50).

This argument for the difference principle surely proves too much, however, because the threat to stability that Rawls is most worried about here can be avoided by guaranteeing a basic minimum in the context of utilitarianism, libertarianism or a sufficientarian version of egalitarianism, without going all the way to the difference principle. But more importantly, concerns about the "strains of commitment" can as easily be turned on "justice as fairness" as its rivals. Nozick led the way here, noting that while Rawls worries about the potential resentment that those who turn out to be worst off would feel about any distributive principle less generous to them than the difference principle, he ignores the potential resentment of those who turn out to be the fortunate and who feel they are being bled dry for the sake of the worst off (*ASU*, 196; *TJ*, 470–71). As Lomasky suggests, one might also worry that everyone other than the worst off would resent the draconian effects of the strict Paretianism built into the difference principle (2005, 185–186).

Finally, in the real world one would have to worry about the strains of commitment not just for those who want to defect from "justice as fairness" once they see how things turn out for them, but also from those who never accept its normative vision to begin with – for example, those who believe that economic liberties are as important as political liberties, or whose conception of the good life is to amass great wealth.

It's hard to say what "justice as fairness" would look like once revised to accommodate the "strains of commitment" that it actually provokes, but one cannot rule out the possibility that it would push Rawls's two principles substantially in the direction of libertarianism.

The second concession Rawls makes is to any inequalities that work to the advantage of the worst off. The consequence of this concession, as G.A. Cohen and others have argued, is to hold the distributive implications of the difference principle hostage to the real-world motivations of the wealthy. *Pace* Cohen, the incentives necessary to induce the well off to work 40 rather than 30 hours a week or shift from painting to doctoring for the benefit of the least well off are unlikely to account for the major inequalities we observe in (say) contemporary American society. But the picture could conceivably change if we took a broader view of labor decisions, to include the sorts of entrepreneurial risks that have arguably contributed the most to raising everyone's standard of living (including that of the least well off) in the industrialized world over the last three centuries. If libertarians were in the end proved right as an empirical matter about the universal advantages of an unregulated market economy, the difference principle would commit Rawls to join in their endorsement of laissez-faire capitalism, and with it a distributive scheme that most libertarians could happily live with.

On libertarians' side, a number of factors could well nudge the programmatic implications of libertarian principles much closer to Rawlsian egalitarianism than libertarians themselves have assumed.

The possibility that has gotten the most attention over the last two centuries is whether and how to restrict individuals from appropriating the commons for their private use. The widely varying answers libertarians have given to this question produce (on their own accounts) widely disparate distributive outcomes.

At one end of the spectrum, libertarians like Rand, Rothbard, Narveson and Mack would allow private appropriation by the first comer, without any obligation to leave a "fair share" for others (Mack 2009, 134). At the other extreme, "joint-ownership" libertarians (e.g., Grunebaum 1987) argue either that no use may be made of natural resources without the unanimous consent of others or that resources may be used but not appropriated for exclusive use.

Most libertarians fall in between these two extremes, recognizing the right to unilateral appropriation of some portion of the commons but subject to some version of the Lockean proviso that we leave "enough, and as good" for others. They have, however, disagreed about what is in the commons, what rights one acquires by virtue of a legitimate act of appropriation, and what it means to leave "enough, and as good" for others.

Right libertarians have typically read the "commons" very narrowly to include only material natural resources, and have read the rights of appropriation broadly, at the extreme to give first appropriators full ownership over natural resources on the basis of token labor. Interpretations of the Lockean proviso, however, have varied more widely even within the right libertarian camp. Nozick famously concludes that later-comers are adequately compensated by the institution of private property, which is made possible by earlier generations' appropriations (*ASU*, 176–177). Sufficientarian libertarians like Simmons (1992) and Lomasky (1987), in contrast, construe the "fair share" obligation to require appropriators to leave others sufficient resources for a decent life.

At the other end of the political spectrum, "left libertarians" have interpreted the "fair share" obligation in a fashion that leads to far more egalitarian results. At the modest end would be Georgist proposals for the state to expropriate land rents and redistribute them equally to all citizens. At the more extreme end, contemporary left libertarians like Michael Otsuka, Peter Vallentyne and Hillel Steiner have read "the commons" broadly, to include not only tangible natural resources but also social capital (language, culture, knowledge, functioning markets, etc.) and (in Steiner's case) even the gene pool from which our genetically determinate selves emerge. At the same time, they have interpreted the requirement to leave "enough, and as good" to authorize the state to levy a confiscatory tax on virtually all incomes and then distribute the proceeds in a fashion that will offset differences in natural endowments. The result is a redistributive scheme at least as egalitarian as Rawls's, and in some cases quite likely more so (Vallentyne and Steiner 2000; Fried 2004).

A number of other less discussed factors could well push libertarianism in the direction of Rawlsianism. The first, reflected in Nozick's Principle of Rectification, is the moral imperative most Lockeans feel to undo the fruits of past injustices. As even Nozick conceded, given the historical record, complying with this duty in the world we actually live in could well have radical implications (starting with returning America to the Native Americans) that swamp in importance all the other distributive implications of libertarianism.

Second, as Lomasky (2005, 195–196) notes, Nozick is a decided outlier among prominent libertarians in denying any societal obligations to the worst off. Most libertarians would guarantee a basic minimum to those who cannot obtain it for themselves, and many regard the refusal to do so as indefensible. In Lomasky's words, "To the extent that successful civility requires the provision of aid, welfare rights merit a place alongside liberty rights" (1987, 126). This concession is enormously significant, both in closing the gap between Rawlsianism and libertarianism and in neutralizing what is, for most people, the most powerful selling point of "justice as fairness": its guarantee that no one will be left destitute in the name of principle, be the principle average utilitarianism or libertarianism.

Third, libertarians who reject the moral purity of anarchy for the pragmatic advantages of a coercive state have just begun to confront the compromises with principle that may be necessary to secure those advantages. Having achieved the minimal state by force in Part I of *ASU*, the Nozick of Part II regains religion on the sanctity of individual consent, famously asserting that compulsory taxation is a form of slavery. But most nonanarchic libertarians recognize that the same collective action problems that necessitate a state in the first place also necessitate giving the state the power to levy compulsory taxes, at a minimum to fund public goods; the power to solve the problems of externalities that cannot realistically be solved by private contract; and the authority to operate through majoritarian or supermajoritarian rule, at the cost of minority interests (Mack 1986; Lomasky 1987; Schmidtz 1991; Epstein 1985; Buchanan 1968, 1975; Buchanan and Tullock 1962; Sugden 1990; Gauthier 1986).

Pragmatic libertarians have spent much of the last century trying to work out principled limits to each of these necessary concessions. Without prejudging the ultimate success of these efforts, I think it is fair to say, once again, that one cannot rule out the possibility that at the end of the day, libertarians will find themselves moving much closer to social welfarists on pragmatic grounds.

Finally, there is the question of what Rawls himself might have made of his two principles of justice, revisiting them at 40 years' distance. Rawls left a number of clues that together suggest he might well have revised them significantly, in a direction congenial to libertarians.[4] Two potential changes in particular are worth noting.

The first concerns individual responsibility. Rawls was famously equivocal in *TJ* about whether individuals' distributive share should be "ambition sensitive" – that is, reflect their work effort and other voluntary choices made against the backdrop of an otherwise just world. The difference principle, however, seems to resolve the question in the negative, basing individuals' distributive shares on the positions individuals find themselves in, without regard to how they got there. (The difference principle would of course allow greater return to greater work effort to the extent necessary to induce effort that redounds to the benefit of the least well off. But the inequalities that result are a forward-looking, instrumental concession, not a backward-looking measure of desert.)

Rawls's apparent position on this issue is anathema to libertarians, who regard the right to the peaceful enjoyment of the fruits of one's labor as "the core prescriptive postulate of libertarianism" (Mack 2011, 673). But libertarians are hardly alone in this regard. Beginning with Ronald Dworkin's ambition-sensitive resource egalitarianism, most contemporary liberal egalitarians have distanced themselves from what they take to be Rawls's position on this point. As G.A. Cohen said of Dworkin's departure, in an oft-quoted passage, it "has, in effect, performed for egalitarianism the considerable service of incorporating within it the most powerful idea in the arsenal of the anti-egalitarian right: the idea of choice and responsibility" (1989, 933).[5]

In the Preface to the 1999 revised edition of *TJ* (*TJ*, xiv–xv), Rawls suggests that if he were writing *A Theory of Justice* anew, he would move much closer to the luck egalitarian position, and stress equal citizenship rather than equality of material goods as the motivation for redistributing wealth. As Andrew Williams (2006) notes, depending on one's empirical assumptions, the shift to ambition-sensitive egalitarianism on the left could well give libertarians most of what they want in terms of outcomes, and would certainly give them the portion of economic rights they most care about in principle.

Second, in writings after the original 1971 publication of *TJ*, Rawls qualified his support for the difference principle significantly. Responding to Arrow's (1973) and an early draft of Harsanyi's (1975) critical reviews of *TJ*, he defended his use of the maximin criterion but conceded that other conceptions of justice might in the end turn out to be more reasonable ("Some Reasons for the Maximin Criterion"). Beginning with "The Idea of an Overlapping Consensus" in 1987, he suggested that the core moral intuition behind the difference principle was a sufficientarian version of egalitarianism that guaranteed "all citizens sufficient material means to make effective use of [their] basic rights," a goal that he acknowledged could be achieved through a wide range of schemes, of which the difference principle was just one example (*PL*, 156–157; "The Idea of Public Reason Revisited," 774). In the Preface to the 1999 revised edition of *TJ*, Rawls acknowledged it might not even be the most plausible example, and gave what was at best a half-hearted and somewhat misleading defense of its relative virtues (*TJ*, xiv).[6]

If one imagines that Rawls circa 2013 would in fact have ditched the difference principle for some version of ambition-sensitive sufficientarianism, it is not out of the question that his disagreements with many libertarians about the just distribution of wealth would be reduced to haggling over numbers – that is, over exactly what level of a basic minimum is sufficient to enable a decent life.

## 5. Conclusion

From the selfish perspective of contemporary readers, it is regrettable that the other *Theory of Justice* – the one framed as a response to the libertarian critique of the actual *Theory of Justice* – will remain unwritten. One can only speculate how engaging with that critique might have moved Rawls to revise "justice as fairness." But there seem to be two obvious directions in which he could have gone, both foreshadowed above. Whether either of them would have left him with what he hoped to achieve – "a viable systematic doctrine" to rival that of utilitarianism – is more doubtful.

The first would have been to ditch any perfectionist notion of the good in favor of the "incommensurable and irreconcilable" ends that determinate individuals actually possess, and to revise the list of primary goods accordingly, to include those things that are essential to attain those ends, whatever (within reason) those ends might be. It seems likely that the resulting principles of justice would have included much broader protections for private property – at least insofar as it resulted from individual effort – and would have ditched the difference principle entirely, in favor of some guaranteed decent minimum for all. Faced with that revised version of "justice as fairness," one imagines that most libertarians would concede, however grudgingly, that it is a plausible interpretation of liberal individualism, even if not theirs.

The second would have been to abandon any pretense of seeking terms of cooperation that would be to the mutual advantage of determinate selves, and to substitute two principles, both unabashedly reflecting Rawls's substantive notion of the good: strong protections for civil and political liberties, coupled with a broad-based, ongoing redistribution of wealth to the least fortunate in accordance with some social welfarist metric. It seems likely that this revised version of "justice as fairness" would look much like the original, with one notable exception: the strict maximin rule built into the difference principle would have to be jettisoned in favor of a more plausible compromise between egalitarian and aggregate social welfarist ends.

It is an open question how different a Rawlsianism that took this second tack would look from average utilitarianism. But there are a couple of reasons to think it wouldn't look all that different, once the implications of average utilitarianism are fleshed out. First, while we tend to focus on what utilitarianism implies about the optimal distribution of wealth, wealth is hardly the only – or in many cases even most important – determinant of happiness, once a subsistence level of income is reached. Insofar as people share a strong preference for protecting basic political and civil liberties, those preferences would count in any utilitarian calculus as well (Arrow 1973; Lyons 1972). Thus, while utilitarians would have very different motivations for protecting basic liberties than did Rawls, the actual protections implied by the two regimes might not look all that different.

Second, as economists have long argued, if (as seems plausible) the marginal utility of income decreases as a person's total income increases, aggregate utility will be maximized by equalizing wealth, all other things held constant (Fried 1998, 152–155). But of course all other things are not held constant. In particular, the optimal distributional scheme from a utilitarian perspective must balance the welfare gains from redistributing wealth from the rich to the poor against the welfare losses from the disincentive effects of an implicit 100 percent marginal tax rate on the rich. Rawls's difference principle of course struck its own version of the trade-off between equality and efficiency. As with protections afforded political liberties, Rawls's motivations for the trade-off are different from utilitarians' – not to maximize aggregate welfare but to maximize the position of the least well off. But once the difference principle is jettisoned for a more plausible compromise between equality and efficiency, it is not clear that the ideal redistributive scheme implied by a Rawlsianism that took this second tack would look very different from the optimal distribution implied by average utilitarianism.

Whether it did or not, this alternative Rawlsianism, unlike the original *TJ*, would share with utilitarianism something perhaps more telling from the libertarian perspective: a frank acknowledgment that the motivation for redistribution is other-regardingness, not mutual disinterest. Whatever libertarians might make of this alternative Ralwsianism on the merits, one imagines they would regard that acknowledgment as a major victory.

# Notes

I am grateful to Joe Bankman, Mark Kelman, Loren Lomasky, Debra Satz and the editors of this volume for their very helpful comments on earlier drafts.

1   I omit consideration of the virtue-based (or teleological) arguments for libertarianism most associ-
    ated with Ayn Rand and (among contemporary writers) Douglas Rasmussen and Douglas Den Uyl.
2   Rawls (*TJ* 1971, 15, 103) does in fact engage the question when he argues that the difference
    principle is necessary to elicit the willing cooperation of the worst endowed. But as discussed below,
    it is not obvious how this argument fits in with the original position, which presupposes that no
    one knows whether they will be the worst off or not when they are asked to sign on to the difference
    principle.
3   As many have noted, equalizing political influence and participation across income and social
    classes, like equalizing fair opportunity under the second principle, potentially entails redistribution
    so extensive as to render the difference principle superfluous. Since neither Rawls nor libertarians
    have focused on this possibility in developing their respective positions, I will set it aside as well.
4   On the evolution of Rawls's thinking after the 1971 original publication of *TJ*, see Sterba 2003,
    62–70.
5   In addition to Dworkin, a list of "ambition-sensitive" egalitarians would include Amartya Sen,
    Philippe van Parijs, Richard Arneson, Eric Rakowski, G.A. Cohen, John Roemer, Peter Vallentyne
    and Brian Barry. For further discussion, see Knight and Stemplowska 2011.
6   I say misleading, because Rawls omits the one comparison that in most people's minds puts the
    difference principle at the greatest relative disadvantage: Rawls's two principles of justice versus the
    first principle plus average utilitarianism with a sufficientarian minimum.

# Works by Rawls, with Abbreviations

"The Basic Liberties and Their Priority," in *The Tanner Lectures on Human Values*, vol. 3, ed. Sterling
    McMurrin (3–87). Salt Lake City: University of Utah Press, 1982. Reprinted in *Political Liberalism*,
    Lecture VIII.
"The Idea of Public Reason Revisited" (IPRR), *University of Chicago Law Review* 64 (1997): 765–807.
"Kantian Constructivism in Moral Theory" (KC), *Journal of Philosophy* 77 (1980): 515–572. (Reprinted
    in *Collected Papers*, ed. Samuel Freeman. Cambridge, MA: Harvard University Press, 2001.)
*The Law of Peoples* (LP). Cambridge, MA: Harvard University Press, 1999.
*Political Liberalism* (PL), expanded edn. New York: Columbia University Press, 2005.
"Social Unity and Primary Goods," in Amartya Sen and Bernard Williams (eds), *Utilitarianism and
    Beyond* (159–186). Cambridge: Cambridge University Press, 1982.
"Some Reasons for the Maximin Criterion," *American Economic Review* 64 (1974): 141–146.
*A Theory of Justice* (TJ 1971), original edn. Cambridge, MA: Harvard University Press, 1971.
*A Theory of Justice* (TJ), rev. edn. Cambridge, MA: Harvard University Press, 1999.

# Other References

Arrow, Kenneth (1973) "Some Ordinalist-Utilitarian Notes on Rawls's Theory of Justice." *Journal of
    Philosophy* 70: 245–263.
Brighouse, Harry (1997) "Political Equality in Justice as Fairness." *Philosophical Studies* 86:
    155–184.
Buchanan, James M. (1968) *The Demand and Supply of Public Goods*. Chicago: Rand McNally.
Buchanan, James M. (1975) *The Limits of Liberty*. Chicago: University of Chicago Press.
Buchanan, James M. (1984) "The Ethical Limits of Taxation." *Scandinavian Journal of Economics* 86:
    102–114.

Buchanan, James M. and Lomasky, Loren (1984) "The Matrix of Contractarian Justice." *Social Philosophy and Policy* 2: 12–32.

Buchanan, James M. and Tullock, Gordon (1962) *The Calculus of Consent.* Ann Arbor: University of Michigan Press.

Cohen, G.A. (1989) "On the Currency of Egalitarian Justice." *Ethics* 99: 906–944.

Epstein, Richard (1985) *Takings.* Cambridge, MA: Harvard University Press.

Fried, Barbara (1998) *The Progressive Assault on Laissez Faire: Robert Hale and the First Law and Economics Movement.* Cambridge, MA: Harvard University Press.

Fried, Barbara (2003) 'If You Don't Like It, Leave It': The Problem of Exit in Social Contractarian Arguments." *Philosophy and Public Affairs* 31: 40–70.

Fried, Barbara (2004) "Left Libertarianism: A Review Essay." *Philosophy and Public Affairs* 32: 66–92.

Fried, Barbara (2011) "Does Nozick Have a Theory of Property Rights?" In Ralf M. Bader and John Meadowcroft (eds), *The Cambridge Companion to Nozick's Anarchy, State, and Utopia* (230–254). Cambridge: Cambridge University Press.

Gauthier, David (1974) "Justice and Natural Endowment: Toward a Critique of Rawls's Ideological Framework." *Social Theory and Practice* 3: 3–26.

Gauthier, David (1986) *Morals by Agreement.* Oxford: Oxford University Press.

Gibbard, Allan (2000) "Natural Property Rights." In Peter Vallentyne and Hillel Steiner (eds), *Left-Libertarianism and Its Critics.* London: Palgrave Macmillan.

Grunebaum, James (1987) *Private Ownership.* New York: Routledge & Kegan Paul.

Harsanyi, John (1975) "Can the Maximin Principle Serve as a Basis for Morality? A Critique of John Rawls's Theory." *American Political Science Review* 69: 594–606.

Hart, H.L.A (1973) "Rawls on Liberty and Its Priority." *University of Chicago Law Review* 40: 534–555. Reprinted in Normal Daniels (ed.), *Reading Rawls (230–252).* Stanford: Stanford University Press, 1989.

Hasnas, John (2008) "The Obviousness of Anarchy." In Roderick T. Long and Tibor R. Machan (eds), *Anarchism/Minarchism.* Farnham, UK: Ashgate.

Hospers, John (2003) "The Libertarian Manifesto." In James Sterba (ed.), *Morality in Practice* (21–27). 7th edn. Belmont, CA: Wadsworth.

Knight, Carl and Stemplowska, Zofia (eds) (2011) *Responsibility and Distributive Justice.* Oxford: Oxford University Press.

Lomasky, Loren (1987) *Persons, Rights and the Moral Community.* New York: Oxford University Press.

Lomasky, Loren (2005) "Libertarianism at Twin Harvard." In Ellen Frankel Paul, Fred D. Miller, Jr, and Jeffrey Paul (eds), *Natural Rights Liberalism from Locke to Nozick, Part I* (178–199). Cambridge: Cambridge University Press.

Lyons, David (1972) "Rawls versus Utilitarianism." *Journal of Philosophy* 69: 535–545.

Mack, Eric (1986) "The Ethics of Taxation." In D. Lee (ed.), *Taxation and the Deficit Economy* (487–514). San Francisco: Pacific Research Institute.

Mack, Eric (2009) "Individualism and Libertarian Rights." In Thomas Christiano and John Christman (eds), *Contemporary Debates in Political Philosophy* (121–137). London: Wiley-Blackwell.

Mack, Eric (2011) "Libertarianism." In George Klosko (ed.), *The Oxford Handbook of the History of Political Philosophy* (673–688). Oxford: Oxford University Press.

Nagel, Thomas (1973) "Rawls on Justice." *Philosophical Review* 82: 220–234.

Narveson, Jan (1988) *The Libertarian Idea.* Philadelphia: Temple University Press.

Nozick, Robert (1974) *Anarchy, State and Utopia.* New York: Basic Books.

Roemer, John (1988) "A Challenge to Neo-Lockeanism." *Canadian Journal of Philosophy* 18: 697

Rothbard, Murray (1977) "Robert Nozick and the Immaculate Conception of the State." *Journal of Libertarian Studies* 1: 45–57.

Rothbard, Murray (1982) *The Ethics of Liberty.* Atlantic Highlands, NJ: Humanities Press.

Rothbard, Murray (2006 [1973]) *For a New Liberty: A Libertarian Manifesto*. 2nd edn. Auburn, AL: Ludwig von Mises Institute.

Schmidtz, David (1991) *The Limits of Government*. Boulder, CO: Westview Press.

Simmons, A. John (1992) *The Lockean Theory of Rights*. Princeton: Princeton University Press.

Simmons, A. John (2005) "Consent Theory for Libertarians." *Social Philosophy and Policy* 22: 330–356.

Sterba, James (2003) "Rawls and a Morally Defensible Conception of Justice." In James Sterba (ed.), *Morality in Practice*, 7th edn (62–70). Belmont, CA: Wadsworth.

Stick, John (1987) "Turning Rawls into Nozick and Back Again." *Northwestern Law Review* 81: 363–416.

Sugden, Robert (1990) "Rules for Choosing Among Public Goods." *Constitutional Political Economy* 1: 63–82.

Vallentyne, Peter and Steiner, Hillel (eds) (2000) *Left-Libertarianism and Its Critics*. London: Palgrave Macmillan.

Williams, Andrew (2006) "Liberty, Equality and Property." In John S. Dryzek, Bonnie Honig, and Anne Phillips (eds), *The Oxford Handbook of Political Theory* (488–506). Oxford: Oxford University Press.

Wolff, Jonathan (1991) *Robert Nozick: Property, Justice and the Minimal State*. Stanford: Stanford University Press.

# 26

# The Young Marx and the Middle-Aged Rawls

## DANIEL BRUDNEY

The standard Marxian criticism of *A Theory of Justice* is that it stresses distribution while the proper stress should be on production.[1] In its usual form this criticism is misguided, yet it does get at a difference between Marx and Rawls. Marx stresses agents' lives as producers and consumers, Rawls their lives as citizens engaged in maintaining a distributively just society. In this essay I compare the 1844 Marx (the Marx of the "Comments on James Mill, *Éléments d'économie politique*" and the *Economic and Philosophic Manuscripts of 1844*)[2] and the Rawls of *A Theory of Justice*. With each writer I invoke other texts but only to explicate those on which I focus. For instance, I make use of Marx's "Critique of the Gotha Programme" and Rawls's *Justice as Fairness*, but only to develop themes present in the writers' earlier works. With each writer I ignore issues of change across their careers. What I show are time-slices but, I hope, revealing ones. My central topic is the young Marx and the middle-aged Rawls.

I start with the standard criticism, then note two ways in which the writers resemble one another. Eventually, I return to the standard criticism, casting it as a difference in the writers' conceptions of "alienation." This leads to what appears to be a key distinction. It might seem that the deepest value in *Theory* is respect, while in the 1844 Marx it is concern – that the first stresses the need to avoid respect-alienation and the second to avoid concern-alienation. However, I argue that Rawls, too, puts weight on something like concern; indeed, that something like that concept is an underground current in *Theory*. At the end, however, and despite these several points of overlap, I argue that if one accepts the Marxian's normative view, one will find some force in the standard criticism.

## 1. The Standard Marxian Criticism

According to many Marxians, any theory of distributive justice begins in the wrong place. It asks about distribution in independence from production, but in fact the former is dependent

---

*A Companion to Rawls*, First Edition. Edited by Jon Mandle and David A. Reidy.

on the latter. If there is to be serious distributive change, we must transform production, that is, we must transform the relations of production.

As applied to Rawls, this criticism may seem off the mark, for his view is not allocative. It does not begin with a fixed pile of goods and ask how to distribute them. His two principles of justice are supposed to regulate the central social institutions of a society ("the basic structure," *TJ*, 6–10), and these include the institutions that, for Marx, constitute the level of production. Rawlsian principles of justice regulate productive as well as distributive arrangements. That said, it is still useful to look more closely at the Marxian criticism.

This criticism rests on a causal thesis, one with a strong and a weak form. The strong thesis says that no serious social change is possible without first transforming the relations of production. The weak thesis says that fundamental distributive change requires transforming the relations of production but, even absent such transformation, useful change – change that affects human lives in significant ways – is possible. The weak thesis seems the more sensible. Liberal reforms have had impact. That is why they evoke conservative resistance.

The strong thesis seems too strong. Nevertheless, suppose it is true. There could still be a role for a theory that specifies the best form of distribution. Suppose (i) the strong thesis is true, (ii) Distribution D is the best feasible distribution, and (iii) Distribution D can be instantiated only if we transform the relations of production. We then have good reason to transform the relations of production. We also have good reason to explore D and to defend the claim that it is in fact the best feasible distribution.

The Marxian tradition has pressed two reasons not to explore D. First, it has claimed that social revolution will produce the best distribution without the need to sketch its content in advance; second, conceptions of the best distribution are said to be determined by existing relations of production, so the exploration of any D will tend to justify existing relations of production.[3]

The first objection seems merely a counsel of faith, one quite unsupported by the history of modern revolutions. The second objection is most plausibly seen as a thesis in social psychology. It says that the social institutions that form beliefs and values – for instance, schools, the media – tend to play a stabilizing role, inculcating beliefs and values that justify existing arrangements, including existing relations of production.[4] However, such a thesis can say at most that it is likely that the exploration of any D will justify existing relations of production. Yet for some D (say, that of the 1844 Marx), this might not be true, and for any D, whatever its content, we can ask whether the proposed justification works. Suppose D supports capitalism but seems to have a cogent justification. That might be a reason for a Marxian to look for further arguments against D. It is hardly a reason to dismiss D. Marxians ought to have the courage of their justifications.[5]

The above issues stem from a causal claim, but one could also make a normative claim: we should not waste time thinking about distribution because what is most important – most central for a good human life – obtains at the level of production. This is the 1844 Marx's point when he condemns capitalism for its deep and multiform alienation of labor.

This criticism misses the fact that a theory of distribution asks, among other things, *what* ought to be distributed. Alienated labor could be seen as a consequence of a failure to make available or properly to distribute certain things – among them, opportunities to have a say in the workplace, for solidaristic relations, for joint control over the products of labor. In assessing a distributive view we can take many variables into account, for instance, the relations among citizens that instantiating the view is likely to generate. An adherent of the 1844

Marx could say that the best D would take proper cognizance of the fact that human beings are, in their essence, cooperative producers. To stress the normative priority of production is merely to assert a criterion for the best D.[6]

There is, then, no good reason not to compare the 1844 Marx and the *Theory* Rawls as writers who present views of what a society with a proper distribution would be like. Incidentally, I use the phrase "proper distribution" to dodge the question of whether Marx has a "theory of justice."[7] The 1844 Marx does seem to think that, along some dimension or dimensions, some patterns of distribution are better than others. For our purposes, that is all we need.

## 2. From Each/To Each and the Two Principles

Rawls's two principles of justice are as follows:

First, each person is to have an equal right to the most extensive basic liberty compatible with a similar liberty for others.

Second, social and economic inequalities are to be arranged so that they are both (a) to the greatest benefit of the least advantaged and (b) attached to offices and positions open to all under conditions of fair equality of opportunity.[8]

One link of the 1844 Marx and the *Theory* Rawls is that the distributive arrangements of a society regulated by Rawls's two principles have parallels, when we take into account real world scarcity, to the situation sketched by Marx at the end of the "Comments on James Mill."[9] There Marx describes a communist society in which agents freely engage in activities that are simultaneously oriented to the agent's individual self-realization and involve the production of goods that others will use for *their* self-realization. Agents choose to produce and what they choose to produce is determined by their individual predilections, but they are also concerned for others' well-being: they want to produce things others will use. One's productive activity expresses both one's attempt to attain one's own self-realization and one's concern that others attain theirs.

An underlying premise here is that society is beyond material scarcity.[10] Now if we grant that premise, the "Comments" picture instantiates the famous slogan from the later "Critique of the Gotha Programme": "From each according to his abilities, to each according to his needs."[11] It does so, however, not as a norm to which people must adhere but simply as a description of communist society.[12]

Taken as a gloss on the 1844 Marx's communism, the "from each" clause presumes the freedom to develop, exercise and choose among one's abilities; the "to each" clause presumes the material conditions that would enable one to have what is needed to pursue one's conception of self-realization. The goal seems similar to Rawls's thought that citizens should have adequate liberty and opportunity to develop their capacities and to pursue their conceptions of the good, as well as sufficient material wherewithal to make such liberty and opportunity more than merely formal.

Let's now drop Marx's assumption that we are beyond scarcity, and see how that might affect his view. Marx, at least in the texts of the 1840s, believes that the worst sort of conflict will result.[13] If he is correct, then there is no point in asking about the best distributive view. If transcending scarcity is a necessary condition not merely for the best society but even for a society without fundamental exploitation and conflict, then humanity is in a very bad way.

So let's assume that we are not beyond scarcity but that Marx's gloomy belief is false. To ensure that agents can develop their various abilities and pursue their various conceptions of self-realization, a constrained 1844 Marx – one who accepts the constraints of scarcity and so the need for political institutions as well as for principles to regulate them – will require something like Rawls's liberty principle. The 1844 Marx complains bitterly about the stultifying impact of the division of labor, and shows great concern for the broad development of human capacities.[14] (He might even be thought to accept Rawls's "Aristotelian Principle," *TJ*, 374.) However, only under conditions of liberty can agents discover which activities they do well and enjoy doing. Must a constrained 1844 Marx adopt a liberty principle of precisely the Rawlsian form (either as stated in *Theory* or as later amended)?[15] Perhaps not; here, it is sufficient that the "from each" clause, as a gloss on the passage from the "Comments," requires some way to protect at least some basic liberties.

How about "to each"? Would a constrained 1844 Marx find some sort of prioritarian distributive principle, even if perhaps not the difference principle itself, appropriate for a constrained communism?[16] Here, the "Gotha Programme" is instructive. In that text Marx examines payment by labor time as the distributive principle for the transitional stage to communism. If I work for an hour, I get X in pay; for two hours, 2X.[17] Marx has two complaints about this standard. First, if labor is "to serve as a measure, [it] must be defined" by both "intensity" and "duration."[18] Labor time must be calibrated to productivity. Those who are more productive, either within a given hour or by working more hours, would receive more pay. Workers' capacities surely differ along these dimensions, a difference that would be reflected in their remuneration. Marx calls this a "defect." He seems to think that wage differentials due to such factors are unjustifiable.[19] This rejection of arbitrary variations among human beings as a basis for differential distribution is of course wholly in line with Rawls's thought.

Marx's second criticism of payment for productivity is more important: it ignores differential need. "[O]ne worker is married, another not; one has more children than another, etc."[20] Differential need is not invoked by Rawls in the intuitive arguments for the difference principle or in the reasons guiding the construction of the original position. Still, the issue is live for him (*TJ*, 244–245, 271). Moreover, it could play a role for the parties behind the veil of ignorance. Awareness that one's needs might be extensive could be among the reasons why the parties opt for the highest possible floor.

The actual 1844 Marx – the unconstrained one – presumes that communism will overcome scarcity. Not surprisingly, he makes no prioritarian proposal. Still, Marx's focus on need suggests giving priority to those most in need, that is, to those who are worst off. In addition, Marx believes that communists would have equal concern for one another's individual wellbeing, and it seems plausible that agents who have such concern will tend to focus on the condition of the worst off. If I care equally about each, the plight of the worst off will probably tug hardest at me.[21] Although the claim is as much speculative as textual, it seems likely that a constrained 1844 Marx would consider some sort of prioritarian principle to be the least bad of the distributive possibilities open to a communist society subject to scarcity.

I leave open what form of prioritarianism Marx would prefer. Interestingly, the difference principle itself poses a possible problem.[22] Marx is not committed to material equality for its own sake.[23] That the difference principle countenances some degree of material inequality would not prompt a Marxian veto. Yet a principle that depends in a central way on individual incentives fits uneasily with the 1844 Marx's view of communists' motivations. Marx has a large place for the individual pursuit of self-realization. He does not stress sacrifice of one's own good. Nevertheless, his communists act in significant part from concern for one another's well-being. Further work in this area would need to pin down the 1844 Marx's form of prioritarianism; more specifically, it would need to determine whether there is a way to make peace with individual incentives (and so perhaps with something like the difference principle) without the social world in question ceasing to be what even a constrained 1844 Marx would find acceptable.[24]

## 3. Shared Ends

My second Marx/Rawls link concerns the way in which agents have shared ends.[25] Here, two distinctions are needed. To begin with, there could be *internally oriented* or *externally oriented* shared ends. With the first, the content of agents' shared end is simply to live in a society structured in a certain way. By contrast, an externally oriented shared end involves attaining some goal held by the collectivity as a whole, for example, attaining God's kingdom on earth. Here, agents wish to promote something beyond the maintenance of a certain structure of living together.

Marx's communists have the shared end of creating and maintaining a society in which each agent can attempt to realize her nature as a being who simultaneously expresses her individuality and produces for others as part of the species' continual joint transformation of itself and the world. There is no shared end beyond this. Similarly, Rawls's citizens, at least qua citizens, wish simply to live in a society whose basic structure is regulated by the two principles of justice. For Rawls, this is a very important end. He calls the maintenance of a just society "the preeminent form of human flourishing" and says that "persons best express their nature" by maintaining just institutions (*TJ*, 463). Yet this involves no end external to the well-ordered society of justice as fairness, no end beyond maintaining that society (*TJ*, 463). For Rawlsian citizens, maintaining just institutions is a shared, internally oriented final end.

The second distinction is between *overlapping* and *intertwined* shared ends. Ends overlap when agents have the same end but need not attain it with and through others. The donors to a fund drive to eradicate diabetes share an end, but they need one another only because a joint effort is required to raise sufficient money. It would not defeat their shared end if one donor gave enough to support all the research or if fortunate circumstances made diabetes disappear. But it is part of Marx's 1844 description of a communist's activities that she is producing *for* other human beings, and that in consuming she appreciates what others have produced *for* her. Her ends in producing would be short-circuited if her products were to rot or God were to rain manna. Persons for whom it is crucial that they help to satisfy one another's ends have intertwined ends.

As for Rawls, his citizens need one another to realize the good of living in a just society. This good involves giving one another justice, that is, giving justice *to* one another. It involves acting toward one's fellow citizens from one's sense of justice and being (at least implicitly) recognized as doing so. The structure is the same as with Marx's communists except that here justice – conduct both in accordance with and from just principles – rather than goods is what citizens give to, receive from, and appreciate about one another.

Communities formed via overlapping, external shared ends are structurally different from those formed via internal, intertwined shared ends. In a community characterized by external, overlapping ends agents are bound to each other through their shared final end. That my actions contribute to attaining your end is a contingent consequence of the nature of my end. It is not part of the content of my end. We do not do things *for* one another. By contrast, with both Marx and Rawls, citizens give and receive from one another (products, justice); they intend to give and receive such things; and all this is generally understood and appreciated. And for both writers, it is through the giving/receiving process that people individually – and so, granted the structure of the activities, also jointly – realize (at least some of) their final ends.

I have noted two connections between the 1844 Marx and the *Theory* Rawls. The writers share a commitment to a society that creates and maintains the conditions in which each agent has the real possibility of pursuing her vision of the good while also seeing herself as sharing with others the goal of maintaining precisely such a society. Still, it is tricky to link these writers. The danger is less that the alleged links aren't there than that they obscure the remaining differences.

I have already noted that the 1844 Marx might have qualms about the difference principle. Another difference is this. For the *Theory* Rawls, the circumstances that make distributive principles necessary involve not only material scarcity and limited benevolence but the fact that under conditions of liberty there will always be diversity in fundamental beliefs, such as religious beliefs and conceptions of the good.[26] Even a constrained Marx would reject this last claim except in the modest form of differences in agents' views about which of their many capacities to develop and exercise (e.g., hunting versus fishing[27]). He would certainly reject the claim that a proper society will contain diverse religious beliefs. Marx's one-time mentor and then target of his polemics, Bruno Bauer, argued that in a proper society religious beliefs and religious institutions would wither away (see Bauer 1843, 72, 67). Marx never doubts that this would be the case under communism. The 1844 Marx would cease to be Marx if he accepted that religion would flourish in a society that increasingly instantiates communism. Even a constrained Marx and the *Theory* Rawls would thus remain importantly different about the circumstances that make distributive principles necessary.[28]

## 4. Alienation

The 1844 Marx is famously focused on the concept of alienation, and although Rawls does not use the term, he is concerned with something in this general area. A further useful comparison of the two writers goes through the difference in their visions of alienation.

For our purposes, alienation can be taken to be a normative concept.[29] If A is alienated from N, there is some sort of problem or deficiency in A's relation to N. The claim that A is alienated from N presumes that the normal A to N relationship is one of closeness or connectedness or trust, etc. Thus not every A can be alienated from every N. As a non-Catholic I can have pro or con attitudes toward the Catholic Church but I cannot be alienated from it.

There is usually a causal explanation for a condition of alienation, a reason or reasons why the normal A to N relationship does not obtain. Alienation might then be seen as a three-part relation: A is alienated from N due to cause X. People do sometimes say merely, "I feel alienated from N," without specifying an X, and this can convey something about the person's attitude toward N. Still, we understand more if we know what has alienated A from N. Someone brought up in the Catholic Church could be alienated from the church because of its current theological dictates or political positions or perhaps because of the behavior of some of its clergy. What would end the alienation might be different in the different cases.

We could also specify an axis along which A is alienated from N, for example, theologically or politically. Alienation would then be a four-place relation: A is alienated from N along axis J due to cause X. It follows that A could be alienated from N along axis J but not along axis K. This tends to be overlooked because we usually take A's alienation from N to mark a pervasive condition. It is rare to be alienated along one axis without this changing for the worse one's general attitude toward N. Yet in principle one could be alienated from the church so far as it takes certain political positions without being alienated from its theological teachings. Strictly speaking, alienation is a four-place relation.[30]

Alienation often involves a felt psychological state, but it need not. This is usually labeled "subjective" versus "objective" alienation. On some accounts, the most extreme form of alienation consists in *not* feeling alienated, in not having a negative feeling under circumstances C when such a feeling would be the rational response to C.[31] The underlying claim is that under other circumstances C', e.g., the 1844 Marx's communism, one would realize one's genuine good, and so C' is the proper benchmark from which to evaluate life under C. Under C, one is detached from one's genuine good – which is why it would be rational to have a negative response to C – and this is the case regardless of one's actual feelings and beliefs.

Subjective alienation is belief-dependent: it involves beliefs about one's proper relation to N. According to the 1844 Marx, workers are subjectively alienated from their labor activity but this is due both to the miserable conditions of the capitalist work process and, crucially, to the workers' belief (understandable given their circumstances) that labor is not the sphere of human self-realization. Their work feels worse, in one way, because work, on their (false) beliefs, is not the sphere of self-realization. Of course, given its degraded condition, their work would feel worse in a different way if they believed (correctly) that it is – ought to be – the sphere of self-realization. Either way, this element of subjective alienation is belief-dependent.

It seems clear that objective without subjective alienation is possible. So is the converse. I might believe that central social institutions don't reflect my concerns and interests, and yet they might do so. Members of the Tea Party movement in the United States seem subjectively alienated from the federal government, yet this could flow from false beliefs, for example, that the new health care law prevents people from using their current physicians (subjective without objective alienation). Moreover, even if central institutions don't reflect my concerns and interests, I could have a false belief about why they fail to do so. Someone might feel alienated from the government because she believes (correctly) that the government ought to be but is not in fact responsive to her basic needs, yet she might believe (falsely) that this failure is due to large amounts of money being spent on welfare (subjective *and* objective alienation but without the proper link).

Back now to Marx and Rawls.

# 5. Rawlsian Alienation

There is a vast literature on Marx on alienation, so I will be brief. The 1844 Marx lists four ways in which the capitalist labor process generates alienation: alienation from one's activity of labor, from other workers, from one's species being, and from the product of one's labor.[32] In each case the cause is the capitalist form of social institutions. Under capitalism, labor, which should count as the sphere of self-realization, is seen as merely a means to leisure-time activity, not valued for its own sake;[33] other workers (a) are seen as competitors rather than as fellow participants in the collective enterprise of transforming nature, and (b) are not seen as intended beneficiaries of one's own productive activity (and, in their activity, as intending to benefit oneself); one fails to identify with the human species, that is, the fact that one is a member of a species that continually transforms the world and itself, constituting its own nature over time, has no resonance in one's life; and one sees the world, including those parts produced and transformed by human labor as merely external to oneself, rather than as the site and product of human activity, as the place where human meaning has been and continues to be imposed.

All of this generates a condition in which what Marx takes to be the real telos of human life is unrecognized and instead we concentrate on narrow and selfish consumption activities with no sense of any larger purpose. It is a condition of apathy and emptiness that, as Allen Wood puts it, involves "a lack of a sense of meaning and self-worth" (1981, 23).[34]

There is obviously more to say about Marx on alienation, but what is relevant is best discussed via comparison and contrast with Rawls. I should note, though, that, for Marx, as Wood insists, objective alienation plays as much of a role as subjective alienation. Capitalism deprives agents of the opportunity properly to exercise their fundamental human capacities (where such proper exercise includes understanding these capacities' proper role in human life) and to relate to one another and their joint social arrangements in the proper way; and this is true regardless of agents' subjective states (Wood 1981, 23). Objective alienation will eventually be relevant to a Marxian criticism of justice as fairness.

Although Rawls does not talk of alienation, at moments the concept appears to play an important role. I focus on the stretch of *Justice as Fairness* in which Rawls argues against the principle of restricted utility. Rawls defines this principle as the two principles of justice except that the "principle of average utility, combined with a suitable social minimum, is substituted for the difference principle" (*JF*, 120). Rawls argues that, under a regime of restricted utility, for some citizens, especially "the least advantaged," the strains of commitment from complying with distributive rules might become so great that they "can no longer affirm the principles of justice" (*JF*, 128). Here, Rawls distinguishes two types of failure of affirmation. The first involves a straightforward rejection of "society's conception of justice." Agents see themselves as "oppressed" and are ready to revolt (*JF*, 128). Rawls does not think this is likely under restricted utility. However, the other failure of affirmation is possible, and, with the least advantaged, even likely: "[W]e grow distant from political society and retreat into our social world. We feel left out; and, withdrawn and cynical, we cannot affirm the principles of justice in our thought and conduct over a complete life . . . those principles are not ours and fail to engage our moral sensibility" (*JF*, 128). We seem asked to imagine a citizen who does not consider her condition so miserable as to revolt but who is unable to see herself as part of the joint political enterprise that goes on around her, an enterprise that most of her fellow citizens affirm, and that sustains, in Mill's phrase, the "groundwork" of her own existence (*Utilitarianism*, ch. 3, see Mill 1985, 251).

Note the following about this second condition:

(i) It can obtain even in the absence of a claim to be oppressed. With restricted utility, those who are withdrawn and cynical have equal liberty and opportunity as well as a social minimum.

(ii) The citizen in question, who can be thought of as alienated from the reigning distributive principles, would *like* to be able to affirm those principles. To feel left out is to want to belong. An Amish farmer, I assume, wishes to be left alone and cares nothing for the principles of the larger society. He is not subjectively alienated from that society. By contrast, our citizen is subjectively alienated.[35]

(iii) Rawls believes that being unable to affirm the principles that regulate one's society is a bad condition. "In a well-ordered society," he writes in *Theory*, "self-respect is secured by the public affirmation of the status of equal citizenship for all" (*TJ*, 478). But merely formal equal status cannot secure one's self-respect. One must also believe one is valued, qua citizen, equally with others. Yet if one's social situation forestalls affirming the reigning principles of justice, one might have equal legal status but feel oneself to be, qua citizen, second-class. One will not feel oneself to be a "full [member] of ... the public world" (*JF*, 130). One's self-respect is then *not* secured through the status of citizen. In this very context something is missing. And without self-respect, "nothing may seem worth doing, or if some things have value for us, we lack the will to strive for them. All desire and activity becomes empty and vain, and we sink into apathy and cynicism" (*TJ*, 386).

(iv) Given that restricted utility protects liberty and equal opportunity and provides a social minimum, disaffection to the point of revolt seems unjustified. Rawls insists that a problem remains: restricted utility lacks the reciprocity instantiated by the difference principle. The least advantaged will see themselves as accepting a worse condition merely to benefit the better off while the condition of the better off does them no good. Rawls worries that this will prevent the least advantaged "from being drawn into the public world and seeing themselves as full members of it" (*JF*, 130). Only with the difference principle could the least advantaged "recognize how the greater advantages achieved by others work to their good [the good of the least advantaged]" (*JF*, 130). Only then could the least advantaged see themselves as treated as fully equal.

For Rawls, alienation is not from one's labor but from the principles that regulate the basic structure. These are what alienated citizens cannot affirm. The *Theory* Rawls should find this deeply problematic. For that Rawls, an agent realizes her nature in significant part through giving and receiving justice, that is, through acting from principles that the agent herself affirms, that are widely affirmed by others, and that are embodied in institutional arrangements.[36] For the *Theory* Rawls, to be alienated from the principles that regulate basic social institutions is to be deprived of the opportunity to realize a fundamental part of one's nature.

Now, our alienated citizen feels herself to be a second-class citizen. This idea is familiar from American constitutional jurisprudence, for instance from the school prayer cases. Justice O'Connor writes that such prayer sends "a message to nonadherents that they are outsiders, not full members of the political community."[37] One seems not to have full standing in the polity, and the bite from this can go deep.

Stephen Darwall (1977) distinguishes between two kinds of respect: appraisal and recognition respect. The first involves respect for a person's character where this can be either under some specific description, say, one's character qua tennis player (one is quiet while one's opponent serves), or more generally one's character qua moral being. The second involves respect for one as having a certain feature, for example, that one is an American or a "person," or as having a certain status (I respect her as the president). In American history this latter form of respect, recognition respect, where the relevant feature or status is that of equal citizen, has often been at issue.

It might seem that Rawlsian alienation, at least in the context discussed, involves an absence of recognition respect, an absence of respect as an equal citizen – at stake would be *respect-alienation*. However, lack of respect is not the only problematic social attitude. Another is lack of concern. This is shown in a passage from Friedrich Engels's 1844 book *The Condition of the Working Class in England*:

> Ultimately it is self-interest, and especially money gain, which alone determines [these English bourgeois]. I once went into Manchester with such a bourgeois, and spoke to him of the bad, unwholesome method of building, the frightful condition of the working-people's quarters, and asserted that I had never seen so ill-built a city. The man listened quietly to the end, and said at the corner where we parted: "And yet there is a great deal of money made here; good morning, sir." It is utterly indifferent to the English bourgeois whether his working-men starve or not, if only he makes money.[38]

Engels's bourgeois shows no contempt for the working-people and takes no satisfaction in their misery. Rather, their condition simply does not register. Their plight does not matter to him.

Our society's history has made us assume that to be treated as second-class is to be the object of disrespect. Yet to be the object of indifference can also count as second-class treatment. Contempt is the negative counterpart to respect; indifference is the negative counterpart to concern.[39] For the 1844 Marx, the worker's subjective alienation involves, among other things, a (justified) belief that he is not the object of others' concern, that others are indifferent to his well-being; for Marx, proper – unalienated – social relationships consist in reciprocal concern for one another's well-being.

Does the Rawlsian alienation sketched above involve a belief in an absence of respect or in an absence of concern? Some commentators have claimed that respect for persons is the central value in justice as fairness, a plausible claim for a Kantian view.[40] And it is easy to imagine arrangements that violate Rawls's two principles where respect-alienation would in fact be at stake, for instance, if there is an absence of equal liberty or equal opportunity.

Here, though, our focus is the reason to reject the principle of restricted utility. In a society regulated by that principle there would be equal liberty and equal opportunity, and all citizens' right to these things would be widely affirmed. Why think that here alienation is respect-alienation? What our second-class citizen feels is not the contempt of the better off but their indifference. If there is an absence of a desirable social attitude here, it would seem to be that of concern rather than respect.

For Rawls, the reason to encourage "the better endowed . . . to seek still further benefits" is maximally to benefit the least advantaged (*JF*, 124). That is the goal of arrangements that instantiate the difference principle. A restricted utility society has no such goal. There, the least advantaged know that their condition could be improved without making anyone else as badly off as they (the least advantaged) are now. The least advantaged are likely to feel that other citizens don't care about their condition, that their lives don't matter to others.

The least advantaged cannot affirm the principles of justice because they have reason to believe that, in a society regulated by restricted utility, their condition does not matter equally. Theirs is *concern-alienation*.[41]

## 6. Rawlsian Fraternity

I have claimed that the alienation associated with the absence of the difference principle in a restricted utility society stems from a perceived deficit of concern rather than respect. This links me to those commentators who urge that *A Theory of Justice* contains a strain that highlights citizens' mutual affection (see Okin 1989; also Mendus 1999). I want to press this thought by looking at the issue of concern in terms of what I take to be the official *Theory* view as well as in terms of moves that seem to go beyond that view. I call the first the "official view" because I suspect that, if pressed, the Rawls of *Theory* would have endorsed it; still, at several points the text seems to go further.

Let's start with Rawls's claim in *Theory* that the difference principle is "an interpretation of the principle of fraternity" (*TJ*, 90). He connects the difference principle to fraternity through analogy to an idealized family.

> Members of a family commonly do not wish to gain unless they can do so in ways that further the interests of the rest. Now wanting to act on the difference principle has precisely this consequence. Those better circumstanced are willing to have their greater advantages only under a scheme in which this works out for the benefit of the less fortunate. (*TJ*, 90)

Interestingly, immediately after invoking family relationships Rawls denies that justice as fairness requires "ties of sentiment and feeling." It is "unrealistic," he thinks, to expect such things among members of a large society (*TJ*, 90). On Rawls's account, commitment to the difference principle merely models what it is like to have family relationships, relationships in which I accept greater advantages only if doing so benefits the less fortunate. The difference principle instantiates distributive relationships that *would be* instantiated by people motivated as family members would be motivated – but the citizens of the well-ordered society need not actually be so motivated.

There are several things to note here.

(i) Were citizens in fact to have ties of sentiment and feelings, they would find the difference principle compelling, at least relative to average utility or even restricted utility.

(ii) The attitudes Rawls invokes in the quoted passage seem similar to those of the 1844 Marx's communists. Those communists' central orientation toward one another is that of equal concern for one another's well-being. That is why they try to facilitate one another's aims and, as Marx puts it, take satisfaction in one another's satisfactions.[42]

(iii) The conception of fraternity that Rawls rejects is one in which fraternal relationships involve robust sentiments and feelings. Rawls thinks it is not realistic to expect such things in a large society. Here, he repeats a common nineteenth-century theme. The classical utilitarians emphasized our capacity to be motivated by sympathy and love. In Mill's *Utilitarianism*, this led to the thought that, with proper moral education, "each individual" would have "a feeling of unity with all the rest; which feeling, if perfect, would make him never think of, or desire, any beneficial condition for himself, in the benefits of which they are not included" (Mill 1985, 232).[43] However, in the nineteenth century, the joint stress on identification with humanity as a whole and on cultivating a desire for general human well-being prompted the widespread attack that such commitment to humanity, such ostensible philanthropy, was in fact a sham, a cover for indifference to actual individuals. "Thy love afar is spite at home," Emerson declared in "Self-Reliance" (Emerson 1980, 30). Hegel and James Fitzjames Stephen, among many others (most famously, Dickens, in his Mrs Jellyby in *Bleak House*), made similar complaints: to love everyone is to love no one; the utilitarian does not actually care about the well-being of individuals (see Hegel 1970, 246–247; Stephen 1990, 238, 241).

Rawls, Mill, and the antiphilanthropists all seem to share the belief that concern for unknown distant others is an extended form of love for those known and near, and that in fact love of this kind simply cannot be extended very far. But I take concern for distant others to be something different from love – to be a distinct attitude. For instance, concern, as I understand it, need not involve much in the way of occurrent feelings for its object. Perhaps this mostly marks a difference from nineteenth-century writers. Recent discussions of love downplay occurrent feelings, and concern does involve some feelings, say, reactive emotions with regard to the object of one's concern. Still, feelings are likely to be less frequent and intense with concern than with love. Like the attitude of trust, the attitude of concern can be present and motivationally efficacious without much, if anything, in the way of occurrent feelings.

The key difference between love and concern probably has less to do with feelings than with the degree of specification of the objects of these attitudes. At issue in political philosophy are our omnipresent relations to people of whose specific lives we will never hear. I don't think the object of love can be someone unspecified in the sense of being seen only under a very general identity (see Frankfurt 1999, 166). Yet it does seem possible to have concern for someone like that – say, for those people who are, and take this as the full available description, the victims of an earthquake in New Zealand. If the concept of concern, where the object is other individuals and their individual well-being, is to do work for political philosophy, we must be able to have a motivationally efficacious attitude – concern, not love – toward individuals about whom we know very little. How far we are likely to have this attitude is of first importance but cannot be dealt with here. Here, I want merely to press for the possibility of such an attitude toward unknown others.

Andrew Mason gives an example of concern that seems unlikely to involve what normally counts as love or even affection. He points out that a physician can have concern for her patient's well-being and be motivated by such concern (say, to stay late at the hospital and monitor her patient's condition), and yet not be said to have love or affection for someone she met that afternoon (see Mason 2000, 29).

Cora Diamond also provides a useful example. She imagines a news report announcing that a Boeing 747 has crashed and everyone aboard has been killed. Diamond then imagines two different news flashes that correct the earlier report. On one corrective flash it turns out that a Boeing 747 crashed but not everyone was killed – there were survivors. The alternative news flash says that the crashed plane turned about to be a Boeing 727, a smaller plane – everyone died, but there were fewer deaths (Diamond 1990, 162). In both corrected scenarios the number of fewer dead is the same. If we respond differently to the two corrections, feel a kind of relief with the first but less so with the second, the difference cannot be due to aggregative considerations.

461

In neither of Diamond's corrected scenarios is a face put on those who do not die. In the first scenario, however, one finds oneself imagining individual people with individual lives. Yet this is entirely an exercise in imagination. Although one's concern here is for individuals, one knows nothing about them. The example suggests that we are capable of concern for the well-being of unknown yet individual human beings. Rawls accepts that there is a way to understand fraternity that does not make it a matter of the feelings and attitudes that are possible only among people who know one another well (*TJ*, 90–91). But he takes such fraternity to consist merely in affirming the difference principle. My claim is that such an affirmation could itself be construed as an expression of concern for distant others' well-being.

On the official *Theory* view, citizens need not have concern for one another's well-being. Yet I suspect that many readers come away believing that Rawls favors – hopes for – less pallid fraternal relations. Consider, for instance, the famous line, "in justice as fairness, men agree to share one another's fate."[44] To agree to share another's fate could mean merely that we agree to have our lives be linked, but that seems far too weak. More plausibly, it could mean that we agree that A will gain only if B gains. I suspect that this would be the official reading. Still, the idea could also be, more robustly, that A and B are not indifferent to one another's fates: what happens to B has an impact on A. To share one another's fate could be to care about one another's well-being.

Think also of the treatment of envy. Rawls believes that he must show that in justice as fairness this vice is unlikely to be widespread. Remarkably, he frames the issue in terms of "excusable envy,"[45] the idea that there might be an excuse for a form of a basic human vice. (Rawls agrees with Kant that envy is a vice "of hating mankind," *TJ*, 466). That a form of envy might be excusable is even more remarkable when, by hypothesis, it would obtain under principles chosen within the original position and so in a social world that ought to count as "just." Of course, Rawls's point is that it might be prudent for the parties behind the veil of ignorance to reconsider the choice of the two principles if these are likely to generate excessive "general envy" (envy of the lives of those in social groups above one's own) (*TJ*, 466). He thinks that under some social circumstances it would be demanding too much of human nature to ask that people not feel such envy, and so not be prompted to destabilizing conduct (*TJ*, 468). The parties might then want to choose principles that would avoid such circumstances.

Yet it is striking that coercion is not mentioned as a response to what seems to be social malevolence. Elsewhere Rawls concedes the need for a police power, but not here (see *TJ*, 505, 237). Officially, that is because the question is whether, given so much general envy that instability cannot be adequately contained, the parties would reevaluate the choice of principles. Still, I think something is flagged by Rawls's failure to talk of the police power, by his readiness to consider a form of envy to be excusable, and by his eagerness to make sure that it would tend not to arise. Something seems at stake beyond the official prudential view.

In fact, I take Rawls to recognize that it is bad for people to live with a self-destructive inner life (to suffer a profound "wound [to one's] self-respect") (*TJ*, 468). Indeed, he remarks that "we may sympathize with [the envious person's] sense of loss" (*TJ*, 468). We – the readers of *Theory* – ask, as the parties do, whether under Rawls's two principles general envy is likely to be so rife as to destabilize social institutions. However, I suspect that we also do not *want* citizens to suffer envy (we "sympathize" with the envious). If in fact we feel a claim against letting citizens' lives be scarred by envy, I think that what is being tugged is our concern for their well-being. Of course, such concern is irrelevant to the deliberations behind the veil.

Nevertheless, I think it does contribute to our – to the reader's – sense that the parties are in fact right to worry so much that citizens might suffer from envy. It seems to play an unacknowledged role in the overall argument.

Consider also the idea of society as a social union of social unions (*TJ*, 456–464). For Rawls, a social union is a group whose members find satisfaction in some form of joint activity (as in a reading group, a weekly basketball game, a chapter of the Elks Club) and recognize and appreciate one another's contributions to the joint activity. The activity need not (though it could) be perfectionist, and in thinking of society as composed of many such unions, these are not to be ranked along any perfectionist axis. Rawls urges that one way to think of society in justice as fairness is as a social union of social unions.

Here, though, we see an uncertainty about connections among distant citizens. The members of a social union of social unions would seem to be not individuals but groups, that is, social unions. Each citizen seems capable of being appreciated by and appreciating only the citizens within those social unions to which she belongs. This would be consistent with Rawls's skepticism about social ties extending across a large society. Yet Rawls appears to take the members of the broader social union to be individuals.

> In much the same way that players have the shared end to execute a good and fair play of the game, so the members of a well-ordered society have the common aim of cooperating together to realize their own and another's nature in ways allowed by the principles of justice. (*TJ*, 462)

The members of the larger social union seem to be individual citizens. Now, suppose two people share the end of a good and fair play of a game. Is each indifferent to the benefits they bestow on one another? They could be indifferent, being merely diligent promise keepers who have promised to play well and fairly and who in some sense enjoy a well-played game. But this seems more bloodless than what Rawls has in mind. In justice as fairness, is the fact that each citizen aims "to realize their own and another's nature" simply a technical feature of Rawls's well-ordered society – or does it point to a widespread concern that one another's lives go well?

Rawls sometimes invokes the thought that in a well-ordered society one will do one's part in the joint social enterprise "provided that others do their part." (See, for example, *LHPP*, 87; *TJ*, 412–413.) As a condition for one's continued willing cooperation, this "provided that" thought is ambiguous. It could mean:

(i) *Fairness "provided that."* Each of us believes that the terms of our relationship are sufficiently fair, and each of us is committed to act as fairness requires. Yet if one of us persistently violates the terms of our relationship, the other might follow suit – she might conclude that we are no longer in a relationship in which each of us is committed to fairness.

(ii) *Gift "provided that."* When I give you a birthday gift, it is not conditional on receiving anything in return. Nevertheless, I expect that when the time rolls around you will give me a gift. Our relationship involves mutual trust whose content is not that each of us believes the other will keep an agreement but that each of us believes we will continue to be friends, that is, continue to have concern for one another's well-being and to act in ways that express this concern. Yet if one of us stops giving gifts, the other might follow suit – she might conclude that our relationship of friendship has ended.

Rawls writes that in the well-ordered society of justice as fairness "mutual trust and the cooperative virtues" are encouraged (*JF*, 126). But trust can be trust that each of us will continue to be committed to fairness or it can be trust that we will continue to be concerned for one another's well-being. What can count as the cooperative virtues is similarly ambiguous.

Both "provided that" models are present in *Theory*. The gift model fits nicely with Rawls's account of the morality of association, the account of the bonds of "friendship and mutual trust" that arise in the context of participation in cooperative groups (*TJ*, 411–412). But in his description of moral development Rawls explicitly moves beyond this to the morality of principles, which fits well with the fairness model. Something like concern for others – a basic feature of friendship – is thus subordinated to commitment to principles. To justify this move Rawls invokes the premise (in effect, the nineteenth-century assumption) that in a large society widespread social affections are not possible – and so only principles can tie us together (*TJ*, 415).

Finally, here is one last way to find in *Theory* (or maybe to read into it) the theme of reciprocal concern. Consider the most ideal instantiation of the difference principle. Imagine that what Rawls calls *chain connectedness* and *close-knittedness* both obtain. (See *TJ*, 69–71.) In that case:

> There is no loose-jointedness, so to speak, in the way expectations hang together. Now with these assumptions there is a sense in which everyone benefits when the difference principle is satisfied. For the representative man who is better off in any two-way comparison gains by the advantages offered him, and the man who is worse off gains from the contributions which these inequalities make. (*TJ*, 70)

We could interpret this as a situation in which each agent's productive activity benefits all other citizens. Whatever I do to increase the social pie moves the entire structure marginally upward. "It is impossible to raise or lower the expectation of any representative man without raising or lowering the expectation of every other representative man" (*TJ*, 70). Given this premise, in our various labors we are all benefiting one another. No doubt, one could see this state of affairs in a self-interested way – I benefit when others benefit, so I have a prudential reason to accept and maintain this arrangement. However, one *could* see it in a concerned way: one could be pleased that all representative spots are at their (increasing, one hopes) maximum, given the priority of the worst off, and that one's activities have contributed to attaining and maintaining this state of affairs. One could interpret this as a state of affairs in which in a sense we work *for* one another, as with Marx's communists.

## 7. The Problem of Alienated Labor

I have argued that the 1844 Marx and the *Theory* Rawls share a further theme – although with Rawls the theme is a bit subterranean – that of concern for others' well-being. Yet we should not lose sight of the differences. For instance, the 1844 Marx cares about bonds among human beings simply as human beings (the sense that we are tied together as a species), a theme absent in Rawls. More important, the source of alienation is quite different for the two writers. So we return to the distinction between production and distribution.

The *Theory* Rawls is, in principle, agnostic between private and public ownership of the means of production. (See *TJ*, 234–251, esp. 242.) In his well-ordered society, what is needed is merely a shared affirmation of principles of distributive justice and the institutions that embody them. Ideally, we will feel and be "at home" in our social world – neither feel nor be alienated – because we can endorse the distributive principles that regulate it. For the 1844 Marx, this is to fail to see the centrality of the production process. For him, we can be at home in our social world only if that process exists within a communist society.

Rawls is certainly aware of how inhuman work under capitalism has often been, as well as that decent work relations must be, in some sense, under the control of those who inhabit them ("What men want is meaningful work in free association with others," *TJ*, 257).[46] Moreover, *Justice as Fairness* rejects both laissez-faire and welfare-state capitalism, remaining agnostic only between property-owning democracy (where there is considerable dispersal of social wealth) and liberal democratic socialism.[47]

Still, there remains a difference between Marx and Rawls, a basic contrast between the view that human self-realization crucially involves producing for others and the view that the maintenance of just institutions is the preeminent form of human flourishing. For Rawls, the cause of alienation is the (problematic) content of distributive principles/ institutions, while for Marx the cause is the (problematic) content of the social structure of production. Rawlsian alienation is from distributive principles/institutions, while, for Marx, alienation is from various dimensions of labor and its product. For Rawls, the alienated citizen cannot see herself as properly engaged in the shared activity of maintaining just institutions, of giving and receiving justice. For the 1844 Marx, the alienated worker cannot see herself as properly engaged in the shared activity of transforming nature with the intent to provide one another with the objects needed to pursue our individual ends.

We can now see a possible Marxian criticism of Rawls. The Marxian might say that justice as fairness could permit – more to the point, it does not stress forestalling – the alienation of labor.

Let's assume that the human good consists in relation R to one's labor, to the product of one's labor, and so forth (something like the 1844 Marx's view of those relations). A focus on distributive principles, making the choice between social institutions into a merely techni- cal question – which arrangement maximizes the economic floor? – might then seem to miss what is crucial.

But this *human good premise* has a strong and a weak form. The strong form says that relation R is the essential and nearly exhaustive feature of the human good. The weak form says that R is an important part of the human good but far from the only part, and that R is scalar. Something like the strong form is probably held by the actual – the uncon- strained – 1844 Marx. It would prompt a condemnation of justice as fairness as failing to put relation R front and center. However, this form is quite suspect. Labor within an appro- priate social structure and with an understanding of its significant value may well be an important component of the human good, but it is far from the only component; nor is it obviously the dominant component. The weak form of the human good premise is much more plausible (and could perhaps be adapted to the work of writers like Axel Honneth, see Honneth 1995).

The actual 1844 Marx would clearly reject justice as fairness. Let's assume, though, that a constrained 1844 Marx would subscribe only to the weak form of the human good premise. Could such a Marx give a qualified acceptance to justice as fairness? After all, in principle, justice as fairness *could be* compatible with relation R, on the weak form of the human good premise. Presumably, relation R (on the weak form of the premise) could be adequately instantiated if justice as fairness is embodied in liberal democratic socialism. Perhaps relation R could even be adequately instantiated in a property-owning democracy if appropriate structures of work are widely available and there is widespread affirmation of labor's significant value.[48] The point is that, for the Marxian, the acceptability of justice as fairness, as embodied in one or another set of social institutions, depends on its ability to satisfy the weak form of the human good premise.

For such a Marxian, the worry about justice as fairness turns out to be this. Such a Marxian acknowledges that, in principle, justice as fairness *could* involve adequate instantiation of relation R, maybe even within a property-owning democracy. Nevertheless, this Marxian says, by starting with a focus on distributive principles a Rawlsian approach is *likely* to give too little weight to proper production relationships – it will *tend* to orient citizens away from a focus on such relationships and so is *unlikely* to push them toward institutional arrangements that do adequately instantiate relation R. Citizens will focus on distributive fairness and so tend not to see the importance of relation R (even on the weak form of the human good premise), and so will tend not to see that instantiating it is a crucial consideration in choosing institutional arrangements. The more important one thinks relation R is in a good human life, the more telling one will find this criticism.

The criticism, then, is that, in practice, justice as fairness might countenance a condition in which citizens are alienated from their labor, certainly objectively and perhaps subjectively. Of course, to accept this as a serious criticism of justice as fairness one would have to accept (at least) the weak form of the human good premise, accept what amounts to a particular substantive view of (at least part of) the human good. Marxians, including a constrained 1844 Marx, would do so.

## 8. Conclusion

I have argued that the *Theory* Rawls and the 1844 Marx share more than has usually been thought. Still, to a Marxian, even a constrained one, some cogency is likely to remain in the standard claim that Rawls goes awry in focusing on principles of distribution rather than on the structure of productive activity. The two writers have different conceptions of how one realizes one's nature. Not surprisingly, this makes for a difference in their views about the proper focus of normative political analysis.

## Notes

I am grateful to Jon Mandle and David Reidy for extremely helpful comments on an earlier version of this article.

1  I use the term "Marxian" rather than "Marxist" to avoid the suggestion that the views I present are "official" or to be associated with the views of an organization or party.
2  Marx and Engels citations are given by the English title of the work and then the volume and page number, first in Karl Marx and Friedrich Engels, *Marx-Engels Werke* (MEW, see Marx and Engels 1956–) and then in *Marx-Engels Collected Works* (MECW, see Marx and Engels 1975–). The translation is sometimes amended. All emphases are in the original.

3   For recent versions and discussions of these criticisms, see the debate about "ideal theory." See Sen 2006; Simmons, 2010; Estlund 2008. See also Mills 2005.

4   In holding that conceptions of proper distribution are determined by the relations of production, Marx is sometimes taken to be claiming that ideas are mere epiphenomena of matter and therefore cannot outrun their time. This claim is in Engels and Lenin. Marx is more subtle, but in a coauthored work such as *The German Ideology* it is difficult to prise apart competing strands. On these issues, see Brudney 1998, ch. 10.

5   At this point in this essay I stop using the phrase "relations of production." In presenting the standard Marxian criticism I have made use of concepts from Marx's work as a whole. From now on my focus is the 1844 Marx, and "relations of production" does not come from that Marx.

6   A different Marxian criticism is that by permitting inequality Rawls is endorsing class divisions. Against this, first, Marx, himself, is not in favor of equality for its own sake (see *Economic and Philosophic Manuscripts of 1844*, in *MEW*, Ergänzungsband, 534–536/*MECW*, vol. 3, 294–296); and second, Rawlsian divisions refer to the distribution of primary goods – Rawls does not think in terms of what Marxians have usually meant by class. (An excellent defense of Rawls here is DiQuattro 1983; I am much indebted to DiQuattro's discussion.) Still, primary goods include not only income but offices, so the difference principle does license some differentials in effective control and authority. But (a) the existence of such differentials is justified solely by its benefit to the worst off and publicly understood to be justified only by that consideration; (b) the extent of inequality is limited to what is *necessary* to maximize the condition of the worst off (in terms of primary goods), and Rawls believes such inequality will not be large; (c) effective voting power is never supposed to mirror these inequalities; and finally (d) Rawls believes that social status will increasingly not mirror them (*TJ*, 477–478). Rawls's well-ordered society will involve some degree of hierarchy, but such hierarchy seems unlikely to match up well with the bulk of what Marxians have meant by class division.

7   For this debate, see Nagel et al. 1980.

8   The statement of the first principle is from *TJ*, 53; the statement of the second principle is from *TJ*, 72. Rawls's final statement of the two principles, at least in *Theory*, is at *TJ*, 266–267.

9   Karl Marx, "Comments," in *MEW*, Ergänzungsband, vol. 1, 462/*MECW*, vol. 3, 227. Here is the complete passage (translation amended, all emphases in original):

> Suppose we had carried out production as human beings. Each of us would have, in his production, *doubly affirmed* himself and the other person. (1) In my *production* I would have objectified my *individuality*, its *specific character*, and therefore enjoyed not only an individual *life-expression* during the activity, but also when looking at the object I would have the individual pleasure of knowing my personality to be *objective, sensuously perceptible* [*sinnlich anschaubare*] and hence a power raised *beyond all doubt*. (2) In your enjoyment or use of my product I would have the *direct* [*unmittelbar*] enjoyment both of being conscious of having satisfied a *human* need by my work, that is, of having objectified *human* nature [*Wesen*], and of having thus created an object corresponding to the need of another *human* being [*Wesen*]. (3) I would have been for you the *mediator* [*der Mittler*] between you and the species, and therefore would become recognized and felt by you yourself as a completion [*Ergänzung*] of your own nature and as a necessary part of yourself, and consequently would know myself to be confirmed both in your thought and your love. (4) In my individual life-expression I would have directly created your life-expression, and therefore in my individual activity I would have directly *confirmed* and *realized* my true nature [*wahres Wesen*], my *human* nature, my *communal* nature.
>
> Our products would be so many mirrors reflecting our nature.
>
> This relationship would moreover be reciprocal [*wechselseitig*]; what occurs on my side has also to occur on yours.

10  There is another (implausible) premise at work here, namely, that under communism the unfettered and unincentivized individual choice of activities will generate not just the quantity but the

variety of goods and services that individuals need in order to pursue their various forms of self-realization. This second premise shows the influence of Fourier. See Schmidt am Busch n.d.

11  See *MEW*, vol. 19, 21/*MECW*, vol. 24, 87.

12  G.A. Cohen also notes that the "from each/to each" phrase is not an obligatory standard but a description of what communism would be like (1990a; 1990b).

13  As he and Engels put it in *The German Ideology*, if there is a scramble for necessities, "die ganze alte Scheiße" is inevitable. See *MEW*, vol. 3, 35/*MECW*, vol. 5, 49.

14  This theme is spread across the *Economic and Philosophic Manuscripts of 1844*, sometimes taking the form of noting that valuable human capacities are either unexercised under capitalism (*MEW*, Ergänzungsband, 517, 537–538, 542/*MECW*, vol. 3, 277, 298, 302) or, if exercised, unrecognized *as* valuable capacities (*MEW*, Ergänzungsband, 542–543, 555/*MECW*, vol. 3, 303–304, 315). In *The German Ideology*, Marx and Engels assert that only communism can produce the conditions for the "all-around realization of the individual" (*MEW*, vol. 3, 273/*MECW* vol. 5, 292).

15  For further discussion of the first principle, see Rawls, "The Basic Liberties and Their Priority."

16  For discussions of distributive prioritarianism, see Parfit 1997; Arneson 2000. For a discussion of distributive sufficiency, see Frankfurt 1987; see also Crisp 2003.

17  See *MEW*, vol. 19, 20/*MECW*, vol. 24, 86.

18  *MEW*, vol. 19, 21/*MECW*, vol. 24, 86.

19  *MEW*, vol. 19, 20–21/*MECW*, vol. 24, 87.

20  "The Critique of the Gotha Programme," in *MEW*, vol. 19, 21/*MECW*, vol. 24, 87.

21  The intuition that equal love or concern draws one to the worst off is urged by Thomas Nagel (1979, 123–124). As Nagel notes, there are complications when the intuition is applied beyond a family to overall social distribution.

22  Might a constrained 1844 Marx be a sufficientarian? It depends on what counts as sufficient. Marx is a progressive. He thinks there will be further improvements in the human lot, and if the level of sufficiency would not rise with these improvements he would not be a sufficientarian. On the other hand, the idea that under communism one will take what one needs suggests that Marx's underlying standard is whatever is sufficient for every agent to have a real chance to pursue her own vision of self-realization. Unfortunately, that standard might require the transcendence of scarcity. It is not clear what standard of sufficiency a constrained 1844 Marx would accept.

23  On this issue, see Marx's criticism of vulgar, leveling communism at *Economic and Philosophic Manuscripts of 1844*, in *MEW*, Ergänzungsband, 534–536/*MECW*, vol. 3, 294–296.

24  One way to make peace would be to distinguish between one's reasons for choosing a distributive principle and one's reasons for action in a society in which that principle is instantiated. Concern for others could prompt the choice of the difference principle even if, within a society regulated by the difference principle, one might often act from self-interest. However, I doubt that the 1844 Marx would approve of such double-mindedness.

25  I discuss this topic at greater length in Brudney 1997.

26  See *TJ*, 110–111. I thank Jon Mandle and David Reidy for pressing me to note this difference.

27  See *The German Ideology*, in *MEW*, vol. 3, 33/*MECW*, vol. 5, 47.

28  In *Political Liberalism* Rawls talks of a "liberal conception of justice" where this is not limited to his two principles (*PL*, 6). Might a constrained 1844 Marx's view fit under this umbrella? The key question concerns Rawls's stress on the priority of liberty. The unconstrained 1844 Marx does not worry about this because he thinks that under communism there will be no temptation to suppress liberty. Would a constrained 1844 Marx affirm the priority of liberty? I suspect that equal concern for individuals' well-being does commit one to the priority of liberty, but to show this would take an extended argument. In general, I think that the conditions for the priority issue to be pressing take us too far from Marx's, even a constrained Marx's, own picture. With regard to the 1844 Marx and the priority of liberty I think there is simply no useful answer. For what it is worth,

however, a small piece of evidence that in the 1840s Marx sees a link between liberty and individual development is *The German Ideology*'s famous hunting, fishing, etc., passage. It puts weight on the fact that under communism I will be able to do things "just as I have a mind" to do them. See *The German Ideology*, in *MEW*, vol. 3, 33/*MECW*, vol. 5, 47.

29   For an overview of the concept of alienation, see Schacht 1971. We owe it to Rahel Jaeggi that "alienation" has been brought back into the political philosopher's lexicon. See her excellent *Entfremdung* (Jaeggi 2005).

30   There is usually a link between cause and axis. The church's assertion of a theological principle one rejects is likely to alienate one along the theological axis. Still, it is worth distinguishing what generates the alienation from the dimension in which it obtains.

31   For claims like this, see Lukács 1971 and Marcuse 1964.

32   *Economic and Philosophic Manuscripts of 1844*, in *MEW*, Ergänzungsband, 514–518/*MECW*, vol. 3, 274–278.

33   *Economic and Philosophic Manuscripts of 1844*, in *MEW*, Ergänzungsband, 514/*MECW*, vol. 3, 274.

34   This is subjective alienation.

35   For the *Theory* Rawls, our alienated citizen is not only subjectively but also objectively alienated from her social world. For as I will shortly note, her condition is one in which she is deprived of an opportunity to realize a fundamental part of her nature.

36   In *Justice as Fairness* the theme of self-realization via maintaining just institutions remains, but such self-realization is diluted to being an aspect of one's life merely qua citizen. (See *JF*, 199.)

37   *Lynch v. Donnelly*, 465 US 688 (1984) (O'Connor, J. concurring).

38   In *MEW*, vol. 2, 487/*MECW*, vol. 4, 563.

39   Lack of respect can lead to lack of concern, but the latter is an independent attitude. Indeed, lack of concern can lead to lack of respect, e.g., my indifference to your misery may eventually lead me to see you as contemptible.

40   Charles Larmore makes this claim about political liberalism (2008, ch. 6). See also Nussbaum 2011.

41   That distributive principles ought to embody equal respect *and* concern has long been emphasized by Ronald Dworkin. See Dworkin 1977, 180–183. At 181, Dworkin ascribes this belief to the Rawls of *A Theory of Justice*.

42   *Economic and Philosophic Manuscripts of 1844*, in *MEW*, Ergänzungsband, 563/*MECW*, vol. 3, 322.

43   Interestingly, Rawls takes this passage to suggest that Mill favors the difference principle. See *LHPP*, 282 n4.

44   See Rawls, *A Theory of Justice*, original edition (*TJ* 1971, 102). In the revised edition, Rawls removes this phrase.

45   See *TJ*, §§80, 81. In *Justice as Fairness*, Rawls says that he "would not change [those sections] substantially" (*JF*, 184).

46   In a well-ordered society, "no one need be servilely dependent on others and made to choose between monotonous and routine occupations which are deadening to human thought and sensibility. Each can be offered a variety of tasks so that the different elements of his nature find a suitable expression" (*TJ*, 464). The underlying thought descends from von Humboldt, but I take Rawls to be aware of the resonances to the famous passage on hunting, fishing, etc. in *The German Ideology*.

47   See *JF*, 135–140. Here, Rawls also rejects state socialism with a command economy. Rawls also refers to property-owning democracy at *TJ*, §42.

48   To an extent, Rawls is aware of this issue. In a brief discussion in *Justice as Fairness*, he considers whether, over time, property-owning democracy would lead to the rise of worker-managed firms

(*JF*, 178–179). A topic for further work is whether this would in fact overcome Marxian alienation.

## Works by Rawls, with Abbreviations

"The Basic Liberties and Their Priority" (1982), Lecture VIII in *Political Liberalism*.
*Justice as Fairness: A Restatement* (*JF*), ed. Erin Kelly. Cambridge, MA: Harvard University Press, 2001.
*Lectures on the History of Political Philosophy* (*LHPP*), ed. Samuel Freeman. Cambridge, MA: Harvard University Press, 2007.
*Political Liberalism* (*PL*), expanded edn. New York: Columbia University Press, 2005.
*A Theory of Justice* (*TJ* 1971), 1st edn. Cambridge, MA: Harvard University Press, 1971.
*A Theory of Justice* (*TJ*), rev. edn. Cambridge, MA: Harvard University Press, 1999.

## Other References

Arneson, Richard J. (2000) "Luck Egalitarianism and Prioritarianism" *Ethics* 110: 339–349.
Bauer, Bruno (1843) *Die Judenfrage*. Braunschweig: Friedrich Otto.
Brudney, Daniel (1997) "Community and Completion." In A. Reath, B. Herman, and C. Korsgaard (eds), *Reclaiming the History of Ethics: Essays for John Rawls*. Cambridge: Cambridge University Press.
Brudney, Daniel (1998) *Marx's Attempt to Leave Philosophy*. Cambridge, MA: Harvard University Press.
Cohen, G.A. (1990a) "Marxism and Contemporary Political Philosophy, or: Why Nozick Exercises Some Marxists More than He Does Any Egalitarian Liberals." *Canadian Journal of Philosophy* (suppl. vol.) 16: 363–387.
Cohen, G.A. (1990b) "Self-Ownership, Communism and Equality." *Proceedings of the Aristotelian Society* (suppl. vol.) 64: 25–61.
Crisp, Roger (2003) "Equality, Priority, and Compassion." *Ethics* 113: 745–763.
Darwall, Stephen (1977) "Two Kinds of Respect." *Ethics* 88: 36–49.
Diamond, Cora (1990) "How Many Legs?" In Raimond Gaita (ed.), *Value and Understanding: Essays for Peter Winch*. London: Routledge.
DiQuattro, Arthur (1983) "Rawls and Left Criticism." *Political Theory* 11: 53–78.
Dworkin, Ronald (1977) *Taking Rights Seriously*. Cambridge, MA: Harvard University Press.
Emerson, Ralph Waldo (1980) "Self-Reliance." In *The Collected Works of Ralph Waldo Emerson*, vol. 2. Cambridge, MA: Harvard University Press.
Estlund, David (2008) "Utopophobia: Concession and Aspiration in Democratic Theory." In Estlund, *Democratic Authority: A Philosophical Framework*. Princeton: Princeton University Press.
Frankfurt, Harry (1987) "Equality as a Moral Ideal." *Ethics* 98: 21–43.
Frankfurt, Harry (1999) *Necessity, Volition and Love*. Cambridge: Cambridge University Press.
Hegel, Friedrich (1970) "The Spirit of Christianity." In Hegel, *Early Theological Writings*, trans. T.M. Knox. Gloucester, MA: Peter Smith.
Honneth, Axel (1995) *The Struggle for Recognition: The Moral Grammar of Social Conflicts*, trans. Joel Anderson. Cambridge: Polity.
Jaeggi, Rahel (2005) *Entfremdung: zur Aktualität eines sozialphilosophischen Problems*. Frankfurt am Main: Campus.
Larmore, Charles (2008) *The Autonomy of Morality*. Cambridge: Cambridge University Press.
Lukács, György (1971) *History and Class Consciousness: Studies in Marxist Dialectics*, trans. Rodney Livingstone. Cambridge: MIT Press.

Marcuse, Herbert (1964) *One Dimensional Man: Studies in the Ideology of Advanced Industrial Society.* Boston: Beacon Press.

Marx, Karl and Engels, Friedrich (1956–) *Marx-Engels Werke.* Berlin: Dietz.

Marx, Karl and Engels, Friedrich (1975–) *Marx-Engels Collected Works.* New York: International.

Mason, Andrew (2000) *Community, Solidarity and Belonging: Levels of Community and their Normative Significance.* Cambridge: Cambridge University Press.

Mendus, Susan (1999) "The Importance of Love in Rawls's Theory of Justice." *British Journal of Political Science* 29: 57–75.

Mill, John Stuart (1985) *Utilitarianism.* In Mill, *Collected Works,* vol. 10. Toronto: University of Toronto Press.

Mills, Charles W, (2005) " 'Ideal Theory' as Ideology." *Hypatia* 20: 165–184.

Nagel, Thomas (1979) "Equality." In *Mortal Questions.* Cambridge: Cambridge University Press.

Nagel, Thomas, Cohen, Marshall, and Scanlon, Thomas (eds) (1980) *Marx, Justice and History.* Princeton: Princeton University Press.

Nussbaum, Martha (2011) "Perfectionist Liberalism and Political Liberalism." *Philosophy and Public Affairs* 39: 3–45.

Okin, Susan Moller (1989) "Reason and Feeling in Thinking about Justice." *Ethics* 99: 229–249.

Parfit, Derek (1997) "Equality and Priority." *Ratio* 10: 202–221.

Schacht, Richard (1971) *Alienation.* Garden City, NY: Anchor.

Schmidt am Busch, Hans-Cristoph (2013) "'The Egg of Columbus?' How Fourier's social theory exerted a significant (and problematic) influence on the formation of Marx's anthropology and social critique." *British Journal for the History of Philosophy,* vol. 21, no. 6.

Sen, Amartya (2006) "What Do We Want from a Theory of Justice?" *Journal of Philosophy* 103: 215–238.

Simmons, John (2010) "Ideal and Nonideal Theory." *Philosophy and Public Affairs* 38: 5–36.

Stephen, James Fitzjames (1990) *Liberty, Equality, Fraternity.* Chicago: University of Chicago Press.

Wood, Allen W. (1981) *Karl Marx.* London: Routledge & Kegan Paul.

# 27

# Challenges of Global and Local Misogyny

## CLAUDIA CARD

*Two main ideas motivate the Law of Peoples. One is that the great evils of human history – unjust war and oppression, religious persecution and the denial of liberty of conscience, starvation and poverty, not to mention genocide and mass murder – follow from political injustice, with its own cruelties and callousness. The other main idea . . . is that once the gravest forms of political injustice are eliminated by following just (or at least decent) social policies and establishing just (or at least decent) basic institutions, these great evils will eventually disappear.*

John Rawls, *The Law of Peoples*, 6–7

John Rawls's hypothesis that grave political injustices underlie the great social evils motivated his life's work, not just his last book. Evils discussed throughout his work include the atrocities of slavery and the Inquisition. Rawls's hypothesis implies that the worst evils that target women and girls will disappear once the gravest political injustices are gone. This idea is hard to assess. Misogynous evils are often rooted in failures of cooperation, enforcement, and perception, rather than in a political constitution, legislation, or foreign policy. Some sexism stems from background cultures not obviously incompatible with (liberal) just institutions. But the worst *evils* are not immune to institutional forces. Often women are left to defend themselves without organized help, not only within societies but in global traffic and in wars. That could change.

Perhaps Rawls was right that *if* the worst political injustices *were* eliminated, the great evils that have plagued humanity would disappear. Yet those worst injustices may not be eliminable unless people are willing to fight back using measures that include force and violence and are willing to do so in nonstate organizations when states fail them, as peoples go to war against unjust aggressors after less drastic measures have failed. If such nonstate organizations were understood to value reciprocity and to be capable of governing themselves by Rawlsian scruples, that thought might be less disturbing than it is otherwise apt to be.

If Rawls's ideas are to be a helpful resource for thinking about women's self-defense and mutual defense, that will probably not be through straightforward applications of his own projects. His projects were, first, what justice means in the basic structure of a society (*A Theory*

*A Companion to Rawls*, First Edition. Edited by Jon Mandle and David A. Reidy.
© 2014 John Wiley & Sons, Inc. Published 2016 by John Wiley & Sons, Inc.

*of Justice* and *Political Liberalism*), and second, what justice means in the foreign policy of a reasonably liberal well-ordered society (*The Law of Peoples*). Justice in foreign policy he divided into "ideal theory" for relations with other well-ordered peoples (governed by shared public conceptions of justice) and "nonideal theory" for relations with states not well-ordered. In nonideal theory we find his principles for war against outlaw states, which "refuse to comply with a reasonable Law of Peoples" (*LP*, 5). Rawls saw need for nonideal theory also within society but never developed that project. Perhaps the nonideal part of his Law of Peoples can be a resource for thinking about responding to evils when the subject is not state-centered, neither a society's basic structure nor its foreign policy. It is plausible that defense against great evils other than those of aggressive states should be governed by analogues of scruples that Rawlsian well-ordered societies observe in defending themselves against outlaw states.

This essay explores those hypotheses in relation to women's self-defense and mutual defense against evils of misogyny. It extrapolates and adapts to this case values, concepts, and methods from Rawls's life's work, especially his writing on war.

## Global and Local Misogyny

Despite its exemplary Constitution, the United States, like most societies, has laws, practices, customs, and attitudes that create environments hostile to women's and girls' development and thriving. In his later work Rawls explicitly addresses the family as a source of female oppression (*CP*, 587, 595–601). In response to protest by Susan Moller Okin (1989) that making parties in the Original Position heads of families left families internally opaque to claims of justice, Rawls changed that aspect of his theory. He also ventured the hypotheses that were women treated equally in the family, population growth would cease to be a major issue and that such a change would have a positive impact on unlawful immigration and the evils attendant upon current policies for dealing with it (*LP*, 9).

Special attention to the family by Rawls and a majority of his feminist critics and defenders is easily justified, as Okin argued, in terms of the early formative impact of families on the child's development of a sense of justice. Yet families are not a centerpiece of my concern. Family is not the stage for many of the worst forms of misogyny. Many victims of the worst misogyny are not particularly attached to men. These victims include women who do not rear children, women with careers (not necessarily as caregivers) and economic independence, and women who are intimate with women. In "Renaissance" Europe, women not attached to men – "dispensable" women, economically independent midwives and healers – were the most vulnerable to being burnt as witches (Daly 1978, 178–222). In India, widows were burnt. Today, many women who resist traditional expectations regarding marriage are vulnerable to "honor killings." Globally, it is very young women who are sold and enslaved for sexual service.[1]

Families are often sexist without being misogynous. "Misogyny" (literally, "woman-hating") is the term feminists apply to the most deeply hostile environments of and attitudes toward women and girls and to the cruelest wrongs to them/us, regardless of whether perpetrators harbor feelings of hatred. Sexism includes misogyny but encompasses a spectrum of bad attitudes and behaviors, including male arrogance, male-centeredness (not only in men), sex discrimination, and female subordination. Not all sexism is culpable. Misogyny tends to be highly culpable and grossly oppressive.

By "misogyny," I have in mind evils perpetrated with aggressive (often armed) use of force and violence against women: rape and domestic battering, kidnap for sexual slavery, forced prostitution, "honor killing," stoning, simulated suicide by burning, widow burning, and horrors without special names, such as throwing acid in a woman's face to disfigure her. Most global are the overlapping evils of rape (including forced prostitution) and domestic battering. More local are the systematic, irreversible, and disabling mutilation of girls (as in clitoridectomy and infibulation), coerced sati (widow burning, not altogether of the past), and "honor killing."

## Evils

My work on evil has been motivated by concerns to identify evils and avoid the perpetration of further evils in responding to them. On what I call "the atrocity paradigm," evils are reasonably foreseeable intolerable harms produced by inexcusable wrongs (Card 2002, 3–26; 2010, 3–35). There is no need for malicious motives, such as sadism or spite. A practice is evil when there is morally no excuse for it and acting in accord with it foreseeably does intolerable harm.

Not all injustices are evils, only those that are inexcusable and do intolerable harm. What makes harms intolerable is not altogether subjective. A reasonable conception of intolerable harm is that it is a significant deprivation of basics ordinarily required for a life (or a death) to be decent for the person whose life (or death) it is. Such basics include nontoxic air, water, and food; sleep; the ability to move one's limbs; the ability to make choices and act on some of them; freedom from severe and unremitting pain and from debilitating humiliation; affective bonds with others; a sense of one's human worth. Although not exhaustive, that list is enough to show that intolerable harm does not totally depend on individual preferences. Intolerable harm interferes with one's ability to function decently as a human being.

A wrong can be inexcusable in two ways, which I call "metaphysical" and "moral." There is metaphysically no excuse when there was no diminished capacity for choice in the wrongdoer (no insanity or other relevant disability, for example). There is morally no excuse when no significant morally good reasons provide a partial defense. When there is some moral excuse, there are significant reasons in favor of the deed that carry moral weight, although not enough to justify it on the whole. Nonmoral reasons may favor the deed. And a reason that might carry moral weight for some deeds may carry none for others. An inexcusable deed or practice is morally indefensible. On the atrocity paradigm, evils are inexcusable in both ways, metaphysically and morally.

On these understandings, rape, domestic battering, and murder (as in "honor killing," simulated suicide, and coerced sati) are generally evils, as social practices and in individual instances. Disfiguring and disabling women or girls can be evils as well, depending on forms, contexts, and consequences. Stoning, like burning, tortures many victims to death, and is especially evil.[2]

## Principles for Individuals

What uses of force and violence are justifiable for defense by women against evils of misogyny? I ask "what is justifiable?" rather than "what is just?" because, as Rawls noted in class lectures, full justice may be unrealizable when currently available options are shaped by past

474

wrongful choices. When no fully just options remain, it may be possible to reduce the amount or seriousness of deprivations of justice, or to contain them, prevent spreading or worsening. A best choice can be the lesser of unjust options or the creation of options that set a course for future justice. Even a best option can leave what Bernard Williams called "remainders," including injustices that can never be adequately redressed (1974, 179).

Uses of force and violence include matters of individual choice and matters of policy or practices involving cooperation. Rawls's theory of justice for society's basic structure includes distinct principles for these different cases: two principles for social practices or institutions and one principle (fair play) for individuals. In *LP*, the distinction between justifying a practice or policy and justifying a particular choice seems not to figure, unless in the "supreme emergency exemption" if that exemption is understood as an unpunishable violation of policy (rather than a policy itself). Rawls's theorizing about the Law of Peoples remains at the level of policies and practices. His principle of fair play presupposes principles at that level. And so the question arises: how are individuals to approximate fairness in the absence of relevant social practices, institutions, or organizations for self-defense?

At the root of Rawls's idea of fair play is the idea of reciprocity. Rawls's principle of fair play, incorporating reciprocity, is borrowed from H.L.A. Hart, who described it as a "mutuality of restrictions" (1955, 185; cf. *TJ*, 96). According to that principle, it is *sufficient* for one's obligation to follow rules of a just practice that one freely accepted benefits of others having done so. This principle leaves much unspecified. It does not say what is *necessary*. It does not say there is no obligation if the practice is unjust (would that depend on how unjust?), if one lacked choice about accepting benefits (would it depend on the nature of the benefits?), or if one did not benefit although it was reasonable to expect that one would, nor does it say how many must cooperate in order to generate duties to reciprocate. It is unclear how much women would be obligated by accepting (without exactly being forced to do so) benefits of existing practices and institutions.

Consider the following true stories, on which I have written elsewhere (Card 2010, 141–145). One is that of Francine Hughes of the "burning bed" who in 1977 poured gasoline on her sleeping former husband and ignited it, killing him, after years of being battered by him despite her efforts to enlist law enforcement protection (McNulty 1980). The other is that of Inez García who in 1974 pursued and shot with intent to kill at two men who had just raped her. Right after the rape (but before the shooting), she received a phone call from one of them warning her to leave the area and threatening her otherwise. She killed one; the other escaped (Salter 1976; Wood 1976).

What these survivors did may have been justified but it is not likely to be described as fair or just (however deserved their actions). Neither does it seem fair or just to evaluate their choices simply by Rawls's principle of fair play, although one could apply it as follows. They had benefited somewhat by living under the rule of law, which argues in favor of letting courts, not victims, decide perpetrators' fates. But the law also failed to protect them well against rape and battery. A more appropriate standard for evaluating their responses might be whether they chose the lesser of injustices. Would it not be a worse injustice to let such evils continue unopposed by anything more than incompetent or unwilling law enforcement agencies? Clearly, there is need for creative thinking on how, using the apparatus of law, to combat such incompetence and unwillingness. That process is slow. Women are poorly represented in it. Meanwhile, many endure irreversible harm or are at risk of being killed. Of options available to them, which represent the lesser injustices?

475

There are also questions of justice regarding how others should respond to what the women did. States may have no choice but to charge and try them for murder. But how should women respond? One, an attorney, responded by successfully defending García.

Hughes and García were each found guilty of murder, with the verdicts overturned on appeal. Hughes (in Michigan) was declared not guilty by reason of insanity. García (in California) was found justified in self-defense. None of these verdicts may be totally satisfying. If "guilty" seems unjust to the women, "not guilty" raises the question whether individuals should be allowed to execute assailants who have not been tried and are not at that moment engaged in an assault. It is tempting to adapt John Stuart Mill's observation: "If society lets any considerable number of its members grow up mere children . . . society has itself to blame for the consequences" (2003, 153). This is interesting from Mill: an argument not from utility but from fairness. Adapting his reasoning, we might argue that a society that fails to protect any considerable number of its members has itself to blame when they do what they judge needful to protect themselves. That does not imply that they act justly. It does suggest where the greater injustice might lie.

## Containing Unavoidable Injustice

In war some agents confront options none of which is fully just. Rawls's LP contains his only extended discussion of war. Here, he invokes the idea of the social contract by way of a "second original position" (LP, 32) to yield a hypothetical agreement that representatives of liberal peoples could make with each other, the content of which could be agreed to also by representatives of nonliberal decent peoples situated within their own appropriate original position. The agreement includes principles for engaging with states that are not well-ordered, including outlaw states. These, Rawls's principles of war, might be best conceived as principles for containing injustice, principles "of" justice only because motivated by concern for justice, hope for future justice, and values underlying justice.

Rawls's approach to war seems actually to respond to these questions: in a people's defense against unjust aggression, (1) what scruples best contain, reduce, or at least do not aggravate injustice? (2) what principles pave the way for outlaw states to become well-ordered so that relationships of justice with them are possible? Rawls uses the language of "just war" (LP, 90 ff.), which sounds as though he thinks war can be just, whether in execution or in cause. Yet that terminology may persist only because of tradition. Both "just war theory" and Rawls's principles are for the conduct of war by societies that value justice. It is consistent with Rawls's best insights to acknowledge that the most to be hoped for in the conduct of war is containment of injustice and movement toward justice. Principles of "just war" then become scruples for managing war's inevitable injustices, identifying the lesser of unjust options and paving the way for (at least, not putting obstacles to) a future in which no states are outlaws.

Suppose we approach Rawls's thoughts on war and justice with the following two ideas. First, there is in reality no such thing as true justice in fighting a war, even if its cause is just; rather, there are degrees of injustice. Second, some wars need to be fought because the alternatives are morally worse. What is justifiable depends on alternatives in a way that what is just does not. Justice is determined more abstractly by relationships that are not always realizable. Fighting a war when alternatives are worse can be a choice of the lesser of unjust options, attempting at least to contain injustice and ideally set a stage for future justice.

So understood, Rawls's thoughts on war are suggestive for addressing a "war" on women.

## "War" on Women

Mary Kaldor argues that the "new wars" – since the Cold War – " involve a blurring of distinctions between war (usually defined as violence between states or organized political groups for political motives), organized crime . . . and large-scale violations of human rights" (2001, 2). Extending her reasoning, one can argue that many ancient massive violations of human rights warrant classification as "wars" at least as much as the Cold War, drug wars, and wars on terrorism. Such classifications change (blur) the meaning of "war" – a price of the moral recognition of relevant analogies. Millennia of global misogyny bear enough analogies to hostilities, aims, and consequences of wars perpetrated by heads of state to warrant speaking of a "war" (or "wars") of aggression against women, some of it consciously organized, some coordinated by way of norms internalized early by individuals. In these ways, sex wars resemble race wars. A decade before Kaldor's work, Harvard Medical School psychiatrist Judith Lewis Herman wrote, "There is a war between the sexes. Rape victims, battered women, and sexually abused children are its casualties. Hysteria is the combat neurosis of the sex war" (1992, 32). She compared female "hysteria" to "shell shock" in soldiers during World War I. Both today are recognized as posttraumatic stress disorder. "War between the sexes," however, suggests a more balanced distribution of responsibility for aggression than we find. For the most part, women have not fought back very aggressively. War *between* the sexes would be progress. What we find is better described as a war on women.

The aggression has been mainly by men (not without female support), and groups instituted by men, against females on account of their sex. As with outlaw states, this aggression is not justifiable self-defense, despite some rhetoric of "honor." It is to advance and secure prudential and other interests that lack moral grounding. Collaborating women are also victims. Some male resisters become victims. Others profit but are not aggressive. Some are bystanders. Some beneficiaries are not very aware that their profits come at women's expense. Those aware who choose to "do nothing" are collaborators; those unaware but who should be are at least complicit. Many men in these categories are intimate with and feel benevolent toward women. The "war" is not by all men as hostile aggressors against all women. Aggressors, however, are mainly men and victims mainly women.

There are environments where women are less likely to be targets of aggressive violence based on their sex. Some men would not knowingly advance themselves at women's expense, let alone do so violently. Still, women court danger when they venture outside those environments. And many men are not very aware of when they advance at women's expense.

Misogynous evils mostly lack national boundaries. With the exception of certain war crimes, such as mass rape, they tend not to victimize entire peoples. Nor are perpetrators always a people. But peoples are guilty of failing to do well at protecting women and girls. Eventually, many women, individually and in groups, confront needs to defend themselves.

Most misogynous practices do not fit the conventional model of war Rawls has in mind in his Law of Peoples. His parties to war are well-ordered peoples and outlaw states, not individuals.[3] Opposing aggressive outlaw states are well-ordered peoples, whose societies are relatively compliant with a shared public conception of justice. So described, well-ordered peoples sound innocent and clearly distinct from their enemies. Women are seldom innocent. They are often sleeping with the enemy. Their loss of innocence is frequently traceable to misogynous evils they have suffered. Many inhabit something like what Primo Levi called "gray zones," in which victims become complicit in the evils from which they, too, suffer (1989, 36–69; Card 2002, 211–234).

Well-ordered peoples, however, are less innocent than they sound when described as above. Even "relatively well-ordered peoples" (*LP*, 89) contain and tolerate what are for women "outlaw environments" in which a commitment to justice for women and girls does not exist or is not very effective.

"Outlaw" here does not mean what gender critics have meant. It does not describe rebels against conventional gender practices. On the contrary, it describes conventional gender practices that are deeply unjust, "noncompliant," as Rawls would put it, with principles of justice.

If global misogyny is not unproblematically conceived as martial, neither are domestic misogynous evils unproblematic as causes for armed humanitarian intervention. What people does such a good job of protecting its females that it would be justified in militarily intervening for that purpose into the affairs of another? Such "glasshouses" questions are raised about humanitarian intervention generally. In response, some propose that international bodies such as the United Nations be given sole power to authorize interventions. But glasshouses questions can be asked of international bodies. At issue are long track records of failing to protect women and girls against inexcusable intolerable harms, not inevitable failures due to error or ignorance.

## Ideal Contracts, Original Positions, and Hypothetical Agreements

Despite analogies between a war where parties are peoples or states and a "war" on women, there are obvious disanalogies. So, I have heretofore put the analogous "war" in scare quotes (dropped hereafter). Fighting back in a war on women is like fighting a war on terrorism in which the terrorists are not states. Some of it *is* war on terrorism that targets women. Unlike states, the sexes are not agents. The sexes might be regarded as groups in virtue of shared interests. But the sexes do not *act* as groups (although subgroups act). Peoples at war, in its conventional sense, act through representatives. Outlaw states act, although they do not represent their peoples. There are no representatives of the sexes, considered as such. Were we to employ Rawls's imaginative device of a veil of ignorance for choosing principles to govern women's responses to misogynous evils, the parties would have to represent individuals, as in Rawls's first use of the idea of the "original position" (hereafter, OP). So, why not simply leave it a task of parties in Rawls's first and second uses of the OP to propose principles for responding to misogyny? Is it helpful to use the OP to generate principles specifically to guide women's responses to misogyny? I will suggest a way that it is.

It should, indeed, be a task of parties in both of Rawls's OPs to propose principles governing responses to misogynous crimes. The Law of Peoples includes the principle: "Peoples are to honor human rights" (*LP*, 37). But there is no enforcement provision other than humanitarian intervention, the particulars of which are not given. Parties in the first OP would want women protected, too. But how would their reasoning go?

When the task is nonideal theory for within a society, parties in the OP must know that their society may be permeated even in law enforcement by misogyny and that many may in reality not be committed to principles reasonable to choose behind the veil. Do circumstances of justice, then, obtain? How should parties conceive the point of their task?

It might be thought that *well-ordered* peoples would not have that problem. But misogynous evils are not confined to outlaw states, burdened states, and benevolent dictatorships. The division of societies into those well-ordered and those not sounds simpler than the reality. Being well-ordered is a matter of degree in how well-governed a people is, how well-developed, well-applied, widely shared, and comprehensive its public conception of justice. Rawls refers to "relatively well-ordered peoples" (*LP*, 89). No society is thoroughly well-ordered. "Relatively" does not even imply "very." Misogynous subcultures exist within many a relatively well-ordered people as do areas of conduct in which an otherwise relatively well-ordered people is not at all well-ordered.

Individuals, too, can be inconsistent. People who try to be guided by justice toward those they respect often treat others as inferiors. This phenomenon applies to race and gender. Many men in relatively well-ordered societies are not motivated to grant women the respect they grant other men (or, *some* other men).

So the question arises: whom would parties in the OP represent when proposing (nonideal theoretical) principles to address such evils as those of misogyny? In what Rawls calls his second use of the OP, parties represent only well-ordered peoples, not outlaw states or burdened societies. Analogously, in Rawls's first OP, if the task were to choose principles for a *partially* compliant society, parties should represent not *all* individuals but only those of presumable compliance. They need to know roughly the collective strength of that group to estimate how much compliance to expect on the other side of the veil, in order to assess whether circumstances of justice obtain, so they can set a realistic task.

Rawls understands circumstances of justice as conditions under which cooperation is both useful and necessary: everyone is vulnerable but no one so powerful as to be able to dominate the rest for long. In ideal theory, parties in the first OP know this about their society. In nonideal theory, must parties know that noncompliance is not so widespread that cooperation is hopeless? Is that enough to give point to their task for parties who know they might turn out to be victims of well-entrenched misogyny? What if cooperation *has been* hopeless? Might the task then shift to proposing principles for coalition building, to ground hope of sufficient cooperation? In any case, victims can be justified as a matter of self-respect in fighting even hopeless battles.[4] If they care about self-respect, presumably they care about principles for fighting even hopeless battles.

Rawls's use of the contract idea in his sketch of a Law of Peoples does not receive the elaboration of reasoning that we find in *A Theory of Justice*. Perhaps the contract idea is less useful for nonideal theory. More interestingly, perhaps the parties' task changes.

Something like Nietzsche's view of early justice is suggestive for nonideal theory: "Justice on this elementary level is the good will among parties of approximately equal power to come to terms with one another, to reach an 'understanding' by means of a settlement – and to *compel* parties of lesser power to reach a settlement among themselves" (Nietzsche 1967, 70–71). Nietzsche, unlike Rawls, presents the compact as historical, not hypothetical, and as among those who know they are powerful, not among parties behind a veil who may know only that cooperation is not hopeless. But Nietzsche also presents his speculative compact as among parties of good will, suggesting that it may not be merely a modus vivendi, and as including provision for coercing others. A Rawlsian hypothetical contract for nonideal theory might likewise be conceived as among parties of goodwill and as including principles for using force against those whose goodwill cannot be presumed. This is how Rawls does conceive it for the case of war.

Rawls admits to a certain agnosticism regarding the likelihood of success in implementing a Law of Peoples and, ultimately, bringing about a world in which all societies are members of a Society of Well-Ordered Peoples. What sustains him is the human possibility of success here. This allows him hope. His agnosticism may derive from doubts about whether circumstances of justice obtain at the global level. His hope may be more an aspect of his nontheistic religion than a sociologically grounded stance (*A Brief Inquiry*, 261–269).

Rawls does not assume that the basic structure of society and relations among peoples are the only subjects of justice. But they are the only ones he addresses. Defense of women should doubtless be incorporated into justice for both subjects. Given the histories of peoples, however, that will not much encourage women. A more promising idea might be to seek circumstances of justice among women, or groups of women, or try to cultivate circumstances in which cooperation among women would be fruitful (as it surely seems necessary).

Women and girls do not form a society. They form a kind of group, joined (if not united) across the boundaries of peoples by common and overlapping interests. This group is not yet capable of action, although subgroups are. What social units are appropriate subjects of principles for the self-defense and mutual defense of women and girls against evils of misogyny? Feminist groups have not achieved stability, let alone membership, comparable to states. An interesting approach embraced by radical feminists of the 1970s, exemplified earlier in Virginia Woolf's "society of outsiders," is separatism. Woolf was moved in her last, most radical book to have her female outsider proclaim, "in fact, as a woman I have no country. As a woman I want no country. As a woman my country is the whole world" (1938, 109). Women need principles for forming social units of defense against global and local misogyny. Meanwhile, women need principles now for defending themselves and each other as individuals.

## Principles for Individual Self-Defense in a War on Women

Instead of going much into the reasoning of parties in his second use of the OP (which generates the Law of Peoples), Rawls sets out a list of principles, including principles for war. Let us consider how adaptable those war principles are to the case of women, when their case is not subsumed under the basic structure of the society of a well-ordered people or its foreign relations.

Following just war theory, Rawls begins his discussion of war by first taking up justifications for going to war (*jus ad bellum*) and states a version of the principle of just cause, in two parts. The first part is negative: "No state has a right to war in the pursuit of its *rational* as opposed to its *reasonable* interests" (*LP*, 91, emphasis in original). His distinction between rational and reasonable interests roughly tracks Immanuel Kant's distinction between merely prudential interests and morally grounded interests.[5] Reasonable interests take others into account; merely rational interests need not. The second part of Rawls's *jus ad bellum* principle is positive: "*any* society that is non-aggressive and that honors human rights has the right of self-defense" (*LP*, 92, emphasis in original). Later he mentions humanitarian intervention but does not elaborate or clarify.

Adapting Rawls's just cause principle to the case of women requires distinguishing women's merely prudential (rational) interests from morally grounded (reasonable) interests and altering the part about a nonaggressive society. The first part of the principle is satisfied when the interests protected are the morally grounded interests of security and freedom. Women are not justified in resorting to violence over conflicts regarding forms of discrimination that hamper their pursuit of merely rational (prudential) interests (say, merely personal ambitions) that are not at the same time reasonable interests (morally grounded). In the second part of the principle, a plausible substitute for "society that is nonaggressive" might be: "one who lacks a history of unjust aggression and whose principles would not permit it" so that the principle becomes: Anyone who lacks a history of unjust aggression, whose principles would not permit it, and who honors human rights has the right of self-defense. Thus, complicity under duress need not negate a justification for self-defense.

Next Rawls offers six principles for the conduct of war (*jus in bello*). The first states that "the aim" is "a just and lasting peace among peoples, and especially with the people's present enemy" (*LP*, 94). Adapting this principle, the plausible aim would be a just and lasting peace between (among) the sexes. But the part about peace with one's current enemies is not clearly adaptable. When the parties are not group agents, one's most obvious current enemies are the individuals one is most likely to harm deliberately in war. Perhaps the aim should be reconceived for both the Law of Peoples and the case of women as a peace that paves the way to reducing significantly the injustices that led to war.

Rawls's second *jus in bello* principle is: "Well-ordered peoples do not wage war against each other . . . but only against non-well-ordered states whose expansionist aims threaten the security and free institutions of well-ordered regimes and bring about the war" (*LP*, 94). This principle seems redundant, given the *jus ad bellum* principle: well-ordered peoples are not aggressively expansionist. Here what Rawls may want to emphasize is that well-ordered peoples resolve conflicts among themselves even over *reasonable* interests without violence. An analogue for women might be that women governed by a sense of justice resolve conflicts with individuals who are not outlaws even over *reasonable* interests without violence. We need, then, to define "outlaw individuals." A plausible approximation is "individuals who are prepared to *use violence*, in a society that fails to restrain them from doing so, in pursuit of interests that are not reasonable."

Rawls's third principle distinguishes degrees of responsibility among three groups: "the outlaw state's leaders and officials, its soldiers, and its civilian population" (*LP*, 94). Adapting it, we can distinguish levels of responsibility for aggressive violence against women. Parallel distinctions might be those who have greatest control over whether, how, and what kinds of aggression are perpetrated (compare "leaders and officials"), those who are instruments of aggression but lack such control (compare "soldiers" who are not leaders or officials), and those under the authority of members of the first group but who are not instruments of violence (compare "civilians"). Further distinctions may be needed regarding bystanders and beneficiaries. Rawls's fourth principle is: "Well-ordered peoples must respect, so far as possible, the human rights of the members of the other side, both civilians and soldiers" (*LP*, 96). This principle seems straightforwardly adaptable and even to follow from the fifth principle.[6]

Rawls's fifth principle is that well-ordered peoples are to foreshadow during war the kind of peace they aim for and the kind of relationships they seek. This duty, he notes, falls largely on leaders and officials. Although there are no current analogues of leaders, the basic idea is important for women. What kinds of relationships with men should women aim for and foreshadow? Women have been steered into relationships that give men constant intimate access to them, often to the detriment of peace. The relationship lacking has usually been one of adequate respect. Women should try to foreshadow a peace in which men have less of that intimate access and are more respectful. This idea rules out sexual seduction by women as a war tactic.

Rawls's sixth principle is that "practical means-end reasoning must always have a restricted role in judging the appropriateness of an action or policy" (*LP*, 96). His intent seems to be to emphasize that the preceding principles restrict the role of means-end reasoning in war. In his gloss on this principle Rawls invokes the exception of "supreme emergency," discussing it only briefly, relying for illustration on Nazism's threats to "civilized life everywhere" (*LP*, 98–99). Like ticking bomb torture, "supreme emergency" is a dangerous idea, liable to gross abuse. If it has validity nevertheless, we should appreciate that it undercuts the human rights of the fourth principle and the "foreshadowing peace" of the fifth. As applied to women's resistance, "supreme emergency" measures, which violate normal restrictions on means–end reasoning, should be not only needed quickly but reasonably judged necessary and, under the circumstances, sufficient for an objective of supreme importance transcending that of any individual and limited in severity by the severity of the evils to be prevented. Still, it is good to be skeptical of the idea of a "supreme emergency exemption."

Insofar as Rawls's principles say not what is *justifiable* but only what is not, they are scruples. Only the second part of the just cause principle and the "supreme emergency exemption" (not a principle but an exception) are explicitly about what is justifiable. The unnamed elephant in the vicinity is the use of force and violence to kill and maim. The idea is that killing and maiming can be justifiable if these principles are observed. Adapting that conclusion to women's resistance yields the idea that killing or maiming perpetrators of the evils of misogyny can likewise be justifiable if analogues of Rawls's principles are observed.

Did the actions of Hughes and García fall within those limits? Did they avoid doing evil in response to evils they faced? They inflicted harm clearly intolerable from their victims' points of view. But were they justified? And if not, had they any moral or metaphysical excuse?

Consider just cause. If the interests defended were the morally grounded interests in security and freedom, not some merely prudential interest (or, say, an interest in revenge), they satisfied the first part of this principle. If the women lacked histories of unjust aggression, were not committed to unjust aggression, and honored human rights, they satisfied the second part. Of course, what is at issue is whether their responses failed to honor human rights. Perhaps it is sufficient for this principle that they lacked histories of commitment to aggressive injustice or of failing to honor human rights.

If Hughes and García are regarded as ordinary civilians (as the courts regarded them), their acts are difficult to construe as self-defense, given how assault and battery are defined in criminal law. Hughes's batterer was asleep. García's rapists had done their deed; she was free to go. But military combat rules are reasonably more permissive. Soldiers can attack at night when the enemy might be asleep. They do not have to retreat whenever retreat is possible. Hughes and García defended against *patterns* of violence, not simply particular episodes. Neither could depend on state protection. Regarding them as more like military combatants than like civilians seems fair. Another way to look at Hughes is that she defended herself against a coerced relationship, which did not dissolve when the enforcer slept.

Were their aims a lasting peace with those who currently terrorize women? The analogy breaks down if the peace at issue is between groups at war. Hughes was not fighting batterers in general, nor was García fighting rapists generally. Each fought only her own assailant(s). Nor was either fighting as a member of a group. Yet, their deeds were potentially precedent setting, sending the message that men cannot be confident of being able to get away with misogynous violence, a message compatible with peace. Whether that is the dominant message depends also on whether women who do likewise are exonerated. Most women who respond as they did go to prison, many for the rest of their lives. Still, the first message remains partially valid (the men killed did not get away with it) and might have a salutary effect.

Did either woman fail to make relevant distinctions regarding responsibility? Hughes tried first to enlist help from law enforcement. Although García succeeded only in killing the 300-pound man who stood guard while the other assaulted her, she tried to kill both and regretted only that she did not succeed in killing the other man. (He was never charged with a crime.) Neither woman harmed others.

Was either woman guilty of a human rights violation? Did Hughes violate the right not to be tortured? As her batterer was asleep in a drunken stupor, there may be no way to know what he felt. She should have been aware of the danger that she might be torturing him.[7] Although she was protecting children also, her objective was, I would say, insufficiently important and transcendent to make plausible a "supreme emergency exemption," that is (here), a violation of restrictions on means-end reasoning that proscribe torture. Further, her incendiary deed, although sufficient, may have exceeded what was needful, a conclusion calling for judgment regarding her long-range options. In any case, it appears not to have been premeditated, which enabled Michigan to find her temporarily insane.

García took advantage of the fact that her rapists would not expect her to pursue them armed. Had they expected that, they would have been armed and she would likely have been the one killed. Given women's socialization to nonviolence and failures in law enforcement, the rapists' expectation was epistemically justified. As combatants in a war on women, they had no moral title to rely on that expectation.

Neither woman's response seems, on these reckonings, inexcusably wrong, morally or metaphysically. In the absence of nongovernmental organizations for defense of women, individuals like these survivors are all we have to consider. But ultimately the more important issue is organizing for effective use of force and violence in women's defense.

## Guerrilla Feminism

In the 1970s and 1980s guerrilla feminists in the United States carried to another level defense of women against misogyny. Typical tactics were property assaults – public graffiti, physical destruction of pornography, trashing pornography shops. There may have been organized violence against targeted individuals. In 1989, the journal *Lesbian Ethics* carried an interesting piece titled "Guerilla Feminism," consisting of information about actions in Massachusetts "from newspaper clippings and other material sent to *LE* anonymously" ("Guerilla Feminism" 1989, 79–90). Reports of violence against persons appear in a concluding paragraph:

In Iowa, a huge group of women kidnapped a man who had raped dozens of women. They castrated him in a cornfield. Closer by, a man who had raped at least 10 women was captured by a band of women. They stamped 'rapist' all over his body. They super-glued his hands to his penis and his balls to his legs. (1989, 90)

This is vigilantism, or freedom-fighting, depending on your perspective.

A pair of short stories by Melanie Kaye/Kantrowitz, "The Day We Didn't Declare War" and "The Day We Did" suggests that more drastic violence against persons may have been contemplated (1990, 85–96), even implemented. The first story describes an organization calling itself "The Godmothers." The Godmothers made services available to women who were being assaulted in their homes. This organization put new and better locks on doors, sent pairs of Godmothers to stay with women in their homes, and put up warning signs on doors that the assailant was being monitored by The Godmothers. And they did monitor assailants. The second story describes a formal meeting at which Godmothers entertained more drastic measures in response to series of rapes in a local park after police failed to arrest anyone. That story ends without revealing what the Godmothers decided. In a later collection of essays, Kaye/Kantrowitz wrote, "In Portland we formed a group called the Godmothers who would protect battered women in their own homes" (1992, 48).

Women in the self-defense movement and in a group called WAR (Women against Rape) organized in many cities to teach women and girls martial arts through groups like Chimera Self Defense, which has active branches today. Chimera was formed in the 1970s by women with black belts in martial arts who were getting raped on Chicago streets. Physical skill, they concluded, was only part of self-defense. Their courses consist of 50 percent attitude training.

These are small-scale organizations compared to political states. But like the Portland Godmothers and guerrilla feminists of Iowa and Massachusetts, they demonstrate sensitivity to reciprocity. When men are trained for combat and taught how to kill, is it not justifiable for women to form groups to teach those skills systematically to women, who might need them for protection against men so trained? Might it be justifiable to teach women to notice when breaking a law might save life or limb (perhaps one's own) without endangering the innocent? Such projects might be regarded as supplements, rather than alternatives, to projects for improving the law, although tension between these kinds of projects is likely.

Yet, a serious issue remains. Civil law has trials to determine who is guilty of an offense, and states have international norms for identifying combatants. Nonstate organizations have only their own relatively subjective improvisations for identifying the enemy, which can make their identifications and subsequent targetings seem to others unpredictable or indiscriminate.[8] The difficulty of identifying enemies fairly is a general problem for terrorists, insurgents, and all who would engage them in scruple-governed combat. Rawls's just war principles need to be supplemented with further principles and discussion to address that issue.

# Notes

Earlier drafts of this essay were read and commented on by Adam Pham, Harry Brighouse, Jeffrey Reiman, Eric Senseman, Regina Schouten, and the editors of this book. I am grateful for their suggestions and also to Jeffrey Reiman for sharing with me in advance his review of my book *Confronting Evils* (2010), in which he comments on my discussion of Hughes and García.

1   "An estimated *2.5 million people* are in forced labour (including sexual exploitation) at any given time as a result of trafficking"; "The majority of trafficking victims are *between 18 and 24 years* of age"; "43% of victims are used for *forced commercial sexual exploitation*, of whom 98 per cent are women and girls" (emphases in the original). For these and more statistics on human trafficking and the proportions of victims who are women and girls, see UN GIFT (Global Initiative to Fight Global Trafficking), at http://www.unglobalcompact.org/docs/issues_doc/labour/Forced_labour/HUMAN_TRAFFICKING_-_THE_FACTS_-_final.pdf (accessed May 2013).
2   A detailed account of a 1986 stoning is in Sahebjam 1990.
3   On why Rawls reserves the term "peoples" for liberal and decent societies and does not apply it to outlaw states, see helpful discussion by Philip Pettit in Martin and Reidy 2006, esp. 42–48.
4   I owe this thought to Richard Mohr's work on gays and dignity (1988, 315–337).
5   For Kant's distinction between prudence and morality, see the first and second sections of his *Groundwork of the Metaphysics of Morals* (Kant 1996, 49–93).
6   It is puzzling that Rawls mentions the human rights only of civilians and soldiers, apparently omitting leaders and officials. Perhaps he was subsuming leaders and officials under "soldiers"?
7   Thanks to Jeffrey Reiman for noting that the possibility that she was torturing him was something she should have known.
8   I discuss this and other issues raised by terrorism in Card 2010, 123–148, which discusses Hughes and García.

## Works by Rawls, with Abbreviations

*A Brief Inquiry into the Meaning of Sin and Faith*, with "On My Religion" (*BI*), ed. Thomas Nagel. Cambridge, MA: Harvard University Press, 2009.
*Collected Papers* (*CP*), ed. Samuel Freeman. Cambridge, MA: Harvard University Press, 1999.
*The Law of Peoples* (*LP*). Cambridge, MA: Harvard University Press, 1999.
*Political Liberalism* (*PL*), expanded edn. New York: Columbia University Press, 2005.
*A Theory of Justice* (*TJ*), rev. edn. Cambridge, MA: Harvard University Press, 1999.

## Other References

Card, Claudia (2002) *The Atrocity Paradigm: A Theory of Evils*. New York: Oxford University Press.
Card, Claudia (2010) *Confronting Evils: Terrorism, Torture, Genocide*. Cambridge: Cambridge University Press.
Daly, Mary (1978) *Gyn/Ecology: The Metaethics of Radical Feminism*. Boston: Beacon Press.
"Guerilla Feminism" (1989) *Lesbian Ethics* 3(3): 79–90.
Hart, H.L.A. (1955) "Are There Any Natural Rights?" *Philosophical Review* 64(2): 175–191.
Herman, Judith Lewis (1992) *Trauma and Recovery*. New York: Basic Books.
Kaldor, Mary (2001) *New and Old Wars: Organized Violence in a Global Era*. Stanford: Stanford University Press.
Kant, Immanuel (1996) *Practical Philosophy*, ed. and trans. Mary J. Gregor. 2nd edn. Cambridge: Cambridge University Press.
Kaye/Kantrowitz, Melanie (1990) *My Jewish Face and Other Stories*. San Francisco: Spinsters/Aunt Lute Books.
Kaye/Kantrowitz, Melanie (1992) *The Issue Is Power: Essays on Women, Jews, Violence and Resistance*. San Francisco: Aunt Lute Books.
Levi, Primo (1989) *The Drowned and the Saved*, trans. Raymond Rosenthal. New York: Vintage.

Martin, Rex and Reidy, David (eds) (2006) *Rawls's Law of Peoples: A Realistic Utopia?* Oxford: Wiley-Blackwell.

McNulty, Faith (1980) *The Burning Bed.* New York: Harcourt Brace Jovanovich.

Mill, John Stuart (2003) *Utilitarianism and On Liberty,* ed. Mary Warnock. 2nd edn. Oxford: Blackwell.

Mohr, Richard (1988) *Gays/Justice.* New York: Columbia University Press.

Nietzsche, Friedrich (1967) *On the Genealogy of Morals,* trans. Walter Kaufmann and R.J. Hollingdale. New York: Vintage.

Okin, Susan Moller (1989) *Justice, Gender, and the Family.* New York: Basic Books.

Pettit, Philip (2006) "Rawls's Peoples." In Rex Martin and David Reidy (eds), *Rawls's Law of Peoples: A Realistic Utopia?* (38–55). Oxford: Wiley-Blackwell.

Sahebjam, Freidoune (1990) *The Stoning of Soraya M.,* trans. Richard Seaver. New York: Arcade.

Salter, Kenneth (1976) *The Trial of Inez García.* Berkeley: Editorial Justa.

Williams, Bernard (1974) *Problems of the Self.* Cambridge: Cambridge University Press.

Wood, Jim (1976) *The Rape of Inez García.* New York: Putnam.

Woolf, Virginia (1938) *Three Guineas.* New York: Harcourt, Brace & World.

# 28

# Critical Theory and Habermas

## KENNETH BAYNES

## 1. Introduction

This essay explores the thesis that Rawls's political philosophy – and indeed his philosophical orientation more broadly – stands much closer to the tradition of critical theory (from Horkheimer to Habermas) than it does to some more recent trends in normative moral and political theory.[1] This might seem surprising since Rawls is usually viewed as a liberal egalitarian who defends the liberal democratic welfare state, while the tradition of critical theory has generally rejected such an institutional arrangement as inadequate for realizing social justice. However, while I think this already mischaracterizes Rawls's first-order normative views – in which he expresses deep reservations about the possibilities of the liberal democratic welfare state – my primary concern in this essay is with Rawls's broader views about how political philosophy should be conducted. (See *TJ*, 241–242; *JF*, 135–137; Krouse and McPherson 1988.) Political philosophy – even at the level of ideal theory – must accept a socially situated and "fact-sensitive" description of its task, even if that does not mean thereby abandoning any claim to objectivity or truth suitably interpreted. "Conceptions of justice must be justified by the conditions of our life as we know it or not at all" (*TJ*, 398). This observation reveals Rawls's proximity at a deep level to what is called "immanent critique" in the tradition of critical theory. It suggests that both the resources for normative critique as well as the constructive aims and goals of critique are limited by judgments and assumptions about what is feasible – "taking people as we know them and laws as they might be," to borrow Rousseau's memorable phrase (Rousseau 2007, 41). For Rawls this idea of immanent critique is expressed most clearly in his conception of philosophy as the defense of a "reasonable faith" and normative theory as the sketch of a "realistic utopia" (*LHMP*, 324; *LP*, 4). But as a general conception of practical philosophy it can also be found throughout his work.

In another sense, the claim about the continuities between Rawls and critical theory should not be so surprising since both are deeply indebted to the critical philosophy of Kant.

*A Companion to Rawls*, First Edition. Edited by Jon Mandle and David A. Reidy.
© 2014 John Wiley & Sons, Inc. Published 2016 by John Wiley & Sons, Inc.

For both Rawls and critical theory – especially Habermas – this implied a "detranscendental-izing" of some central Kantian insights while also preserving his ideas about the autonomy of morality and the "primacy of practical reason" (Habermas 2008, 53; Baynes 2004). For both Rawls and Habermas it also meant incorporating important Wittgensteinian insights about the central role of practices – in Rawls's case specifically via the influence of H.L.A. Hart. (See, for example, "Two Concepts of Rules" in *CP*.) For Rawls, this appropriation of Kant is reflected in his own version of "philosophy as defense" and his notion of a "reasonable faith," not in God but in the powers of human reason and in a world that need not be indifferent to our moral efforts (*LP*, 128). In Habermas, it is found in a chastened conception of philosophy in a dual role as "stand-in" and "interpreter" – that is, in the more limited role for philosophy as the defender of rationality claims rooted in our social practices and as an interpreter of those practices (Habermas 1990 and 2003b). In a provocative reading of Kant's philosophy of religion, Habermas (like Rawls) also articulates the idea of philosophy as a defense of our more mundane social practices (and their internal rationality) against the assaults of both a distorted reason and religious fanaticism (Habermas 2008, ch. 8). In the following I will first briefly outline this broadly "practice-based" approach in early critical theory, Rawls and Habermas (section 2). Then I will examine the "family quarrel" between Habermas and Rawls to illustrate some of their deeper affinities (section 3). I will conclude with some remarks about their respective views on the public role of philosophy especially in connection with the debate about the place of religion in the public square (section 4).

## 2. Immanent Critique and the Primacy of Practices

(1) One provocative idea found among the early critical theorists (especially Horkheimer and Marcuse) is their view that in an important sense philosophy reached its culmination in Kant's critical philosophy, especially in his idea of the freedom and equality of each person. Metaphysics for them comes to an end with Kant, and the post-Kantian project is rather how best to realize the ideals of the Enlightenment with the aid of a critical social theory. Of course, this idea also echoes Marx's Feuerbachian thesis that the important point is no longer to interpret the world, but to change it (Marx 1994, 101). The early critical theorists were equally emphatic that the primary challenge was not to establish the "truth content" of bourgeois philosophy but rather to bring about the "rational social order" it had promised. As Max Horkheimer expressed it,

> Today it is claimed that the bourgeois ideals of Freedom, Equality, and Justice have proven them-selves to be poor ones; however, it is not the ideals of the bourgeoisie, but conditions which do not correspond to them, which have shown their untenability. The battle cries of the Enlighten-ment and of the French Revolution are valid now more than ever. (1993, 37)

Herbert Marcuse held a similar view and further claimed (again echoing Marx): "If reason means shaping life according to men's free decision on the basis of their knowledge, then the demand for reason henceforth means the creation of a social organization in which individu-als can collectively regulate their lives in accordance with their needs. With the realization of reason in such a society philosophy would disappear" (1968, 141–142). Of course, it remained a difficult challenge for early critical theorists to balance this commitment to the social character of reason (and norms) while resisting the more relativist consequences drawn by those found, for example, among the sociologists of knowledge (see Hoy and McCarthy 1994, ch. 1). And their varied attempts to maintain this balance were of mixed success (see Habermas 2003b). Marcuse, for example, was compelled to speak of a "truth that is more than the truth of what is" without however falling back into a speculative meta-physics that was no longer defensible (1968, 149). Like his other colleagues at the Institute for Social Research, he sought to maintain the idea of immanent critique without, however, accepting the existing social world as (fully) rational:

> Like philosophy, [critical theory] opposes making reality into a criterion in the manner of com-placent positivism. But unlike philosophy, it always derives its goals only from present tendencies of the social process. . . . The utopian element was long the only progressive element in philoso-phy, as in the constructions of the best state and the highest pleasure, of perfect happiness and perpetual peace. The obstinacy that comes from adhering to truth against all appearances has given way in contemporary philosophy to whimsy and uninhibited opportunism. Critical theory preserves obstinacy as a genuine quality of philosophical thought. (Marcuse 1968, 143)

It would not take a great deal of interpretive work to show that this view is not far removed from Rawls's idea of a "realistic utopia" – that is, "as probing the limits of practicable political possibility" (JF, 4).

(2) Since the publication of *A Theory of Justice* there have been competing interpretations of Rawls's broader philosophical method and commitments. These range from claims that he sought to deploy the minimal assumptions of rational choice theory in order to arrive at substantive principles of justice to claims that he was (simply) setting out the deeper assump-tions of our liberal democratic culture without offering any further argument for them (Rorty 1991). These debates became further complicated by Rawls's turn to "political liberalism" with its "method of avoidance" with respect to deeper metaphysical claims and comprehen-sive doctrines. Many sympathetic with his earlier project believed he yielded too much to critics who charged he made excessively controversial assumptions about, say, the nature of the person (Hampton 1993). Finally, and more recently, discussion about his distinction between ideal and nonideal theory have raised questions both about how ideal ideal theory should be – should his ideal theory be rendered even more "fact-insensitive" or should the usefulness of the distinction be cast into doubt (Simmons 2010)?

An important but often overlooked aspect of Rawls's approach is the way in which his theorizing takes for granted the existence of background institutions and practices and does not attempt to offer an independent justification for them (but see importantly James 2005 and Sangiovani 2008). To cite Burton Dreben's apt remark, "Rawls always begins *in mediis rebus*, quite explicitly so" (2003, 322) – that is, "in the middle of things." On the reading I am proposing, this means that Rawls's reflections always take place with reference to specific practices and the principles he proposes are always in the context of a given set of practices. This feature of his philosophical approach is most visible in his claim that social justice may have distinct principles and a distinct "subject," namely, the "basic structure" of society – that is, the set of basic institutions of a liberal democratic society and the way in which, taken together, these institutions shape the expectations of its members. However, it is also clearly a prominent feature in his writings from "Two Concepts of Rules" (1955) through *The Law of Peoples* with its emphasis on a "realistic utopia." Borrowing Dworkin's notion of "constructive interpretation," Aaron James notes three steps in Rawls's own approach: first, he identifies a particular practice (or set of practices) he assumes will be widely recognized; next, he offers an interpretation of their underlying point or purpose; and, finally, he specifies the regulative principles that are most appropriate for those practices given their underlying point or purpose (James 2005, 22).

I think there is much to be said in support of this reading. It is important though to emphasize the fundamental role practices assume throughout Rawls's thought. For example, in "Justice as Fairness" (1958) Rawls argues that the parties to his "conjectural account" – what will eventually become the "original position" – are to consider what principles they can acknowledge as fair for a practice. Rawls continues:

> A practice will strike the parties as fair if none feels that, by participating in it, they or any of the others are taken advantage of, or forced to give in to claims which they do not regard as legitimate. . . . A practice is just or fair, then, when it satisfies the principles which those who participate in it could propose to one another for mutual acceptance under the aforementioned circumstances. Persons engaged in a just, or fair, practice can face one another openly and support their respective positions, should they appear questionable, by reference to principles which it is reasonable to expect each to accept. (*CP*, 59)

Here the rules (or principles) in question are internal to a practice and they define the "legitimate expectations" the parties are to consider. What is especially striking about this passage, however, is that the idea of reciprocity invoked is not limited to the situation of the parties in his "conjectural account." Rather, it is the same principle of reciprocity that in *PL* and elsewhere Rawls also claims is connected with the fundamental idea of society as a system of cooperation found in our own social practices and in our own political culture:

> Fair terms of cooperation specify an idea of reciprocity: all who are engaged in cooperation and who do their part as the rules and procedure require, are to benefit in an appropriate way as assessed by a suitable benchmark of comparison. . . . Since the primary subject of justice is the basic structure of society, these fair terms are expressed by principles that specify basic rights and duties within its main institutions and regulate the arrangements of background justice over time. (*PL*, 16; cf. *JF*, 48 n14)

In short, according to Rawls, the same idea of reciprocity that governs the practices considered by the (hypothetical) parties in the original position is also contained within a set of practices – the basic structure – of our own society and is accordingly described as a "fundamental intuitive idea" of our own political culture. This reading of the idea of reciprocity (and its relation to social practices) also suggests, following "constructive interpretation," that "justice as fairness" (with its two principles) can be viewed as a proposal about the most appropriate regulative principles for our own society conceived as a fair system of cooperation.

Of course, this reading of Rawls's philosophical method gives rises to some serious challenges – ones not unlike those that confront the method of immanent critique in early critical theory. For example, won't such an approach either defer too much to the status quo or, alternatively, leave any external normative critique of social practices too removed and detached – an instance of what Hegel called an "empty ought"? I can't pursue these questions further here (see briefly below; and see also James 2005). It is worth noting, though, that this reading also has some interpretive advantages. For example, since the background practices they assume differ, it helps explain why Rawls's global original position differs from the domestic case. (See *LP*.)

(3) Habermas also employs an interpretive approach as evidenced by his indebtedness to the work of Gadamer and Wittgenstein. Others, however, have read Habermas as having abandoned immanent critique and in an influential essay from the mid-1970s Habermas did claim that "bourgeois consciousness has become cynical" (1976, 97; see Geuss 1981, 67). But this juxtaposition of immanent and transcendent criticism is too crude to capture Habermas's own view and his so-called "transcendental turn" did not signal the rejection of an interpretive approach but rather highlighted the importance of deeper reconstructive efforts to identify precisely the norms and rules implicit in various social practices. Of course, as is also the case for Rawls, our reconstructive efforts are fallible and so open to the same type of criticism that faces similar forms of (weak) transcendental argument: There is always the possibility that other reconstructions can offer a competing and equally compelling account of the assumptions constitutive for a practice (Power 1993).

Habermas's approach is also "practice-based" as can be seen from some of his earliest writings that focused on what he called the "institutional framework" of a society (1970; 1973). Summarizing briefly, the "institutional framework" is Habermas's more general term for what Marx called the "social relations of production." Thus societies for him can still be fruitfully analyzed in terms of conflicts between an existing society's institutional framework and its expanding productive forces (i.e., labor power and technology). But Habermas's suggestion was that Marx's restriction of the institutional framework to the specific relations of wage labor and private ownership made it difficult to analyze developments in "late capitalism" and, in particular, new forms of crisis that emerge with the interventionist welfare state (Habermas 1973; Postone 1993, ch. 6). Further, this restriction of the "institutional framework" hindered subsequent critical theorists from identifying new rational potentials – communicative reason – contained within the modern or posttraditional institutional framework (or in what Habermas later called the lifeworld) able to counter the instrumental rationality that prevailed in the social subsystems of the market economy and bureaucratic state. Finally, in *Between Facts and Norms* (1996) (hereafter, *BFN*) Habermas limited his attention to the question of how modern complex societies could be legitimated through the medium of modern law given what Rawls calls the fact of reasonable pluralism. The guiding question for Habermas thus becomes that of what system of rights must legal consociates mutually confer upon one another if they want to regulate their life under positive law (*BFN*, 82, 118, 127). The important point in all this for our own purposes is that Habermas does not attempt to bring normative standards from the outside to bear on a set of institutional practices but rather seeks to reconstruct what is already implicit in those practices or in the "lifeworld." Though he offers a broad sociological account of the emergence of what Rawls calls the fact of reasonable pluralism – one that roughly parallels Weber's own account of secularization – the conclusion he reaches in *BFN* is not substantially different from Rawls's case for a freestanding account of political legitimacy. It also continues at a deeper level a method of immanent critique in that it inquires into the rational potential for critique (available to the participants themselves) already contained within social institutions.

# 3. The Habermas/Rawls Exchange: On the Relation between Justice and Democracy

The 1995 exchange between Habermas and Rawls was important at least for stimulating discussion about the views of these two leading political theorists.[2] It also helped to make more explicit the ways in which Rawls's own thought was shaped by democratic commitments that were less evident in *TJ*. In fact, Rawls subsequently endorsed a deliberative conception of democracy as most adequate to his own theory of justice (*JF*, 148, 150; cf. J. Cohen 2003). At another level, however, the exchange was disappointing. On the one hand, though Habermas described his disagreement with Rawls as a "family quarrel" (1998a, 50), he offered a reading of "justice as fairness" that still inclined to view *TJ* as an attempt to derive substantive principles of justice from more minimal principles of rational choice (1998a, 52). At the same time, he suggested that Rawls's later concerns about political stability undermined the possibility of a more robust normative justification rooted in a more systematic account of practical reason. He also suggested that Rawls's own attempt to integrate the civil and political liberties tended to downplay the value of democracy since, as he put it, it deprived citizens of the "radical democratic embers" required for them to view their constitution as an ongoing project (1998a, 69). On the other hand, Rawls's engagement with Habermas's work also revealed some important misunderstandings – most notably, perhaps, his claims that Habermas's project represented a "comprehensive doctrine" rather than a "political conception" and that it was misguidedly too "procedural." I will address these mutual misunderstandings in the following and show why I think their positions are in fact much closer to each other than often assumed.

## 3.1 Democracy and "Co-originality"

(a) Habermas's conception of a "procedural democracy" and "deliberative politics" shares the same core features as other recent accounts of deliberative democracy (see J. Cohen 1997): Politics is concerned, at least in part, with the common good and deliberation has as its primary focus the common good (or "generalizable interests"). This conception of democracy is also "cognitive" or "epistemic" in that it is concerned with specifying procedures for collective decision-making that have a presumption of rational outcomes (*BFN*, 285). Habermas also argues that democratic procedures should specify not simply a means for aggregating prepolitical preferences but the conditions of deliberation in which collective reasoning about "generalizable interests" can be pursued, at least in part through the transformation of preferences. Finally, this conception of a deliberative politics assumes that individuals will not be motivated exclusively by self-interest. Rather, democratic procedure requires a "rationalized lifeworld" including a liberal political culture and corresponding civic virtues that, as he puts it, "meets it halfway" (*BFN*, 302).

Within the wider context of legal and democratic theory, the term "procedural" is ambiguous and is often used in connection with very different conceptions of philosophy. For example, Habermas's view differs importantly from the procedural conceptions offered by Jeremy Waldron and Peter Singer that are much more minimalist and majoritarian in character (Waldron 1999; Christiano 1998). For these conceptions, the democratic process consists in a set of rules and procedures intended to capture a more general idea of the equal consideration of interests. Each person should be granted the opportunity to express her preference and no person's preference should count for more than another's. These conceptions often assume an ideal of political equality understood in terms of the equal opportunity to influence political outcomes. A procedure is fair if it captures this notion of equal influence. The difficulty with such conceptions, however, is that they remain relatively indifferent to the quality and/or urgency of preferences that enter into the procedure (Beitz 1989, 82).

Habermas's conception of democracy, by contrast, assumes a more abstract ideal of political equality and the aim is to mirror this abstract ideal in a set of ideal procedures thereby considered fair. "The claim that a norm lies equally in the interest of everyone has the sense of rational acceptability: all those possibly affected should be able to accept the norm on the basis of good reasons" (*BFN*, 103). In this sense, Habermas's procedural conception is closer to what Charles Beitz has called "complex proceduralism":

> Like other forms of proceduralism, [complex proceduralism] holds that democratic procedures should treat *persons* as equals; but it will not follow that the appropriate criterion for assessing procedures is the simple principle of equal power over outcomes. Instead, complex proceduralism holds that the terms of democratic participation are fair when they are reasonably acceptable from each citizen's point of view, or more precisely, when no citizen has good reason to refuse to accept them. (Beitz 1989, 23)

In Habermas's conception too there are certain abstract ideals – and ultimately the idea of communicative freedom (or capacity of each person to take a "yes" or "no" position on a speech act offer) – that are identified prior to any proposed set of (ideal) procedures. Habermas nonetheless refers to his conception as "procedural" for two reasons: First, he claims that the fundamental ideal that forms the "dogmatic core" of his theory is not itself simply one value among others, but reflects a basic norm implicit in the very idea of communicative action (*BFN*, 445–446). Second, he claims that this ideal – developed in *BFN* in connection with the co-equal and mutually interdependent ideas of public and private autonomy – can in turn be used to describe a set of (ideal) democratic procedures. It is because the procedures sufficiently mirror this basic ideal, however, that we are entitled to confer a presumption of reasonableness or fairness upon them (*BFN*, 295). In sum, then, for Habermas, ideal procedures attempt to capture or express an ideal of citizens as free and equal engaged in reasoning about their common good.

(b) Habermas's conception of democracy also provides a basis for reconsidering the longstanding dispute concerning the relation between democracy and other liberal values or, in Benjamin Constant's phrase, the liberty of the ancients and the liberty of the moderns. In *BFN* Habermas argues that neither the "principle of democracy" nor the basic scheme of (liberal) rights should be seen as primary. Rather, as he puts it, the principle of democracy and the basic scheme of rights are "co-original" and emerge together via the "interpenetration of the discourse principle and the legal form" (*BFN*, 121). As Habermas sees it, this enables his conception to avoid the two extremes of a legal positivism that leaves basic rights up to the political sovereign, on the one hand, and a subordination of popular sovereignty to a prior moral principle as in, for example, Kant and the natural law tradition, on the other. "The universal right to equal liberties may neither be imposed as a moral right that merely sets an external constraint on the sovereign legislator, nor be instrumentalized as a functional prerequisite for the legislator's aims" (*BFN*, 104). Thus, the "co-originality thesis" regards public autonomy (roughly, the idea that citizens can be bound only by laws that they give to themselves) and private autonomy (roughly, civil and expressive liberties) as reciprocally dependent on each other such that neither can claim a prior or independent status.

In an extended comparison between Habermas's views and his own, Joshua Cohen endorses (as does Rawls) this idea of the "co-originality" of public and private autonomy (1999; *PL*, 412). However, he is less convinced by the specific arguments in support of it. In particular, he suggests, first, that Habermas's account appeals to a "comprehensive doctrine" or philosophy of life that is inappropriate given the "fact of reasonable pluralism" and, second, that it is deficient in its support for an equal right to (nonpolitical) expressive liberties. Cohen's alternative account of the relation between basic liberties and democracy is highly instructive and strengthens the co-originality thesis. However, since Habermas grants that there is a "dogmatic core" to his theory, I think it is incorrect to read him in the more procedurally minimalist manner that Cohen proposes. In fact, my account of Habermas's conception of procedural democracy above is intended to counter such an interpretation.

Cohen's first reservation – that it is a comprehensive doctrine – is initially plausible in that Habermas's account of political legitimacy is presented within the wider framework of his theory of communicative action. However, an alternative reading is possible: The "interpenetration of the discourse principle and the legal form" can itself be seen as a restriction of the more abstract conception of autonomy to the political-legal context and thus as first introducing the idea of "legal consociates." In Habermas's own variation on the social-contract tradition, the guiding question thus becomes, "What basic rights must free and equal citizens mutually accord one another if they want to regulate their common life legitimately by means of positive law?" (*BFN*, 82, 118). Further, this question must finally be addressed from the internal perspective of legal consociates (or citizens) committed to regulating their lives in common and not only from the external standpoint of one preferred philosophical theory. Thus, unlike earlier contract theorists (including at least some readings of Rawls), this question cannot be settled by appeal to particular interests of hypothetical parties nor by appeal to a set of "natural" (prepolitical) rights, but, in the final analysis, to considerations about what citizens would consent to in view of their status as free and equal persons:

> Under conditions of postmetaphysical thinking, we cannot expect a further-reaching consensus that would include substantive issues. This restriction to presuppositions that are formal in this sense is tailored for the specifically modern pluralism of worldviews, cultural forms of life, interest positions, and so forth. Naturally, this does not mean that a constitution-making practice of this kind would be free of all normative content. On the contrary, the performative meaning of this practice, which is merely set forth and explicated in constitutional principles and the system of rights, already contains as a doctrinal core the (Rousseauian-Kantian) idea of the self-legislation of voluntarily associated citizens who are both free and equal. (Habermas 1998b, 406)

According to Cohen's second reservation, Habermas's commitment to equal liberties is deficient since it rests on a claim that the system of rights can be derived *exclusively* from "the interpenetration of the discourse principle and the legal form." Since, on his view, the discourse principle imposes a fairly general requirement of impartiality, Cohen is doubtful that its conjunction with the idea of the "rule of law" (or "legal form") will yield a sufficiently broad set of liberal rights (including rights to conscience, bodily integrity, privacy, property, etc.). Although it must be admitted that Habermas's argument here is not as clear as it might be, Cohen reads Habermas's proceduralism in an excessively minimalist manner. If, as I have argued, the discourse principle itself presupposes an (abstract) ideal of persons as free and equal, then it may impose more constraints than Cohen assumes. Further, the notion of the "legal form" that Habermas invokes, derived from legal debates in twentieth-century German law, is also more substantive in character than the idea of the "rule of law" more narrowly conceived and already includes something like the idea of equal subjective liberties (*BFN*, 84–89; Baynes 2012, 134–136). Thus, the "interpenetration" strategy could arguably generate something like the liberties specified, for example, in Rawls's Principle of Equal Liberty. On the other hand, however, Cohen is correct to note that, on Habermas's account, the "interpenetration of the discourse principle and legal form" yields only a general scheme of basic rights and not a concrete set of liberties (J. Cohen 1999, 393). Although this scheme is more detailed than Cohen assumes, it does not by itself provide the means for assigning specific weight to the reasons that citizens must consider when determining the more specific scope of the basic liberties – it will arguably leave open, for example, the question of whether the scope of liberty (or equality) requires a legal right to abortion. On Habermas's account, these are questions that citizens within a given polity must determine for themselves within the framework of a deliberative politics. Of course, citizens would have to give consideration to precisely the kinds of reasons – and the appropriate weighting among them – that Cohen raises in his own reflections on the relation between democracy and rights to civil and expressive liberties – including religious liberty. (See J. Cohen 1998.)

## 3.2 The Idea of Public Reason

The idea of public reason figures prominently in the conceptions of political legitimacy proposed by both Rawls and Habermas. However, in their exchange each criticizes the other for shortcomings in their respective approach. Rawls suggests that Habermas's idea of public reason is part of a comprehensive philosophical doctrine and thus unacceptable as a basis of political legitimacy in a society characterized by a plurality of comprehensive views. Habermas, by contrast, suggests that Rawls's model of public reason, with its reliance on the idea of an overlapping consensus, remains too beholden to the contingencies of a de facto agreement to serve as a suitable basis of political legitimacy (Habermas 1998a, 84). While Rawls is not always as clear about his conception of public reason as he might be, I believe that again their positions are not as far from one another as is often supposed. In particular, though Rawls suggests that his model of public reason is circumscribed and perhaps even constituted by what he calls the "domain of the political," I believe that when his conception of the political is properly understood – when, that is, it is not "political in the wrong way" – it does not differ significantly from Habermas's own account of public reason. In the end, both accounts of public reason incorporate a core set of liberal values tied, in

Rawls's case, to the notion of citizens as free and equal persons with the two basic moral powers and, in Habermas's case, to a notion of communicative autonomy.

To begin, the idea of public reason also plays a crucial role in Habermas's account of political legitimacy. Basic political norms (e.g., what Rawls calls the "constitutional essentials" and matters of basic justice) are legitimate only if they conform to a demanding ideal of public reason, that is, only if they could be agreed to by all citizens as participants in a practical discourse for the same (publicly available) reasons. Thomas McCarthy and others have argued that this conception of political legitimacy, together with the idea of public reason, is too strongly oriented to the idea of consensus or "rational agreement" and that he should move more in the direction of Rawls's notion of an overlapping consensus which allows for "reasonable disagreement" and "reasonable pluralism" within a public culture (McCarthy 1998). Political legitimacy neither can nor should depend on such a demanding idea of rational agreement but rather should draw upon the idea of a "mutual accommodation" among diverse worldviews and corresponding forms of life. This revision also entails a more thoroughly "proceduralist" interpretation of political legitimacy.

On the other hand, in his own contribution to the exchange Habermas argued that Rawls's notion of an overlapping consensus cannot serve the purpose to which he puts it and that he needs a stronger, more systematically grounded notion of practical reason to support his own liberal principle of legitimacy (Habermas 1998a, chs 2 and 3). This principle reads as follows: "Our exercise of political power is fully proper only when it is exercised in accordance with a constitution the essentials of which all citizens as free and equal may reasonably be expected to endorse in the light of principles and ideals acceptable to their common human reason" (PL, 137). According to Habermas, however, Rawls interprets this principle of legitimacy in connection with the de facto emergence of an overlapping consensus rather than, as one should, in terms of a more abstract and normatively secure (communication-theoretical) idea of rational agreement or acceptability (appropriately tailored or restricted to the domain of legal consociates). In contrast, then, to both McCarthy and Habermas, I want to give some reasons for suggesting that the views of Rawls and Habermas on public reason are closer to one another than is often supposed.

First, according to McCarthy, Habermas has not offered a conception of public reason (and, hence, political legitimacy) that can adequately respond to the value pluralism that characterizes liberal democratic societies. On the one hand, there typically is no homogeneous ethico-political culture that could provide the necessary background for an agreement on "constitutional essentials and matters of basic justice." On the other hand, the model of discourse that Habermas proposes does not make sufficient allowance for "reasonable disagreements" about moral/ethical questions. Rather, cases supporting the idea of a reasonable value pluralism are either interpreted as "interim reports" on an ongoing moral disagreement, where it is claimed there is only one right answer, or they are too quickly treated as a matter of negotiation and compromise, in just the way that conflicts of "interest" are to be handled (McCarthy 1998, 150). The result is a certain inadequacy within Habermas's theory in responding to the value pluralism characteristic of modern societies. McCarthy's suggestion is that, to accommodate the fact of reasonable pluralism, Habermas must relinquish the strong claims concerning rational agreement (Einverständnis), make room for a notion of mutual accommodation and, consequently, give his theory a still more "procedural twist" (McCarthy 1998, 151). By making greater use of his own distinction between direct and indirect justification of a norm, for example, Habermas could allow for the idea of a "reasonable disagreement" on values, while nonetheless still providing citizens with a strong procedural reason for accepting as legitimate those norms and decisions they oppose at a substantive level (McCarthy 1998, 128).

As I have attempted to show above, however, despite his own frequent use of the term procedural, neither Habermas (nor Rawls) are proceduralists "all the way down." (See also J. Cohen 1994.) Rather, both attempt to mirror in a set of procedures a prior substantive value or set of values – autonomy, in the case of Habermas, and the idea of citizens as free and equal persons, in the case of Rawls. It is these values or ideals that then confer a presumption of reasonableness or fairness on the proposed procedures (*BFN*, 266, 295; and Habermas 1998b, 406). More important, however, is the question of the conditions under which an agreement should count as reasonable. But here too the differences may not be so great as first appears. The idea of the reasonable is invoked at many levels within Rawls's theory, but its most basic use is with respect to persons: a citizen is reasonable if she is willing to accept and abide by fair terms of cooperation and willing to accept the "burdens of judgment," that is, to acknowledge and abide by the limits of public reason (*PL*, 49 n1). These two basic virtues of the citizen are themselves understood in connection with what Rawls calls the basic moral powers of the person: the capacity for a sense of justice and the capacity for a conception of the good. These moral powers (or basic human capacities) are part of a moral psychology or conception of the person that, along with the idea of social cooperation, form one of the "fundamental intuitive ideas" found in a liberal political culture and from which his political conception is drawn. According to Rawls, although this idea is not itself part of a comprehensive doctrine or theory of human nature, it is nonetheless part of a general set of normative reflections, informed as well by moral and social-scientific theory, on the basic capacities of human agency (*PL*, 86–87). The further notions of a "reasonable comprehensive doctrine," a "reasonable overlapping consensus," and "reasonable pluralism" all draw upon this prior notion of reasonable persons: a doctrine, for example, is reasonable if its more specific elements fall within the "burdens of judgment" of reasonable citizens and an overlapping consensus is reasonable just in the case it is a consensus among reasonable comprehensive doctrines. Finally, a reasonable disagreement is a disagreement that persists even after reasonable people, exercising good faith and recognizing the "burdens of judgment," nonetheless fail to agree on a particular matter. According to Rawls, such disagreements will be a permanent feature of a liberal democratic society.

Even with these brief remarks, it is important to emphasize that what Rawls describes as the reasonable is *not* the conclusion or outcome of an agreement or overlapping consensus that just happens to exist. Rather, the prior idea of the reasonable informs what can count as a reasonable comprehensive doctrine and thus what could finally be part of a (reasonable) overlapping consensus. The idea of the reasonable, in other words, is something that must in this sense be specified in advance of any existing overlapping consensus, rather than something that results from it. It might be objected, in response, that this reading does not follow Rawls's own recent distinction between "moral autonomy" and "political autonomy" (or, relatedly, between "persons" and "citizens") and thus still gives Rawls's position a too Kantian interpretation – one that his "freestanding" political conception is meant to avoid. (But see Forst 2011, 158.) However, though Rawls's own formulations sometimes lend support to such a reading, this cannot be his considered position. He is himself explicit that a "political" conception is still a "moral conception" (*PL*, xxxix, xliii). In short, even his conception of the political autonomy of citizens still assumes the "fundamental intuitive ideas," including the idea of citizens as free and equal with their two basic moral powers – and these fundamental ideas are themselves contained in (Rawls's idealized version) of our own practice of fair social cooperation with its guiding principle of reciprocity.

In his own interpretation of Rawls, however, Habermas takes a different tack. That is, he attributes a *more* significant justificatory role to the idea of an overlapping consensus than, I believe, Rawls has in mind. Habermas apparently does not consider that the idea of the reasonable must already be presupposed prior to the identification of those comprehensive doctrines that might be eligible candidates for a reasonable overlapping consensus. Rather he regards the notion of the reasonable as itself the outcome of a contingent or "lucky" convergence: "Only the lucky convergence of the differently motivated nonpublic reasons can generate the public validity or 'reasonableness' of the content of this 'overlapping consensus' that everyone accepts. Agreement in conclusions *results* from premises rooted in different outlooks" (Habermas 1998a, 84). Now, while it is true that each citizen may and even should look to his or her own comprehensive doctrine to see whether he or she has reason to affirm the content of the overlapping consensus, it is not the case either that the justification of the content rests solely upon these "nonpublic" reasons or that a contingent overlapping consensus produces or defines the "reasonableness" of that content. Interestingly, in a later essay on the place of religion in the public square Habermas himself endorses a position essentially the same as Rawls's own idea of a freestanding political conception as a "module" that can be embedded in a person's own comprehensive doctrine but that does not need that doctrine for its own justification (Habermas 2008, 112).

This (modest) repositioning of the reasonable within Rawls's conception of political liberalism suggests how Rawls may in fact be closer to Habermas's own position. It is the basic idea of the citizen as reasonable and rational and, behind this, the idea of the basic moral powers of the person that importantly shapes the subsequent employment of the reasonable in Rawls's work. In ways that closely resemble Habermas's basic assumptions about communicative freedom – the capacity to take a position on a speech act offer – Rawls's idea of the reasonable acquires at least some of its normative authority from the fundamental human capacity to respond to and act from reasons: the legitimacy of a political order depends on what citizens can endorse in view of their "common human reason" (though a great deal of further philosophical argument – contained in *TJ* and *PL* – is required to show what kind of political order might possibly satisfy this requirement).

An important consequence of the Rawls–Habermas exchange is that it highlights the importance of democratic theory for Rawls's own reflections about justice. As Cohen has argued in another instructive essay, the principles of justice – or "justice as fairness" – are in an important sense principles "for a democratic society" (J. Cohen 2003). By this Cohen means not only that they are appropriate (and perhaps even required) for a society that is democratically organized; rather, he means that they are principles that in their content reflect the idea of society among free and equal citizens who are prepared to publicly acknowledge and affirm the principles governing the basic institutions in which they live. Further, they are principles that can appropriately guide the deliberations of citizens in their attempts to publicly recognize and affirm their equal status. Here it is perhaps especially significant that Rawls describes his difference principle as a principle of "democratic equality" (*TJ*, 65). To insist that inequalities in some primary social goods are only permissible if they work to the advantage of the least well off is one way in which the equal status of citizens can be affirmed and so serves to express the idea of democratic society as a society among equals.

Such an interpretation of Rawls's democratic commitments offers some resources for Rawls to respond to the final criticism offered by Habermas mentioned above. Habermas suggests that since on Rawls's account the citizens have a fully developed theory of justice delivered to them (by the philosopher?) they "cannot reignite the radical democratic embers of the original position within the civil life of their society" (Habermas 1998a, 169; see also, more forcefully on this point, Wolin 1996). Rather, since they are constrained from the outset by the prior agreement of the parties, they cannot conceive their own democratic constitution as an ongoing project. However, based on his reply, I think we are not required to accept Habermas's reading of Rawls on this point. Though it is true that his two principles are more determinate than Habermas's own structurally analogous "system of rights," they are offered not from the perspective of an expert philosopher, but as an attempt by a philosopher to make a substantive contribution to a public debate among citizens about appropriate principles for a democratic society. Moreover, even Habermas's own conception of deliberative democracy does not mean that citizens (with each new generation?) start from scratch. Rather, they too must presuppose the "system of rights" and are guided in their collective deliberations by a given constitutional tradition in arguing for their respective claims about what is for the common good. It thus does not seem that acknowledging the constraints of justice in their deliberations must necessarily denigrate its democratic character or prohibit them from seeing their constitution as an ongoing project. (See Habermas 2001.)

## 4. Conclusion: The Public Role and Character of Philosophy; Religion in the Public Square

I have attempted to outline some of the deeper affinities in the approach to practical philosophy in Rawls and the tradition of critical theory, especially Habermas. But the discussion has thus far remained at a fairly abstract level. By way of conclusion I would also like to compare their views on the public role and public character of philosophy, and illustrate it briefly in connection with some recent debates on the place of religion in the public square. Even though Rawls never assumed the role of a public intellectual in the way that Habermas has, they both embrace a very public conception of philosophy – perhaps, in both cases, due to the influence of John Dewey.

Habermas's role as a public intellectual is of course well known (see Pensky 1999). As interesting, however, is the way in which he considers philosophy to be public at its core. Alluding to their common origin in ancient Athens, he writes: "Philosophy and democracy not only emerge from the same historical context; they are also structurally dependent on each other" (Habermas 2003b, 290). He means by this not only that philosophy should assume the role of the "public guardian of rationality" but, more importantly, that it is essentially bound to "democratic common sense" (Habermas 2003a, 105; and compare Rawls on "common sense," CP, 306). Philosophy has no special access to or claim upon truth as Plato thought; rather in its role as "stand-in" for empirical theories accompanied by normative and universal claims, it strives to "reconstruct pretheoretical knowledge" (Habermas 2003b, 286). In this effort, too, it can claim no special expertise. Rather, given its own history and location within the academy, it can at most claim a "polyglot trait" that enables it to propose interpretations across disciplinary boundaries and to the wider public as well. However, unlike religion and in contrast to its earlier ambitions, it cannot hope to provide an answer to the "meaning of life" or even concrete advice on how to live (Habermas 2003b, 289). Its attempt to describe "how things hang together" (Sellars 1963, 1) remains, in that sense, extremely "ascetic." Nonetheless, as Habermas has also exhibited in his own public role, philosophers need not shy away from making contributions to a wider public debate even if they can claim only a modest and limited expertise – such as a professional familiarity with normative debates (Habermas 2003b, 287).

Rawls, by contrast, did not assume the role of a public intellectual apart from some brief and limited antiwar protest during the Vietnam period. (See Pogge 2007, 18f.) This may speak more to his own personal temperament but it does not detract in any way from the public character of his philosophical method (Laden 2011). On the contrary, as became evident in his Dewey Lectures, even the theoretical construction of the "original position" must, in the last analysis, be acceptable to each citizen viewed as a free and equal member of society. (See, for example, his important distinction among the three different points of view – that of the parties in the original position, the citizens in a well-ordered society and us; CP, 321). More poignantly, in his response to Habermas's suggestion that he had assigned a less modest role to philosophy than Habermas himself, Rawls replied, "In justice as fairness there are no experts. Heaven forbid" (PL, 427). Rawls too maintains that ultimately any contributions offered by "students of philosophy" must be received as that of one citizen among others (PL, 427). Just as for Habermas "quasi-transcendental" reconstructions cannot displace commonsense knowledge but at most help to guide it, for Rawls "philosophy as defense" can only hope to make explicit what is found in common human reason, defending it against more pretentious attempts in grounding (CP, 306; cf. Laden 2011).

In the recent debate about the limits of religious contributions to public reason, Habermas and Rawls each exhibit this deeply public and democratic character of their thought. Both insist that a duty of civility requires that at least in the more formal context of political deliberation (though arguably also when they vote) citizens make their claims on the basis of considerations others can be expected to recognize as reasonable – that is, they should not be sectarian (PL, 219). In response to criticisms, both have both resisted the charge that their ideas of public reason are hostile to religious believers and reflect a bias toward a form of secular reason (or what Habermas calls "secularism"). Rawls proposed a "wide" view of public reason with a "proviso" that permits religious believers to introduce claims into the public so long as they do so in good faith that their claims can be translated into public reasons (PL, 453). Though Habermas has expressed some sympathies for the asymmetrical burdens this imposes on a religious believer, he has essentially endorsed the same position (Habermas 2003a and 2008, ch. 5). Habermas also now accepts Rawls's idea of political conception as a freestanding module that can and should be embedded within a citizen's (reasonable) wider comprehensive worldview as long as this does not disturb their commitment to argue with one another as citizens on the terrain of public reason (Habermas 2008, 112). Finally, like Rawls's own understanding of a "freestanding" political conception based on shared values in the political public culture, Habermas also refers to the "independence" of "democratic common sense" from all comprehensive doctrines (Habermas 2003a, 105). Space does not permit a further discussion of the nuances in their respective views here, but their basically similar approach again reveals their common "practice-based" conception of public reason, focused on what citizens should reasonably expect given the fact of reasonable pluralism. Each in their own way also views philosophy (like Kant) as the articulation and defense of a "reasonable faith" against the dangers of both religious fanaticism and an encroaching naturalism or "scientism" that threatens "democratic common sense."

## Notes

1   I have in mind especially G.A. Cohen's claim that normative theory should be "fact-insensitive" and related views about ideal theory (see G.A. Cohen 2008; Parfit 2011; Estlund 2011).
2   Originally in the *Journal of Philosophy* 92 (1995). Habermas's contribution can also be found in Habermas 1998a; Rawls's "Reply" is also *PL*. On the exchange see also Finlayson and Freyenhagen 2011 and Hedrick 2010.

## Works by Rawls, with Abbreviations

*Collected Papers* (CP), ed. Samuel Freeman. Cambridge, MA: Harvard University Press, 1999.
"Justice as Fairness" (1958), in *Collected Papers* (47–72).
*Justice as Fairness: A Restatement* (JF), ed. Erin Kelly. Cambridge, MA: Harvard University Press, 2001.
*The Law of Peoples* (LP). Cambridge, MA: Harvard University Press, 1999.
*Lectures on the History of Moral Philosophy* (LHMP), ed. Barbara Herman. Cambridge, MA: Harvard University Press, 2000.
*Political Liberalism* (PL), expanded edn. New York: Columbia University Press, 2005.
*A Theory of Justice* (TJ), rev. edn. Cambridge, MA: Harvard University Press, 1999.
"Two Concepts of Rules" (1955), in *Collected Papers* (20–46).

## Other References

Baynes, Kenneth (2004) "The Transcendental Turn: Habermas's 'Kantian Pragmatism.'" In Fred Rush (ed.), *The Cambridge Companion to Critical Theory*. Cambridge: Cambridge University Press.
Baynes, Kenneth (2012) "Making Global Governance Public: Habermas's Model for a Two-Track Cosmopolitan Order." In Ludvig Beckman and Eva Erman (eds), *Territories of Citizenship*. New York: Palgrave.
Beitz, Charles (1989) *Political Equality*. Princeton: Princeton University Press.
Christiano, Thomas (1998) *The Rule of the Many*. Boulder, CO.: Westview Press.
Cohen, G.A. (2008) *Rescuing Justice and Equality*. Cambridge, MA: Harvard University Press.
Cohen, Joshua (1994) "Pluralism and Proceduralism." *Chicago-Kent Law Review* 69: 589–618.
Cohen, Joshua (1997) "Deliberation and Democratic Legitimacy." In James Bohman and William Rehg (eds), *Deliberative Democracy*. Cambridge, MA: MIT Press.
Cohen, Joshua (1998) "Democracy and Liberty." In Jon Elster (ed.), *Deliberative Democracy*. Cambridge: Cambridge University Press.
Cohen, Joshua (1999) "Reflections on Habermas on Democracy," *Ratio* 12: 385–416.
Cohen, Joshua (2003) "For a Democratic Society." In Samuel Freeman (ed.), *The Cambridge Companion to Rawls*. Cambridge: Cambridge University Press.
Dreben, Burton (2003) "On Rawls and Political Liberalism." In Samuel Freeman (ed.), *The Cambridge Companion to Rawls*. Cambridge: Cambridge University Press.
Estlund, David (2011) "Human Nature and the Limits (If Any) of Political Philosophy." *Philosophy and Public Affairs* 39: 207–237.

Finlayson, James Gordon and Freyenhagen, Fabian (eds) (2011) *Habermas and Rawls: Disputing the Political*. New York: Routledge.

Forst, Rainer (2011) "The Justification of Justice." In James G. Finlayson and Fabian Freyenhagen (eds), *Habermas and Rawls: Disputing the Political*. New York: Routledge.

Geuss, Raymond (1981) *The Idea of Critical Theory*. Cambridge: Cambridge University Press.

Habermas, Jürgen (1970) *Toward a Rational Society*, trans. J. Shapiro. Boston: Beacon Press.

Habermas, Jürgen (1973) *Legitimation Crisis*, trans. Thomas McCarthy. Boston: Beacon Press.

Habermas, Jürgen 1976) *Communication and the Evolution of Society*, trans. Thomas McCarthy. Boston: Beacon Press.

Habermas, Jürgen (1990) "Philosophy as Stand-In and Interpreter." In Habermas, *Moral Consciousness and Communicative Action*, trans. Christian Lenhardt and Shierry Weber Nicholsen. Cambridge, MA: MIT Press.

Habermas, Jürgen (1996) *Between Facts and Norms*, trans. William Rehg. Cambridge, MA: MIT Press.

Habermas, Jürgen (1998a) *The Inclusion of the Other*, trans. Ciaran Cronin and Pablo de Greiff. Cambridge, MA: MIT Press.

Habermas, Jürgen (1998b) "Reply." In Michel Rosenfeld and Andrew Arato (eds), *Habermas on Law and Democracy*. Berkeley: University of California Press.

Habermas, Jürgen (2001) "Constitutional Democracy: A Paradoxical Union of Contradictory Principles?" *Political Theory* 29: 766–781.

Habermas, Jürgen (2003a) "Faith and Knowledge." In Habermas, *The Future of Human Nature*. Cambridge: Polity.

Habermas, Jürgen (2003b) "The Relationship between Theory and Practice Revisited." In Habermas, *Truth and Justification*, trans. Barbara Fultner. Cambridge, MA: MIT Press.

Habermas, Jürgen (2008) *Between Naturalism and Religion*. Cambridge: Polity.

Hampton, Jean (1993) "The Moral Commitments of Liberalism." In D. Copp, J. Hampton, and J. Roemer (eds), *The Idea of Democracy*. Cambridge: Cambridge University Press.

Hedrick, Todd (2010) *Rawls and Habermas*. Stanford: Stanford University Press.

Horkheimer, Max (1993) *Between Philosophy and Social Science*. Cambridge, MA: MIT Press.

Hoy, David and McCarthy, Thomas (1994) *Critical Theory*. Oxford: Blackwell.

James, Aaron (2005) "Constructing Justice for Existing Practice: Rawls and the Status Quo." *Philosophy and Public Affairs* 33: 1–36.

Krouse, Richard and McPherson, Michael (1988) "Capitalism, 'Property-Owning Democracy,' and the Welfare State." In Amy Gutmann (ed.), *Democracy and the Welfare State*. Princeton: Princeton University Press.

Laden, Anthony (2011) "The Justice of Justification." In James G. Finlayson and Fabian Freyenhagen (eds), *Habermas and Rawls: Disputing the Political*. New York: Routledge.

Larmore, Charles (1996) *The Morals of Modernity*. Cambridge: Cambridge University Press.

Marcuse, Herbert (1968) "Philosophy and Critical Theory." In Marcuse, *Negations*. Boston: Beacon Press.

Marx, Karl (1994) *Selected Writings*, ed. Lawrence Simon. Indianapolis, IN: Hackett.

McCarthy, Thomas (1998) "Legitimacy and Diversity." In Michel Rosenfeld and Andrew Arato (eds), *Habermas on Law and Democracy*. Berkeley: University of California Press.

Parfit, Derek (2011) *On What Matters*. New York: Oxford University Press.

Pensky, Max (1999) "Habermas and the Antinomies of the Intellectual." In Peter Dews (ed.), *Habermas: A Critical Reader*. Oxford: Blackwell.

Pogge, Thomas (2007) *John Rawls: His Life and Theory of Justice*. New York: Oxford University Press.

Postone, Moishe (1993) *Time, Labor and Social Domination: A Reinterpretation of Marx's Critical Theory*. Cambridge: Cambridge University Press.

Power, Michael (1993) "Habermas and Transcendental Arguments." *Philosophy of Social Science* 26: 1–23.

Rorty, Richard (1991) "The Priority of Democracy to Philosophy." In Rorty, *Objectivity, Relativism, and Truth*. Cambridge: Cambridge University Press.

Rousseau, Jean-Jacques (2007) *"The Social Contract" and Other Later Political Writings*, ed. Victor Gourevitch. Cambridge: Cambridge University Press.

Sangiovani, Andrea (2008) "Justice and the Priority of Politics to Morality." *Journal of Political Philosophy* 16: 137–164.

Sellars, Wilfrid (1963) "Philosophy and the Scientific Image of Man." In Sellars, *Science, Perception and Reality*. New York: Humanities Press.

Simmons, A. John (2010) "Ideal and Nonideal Theory." *Philosophy and Public Affairs* 38: 5–36.

Waldron, Jeremy (1999) *Law and Disagreement*. New York: Oxford University Press.

Wolin, Sheldon (1996) "The Liberal/Democratic Divide: On Rawls's *Political Liberalism*." *Political Theory* 24: 97–142.

# 29

# Rawls and Economics

## DANIEL LITTLE

Rawls's theory of justice has played a prominent role in a number of academic fields beyond philosophy, and one of these is the field of economics.[1] The theory of justice includes many assumptions about how a modern economy works, and it has normative implications for the results of those workings. So it is reasonable to ask whether and in what ways Rawls's thinking was seriously influenced by academic economic theory. A second issue is more substantive. *A Theory of Justice* is advanced as an ideal theory, abstracted from specific empirical details about modern society. Nonetheless, the basic institutions of a democratic capitalist society are plainly present in Rawls's mind as he develops his theory of justice. So it is worthwhile to consider whether Rawls's theory of justice permits moral assessment of these basic political and economic institutions. Does Rawls's corpus allow us to derive some conclusions about his own considered judgments of the justice and humanity of the institutions of democratic capitalism? This chapter undertakes to examine both aspects of this relationship between moral theory and economics. What role did serious engagement with economic theory play in the formation and development of Rawls's thought? And what concrete assumptions and judgments did Rawls make about liberal capitalism? I will argue that the economic influences on Rawls were fairly narrow – largely the important developments in social choice theory, welfare economics, game theory, decision theory, and microeconomics that emerged in the 1950s. Second, I will argue that his stance toward existing democratic capitalism is more radical than was generally recognized in the two decades following publication of *A Theory of Justice*.

This chapter has a great deal to do with the question of intellectual influence. Rawls was a "social contract theorist"; to what extent were his theories shaped and framed by his reading of the great contract theorists such as Locke, Rousseau, or Kant? He was also influenced by the history of economic thought; so is it possible to find parallels or echoes of the thought systems of Adam Smith or Karl Marx in Rawls's thinking? And to what extent were there more local influences in the 1940s and 1950s that created fairly specific directions and characteristics in Rawls's thinking? These are interesting questions in application to one

*A Companion to Rawls*, First Edition. Edited by Jon Mandle and David A. Reidy.

particular philosopher. But they also raise more general questions: Where do philosophical theories come from? To what extent is it the case that a given philosopher is working within a "micro-tradition" – a particular and specific field of influence – and to what extent is the thinker "original," bringing forward new ideas on a topic? And once a fundamental topic has been established for a thinker – for example, "What defines the principles of justice for a market-based democracy?" – to what extent does the theory then develop autonomously according to the arguments and analysis of the philosopher? The question of the economic influences on Rawls's thought sheds some light on these more general questions as well.

Rawls was explicit in addressing the relationship between his own theorizing and the theories of the economists:

> It is essential to keep in mind that our topic is the theory of justice and not economics, however elementary. We are only concerned with some moral problems of political economy. For example, I shall ask: what is the proper rate of saving over time, how should the background institutions of taxation and property be arranged, or at what level is the social minimum to be set? In asking these questions my intention is not to explain, much less to add anything to, what economic theory says about the working of these institutions . . . Certain elementary parts of economic theory are brought in solely to illustrate the content of the principles of justice. (*TJ*, 234)

So Rawls is clear in distinguishing the analytics of his own work from that of contemporary economics. At the same time, he is committed to discussing the workings of existing and hypothetical economic arrangements, and this requires a foundational understanding of current thinking in economic theory.

One of the primary goals of Rawls's theory of justice is directly relevant to economic policy. He specifically wanted to work out the implications of the theory of justice for the justice of fundamental economic institutions:

> My aim in this chapter is to see how the two principles work out as a conception of political economy, that is, as standards by which to assess economic arrangements and policies, and their background institutions. (Welfare economics is often defined in the same way. I do not use this name because the term "welfare" suggests that the implicit moral conception is utilitarian; the phrase "social choice" is far better although I believe its connotations are still too narrow.) A doctrine of political economy must include an interpretation of the public good which is based on a conception of justice. It is to guide the reflections of the citizen when he considers questions of economic and social policy. (*TJ*, 228–229)

Or in other words, philosophy and economics intersect when it comes to analyzing, evaluating, and implementing economic institutions and policies. The subject matter of the theory of justice forces us to pay attention to the actual dynamics and outcomes of existing and hypothetical economic arrangements and the inequalities that they may create. This chapter will attempt to discover the intellectual and theoretical relationships that existed between economic theory and the formation and development of Rawls's thought.

## Rawls's Sources in Economics

One way of beginning to address these questions is to survey the uses that Rawls made of economic literature throughout his corpus. We can look at Rawls's major papers between

1955 and 1971 as a reasonable sample of the intellectual influences that affected the development of his thought. His first major paper, "Two Concepts of Rules," appeared in 1955,[2] and *A Theory of Justice* appeared in 1971. All of his major papers during this formative period are included in his *Collected Papers*, so this is a convenient way of surveying his thought during this portion of his career. What can we learn from these papers when it comes to the influence of the economists on Rawls? Table A in the appendix below provides an inventory of Rawls's references to economists in articles published from 1955 to 1971. Tables B and C provide a similar analysis of *A Theory of Justice*.

Several things are noteworthy in this inventory. First, Rawls's references are highly contemporary to the 1950s. He appears to have had a high level of acquaintance with what was happening in economics in that decade. But there are virtually no references to earlier figures in the history of economics; Pareto is virtually the only repeat entry in the index from any time prior to 1940 (Pareto principle).

Second, there is a decided focus on several areas of then-contemporary economic theory: welfare economics, social choice theory, and game theory. Von Neumann and Morgenstern are cited numerous times, as are Luce and Raiffa. Kenneth Arrow and John Harsanyi are repeat references as well. (It is interesting to observe that Amartya Sen is cited in later essays, but not prior to 1971.) Keynes is not mentioned in these early articles, and only tangentially in *TJ*. And there is no mention of general equilibrium theory. Rawls was interested in the areas of economics in the 1950s and 1960s that were relevant to the assessment of social welfare, the formal procedures of democracy, and the theory of rational decision-making in the presence of multiple rational agents. He was evidently not interested in microeconomics, equilibrium theory, or macroeconomics.

Third, none of these citations reflect a significant or substantive discussion of the economist's views. There are virtually no extended passages in these articles from 1955 to 1971 in which Rawls offers a substantive discussion of a point of economic theory. Rather, Rawls tends to illustrate a philosophical point by finding a relevant theoretical claim in one economist or another. This indicates a degree of familiarity with the contemporary literature, but a fairly low level of intellectual engagement with the debates and analytical approaches. In contrast to his treatment of utilitarianism, Kant, or Rousseau, Rawls's treatment of economic theory is brief and nonsubstantive.

Significantly absent from this inventory of references is any mention of the classical political economists. The index of *Collected Papers* contains no references to Ricardo, Quesnay, or Malthus, and only one reference to Adam Smith (ideal spectator theory; *CP*, 201). John Stuart Mill is discussed in some detail, but always as a utilitarian philosopher, not as an economist. Marx is mentioned briefly (*Critique of the Gotha Programme*; *CP*, 252). The labor theory of value – the central construct of classical political economy – is not mentioned once.

We can also examine the economic content of *A Theory of Justice* itself for an indication of Rawls's intellectual itinerary. Tables B and C provide lists of economists and topics included in the index of *TJ*. Table B provides a list of the economists cited in *A Theory of Justice* ordered by approximate date of their works. The economists cited are disproportionately drawn from 1950–1970. Out of the 36 economists cited, 25 fall in this period. Essentially, these are economists who published their work from the time of Rawls's graduate studies at Princeton through publication of *A Theory of Justice*. Only five economists prior to 1900 are cited, and six are cited from between 1900 and 1950. (Karl Marx is cited in six places, but none of these citations include his economic writings.) There are a few references to Smith in *A Theory of Justice*, but they are superficial and incidental. Smith is discussed as a utilitarian, an advocate for the concept of the invisible hand (*TJ*, 49), and a student of the moral sentiments (*TJ*, 161, 419) and impartial spectator theory (*TJ*, 233). There is nothing to confirm a careful or extensive reading of Smith, Ricardo, Malthus, or Marx as economists in *A Theory of Justice*. This distribution implies fairly clearly that the primary influences on Rawls from economic theory were drawn from mid twentieth-century economics.

A second question that arises is whether we can identify clusters of economic topics in Rawls's discussions and references in *TJ*. Do the citations included in *TJ* allow us to do a content analysis of the areas of economics that were of interest to Rawls? Here again the index to *TJ* is a valuable lens for analyzing Rawls's areas of interest. Table C provides a listing of the topics included in the index to *TJ* that have clear connection to economics. As the table suggests, these topics fall into four specific areas: a few topics from classical economics; topics associated with the theory of markets and prices; topics associated with decision theory and game theory; and topics associated with social choice theory and social welfare theory. The most frequently cited economists in *TJ* are Amartya Sen (social choice theory), Kenneth Arrow (social choice theory), F.Y. Edgeworth (utility theory), and Luce and Raiffa (game theory).

In sum, Rawls was reasonably well acquainted with contemporary economics as of the 1950s and plainly found some aspects relevant to his philosophical agenda (Arrow, Harsanyi, von Neumann). Contemporary economists appear to have had significant influence on the formation of Rawls's thought – decision theory, game theory, and social choice theory in particular. But there is little evidence to suggest that Rawls's important philosophical insights on justice were very much shaped by a reading of the history of economics. We will return to Rawls's knowledge of the history of economic thought in the next section.

## Rawls and the History of Economics

This review suggests that the most visible economic influences on Rawls fell in the field of modern economics. What about earlier economists such as Adam Smith or Karl Marx? What did Rawls know about the history of classical political economy as he formulated his ideas about social and economic justice, including especially the theories of Smith, Ricardo, Malthus, Marx, or Mill?

It is clear from his lectures on ethics and social and political philosophy (*LHMP*; *LHPP*) that Rawls was generally familiar with the basic theoretical positions and debates in classical political economy – the labor theory of value, the invisible hand, the theory of land rent, and the simple theory of a competitive market. And beginning with the marginalist revolution (Jevons, Pareto, and Marshall), he seems to have studied economic theory more carefully. But we do not find any evidence in his corpus of a careful reading of Smith, Ricardo, or Malthus. So what was the source of his knowledge of classical political economy?

One source of exposure to the history of economics occurred during Rawls's first two years of teaching as a lecturer at Princeton. Thomas Pogge indicates in *John Rawls: His Life and Theory of Justice* that Rawls did significant reading and study of political economy during 1950–1952:

507

In the fall of 1950, he attended a seminar of the economist William Baumol, which focused mainly on J.R. Hicks's *Value and Capital* and Paul Samuelson's *Foundations of Economic Analysis*. These discussions were continued in the following spring in an unofficial study group. Rawls also studied Leon Walras's *Elements of Pure Economics* and John von Neumann and Oskar Morgenstern's *Theory of Games and Economic Behavior*. (Pogge 2007, 16)

W.J. Baumol's 1950 seminar included study of current work in modern economics, but included as well classics in the history of political economy, including some of Marx's writings. Samuel Freeman describes this encounter and quotes from Rawls in these terms:

Rawls says in his 1990 interview with *The Harvard Review of Philosophy* that he started collecting notes that later evolved into *A Theory of Justice* in Fall 1950, after completing his thesis. During this period he studied economics with W.J. Baumol, and read closely Paul Samuelson on general equilibrium theory and welfare economics, J.R. Hicks's *Value and Capital*, Walras's *Elements*, Frank Knight's *Ethics of Competition*, and von Neumann and Morgenstern's seminal work in game theory.

"As a result of all these things somehow – don't ask me how – plus the stuff on moral theory which I wrote my thesis on – it was out of that, in 1950–51, that I got the idea that eventually turned into the original position. The idea was to design a constitution of discussion out of which would come reasonable principles of justice. At that time I had a more complicated procedure than what I finally came up with." (Freeman 2007, 13)

We can get some idea of the views of classical political economy that were current in the 1950s and would likely have been conveyed by Baumol by examining Paul Samuelson's writings on this field. In his 1978 article about classical political economy, Samuelson credits Baumol for his careful reading of the manuscript along with George Stigler and Mark Blaug – each an expert on the history of economic thought. Samuelson's goal in this article is to provide a mathematical formulation of the core postulates of classical political economy (Smith, Ricardo, Malthus, Mill, and Marx) and to demonstrate their correspondence to "modern" economics. Samuelson wrote a series of essays on this theme in the 1950s and 1960s and demonstrates a detailed knowledge of the theories offered by the classical political economists. He makes substantial use of Mark Blaug's history of economic thought, as well as works by Michio Morishima and Piero Sraffa.

Another way in which Rawls might have gained a speaking acquaintance with the history of economics is through secondary surveys of the field. Were there standard histories of political economy in Rawls's formative years from 1950 to 1965? Mark Blaug's *Economic Theory in Retrospect* (1985 [1962]) was well known to Rawls by the time he wrote *A Theory of Justice*, and it provides extensive and technical discussions of the classical political economists. There are two references to Blaug in *A Theory of Justice*, and a heavily annotated copy of *Economic Theory in Retrospect* is contained in Rawls's collection of books in political economy (Schliesser 2011b).[3] So there is direct and indirect evidence of Rawls's reading in economics, including acquaintance with this detailed historical analysis of central theories within classical political economy.

One of the great historians of economic thought during those years was Joseph Schumpeter. Schumpeter's *Ten Great Economists* appeared in 1951. This book focuses largely on postclassical political economy. After a long chapter on Marx, Schumpeter provides short discussions of Walras, Menger, Marshall, Pareto, von Böhm-Bawerk, Taussig, Fisher,

Mitchell, and Keynes. More important than *Ten Great Economists* is Schumpeter's major contribution to the history of economic thought, *History of Economic Analysis*, which appeared posthumously in 1954. It is possible that Rawls used these books as a sort of intellectual guide to his understanding of the history of economic thought. The only reference to Schumpeter in Rawls's corpus is a single citation of *Capitalism, Socialism, and Democracy* (Schumpeter 1947) in *A Theory of Justice*. This does not preclude the possibility that he read Schumpeter's histories of economics. But is there any basis for supposing that Rawls was in fact acquainted with Schumpeter's work?

Here is a clue worth pursuing. Thomas Pogge notes that Rawls spent a final year of fellowship at Princeton in 1949–1950, and that he spent part of this time in an economics seminar with Jacob Viner, a distinguished Princeton economics professor (Pogge 2007, 15). (The other main area of study during that year was in the history of US political thought with Alpheus Mason.) This serves to establish a tenuous connection to Schumpeter and the history of economic thought. Viner was a significant contributor to economic theory and policy in the 1930s and 1940s at the University of Chicago and Princeton, and he also had a sustained interest in the history of economic thought. In 1954 he wrote one of the first (and most prominent) reviews of Schumpeter's *History of Economic Analysis* in *American Economic Review*.

So here is a hypothesis: it seems likely enough that part of the work that Rawls did in 1949–1950 with Viner was concerned with the history of economic thought, and it seems possible as well that he would have learned of Schumpeter's ambitious research on the history of economics from Viner. Schumpeter's book existed only in extensive notes and drafts at the time of his death in 1950 and was edited for publication by his wife, Elizabeth Boody Schumpeter, following his death. Exposure to Schumpeter through Viner would have given Rawls the motivation to study *History of Economic Analysis* carefully when it appeared in 1954. Rawls was an assistant professor of philosophy at Cornell by that time, and Pogge emphasizes his discipline when it came to reading and reflecting on the materials that he found relevant to his philosophical work. It seems likely, then, that Rawls had engaged in a moderate degree of study of the founders of classical political economy through secondary sources.

## Rawls and Decision Theory

I turn now to the influence of "modern" economic theory on Rawls's development. Decision theory and game theory were two areas of economics that Rawls plainly cared about in detail. In fact, one of the most original aspects of Rawls's arguments in *A Theory of Justice* was his use of the tools of decision theory to help refine and justify his theory of justice. Against the prevailing preference for "metaethics" in the field of philosophical ethics, Rawls made an effort to arrive at substantive, nontautological principles that could be justified as a sort of "moral constitution" for a just society. As is explained more fully in other chapters in this volume, the theory involves two fundamental principles of justice: the liberty principle, guaranteeing maximal equal liberties for all citizens, and the difference principle, requiring that social and economic inequalities should be the least possible, subject to the constraint of maximizing the position of the least well off. (The principle also requires equality of opportunity for all positions.)

509

Two elements of Rawls's philosophical argument for these principles of justice were particularly striking. The first was his adoption of the antifoundationalist coherence epistemology associated with W.V.O. Quine and Nelson Goodman. Rawls recognized that it is not possible to provide logically decisive arguments for moral positions. Though his theory of justice has much in common with the ideas of Kant and Rousseau, Rawls rejected the Kantian idea that moral theories could be given secure philosophical foundation. It is rather a question of the overall fit between a set of principles and our "considered judgments" about cases and mid-level moral judgments. He refers to the situation of "reflective equilibrium" as the state of affairs that results when a moral reasoner has fully deliberated about his or her considered moral judgments and tentative moral principles, adjusting both until no further changes are required by the requirement of consistency.[4]

Another and perhaps even more distinctive part of Rawls's approach is his use of the framework of decision theory to support his arguments in favor of the two principles of justice against plausible alternatives (including especially utilitarianism). Essentially the argument goes along these lines. Suppose that representative individuals are brought together in a situation in which they are expected to make a unanimous and irreversible decision about the fundamental principles of justice that will regulate their society; and suppose they are profoundly ignorant about their own particular characteristics. Participants do not know whether they are talented, strong, intelligent, or eloquent; and they do not know what their fundamental goals are (their theories of the good). Rawls refers to this situation of choice as the original position; and he refers to the participants as deliberating behind the veil of ignorance.

Once we connect the question "what is the best theory of justice?" with the question "what principles of justice would rationally self-interested persons choose?" there are various ways we might proceed. Rawls's description of the original position is just one possible starting point out of several. But if we begin with Rawls's assumptions, then it is natural to turn to formal decision theory as a basis for answering the question. How should rational agents reason in these circumstances? How should they decide which of several options will best serve their future interests? One point becomes clear immediately in this context: the choice of a decision rule makes a critical difference for the ultimate choice. If we were to imagine that decision-making under conditions of uncertainty depends upon the "expected utility" rule, then one choice follows (utilitarianism). But Rawls argues that the expected utility rule is not rational in the circumstances of the original position. The stakes are too high for each participant. Therefore he argues that the "maximin" rule would be chosen by rational participants in the circumstances of the original position. The maximin rule requires that we rank options by their worst possible outcome, and we choose that option that comes with the least bad outcome. In other words, we "maximize the minimum." (The maximin rule was described by von Neumann and Morgenstern in 1944 in their *Theory of Games and Economic Behavior*.)

Rawls argues that rational individuals in these circumstances would unanimously choose the two principles of justice over utilitarianism. The reason is that the two principles of justice offer a guaranteed high-minimum outcome, no matter what one's initial endowments of talents and resources are. We should be risk-averse about the most life-determining choices that we make; and the two principles represent less risk to the participants in the original position than any other alternative. This assumption does not reflect a general point about human decision-making, it should be noted, but rather a point about the fundamental seriousness of the choices made in the original position. The maximin principle is the most rational decision rule to employ in these life-determining circumstances. This conclusion is taken to be a strong basis of support for the two principles as correct. This is what qualifies Rawls's theory as falling within the social contract tradition; the foundation of justice is the fact of unanimous rational consent (albeit hypothetical consent by abstractly characterized individuals).

Notice that this analysis involves a question of second-order rationality: not "what outcome would the rational agent choose?" but rather "what decision rule would the rational agent follow?" So it is the rationality of the decision rule rather than the rationality of the choice that is at issue.

Another important qualification has to do with defining more carefully what part of the theory of rationality Rawls is using in this argument. It is sometimes thought that Rawls applies game theory to the situation of the original position, and there is a certain logic to this interpretation. Game theory is the theory of strategic rationality; it pertains to that set of situations in which the payoff for one participant depends on the rational choices of other participants. And the original position seems to embody this condition. However, the requirement of unanimity and the complete absence of a context of bargaining makes the situation nonstrategic. So Rawls's use of rational choice theory does not involve game theory or bargaining theory per se, and he is not interested in demonstrating a Nash equilibrium in the original position. Instead, he believes that there is a single best strategy that will be chosen by each individual – the two principles of justice.

One might question whether the two features singled out here – antifoundationalism and decision theory – are consistent. If Rawls's theory of justice depends on an argument within formal decision theory, then why is it not a foundationalist argument? (In fact, Rawls on occasion refers to his argument as reflecting a "kind of moral geometry"; *TJ*, 105.) What makes Rawls's use of decision theory "antifoundationalist" is the fact that this argument itself is philosophically contestable. Reasonable decision theorists may differ about the rationality of the maximin rule (as John Harsanyi argued against Rawls). So the appeal to decision theory does not obviate the need for a balance of reasons in favor of the approach and the particular way in which it is specified in this situation; and this in turn sounds a great deal like the role of physical theory and methodology within Quine's notion of "The Web of Belief" (Quine and Ullian 1970).

## Subjective Preferences and Primary Goods

Throughout the discussion above there has been a back-and-forth between classical political economy and "modern economics." Classical political economy was premised on the labor theory of value – the idea that there is a concrete, economically meaningful measure of value that guides economic organization. Use value was prior to exchange value. Further, there was the idea that the economic needs that individuals had were also concrete – the consumption goods that permitted life to proceed. So economic activity, according to the classical economists, was about something objective. Neoclassical economy, by contrast, rejected even the idea of utility as a concrete or objective human reality. Instead, modern economics bracketed the reality of needs in favor of an ontology of subjective preference. Economists no longer needed to think about what people needed, but rather simply what they preferred; so the utilities they ascribed to outcomes could be discovered by the quasi-experiments of "revealed preference." Welfare was then defined as the degree to which the individual can satisfy the range of subjective preferences he or she happens to have.

A major thrust of the twentieth-century critique of neoclassical economics arises at just this point. Development thinkers and economists like Amartya Sen and Martha Nussbaum have put forward fundamentally different ideas about human well-being. Thinkers like Paul Streeten introduced the idea of basic needs into the discussion of development priorities: they disputed that the goal of economic development in poor countries should be defined in terms of subjective preferences or utilities and argued instead for achieving a decent minimum for whole populations in the satisfaction of basic needs (Streeten et al. 1981). Amartya Sen went a step further, by introducing a more adequate theory of the human person in terms of capabilities and functionings, and argued for a conception of well-being that is defined in terms of the ability of individuals and populations to realize their capabilities (Sen 1999). These are objective criteria of well-being, not simply summations of subjective preference satisfaction.

In light of these comments, it is significant to observe that Rawls defined the situation of deliberation within the original position as one that focuses on primary goods, not subjective utilities. In fact, it might be argued that one of the large contributions Rawls made to contemporary economics is his strong and philosophically convincing case for primary goods. His rationale is that a person's ultimate goals are set by his or her conception of the good, and there is no reason to expect there to be a common agreed-upon standard for the conception of the good. It is logical, however, to observe that there are some goods that every individual requires in order to pursue any conception of the good: access to material resources and liberties. So Rawls's description of the original position stipulates that individuals pay attention to their access to primary goods, and this has more in common with classical political economy than with neoclassical economics.

## Rawls and Marx

So far we have considered the possible relationships between Rawls and classical or neoclassical economics. What about his relationship to Karl Marx? Rawls and Marx shared a number of core intellectual concerns. Each was interested in the question of what features a decent society should have; each had theories about the good human life; and each understood that the benefits of modern life depend upon social cooperation. So it is interesting to ask whether Marx's thought had an influence on Rawls. In brief, the answer seems to be largely "no." In particular, Marx's economic writings and his theory of exploitation seem to have been of no special interest to Rawls during the period leading up to the publication of *A Theory of Justice* in 1971, judging from the lectures on Marx that Rawls delivered in 1971 through 1973 in his course on the history of political philosophy. My primary evidence for this conclusion is a close reading of the lectures that Rawls offered on Marx in the early 1970s.

Rawls's two primary lecture series have been compiled by former students of his: Samuel Freeman's edition of *Lectures on the History of Political Philosophy* and Barbara Herman's edition of *Lectures on the History of Moral Philosophy*. The lectures continued into the 1990s, and they certainly evolved significantly during that time. In particular, the lectures on Marx are substantially more extensive by the time of the 1990s than they were in the 1970s. Like many other Harvard graduate students in philosophy in the 1970s, I attended both of Rawls's lecture series on the history of moral philosophy and the history of social and political thought in 1972 and 1973, and I served as a graduate assistant in the latter course. In what follows I have reviewed my notes from the 1973 version of the course to attempt to assess the degree of acquaintance Rawls had with Marx at the time of the publication of *A Theory of Justice* and to ascertain which aspects of Marx's thought were of the greatest interest to Rawls.

In brief, I find that Rawls knew the "humanist" Marx well and had some affinity with this part of his thought, including particularly the theory of human nature and alienation developed in Marx's early writings. His acquaintance with Marx's economic writings (*Capital*) was much more limited, however, and this part of Marx's thought seemingly had little appeal to him.

Rawls's teachings about Marx in his courses on ethics and social and political philosophy focused primarily on the early Marx – the "philosophical Marx." He taught and reflected upon the theory of alienation and species being, and the main texts he focused on were the *Economic and Philosophical Manuscripts*, *On the Jewish Question*, and *Contribution to a Critique of Hegel's Philosophy of Right*. He gave little serious attention to *Capital* or Marx's own economic theories. (Rawls used Robert Tucker's *Marx-Engels Reader* (Marx and Engels 1972) as the primary source of Marx's writings in his course. He also used Tom Bottomore's collection, *Karl Marx: Early Writings* (Marx 1964).)

There is only one substantive comment about Marx in the lectures on moral philosophy:

> A difference between Hegel and Marx in this respect is that Hegel thinks that the citizens of a modern state are objectively free now, and their freedom is guaranteed by its political and social institutions. However, they are subjectively alienated. They tend not to understand that the social world before their eyes is a home . . . By contrast, Marx thinks that they are both objectively and subjectively alienated. For him, overcoming alienation, both subjective and objective, awaits the communist society of the future after the revolution. (*LHMP*, 336)[5]

Rawls gave more extensive attention to Marx in his lectures on the history of social and political philosophy. (This material occupied roughly two weeks of the 12-week course.) Here are the selections of Marx's writings that Rawls assigned in this course: *On the Jewish Question*; *Contribution to the Critique of Hegel's Philosophy of Right*; selections from *The German Ideology*; selections from the *Economic and Philosophic Manuscripts*; *Capital*, vol. I, chs I, sec. 4; VI–VII; IX, sec. 1; X, sec.1; XIII–XIV; and *Critique of the Gotha Program*.[6]

The materials assigned from the early Marx in this syllabus provide a fairly complete exposure to Marx's theories of species being, true human emancipation, and alienation. *On the Jewish Question* and the *Economic and Philosophic Manuscripts* contain rich bodies of argument in which Marx lays out his conception of human activity and freedom. Sections from *The German Ideology* provide some exposure to the theory of historical materialism. And the *Critique of the Gotha Program* is a vehicle for discussing Marx's ideas of a socialist society. So this batch of materials offers a reasonably thorough exposure to Marx's thought prior to his political economy and his formulation of an economic theory of capitalism.

By contrast, the imprint of Marx's political economy in this set of lectures is very limited. The readings from *Capital* break out this way:

- Vol. I, ch. I, sec. 4: The Fetishism of Commodities and the Secret Thereof
- VI: The Buying and Selling of Labour-Power
- VII, sec. 1: The Labour-Process or the Production of Use-Values
- X, sec.1: The Limits of the Working-Day
- XIII: Co-operation
- XIV: Division of Labour and Manufacturing

This amounts to about 55 pages of reading from *Capital*, out of the 774 pages of volume I. These readings introduce a few fundamental ideas such as the fundamentals of the labor theory of value, the idea of commodity fetishism, and some of the basics of Marx's sociological description of capitalist society and the economic process within capitalism. But this set of readings provides only a very sketchy introduction to Marx's thinking in *Capital*. And the most extensive discussion that Rawls provided of any ideas from *Capital* in his 1973 course – the discussion of Marx's conception of justice in the 1973 lectures – is largely a paraphrase of Allen Wood's analysis in "The Marxian Critique of Justice" (1972). This is true all the way down to the two passages that Rawls mentions from *Capital* in the course of this lecture; both were previously quoted in Wood's article. So there is nothing original in the 1973 lecture in its interpretation of Marx's thought. Rawls has largely adopted Wood's frame of analysis in treating the question of Marx's conception of justice. This is not surprising, in that Wood's article was itself highly original and rigorous, and opened up a largely new line of interpretation of Marx's theories. But Rawls did not have much to add to the debate in this lecture.

In other words, as of 1973, two years after the publication of *A Theory of Justice*, Rawls's references to the economic theories and sociological descriptions contained in *Capital* were very slender indeed. It is justified to conclude that Rawls had not been significantly immersed in a reading of Marx's economic and sociological writings during the formative period of his development of the theory of justice.

This breakdown of topics and readings gives a clue to what Rawls found appealing about Marx. The conception of individuals forging themselves through labor is central; it reflects a line of thought extending from Aristotle to Hegel to Marx, and it seems to be foundational for Rawls himself when he describes his theory of the good. But there are other core ideas in Marx's thought that plainly did not appeal to Rawls. Central is the idea of exploitation. This idea is absolutely core to Marx; but it seems to have played little role in Rawls's theories, by the evidence of his written work and lectures.

## Rawls and Capitalism

Let us turn now to the relation between Rawls's theories of justice and the realities of existing economic institutions. How does *A Theory of Justice* work out as a critique of contemporary economic and political institutions? What can we infer from his writings about how Rawls viewed the society around him? Perhaps surprisingly, Rawls's critique of capitalism now seems deeper than has been commonly recognized. This is a central thrust of quite a bit of important recent work on Rawls's theory of justice. Much of this recent discussion focuses on Rawls's idea of a "property-owning democracy" as an alternative to both laissez-faire and welfare-state capitalism. This more disruptive reading of Rawls is especially important today,

40 years later, given the great degree to which wealth stratification has increased and the political influence of wealth has mushroomed in the United States and Great Britain.

## Rawls and Exploitation

We can begin to approach Rawls's view of capitalism by asking what the implications of Rawls's theory of justice are for the concept of exploitation. Is exploitation possible within a society that is just according to the two principles of justice? The concept of exploitation is key to Marx's theory of the capitalist economy. Marx believed, as a matter of objective economic analysis, that capitalism is a system of exploitation in a specific technical sense: the capitalist is enabled to expropriate the unpaid surplus labor of the worker. This perspective on modern economic relations as representing a set of fundamentally unfair economic relations between the powerful and the weak is not one that Rawls found compelling, apparently. And the fundamental ontological framework of Marx's thinking – the idea of capitalism as a system of relations of production through which economic activity transpires – never comes in for detailed description or discussion in Rawls.

Marx's argument that capitalism is inherently exploitative became central in the debate in the 1970s and 1980s over "Marx's theory of justice" (for example, Buchanan 1982 and Wood 1981). If capitalism is exploitative in its most fundamental institutions, then presumably Marx would judge that capitalism is unjust. An extensive debate ensued over the relationship between Marx and justice. These discussions developed quickly into an explosion of interest in Marx by analytic philosophers that took place in the early 1970s. Philosophers such as Allen Wood, George Brenkert, Allen Buchanan, John McMurtry, and Gerald Cohen, political scientists Jon Elster and Adam Przeworski, and economist John Roemer began taking Marx's writings seriously and offering extensive analysis and criticism of his theories. This resurgence began in discussions of "Marx's theory of justice," but extended quickly into many other areas of Marx's thought – the theory of exploitation, the labor theory of value, the theory of historical materialism, and his theory of capitalism as a distinctive mode of production. Examples of some of this work are included in John Roemer's edited *Analytical Marxism: Studies in Marxism and Social Theory* (1986). This work was referred to as "rational choice Marxism" or "analytical Marxism," and it represented an intellectual agenda that took Marx seriously as a thinker but often came to conclusions that jarred the sensibilities of more traditional Marxist thinkers.

It is interesting, then, to consider whether the principles that Rawls describes would in fact permit exploitation in Marx's sense of the term. Marx's concept of exploitation is formulated in the language of labor value and surplus value. Capitalists own the means of production and workers own only their labor power. The capitalist purchases the worker's labor time for a wage that is the equivalent of a certain number of labor hours X. The length of the working day is greater than X. The capitalist subtracts the cost of constant capital (machinery depreciation, space, and raw materials), and is left with a positive sum of value in the form of profit. Marx describes this as extraction of surplus value and as exploitation by the capitalist of the worker.

Do the two principles of justice permit what Marx would call systemic exploitation? It might appear that Rawls's two principles do in fact permit Marxian exploitation. It would seem apparent that the liberty principle creates a basis for the economic arrangements involved in wage labor, in which the labor time of the worker is purchased on the basis of a

515

wage set by a competitive labor market. The worker is at liberty to sell his or her labor power as she chooses.

The critical question is whether the two principles of justice permit private ownership of property in the means of production. There are two plausible approaches we can take on this question, leading to different results. The answer, it would appear, does not depend on the second principle of justice (the difference principle) but rather on the first principle of justice (the liberty principle). This, then, is the central point: does the liberty principle include protection of economic rights, including the right to own the means of production and the right to buy and sell labor power?

It is possible to read the liberty principle as representing a form of Lockean liberalism, with rights of life, liberty, and property to be protected above all else. And in fact, Rawls explicitly includes the right to hold (personal) property as a right protected by the liberty principle. It is only a small step to argue that ownership of property extends to all potential things. On this interpretation, some form of capitalism follows. If the first principle permits private ownership of property, including property in the means of production, then it is not inherently unjust to derive income from ownership of property and to hire workers to make one's property "productive." Further, if the first principle entails the right to use one's labor as one chooses, then presumably one has the right to sell one's labor time. This is the essence of capitalism. The second principle may moderate the effects of this system; but at best we get welfare capitalism instead of laissez-faire capitalism, and we get exploitation in the technical sense. A surplus is transferred from the workers who create it to the owners of capital. Therefore Rawlsian justice tolerates exploitation, on this interpretation of the liberty principle.

But perhaps the liberty principle does not in fact support these unlimited economic rights after all. This is the view that Samuel Freeman explores in depth in his book *Rawls.* (2007). In a nutshell, Freeman gives an extensive argument for concluding that Rawls does not include these economic rights under the liberty principle (the right to own and accumulate capital and the right to buy and sell labor time). Here is Freeman's position:

> Then again, Rawls resembles Mill in holding that freedom of occupation and choice of careers are protected as a basic freedom of the person, but that neither freedom of the person nor any other basic liberty includes other economic rights prized by classical liberals, such as freedom of trade and economic contract. Rawls says that freedom of the person includes having a right to hold and enjoy personal property. He includes here control over one's living space and a right to enjoy it without interference by the State or others. The reason for this right to personal property is that, without control over personal possessions and quiet enjoyment of one's own living space, many of the basic liberties cannot be enjoyed or exercised. (Imagine the effects on your behavior of the high likelihood of unknowing but constant surveillance.) Moreover, having control over personal property is a condition for pursuing most worthwhile ways of life. But the right to personal property does not include a right to its unlimited accumulation. Similarly, Rawls says the first principle does not protect the capitalist freedom to privately own and control the means of production, or conversely the socialist freedom to equally participate in the control of the means of production [*TJ*, 54; *PL*, 338; *JF*, 114]. (Freeman 2007, 48)

Unlike John Locke, then, John Rawls does not accept the property rights that give rise to capitalism as basic rights of liberty. If these rights are to be created within a just society, they must be governed by the difference principle. Or in more contemporary terms: Rawls and

Nozick (Nozick 1974) part ways on liberties even more fundamentally than they do on distributive justice.

If we accept Freeman's argument, then the answer to the question posed above is resolved. The two principles of justice are not a priori committed to the justice of the basic institutions of capitalism; and therefore Rawls's system is not forced to judge that exploitation is just. Or more affirmatively: exploitation is unjust in this interpretation of the liberty principle.

## A Property-Owning Democracy

These arguments have very direct implications for one of Rawls's most important discussions of economic institutions, his idea of a property-owning democracy. (The concept of a property-owning democracy seems to originate in writings by James Meade, including his *Efficiency, Equality, and the Ownership of Property,* 1964.) Rawls offered a general set of principles of justice that were formally neutral across specific institutions. However, he also believed that the institutions of a property-owning democracy are most likely to satisfy the two principles of justice. So what is a property-owning democracy?

Martin O'Neill and Thad Williamson's volume *Property-Owning Democracy: Rawls and Beyond* (2012) provides an excellent and detailed discussion of the many dimensions of this idea and its relevance to the capitalism we experience now. O'Neill and Williamson argue that the arguments underlying the idea of a property-owning democracy have the potential for resetting practical policy and political debates on more defensible terrain, and they establish the basis for a more radical reading of Rawls.

The core idea is that Rawls believes that his first principle establishing the priority of liberty has significant implications for the extent of wealth inequality that can be tolerated in a just society. The requirement of the equal worth of political and personal liberties implies to Rawls that extreme inequalities of wealth are unjust, because they provide a fundamentally unequal base to different groups of people for the exercise of their political and democratic liberties. As O'Neill and Williamson put it in their introduction, "Capitalist interests and the rich will have vastly more influence over the political process than other citizens, a condition which violates the requirement of equal political liberties" (2012, 3). A welfare capitalist state that succeeds in maintaining a tax system that compensates the worst off in terms of income will satisfy the second principle, the difference principle. But in these recent interpretations of Rawls's thinking about a property-owning democracy, a welfare state cannot satisfy the first principle. (It would appear that Rawls should also have had doubts about the sustainability of a welfare state within the circumstances of extreme inequality of wealth: wealth-holders will have extensive political power and will be able to effectively oppose the tax policies that are necessary for the extensive income redistribution required by a just welfare capitalist state.) Instead, Rawls favors a form of society that he describes as a property-owning democracy, in which strong policies of wealth redistribution guarantee a broad distribution of wealth across society. Here is how Rawls puts it in *Justice as Fairness: A Restatement*:

> Property-owning democracy avoids this, not by the redistribution of income to those with less at the end of each period, so to speak, but rather by ensuring the widespread ownership of assets and human capital (that is, education and trained skills) at the beginning of each period, all this against a background of fair equality of opportunity. The intent is not simply to assist those who lose out through accident or misfortune (although that must be done), but rather to put all

citizens in a position to manage their own affairs on a footing of a suitable degree of social and economic equality. (*JF*, 139)

*Justice as Fairness* offers a more explicit discussion of this concept than was offered in *A Theory of Justice*. In *JF* he describes five kinds of regimes: "Let us distinguish five kinds of regime viewed as social systems, complete with their political, economic, and social institutions: (a) laissez-faire capitalism; (b) welfare-state capitalism; (c) state socialism with a command economy; (d) property-owning democracy; and finally, (e) liberal (democratic) socialism" (*JF*, 136–137). There is similar but less developed language in *A Theory of Justice* (*TJ*, 228).

Rawls argues that the first three alternatives mentioned here (a–c) fail the test of justice, in that each violates conditions of the two principles of justice in one way or the other. In particular, laissez-faire capitalism fails because it slights the "fair value of the equal political liberties and fair equality of opportunity" (*JF*, 137). So only a property-owning democracy and liberal socialism are consistent with the two principles of justice (*JF*, 138). Another way of putting this conclusion is that either regime can be just if it functions as designed, and the choice between them is dictated by pragmatic considerations rather than considerations of fundamental justice.

Here is how Rawls describes the fundamental goal of a property-owning democracy:

> In property-owning democracy . . . the aim is to realize in the basic institutions the idea of society as a fair system of cooperation between citizens regarded as free and equal. To do this, those institutions must, from the outset, put in the hands of citizens generally, and not only of a few, sufficient productive means for them to be fully cooperating members of society on a footing of equality. (*JF*, 140)

Rawls is not very explicit about the institutions that constitute a property-owning democracy, but here is a general description:

> Both a property-owning democracy and a liberal socialist regime set up a constitutional framework for democratic politics, guarantee the basic liberties with the fair value of the political liberties and fair equality of opportunity, and regulate economic and social inequalities by a principle of mutuality, if not by the difference principle. (*JF*, 138)

This last point is important:

> For example, background institutions must work to keep property and wealth evenly enough shared over time to preserve the fair value of the political liberties and fair equality of opportunities over generations. They do this by laws regulating bequest and inheritance of property, and other devices such as taxes, to prevent excessive concentrations of private power. (*JF*, 51)

And concentration of wealth is one of the deficiencies of a near-cousin of the property-owning democracy, welfare-state capitalism:

> One major difference is this: the background institutions of property-owning democracy work to disperse the ownership of wealth and capital, and thus to prevent a small part of society from controlling the economy, and indirectly, political life as well. By contrast, welfare-state capitalism permits a small class to have a near monopoly of the means of production. (*JF*, 139; cf. *CP*, 419)

How would the wide dispersal of wealth be achieved and maintained? Evidently this can only be achieved through taxation, including heavy estate taxes designed to prevent the "large-scale private concentrations of capital from coming to have a dominant role in economic and political life" (JF, 5).

A property-owning democracy, then, is fundamentally different from virtually any version of modern capitalism. It is an economic system in which there is not a fundamental separation of society into wealth-holders and non-wealth-holders. It is one in which virtually every citizen has access to productive wealth. Consequently it is a system in which capitalist exploitation cannot occur, since workers are not "freed" from direct access to productive property. Workers are therefore not compelled to accept exploitative wage relations. It is a system in which political liberties are substantively equal, in that all citizens have roughly comparable abilities to influence and to participate in political debates. So when Rawls suggests that a property-owning democracy (or else democratic socialism) is the only system genuinely compatible with the two principles of justice, he is making a strong claim indeed about the status of existing economic institutions.

## Rawls's Later Cultural Critique of Capitalism

During the final preparation of The Law of Peoples, Rawls had extensive interaction with Philippe van Parijs. Van Parijs was particularly interested in the political and legal circumstances surrounding the establishment of the legal structure of the European Union and the obligations states and their citizens would have to each other within the EU. A key question is whether a political body – a state or confederation – needs to encompass a single unified "people" (whether by language, traditions, or culture); or if, on the contrary, such a body can consist of multiple peoples who nonetheless have duties of justice to each other.

What turns on this from a moral point of view is the level of moral concern that members of this kind of union owe each other. Are their obligations limited to the domain of "concern" that gives rise to some obligations of charity? Or are they closely enough interconnected that they are subject to the demands of justice toward each other? If the latter then the difference principle applies to them when inequalities of life circumstances are apparent. If the former then only weaker principles of assistance apply. For van Parijs this question is particularly acute in the case of Belgium, which was even then subject to fissional pressures along linguistic-cultural lines between Flemings and Walloons.

Van Parijs and Rawls exchanged several careful and thoughtful letters on these issues in 1998, and these letters were published in their entirety in Revue de Philosophie Économique in 2003 (Rawls and Parijs 2003). The disagreements between van Parijs and Rawls are very interesting to follow in detail. There is one aspect of the exchange that is particularly intriguing on the subject of Rawls's own assessment of modern capitalism. The passage is worth quoting. Here is an excerpt from Rawls's letter:

> One question the Europeans should ask themselves, if I may hazard a suggestion, is how far-reaching they want their union to be. It seems to me that much would be lost if the European union became a federal union like the United States. Here there is a common language of political discourse and a ready willingness to move from one state to another. Isn't there a conflict between a large free and open market comprising all of Europe and the individual nation-states, each with

its separate political and social institutions, historical memories, and forms and traditions of social policy. Surely these are great value to the citizens of these countries and give meaning to their life. The large open market including all of Europe is the aim of the large banks and the capitalist business class whose main goal is simply larger profit. The idea of economic growth, onwards and upwards, with no specific end in sight, fits this class perfectly. If they speak about distribution, it is [al]most always in terms of trickle down. The long-term result of this – which we already have in the United States – is a civil society awash in a meaningless consumerism of some kind. I can't believe that that is what you want.

So you see that I am not happy about globalization as the banks and business class are pushing it. I accept Mill's idea of the stationary state as described by him in Bk. IV, Ch. 6 of his *Principles of Political Economy* (1848). (I am adding a footnote in §15 to say this, in case the reader hadn't noticed it). I am under no illusion that its time will ever come – certainly not soon – but it is possible, and hence it has a place in what I call the idea of realistic utopia.

Several aspects of this excerpt are noteworthy. The first is a tentative skepticism about the goal of creating a European community in a strong sense – a polity in which individuals have strong obligations to all other citizens within the full scope of the expanded boundaries. Rawls seems to equate this goal with the idea of creating a somewhat homogeneous and pervasive European culture, replacing German, French, or Italian national cultures. And he offers the idea that the traditions, affinities, and loyalties associated with national identities are important aspects of an individual's pride and satisfaction with his or her life.

What is surprising about these views is that Rawls seems to overlook the polyglot, polycultural character of the United States and Canada themselves. Both North American countries seem to have created some durable solutions to the problem of "unity with difference." It is possible to be a committed United States citizen but also a Chicago Polish patriot, a Los Angeles Muslim, or a Mississippi African-American. Each of these is a separate community with its own traditions and values. But each can also embody an overlay of civic culture that makes them all Americans. It certainly doesn't seem impossible to imagine that Spaniards will develop a more complex identity, as both Spaniard and European. So Rawls's apparent concerns about homogenization and loss of collective meaning seem ill founded.

Even more interesting, however, are his several comments about globalization and capitalism. As we observed above in discussion of the idea of a property-owning democracy, Rawls has already expressed the idea that capitalism has a hard time living up to the principles of justice because of the inequalities of wealth that it tends to create. Here he goes a step further and reveals a significant mistrust of the value system created by capitalism. He refers to the world the "bankers and capitalists" want to create – one based on acquisitiveness and the pursuit of profit – and he clearly expresses his opinion that this is incompatible with a truly human life.

The goal of perpetual growth expresses this capitalist worldview, and Rawls reveals his skepticism about this idea as well. He offers the opinion that the pursuit of growth by this class is no more than the pursuit of greater wealth and more meaningless consumption. And he clearly believes this is a dead-end. Instead, he endorses J.S. Mill's idea of a steady-state.

Here Rawls seems to express a cultural critique of capitalism: the idea that the driving values of a market society induce a social psychology of consumerism – a "meaningless consumerism" – that overrides the individual's ability to construct a thoughtful life plan of his or her own.

Finally, Rawls criticizes the neoliberal dogmas about distribution of income that had dominated public discourse in the United States almost since the publication of *A Theory of Justice*: the theory of trickle-down economics. That theory holds that everyone will gain when businesses make more profits. And, of course, the data on income distribution in the United States since 1980 has flatly refuted that theory.

# Conclusion

Several points emerge from this discussion concerning the relationship between economics and Rawls's thinking about justice. First, we can draw some conclusions about what aspects of economics seem to have played a formative role in Rawls's thinking. The economists whose ideas show up in Rawls's arguments are largely those whose work appeared during the 1940s, 1950s, and 1960s. The topics that Rawls seems to have followed most closely are only a subset of the field of economics: social choice theory, decision theory, game theory, and social welfare theory. The history of economic thought seems not to have played much of a role in the formation of Rawls's key ideas. Smith, Ricardo, Malthus, and Marx were epochal founding theorists of political economy; but their ideas do not appear to have influenced the course of Rawls's theorizing about justice. He was aware of this tradition of thought, but it does not seem to have exerted substantial intellectual influence on his theories.

Second, Rawls had several specific reasons to be interested in decision theory, game theory, and social choice theory. These fields of economics in the 1950s and 1960s offered a technical apparatus in terms of which to think about justice, democracy, and institutional design, and Rawls plainly expended the effort needed to understand these fields in some detail. Further, he adopted decision theory as a technical resource within his argument from the original position. It is therefore unsurprising that the most common references in Rawls's corpus are to Amartya Sen, Kenneth Arrow, John Harsanyi, Luce and Raiffa, and Morgenstern and von Neumann.

Finally, Rawls's system has definite economic implications, especially when it comes to economic institutions and their consequences. He wants to know how various sets of institutions and rules work to manage the set of opportunities, liberties, and incomes that ordinary citizens possess in a modern society. Furthermore, the two principles of justice, including both the liberty principle and the difference principle, have very specific consequences for how we should judge the justice of various possible institutional arrangements. The ideal of a property-owning democracy provides a basis for a deep critique of the systemic inequalities that contemporary capitalism has created.

The past 40 years have taken us a great distance away from the social ideals represented by Rawls's *A Theory of Justice*. The acceleration of inequalities of income and wealth in the US economy is flatly unjust by Rawls's standards. The increasing – and now by Supreme Court decision, almost unconstrained – ability of corporations to exert influence within political affairs has severely undermined the fundamental political equality of all citizens. And the extreme forms of inequality of opportunity and outcome that exist in our society – and the widening of these gaps in recent decades – violate the basic principles of justice, requiring the full and fair equality of political lives of all citizens. This suggests that Rawls's theory provides the basis for a very sweeping critique of existing economic and political institutions. In effect, the liberal theorist offers the basis for a radical criticism of the modern order.

# Appendix Tables

**Table A**  Economists cited in essays from 1955 to 1971 included in John Rawls, *Collected Papers*

| Source date | Reference | Cited in |
|---|---|---|
| 1888 | F.Y. Edgeworth, "The Pure Theory of Taxation" | "Justice as Reciprocity" (1971) |
| 1909 | Wilfredo Pareto, *Manuel d'économie politique* | "Distributive Justice" (1967) |
| 1946 | J.R. Hicks, *Value and Capital* | "Justice as Fairness" (1958), "Justice as Reciprocity" (1971) |
| 1947 | John von Neumann and Oskar Morgenstern, *The Theory of Games and Economic Behavior* | "Justice as Fairness" (1958), "Justice as Reciprocity" (1971) |
| 1951 | K.J .Arrow, *Social Choice and Individual Values* | "Justice as Fairness" (1958), "Legal Obligation and the Duty of Fair Play" (1964), "Justice as Reciprocity" (1971) |
| 1952 | Tibor Scitovsky, *Welfare and Competition* | "Justice as Fairness" (1958) |
| 1952 | W.J. Baumol, *Welfare Economics and the Theory of the State* | "The Sense of Justice" (1963) |
| 1952 | Lionel Robbins, *The Theory of Economic Policy in English Political Economy* | "Two Concepts of Rules" (1955) |
| 1953 | J.C. Harsanyi, "Cardinal Utility," "Cardinal Welfare" | "Justice as Fairness" (1958), "Distributive Justice: Some Addenda" (1968), "Justice as Reciprocity" (1971) |
| 1955 | Nicholas Kaldor, *An Expenditure Tax* | "Distributive Justice" (1967) |
| 1955 | R.B. Braithwaite, *Theory of Games as a Tool for the Moral Philosopher* | "Justice as Reciprocity" (1971) |
| 1957 | I.M.D. Little, *A Critique of Welfare Economics* | "Justice as Fairness" (1958), "Justice as Reciprocity" (1971) |
| 1957 | R. Duncan Luce and Howard Raiffa, *Games and Decisions* | "Justice as Fairness" (1958), "The Sense of Justice" (1963), "Distributive Justice" (1967), "Justice as Reciprocity" (1971) |
| 1961 | Jerome Rothenberg, *The Measurement of Social Welfare* | "Justice as Fairness" (1958) |
| 1963 | Tibor Scitovsky, *Welfare and Competition* | "Justice as Reciprocity" (1971) |

**Table B**  Economists cited in *A Theory of Justice* (1971)

| Source date | Reference | Number of citations |
|---|---|---|
| 1776 | Smith, Adam | 7 |
| 1863 | Mill, J.S. | Frequent |
| 1871 | Jevons, W.S. | 1 |
| 1874 | Walras, Leon | 1 |
| 1888 | Edgeworth, F.Y., "The Pure Theory of Taxation" | 8 |
| 1909 | Pareto, Wilfredo, *Manuel d'économie politique* | 2 |
| 1921 | Keynes, J.M. | 2 |
| 1932 | Pigou, A.C. | 3 |
| 1935 | Knight, F.H. | 4 |
| 1939 | Hicks, J.R., *Value and Capital* | 1 |
| 1949 | Viner, Jacob | 1 |
| 1950 | Nash, J.F. | 1 |
| 1950 | Schumpeter, J.A. | 1 |
| 1951 | Arrow, Kenneth J., *Social Choice and Individual Values* | 8 |
| 1952 | Baumol, W.J., *Welfare Economics and the Theory of the State* | 6 |
| 1953 | Myrdal, Gunnar | 1 |
| 1953 | Harsanyi, J.C., "Cardinal Utility," "Cardinal Welfare" | 3 |
| 1954 | Georgescu-Roegen, Nicholas | 1 |
| 1954 | Savage, L.J. | 1 |
| 1955 | Braithwaite, R.B., *Theory of Games as a Tool for the Moral Philosopher* | 1 |
| 1955 | Kaldor, Nicholas, *An Expenditure Tax* | 1 |
| 1955 | Simon, H.A. | 2 |
| 1957 | Koopmans, T.C. | 4 |
| 1957 | Little, I.M.D., *A Critique of Welfare Economics* | 5 |
| 1957 | Luce, R. Duncan and Howard Raiffa, *Games and Decisions* | 7 |
| 1961 | Sen, A.K. | 16 |
| 1962 | Buchanan, J.M. | 3 |
| 1963 | Marglin, S.A. | 2 |
| 1965 | Olson, Mancur | 1 |
| 1965 | Fellner, William | 3 |
| 1966 | Tobin, James | 1 |
| 1966 | Bergson, Abram | 2 |
| 1968 | Blaug, Mark (2nd edn) | 2 |
| 1969 | Chakravaraty, Sukamoy | 2 |
| 1970 | Vanek, Jaroslav | 1 |

**Table C**   Economics topics cited in index, *A Theory of Justice* (1971)

| Classical political economy | Microeconomics | Decision theory, game theory | Social choice, social welfare theory |
|---|---|---|---|
| Division of labor | Contribution curve | Bargaining | Social minimum |
| Economic systems | Economic theory of democracy | Cardinal utility | Socialism |
| Exploitation | Efficiency, principle of | Coordination, problem of | Standard assumptions of utilitarianism |
| Political economy | Equilibrium | Counting principles of rational choice | |
| | Fuchs criterion | Free-rider, problem of | Transfer branch |
| | Ideal market process | Games as examples of social unions | Wages, fair |
| | Indifference curves | | Taxation |
| | Isolation problem | Interpersonal comparisons of well-being | |
| | Markets, use of in economic systems | Lexical order | |
| | Prices, allocative and distributive functions of | Maximin rule | |
| | Private property economy | Method of choice, first-person | |
| | Quasi-stability | Prisoner's dilemma | |
| | | Public goods | |
| | | Rational choice, principles of | |
| | | Time preference | |
| | | Uncertainty, choice under | |

# Notes

1   Rawls's theory of justice was formulated initially in *A Theory of Justice* (1971) and was refined and clarified in *Justice as Fairness: A Restatement* (2001).

2   This was preceded by the publication of "Outline of a Decision Procedure for Ethics" (1951), in *CP*, which was based largely on his dissertation.

3   Eric Schliesser documents Rawls's use of Mark Blaug in his blog, New APPS: Politics, Philosophy, Science, which has images of several pages including Rawls's annotations and notes (Schliesser 2011b). Schliesser's obituary of Mark Blaug provides more context on Blaug's writings (Schliesser 2011a).

4   See Freeman 2007, Daniels 1996, and Little 1984 for more discussion of the moral epistemology underlying Rawls's theory of justice.

5   Shlomo Avineri's *Hegel's Theory of the Modern State*, which appeared in shortly after *TJ*, provides a similar treatment of Hegel view of the modern state and the citizen's freedom (Avineri 1972).

6   These are the assignments listed in the syllabus for Philosophy 171, fall 1973–1974; author's file.

# Works by Rawls, with Abbreviations

*Collected Papers* (CP), ed. Samuel Freeman. Cambridge, MA: Harvard University Press, 1999.
*Justice as Fairness: A Restatement* (JF), ed. Erin Kelly. Cambridge, MA: Harvard University Press, 2001.

*The Law of Peoples, with "The Idea of Public Reason Revisited"* (*LP*). Cambridge, MA: Harvard University Press, 1999.

*Lectures on the History of Moral Philosophy* (*LHMP*), ed. Barbara Herman. Cambridge, MA: Harvard University Press, 2000.

*Lectures on the History of Political Philosophy* (*LHPP*), ed. Samuel Freeman. Cambridge, MA: Harvard University Press, 2007.

*A Theory of Justice* (*TJ*), rev. edn. Cambridge, MA: Harvard University Press, 1999.

# Other References

Avineri, Shlomo (1972) *Hegel's Theory of the Modern State*. Cambridge: Cambridge University Press,.

Blaug, Mark (1985 [1962]) *Economic Theory in Retrospect*. 4th edn. Cambridge: Cambridge University Press.

Buchanan, Allen E. (1982) *Marx and Justice: The Radical Critique of Liberalism, Philosophy and Society*. Totowa, NJ: Rowman & Littlefield.

Daniels, Norman (1996) *Justice and Justification: Reflective Equilibrium in Theory and Practice*. Cambridge: Cambridge University Press.

Freeman, Samuel (2007) *Rawls*. London: Routledge.

Little, Daniel (1984) "Reflective Equilibrium and Justification." *Southern Journal of Philosophy* 22: 373–387.

Marx, Karl (1964) *Karl Marx: Early Writings*, ed. Tom Bottomore. New York: McGraw-Hill.

Marx, Karl and Engels, Friedrich (1972) *The Marx-Engels Reader*, ed. Robert Tucker. New York: Norton.

Meade, J.E. (1964) *Efficiency, Equality, and the Ownership of Property*. London: Allen & Unwin.

Nozick, Robert (1974) *Anarchy, State, and Utopia*. New York: Basic Books.

O'Neill, Martin and Williamson, Thad (eds) (2012) *Property-Owning Democracy: Rawls and Beyond*. Oxford: Wiley-Blackwell.

Pogge, Thomas (2007) *John Rawls: His Life and Theory of Justice*. Oxford: Oxford University Press.

Quine, W.V. and Ullian, J.S. (1970) *The Web of Belief*. New York: Random House.

Rawls, John and Van Parijs, Philippe (2003) "Three Letters on The Law of Peoples and the European Union." *Revue de Philosophie Économique* 8: 7–20.

Roemer, John (ed.) (1986) *Analytical Marxism: Studies in Marxism and Social Theory*. Cambridge: Cambridge University Press.

Samuelson, Paul (1978) "The Canonical Classical Model of Political Economy." *Journal of Economic Literature* 16: 1415–1434.

Schliesser, Eric (2011a) "Mark Blaug (1927–2011)." In New APPS: Art, Politics, Philosophy, Science, at http://www.newappsblog.com/2011/11/weekly-philo-economics-mark-blaug-1927-2011.html (accessed May 2013).

Schliesser, Eric (2011b) "Rawls, Robbins, and Blaug." In New APPS: Art, Politics, Philosophy, Science, at http://www.newappsblog.com/2011/11/rawls-robbins-and-blaug.html (accessed May 2013).

Schumpeter, Joseph (1947) *Capitalism, Socialism, and Democracy*. 2nd edn. New York: Harper.

Schumpeter, Joseph (1951) *Ten Great Economists, from Marx to Keynes*. New York: Oxford University Press.

Schumpeter, Joseph (1954) *History of Economic Analysis*. New York: Oxford University Press.

Sen, Amartya Kumar (1999) *Development as Freedom*. New York: Knopf.

Streeten, Paul, Burki, Shahid Javed, ul Haq, Mahbub, Hicks, Norman, and Stewart, Frances (1981) *First Things First: Meeting Basic Human Needs in Developing Countries*. New York: Oxford University Press.

von Neumann, John and Morgenstern, Oskar (1944) *Theory of Games and Economic Behavior*. Princeton: Princeton University Press.

Wood, Allen (1972) "The Marxian Critique of Justice." *Philosophy and Public Affairs* 1: 244–282.

Wood, Allen W. (1981) *Karl Marx* London: Routledge & Kegan Paul.

# 30

# Learning from the History of Political Philosophy

## S.A. LLOYD

The theory of justice that John Rawls developed and elaborated across his major writings is widely acknowledged to be a boldly original work of creative power. Yet no one who studies the theory can come away without feeling Rawls's deep sense of indebtedness to his predecessors in the annals of Western moral and political philosophy. Rawls learned from great writings in the history of political philosophy and moral philosophy – incorporating, developing, refining, correcting, contrasting with and situating his own work in relation to them. Attention to Rawls's explicit use of works in the history of political philosophy, and particularly to his teaching lectures on those works, reveals the absolutely staggering depth of his understandings of the political philosophies of Hobbes, Locke, Hume, Rousseau, Mill and Marx, among others. Not content with textbook accounts of these figures, Rawls worked through his own, in many cases quite original, interpretations of their writings, employing his own method of contextually situated and charitable interpretation.

In this chapter I offer support for three distinct but related claims about the significance of Rawls's attention to the history of political philosophy: that such attention offers the most fecund approach to questions of contemporary political philosophy, that it is not objectionably conservative, and that neglecting to learn how Rawls understood the great systems of the past places one at a severe disadvantage in interpreting Rawls's own theory of justice. In the course of making this case I offer brief general introductions to Rawls's approach to the history of political philosophy, and his advice on how to learn from it through comparative study of complex systems; his views about the independence of political from other sorts of philosophy, and the relationship of his thinking to the social contract tradition and to the history of liberalism. I review some features of his interpretations of various historical political philosophies to show how knowing these is needed to guide proper interpretations of Rawls's own theory of justice.

*A Companion to Rawls*, First Edition. Edited by Jon Mandle and David A. Reidy.
© 2014 John Wiley & Sons, Inc. Published 2016 by John Wiley & Sons, Inc.

# The Questions of Political Philosophy

Rawls taught that political philosophy was not the story of varying answers across time to a single question, analogous to ontology's question "What exists?" or epistemology's question "What can we know?" While it does find general themes in such topics as political legitimacy, political obligation, social stability and the public good, the various questions of political philosophy addressed by its major historical practitioners are often occasioned by practical problems and historical events, and reflect their understanding of the state of political philosophy when they were writing. Hobbes's revision of his inherited natural law tradition in order to provide a basis for social stability among many religious and political factions in the wake of the English civil wars could hardly be further from Marx's critique of the capitalist mode of production with its supporting contractarian ideology at the height of the Industrial Revolution. (Rawls's lectures on these authors to students at Harvard University from the 1960s through 1995 are collected in *Lectures on the History of Political Philosophy*.)

Learning from historical works thus required particular attention to the context of those writings, even down to the evolution of the meanings of terms over time. Rawls evoked delighted laughter from his students whenever he recounted, in the context of introducing Hume's artificial virtues but also as a cautionary tale, the story of King Charles II's pronouncing Sir Christopher Wren's design for rebuilding the dome of St Paul's Cathedral after the Great Fire of 1666 to be "awful and artificial," meaning, in the language of the time, "awe-inspiring and a work of human artifice," a great compliment.

Rawls described his approach to interpreting works in the history of political or moral philosophy, and to teaching them, as involving two quite conscious efforts. The first was to understand the particulars of their respective projects:

> One thing was to pose their philosophical problems as they saw them, given what their understanding of the state of moral and political philosophy then was. So I tried to discern what they thought their main problems were. I often cited the remark of Collingwood in his *An Autobiography*, to the effect that the history of political philosophy is not that of a series of answers to different questions, or, as he actually put it, it is "the history of a problem more or less constantly changing, whose solution was changing with it." This remark is not quite right, but it tells us to look for a writer's point of view on the political world at that time in order to see how political philosophy develops over time and why.[1]

# How to Learn from History

Despite the differences in earlier writers' projects and philosophical and historical contexts, Rawls insisted that there was much to be learned from them. Thomas Pogge rightly notes that "unlike other great philosophers in history, Rawls regarded his work neither as a revolutionary new beginning nor as the definitive treatment of a topic area. Rather, he studied his predecessors . . . very carefully and tried to develop their best ideas in his own work" (Pogge 2007). But doing so required both a stringent fidelity to the principle of charity in interpretation, and the mastery of several complex philosophical systems, the more the better, for purposes of comparative study. Referring to his method of interpreting and teaching the philosophies of past greats, Rawls wrote:

> Another thing I tried to do was to present each writer's thought in what I took to be its strongest form. I took to heart Mill's remark in his review of [Alfred] Sedgwick: "A doctrine is not judged at all until it is judged in its best form" ... So I tried to do just that. Yet I didn't say, not intentionally anyway, what to my mind they should have said, but what they did say, supported by what I viewed as the most reasonable interpretation of their text. The text had to be known and respected, and the doctrine presented in its best form. Leaving aside the text seemed offensive, a kind of pretending. If I departed from it – no harm in that – I had to say so ... Several maxims guided me in doing this. I always assumed, for example, that the writers we were studying were always much smarter than I was ... If I saw a mistake in their arguments, I supposed they [the philosophers] saw it too and must have dealt with it, but where? So I looked for their way out, not mine. Sometimes their way out was historical: in their day the question need not be raised; or wouldn't arise or be fruitfully discussed. Or there was a part of the text I had overlooked, or hadn't read ... My task was to explain Hobbes, Locke, and Rousseau, or Hume, Leibniz, and Kant as clearly and forcefully as I could, always attending carefully to what they actually said. (*LHPP*, xiii–xvi)[2]

Rawls scrupulously practiced this method of charitable interpretation, and required it of his graduate students as well. Despite its commonsense appeal, such a method is not without its critics. Some have suggested that without much more detailed knowledge of the historical and intellectual context of a written text than Rawls typically collected there is no way to make out what the writer "actually said."[3] Others have seen such a method as stunting philosophical creativity. This is one version of the charge of conservatism. One aspiring tastemaker reviewing *LHPP* opined that Rawls's "very modesty and lack of speculative curiosity are what exclude him from the ranks of the great philosophers." Noting that "Rawls typically wrote in a gray bureaucratic prose," he asserts that unlike the epic ambitions of the great philosophers, Rawls sought merely to "rationalize" the "dogmas and preconceptions" of his age (Smith 2007). Other commentators have worried that there may be a tension between Rawls's interpretive charity (insisting that a text must be read in its intellectually strongest form) and his interpretive humility (assuming that the canonical philosophers are smarter than he) (Frazer 2010).[4] Most of those who knew Rawls personally would, I think, agree with Thomas Pogge's judgment: "Rawls's astonishing modesty was not due to ignorance. He knew very well that he had written a classic that would be read for decades to come, while most other academic authors fall far short of such achievement. But the comparison he found relevant was not to others, but to the task of political philosophy. And this comparison must always be in some degree humbling" (2007, ix).

Beyond his approach to interpreting texts, Rawls gave careful consideration to which texts he studied. The value of studying a philosophical *system* – a full and complete system, articulating and organizing each of the elements necessary to any such system – and in particular the value of *comparatively evaluating multiple systems*, could not be emphasized enough. In comparative study of complete political-philosophical conceptions we can see the working elements of any functional system in action. We can view the interaction and interdependence of the parts of a social system – law, education, family, associations both secular and religious, political rights and responsibilities – and, at least potentially, abstract from them a template for designing our own, new and improved, society. The philosophers Rawls selected for study tended either to have full systems worth mining, or to be ripe candidates for extending their thought into a fuller system. Rawls viewed political philosophy through the selective lens of "exemplars." In line with this attitude, Rawls explained how he followed what Kant says in the *First Critique* at B866. He says that Philosophy is a mere idea of a possible science and nowhere exists *in concreto*. So how can we recognize and learn it? ". . . we cannot learn philosophy, for where is it, who is in possession of it, and how shall we recognize it? We can only learn to philosophize, that is, to exercise the talent of reason in accordance with universal principles, on certain actually existing attempts at philosophy, always, however, reserving the right of reason to investigate, to confirm, or to reject these principles at their very sources." So we learn moral and political philosophy, and indeed any other part of philosophy by studying the exemplars – those noted figures who have made cherished attempts – and we try to learn from them, and if we are lucky to find a way to go beyond them. (*LHPP*, xiv)

Connecting this attention to comparative study of entire philosophical systems to his commitment to charity in interpretation, Rawls reveals:

> The result was that I was loath to raise objections to the exemplars – that's too easy and misses what is essential – though it was important to point out objections that those coming later in the same traditions sought to correct, or to point to views those in another tradition thought were mistakes. (I think here of the social contract view and utilitarianism as two traditions.) Otherwise philosophical thought can't progress and it would be mysterious why later writers made the criticisms they did. (*LHPP*, xiv)

Rawls regretted the tendency of much philosophical training to encourage students to attempt refutations of fragmentary arguments rather than to seek to understand the overall design of the philosophers' work, and to mine it for elements of truth useful in building our own theories.

An important part of the value of comparative study of philosophical systems, whether moral or political, lies in how it focuses our attention on the many elements, or moving parts crucial to a complete system and to the different ways of settling them. Human motivation, notions of goodness and principles of right, feasible institutions, a conception of law, and of political legitimacy, mechanisms for stability, the role of education, the ordering of public and associational or personal roles, the relation of political life to religion are a few of the elements systematized by the main political philosophies Rawls studied as exemplars. Rawls often explicitly commented on how the characterizations of these elements within Justice as Fairness differed from those of earlier systems.

Rawls emphasized the importance of comparative study of substantive moral systems and of the priority and independence of such study from other questions one might pursue within moral philosophy: questions of (moral) epistemology, the theory of meaning (of moral terms), and the philosophy of mind (e.g., the nature of personal identity). In his 1975 address to the American Philosophical Association on "The Independence of Moral Theory," Rawls writes:

> The fault of methodological hierarchies is not unlike the fault of political and social ones: they lead to a distortion of vision with a consequent misdirection of effort. In the case we have discussed, too many questions about the substantive structure of moral conceptions, and their comparative differences, are postponed. (*CP*, 302)

The substantive structure of moral conceptions and the judgments on which they rely provide data, as it were, about the practice of moral reasoning. Rawls had already rejected as barren the approach of conceptual analysis, and saw the futility of trying to understand the practice of moral judgment apart from the known serious efforts to give substantive structure to our moral conceptions. The idea Rawls introduced as "reflective equilibrium," a state in which our considered moral convictions had been brought into line (through a process of revision both of principles and practical judgments) with the best moral theory we have, was sometimes criticized as being too conservative to arrive at the truth about morality. Achieving coherence between our cherished judgments and our favored principles seemed to some merely to rationalize our parochial prejudices. Rawls addressed this worry with his notion of "wide" reflective equilibrium, which takes into account all competing moral conceptions we can imagine. But he would not accept his critics' notion that moral philosophy should or even could possibly be done without reliance on some or another moral theory systematizing moral judgments.

# The Roles of Political Philosophy

Although Rawls did not regard the history of political philosophy as a continuous debate on a single topic, he did see political philosophy as capable of performing a set of important functions, tasks, or as he termed them "roles" in a society's public political culture. These are set out in course lectures given over the 1980s and published as *Justice as Fairness: A Restatement.*[5] The first role is that of investigating whether some underlying basis of moral or philosophical agreement can be found to bridge divisive political conflict over deeply disputed questions, or at least to narrow the gap enough that willing and mutually respectful social cooperation can be maintained. Such divisive conflict calls forth a need for political philosophy, and in answering that need philosophy may serve a *practical role*. Rawls offered as examples of works performing this role Hobbes's *Leviathan* and Locke's *Second Treatise* and *Letter on Toleration*. In the American case he cited the debates between Federalists and Anti-Federalists over ratification of the constitution, and the discussions of slavery and of the nature of the union between the states called forth by the question of the extension of slavery that preceded the Civil War. Rawls saw his own theory of justice as addressing the practical need to adjudicate the conflicting claims of equality and liberty in our democratic tradition, a tradition which pits the liberties of the ancients, stressed by Rousseau, against the liberties of the moderns, traced to Locke, rooted in sharp disagreements over how the claims of liberty and equality are to be understood, weighed, and ordered.

Rawls termed the second role of political philosophy *orientation*, that of helping individuals to situate themselves as citizens within their own social and political institutions, and to think about their aims and purposes as members of a society with a history. This sort of orientation is distinguished from the way we ordinarily locate ourselves as members of families, or of churches or other associations. Philosophy, as an exercise of both theoretical and practical reason and reflection, orients us by showing how reasonable and rational ends – individual, associational, political and social – can be harmonized within a united framework of a just or reasonable society.

A third role of political philosophy is to reconcile us to our social world so that we may view it positively, rather than merely resign ourselves to it. In its role of *reconciliation*, stressed by Hegel in his *Philosophy of Right*, "political philosophy may try to calm our frustration and rage against our society and its history by showing us the way in which its institutions, when properly understood from a philosophical point of view, are rational, and developed over time as they did to attain their present, rational form." Rawls continues, "This fits one of Hegel's well-known sayings: 'When we look at the world rationally, the world looks rationally back'" (*JF*, 3).

Rawls saw the dangerous potential for philosophy to abuse its role of reconciliation by instead providing ideological support for an indefensible social system, by encouraging the illusions and delusions citizens must embrace if such a system is to be stable (*LHPP*, 10). He offers as an example of the kind of vigilance we should maintain in examining the ideas of our own theories Marx's critique of classical political economy as an ideology obscuring the exploitative nature of capitalism.

Related to reconciliation is political philosophy's role of probing the limits of practical political possibility; in this sense, political philosophy should be "realistically utopian." Is a just social world possible under reasonably favorable but still possible historical conditions? Social conditions vary across time, and the limits of the possible are not given by the actual, so judging the practicable is not a simple matter. But if, say, Justice as Fairness explains how a reasonably just democratic regime is realistically possible even given the fact of reasonable pluralism, it may serve to reconcile us to what we might otherwise have regretted as a sad loss of a simpler (if imagined) time in which society enjoyed consensus in values.

We can see all four of these roles being carried out in Rawls's political philosophy. Citizens find themselves born into ongoing societies. Because political society is not an association we freely choose to enter or exit – we are born into a political society and our exit options are typically quite limited and do not include the option of exiting political society altogether (where would we go to live outside the jurisdiction of some political society or other?) – we may feel trapped, or not free, by membership in our political society. In Justice as Fairness, we view political society as a system of fair social cooperation among free and equal persons and formulate principles of justice to order its basic structure. We can then reasonably view citizens living in a society the basic structure of which satisfies these principles as truly being free and equal citizens. Of course, such a society might not be realistic. Perhaps citizens living in such a society will find themselves too deeply divided over too many fundamental questions of religious or philosophical doctrine to sustain, especially to sustain democratically, fair and peaceful social cooperation. But suppose we can show that it is not unrealistic, notwithstanding the inevitability of such doctrinal diversity. Then Justice as Fairness can reconcile us to reasonable pluralism as a permanent feature of any free society that poses no necessary threat to its justice and even offers its own benefits. By so doing it can also orient us by showing us how to square our diverse individual aims and associational commitments with our basic end as citizens, organizing and maintaining political society as fair or just social cooperation. Knowing that the main religious, moral and philosophical doctrines likely to persist in a society well-ordered by Justice as Fairness could be part of an overlapping consensus on its principles of justice may provide us with the confidence we need to act responsibly as citizens in a democracy. Because the well-ordered society allows scope for the pursuit of a wide range of individual ends, and guarantees free choice of occupation and fair equality of opportunity to individuals, while holding individuals responsible for adjusting their ends to their legitimate expectations under that system, and allows us to view society as a social union of social unions, it becomes possible for us to orient and reconcile ourselves to our political society as a democratic union of free and equal citizens. Justice as Fairness harmonizes historically competitive values within a systematically worked out political conception of our freedom and equality as citizens.

# The Independence of Political Philosophy

Starting in the 1980s, Rawls began developing a view of the independence of political philosophy from moral philosophy (expressed in *Political Liberalism*) that was in some ways parallel to his earlier argument for the independence of moral theory from speculative philosophy. The political realm had its own distinctive set of political values, a conception of the person *qua* citizen, and its own norms of public reason. His presentation of Justice as Fairness as a "freestanding" political conception that, although not dependent on any comprehensive moral, religious, or philosophical doctrine, might nonetheless receive the support of an overlapping consensus among such doctrines seemed to some critics to divest his theory of its philosophical bona fides. The ideas that political philosophy serves as part of the general background culture of our society, that it should seek principles of justice whose application is limited to a pluralistic, democratic society such as our own, and that it relies on no deep roots in moral philosophy provoked indignant criticism from some. Again, the theory was accused of being too conservative.

Joseph Raz (1990) faulted Rawls for his "epistemic abstinence," while Jean Hampton (1989) went so far as to insist that Rawls was not a philosopher at all, because philosophers want truth, while Rawls looked only for agreement among existing political opinion. Habermas led the charge: "Surely you, as a philosopher, must claim truth for your theory." Rawls replied, "I think that we, as students of philosophy, should be allowed to claim for our theories whatever we think most appropriate."[6] Once Rawls had reclaimed political philosophy as an important field, his resistance to reducing it to a central but overly abstract organizing question, such as "What is justice?" for any and every object of consideration (and not just for organizing the basic structure of modern, industrial, democratic, pluralistic societies) frustrated those who saw philosophy's role as uncovering deep, timeless, universal truths. Those critics embracing a conception of cosmic justice according to which no one's distributive share in any context should reflect any morally undeserved characteristic thought Rawls's political liberalism so incomplete as to be inadequate even within its specified political sphere (G.A. Cohen 1997). Cosmopolitan critics of Rawls's refusal to extend Justice as Fairness to order international society expressed similar frustration with the perceived parochialism of Rawls's political liberalism (Buchanan 2000; Pogge 2004). It is too conservative, paying too much deference to the illiberal practices of decent but nonetheless nonliberal societies, depriving their members of full justice. A similar complaint reverberated throughout sectors of the feminist community: because justice as fairness respects, on grounds of freedom of conscience, association and exercise of religion the liberty of families and churches to order their internal life on less egalitarian principles than Rawls's own, it is too conservative to secure substantive justice for girls and women. It is ironic that some communitarian critics (mistakenly) objected to Justice as Fairness precisely on the ground that it would extend political principles of justice to internally order families, replacing the proper familial bonds of affection and benevolence (Sandel 1982).

In a nutshell, the downside to using existing practical judgments and influential historical moral theories as data in the development of our own theories is that doing so puts some conservative pressure on how large our leaps of moral imagination can be. But Rawls insisted that we cannot just make it all up.

As compared with the alternatives, Rawls's approach is defensible. Were we to ignore all prior moral beliefs on the ground that to take them into account would conserve prior biases, it would be difficult to know how even to begin the political philosopher's task. If it seems silly to begin by simply affirming the negation of all of our considered convictions, and repudiating all the historical systems we find most promising – and that really does seem ridiculous – Rawls's own approach merits serious scrutiny. Of course our best theories are likely to be wrong on many points, and certainly incomplete, and even considered judgments are not guaranteed to be true. But here it actually helps to defend against the charge of conservativism that we are seeking principles of justice to order the basic structure of a *pluralistic* society, in which the differences among citizens' considered convictions of, for example, the justice of denying marriage rights to homosexuals, or historically, the justice of Negro slavery, allow for the progressive evolution of our political culture.

## Rawls in the Social Contract Tradition

Rawls announces in the opening paragraph of *A Theory of Justice* that it is his intention to generalize and carry to a higher level of abstraction the traditional conception of the social contract. The social contract tradition, which in its modern form had run from Hobbes through Locke, Rousseau, and Kant, had been eclipsed by the utilitarianism of Bentham and Mill and its absorption into twentieth-century economic and social theory. Utilitarianism had lost sight of the fundamental distinctness of persons, said Rawls, treating individuals as fungible receptacles of good. Social contract theory offered a more fitting framework for identifying a basic social structure to sustain the rights and liberties of individuals in an increasingly and permanently pluralistic society. By tying the justification of social arrangements, whether forms of political society or principles of justice to order them, to the agreements that properly informed, properly motivated, free and equal individuals deciding within a fair deliberative situation would make, contractarianisms promised a nonaggregative way of taking each person seriously. Unfortunately, existing social contract theories had not delivered on that promise, precisely because of faults in their characterizations of contractors and their situations.

Although Hobbes recognized reasonable constraints on human behavior in his laws of nature (requiring equity, gratitude, submission of disputes to arbitration, and generally, reciprocity in our dealings with others), his argument for the narrow rationality of accepting these reasonable constraints neither acknowledged nor deployed our social capacity for treating others fairly. What Rawls described in his own theory as our "highest order capacity to have and act from a sense of justice" is, on his interpretation of Hobbes, absent from Hobbes's view. Hobbes supplies a framework for the social contract, but his conception of human motivation proves inadequate. Locke does better on that front.

Rawls described Locke's political philosophy as largely right. Comparing Locke's work to Hobbes's *Leviathan*, Rawls wrote that "Locke's *Second Treatise* may be more reasonable, more sensible, in some ways, and one might think closer to being accurate, or true" (*LHPP*, 23). But Locke's contractarianism contained two difficulties. First, Locke specified no mechanism for the people to exercise their constitutive power to seat a new government. Once a government had put itself into a state of war with the people by, say, abusing its prerogative or taxing without consent, it became illegitimate and citizens were freed of any obligation to it. They could then "appeal to heaven" to favor their side in an armed insurrection to establish a new, legitimate government. This unsatisfactory suggestion to appeal to heaven had found an historical replacement in the American innovation of the constitutional convention. Rawls saw the constitutional convention as the appropriate method for the people's exercise of their constitutive power. There was no reason in principle why such a mechanism could not be accepted into Locke's political philosophy.

The second difficulty was much more serious. Locke's state of nature, in which the institution of money allowed for large differentials in private property holdings, permitted differences in economic bargaining power to affect the terms of the social contract. Those with more property could exact greater political rights, resulting in the 40 shilling freehold property qualification for voting rights. Rather than reflecting an illegitimate exercise of force, the agreement to afford voting rights only to those with significant property holdings was rational even from the point of view of those without property.[7] It was perhaps rational, considering their inferior bargaining position, but not reasonable, precisely because reflecting their inferior bargaining position. Rawls's solution to this problem, which cannot be handled within Locke's own theory, is, of course, the original position with its veil over economic and all other bargaining advantages:

> If we are unhappy with Locke's class state, and still want to affirm some form of contract doctrine, we must find a way to revise the doctrine so as to exclude the unwanted inequalities in basic rights and liberties. Justice as fairness has a way of doing this: it uses the original position as a device of representation. The veil of ignorance limits information about bargaining advantages outside that contractual situation. (*LHPP*, 139)[8]

Rousseau's social contract introduces the idea of voting our judgments of what conduces to the public good, rather than merely voting our personal or associational interests. There is something appealing about the three aspects of generality of the general will Rawls distinguishes: Roughly, everyone votes, they vote on rules affecting everyone, and they vote their opinion on whether the rule serves the general good. But maintaining this strict discipline against the pull of private and associational interests poses a serious challenge, as Rousseau himself recognized in writing that if factions are inevitable, there should be lots and lots of them to counterbalance one another. Here again, Rawls's veil of ignorance in the original position enables contractors to abstract from rather than to hope to counterbalance private prejudices. Further, it makes rational the selection of a principle settling equal basic rights and liberties for all citizens, regardless of their membership in the majority opinion.

Along with the great works of social contract theory, Rawls taught Marx's critique of capitalism and of its underlying contractarian ideology. He accepted Marx's claim that class systems must rely for their stability on illusions about how those systems work, and delusions on the part of their participants about their own interests. In particular, if we think of labor contracts between owners of capital and owners only of their own labor power as free and as legitimating the resultant distributive shares, we will miss, as Marx said we would, the element of exploitation necessary for profit creation. In contrast, a system of reciprocal advantage, such as is Justice as Fairness, in which the greatest benefit of the least well-off in a system yielding unequal benefits of cooperation is required as a condition for the better off to enjoy that position, and especially against the background of genuinely fair equality of opportunity, immunizes citizens from exploitation. Rawls left undecided the question whether Justice as Fairness could best be realized by a system of private property democracy or by a system of democratic socialism, but he ruled out laissez-faire capitalism, welfare-state capitalism, and state socialism with a command economy.

Rawls's requirement of publicity meets Marx's complaint of ideological obfuscation head on. In the well-ordered society of Justice as Fairness the principles ordering its basic structure are known, and known to be known by all citizens; its institutions conform to those principles, and can be seen to do so. Most importantly, Rawls took seriously Marx's charge that liberal freedoms were almost purely formal. In the absence of material means to exercise them, they were worthless imaginary comforts. An adequate scheme of primary goods, including income and wealth, a guaranteed social minimum including health care, and assurance of the fair value of the political liberties, along with fair equality of opportunity, and income differentials constrained by the difference principle – all these play a part in eliminating the workplace bargaining disadvantage that feeds capitalist exploitation.

One may speculate that Rawls embraced some more positive ideas from his study of Marx. Marx's ideal of individual development of undetermined personal capacities finds expression in Rawls's insistence that we should not regret the limitedness of our capacities to develop our individual talents, but rather take satisfaction from living in a social world organized to allow us to participate in different social unions, and in our society as a "social union of social unions."

## Rawls in the History of Liberalism

Rawls's effort to refine the social contract tradition can be viewed as his way of pursuing the best method for advancing liberal political theory.[9] Justice as Fairness lies squarely within liberalism, understood as a movement toward constitutional democracy accommodating pluralism. It is meant to defend principles of justice appropriate to order the basic structure of a modern, industrial, democratic but pluralistic society, where rights, liberties and opportunities are secured to every citizen, along with adequate material means to make use of those. Rawls identified the historical origins of liberalism in the acceptance of religious tolerance after the European wars of religion, the establishment of constitutionally limited regimes, and the rise of democracy. "Expressed in broad terms, the content of a liberal political conception of justice has three main elements: a list of equal basic rights and liberties, a priority for these freedoms, and an assurance that all members of society have adequate all-purpose means to make use of these rights and liberties" (*LHPP*, 12).

Rawls saw Justice as Fairness as building on the liberal tradition, but also recognized that no existing liberal democracy comes anywhere close to implementing its requirements. His enumeration of several of the reforms still needed in the United States to bring its liberalism closer to the ideal (a prescient list in today's political climate) included:

> Campaign finance reform to overcome the present system of money buying access to power; fair equality of educational opportunity; some form of assured health care for all; some form of guaranteed and socially useful work; and equal justice for and equality of women. These reforms would greatly mitigate if not remove the worst aspects of discrimination and racism. (*LHPP*, 12)

This leads us to consider what role Rawls thought political philosophy could realistically play in democratic politics. The role he assigns to it, as serving an educational role as part of the "background culture," has been criticized as underambitious. Surely, philosophy should play a grander role in public life. But, says Rawls, unless citizens come to democratic politics with fundamental conceptions and ideals of justice, equality, basic rights and liberties of the sort political philosophy provides – ideals that endorse and strengthen their democracy's basic political institutions – their democracy may not last long. Rawls suggests that among the reasons the Weimar constitution failed was that the leading German philosophers and intellectuals were not willing to defend it (*LHPP*, 6). This, then, is quite a significant role. Furthermore, in a constitutional democracy, philosophers may play a more direct role by seeking to influence the deliberations of the Supreme Court. Rawls himself participated in one such project as signatory to "The Philosopher's Brief" to the Supreme Court in 1996 concerning assisted suicide. *A Theory of Justice* contained clarification and justification for the practices of conscientious refusal and civil disobedience, a topic with great practical importance during the Vietnam War era. On the fiftieth anniversary of the bombing of Hiroshima, Rawls appealed to his conception of a decent democratic society to support constraints on the just conduct of war that condemned that bombing. These exceptions aside, Rawls usually resisted requests that he apply his theory of justice to settle practical political disputes. He would say that he had enough on his plate just to think through and work out the theory itself – applying it would have to be left to others with the time and ability to gather and sort all the relevant facts and so on.

## What Rawls Learned from Some of the Greats

John Locke, himself a political activist during the Exclusion Crisis of 1679–1681, sought to justify resistance to a crown attempting to exercise unlimited rule within a mixed constitution in which the crown enjoys a share of legislative authority. The fear of the Earl of Shaftesbury (Locke's patron), the Whig party, and of Locke with them was that were the Catholic James to succeed Charles II, he would attempt to restore Catholicism and to establish royal absolutism in England. Locke's project in *Two Treatises of Government* was to demonstrate the illegitimacy of royal absolutism as a form of regime, hence justifying resistance to it, by arguing that it could not have been agreed to by free and equal people without irrationality, coercion, or violation of their duties to God under the Fundamental Law of Nature. Locke's intense engagement with Sir Robert Filmer's defense of divinely authorized royal absolutism clears the deck for his own positive accounts of political legitimacy and political obligation. These accounts are distinct on Rawls's interpretation of Locke's view: a person is obligated to obey a regime only if (a) it is of a legitimate form, and (b) he or she has actually consented, whether expressly or tacitly, to do so; while a form of regime is legitimate only if it could have been contracted into from the Lockean state of nature. Joining consent is necessary for political obligation, but even consent cannot bind one to obey an illegitimate form of regime.

Rawls speculated that the missing middle section of *Two Treatises* referred to by Locke in his preface to the work may have contained "constitutional doctrines that might have cost him his head."

A list of books in Locke's library suggests that to mislead the King's agents he may have called the whole work *De Morbo Gallico* (the French disease), in those days a name for syphilis. Locke and Shaftesbury did think of royal absolutism as a French disease, and certainly the French had a bad case of it under Louis XIV. (*LHPP*, 108–109)

Although Locke, like Hobbes, spent time in self-imposed exile for the sake of his safety, Hobbes was with the court of the future Charles II, while Locke became a fugitive after the discovery of the Rye House (Assassination) Plot. Recounting Locke's political activism, Rawls noted "it is quite remarkable that anyone could write such a reasonable work, one of such imperturbable good sense, while actively engaged, at great personal risk, in what may have been treason" (*LHPP*, 108).

Rawls viewed David Hume as a naturalist observing the role of moral concepts, judgments, and feelings or sentiments within the human institutions and practices regulating our conduct. Hume brings an experimental or scientific explanatory model to bear on the subject of morality, understood in his time to include psychology and social theory. Rawls described the utilitarian tradition in which Hume participated as "probably the most impressive tradition in moral philosophy" and "perhaps unique in its collective brilliance" (*LHPP*, 162). Broadly concerned with organizing society to secure the general well-being of the people, utilitarianism lacked the backward-looking dimension of a social contract theory like Locke's. In his essay "Of the Original Contract" Hume argues that while consent might in principle found a government, virtually no existing governments came into being this way, and it is not as if those of us currently living under governments could refuse our "consent" without suffering hardships so extreme that such coerced consent would not create bonds of obligation. More to the point, consent theories introduce an otiose element in their account of political obligation, because the explanation for why we ought to honor our consent, that is, keep our promises, is the social utility of the practice of doing so, the very same ground for submitting to political authority. "Society cannot possibly be maintained without the authority of magistrates," Hume maintained. Rawls characterized Hume's critique of Locke's view as imposing an "unnecessary shuffle" that obscures the fact that considerations of utility underlie all artificial duties. He judged this critique only partially successful against Locke, because it does not touch Locke's criterion for political legitimacy, but only his criterion for political obligation to a legitimate regime. Nevertheless, as a historical matter, Rawls noted that Hume's essay, along with Bentham's work, successfully weakened attachment within England to the social contract view.

John Stuart Mill, in what Rawls described as his "incessant lofty style and sermonizing tone untroubled by self-doubt," developed arguments to encourage expansion of opportunity to more of society's members and to propel progressive innovation. He saw himself, Rawls thought, as an educator of enlightened opinion trying to articulate the fundamental principles for an "organic" as opposed to "critical" age – an age in which society would be secular (without a state religion), democratic, and industrial. He was trying to sway those who had political and social influence, accounting for his nonscholarly, easy-reading and seemingly nonpioneering writings. Rawls expressed some skepticism that Mill's self-proclaimed utilitarianism really preserved the essential elements of the classical tradition. At times Mill sounded more like a perfectionist than a utilitarian. In contrast with Bentham's narrow psychological egoism, Mill built on Humean ideas of natural sympathy and a primitive form of fellow-feeling to imagine how an interest in pursuing utilitarian moral principles could be incorporated into the motivation of moral agents. Mill expanded the place of individual liberties as a higher-order, or at least longer-run method for pursuing the greatest good. Mill paid attention to pluralism and trumpeted the value of people's conducting experiments in living. Importantly, Mill sought to expand the rights of women. He did so not only through his writing, but also during his term as a Member of Parliament. He pressed for voting rights for women, rights within marriage and to divorce, rights to control their own money and reproductive activity, and rights to education and to compete for employment. Rawls accepted Mill's contention that the family is the first school of social justice, and wrote that "except for the great John Stuart Mill, one serious fault of writers in the liberal line is that until recently none have discussed in any detail the urgent questions of the justice of the family, the equal justice of women and how these things are to be achieved."[10] Rawls continued till the end of his life to think through the practical implications for a just political society of how to make women's equality real.

Rawls wrote of the self-taught Karl Marx that "his achievement as an economic theorist and political sociologist of capitalism is extraordinary, indeed heroic" (*LHPP*, 319). Marx demonstrated the inadequacy of merely formal freedoms to secure human well-being, criticized liberalism's securing only negative and not positive liberty, and exposed the alienating, dehumanizing effect of production under a capitalist division of labor. Marx unmasked the exploitation inevitable in an unconstrained market system operating with a merely formal notion of equality of opportunity. Taking these criticisms of liberalism seriously, Rawls explained how features of justice as fairness provided a response. In a well-ordered property-owning democracy (or democratic socialism) securing the fair value of the political rights and liberties, along with fair equality of opportunity, the difference principle, and an adequate material minimum needed to exercise the equal basic rights and liberties, Marx's objections will not arise.

## Interpreting Rawls Using Rawls's Interpretations of the Exemplars

Seeing what Rawls learned from his study of the history of political philosophy is tremendously helpful in grasping central ideas in Rawls's own philosophy. I'll illustrate this with examples drawn from his interpretations of Hobbes and Rousseau.

Knowing how Rawls interpreted what he called "Hobbes's secular morality" proves crucial to understanding Rawls's own approach in Justice as Fairness to public reason, to the depth of the problem of stability, and to the need for a political rather than comprehensive liberalism. Hobbes's project was to address the internal sources of disruption and corruption that, considering human nature and human circumstance, are apt to lead to divisive social conflict. Writing in the time that he did, Hobbes viewed factional religious disagreement and competition for authority over Christian subjects between secular and religious authorities as prominent among those sources of discord and instability. Rawls contextualized Hobbes's political philosophy by noting that Hobbes

> is concerned with the problem of civil war between contentious religious sects, made worse by conflict between political and class interests. In his contract doctrine Hobbes argues that everyone

has sufficient rational grounds, rooted in their most basic interests, for creating, by agreement among themselves, a state, or Leviathan, with an effective sovereign with absolute powers, and for supporting such a sovereign whenever one exists. These basic interests include not only our interest in preserving ourselves and obtaining the means of a commodious life, as Hobbes says, but also, and this is important for Hobbes, who was writing in a religious age, our transcendent religious interest in our salvation. (A transcendent religious interest is one that may override all secular interests.) Taking these interests as basic, Hobbes thinks it rational for everyone to accept the authority of an existing and effective absolute sovereign. He views such a sovereign as the only sure protection against destructive civil strife and the collapse into the state of nature, the worst condition of all. (*LHPP*, 105)[11]

Comprehensive religious or moral doctrines often take the form of transcendent interests, which means that those holding them afford them priority over mundane interests in political stability or perhaps even fairness. They are not reliably contained by mere exercise of force, and so those who hold them must be given reasons in terms of those interests for supporting political arrangements if the society is to remain stable over time and not to be, in Rawls's phrase, a mere "modus vivendi." Those with transcendent interests in satisfying the requirements of their comprehensive doctrines must be able to form a principled attachment to the principles of justice ordering their society if it is to remain stable; and that attachment requires a showing that their comprehensive doctrine affirms those principles, or at least that it is not incompatible with them.

However, when different groups hold divergent doctrines transcendently, they may not all affirm the same principled reason to adhere to common principles of justice (or in Hobbes's case, of political obligation). This is why the basic or common argument for such principles must be "freestanding" of sectarian doctrines, and rely only on the shared premises of a "secular morality." Hobbes's laws of nature, the core of which is a principle of reciprocity requiring that we do not reserve to ourselves any right we are not willing to allow to all others, are reasonable principles, rationally justified, according to Rawls. He terms them "articles of civic concord" and they "define a family of *reasonable* principles so far as their content and role discern, the *general* compliance with which is *rational* for each and every person" (*LHPP*, 64). Rawls took Hobbes's primary argument for these reasonable principles to be that rational parties would affirm them as the basis of social cooperation. That argument relies only on a partial, political conception of human nature: "Hobbes's psychological and other assumptions need not be strictly true of all human conduct . . . On the interpretation proposed, Hobbes's secular moral system is meant as a political doctrine; and as such, it is appropriate that it stress certain aspects of human life" (*LHPP*, 50–51). But of course, because the cooperative principles adopted need to enjoy principled compliance from actual citizens with potentially transcendent comprehensive doctrines if the society is to remain stable, Hobbes must establish the possibility of something like an overlapping consensus on those principles. This is what Hobbes attempted in the second half of *Leviathan*, and although his approach to doing so differs significantly from Rawls's (Lloyd 1992, 271–280), Hobbes's insight struck Rawls as clearly correct, and his evolving interpretation of Hobbes's strategy affected his development of the idea of overlapping consensus as the best means of securing stability in a pluralistic society.

It also affected Rawls's discussion of the requirements of public reason. Initially, Rawls held that public discussions of questions of basic justice and constitutional essentials ought (morally though not legally) to *exclude* sectarian considerations based on comprehensive doctrines. He subsequently modified his position so as to allow arguments based on sectarian considerations provided that "in due course" arguments to those same conclusions were provided in terms of purely public reasons. Why did Rawls revisit his views on public reason? And why did he limit "wide public reason" (*JF*, 90 n12) the way he did?

Part of the answer to the first question has to do with his appreciation of instances in which important advances in the justice of American society had been driven by religious public discourse – for instance the abolitionist and civil rights movements, and also a desire to avoid inauthenticity and factional frustration in public discourse. Why then insist that every conclusion reached on the basis of argument from a comprehensive doctrine also be reachable from an argument based solely on public reasons? If you're going to include sectarian arguments because of their efficacy, or to avoid inauthenticity, or frustration, why not go in all the way?

Hobbes held that such a limitation on public reasons is the only way to have confidence that sectarian reasons are not strictly incompatible with the minimal secular morality supporting the principles ordering our political life. Hobbes offered a robust argument that reasons based on alleged divine personal revelations should be discounted in public discourse unless they could also be supported by natural reasoning on the basis of the laws of nature. It was relatively easy for Hobbes to show this because he could tap his readers' confidence in the unity of practical reason – that because of God's design, all practical truths – prudential, moral, and religious – must cohere. Rawls dealt with this threat of strict incompatibility by counting appeals to comprehensive doctrines outside his limits of wide public reason as *unreasonable*. It is unreasonable to attempt to use the coercive power of the state (which is, for both Rawls and Hobbes, the power of citizens collectively) to enforce disadvantageous rules on others on grounds not justifiable to them.

Turning now to Rawls's interpretation of Rousseau, we can see how it influences his inclusion of "the social bases of self-respect" in his list of primary social goods, and why he gives that good such an important place. Many have found this puzzling. His interpretation of Rousseau also sheds light on Rawls's insistence on distinguishing three points of view – ours as philosophers designing the theory, the point of view of parties in the original position, and the point of view of citizens in the well-ordered society of justice as fairness.

Rawls said that, taken together, Jean-Jacques Rousseau's *On the Social Contract, Second Discourse*, and *Emile* might reasonably be claimed to be the greatest work of political philosophy in French, on a par with Hobbes's *Leviathan* in English. But Rousseau's project was much broader than those of Hobbes or Locke:

> [Rousseau] seeks to diagnose what he sees as the deep-rooted evils of contemporary society and depicts the vices and miseries it arouses in its members. He hopes to explain why these evils and vices come about, and to describe the basic framework of a political and social world in which they would not be present. Rousseau, like Hume, is of another century than Hobbes and Locke. He represents the generation that . . . prepared the way for the coming French Revolution. Established traditions were being questioned, and the sciences were developing rapidly. (*LHPP*, 192)

Rawls saw Rousseau's work as performing one of the historic tasks of political philosophy: providing a template for the design of a realistic utopia and reassurance that there is nothing in human nature that precludes our realizing a system that depends on humanity's potential for goodness. Rousseau's work stressed the values of authenticity and integrity, and, Rawls thought, laid a foundation for Mill's justifications of the liberties of thought and conscience (*LHPP*, 194), as well as Marx's attention to the problem of alienation.

Rousseau's idea that people are naturally good and become less so under the influence of malformed social institutions, along with his confidence in the possibility of structuring a social system that would not have this degrading effect, should give us some hope. One of Rawls's significant innovations in the interpretation of Rousseau was to distinguish between "proper" and "improper" forms of *amour-propre*, as opposed to simple *amour de soi*. Improper *amour-propre*, or vanity, demands that others acknowledge our superiority over them, and our natural dominance or excess of excellence. The proper form of *amour-propre* acknowledges our need to secure equal standing with others in our society, and is thus open to the requirements of reciprocity – of accepting fellowship on equal terms with others. It is not unnatural to see ourselves through the eyes of others; on Rawls's account of moral learning it is all but inevitable. The healthy way of doing this is by requiring that others regard us as equals. The corrupt and unhealthy way is by insisting that they acknowledge our superiority, or accede to our dominance.[12] This idea is evidently at work in Rawls's counting the social bases of self-respect as among the primary goods. These social bases include the fact that citizens recognize the fact that all enjoy equal basic rights and that everyone endorses the principle of reciprocity represented by the difference principle. This is a structural rather than psychological good, but it does support the attitude of self-respect.

Rousseau's famous solution to the problem of how we may "find a form of association that defends and protects the person and good of each associate" while "each one, uniting with all, nevertheless obeys only himself and remains as free as before," namely, the social contract, stressed the idea of equality at the highest level of how political society itself is to be understood, of the equality of citizens in virtue of their fundamental capacities for moral and civil freedom and their fundamental interests, and of general laws to preserve the conditions for personal independence by moderating lower-level inequalities. These measures provide social bases for self-respect.

But some of what Rawls learned from Rousseau shows up more specifically in his insistence on distinguishing three distinct points of view in the reasoning supporting his version of social contract theory. Many critics have conflated the points of view of parties in the original position with those of citizens in society.[13] They find his separation of these deliberative perspectives mysterious. Yet if we read Rawls's interpretation of Rousseau, this segregation seems to have been partly intended to remedy a problem in Rousseau's own theory. Any citizen occupies multiple roles, as a private person, as a member of various associations, and as a citizen responsible for deliberating about the general good of the society. Rousseau required an act of will on the part of the individual to don the proper hat for the deliberative question at hand. Ideally, citizens would preclude their personal and associational perspectives from their deliberations on matters of the public good. But Rousseau recognized that weak as we are, these lines will be blurred, and thus recommended that if public deliberations are to be corrupted by factional interests, they should be corrupted by as many factional interests as possible – the more the merrier.

Rawls devised a better solution to the problem of the infection of our public reasoning by personal and associational interests. Impose informational constraints that force deliberators to wear the proper hats. Parties in the original position pursue the personal interests of those they represent but have no possibility of doing so in a way that compromises the fair terms of social cooperation that comprise the general good in a just society. Citizens in the well-ordered society pursue their associational interests against the background of a just basic structure that prevents them from corrupting fair terms of cooperation. You and I deliberate directly over fair terms of our political cooperation and, taking a philosophical perspective, collectively design the deliberative process that justifies Justice as Fairness. Recognizing our various roles in political life, Rawls introduces a four-stage sequence – from the original position designed to pick out first principles of justice to constitutional, legislative and judicial stages at which the first principles are applied to and embodied in institutions. At each stage Rawls allows reasoning from a wider range of available facts since the results reached at earlier stages remove some of the risk of unfair biases distorting our reasoning. Constrained by a constitution that itself adheres to first principles of justice, legislators may be allowed to draw in their reasoning on a wider range of facts than would be appropriate for parties settling on first principles of justice. Rawls's idea here, that we each wear or may be called to wear multiple hats in political life, is best understood, perhaps only understood, in light of his interpretation of Rousseau. Many more examples could be produced to support the claim that to try to understand Rawls without understanding Rawls's understanding of the exemplars in the history of political (and moral) philosophy is to decipher without a key.

## Rawls in the History of Political Philosophy

With *A Theory of Justice* now more than 40 years old, still widely taught and with a steady stream of new volumes devoted to discussion of it, we can safely say that the political philosophy of Rawls belongs to the canon of Western political thought. It is not just that attention to his work has turned the corner from the twentieth to the twenty-first centuries, or that his work has been translated into at least 27 languages. Nor is it just that many of the generations of his students are still alive and teaching his work to their students, and teaching it in the way they learned it from Rawls. Since the publication of *TJ* it has often been said that we must either work within Rawls's theory or explain why not. Rawls dealt utilitarianism a formidable blow. Social contract doctrine has been corrected and refined. In the words of one of his expositors

> *A Theory of Justice* was a formative event for twentieth-century philosophy. It showed how philosophy can do more than play with its own self-invented questions . . . that it can work thoroughly and creatively on important questions that every adult citizen is or should be taking seriously. Many thought, after reading this book, that it was worthwhile again to read, study, teach, and write philosophy. It became a paradigm, within academic philosophy, of clear, constructive, useful work, a book that made the profession proud, especially also because its author was such a thoroughly good and likeable person. (Pogge 2007)

It is difficult to imagine Rawls's work ever becoming an obscure footnote in the history of political philosophy. It is almost certainly destined to become one of the "exemplars." And if we adopt Rawls's approach to doing political philosophy – contextual and charitable interpretation in comparative study of prior systems of political and moral philosophy – as I have argued we should, we will be mining Justice as Fairness for insights into our own philosophical projects for a long time to come.

# Notes

1   "Some Remarks about My Teaching" (1993). Nearly identical to his 1993 remarks are those in his 1997 paper "Burton Dreben."

2   This and other extracts from *LHPP* reprinted by permission of the publisher from *Lectures on the History of Political Philosophy* by John Rawls, edited by Samuel Freeman (Cambridge, MA: Belknap Press of Harvard University Press), pp. xiii–xiv, 11–12, 51, 64, 105, 108–109, 139, 162, 192, 319. Copyright © 2007 by the President and Fellows of Harvard College.

3   One well-known intellectual historian (who shall remain nameless) actually characterized Hobbes's *Leviathan* as "a particularly well-judged contribution to the ship money debate." Contrast this deflationary assessment with Rawls's own description: "Hobbes's *Leviathan* is the greatest single work of political thought in the English language . . . [T]aking everything together – including its style and its language, its scope and its acuteness and interesting vividness of observation, its intricate structure of analysis and principles, and its presentation of what I think is a dreaded way of thinking about society which almost might be true and which is a quite frightening possibility – adding all those together, the *Leviathan* makes, to me, a very overwhelming impression. Taken as a whole, it can have a very overwhelming and dramatic effect on our thought and feeling . . . There isn't anything [J.S. Mill] did that begins to have this overall effect. Locke's *Second Treatise* . . . lacks the scope and power of presentation of a political conception on the order of Hobbes" (*LHPP*, 23).

4   Frazer encapsulates his argument this way: "despite his commitment to interpretive humility in principle, Rawls often adopts a mode of interpretive charity which reveals a lack of interpretive humility in practice. Yet this thesis is not meant to accuse Rawls of a lack of humility as such. To the contrary, it is Rawls's great personal and political-philosophical humility which often leads him to practice an insufficient degree of interpretive humility" (2010, 219).

5   Rawls discusses these roles in *JF*, 1–5, and again in abbreviated form in *LHPP*, 10–11.

6   Oral exchange between John Rawls and Jürgen Habermas, Harvard University, Oct. 1986.

7   Rawls credits Joshua Cohen with having demonstrated this in his essay "Structure, Choice and Legitimacy" (J. Cohen 1986).

8   Rawls continues, "Of course, other ways may be superior; or perhaps no revisions of the social contract view will prove satisfactory, once we have considered them thoroughly."

9   Two helpful discussions of this topic are Nagel 2003 and Gutmann 2003.

10   Quoted from an unpublished manuscript of 1994 by Martha Nussbaum (2003). Nussbaum's paper carefully traces and assesses the development of Rawls's efforts to remedy this failure in the liberal tradition.

11   Interestingly, this characterization of Hobbes's project appears not in Rawls's lectures on Hobbes, but rather in his introductory lecture on Locke, by way of drawing attention to the quite different aims of their respective political philosophies. I speculate that this religion-heavy specification of Hobbes's project does not appear in the Hobbes lectures because those were transcribed from audio recordings of his lectures of 1983 in which he presents only Hobbes's secular arguments, whereas the description of Hobbes's project in his much later revised Locke lectures reflected a change in his thinking in the later 1980s from supervising a doctoral dissertation on Hobbes. Rawls's course outline (syllabus) from Spring 1983 assigns no readings from parts 3 or 4 of *Leviathan*, the half of the book in which Hobbes deals with his readers' transcendent religious interests. See *LHPP*, 459.

12    Elizabeth Anderson, also a student of Rawls, has written helpfully on the importance of the avoid-
      ance of relations of domination, and the good of the social bases of self-respect. See, e.g., Anderson
      1999, 287.
13    Michael Sandel's claim that Rawls sees actual citizens as fundamentally "disembodied selves"
      because of the way he represents parties in the original position is a prime example of this sort of
      confusion (Sandel 1982).

# Works by Rawls, with Abbreviations

"Burton Dreben: A Reminiscence" (1997), in Juliet Floyd and Sanford Shieh (eds), *Future Pasts: Perspec-
     tives on the Place of the Analytic Tradition in Twentieth-Century Philosophy*. New York: Oxford University
     Press, 2000.
*Collected Papers* (CP), ed. Samuel Freeman. Cambridge, MA: Harvard University Press, 1999.
"The Independence of Moral Theory" (1975). In *Collected Papers* (286–302).
*Justice as Fairness: A Restatement* (JF), ed. Erin Kelly. Cambridge, MA: Harvard University Press, 2001.
*Lectures on the History of Political Philosophy* (LHPP), ed. Samuel Freeman. Cambridge, MA: Harvard
     University Press, 2007.
*Political Liberalism* (PL), expanded edn. New York: Columbia University Press, 2005.
"Some Remarks about My Teaching" (1993), unpublished but quoted in *Lectures on the History of Politi-
     cal Philosophy*.
*A Theory of Justice* (TJ), rev. edn. Cambridge, MA: Harvard University Press, 1999.

# Other References

Anderson, Elizabeth (1999) "What is the Point of Equality." *Ethics* 109(2): 287–337.
Buchanan, Allen (2000) "Rawls's Law of Peoples: Rules for a Vanished Westphalian World." *Ethics* 110:
     697–721.
Cohen, G.A. (1997) "Where the Action Is: On the Site of Distributive Justice." *Philosophy and Public
     Affairs* 26(1): 3–30.
Cohen, Joshua (1986) "Structure, Choice and Legitimacy: Locke's Theory of the State." *Philosophy and
     Public Affairs* 15(4): 301–324.
Frazer, Michael L. (2010) "Review Article: The Modest Professor: Interpretive Charity and Interpretive
     Humility in John Rawls's Lectures on the History of Political Philosophy." *European Journal of Political
     Theory* 9(2): 218–226.
Gutmann, Amy. 2003. "Rawls on the Relationship between Liberalism and Democracy." In Samuel
     Freeman (ed.), *The Cambridge Companion to Rawls*. Cambridge: Cambridge University Press.
Hampton, Jean (1989) "Should Political Philosophy Be Done without Metaphysics?" *Ethics* 99(4):
     791–814.
Lloyd, S.A. (1992) *Ideals as Interests in Hobbes's Leviathan*. Cambridge: Cambridge University Press.
Nagel, Thomas (2003) "Rawls and Liberalism." In Samuel Freeman (ed.), *The Cambridge Companion to
     Rawls*. Cambridge: Cambridge University Press.
Nussbaum, Martha (2003) "Rawls and Feminism." In Samuel Freeman (ed.), *The Cambridge Companion
     to Rawls*. Cambridge: Cambridge University Press.
Pogge, Thomas (2004) "The Incoherence between Rawls's Theories of Justice." *Fordham Law Review*
     72(5): 1739–1759.

Pogge, Thomas (2007) *John Rawls*. New York: Oxford University Press.

Raz, Joseph (1990) "Facing Diversity: The Case for Epistemic Abstinence." *Philosophy and Public Affairs* 19(1): 3–46.

Sandel, Michael J. (1982) *Liberalism and the Limits of Justice*. Cambridge: Cambridge University Press.

Smith, Steven B. (2007) "Review of John Rawls's *Lectures in the History of Political Philosophy*." *New York Sun*, May 11.

# 31

# Rawls and the History of Moral Philosophy

## *The Cases of Smith and Kant*

### PAUL GUYER

## Introduction

My brief for this chapter is Rawls and the history of moral philosophy. That is a very large subject. Rawls's magnum opus in political philosophy, *A Theory of Justice*, was deeply informed and to a considerable extent structured by conceptions of utilitarianism, perfectionism, and Kantianism, understood as the culmination of what Rawls called contractarianism, as the chief approaches not just to political philosophy but to moral philosophy as well since the beginning of the eighteenth century to his own time in the middle of the twentieth. Recounting Rawls's use of the history of moral philosophy in *TJ* – above all his complicated relationship to Henry Sidgwick, who provides a model in his defense of utilitarianism for what Rawls wants to do for contractarianism, but who also, precisely because he defends utilitarianism so effectively, is the major historical antagonist for Rawls in this work – would certainly be one way to present Rawls's relationship to the history of moral philosophy.

Rawls also lectured directly on the history of modern moral philosophy throughout his 30-year teaching career at Harvard, and his lectures from the final version of the course, given in 1991, were published in 2000 as *Lectures on the History of Moral Philosophy*. (Five lectures on the moral philosophy of Joseph Butler from Rawls's course on moral philosophy in 1982, not included in the 1991 course and thus not included in *LHMP*, were included in Rawls's *Lectures on the History of Political Philosophy* published in 2007.) In his lectures on the history of moral philosophy, Rawls largely confined himself to the eighteenth century, passing beyond the boundary of 1800 only to discuss Hegel, whose own views on moral philosophy were in any case largely formed within the first decade of the new century, and in response to eighteenth-century views, above all, of course, Kant's. Writing about these lectures alone might also be a reasonable task for a single essay, and indeed it might be argued that examining Rawls's treatment of eighteenth-century moral philosophy would be a way to examine his conception of the whole history of modern moral philosophy, since it could be argued with some plausibility that the main forms of ethical theory since the eighteenth

*A Companion to Rawls*, First Edition. Edited by Jon Mandle and David A. Reidy.
© 2014 John Wiley & Sons, Inc. Published 2016 by John Wiley & Sons, Inc.

century – varieties of utilitarianism, Neo-Kantianism, perfectionism, intuitionism, even virtue ethics – have been nothing but refinements of views already developed during that fertile period for modern philosophy in general.

But I will take neither of these obvious and sensible approaches. Instead, I will attempt to cast some light on Rawls's central attempt to demonstrate the superiority of a position inspired by Kant over utilitarianism by focusing on Rawls's treatment of Kant in both *TJ* and *LHMP*, as well as in the eponymous 1980 Dewey Lectures on "Kantian constructivism" (reprinted as "Kantian Constructivism in Moral Theory" in *CP*, 303–358). But I will also raise a question about Rawls's conception of the grounds for utilitarianism by discussing a figure whom Rawls touches upon in *TJ* but to my mind unfortunately neglects in his lectures, namely Adam Smith, in particular the Smith not of *The Wealth of Nations* but of *The Theory of Moral Sentiments* – an Adam Smith who was of course inspired by his friend David Hume but also by Hume's cousin but critic Henry Home, Lord Kames, and a Smith who, in my estimation, should be considered the most important of all the moral sense theorists of the eighteenth-century and their twentieth-century heirs, such as Peter Strawson.[1] And what I want to argue by focusing on Rawls's treatment of Smith on the one hand and Kant on the other is that in both of those authors the relation between deontological and teleological approaches is more complex than Rawls sometimes suggests, but that while this may be something of a criticism of Rawls the historian it is not a criticism of Rawls the political philosopher, for in his own theory there is a subtle relation between deontological and teleological considerations that is more of a continuation of than a departure from the approach of his two great predecessors.

The interpretation of Rawls's treatment of Kant is of course complicated precisely by the fact that Kant was a central figure for Rawls for so much of his career: he was the inspiration for the contractarianism of *TJ*; he was the subject of Rawls's Dewey Lectures on Kantian constructivism; and he was the figure who received the most attention in Rawls's course on the history of moral philosophy in all its versions, but particularly the version from 1991 that was printed in *LHMP*.[2] Rawls's interpretation of Kant could have changed over those years. But of course there is a more fundamental source of complexity here, namely that while in *TJ* Rawls was interested in *using* the history of moral (and political) philosophy only in order to develop his own theory of justice, in *LHMP* his aim was avowedly pedagogical – as he described it, his aim in his discussion of the historical figures he treated was "to pose their problems as they themselves saw them, given what their understanding of these problems was in their own time," and "to present each writer's thought in . . . its strongest form" rather than "to raise objections to the exemplars," which would have been "too easy" and all too likely to miss "what is essential" (*LHMP*, xvi–xvii). This point bears particularly on the interpretation of Rawls's attitude toward Kant's *method* for practical philosophy. There is some difference in what Rawls emphasizes in his accounts of Kant's central normative notions between *TJ* and *LHMP*, the former emphasizing Kant's conception of *freedom* as his foundational notion and the latter emphasizing his conception of *rationality* and treating freedom as an aspect of rationality. But the greater difference between the two works is that in the earlier book Rawls combines a Kantian notion of freedom as the fundamental human value to be reflected in a theory of justice with a post-Quinean methodology, his method of "reflective equilibrium," which aims to remain acceptable to the audience that accepted the idea of "epistemology naturalized,"[3] while in *LHMP* Rawls emphasizes and does not criticize Kant's ambition to ground morality entirely on a priori cognition of a truly universal and necessary fundamental principle valid for any rational being. In what Rawls dubs Kant's "constructiv-ism" in his Dewey Lectures and in his 1989 "Themes in Kant's Moral Philosophy" (in *CP*, 497–528) as well as *LHMP*, this strictly a priori principle is supposed to be *applied* to certain empirical assumptions about the human condition – for example, that in addition to having pure reason human beings also have sensible desires and needs the fulfillment of which would constitute happiness – in order to "construct" the "object" of morality, the realm of ends, a state of affairs to be (imperfectly) realized in nature through morally mandated and moti-vated human actions. A crucial part, but not the whole, of this realm of ends is the domain of the duties of right, Kant's version of the just "basic structure of society" described by Rawls in *TJ*.[4] But this "construction" is supposed to begin with a principle known strictly a priori, not a principle known or justified by the fact that it brings a set of empirical assumptions and intuitions about what is right and wrong into "reflective equilibrium."[5] The difference in purpose between Rawls's use of Kantian ideas in *TJ* and his interpretation of Kant in *LHMP* makes it less than obvious whether Kant's apriorism became clearer to Rawls between 1971 and 1991 or whether it was just something of little interest to him for his own purposes as a political philosopher but important for his purposes as a pedagogue.

More generally, while Rawls often presented his aim as that of doing "moral theory" inde-pendently of substantive assumptions from other parts of philosophy ("The Independence of Moral Theory," in *CP*, 286–302), thus independently of much of traditional metaethics, in fact Rawls's critique of utilitarianism and his defense of his version of Kantianism is embed-ded in a complex model of the relation between normative ethics and metaethics which further complicates interpreting his own conception of his relation to Kant. In *TJ* Rawls dis-tinguishes three main normative theories in modern moral philosophy, namely utilitarianism (which comes in both "classical" or aggregative as well as averaging versions), perfectionism, and the contractarian approach of Locke, Rousseau, and Kant; and this threefold distinction is mirrored in his choice of the major figures for *LHMP*, namely Hume, a utilitarian of a certain sort, Leibniz, a perfectionist of a certain sort, and Kant, although it is Kant's advocacy of autonomy rather than contractarianism that is emphasized in *LHMP*. In *TJ*, Rawls also distinguishes three main metaethical approaches, namely empiricism, intuitionism, and his own method of reflective equilibrium. However, he does not strictly align these with the substantive normative approaches. In fact, the method of reflective equilibrium seems to be a variant of empiricism rather than an alternative to it, or even better a more sophisticated version of empiricism, which does not purport simply to draw a utilitarian principle from moral sentiments but which rather attempts to bring a variety of our moral sentiments and principles, all given empirically, into harmony. Thus, at a methodological level, the debate in *TJ* seems to be between versions of empiricism on the one hand and intuitionism on the other. In particular, the Kantian contractarianism that Rawls advocates in *TJ* is by no means entirely independent of empiricism, for Rawls presents his own method of reflective equilibrium as empiricist in spirit; thus the battle between the normative theories of utilitarianism and con-tractarianism that plays out in *TJ* could be seen as intended to be a family fight within a generally empiricist metaethical framework. In *LHMP*, however, while Hume, the utilitarian, is obviously an empiricist, in particular a moral sense theorist, who holds that right and wrong are not merely evidenced by our feelings of approbation and disapprobation but con-stituted by those feelings, the perfectionist Leibniz is a rational intuitionist, and Kant is pre-sented as a rationalist, although not a rational intuitionist, for whom reason would give insight into an order of moral reasons or values independent of itself. Instead, he is presented as a constructivist, for whom reason begins with an insight into its own structure that yields the fundamental principle of morality, which can then be applied to empirical conditions to yield the particular duties of human beings as opposed to the general principle of duty valid for any rational being. What may be unclear in *LHMP*, however, is whether Rawls's insistence that Kant's constructivism is a form of rationalism rather than empiricism is simply a historiographical point, emphasized for his pedagogical purposes, that leaves Rawls's own commitments as a political philosopher unchanged, or is meant to signal a change in his own conception of the best method for practical philosophy, political or more generally moral. The further development of Rawls's own philosophy in *Political Liberalism* probably suggests the former, but some obscurity remains about the relation between Rawls's interpretation of Kant's philosophical method and Rawls's own philosophical method.

The relation of Rawls's own constructivism to Kant's philosophical method would perhaps be the fundamental one for any discussion of Rawls's own relation to the history of moral philosophy. But I have discussed this issue elsewhere and will not focus on it here.[6] Instead, what I want to focus on is the contrast between utilitarianism (and indeed perfectionism) on the one hand and Kantianism on the other, a contrast that Rawls often presents as a straightforward contrast between teleological approaches to ethics on the one hand and a deontological approach on the other. What I want to argue is that the Kantianism that Rawls himself employs, particularly in *TJ*, is actually a complex theory that incorporates elements of its supposedly teleological opponents, and indeed at two levels. As Rawls's *LHMP* clearly suggests, there are elements of both teleological theories, utilitarianism and perfectionism, in the doctrine of specifically human duties that Kant constructs on the basis of his fundamental, deontological principle of morality: after all, as Kant makes plain in the "Doctrine of Virtue" of the 1797 *Metaphysics of Morals* (Kant 1996c), and as Rawls faithfully reports, the ends that are also duties are nothing less than our own perfection and the happiness of others, thus we are in fact to be perfectionists with regard to ourselves and, to some extent at least, utilitarians with regard to others – although of course the duties to adopt the ends of self-perfection and the happiness of others are subordinated to the duties of right and to our perfect duties to self and others more generally (not all of which are duties of right)[7] and thus the teleological elements in Kant's system of duties may be seen as being constrained by deontological ones. But further, as perhaps *TJ* makes clearer than does *LHMP*, there is a teleological aspect not just to the *application* of Kant's fundamental principle of morality to the specifics of the human condition but also to its *foundation*: while *LHMP* emphasizes that acting in accordance with the requirement of universalizability gives rise to autonomy but takes reason's commitment to universalizability as a nonderivable "fact of reason," *TJ* suggests that Kantian contractarianism is rooted in a fundamental commitment to the insuperable *value* of freedom, and the equal value of the freedom of all. In my view, this is a teleological foundation for a deontological principle: a conception of the good, or of value, is in fact being presupposed by a theory of the right, although to be sure no objects of ordinary *inclination* are being allowed to precede the deontological principle of the categorical imperative, and thus what Rawls calls a thick theory of the good is not being allowed to precede the theory of the right.

Further, although Rawls often masks this fact by presenting the theory of justice as beginning simply from a *conception* of ourselves as moral persons, in its famous section on the "Kantian Interpretation" *TJ* also argues that our commitment to equal freedom for all can only be rooted in the structure of our *desire* to be reasonable, not in any mere *concept*. This is one idea that Kant himself explored in his earliest writings on moral philosophy in the 1760s. As he developed his "critical" philosophy from 1770 onward, he did indeed seek a foundation of his practical philosophy in pure reason, not in any form of feeling or desire, although, faced with the attractive and popular alternative of moral sense theory, he had to make room for a moral feeling "self-wrought" by reason if not antecedent to reason, namely the feeling of respect, as a moment in the phenomenal etiology of moral action; and Rawls's account of Kant in *LHMP* faithfully reflects this aspect of Kant's mature, published views. But in recognizing that practical philosophy must begin from a *desire* for the freedom of all, the Kantianism of *TJ* may be closer to Kant's original inspiration than is Kant's published doctrine of the 1780s and Rawls's interpretation of it in *LHMP*.

In the discussion of Rawls and Kant that follows, I will focus on this last claim: Rawls's deontological conception of the principles of justice is founded on a teleological theory of the good founded on a fundamental human desire for freedom; and Kant's original deontology is likewise founded on an underlying teleology, in one version that Kant considers a teleology also founded upon a fundamental human desire, in other versions one founded more metaphysically upon a conception of freedom as the essence of human beings. But before turning to Kant, I will make a comment about Rawls's treatment of utilitarianism and its connection to moral sense theory. What I now want to argue, in contrast to what Rawls seems to suggest at least in *TJ*, is that moral sense theory does not directly imply utilitarianism, particularly "classical" or aggregative utilitarianism.[8] I want to argue this point with reference primarily to Adam Smith, upon whom Rawls briefly touches in *TJ* but who, to my mind unfortunately, was not part of Rawls's canon of figures in the history of ethics and who is not treated in *LHMP*.[9] In fact, in the table of "Schools of modern moral philosophy" that Rawls presents in his introductory lecture, he does not even list Smith among the moral sense theorists, listing instead only Shaftesbury, Hutcheson, Butler, and Hume (*LHMP*, 9). Rawls is right to include Butler on this list, because there is really not much difference between Butler's "conscience" and Shaftesbury's or Hutcheson's "moral sense," Butler's importance lying rather in his argument that the pleasure of attempting to do good for others does not change the fact that it is the good of others rather than one's own pleasure that one has aimed at, and indeed depends upon that fact.[10] But Rawls's omission of Smith in *LHMP* and his misinterpretation of Smith, at least the Smith of *The Theory of Moral Sentiments*, in *TJ* has serious consequences for his depiction of utilitarianism and of the difference between Kantian contractarianism and utilitarianism.

## Adam Smith and Utilitarianism

Rawls does mention Smith's earlier work in *TJ*, but the problem I have in mind arises from a misinterpretation of one of Smith's key ideas and of a related idea of Hume's.[11] Rawls invokes what is supposed to be a conception of the "impartial spectator" common to Hume and Smith in his analysis of the attraction but central flaw of classical, aggregative utilitarianism. Since the attraction of utilitarianism is itself supposed to be founded in empiricism, this is essentially a claim that their argument for utilitarianism is a flawed application of empiricism, leaving the way open for the argument that contractarianism is ultimately grounded in a better empiricism. Rawls argues that as conceived by Hume and Smith the impartial spectator sympathizes with the preferences of all others. Were the impartial spectator to sympathize with the preference of each to be treated as equal to all others with regard to freedom, he might come up with Rawls's principles of justice as fairness. But Rawls thinks that Hume and Smith conceived of the impartial spectator as a "perfectly sympathetic being" who, feeling the pleasures in the satisfaction of their preferences of all others, comes up with the principle that to the extent possible all these preferences should be satisfied, and, short of that, the more preferences are satisfied, the better. Thus this impartial spectator is supposed to come up with classical utilitarianism, thinking that all that counts is how many preferences are satisfied, and not whose preferences they are, thus not whether a gain in the satisfaction of the preferences of some is produced at the cost of a loss to others. Classical utilitarianism, motivated by the idea of the impartial spectator, thus fails to honor the numerical difference among persons and the thought that a principle of justice ought to give great weight to this difference. "Thus an impartial spectator experiences . . . pleasure in contemplating the social system in proportion to the net sum of pleasure felt by those affected by it," and "The strength of his approval corresponds to, or measures, the amount of satisfaction in the society surveyed," but only collectively, not individually; "Sympathetically imagined pains cancel out sympathetically imagined pleasures, and the final intensity of approval corresponds to the net sum of positive feeling" in the society as a whole (*TJ*, 162–163, 233). Indeed, it could be argued that since we have no empirical evidence for the existence of such an ideal spectator, this conception of the impartial spectator and the argument for utilitarianism grounded upon it betrays the spirit of empiricism.

But while this was the conception of the impartial spectator held by Rawls's Harvard colleague Roderick Firth (see Firth 1952 and *TJ*, 161 n34), it is certainly not Smith's. His impartial spectator is not an ideal aggregator of human preferences, who might be tempted to overlook the numerical difference between persons in his aggregation of satisfactions, but is, essentially, nothing other than conscience. We adopt the standpoint of an impartial spectator on our own motivations and intentions when we consider how another – *any* disinterested other – would evaluate our motivations and intentions if he knew what they were – which of course actual others might not.[12] Only when we consider what others who would not themselves be directly benefited or harmed by our acting upon them would think of our motives and intentions – only when we adopt the standpoint of an impartial spectator of our own inmost sentiments – can we properly assess the propriety of acting upon them, an assessment which would otherwise be affected by our natural interest in our own good. And this is to say that Smith's impartial spectator is not an aggregator of preferences at all, but a scrutinizer of motives from a disinterested point of view. And since such an impartial spectator is not aggregating the satisfactions of *all*, but rather watching out for the natural human tendency of *each* to give preference to herself over others, we might infer that the impartial spectator has a natural preference for equality, not for total satisfaction. In other words, there is a distributive constraint built into Smith's conception of the impartial spectator that is missing from Firth's and from the conception that Rawls supposes to underlie classical utilitarianism.

Smith's conception of the impartial spectator is thus not a philosophical abstraction, like Firth's idea of an ideally well-informed aggregator of preferences, but flows naturally from the empirical starting-point of Smith's theory of moral sentiments. For Smith, the moral sentiments are in the first instance those that *any* impartial – disinterested, uninvolved, not personally affected – spectator naturally experiences in response to the observation of how a second person treats a third. When one disinterested person observes a second conferring a benefit, not from self-interest and without excessive self-congratulation, upon a third, who receives the benefit with due gratitude but without excessive self-deprecation, he sympathetically enjoys the pleasure of the third person and approves of the action, or the intention to perform such an action. When such a person observes a second inflicting an unprovoked injury upon the other, he shares the hurt and resentment of the third and disapproves of the action. As Smith says,

> these, as well as all the other passions of human nature, seem proper and are approved of, when the heart of every impartial spectator entirely sympathizes with them, when every indifferent by-stander entirely enters into, and goes along with them. He therefore, appears to deserve reward, who, to some person or persons, is the natural object of a gratitude which every human heart is disposed to beat time to, and thereby applaud; and he, on the other hand, appears to deserve punishment, who in the same manner is to some person or persons the natural object of a resentment which the breast of every reasonable man is ready to adopt and sympathize with. (Smith 1979, 69–70)

The impartial spectator is not an abstraction bestowed with unnatural powers of insight into preferences while deprived of the ordinary human sense of the numerical difference between persons; in Smith's view, every actual human being is naturally an impartial spectator when her own interests are not involved, and her moral sentiments are grounded precisely in her natural sense of the difference between persons, for example between one who inflicts an injury and one who suffers it. To take the stance of an impartial spectator toward oneself is then to limit one's actions in one's own interest by one's awareness – naturally generated in the course of maturation and socialization[13] – of how others would feel about one if they knew one's motivations – something people normally and naturally do because they care about how others would judge them, indeed they normally and naturally care more about this than about the gratification of their more particular desires and interests. In order to attain the satisfaction of knowing that we are approved of and admired by others, "we must become the impartial spectators of our own character and conduct" (Smith 1979, 114). And the difference between persons is essential to this, for when a person

> views himself in the light in which he is conscious that others will view him, he sees that to them he is but one of the multitude in no respect better than any other in it. If he would act so as that the impartial spectator may enter into the principles of his conduct, which is what of all things he has the greatest desire to do, he must, upon this, as upon all other occasions, humble the arrogance of his self-love, and bring it down to something which other men can go along with. (Smith 1979, 83)

We can personify this natural tendency to examine our own character and conduct from the point of view of other, impartial spectators by speaking of it as "the supposed impartial and well-informed spectator . . . the man within the breast, the great judge and arbiter" of one's own conduct, and Smith does (1979, 130). But even then what he is talking about is only the natural human tendency to look out for excessive self-interest and dampen it down for the sake of the approbation of others.

In fact, what the Smithian impartial spectator is especially on the lookout for is self-interested but unwarranted *injury* to others, even before he worries about *benefits* to others; and this means that the Smithian impartial observer is more concerned with justice than with additions to utility, aggregate or average. On Smith's account, human beings have a natural sentiment of approbation toward benevolent actions toward others, that is, actions that reduce the suffering and/or increase the satisfaction of others, but also a natural sentiment of resentment toward unprovoked injuries to others and a natural tendency in favor of the punishment of such injuries, all of which expresses itself as the "virtue" of "justice" (Smith 1979, 79). Everyone resents injuries to themselves, of course, but we also naturally resent unprovoked injuries to others when our own interests are not involved. Moreover, our feelings are such that we place the virtue of justice ahead of the virtue of benevolence – we feel that unprovoked harms must be prevented or punished before we can go ahead and provide positive benefits to others – and that we demand strict rather than loose compliance with the demands of virtue. In Smith's words,

> we feel ourselves to be under a stricter obligation to act according to justice, than agreeably to friendship, charity, or generosity; that the practice of these last mentioned virtues seems to be left in some measure to our own choice, but that, somehow or other, we feel ourselves to be in a peculiar manner tied, bound, and obliged to the observation of justice. (Smith 1979, 80)

Smith reiterates this point in a subsequent discussion of duty. Here he first anticipates a point that has been emphasized in recent discussions of Kant's account of acting out of the motive of duty (see esp. Herman 1981), namely "That the sense of duty should not be the sole principle of our conduct . . . but . . . should be the ruling and governing one, as philosophy, and as, indeed, common sense directs" (Smith 1979, 171). He then says: "The general rules of almost all the virtues . . . of prudence, of charity, of generosity, or gratitude, of friendship, are in many respects loose and inaccurate, admit of many exceptions, and require so many modifications, that it is scarce possible to regulate our conduct by a regard to them" (Smith 1979, 174). "There is, however," he continues, "one virtue of which the general rules determine with the greatest exactness, every external action which it requires. This virtue is justice. The rules of justice are accurate in the highest degree, and admit of no exceptions or modifications, but such as may be ascertained as accurately as the rules themselves" (Smith 1979, 175). In Kant's terms, the duty of justice is strict or perfect, while other-regarding duties of love, such as beneficence and gratitude, are imperfect or wide.

As he acknowledges (Smith 1979, 80), Smith learned this point not from his teacher Francis Hutcheson but from his patron Henry Home, Lord Kames, who launched Smith's career by arranging for him to give subscription lectures on rhetoric and *belles lettres*, history of philosophy, and law in Edinburgh, beginning in 1748, before Smith was appointed Professor of Logic and Metaphysics in Glasgow in 1751, from which position he moved to Hutcheson's former Chair in Moral Philosophy the following year (Ross 2010, 75–107). Also in 1751, Kames had argued against Hutcheson's attempt to derive the requirements of justice from our approbation of benevolent intentions, the foundation of Hutcheson's formulation of utilitarianism, that justice is a "primary virtue," "more essential to society than generosity, benevolence, or any other secondary virtue," and that a sense of justice naturally "belongs to man as such" as a condition of the possibility of human beings living together in society, necessary "to provide against mutual injuries" (Kames 2005, 35–36). Kames had distinguished between the duty of justice as "essential to society" and thus "entirely withdrawn from our election and choice," while the "secondary virtues, which contribute to the improvement" and "moral beauty" "of society, are not strictly necessary to its subsistence," and are thus "left to our own choice" (2005, 37). What Smith adds to this is essentially his conception of the internalization of the standpoint of the impartial spectator: our resentment at injuries is unconflicted when our own interests are not involved, but of course they often are involved, and we might be tempted to overlook or even ourselves commit injustices to others for the sake of our own interest; but our naturally internalized concern for the approbation of others, which has led to the internalization of the standpoint of the impartial spectator, will strengthen our sense of justice sufficiently to allow it to overcome the temptations of self-interest (or at least it will do so for most of us most of the time).

I have disputed Rawls's interpretation of the Smithian conception of the impartial specta-tor and referred to the Kamesian-Smithian account of the sense of justice not merely to point to a shortcoming in Rawls's historiography of moral philosophy, but to make the point that the empiricist methodology of the moral sense school, which is ordinarily associated with the origins of utilitarianism and was so by Rawls, does not, at least in the hands of its most sophisticated practitioners, lead to what Rawls considers classical utilitarianism, concerned only with the sum total of satisfaction without regard to distributive constraints. Kames and Smith, just like Hutcheson and Hume, thought that we naturally approve of utility and that all virtues and our natural approbation thereof are to be explained by utility to society in some very broad sense; but certainly for Kames and Smith this did not mean that the sum total of satisfaction trumps all other concerns. On the contrary, they made it very clear that we have a fundamental aversion to the infliction of injury on anyone not provoked by their own misconduct, indeed that the very possibility of human social existence, which is to say of human existence at all, depends on this; and our natural approbation of attempts to benefit others works only within the constraint provided by the "primary" and essential virtue of justice. The idea that some might be made to suffer in order to provide benefits to others that might increase the sum total of satisfaction in society is simply a nonstarter for these moral sense theorists. This is to say that moral sense metaethical theory had room for a deontologi-cal rather than simply teleological normative theory of duty and virtue, or more precisely a mixed theory in which the deontological constraint of justice has lexical priority over the teleological virtue of beneficence. As we will now see, Kant's own theory also involves a subtle relation between deontology and teleology.

## Kant, Deontology and Teleology

Rawls always stressed that Kant's approach to morality was deontological rather than tele-ological, and argued that a theory of justice should be so too: that was why he defended his theory of justice as fairness by means of his argument that neither utilitarianism nor perfec-tionism, both teleological theories, included adequate distributive constraints. He devoted one of the lectures on Kant to "The Priority of Right and the Object of the Moral Law" (*LHMP*, "Kant V," 217–234), and the gist of Rawls's version of constructivism is that our most fun-damental conception of the good, that of a just society in which each is free to develop his or her natural and moral capacities, is constructed on the basis of our commitment to the fundamental principle of the right expressed by the several formulations of the categorical imperative. (Rawls always neglected Kant's own development of his "Doctrine of Right" from the foundations of his practical philosophy, and did not explicitly discuss Kant's own "Uni-versal Principle of Right" as the principle that everyone must be allowed the maximally compossible external use of their freedom of choice, that is, freedom of action; see Kant 1996c [1797], 6:230–231). But *TJ* makes it clear that the commitment to the principles of justice that emerge from the "original position" is an expression of a fundamental *desire*, namely the desire to express our "nature" as free and equal persons, or a fundamental valuation, namely our commitment to the value of persons as free and equal. This is not a value "constructed" on the basis of commitment to the moral law, but a value that *explains* and *grounds* our commitment to the moral law; as such, it places a layer of teleological justification beneath the deontological constraint that Rawls argues is essential to our conception of justice. And not only does Rawls call this a "Kantian Interpretation of Justice as Fairness" (*TJ*, §40, 221–227), he is also right to do so. In *LHMP*, Rawls stresses the teleological elements built into Kant's conception of duties of virtue as "ends that are also duties," the two general duties to promote self-perfection and the happiness, perfectionist and utilitarian elements that Kant allowed into his theory of specifically human duties after he had secured the validity of the fundamental principle of morality for all rational beings in his foundational writings in practical philosophy. In this part of his work on Kant Rawls thus stresses that there is a teleological aspect to the *application* of Kant's deontological fundamental principle of morality. But in what follows, I will outline Rawls's own position on the teleological *foundation* of deontology and correlate it to what I take to be the teleological element underlying rather than following Kant's deontology. To be sure, Rawls's own "Kantian Interpretation," as I will argue, ultimately has an empirical rather than a priori foundation. However, at least from my own point of view, this is no ground for a criticism of Rawls, since I have long argued that Kant's deepest claims about the conditions of possibility of human cognition must be seen as empirical, and I have no qualms about extending this to the case of human practical reason as well (see Guyer 1987, 417–428).

Rawls lays out the general structure of his theory of justice in "The Main Idea of the Theory of Justice" (*TJ*, §3) when he states that the principles of justice are ones to which people "would agree if they were free and equal persons whose relations with respect to one another were fair," or "principles which free and equal persons would assent to under circumstances that are fair." The Kantian provenance of this conception is clear from his further statement: "In this sense" the members of a just society "are autonomous and the obligations they recognize self-imposed" (*TJ*, 12). The determination of what principles such persons would assent to under such conditions is made through the thought experiment of the "original position," where "representative" persons are imagined as choosing principles of justice behind a "veil of ignorance" about their own specific interests, advantages, and resources. In the next section, Rawls continues that the purpose of the conditions specified in the definition of the original position "is to represent equality between human persons as moral persons, as creatures having a conception of their good and capable of a sense of justice" (*TJ*, 17). He stresses that the persons imagined to be *in* the original position, agreeing about specific principles of justice, must be thought of "as rational and mutually disinterested" (*TJ*, 12), but it seems clear that *real people* who would assent to be governed by the principles of justice that would be accepted by the persons *imagined* to be in the original position cannot be "mutually disinterested" but must in fact have a *fundamental normative commitment* to the equal value of "human beings," themselves and others, "as moral persons" (*TJ*, 17): otherwise they would have no reason to be moved by the principles that would be chosen by the imaginary persons in the original position. This is what I mean by saying that in Rawls's own position the deontological constraints of justice are themselves grounded in a foundational level of teleology.

That this is so is further illustrated by Rawls's account of the "Kantian Interpretation," which also makes clear that for Rawls in *TJ* there can only be an empirical and not an a priori foundation for the teleological claim on which his entire approach rests. Rawls argues that Kant "begins with the idea that moral principles are the object of rational choice," defining "the moral law that men can rationally will to govern their conduct in an ethical common-wealth." He adds to this that "Kant supposes that this moral legislation is to be agreed to under conditions that characterize men as free and equal rational beings." These claims manifest Kant's belief "that a person is acting autonomously when the principles of his action are chosen by him as the most adequate possible expression of his nature as a free and equal rational being." Rawls understands his own view that principles of justice are those that would be chosen by parties in an original position of mutually disinterested representatives behind a veil of ignorance about their own particular situations and advantages as a version of this Kantian idea of free and equal persons agreeing upon moral principles under condi-tions that characterize them as free and equal persons – persons in such a condition must choose principles of autonomous action because "the veil of ignorance deprives the persons in the original position of the knowledge that would enable them to choose heteronomous principles" – but adds that his own model of justice as fairness "adds the feature that the principles chosen are to apply to the basic structure of society" rather than to moral life in general (*TJ*, 221–222). One might object that persons who are forced into choosing principles by deprivation of information cannot really be choosing autonomously, that is, choosing to commit themselves to moral principles in spite of their inclinations to do otherwise, but remember that the persons in Rawls's original position are imaginary: the real people are those who *do* choose to govern themselves by the principles that *would be* chosen by people in the thought experiment of the original position, and the former, the real people, must indeed freely choose to abide by these principles in the face of inclinations to do otherwise. So the choice by real people to govern themselves by the principles that would be chosen by imaginary people in the original position would indeed be an expression of their autonomy.

Nevertheless, it seems to be a fundamental difference between Rawls's position and Kant's own that Rawls characterizes the choice of real people to express their nature as free and equal beings through their choice of principles of justice as grounded in *desire* rather than something else, a pure will or pure practical reason. Rawls says that "one reason" for delib-erately assuming the limitations of the original position "is to give expression to one's nature," but also says that this is a reason "for persons who can do so and want to" (*TJ*, 222): there is nothing that can be said about why persons would choose to express their nature as free and equal beings except that they *want* to do so. Indeed, even when he characterizes Kant's own model of free, supposedly noumenal choice, Rawls treats the choice of the principles of justice as grounded in a desire. In response to Henry Sidgwick's famous objection to Kant's supposed position that only the choice to abide by the moral law realizes an agent's "true self" and thus a choice to be immoral does not (Sidgwick 1907, Appendix), Rawls says:

> Kant's reply must be that though acting on any consistent set of principles could be the outcome of a decision on the part of the noumenal self, not all such action by the phenomenal self expresses this decision as that of a free and equal rational being. Thus if a person realizes his true self by expressing it in his actions, *and he desires above all else to realize this self*, then he will choose to act from principles that manifest his nature as a free and equal rational being. (*TJ*, 224, emphasis added)

Rawls then uses the image of choice in a noumenal world to characterize his own model of the choice of principles of justice in the original position:

> My suggestion is that we think of the original position as in important ways similar to the point of view from which noumenal selves see the world. The parties qua noumenal selves have complete freedom to choose whatever principles they wish; but they also have a desire to express their nature as rational and equal members of the intelligible realm with precisely this liberty to choose, that is, as beings who can look at the world in this way and express this perspective in their life as members of society. (*TJ*, 225)

Here Rawls conceives of noumenal choice as based on desire, the desire to express our nature as free and/or rational and equal beings, although from Kant's point of view desire is paradigmatically phenomenal rather than noumenal. Rawls is on the same page as Kant, however, in conceiving of the noumenal choice of principles as governing our conduct in the phenomenal world, where "society" exists: Kant himself sometimes characterizes our moral task as that of transforming the natural world into a moral world (Kant 1998 [1781/1787], A 808/B 836), which would not be a matter of transforming the phenomenal world into a noumenal world (whatever that would mean), but rather of making it live up to the demands of the moral law – by making our natural, empirical selves live up to those demands.

As I suggested earlier, Rawls may mask the point that the choice of principles of justice through the device of the original position must ultimately be grounded in a claim about what human beings *want, desire, or value* by speaking of the principles of justice as constructed on the basis of our *self-conception* as free and equal persons, as parties who "view themselves as free persons who have fundamental aims and interests in the name of which they think it legitimate for them to make claims on one another concerning the design of the basic structure of society" or who "conceive of themselves as beings who can revise and alter their final ends and give first priority to preserving their liberty in these matters" (*TJ*, 131–132) – although perhaps here the contrast between a *self-conception* and a mere *concept* is precisely that a self-conception has a conative element built into it that a concept does not. In any case, Rawls's own theory of justice, in spite of its emphasis on deontological constraints in contrast to perfectionism and utilitarianism, has a teleological foundation. That human beings have a desire to express their nature as – or perhaps better having the potential to be – free and equal persons is presumably also a matter of fact that (if true) can be known only empirically. From Kant's point of view, it would be a matter of fact about human sentiment, and thus Rawls's teleological foundation for the principles of justice would be a form of moral sense theory, which in Kant's own classification of moral theories is emphatically an empirical theory.[14] All this raises two questions. First, what becomes of Rawls's distinction of his own method of "reflective equilibrium" from the straightforwardly empirical method of utilitarianism? Second, how can a theory so explicitly founded on an obviously empirical claim about human sentiment or desire, even if it be some profoundly deep and widespread human desire, seriously claim a Kantian heritage?

I will comment only briefly on the first, less historical question, and then discuss the second, more historical question somewhat more fully. On the first question, two things might be said. On the one hand, I think one could reasonably conclude that Rawls's position is that (at least classical) utilitarianism is not in fact empirically well-grounded, while his own theory of justice as fairness has a better empirical foundation: the argument would be that the derivation of the classical utilitarian principle from the conceit of a well-informed impartial observer who amalgamates all human preferences as if they were those of a single person has little or no foundation in the actual sentiments or desires of normal human beings, but is instead an invention of philosophers. On the other hand, it could also be argued that Rawls's own method of reflective equilibrium is an empirical method, but a sophisticated one because it does not appeal to a single moral sentiment, but to a variety of facts about our desires and beliefs and to our, presumably also empirically established, desire to reconcile them. Rawls describes his method as attempting "to accommodate within one scheme both reasonable philosophical conditions on principles as well as our considered judgments of justice" (*TJ*, 19). I think we should understand this as saying that it is an empirically known fact that humans generally desire to express their nature (or potential) as free and equal beings, that as a matter of empirically known fact human beings have both a variety of more specific beliefs about justice and a desire to reconcile their deep-seated desires, such as the desire to express their own nature as free and equal persons, with their beliefs, including their more specific beliefs about the contents of principles of justice. If the method of reflective equilibrium is to be so understood, then it could be considered an empirical theory without collapsing into either the supposedly empirical method of classical utilitarianism as Rawls describes it or into any of the actual moral sense theories of the eighteenth century, different as we have seen some of these to be from classical utilitarianism as Rawls characterizes it.

But now what about our second question, that is, whether Rawls's foundation of his own theory of justice as fairness on a fundamental human desire to express our nature as free and equal beings can possibly be considered a genuinely Kantian method? After all, Kant is the philosopher who seems to deny above all else that the fundamental principle of morality can ever be grounded on any kind of feeling, no matter how refined or elevated, and who argues that the genuinely moral feeling of respect can only be "self-wrought" by pure practical reason, not a datum for it. Kant's statements of the former position are too numerous to list, but this famous statement could stand for many others:

> An action from duty is to put aside entirely the influence of inclination and with it every object of the will; hence there is left for the will nothing that could determine it except objectively the *law* and subjectively *pure respect* for this practical law, and so the maxim of complying with this law even if it infringes upon all my inclinations. (Kant 1996b [1785], 4:400–401)

And his statement of the second thesis comes in his footnote to this passage, where, although the "pure respect" just referred to is not explicitly characterized as a feeling, he admits that it is, but "not one *received* by means of influence; it is, instead, a feeling *self-wrought* by means of a rational concept and therefore specifically different from all feelings . . . which can be reduced to inclination" (4:401n). It does not seem, then, as if Kant's own ethics could be founded on anything like a *desire* to express our nature as free and equal persons, as Rawls's theory of justice is.

But matters are not so simple here, for there are two different questions to consider. One is whether Kant's theory has a structure similar to that of Rawls's "Kantian Interpretation," on which the deontological constraint expressed by the categorical imperative is itself grounded on an antecedent valuation of freedom in all persons, and so has a teleological foundation. The other question is whether this valuation can be considered as resting on a desire. In my view, the answer to the first question is clearly "yes," thus there is indeed a teleological foundation for deontology in Kant as in Rawls. As to the second question, Kant clearly at least entertained the idea of something like a desire for freedom as the foundation for morality in his earliest reflections on moral philosophy, and later tried to find an alternative to this; but in my view it is not clear whether he ever succeeded. So something like Rawls's desire to express our nature as free and rational beings may not have been the purely rational foundation for practical philosophy that the mature Kant hoped to find, but it may be the best he could have come up with.

I have dealt with these matters at length elsewhere, so will be brief about them here.[15] I can start by saying that neither the *Groundwork* nor the *Critique of Practical Reason* is entirely clear on the relation between deontology and teleology.[16] The argument of section I of the *Groundwork*, the key passage of which was just quoted, and the argument leading up to the first formulation of the categorical imperative in its section II, the "formula of universal law," as well as the opening argument of the *Critique of Practical Reason*, infer a deontological constraint directly from the exclusion of inclination and its objects as a possible foundation for morality. Kant's move in *Groundwork* II from the first to the second formulation of the categorical imperative, the "formula of humanity as an end in itself," might then be interpreted as an attempt to define an end *compatible* with or *acceptable* under the formula of universal law, a step that it is necessary to take because all rational action must have some end, but a step that is subsequent rather than antecedent to the foundation of the moral law itself. But Kant himself introduces the formula of humanity by saying: "But suppose there were something the *existence of which in itself* has an absolute worth, something which as *an end in itself* could be a ground of determinate laws; then in it, and in it alone, would lie the ground of a possible categorical imperative" (1996b [1785], 4:428). This suggests that the teleological value of humanity as an end in itself is antecedent to the deontological constraint of the categorical imperative, not subsequent to or constructed from it – thus that whatever teleological elements might subsequently be incorporated into Kant's theory of specifically human duties, the fundamental principle of morality itself also has a teleological foundation.

Now the *Groundwork* is notoriously obscure about both just what it means for humanity to be an end in itself and about why humanity should count as an end in itself. In other sources from the period around the *Groundwork*, however, Kant makes it clear that *freedom* is our most fundamental end and an end in itself, and in later texts he identifies humanity with the capacity to set our own ends freely, thus suggesting that it is humanity understood as the capacity to set our own ends freely that is the fundamental value on which his practical philosophy is grounded, the teleological value that grounds his deontology. Thus in his lectures on ethics as recorded in various transcriptions from that of Johann Friedrich Kaehler (1777) to that on which Georg Ludwig Collins inscribed his name in the winter semester of 1784–1785,[17] thus during the period of the completion and publication of the *Groundwork*, Kant is reported as saying that "the inner worth of the world, the *summum bonum*, is freedom according to a choice that is not necessitated to act. Freedom is thus the inner worth of the world" (Kant 1997, 125 (Collins 27:344); Kant 2004, 177). Kant goes on to argue that this value can be fully realized only by the intra- and interpersonally consistent use of freedom, thus that this value is the source of all duties to oneself and to others: any treatment of oneself or others that "abolishes" freedom "and all use of it, as the highest *principium* of life," "conflicts with the greatest use of freedom"; "Only under certain conditions can freedom be consistent with itself" (Kant 1997, 126 (Collins 27:346); Kant 2004, 180). This makes it clear that it is not just *one's own* freedom that is the "inner worth of the world," but the "greatest use of freedom" or the greatest possible freedom of *all*; and it also makes clear that the purpose of the rule of consistency, or universalizability, a rule that must of course be discerned by reason, is to make the "greatest use of freedom" possible. Kant makes this point explicit in a contemporaneous lecture course on political philosophy, *Naturrecht Feyerabend*, when he states: "If only rational being can be an end in itself, this is not because it has reason, but because it has freedom. Reason is merely a means" (Kant 1979, 27:1321). Freedom is the end, reason merely the means: that is, human freedom is an or rather *the* end in itself, the only thing of intrinsic and unconditional value, and reason and its rules are only the means to the realization of this end. The categorical imperative as a deontological constraint is founded upon the teleological claim that the greatest possible use of human freedom is the only end in itself.

Thus the general structure of Rawls's "Kantian Interpretation" does mirror what seems to be the underlying structure of Kant's own practical philosophy, even if this structure is not immediately obvious in the argument from the exclusion of inclination to the formality of the categorical imperative by which Kant introduces his initial formulations of the categorical imperative in both the *Groundwork* and the second *Critique*. But now what about the second question I raised, the question about the foundation of this teleology itself? For Rawls, the theory of justice is ultimately founded upon our *desire* to express our nature as free and equal persons. Can Kant's thesis that the greatest possible intra- and interpersonal use of freedom is the inner worth of the world be founded upon anything similar, a *desire* for maximal freedom for oneself and others?

In his earliest reflections on moral philosophy, Kant seems to have thought precisely that (Guyer 2012a). In one of his notes in his own copy of the 1764 *Observations on the Feeling of the Beautiful and Sublime*, Kant says, in terms similar to those of his later lectures, that "freedom in the proper sense (the moral, not the metaphysical) would be the supreme *principium* of all virtue and also of all happiness" (Kant 2011, 87, Remark 25). In several other notes, Kant suggests that the status of freedom as our most fundamental value is simply a matter of human psychology: human beings learn to accommodate themselves to the constraints of nature, because there is nothing they can do about them,

> But what is much harder and more unnatural than this yoke of necessity is the subjection of one human being under the will of another human being. There is no misfortune more terrible to him who would be accustomed to freedom – who would have enjoyed the good of freedom – than to see himself delivered to a creature of his own kind . . . It also requires a very long habituation to make the terrible thoughts of subservience tolerable. (Kant 2011, 128–129, Remark 72)

Here Kant suggests that those who have experienced freedom value it above all else, although he makes no claim that in actual human history everyone necessarily experiences freedom, thus that in actual human history every human being will arrive at this valuation, and he also suggests that it is at least possible that by suitable conditioning people can be weaned from their love of freedom. Thus he treats the love of freedom as a contingent although widespread and deep-seated fact about human beings – a fact about their most fundamental desire. Here Kant seems to be thinking along the same lines as Rawls.

It should be noted, however, that in these passages Kant makes no attempt to explain how humans would get from a love of their own freedom to a love of the freedom of all. His remarks leave open the possibility that each human does not desire the freedom of all, only his own, and recognizes only through the instrumental use of reason that he must concede to others a freedom equal to his own if he is get them to allow him to enjoy his own. Perhaps for this reason Kant was never very happy with this account of the desire for freedom as a foundation for morality, and we find him quickly searching for something else. Even in these early notes, he writes a few pages later: "In subjection there is not only something externally dangerous but also a certain ugliness and a contradiction that at the same time indicates its unlawfulness" (Kant 2011, 129, Remark 75). In a note from another source but from around the same time he remarks that "The essential perfection of a freely acting being depends on whether this freedom is not subject to inclination or in general would not be subject to any foreign cause at all" (Kant 2005, 422, Note 6605). These sorts of remarks suggest that Kant is hoping for a metaphysical argument for rather than a psychological explanation of the fundamental value of freedom, an argument that it is of the essence of human beings to be free and thus that to deprive human beings of their freedom is to contradict something essential to them. Kant makes it clear that such a basis for the value of freedom would immediately imply the equal value of the freedom of all, not just the value of one's own freedom: "Nothing is absolutely good (unconditional in every respect)," he says, "except the existence of freely acting beings" (Kant 2005, 414, Note 5444), not merely one's own freely acting self. Of course such a metaphysical account of the value of the expression of our nature as free and equal, or equally free, persons would be remote from Rawls's desire-based foundation for the principles of justice.

It will have been noted that one of the passages just cited uses perfectionist language (see Guyer 2011), although the kind of perfectionism that Kant is espousing here, contrary to Rawls's conception of perfectionism, seems to have a distributive constraint built into it, since it seems to be the idea that since freedom is of the essence of every human being, the freedom of every human being should be equally perfected. Kant does not use perfectionist language in the *Groundwork*, but his argument in its section III that at the noumenal level we *are* free and can express that freedom *only* by adherence to the moral law, that only the moral, noumenal self is our "proper self," also seems to make it a matter of metaphysical fact that it is our essence to be free rather than a merely empirical fact that we desire to be free, and thus that it would be a contradiction with its essence to deny any human being freedom (or freedom equal to all others) – although Kant's treatment of the moral law as the *causal* law of the proper, noumenal self of all human beings in *Groundwork* III (Kant 1996b [1785], 4:446) also seems to make *immoral* action impossible, as several critics such as Carl Christian Erhard Schmid and Karl Leonhard Reinhold seemed to have recognized very quickly. Kant responded to this difficulty in his *Religion within the Boundaries of Mere Reason* by treating noumenal freedom not as a form of causality inexorably governed by the moral law but rather as the "inscrutable" possibility of making a nondetermined choice *between* the moral law and the principle of self-love, more precisely as the ability to choose between subordinating self-love to the moral law or subordinating adherence to the moral law to the satisfaction of self-love (Kant 1996d, 82–83). Of course, because this inscrutable choice is made at the noumenal level, it cannot be equated with something empirical like a desire, but it is certainly something more than merely having a reason to be moral – for Kant, everyone has that – so it must be something like having the noumenal analogue of a desire to be moral, and thus allow the greatest possible use of freedom to all, in addition to having a reason to do so, namely, knowledge of the moral law. Of course, Kant might have spared us all a lot of metaphysical obscurity if he had simply conceded that morality and the principles of right or justice that follow from it are ultimately based in a desire to express our nature as free and equal beings, or a love equally for the freedom of all and not just oneself. And that of course would have been Rawls's "Kantian Interpretation" of the teleological foundation of the deontological principles of justice.

I have tried to suggest that Kant's foundation of the categorical imperative upon the value of freedom as the inner worth of the world has the same structure as Rawls's "Kantian Interpretation" of justice as fairness, although Kant was much more ambivalent than was Rawls about grounding his teleology on a straightforward, empirically evidenced desire to express our nature as free and equal beings. I suggested earlier that Kant's foundation for morality can also be considered as a kind of perfectionism, although one that, unlike Rawls's examples of perfectionism such as Nietzsche's, has a distributive constraint built into it. I also mentioned earlier that we should not follow Rawls in drawing the lines between a Kantian moral and political theory, perfectionism, and utilitarianism too rigorously because there are perfectionist and utilitarian elements in Kant's *applications* of the fundamental principle of morality as well as a perfectionist element in his foundation of it. As I have already suggested, I just have in mind Kant's view that the (imperfect) duties of virtue – which cannot be coercively enforced and are thus not duties of justice, to be incorporated into the political and juridical "basic structure of society" – are self-perfection and the happiness of others. That is, for Kant, once we have got past the fundamental principles of morality, we should be perfectionists toward ourselves and a certain kind of utilitarian toward others – although since we have duties to show respect toward others as well as to be beneficent toward them, we should presumably not be classical utilitarians toward them, concerned only with the aggregate of benefits conferred and not with some level of equality in benefits conferred sufficient to assure all that they are being treated with equal respect. And all I have room to say about this is that while particularly in his lectures Rawls recognizes the importance of the concept of the highest good in Kant's ethics (see Lectures V and X, *LHMP*), and thus recognizes in general terms the importance to Kant of ultimately combining teleological and deontological elements into an overarching conception of human good, he does not acknowledge the perfectionist and utilitarian strands in Kant's own doctrine of virtue as explicitly as he might have had he paid more attention to the *Metaphysics of Morals* – just as he never made as much use of Kant's doctrine of right as he might have in constructing his own theory of justice. In fact, I would suggest that there is considerable similarity especially between Rawls's conception of the "moral powers" of persons that are to be developed within the basic structure of society ensured by the principles of justice and the powers of "body," "mind" or intellect and nonmoral rationality, and "spirit" or moral rationality that are for Kant included in "A human being's duty to himself to develop and increase his *natural perfection*" (Kant 1996c [1797], Doctrine of Virtue, §19, 6:565). Alas, there is no room here to develop this point more fully. But the more fundamental point that I have wanted to make, that both Rawls (at least the Rawls of *TJ*) and Kant actually construct their deontologies upon an antecedent teleology, a theory of the good that takes the equal value of freedom in all human beings as its starting point, should by now be clear.

# Notes

I am grateful to David Reidy and Jon Mandle for the invitation to write this paper, and to David Reidy and Christopher Melenovsky for helpful discussion of its first draft.

1   See P.F. Strawson, "Freedom and Resentment" (1962), in Strawson 1974. Neither Strawson himself nor the author who most thoroughly developed Strawson's version of a theory of moral sentiments, namely R. Jay Wallace (see Wallace 1994), so much as nod in the direction of Smith.

2   Although the revised version of *TJ* came out in 1999, thus eight years after the version of the course on which the publication of the *LHMP* was published and (obviously) one year before that publication, Rawls's revisions to *TJ*, themselves mostly made years earlier for the German version, did not affect his treatment of the history of moral philosophy.

3   The title, of course, of Quine's 1969 paper, published along with his own Dewey Lectures in Quine 1969, 69–90.

4   For my earlier comparisons of Kant's and Rawls's versions of the just political order, see my articles "Kantian Foundations for Liberalism" and "Life, Liberty, and Property: Kant and Rawls," in Guyer 2000, 235–61 and 262–86.

5   Rawls introduced the term "constructivism" in his 1980 Dewey Lectures, reprinted in *CP*, 303–358; he further developed this conception of Kant in his 1987 Stanford University Centennial Lecture, published in 1989 as "Themes in Kant's Moral Philosophy" and reprinted in *CP*, 497–528. This is close in time to the 1991 lectures printed in *LHMP*.

6   For my treatment of this issue, see Guyer 2013. The literature on the relation of Rawls's "Kantian constructivism" to Kant's own conception of his method is extensive. Besides Stern 2012, see also Davidson 1985, McCarthy 1994, Krasnoff 1999, Rauscher 2002, Ameriks 2003, O'Neill 2003, Kain 2006, Hills 2008, and Wood 2008.

7   Kant includes the duty to refrain from suicide among the duties of virtue rather than right in the *Metaphysics of Morals* because even though it is a perfect duty, the state has no title to enforce it coercively. Kant includes the duties to avoid arrogance, defamation, and ridicule among the imperfect duties to others, although, as duties of omission rather than commission, they might well seem to be perfect rather than imperfect duties; but again, there is (at least for Kant) no right to the coercive enforcement of these duties.

8   David Reidy has pointed out to me that in a note in Rawls's 1958 article "Justice as Fairness" Rawls recognizes that Hume includes a distributive constraint in his version of utilitarianism, and thus does not attribute classical or aggregative utilitarianism to Hume (see *CP*, 51 n5). However, the treatment of Hume along with Smith in *TJ* that I am about to describe seems to depart from this earlier account.

9   Nor has Rawls's view of Smith been much treated in secondary literature; for a rare exception, see Frazer 2007 and 2010, 90–97.

10  Rawls brings this point out clearly in Lecture IV on Butler in *LHPP*, esp. 441–446.

11  See Frazer 2010, 92–93.

12  Smith does not worry, as Kant does, that we might not know our *own* motivations and intentions very well; he assumes that they are relatively transparent to us, but also, or even precisely *because* of that, we tend to overweight them; we need to think about them as someone else might to reach a sounder assessment of the propriety of acting on them.

13  Though in his *Lectures on Jurisprudence*, in discussing attitudes toward "public jurisprudence," or forms of government, Smith suggests that people may be differently inclined by nature toward governments based on the principle of authority or utility, i.e., monarchy or democracy; see Smith 1978, 402. (I owe this reference to Christopher Melenovsky.) However, I do not think that Smith allows a similar natural variation among individuals in their moral sentiments toward injustice in *The Theory of Moral Sentiments*.

14  At Kant 1996b [1785], 5:40, Kant classifies the theory of "moral sense (according to Hutcheson)" as an "internal" and "subjective" theory, meaning that moral standards are set by something internal rather than external to us, but something subjective, namely our own sentiments, rather than something purportedly objective, such as a conception of perfection. But he also says that determining grounds of the will that are "merely *subjective*" are "empirical," presumably meaning

by this that they are known only empirically (5:39). In a similar classification of moral theories in his lectures on ethics, he immediately contrasts moral theories as "empirical or intellectual," and counts the theory that the ground for moral principles "is posited in the moral feeling whereby we can discriminate what is good or bad" of Shaftesbury and Hutcheson as an empirical theory. See Kant 1997, 48–49, from the transcription belonging to Georg Ludwig Collins (27:252–253).

15 See Guyer 1993; 1995; 2002; 2012a; 2012b.

16 Kant 1996a [1788]; 1996b [1785]. See the useful discussion of this issue in Stern 2012, 35–37.

17 I describe the Collins transcription in this somewhat convoluted way because it is so close in wording to earlier transcriptions such as the Kaehler lectures and also sufficiently different from the Mrongovius transcription dated January 3, 1785 (see Kant 1997, 223–248) as to raise the suspicion that the Collins transcription is actually a copy of an earlier set of notes, not notes actually taken by Collins when he was taking the class.

## Works by Rawls, with Abbreviations

*Collected Papers* (CP), ed. Samuel Freeman. Cambridge, MA: Harvard University Press, 1999.

"The Independence of Moral Theory," *Proceedings and Addresses of the American Philosophical Association* 48 (1975): 5–22. Reprinted in *Collected Papers* (286–302).

"Justice as Fairness," *Philosophical Review* 67 (1958): 164–94. Reprinted in *Collected Papers* (47–72).

"Kantian Constructivism in Moral Theory" (KC), *Journal of Philosophy* 77 (1980): 515–572. The Dewey Lectures. Reprinted in *Collected Papers* (303–358).

*Lectures on the History of Moral Philosophy* (LHMP), ed. Barbara Herman. Cambridge, MA: Harvard University Press, 2000.

*Lectures on the History of Political Philosophy* (LHPP), ed. Samuel Freeman. Cambridge, MA: Harvard University Press, 2007.

"Themes in Kant's Moral Philosophy" (1989), in Eckart Förster (ed.), *Kant's Transcendental Deductions: The "Three Critiques" and "Opus Postumum"* (81–113). Stanford: Stanford University Press. Reprinted in *Collected Papers* (497–528).

*A Theory of Justice* (TJ), rev. edn. Cambridge, MA: Harvard University Press, 1999.

## Other References

Ameriks, Karl (2003) "On Two Non-realist Interpretations of Kant's Ethics." In Ameriks, *Interpreting Kant's Critiques*. Oxford: Oxford University Press.

Davidson, Arnold (1985) "Is Rawls a Kantian?" *Pacific Philosophical Quarterly* 66, 48–77.

Firth, Roderick (1952) "Ethical Absolutism and the Ideal Observer." *Philosophy and Phenomenological Research* 12, 317–345.

Frazer, Michael (2007) "Between Two Enlightenments." *Political Theory* 35: 756–780.

Frazer, Michael (2010) *The Enlightenment of Sympathy: Justice and the Moral Sentiments in the Eighteenth Century and Today.* Oxford: Oxford University Press.

Guyer, Paul (1987) *Kant and the Claims of Knowledge.* Cambridge: Cambridge University Press.

Guyer, Paul (1993) "Kant's Morality of Law and Morality of Freedom." In R.M. Dancy (ed.), *Kant and Critique: New Essays in Honor of W.H. Werkmeister* (43–89). Dordrecht: Kluwer. Reprinted in Guyer, *Kant on Freedom, Law, and Happiness* (129–171). Cambridge: Cambridge University Press, 2000.

Guyer, Paul (1995) "Freiheit als 'der innere Werth der Welt.'" In Christel Fricke, Peter König, and Thomas Petersen (eds), *Das Recht der Vernunft: Kant und Hegel über Denken, Erkennen und Handeln*

(231–262). Stuttgart-Bad Canstatt: Fromann-Holzboog. In English as "Freedom as the Inner Value of the World," in Guyer, *Kant on Freedom, Law, and Happiness* (96–125). Cambridge: Cambridge University Press, 2000.

Guyer, Paul (2000) *Kant on Freedom, Law, and Happiness.* Cambridge: Cambridge University Press.

Guyer, Paul (2002) "Ends of Reason and Ends of Nature: The Place of Teleology in Kant's Ethics." *Journal of Value Inquiry* 36: 161–186. Reprinted in Guyer, *Kant's System of Nature and Freedom: Selected Essays* (168–197). Oxford: Clarendon Press, 2005.

Guyer, Paul (2005) *Kant's System of Nature and Freedom: Selected Essays.* Oxford: Clarendon Press.

Guyer, Paul (2011) "Kantian Perfectionism." In Lawrence Jost and Julian Wuerth (eds), *Perfecting Virtue: New Essays on Kantian Ethics and Virtue Ethics.* Cambridge: Cambridge University Press.

Guyer, Paul (2012a) "Freedom as the Foundation of Morality: Kant's Early Efforts." In Susan Shell and Richard Velkley (eds), *Kant's Remarks in the Observations on the Beautiful and Sublime: A Critical Guide.* Cambridge: Cambridge University Press.

Guyer, Paul (2012b) "Passion for Reason: Hume, Kant, and the Motivation for Morality." *Proceedings and Addresses of the American Philosophical Association* 86: 4–21.

Guyer Paul (2013) "Constructivism and Self-Constitution." In Mark Timmons and Sorin Baiasu (eds), *Kant on Practical Justification* (176–200). Oxford: Oxford University Press.

Herman, Barbara (1981) "On the Value of Acting from the Motive of Duty." *Philosophical Review* 90: 359–82. Reprinted in Herman, *The Practice of Moral Judgment* (1–22). Cambridge, MA: Harvard University Press, 1993.

Hills, Alison (2008) "Kantian Value-Realism." *Ratio* 212: 182–200.

Kain, Patrick (2006) "Realism and Anti-realism in Kant's Second *Critique*." *Philosophy Compass* 1: 449–465.

Kames, Henry Home (Lord) (2005) *Essays on the Principles of Morality and Natural Religion.* 3rd edn, ed. Mary Catherine Moran. Indianapolis: Liberty Fund.

Kant, Immanuel (1979) *Naturrecht Feyerabend.* In *Kant's gesammelte Schriften*, vol. 27.2 (1319–1394), ed. German Academy of Sciences. Berlin: Walter de Gruyter.

Kant, Immanuel (1996a [1788]) *Critique of Practical Reason.* In Kant, *Practical Philosophy*, ed. and trans. Mary J. Gregor. Cambridge: Cambridge University Press.

Kant, Immanuel (1996b [1785]) *Groundwork of the Metaphysics of Morals.* In Kant, *Practical Philosophy*, ed. and trans. Mary J. Gregor. Cambridge: Cambridge University Press.

Kant, Immanuel (1996c [1797]) *Metaphysics of Morals.* In Kant, *Practical Philosophy*, ed. and trans. Mary J. Gregor. Cambridge: Cambridge University Press.

Kant, Immanuel (1996d) *Religion and Rational Theology*, ed. Allen W. Wood and George Di Giovanni. Cambridge: Cambridge University Press.

Kant, Immanuel (1997) *Lectures on Ethics*, ed. Peter Heath and J.B. Schneewind, trans. Peter Heath. Cambridge: Cambridge University Press.

Kant, Immanuel (1998 [1781/1787]) *Critique of Pure Reason*, ed. and trans. Paul Guyer and Allen W. Wood. Cambridge: Cambridge University Press.

Kant, Immanuel (2004) *Vorlesung zur Moralphilosophie*, ed. Werner Stark. Berlin: Walter de Gruyter (the 1777 Kaehler transcription).

Kant, Immanuel (2005) *Notes and Fragments*, ed. Paul Guyer, trans. Curtis Bowman, Paul Guyer, and Frederick Rauscher. Cambridge: Cambridge University Press.

Kant, Immanuel (2011) *Observations on the Feeling of the Beautiful and Sublime and Other Writings*, ed. Patrick Frierson and Paul Guyer. Cambridge: Cambridge University Press.

Krasnoff, Larry (1999) "How Kantian Is Constructivism?" *Kant-Studien* 90: 385–409.

McCarthy, Thomas (1994) "Kantian Constructivism and Reconstructivism: Rawls and Habermas in Dialogue." *Ethics* 105 44–63.

O'Neill, Onora (2003) "Constructivism in Rawls and Kant." In Samuel Freeman (ed.), *The Cambridge Companion to Rawls* (347–367). Cambridge: Cambridge University Press.

Quine, W.V.O. (1969) *Ontological Relativity and Other Essays*. New York: Columbia University Press.

Rauscher, Frederick (2002) "Kant's Moral Anti-realism." *Journal of the History of Philosophy* 40: 477–499.

Ross, Ian Simpson (2010) *The Life of Adam Smith*. 2nd edn. Oxford: Oxford University Press.

Sidgwick, Henry (1907) *The Methods of Ethics*. 7th edn. London: Macmillan.

Smith, Adam (1978) *Lectures on Jurisprudence*, ed. R.L. Meek, D.D. Raphael, and P.G. Stein. Oxford: Oxford University Press.

Smith, Adam (1979) *The Theory of Moral Sentiments*, ed. D.D. Raphael and A.L. Macfie. Corrected edn. Oxford: Oxford University Press.

Stern, Robert (2012) *Understanding Moral Obligation: Kant, Hegel, Kierkegaard*. Cambridge: Cambridge University Press.

Strawson, P.F. (1974) *Freedom and Resentment and Other Essays*. London: Methuen.

Wallace, R. Jay (1994) *Responsibility and the Moral Sentiments*. Cambridge, MA: Harvard University Press.

Wood, Allen W. (2008) *Kantian Ethics*. Cambridge: Cambridge University Press.

# Index

*A Companion to Rawls*, First Edition. Edited by Jon Mandle and David A. Reidy.
© 2014 John Wiley & Sons, Inc. Published 2016 by John Wiley & Sons, Inc.

# Download a free PDF copy of this book

Thanks for purchasing this book!

Do you like to read on the go but are unable to carry your print books everywhere? Is your eBook purchase not compatible with the device of your choice?

Don't worry, now with every Packt book you get a DRM-free PDF version of that book at no cost.

Read anywhere, any place, on any device. Search, copy, and paste code from your favorite technical books directly into your application.

The perks don't stop there, you can get exclusive access to discounts, newsletters, and great free content in your inbox daily

Follow these simple steps to get the benefits:

1. Scan the QR code or visit the link below

https://packt.link/free-ebook/9781835469958

2. Submit your proof of purchase

3. That's it! We'll send your free PDF and other benefits to your email directly